A Commentary on the General Instruction of the Roman Missal

A Commentary on the General Instruction of the Roman Missal

Developed under the Auspices of the
Catholic Academy of Liturgy and Cosponsored by the
Federation of Diocesan Liturgical Commissions

Edited by

Edward Foley
Nathan D. Mitchell
Joanne M. Pierce

Foreword by the

Most Reverend Donald W. Trautman, S.T.D., S.S.L.
Chairman of the Bishops' Committee on the Liturgy
1993–1996, 2004–2007

A PUEBLO BOOK

Liturgical Press Collegeville, Minnesota

A Pueblo Book published by Liturgical Press

Cover design by David Manahan, OSB. Illustration by Frank Kacmarcik, OblSB.

1 2 3 4 5 6 7 8 9

Library of Congress Cataloging-in-Publication Data

A commentary on the general instruction of the Roman Missal : developed under the auspices of the Catholic Academy of Liturgy and co-sponsored by the Federation of Diocesan Liturgical Commissions / edited by Edward Foley, Nathan D. Mitchell, Joanne Pierce ; foreword by Donald W. Trautman.

p. cm. — (A Pueblo book)

ISBN-13: 978-0-8146-6017-1

1. Catholic Church—Liturgy—Texts—Rubrics. 2. Catholic Church. General instruction of the Roman missal. 3. Missals—Texts. 4. Lord's Supper—Catholic Church—Liturgy—Texts. 5. Mass—Celebration. I. Foley, Edward. II. Mitchell, Nathan. III. Pierce, Joanne M. IV. Catholic Academy of Liturgy. V. Federation of Diocesan Liturgical Commissions.

BX2015.3.C66 2008
264'.02036—dc22 2007030130

Contents

Foreword by the Most Reverend Donald W. Trautman vii

Introduction ix

Abbreviations and Acronyms xiii

Institutio Generalis Missalis Romani and the Class of Liturgical Documents to Which It Belongs 1
Nathan D. Mitchell and John F. Baldovin

Liturgy and Ecclesiastical Law 28
R. Kevin Seasoltz

Theological and Pastoral Reflections 46
David N. Power and Catherine Vincie

Preamble 73
Margaret Mary Kelleher

Chapter I: Importance and Dignity of the Eucharistic Celebration 99
Keith F. Pecklers

Chapter II: The Structure of the Mass, Its Elements and Its Parts 113
Edward Foley

Chapter III: The Duties and Ministries in the Mass 199
Bruce T. Morrill and Susan K. Roll

Chapter IV.I: The Different Forms of Celebrating Mass 224
Martin Connell and Sharon McMillan

Chapter IV.II: Concelebrated Mass 279
Gilbert Ostdiek and Andrew Ciferni

Chapter IV.III: Mass at Which Only One Minister Participates 310
Mary Shaefer and Joanne M. Pierce

Chapter IV.IV: Some General Norms for All Forms of Mass 325
Mary Shaefer and Joanne M. Pierce

Chapter V: The Arrangement and Furnishings of Churches for the Celebration of the Eucharist 351
Mark E. Wedig and Richard S. Vosko

Chapter VI: Requisites for the Celebration of Mass 383
Richard E. McCarron and Anne C. McGuire

Chapter VII: The Choice of the Mass and Its Parts 405
Joyce Ann Zimmerman

Chapter VIII: Masses and Prayers for Various Circumstances and Masses for the Dead 423
Joanne M. Pierce and Richard Rutherford

Chapter IX: Adaptations Within the Competence of Bishops and Bishops' Conferences 447
Mark Francis and Gary Neville

List of Contributors 468

Index 471

Foreword

The celebration of the Eucharist is the sacred action of Christ and his people. Through the centuries the Church has reformed and regulated, restored and refocused the way of celebrating Eucharist. The *General Instruction of the Roman Missal,* authorized by Pope John Paul in 2002, represents the latest effort of the magisterial office of the Church to guide and govern eucharistic ritual.

The *General Instruction* forms the preface to the Roman Missal and not only contains the rules and rubrics for the celebration of the Eucharist but also expresses the Church's understanding of the Mass. This document offers new insights and new emphasis; it corrects and updates previous general instructions. It seeks to restore the eucharistic rites to ancient norms.

To grasp the deeper meaning of liturgical rites and norms, a commentary is essential. To grasp the pastoral, catechetical, and theological implications and nuances of the *General Instruction*, a commentary is essential. Liturgical norms and guidelines by themselves do not convey their full rationale or historical background. Only a studied analysis can produce the proper perspective and theological insight necessary for a comprehensive understanding.

This present commentary represents the best in liturgical scholarship. It answers a critical need for a detailed study of the *General Instruction*, explaining its pastoral and theological dimensions, especially its ecclesiological implications, in view of contemporary issues. Each chapter shows how eucharistic ritual has developed and adapted to changing cultural circumstances, while preserving its innate Catholic tradition and the biblical teaching on Eucharist. The editorial team, headed by Edward Foley, O.F.M. Cap., has assembled liturgical scholars representing the Catholic Academy of Liturgy and the Federation of Diocesan Liturgical Commissions. These scholars offer a balanced, reliable, and unparalleled resource for all who seek a deeper understanding of the celebration of the Eucharist. No single liturgical viewpoint can ever express the full mystery of the Eucharist. Varying viewpoints give us a broader and deeper comprehension of ritual reform.

The *Constitution on the Sacred Liturgy* gives us appropriate guidance for judging the directives of the *General Instruction*:

> Pastors must therefore realize that, when the liturgy is celebrated, more is required than mere observance of the laws governing valid and licit celebration. It is their duty also to ensure that the faithful take part knowingly, actively, and fruitfully. (no. 11)

These words of the council fathers frame the approach of this commentary. Rubric literalism is never the goal. Pastoral prudence and the spirit of liturgical law must prevail. The "more" the council fathers mention is the goal.

We can understand our eucharistic celebration only if we know the meaning of the eucharistic ritual. Recall the principle: *lex orandi, lex credendi.* What we pray is what we believe. The rule of prayer is the rule of belief. Bows and genuflections, the use of incense and sprinkling with holy water, posture and gestures, singing and silence, processions and presenting gifts—all have doctrinal implications. The liturgy is catechesis. This commentary explains the relationship between ritual and doctrine.

The last *General Instruction* was issued in 1975 shortly after the end of the Second Vatican Council. Many new Church documents have been promulgated since that time, including the Rite of the Dedication of a Church and Altar (1977), the Code of Canon Law (1983), and the Ceremonial of Bishops (1984). These major documents had a direct bearing on the celebration of the Eucharist and hastened the most recent revision of the *General Instruction*. The changes in the Roman Missal as reflected in the *General Instruction* must be seen as something more than a refining of rubrics. These changes must lead to a new commitment to foster full, conscious, and active participation in the Mass. Celebrating Eucharist can never be reduced to a mere enacting of rituals. Some rubrics stress the role of the clergy; other rubrics emphasize the role of the assembly. The GIRM in paragraph 18 stresses that full, conscious, and active participation in the Mass is "demanded by the very nature of the celebration, and to which the Christian people have a right and duty by reason of their Baptism." These are strong words reminding us that all the baptized followers of Jesus share by varying degrees in his priesthood. The Mass is the action of all the members of the assembly, including the priest celebrant and other liturgical ministers. Liturgical laws must never "clericalize" the lay participants.

Transformation is the goal of all liturgical celebration. We must always have before us the ultimate questions: Has the renewed liturgy renewed us? Have the revised rites and liturgical norms led to a transformation of people?

Too often rubrical changes have been viewed as only surface remodeling of our eucharistic celebration. This commentary dispels that notion, penetrating below the surface to give the full context and offering us pastoral, catechetical, and theological insights into the source and summit of our Christian lives.

Most Rev. Donald W. Trautman, S.T.D., S.S.L.
Bishop of Erie
Chairman of the Bishops' Committee
on the Liturgy, 1993–1996, 2004–2007

Introduction

Liturgical renewal is an ongoing process, more energetic at some points in Christian history than in others. The year 2008 marks the fiftieth anniversary of the election of Blessed John XXIII, and the beginning of the most recent active renewal period. These liturgical reforms, supported by the intensive historical and textual research of the nineteenth and twentieth centuries and sparked by the publication of the Vatican II constitution *Sacrosanctum Concilium* (*SC*), reached a kind of crest with the first edition of the *Institutio Generalis Missalis Romani* (*IGMR*) and the *Missale Romanum* (*MR*). This first wave of liturgical reform after Vatican II brought momentous change to the Eucharistic liturgy of the Roman Catholic Church, but it was not in any sense the last word. In fact, later editions of the *IGMR* and *MR* continued to elaborate and refine the post-conciliar celebration of the Eucharist.

The publications of *IGMR2002* and *MR2002* mark the crest of a fresh wave, a significant moment in the flow of Roman Catholic liturgical life at the turn of the new millennium. Based on the experience of thirty years of "living in and through" the liturgical reforms of Vatican II, and grounded in further study and reflection, the directives and insights presented in *IGMR2002* are symbolic of contemporary developments in pastoral practice and theology, as well as symbolic of some of the past tensions that continue in the dynamic of liturgical reform. Therefore, *IGMR2002* needs to be understood as an ecclesially potent document that should be read not only from the viewpoint of liturgical history, theology, and practice, but also through other key "lenses" of the contemporary period, e.g., ecclesiology, Christology, missiology, and theologies of inculturation. In this commentary, the primary "lens" for reading this new edition of *IGMR* is *SC* itself, which provides the guiding hermeneutic for understanding and crafting the Church's worship.

Against the backdrop of these observations, the goals of this commentary can be understood more clearly. The first goal is to set *IGMR2002* in context; thus, the first three essays presented in the volume offer an historical, a theological, and a canonical introduction to the document. The next goal, to provide careful analysis of the text of the document itself, is realized through the design of the rest of the volume, which provides specific theological, historical, and pastoral commentary on each chapter and number of *IGMR2002*. The third goal concerns the future of the document; this commentary is offered not only to enhance understanding of the current *IGMR2002*, but also to anticipate future directions. This is the fifth *IGMR* (and the third *MR*) to be published since 1969, and Catholics will undoubtedly see further editions in the years and decades to come. Clearly, there has been enormous development and improvement through the various stages of *IGMR*, and we expect that to continue in subsequent editions. In some small way, we hope that this commentary contributes to the fruitfulness of that future development.

This commentary was prepared primarily for those in positions of leadership in the Church. We hope that bishops, teachers of liturgy, members of diocesan liturgical staffs, pastors, and those who exercise other roles of ministerial leadership in liturgy will find this volume a rich source of historical background and contemporary theological reflection to assist them in their work. At the same time, we have tried to make the commentary an accessible resource for others interested in learning more deeply about the liturgy, especially students engaged in more formal study; thus, while offering a commentary on the official Latin text of *IGMR2002*, we have also provided translations of texts and other tools to assist a wider range of readers.

Because of the liturgical and ecclesial significance of *IGMR2002*, this project has deliberately been a collegial one from the beginning. Therefore, the organization of this volume was undertaken by the members of the Catholic Academy of Liturgy (CAL), an association of Roman Catholic specialists in liturgy, music, art, and architecture; the organization is connected with the ecumenical and interfaith North American Academy of Liturgy, composed of liturgical specialists active in the United States, Canada, and other western countries. Three members of CAL served on the editorial board for the commentary, with Edward Foley serving as overall director. The authors contributing to the work were also drawn largely from its membership, and CAL as an organization serves as one cosponsor of the project. However, from the start, this project was not designed to be a purely academic exercise, but one generated from the meeting of scholarship and pastoral concern; the editors and authors are active in teaching, ministerial training, and pastoral leadership as well as liturgical scholarship.

The second cosponsor of this project is the Federation of Diocesan Liturgical Commissions (FDLC), the professional organization for members of Roman Catholic diocesan Liturgical Commissions and Offices of Worship in the United States. The FDLC understands its more general mission as one of support for all those engaged more generally in the liturgical apostolate. Their commitment to this project springs naturally from their deep concern about the importance of having a strong resource work, grounded in careful scholarship and pastoral reflection, that will aid pastoral leaders in understanding and interpreting *IGMR2002* to the benefit of their worshiping communities.

In keeping with this pattern of professional collaboration, the writing of the commentary itself was collegial. The volume contains the work of twenty-five contributors. The work of all the authors, including that of the editors, was continually placed in dialogue with that of the other contributors. Insights from one author have often influenced the writing of other sections, and sometimes material originally written for one chapter has even been moved to a more appropriate location. In this way, while composed of the work of individual specialists, this volume also reflects the work of a community of liturgical scholars and practitioners.

We would like to express our gratitude to the various authors whose articles appear in this commentary. In addition, we would also like to express our gratitude to other contributors: to J. Michael Joncas, who shared in the early work of the editorial team; to Gilbert Ostdiek, OFM, Mary Collins, OSB, and Bishop Donald Trautman, each of whom read various sections of the commentary and offered comments and suggestions; to the leadership of CAL and FDLC who spearheaded the cosponsorship of this volume; and finally, to Peter Dwyer and our collaborators at Liturgical Press, for their great interest in the project, unflagging support through the writing and editing of the work, and careful professionalism in bringing it to publication.

The liturgical reforms of Vatican II and the books that resulted from them and give form to our twenty-first century worship, have been inspired by the principle articulated so clearly in *SC*, no. 14, full, conscious, and active participation by the laity. This luminous vision, already widely embraced, animates every edition of the *IGMR* and beckons us further into the mystery of Incarnation, Eucharist, Church, and Mission. As Augustine of Hippo preached one Easter to the neophytes and the faithful:

> "You are there on the table; you are there in the chalice. You are this body with us, for, collectively, we are this body. We drink of the same chalice because we live the same life." (Sermon 229)

Edward Foley
Nathan D. Mitchell
Joanne M. Pierce
7 March 2007
Feast of SS. Felicity and Perpetua

Abbreviations and Acronyms

AAS	*Acta Apostolicae Sedis* (Rome: 1909 to present)
AG	*Ad Gentes*, Vatican II "Decree on the Missionary Activity of the Church," 1965
Appendix1969	1969 Appendix to the General Instruction for the Dioceses of the United States
ApTrad	Apostolic Tradition
BCL	Bishops' Committee on the Liturgy of the USCCB
BLS	Built of Living Stones: Art, Architecture, and Worship, issued by NCCB/USCC (now USCCB), 2000
Book of Blessings	Approved for use in Dioceses of the United States by the NCCB, 1987
Bugnini	Annibale Bugnini, *The Reform of the Liturgy 1948–1975*, trans. Matthew J. O'Connell (Collegeville, MN: The Liturgical Press, 1990)
c., cc.	canon, canons
ca.	*circa*
CDF	Congregation for the Doctrine of the Faith
CDWDS	Congregation for Divine Worship and the Discipline of the Sacraments
C.E.	Common Era
CEC	*Catholicae Ecclesiae Catechismus*, 2nd edition (*editio typica*), 1997
CaerEp	*Caeremoniale Episcoporum*, 1984
ch., chs.	chapter(s)
ChrDom	*Christus Dominus*, Vatican II "Decree concerning the Pastoral Office of Bishops in the Church," 1965
CIC1917	*Codex Iuris Canonici*, 1917
CIC1983	*Codex Iuris Canonici*, 1983
d.	died
DOL	International Commission on English in the Liturgy, *Documents on the Liturgy 1963–1979: Conciliar, Papal, and Curial Texts* (Collegville, MN: The Liturgical Press, 1982). All numbers refer to the marginal numbers running sequentially throughout that volume.

DPPL	Directory on Popular Piety and the Liturgy, issued by the CDWDS, 2001
DV	*Dei Verbum*, Vatican II "Dogmatic Constitution on Divine Revelation," 1965
EACW	Environment and Art in Catholic Worship, issued by the BCL, 1978
EccMys	*Ecclesia de mysterio*, issued by the Congregation for the Clergy and seven other dicasteries of the Holy See, 1997
GCE	Guidelines for Concelebration of the Eucharist, issued by the USCCB, 2003
GDC	General Directory for Catechesis, issued by the Congregation for the Clergy, 1997.
Gelasianum	*Liber Sacramentorum Romanae Aeclesiae Ordinis Anni Circuli* (Vat. Reg. lat. 316), ed. Leo Cunibert Mohlberg, *Rerum Ecclesiasticarum Documenta, Series Maior, Fontes* IV (Rome: Herder, 1960)
GIRM1970	ICEL translation of *IGMR1970*
GIRM1975	ICEL translation of *IGMR1975*
GIRM2003	ICEL translation of *IGMR2002*, incorporating adaptations approved for dioceses of the United States
GNLYC	General Norms for the Liturgical Year and the Calendar, issued by the Sacred Congregation of Rites, 1969
GradRom	*Graduale Romanum*, prepared by the monks of Solesmnes (Tournai: Desclée & Co., 1974)
GradSimp	*Graduale Simplex* (Vaticana: Libreria Editrice, 1999)
Hadrianum	Jean Deshusses, *Le Sacramentaire Grégorien d'après ses principaux manuscrits*, 2me ed., Spicilegium Friburgense 16 (Fribourg: Éditions Universitaires, 1979)
ICEL	International Commission on English in the Liturgy
IGLH	*Institutio Generalis de Liturgia Horarum*, 1971
IGMR1969	*Institutio Generalis Missalis Romani*, 1969, the first edition associated with *OM1969*
IGMR1970	*Institutio Generalis Missalis Romani*, 1970, the second edition associated with *MR1970*
IGMR1972	*Institutio Generalis Missalis Romani*, 1972, the third edition issued in light of *Ministeria quædam*
IGMR1975	*Institutio Generalis Missalis Romani*, 1975, the fourth edition associated with *MR1975*
IGMR2000	*Institutio Generalis Missalis* Romani, 2000, a preliminary form of the fifth edition
IGMR2002	*Institutio Generalis Missalis* Romani, 2002, the promulgated form of the fifth edition associated with *MR2002*

IntOec	*Inter Oecumenici*, issued by the Sacred Congregation of Rites, 1964
ITTOM	Introduction to the Order of Mass, issued by the BCL, 2003
Jungmann	Josef Jungmann, *The Mass of the Roman Rite*, trans. Francis Brunner, 2 vols. (Westminster: Christian Classics, 1986 [1951 and 1955])
LG	*Lumen Gentium*, Vatican II "Dogmatic Constitution on the Church," 1964
LitAuth	*Liturgiam Authenticam*, issued by CDWDS, 2001
LMT	Liturgical Music Today, issued by the BCL, 1982
MCW	Music in Catholic Worship, issued by the BCL, rev. ed., 1983 (1972)
MQ	*Ministeria quaedam*, issued *motu proprio* by Paul VI, 1972
MR1474	*Missale Romanum, editio princeps* (Milan, 1474)
MR1570	*Missale Romanum*, promulgated by Pius V, 1570
MR1962	*Missale Romanum*, promulgated by John XXIII, 1962
MR1970	*Missale Romanum, editio typica*, promulgated by Paul VI, 1970
MR1975	*Missale Romanum, editio typica altera*, promulgated by Paul VI, 1975
MR2002	*Missale Romanum, editio typica tertia*, promulgated by John Paul II, 2002
MusSac	*Musicam Sacram*, issued by the Sacred Congregation of Rites, 1967
n., nn.	note, notes
no., nos.	number, numbers
OCF	Order of Christian Funerals, issued by the NCCB, 1989
OrdEx	*Ordo Exsequiarum* 1969
OLM1970-Pr	Introduction (*Proemium*) of the *Ordo Lectionum Missae, editio typica*, 1970
OLM1981-Pr	Introduction (*Proemium*) of the *Ordo Lectionum Missae, editio typica altera*, 1981
OM1969	*Ordo Missae*, 1969
OR I	*Ordo Romanus Primus*
PG	*Patrologia Graeca*
PL	*Patrologia Latina*
PO	*Presbyterorum Ordinis*, Vatican II "Decree on the Ministry and Life of Priests," 1965
RitCon	*Ritus Concelebrationis*, promulgated by the Sacred Congregation of Rites, 1965
RDCA	Rite of Dedication of a Church and an Altar, 1977
Rites I and II	*The Rites of the Catholic Church*, 2 vols. (New York: Pueblo, 1990)

RedSac	*Redemptionis Sacramentum*, issued by CDWDS, 2004
SC	*Sacrosanctum Concilium*, Vatican II "Constitution on the Sacred Liturgy," 1963
TAA	*Tres abhinc annos*, issued by the Sacred Congregation of Rites, 1967
TLS	*Tra le sollecitudini*, issued *motu proprio* by Pius X, 1903
USCC	United States Catholic Conference (until 1 July 2001)
USCCB	United States Conference of Catholic Bishops (from 1 July 2001)
Veronense	*Sacramentarium Veronense*, ed. Leo Cunibert Mohlberg, *Rerum Ecclesiasticarum Documenta, Series Maior, Fontes* I (Rome: Herder, 1966)
VarLeg	*Varietates Legitimae*, issued by CDWDS, 2004

Institutio Generalis Missalis Romani and the Class of Liturgical Documents to Which It Belongs

Nathan D. Mitchell and John F. Baldovin

The purpose of this introductory essay is to outline the history of documents that, over two millennia, have sought to ensure the good order or proper celebration of Christian liturgy—especially the Eucharist—in churches of the Latin West. The essay begins with a discussion of liturgical *ordines* and how they developed from the first centuries C.E. through the medieval epoch (part 1). We turn, then, to the drive for liturgical uniformity as it gained momentum in the Latin West (part 2), particularly during the first half of the second millennium, beginning with the "Gregorian Reform" of the eleventh century and concluding with the publication of the *Missale Romanum* of 1570 *(MR1570)*. In the final portion of the essay, our attention turns to the evolution of those documents variously called *ritus servandus, rubricae generales,* and more recently, "general instructions," whose purpose is to provide normative, detailed prescriptions for the celebration of the Eucharist in the Roman Rite (part 3).

Liturgical *ordines* and How They Grew: Liturgy as an Object of Correction and Regulation in the First Millennium

Descriptions of Christian ritual and instructions for its proper performance already existed by the middle of the first century C.E. St. Paul, for example, sought to correct and regulate liturgical assemblies at Corinth, where the issues included participants' grooming and dress (1 Cor 2–16), disorder vs. decorum in the display of charismatic gifts (1 Cor 14:26-40), and deportment at the Lord's Supper (1 Cor 11:17-34).[1] A generation or two later, the *Didache* or "Teaching of the Twelve Apostles," a short treatise on Christian faith, life, and practice that belongs to a larger class of documents known as "church orders," outlines brief ritual patterns for Sunday worship (ch. 14), baptism (ch. 7), and Eucharist (chs.

1. See the discussion by Jerome Murphy-O'Connor, "The First Letter to the Corinthians," in Raymond E. Brown, Joseph A. Fitzmyer, and Roland E. Murphy, eds., *The New Jerome Biblical Commentary* (Englewood Cliffs, NJ: Prentice-Hall, 1990), 49:51–64.

9–10). It also offers guidelines for receiving itinerant ministers (e.g., teachers, prophets, apostles) and for choosing residential leaders (e.g., bishops and deacons).[2]

The *Didache* was more than a book of ceremonies or *rituale;* its first six chapters constitute a short catechism on "the two ways of life" (light vs. darkness) aimed at shaping the Christian convert's belief and behavior. Church orders were thus "collections of practical directives concerning Christian living; and as these include regulations concerning the method of performing the Church's rites, and some of the texts of the rites themselves, the Church Orders are liturgical books, codes of canon law, and moral treatises combined."[3] Perhaps the most important example from this class of documents is the well-known Apostolic Tradition (ApTrad), sometimes referred to by the Latin title, *Traditio apostolica,* because it exists in an incomplete Latin manuscript (*Veronense,* LV 53), contained in the Verona Cathedral library. ApTrad is often ascribed to a third-century Roman churchman, Hippolytus (d. ca. 236). Its actual origins, date, transmission, and provenance are still debated by scholars.[4] Other notable church orders (some of them incorporating material from ApTrad) include the *Didascalia Apostolorum* (ca. 230), the *Constitutiones Apostolorum* (ca. 380), the

2. For the Greek text of the *Didache,* see Wily Rordort and Andre Tuilier, eds., *La doctrine des douze apotres (Didachè),* Sources Chrétiennes 248 (Paris: Éditions du Cerf, 1978), 140–98. For a recent translation into English, see Aelred Cody, "The *Didache*: An English Translation," in Clayton N. Jefford, ed., *The* Didache *in Context: Essays on Its Text, History, and Transmission* (Leiden: E.J. Brill, 1995), 3–14. On the baptismal rite in *Didache,* see Nathan Mitchell, "Baptism in the *Didache,*" in Jefford, *op. cit.,* 226–55. On the table prayers of *Didache* 9–10 and their relation to Eucharist, see John W. Riggs, "From Gracious Table to Sacramental Elements: The Tradition-History of Didache 9 and 10," *Second Century* 4 (1984) 83–101. See also idem, "The Sacred Food of *Didache* 9–10 and Second-Century Ecclesiologies," in Jefford, *op. cit.,* 256–83. For itinerant and residential ministers in *Didache,* see Jonathan A. Draper, "Social Ambiguity and the Production of Text: Prophets, Teachers, Bishops, and Deacons and the Development of the Jesus Tradition in the Community of the *Didache,*" in Jefford, *op. cit.,* 284–311, and Stephen J. Patterson, "*Didache* 11–13: The Legacy of Radical Itinerancy in Early Christianity," in Jefford, *op. cit.,* 313–29.

3. Edward J. Yarnold, "Church Orders," in Cheslyn Jones, Geoffrey Wainwright, Edward Yarnold and Paul Bradshaw, eds., *The Study of Liturgy,* rev. ed. (New York: Oxford University Press, 1992), 89. See further, Maxwell E. Johnson, "The Apostolic Tradition," and John F. Baldovin, "The Empire Baptized," in Geoffrey Wainwright and Karen B. Westerfield Tucker, eds., *The Oxford History of Christian Worship* (New York: Oxford University Press, 2006), 32–75; 77–130.

4. See Paul F. Bradshaw, Maxwell E. Johnson, and L. Edward Phillips, *The Apostolic Tradition,* Hermeneia Commentary Series (Minneapolis: Fortress Press, 2002). The Eucharistic Prayer found in ApTrad was a remote source for parts of Eucharistic Prayer II in *MR1970;* similarly, ApTrad's prayer for ordaining a bishop was the principal source for the postconciliar prayer of episcopal ordination in the Roman Rite. See Annibale Bugnini, *The Reform of the Liturgy, 1948–1975,* trans. Matthew J. O'Connell (Collegeville, MN: The Liturgical Press, 1990), 456; 714–15.

Canons of Hippolytus (336–340), and the *Testamentum Domini* (fifth century?).[5] As the names indicate, the ritual forms and prayer texts contained in these documents typically claim to have come either from the apostles or directly from the risen Christ himself, who is depicted as dictating detailed liturgical instructions to the church shortly before his ascension. In point of fact, however, few of these documents existed prior to the mid-fourth century. They are not, moreover, "the official manuals of any local church, but rather collections of material deriving from various sources, and perhaps various places and times, and generally showing the idiosyncratic hands of their compilers. They cannot, therefore, be safely used without other corroboration as firm evidence for the actual liturgical practices of any particular Christian group."[6]

Besides these church orders, we also possess a variety of fourth-century Christian documents that describe liturgical practice and custom in the period after the legalization of Christianity (in 312)[7]: prayer books (such as the *Euchologium* or "sacramentary" of Sarapion, bishop of Thmuis [d. after 360][8]); baptismal catecheses from both Eastern and Western churches (e.g., St. Ambrose's [d. 397] *De sacramentis* and John Chrysostom's [d. 407] *Baptismal Instructions*)[9]; and travel diaries (such as that of Egeria, a pilgrim who described liturgies she witnessed in late-fourth-century Jerusalem).[10]

Church orders, prayer books, sacramental catecheses, and travel diaries provide important glimpses into local liturgical practice in the first centuries of Christian history. In the three hundred years between the *pax Constantina* and the birth of Islam (in 612), several additional categories of documents important for understanding the ritual shape and content of liturgy in the Latin West emerged.[11] The origins of these sources are diverse. Some originated as monastic legislation (e.g., the *Rule of the Master* [ca. 525] and the *Rule of St.*

5. For more on these and later documents, see the entry, "Books, Liturgical," in Paul F. Bradshaw, ed., *The New Westminster Dictionary of Liturgy and Worship* (Louisville: Westminster John Knox Press, 2002), 66–86. See also Yarnold, "Church Orders," in *The Study of Liturgy*, 89–91.

6. See "Books, Liturgical," in *The New Westminster Dictionary of Liturgy and Worship*, 67.

7. See John F. Baldovin, "The Empire Baptized," in *The Oxford History of Christian Worship*, 77–130.

8. For the liturgical importance of Sarapion's work, see Maxwell E. Johnson, *The Prayers of Sarapion of Thmuis: A Literary, Liturgical, and Theological Analysis*, Orientalia Christiana Analecta 249 (Rome: Oriental Institute, 1995).

9. See E.C. Whitaker, *Documents of the Baptismal Liturgy*, 3rd ed., revised and expanded by Maxwell E. Johnson (Collegeville, MN: The Liturgical Press, 2003), especially 176–83 and 40–47, with the text selections and bibliographies given there.

10. For Egeria's text, see Pierre Maraval, *Journal de Voyage*, rev. ed., with additions and corrections, Sources Chrétiennes 296 (Paris: Éditions du Cerf, 1997). For an English translation, see John Wilkinson, *Egeria's Travels*, 3rd ed. (Warminster: Aris and Phillips, 1999).

11. For a succinct summary of these sources, see Cyrille Vogel, *Medieval Liturgy: An Introduction to the Sources*, trans. and rev. by William Storey and Niels Rasmussen (Washington, DC: The Pastoral Press, 1986), 10–11; 31–38.

Benedict [ca. 540][12]); some, as sermons, letters, or commentaries (e.g., the homilies of St. Augustine [d. 430], the letters of St. Leo the Great [d. 461], the scriptural commentaries of St. Gregory the Great [d. 604]); some, as a result of conciliar consensus (whether ecumenical, such as Nicaea [in 325], or local, such as the Spanish councils held in Toledo [e.g., in 400, 589, 633 and 681], Gerona [in 517], and Braga [e.g., in 563, 572, and 675][13]); others arose from Latin but not "Roman" practice (e.g., the *Expositio brevis antiquae liturgiae gallicanae* of Germanus of Paris [d. 576]); and still others from Roman and/or papal pronouncements (e.g., the letter of Pope Innocent to Decentius in 416, concerning the postbaptismal laying on of hands and chrismation; the letter of the Roman deacon John to Senarius, *ca.* 500).[14]

For anyone interested in the evolving history of the eucharistic *ordo* and its euchology in the Latin West, however, the sacramentaries are the sources that provide the preeminent documentation. Space does not permit a detailed narrative about how the sacramentaries developed, especially during the seventh

12. Both these Latin rules date from the first half of the sixth century, though the *Rule of the Master* is probably earlier (ca. 525) than the *Rule of Benedict* (*ca.* 540). For a summary discussion of liturgy in the *Rule of the Master*, see Adalbert de Vogüé, "Liturgy," in Luke Eberle and Charles Philippi, trans., *The Rule of the Master* (Kalamazoo, MI: Cistercian Publications, 1977), 26–42. For liturgical practice in the *Rule of Benedict*, see Nathan D. Mitchell, "The Liturgical Code in the Rule of Benedict," Appendix 3 in Timothy Fry, ed., *The Rule of St. Benedict in Latin and English* (Collegeville, MN: The Liturgical Press, 1981), 379–414.

13. For examples of the liturgical decisions reached by some of these councils (especially as regards Christian initiation), see Whitaker, *Documents of the Baptismal Liturgy*, 153–58.

14. As Cyrille Vogel observed, "the decretals of some of the early popes" should be added to the list of liturgical sources for this historical period, because "some of them are essential to any understanding of liturgical history" (*Medieval Liturgy*, 11). See the chronological list in Eligius Dekkcrs, *Clavis Putrum Lationrum,* Editio tertia, aucta et emendata, Corpus Christianorum, Series Latina (Streenbrugge: Abbatia Sancti Petri, 1995). Section VII, "Romanorum Pontificum Opuscula, Acta, Epistulae Genuinae ac Spuriae," nos. 1568–1744. It is important to recognize, however, that at this earlier stage of history, a pastoral decision by the bishop of Rome regarding a liturgical practice (e.g., Innocent's instructions about postbaptismal chrismation in his letter to Bishop Decentius of Gubbio) may well have been required for churches within the pope's ecclesiastical province, but did not necessarily constitute "universal" legislation obliging conformity from *all* Latin churches of the West. Thus, for instance, in spite of Innocent's letter (which appears to prohibit presbyters from performing the second, peculiarly Roman, postbaptismal anointing on the forehead with oil consecrated by the bishop), Gregory the Great allowed that "where bishops are absent, even presbyters ought to anoint the baptized with chrism on their foreheads" (trans. in Whitaker, *Documents of the Baptismal Liturgy*, 206). One is reminded, as well, of the difference between Milan and Rome over the matter of footwashing as part of the baptismal liturgy. Rome seems never to have had this custom, though Milan did, as Ambrose indicates in Book 3, ch. 5, of his *De sacramentis*: "We are aware that the Roman Church does not follow this custom [of footwashing], although . . . we follow her rite in everything. . . . I wish to follow the Roman Church in everything; but we too are not devoid of common sense. When a better custom is kept elsewhere, we are right to keep it here also" (trans. in Whitaker, *Documents of the Baptismal Liturgy*, 180).

and eighth centuries,[15] but the highlights of that history may be briefly summarized.

1. Most modern scholars agree that the complex liturgical book we call the sacramentary "did not appear at once in its developed form," but

> was preceded and prepared by the *libelli missarum* which were leaflets or small booklets, containing the *formulae* of one or more masses (prayers, preface, introductory formula for the *Hanc igitur* [of the "old Roman canon," now Eucharistic Prayer I]; they did not include the fixed Canon of the mass (whose history poses special problems all its own) or the readings and chants belonging to the other ministers.[16]

The *libelli* were "the link between [the earlier liturgical practice of] 'structured improvisation' and the fixed texts of later sacramentaries."[17] The *Sacramentarium Veronense* (hereafter *Veronense,* also called the Leonine Sacramentary because eighteenth-century scholars thought its contents came principally from Leo the Great) is "a private collection of Roman *libelli,* which before their compilation in this book, were collected and kept in the Lateran archives."[18] The manuscript of the *Veronense* dates from ca. 600–625. Some scholars view it as less a true sacramentary than a pastiche of texts compiled under private (rather than official) auspices, which was originally a papal book adapted for presbyteral use.[19] Notable, too, is the fact that the *Veronense* often provides multiple formulas for the same liturgical day (e.g., the Ascension). This is a clue that the presiding "celebrant had a wide selection to chose from," and that this sacramentary was

15. Good introductions, with references and bibliographies, may be found in the following: Vogel, *Medieval Liturgy*, 31–134; Jones, Wainwright, Yarnold, and Bradshaw, *The Study of Liturgy*, 264–85; Cassian Folsom, "The Liturgical Books of the Roman Rite," in Anscar J. Chupungco, ed., *Handbook for Liturgical Studies,* Vol. I: *Introduction to the Liturgy* (Collegeville, MN: The Liturgical Press, 1997), 245–54; Eric Palazzo, *A History of Liturgical Books from the Beginning to the Thirteenth Century*, trans. Madeleine Beaumont (Collegeville, MN: The Liturgical Press, 1998), 21–61. See also Eligius Dekkers, ed., *Clavis Patrum Latinorum*, 3rd ed. (1995), XII, "Sacramentaria," nos. 1897–1932.

16. Vogel, *Medieval Liturgy*, 37–38. As Vogel noted, one should not confuse these leaflets (*libelli*) containing (some or all of) the presidential prayers at Mass with the *libellus officialis,* a forerunner of the *rituale,* which the Fourth Council of Toledo (633) required every parish priest to possess, or with the *libellus ordinis* ("a ceremonial agenda"), or with the Mozarabic *libellus orationum* (containing prayers said at the Liturgy of the Hours). See ibid., 38. On the *libelli*, see also Folsom, "The Liturgical Books of the Roman Rite," 246–48; Palazzo, *A History of Liturgical Books*, 37–42.

17. Folsom, "The Liturgical Books of the Roman Rite," 246. On the history of the important transition from improved prayer to fixed formula, especially in celebrations of the Eucharist, see Allan Bouley, *From Freedom to Formula. The Evolution of the Eucharistic Prayer from Oral Improvisation to Written Texts,* Catholic University of America Studies in Christian Antiquity (Washington, DC: The Catholic University of America Press, 1981), especially 159–215.

18. Ibid. The manuscript of the *Veronense* appears to follow the civil calendar, but is incomplete, with the material for January through March (and part of April) missing.

19. Palazzo, *A History of Liturgical Books*, 40.

in fact a "liturgical resource book" rather than a canonically required set of texts.[20]

2. Several types of sacramentaries are to be found in the Latin West.[21] In addition to the earlier *Veronense,* there are, (a) the old Gelasian Sacramentary, whose manuscript (*Vaticanus reginensis latinus* 316) dates back to ca. 750 C.E. and whose core contents were Roman, as revised on Gallican soil;[22] (b) the Gelasian sacramentaries of the eighth century, most of which show the influence of monastic centers in Frankish territory; and (c) the Gregorian sacramentaries, whose most important manuscript (known as the *"Hadrianum,"* sent by Pope Hadrian I [d. 795] to Charlemagne [d. 814]) dates from ca. 811–812. While the old Gelasian Sacramentary appears to have been a presbyteral book, originally intended for use by a parish priest serving a Roman titular church,[23] the *Hadrianum* was a book designed "for the personal use of the pope, or his representatives, organized with a view toward the liturgical celebrations in the stational churches of Rome."[24] It had to be adapted and supplemented in order to meet the ordinary needs of parishes in Charlemagne's kingdom.[25]

3. In addition to these Roman or Romano-Frankish sacramentaries, other churches of the Latin West (in Italy, Gaul, Germany, Spain, and the British Isles) developed their own distinctive, non-Roman sacramentaries.[26]

4. The persistence of non-Roman, Latin liturgies in the West, as well as the coexistence of numerous forms of the sacramentary in eighth and ninth century Europe, reveal that during the first millennium what we now call "the Roman liturgy" had not yet gelled into a uniform, universally accepted, standard and official form. Textual variation remained the rule, even though an identifiable *ordo* (ritual shape and sequence) for the Roman eucharistic liturgy had certainly emerged.[27] Still, it is also clear that, even within Rome itself, two liturgical tradi-

20. Folsom, "The Liturgical Books of the Roman Rite," 246. For the *Veronense*'s texts for Ascension Day, see Leo Cunibert Mohlberg, ed., *Sacramentarium Veronense*, Rerum Ecclesiasticarum Documenta, series major, Fontes, I (Rome: Herder, 1956), nos. 169–186. One of these formulas (no. 186) eventually made its way into the *Missale Romanum*, as reformed after the Council of Trent and published in 1570.

21. For details, see Vogel, *Medieval Liturgy*, 61–134.

22. See Whitaker, *Documents of the Baptismal Liturgy*, 212.

23. Palazzo, *A History of Liturgical Books*, 45.

24. Folsom, "The Liturgical Books of the Roman Rite," 251.

25. When the *Hadrianum* arrived in Aachen, the Carolingian liturgists were dismayed to find that its Latin needed correcting, and that it seemed "incomplete" and in need of a supplement to meet the needs of parishes in that part of Europe. See Folsom, "The Liturgical Books of the Roman Rite," 253.

26. For details, see Vogel, *Medieval Liturgy*, 107–110. See also Gabriel Ramis, "Liturgical Books of the Non-Roman West," in Anscar J. Chupungco, ed., *Handbook for Liturgical Studies*, Vol. I: *Introduction to the Liturgy* (Collegeville, MN: The Liturgical Press, 1997), 315–327.

27. As Eric Palazzo observes, "It is in the Carolingian and particularly the Ottonian periods that the *Ordo Missae* developed in an important way; it contains all the prayers said by the

tions were developing side-by-side, one papal/episcopal (represented by the *Hadrianum*), the other presbyteral (represented, e.g., by the old Gelasian Sacramentary).[28]

5. Over the course of the first millennium, then, the eucharistic liturgy of the Roman Rite became a cultural and euchological hybrid. As Cyrille Vogel summarized:

> the Roman liturgy assimilated many older liturgical usages native to Gaul . . . and ended by producing a type of hybrid or mixed liturgy which may be termed Romano-Frankish. This is the liturgy we find preserved in the earliest surviving liturgical MSS, all of which were redacted in Frankish Gaul. This is also the liturgy which was explained and commented upon by such prominent figures as Walafrid Strabo (d. 849), Amalarius of Metz (d. 850/851) and Rabanus Maurus (d. 856) and which was definitively regulated—as regards the Eucharist—by St. Benedict of Aniane (d. 821) in the corrected *Hadrianum* and its famous *Supplement* . . .
>
> In a second stage of its evolution, this mixed liturgy spread with surprising but understandable speed to all the churches of Northern Europe and, after the *Renovatio imperii* (962), established itself without difficulty at Rome under the patronage of the Ottonian emperors.[29]

As we will see in part 3 of this introduction, such an evolution continued during the second millennium, particularly in the thirteenth and fourteenth centuries. It was then, with the rise of the mendicant orders, that the Romano-Frankish liturgy—especially as it was celebrated at the papal court—became the Romano-Frankish-Franciscan liturgy. The entire process that shaped the liturgical usage we now call the Roman Rite

> was one of osmosis, amalgamation, and hybridization; liturgies were never simply substituted for one another; they influenced and modified one another, and even the dominant Roman liturgy issued from the process changed and enhanced. As Theodor Klauser says so well: *Romana est sed etiam nostra.* "The Liturgy which is performed by us today, is therefore, truly Roman, but it is at the same time also our own."[30]

---

priest during Mass, in general before the Eucharistic Prayer;" still there were significant variables, and "the study of the *Ordo Missae* often uncovers the liturgical geography proper to a specific sacramentary, demonstrating liturgical exchanges between important monasteries [where most manuscripts were copied], as happened in the course of the ninth and tenth centuries." *A History of Liturgical Books*, 24.

28. Folsom, "The Liturgical Books of the Roman Rite," 249.

29. Vogel, *Medieval Liturgy*, 2.

30. Ibid., 3. Vogel is citing Klauser's *A Short History of the Western Liturgy* (New York: Oxford University Press, 1982), 84.

6. Most of the sources mentioned thus far, particularly the sacramentaries, provided presider's prayers for the celebration of the Eucharist and often included a text for the Eucharistic Prayer (the Roman Canon). Yet these documents provided little by way of rubrics, descriptions, or directives for the proper performance of the rites. Thus, for instance, within a series of presidential prayers "*per dominicis diebus* [*sic*]," the old Gelasian Sacramentary (*Vaticanus reginensis latinus* 316) provides a text of the Roman Canon, but accompanies it with very few ritual details.[31] Twice, the word "*respondetur*" is placed before the people's responses in the preface dialogue,[32] and there are crosses (probably indicating the place where the presider should sign the elements, prior to the consecration).[33] In the same document, after the Lord's Prayer and its embolism, a rubric directs: "*Post haec communicat sacerdos cum ordinibus sacris cum omni populo.*"[34] But again, precisely *how* this communion rite is to be conducted is left to the reader's imagination.

7. The reason why rubrical directives are omitted is fairly simple. The sacramentary was not intended to be a *rituale.* "How-to" procedures were, for the most part, confined to three other categories of Western liturgical books, viz., the *ordines,* the ordinals and the ceremonials. "Strictly speaking," writes Cyrille Vogel, "an *ordo* is a description of a liturgical action *(actio liturgica),* a directory or guide for the celebrant and his ministers setting forth in detail the arrangement of the entire ritual procedure and how to carry it out."[35]

The *Ordines Romani,* fifty of which were edited by Michel Andrieu between 1931 and 1961, began to appear in the middle of the seventh century.[36] Like the sacramentaries, these *ordines* are hybrids; thus, like the sacramentaries, "the oldest collections of *ordines,* even those of purely Roman origin are all of Frankish or Germanic composition."[37] As liturgical documents, the *ordines* "permit us to witness a liturgy as it was actually celebrated" at the time when the work was drawn up.[38] Thus, for example, *Ordo Romanus I* (*OR I,* first analyzed in the late seventeenth century by the Benedictine scholar, Jean Mabillon [d. 1707]) provides "the first full description of Eucharistic worship at Rome" and contains

31. L. Cunibert Mohlberg, ed., *Liber sacramentorum Romanae aeclesiae ordinis anni circuli,* Rerum ecclesiasticarum documenta, Series maior, Fontes, IV (Rome: Herder, 1960), nos. 1242–1255.

32. Ibid., no. 1242.

33. Ibid., no. 1244.

34. Ibid., no. 1260.

35. Vogel, *Medieval Liturgy,* 135. The use of the word "ordo" for a description of a liturgical rite appears to have become common "sometime after Gregory the Great (d. 604), i.e., after the period of liturgical improvisation was over. It does not seem to have been much used before the VIII century." Ibid.

36. Michel Andrieu, *Les Ordines romani du haut moyen âge,* 5 vols., Spicilegium Sacrum Lovaniense 11, 23, 24, 28, 29 (Louvain, 1960).

37. Vogel, *Medieval Liturgy,* 145.

38. Ibid.

not only our oldest ritual description of a solemn papal Mass, but details about the "major structures of the Roman Church and its internal organization: the seven ecclesiastical precincts of the City, the *tituli*, the deaconries, the *episcopium* or *partriarchium Laternanense*, the stational liturgies, the precedence among the various dignitaries and a description of the papal cavalcade."[39] Here, for example, is a portion of *OR I*'s very detailed description of the ritual for the preparation of the gifts:

> Then as the deacon goes to the altar, an acolyte comes with a chalice and a corporal over (it), raises the chalice in his left hand and hands the corporal to the deacon. He takes it off the chalice and lays it on the right side of the altar, throwing the other end to the second deacon so that they can spread it out . . .
>
> The pope, after saying *Let us pray*, goes down at once to the senatorial area, the chancellor holding his right hand and the chief counselor his left, and receives the offerings of the princes in the order of their authorities. After him the archdeacon receives the flasks and pours them into a larger chalice held by the district subdeacon. He is followed by an acolyte with a bowl outside his cope into which the chalice is poured out when it is full. The district subdeacon receives the offerings from the pope and hands them to the subdeacon in attendance, and he puts them in a linen cloth held by two acolytes. After the pope, a hebdomadary bishop receives the rest of the offerings, so that he may put them with his own hand in the linen cloth which follows him. After him the deacon who follows the archdeacon receives (the flasks) and pours them into the bowl with his own hand.[40]

Similarly, *OR XI* provides us with a Roman directory for celebrating the liturgies of Christian initiation, including rites for the Lenten scrutinies and a full baptismal ceremony celebrated during the Easter Vigil.[41]

The *Ordines Romani* are clearly one of the principal forebears of the *IGMR*, but two other categories of "how-to" books aimed at the "good ordering of the liturgy" are also worth mentioning, viz., the ordinals and ceremonials. While *ordines* tend to confine their content to a description of one particular liturgical rite (e.g., Christian initiation, a papal Mass), ordinals typically describe "the entire course of the liturgical year, with the intention of establishing a certain uniform usage," but "because the ordinal is concerned with local and not universal custom, there

39. Ibid., 155.

40. The English translation is taken from R.C.D. Jasper and G.J. Cuming, eds., *Prayers of the Eucharist Early and Reformed*, 2nd ed. (New York: Oxford University Press, 1980), 125–26. In the Latin edition of Andrieu (*Les Ordines romani du haut moyen âge*), the text of *OR I* is found in Vol. 2 (1948), 74–108.

41. Ibid., 164–66. See also Whitaker, *Documents of the Baptismal Liturgy*, 244–51. Since our knowledge of *OR XI* comes from ninth century manuscripts that were produced in France, it is not completely clear how much of this baptismal liturgy represents Roman (rather than Frankish) practice.

is no standard collection of texts comparable to Andrieu's edition of the Ordines."[42] For example, monastic ordinals—such as the *Monastic Constitutions of Lanfranc* or the *Ordinary of the Royal Abbey of St.-Denis*—usually provided descriptions for both the Hours and Mass, plus other rites specific to the communities for which they were written.[43] But especially notable, "because of its influence on the Roman rite," was the ordinal composed by the Franciscan Haymo of Faversham (d. 1244) in 1243–44; "Haymo wrote both an *Ordo breviarii* and an *Ordo missalis;* when both were issued together the document was called *Ordinarium secundum consuetudinem Romanae curiae.*"[44] Haymo's work thus contributed enormously to the consolidation of the medieval Roman Rite (the papal liturgy of the Roman Curia) and to the creation of a ritual pattern that would shape the development of the modern Roman Rite.[45]

Finally, ceremonials were books that described "with greater precision than the ordinal," the ritual customs and practices of a community "throughout the liturgical year."[46] Though the roots of the ceremonial are medieval, it became far more conspicuous as a book aimed at the "good ordering of the liturgy" during the early Renaissance, when two important papal ceremonials were produced: the *Caeremoniale Romanum* of Peter Burgos, who served Nicholas V (d. 1455) as papal Master of Ceremonies (1447–1455), and the *De caeremoniis Curiae Romanae libri tres* (1485) of Agostino Patrizi Piccolomini and John Burckard (sometimes spelled Burckhard, d. 1506).[47] It was Burckard's treatise on the *Ordo Missae* that served as one of the chief sources for the eucharistic rite found in the *Missale Romanum* of 1570 (the so-called "Pian" or "Tridentine" missal, hereafter *MR1570*).[48]

Neither the sacramentaries (with their presidential prayer texts) nor the *ordines,* ordinals, and ceremonials (with their rubrics and ritual descriptions) claimed to establish a definitive *Ordo Missae* that was obligatory for all churches of the Roman Rite in the Latin West. Nor did these documents attempt to provide a pastoral-theological commentary on the rites. Their purpose was descrip-

42. Folsom, "The Liturgical Books of the Roman Rite," 292–93.

43. See *The Monastic Constitutions of Lanfranc,* rev. ed., by Christopher N. L. Brooke (Oxford: Clarendon Press, 2002); Edward B. Foley, *The First Ordinary of the Royal Abbey of St.-Denis in France: Paris, Bibliothèque Mazarine 526,* Spicilegium Friburgense, 32 (Fribourg: University Press, 1990).

44. Folsom, "The Liturgical Books of the Roman Rite," 294.

45. See Stephen J. P. van Dijk, *The Sources of the Modern Roman Liturgy,* Studia et Documenta Franciscana, 1–2 (Leiden: Brill, 1963), Vol. 1, 1–109; 156–206; Vol. 2, 1–331 (along with the introduction).

46. Folsom, "The Liturgical Books of the Roman Rite," 295. Folsom suggests that the ceremonials originated during the twelfth and thirteenth centuries, when the need arose, especially within the Roman curia, for "writing down the rubrics for the complicated ceremonies and court etiquette of papal functions."

47. Ibid., 296.

48. For the text of Burckard's *Ordo,* see J. Wickham Legg, ed., *Tracts on the Mass,* Henry Bradshaw Society, Vol. 27 (London: Harrison and Sons, 1904), 120–78.

tive rather than prescriptive; exemplary rather than obligatory. It was understood, for instance, that a papal rite such as the one outlined in *OR I* would need to be tweaked and adjusted, perhaps quite significantly, if Mass were being celebrated by another bishop or by a presbyter serving a parish. But it is also clear that, during the second millennium, ritual *ordines* once considered authoritative "models" or *exempla* gradually came to be seen as juridically obligatory and canonical. Thus, before proceeding in Part III to a discussion of the immediate predecessors of *IGMR*, some remarks must be made about how and why this fateful shift from authoritative *exemplum* to obligatory *ordo* occurred.

The Drive Toward Liturgical Uniformity in the Latin West

In the second part of this essay we seek to show how the ideal of a single, invariable, uniform Roman Rite, obligatory for virtually all churches in the Latin West, arose.

For most of the first millennium, the person responsible for overseeing ritual matters in a local church was the chief liturgist of the diocese, the bishop. Even the Roman bishop was reluctant to impose liturgical uniformity, preferring instead to respect the distinctive ritual practices of diverse peoples and cultures, as we learn from Bede's (d. 735) report of Gregory the Great's responses to Augustine of Canterbury (d. ca. 605).[49] Scholars have long assumed that these arrangements began to change after the election in 1073 of the reform-minded pope, Gregory VII (d. 1085), for it is at this point in history that we seem to encounter the first systematic papal program to establish a uniform liturgical "rite" for all Christians of the Latin West.[50] Indeed, in *Quod a nobis* (9 July 1568), his introductory decree to the Roman breviary as reformed after the Council of Trent (1545–63), Pope Pius V (d. 1572) cited Gregory VII as responsible for restoring the *"divini officii formula"* originally "established, wisely, by the supreme pontiffs Gelasius I and Gregory I."[51] The implication is that Gregory VII

49. See Bede, *A History of the English Church and People*, Book 1, ch. 27.

50. In view of his later emphasis on legal precedent, Gregory's own election to the papacy was, ironically, irregular, for it failed to meet the conditions that had been drawn up under Nicholas II in 1059. See Colin Morris, *The Papal Monarchy: The Western Church from 1050 to 1250* (Oxford: Clarendon Press, 1989), 109.

51. *"Quae divini officii formula pie olim ac sapienter a summis pontificibus, praesertim Gelasio ac Gregorio primis constituta, a Gregorio autem septimo reformata."* For text, see Reinhard Elze, "Gregor VII. und die Römische Liturgie," *Studi Gregoriani*, XIII (1989): 179, n. 3. Elze notes (ibid., 180) that Gregory VII's reputation as a liturgical reformer may owe a great deal to the work of Bernold of Constance, whose liturgical treatise, *Micrologus de ecclesiasticis observationibus*, was described by its modern editor, V. L. Kennedy, as "probably the best of the many medieval commentaries on the liturgy." See V. L. Kennedy, "For a new edition of the *Micrologus* of Bernold of Constance," in *Mélanges en l'honneur de Mgr. M. Andrieu*, Revue de sciences religieuses, volume hors série (Strassbourg: University Press, 1956), 229–41; here, 229. Elze seems to be unaware that Kennedy died (in 1974) before this edition of the *Micrologus* could be

had devised a single ritual schema for the Hours by restoring an ancient and uniform Roman Rite for use throughout the Latin West.[52]

But is the portrait of Gregory VII as a liturgical reformer reliable? Our historical outline in part 1 shows how diverse and hybridized the eleventh century liturgies Gregory knew actually were.[53] In the first century of the second millennium, the Roman liturgy was in fact a multicultural amalgam of diverse usages, many from north of the Alps, imported into the city of Rome by the Ottonian emperors during the mid- to late-tenth century.[54] It is probably true that "for Gregory the usage of the Roman church was to be the standard for universal imitation following a liturgical conservatism that sought to exclude what was not ancient and to promote what was believed to be the usage of Pope Gregory the Great." At the same time it seems "Gregory was content to leave the worship of the Roman churches little disturbed, while he enunciated traditional principles that may have been congenial to many clergy and laity."[55] So while Gregory may well have wished to purge the late-eleventh-century liturgy in Rome of "accretions of foreign . . . especially German, traditions," his approach to the task appears to have been gradual and "piecemeal."[56] Moreover, because the pope's pastoral responsibilities included "an ancient round of worship which was by no means confined to the Lateran but which included the other great basilicas and the stational churches of Rome," Gregory would have found it necessary to accommodate himself to "a complex of rites and customs . . . cherished and guarded" in Rome's numerous urban and suburban

completed. See Vogel, *Medieval Liturgy*, 28, n. 22. On the limitations of Bernold's understanding of what he may have experienced in Rome, see Stephen van Dijk and Joan Hazelden Walker, *The Origins of the Modern Roman Liturgy* (Westminster, MD: The Newman Press, 1960), 49–50, 74, 248–49.

52. For more on Gregory VII's "reform" of the "Roman" office, see Elze, "Gregor VII. und die Römische Liturgie," 181–82.

53. See H. E. J. Cowdrey, "Pope Gregory VII (1073–85) and the Liturgy," *Journal of Theological Studies* 55, no. 1 (April 2004): 55–83. Cowdrey observes that in Gregory's time, "at Rome itself no less than elsewhere in Latin Christendom, there was a wide and consciously sustained difference of observances amongst different churches of the city" (ibid., 56). Cowdrey goes on to quote a letter written in 1131 by Peter Abelard (d. 1142) to Bernard of Clairvaux (d. 1153) in which the writer remarked that "not even the very City [of Rome] holds to the ancient custom of the Roman see, but only the Lateran church, which is the mother of all, holds to the ancient office; none of its daughters follows it in this respect—not even the very basilica of the Roman palace" (cited in ibid., 57). Cowdrey notes that Abelard's comments "would also have applied in the previous century" (ibid., 56). "The separation of the papal household and the Lateran basilica gave rise to a gathering duality of observance which, in the thirteenth century, under Franciscan influence, led to the liturgy of the papal court's becoming the general standard for the Western Church" (ibid., 57).

54. The Mainz Pontifical (the so-called "Romano-Germanic Pontifical," ca. 950) was established at Rome under Otto I in the mid-tenth century. Despite its provenance, this book came to be regarded as an *Ordo Romanus*. See Vogel, *Medieval Liturgy*, 238–39.

55. H. E. J. Cowdrey, *Pope Gregory VII: 1070–1085* (Oxford: Clarendon Press, 1998), 320.

56. Ibid.

churches. To this must be added the fact that the sixty or so "central Italian bishoprics . . . directly subject to the bishop of Rome as head of what is sometimes called . . . the Roman church province," also had their own distinct liturgical "traditions and loyalties" which "it would be unwise lightly to offend."[57] Any initiatives toward ritual reform or restoration which Gregory VII might have launched had to take into account a city and an ecclesiastical province where liturgical diversity was the norm rather than the exception.

Historian H. E. J. Cowdrey has thus concluded that the "parameters within which liturgical changes might be introduced in late eleventh-century Rome" were rather narrow.[58] It is true that Bernold (Bernhold) of Constance (d. 1100), who attended a Lenten synod in Rome in 1079, wrote his treatise *Micrologus de ecclesiasticis observationibus* to help "propagate Roman customs and observances in all matters of liturgy," especially the *Ordo Missae,* and that he portrays Gregory VII as a restorer of the ancient Roman customs.[59] Yet Bernold himself was "well aware of the extent and tenacity of other conventions at Rome and elsewhere," and he seems to have had "some appreciation of the reasons for them."[60]

While a careful examination of sources reveals that Gregory VII did promote (or permit) liturgical changes in several areas—e.g., the structure and content of the Liturgy of the Hours, the principal liturgical seasons (e.g., Lent, Eastertide, Pentecost), the commemoration of saints, the offerings to be made by all participants at Mass—his instincts were deeply conservative.[61] There is good reason to believe that Gregory saw himself as a liturgical reformer or restorer strictly in terms of the profession that popes of his time made prior to entering office. In words addressed to St. Peter, each of them promised "to diminish or to change nothing of what I have found to be handed down and preserved by my most approved predecessors and to admit no novelty; but fervently as their true disciple and follower with every endeavour of my mind to conserve and venerate whatever I find to be canonically handed down."[62] Given his commitment to these ideals, it is easy to understand why Gregory VII's contemporaries looked, increasingly, "to the apostolic see in liturgical matters in order to establish both the authentic legacy of the ancient past and, in the light of it, the best practice of the present."[63]

The central concern of Gregory VII's "liturgical reform" was thus to preserve and safeguard what he regarded as the ancient patrimony of his papal

57. Cowdrey, "Pope Gregory VII and the Liturgy," 58.

58. Ibid., 61. See also n. 50 above.

59. Elze, "Gregor VII. und die Römische Liturgie," 180–81.

60. Cowdrey, "Pope Gregory VII and the Liturgy," 62.

61. For an excellent summary of the sources and subjects of Gregory's liturgical work, see Cowdrey, "Pope Gregory VII and the Liturgy," 61–78.

62. For the formula of this papal profession, see Hans Foerster, ed., *Liber diurnus Romanorum pontificum* (Berne: Francke, 1958), 429–31.

63. Cowdrey, "Pope Gregory VII and the Liturgy," 74–75.

predecessors "by pruning away the results of latter-day and extraneous intervention by foreign rulers and influences."[64] Within the city of Rome, as we have seen, Gregory used caution in introducing change; outside the city and its ecclesiastical province, Gregory seems to have been a more vigorous advocate of conformity to Roman usage. "Within Latin Christendom, wherever Gregory regarded a regional liturgy as seriously deviant from Roman usage in character and language . . . he was liable to proceed against it with resolution and vigour."[65] While there is no clear evidence that Gregory sought to repress other ancient liturgies in Italy (e.g., those of Milan and Benevento), such is not the case when we turn to Spain and the Mozarabic rite.

Early in his papacy, Gregory VII began seeking ways to integrate Spain more fully into the rest of medieval Europe. This was done, in part, through the suppression of the liturgical rival of the ancient, indigenous liturgy of the Spanish churches, especially that of Toledo (which the pope called "*superstitio toletana*").[66] Gregory's initiative met stiff resistance. Especially controversial was his claim, in a letter of 28 June 1077, that "the kingdom of Spain belongs to St. Peter and the Holy Roman Church, as handed down in ancient grants."[67] This would have meant that Spanish kings were papal vassals, required to pay annual tribute. King Alphonso VI of León-Castile (d. 1109) did capitulate to Gregory's will in the matter of liturgy, but even after the Mozarabic rite was "suppressed," it persisted.[68]

64. Ibid., 71.

65. Ibid., 78. In contrast, Gregory's dealings with the Greek church of Constantinople, as well as with the Armenians, was largely irenic and accommodating. He "nowhere suggested that the Greek liturgy was radically objectionable, let alone that it was heretical and should therefore be abandoned," although he did accuse the Greeks of presumption (*temeritas*) because they had objected to the Armenians' use of unleavened bread in the Eucharist (ibid., 80).

66. See Joseph F. O'Callaghan, "The Integration of Christian Spain into Europe: The Role of Alfonso VI of León-Castile," in Bernard F. Reilly, *Santiago, Saint-Denis, and Saint Peter: The Reception of the Roman Liturgy in León-Castile in 1080* (New York: Fordham University Press, 1985), 101–20. See also, in the same volume, Ramón Gonzálvez, "The Persistence of the Mozarabic Liturgy in Toledo after A.D. 1080," 157–85. (See Gonzálvez, 163, for the phrase "*superstitio toletana*.") It should be remembered that at this time Spain was not yet a single, unified nation, but rather a collection of separate kingdoms. Catalonia and Aragón, as O'Callaghan notes, had already adopted the Roman liturgy prior to the election of Gregory VII in 1073. León-Castile held out longer against Roman pressure to conform. It should be pointed out that Gregory made similar moves against his "Slavonic competitors" by categorically refusing the petition of Duke Wratislav II of Bohemia to "permit performance of divine service . . . in the Slav tongue," arguing that God had left parts of the Bible obscure lest, "if it were clear to all," it might be misunderstood and so lead the simple astray. See Cowdrey, "Pope Gregory VII and the Liturgy," 79.

67. A partial English translation of Gregory's "pastoral letter to the rulers of Spain" may be found in Ephraim Emerton, trans. and ed., *The Correspondence of Pope Gregory VII* (New York: Norton, 1969), 123–125. The quotation is from Emerton's translation. Emerton provides the appropriate reference to Gregory's Latin letters in the *Registrum* on p. 123. The sources on which Gregory's claims to legal authority over Spain were based are in fact largely spurious.

68. See O'Callaghan, "The Integration of Christian Spain," 107.

What was novel about Gregory VII's approach to the liturgy in Spain (and in Slavic territories) was his attempt to extend Roman (i.e., papal) authority over worship in local churches outside the ecclesiastical province of Rome by transforming questions of liturgical custom or practice into matters of legal precedent (based on his argument that the kingdom of Spain belonged to the patrimony of Peter).[69] Although much of the Iberian peninsula had been under Islamic control for centuries, Gregory argued that it was now high time to restore the "tribute *[servitium]* formerly paid to St. Peter [but] so long . . . withheld from us on account of their [i.e., the Islamic rulers'] lack of faith and their tyranny."[70]

There can be little doubt that the Gregorian reform of worship in the Latin West cast a long shadow. Two crucial consequences for liturgy flowed from that reform:

1. First, Gregory VII's effort to suppress the Mozarabic rite helped redefine the complex relations between doxology, doctrine, liturgy, and law. The Gregorian reform began to reinterpret the liturgical *Ordo Romanus* as obligatory legal precedent. Increasingly, liturgical liceity and doctrinal orthodoxy meant conformity, at least in the Latin West, with the liturgical customs of neither the Roman *tituli* nor the "mother church" (St. John Lateran), but of the papal household, whose liturgy was in fact a multicultural amalgam codified largely in transalpine books such as the *Romano-Germanic Pontifical*, brought to Rome under imperial, rather than papal, auspices.

69. Ramón Gonzálvez ("The Persistence of the Mozarabic Liturgy," 159–63) argues that the Gregorian Reform was based on three legal and dogmatic principles. The first of these was "the proprietary right of the Holy See over the 'realm' of Spain" (159); the second was the pope's insistence that any deviation from the "Roman Rite" meant deviation from "right (i.e., correct) doctrine" (160–61); the third flowed from Gregory's conviction that no local church has autonomy in matters liturgical, and hence that a difference in *rite* is tantamount to *schism* (161–62). A local Latin church with its own "rite" would become, in a quasi-legal manner, a schismatic church. Yet curiously, Gregory seems not have applied these same principles to the indigenous rites of Milan or Benevento.

70. Gregory VII, "Pastoral Letter to the Rulers of Spain," in Emerton, *The Correspondence of Pope Gregory VII*, 124. History reveals that the deeds and charters Gregory used to support his claim of sovereignty over Spain are largely spurious. The use of such forgeries to support papal claims prompted Cardinal Yves Congar, the Dominican ecclesiologist and peritus at the Second Vatican Council, to conclude that the eleventh century was "the great turning point in ecclesiology." For by seeking to eradicate simony, nepotism, clerical concubinage, lay investiture, and a host of other pastoral problems through an appeal to legal precedent, Gregory VII wound up, in Congar's words, "making the Church itself into a legal institution" rather than a spiritual *communio*. See Bernard Lauret, ed., *Fifty Years of Catholic Theology: Conversations with Yves Congar* (Philadelphia: Fortress Press, 1988), 40 and 42. Gregory's action, Congar claimed, led the church "to adopt very much the same attitudes as the temporal power itself, to conceive of itself as a society, as a power, when in reality it is a communion, with ministers, servants" (ibid., 42). Paradoxically (and probably unintentionally), the Gregorian reform thus resulted in a massive secularization of the Petrine ministry and the ecclesiology of *communio* that was intended to support it.

2. Second, the Gregorian reform held that the "Roman Rite" creates a legal and doctrinal *norma non normata* from which there can be neither variance nor appeal, and hence, any deviation from the Roman liturgy constitutes a virtual deviation from dogma (and so is tantamount to heresy). To employ any other rite in the liturgy is to risk heterodoxy—or, at the very least, schismatic idiosyncrasy. A local church choosing to follow its own native rite would in effect be choosing schism. Yet, as we have seen, Gregory VII himself seems to have regarded the Milanese rite, for example, as unobjectionable, and Gregory's own predecessors had approved the Mozarabic rite.[71]

The results of the Gregorian reform were thus ambivalent. In dealing with Milan and Benevento, Gregory VII appeared to reaffirm the ancient tradition of local liturgical autonomy and regional variation in the Latin West; in dealing with Spain (and the Slavs), he seemed to claim a legal basis *(in jus et proprietatem)*[72] for insisting on adherence to the *Ordo Romanus* and for denying liturgical autonomy or variation.

More important, however, was the way the Gregorian liturgical reform was later interpreted in the West. "Since the later sixteenth century the prevailing view has been that the pontificate of Gregory VII represents a new departure in the liturgical history of the Western Church."[73] Intentionally or not, Gregory's claims against Spain put into play a principle which held that the Roman Rite enjoys preemptive legal status that undercuts the liceity and legitimacy of any other liturgy in the Latin West. That is why, as noted above, Pope Pius V could preface his publication of the reformed Roman Breviary of 1568 with the claim that Gregory VII was the great "restorer" of Roman liturgical order. Gregory's actions "implied a rejection of unwarranted imperial and royal intervention in spiritual matters and a vindication of papal authority according to the model of the ancient church as Gregory conceived it"; they also "announced the end of 'Franco-German' leadership and the unification of the Christian order under papal headship."[74] As a result of the Gregorian reform, exclusive papal authority over liturgy in the Latin West had been boldly asserted as a matter of law,

71. Gonzálvez, "The Persistence of the Mozarabic Liturgy," 163. In 1080, the Spanish Council of Burgos capitulated to papal pressure and made the "Roman Rite" the official liturgy for all of Spain. As Gonzálvez (164–65) notes, the decisions of Burgos may have made a difference to the *northern* Spanish kingdoms, but probably had little impact on "the other half of Spain, in which the Mozarabs constituted a sizable Christian minority" and where "the mandate of Rome and the decree of Burgos were simply ignored. The Mozarab communities simply continued in the peaceful possession of their particular liturgy . . . Moreover, none of the kings and bishops of the northern peninsula, to whom Rome had peremptorily directed a change of ritual, made the least gesture of instituting liturgical reform beyond the area in which they exercised jurisdiction." Since the Second Vatican Council, a modern version of the ancient Mozarabic liturgy has been prepared and approved. See *Missale hispano-mozarabicum*, 2 vols. (Barcelona: Conferencia Episcopal Espanola, 1991–1994).

72. See Cowdrey, "Pope Gregory VII and the Liturgy," 78 (and n. 83).

73. Ibid., 81.

74. Ibid., 83.

if not everywhere established as a matter of fact. In principle, at least, the Roman church's legal right to insist on liturgical uniformity—even outside its ecclesiastical province—had been set in motion.

The Evolution of *IGMR*

Remote Ancestors of IGMR

To assert a legal right is one thing; to implement it, quite another. Despite the increasing influence of the "Roman liturgy" (the *ordo* of the papal court as reorganized in the mid-thirteenth century[75]), diversity and local variation (in matters of calendar, liturgical custom, and ritual detail) continued to characterize public worship in Latin churches of the medieval West. Even within a relatively small country such as England, multiple usages abounded, as Thomas Cranmer (d. 1556) famously complained in the preface to the 1549 *Book of Common Prayer:* "Heretofore, there hath been great diuersitie in saying and synging in churches within this realm: some folowyng Salsbury use, some Herford use, some the use of Bangor, some of Yorke, and some of Lincolne: now from he[n]cefurth, all the whole realme shall haue but one use."[76] The quote reveals that in the mid-sixteenth century a Reformer (like Cranmer) and a pope (like Pius V) could, for perhaps very different reasons, subscribe to a common goal of liturgical uniformity.[77]

The technology of printing made achievement of this goal feasible. As our discussion in part 1 shows, the sacramentaries (containing the presider's prayers at Mass) were of several different types; moreover, they circulated as manuscripts and hence were open to tampering, revision, and scribal error. Much the same situation obtained in the era when "missals" (containing not only the presider's prayers, but also the readings and chants assigned to the eucharistic liturgy for each day) began to replace the sacramentary as the "presider's

75. It is important to note that even in the latter part of the thirteenth century the "Roman liturgy" was not yet one single, uniform rite. By 1275, "the city of Rome knew four liturgical customs: the papal court, St. Peter's in the Vatican, the reform of Cardinal Orsini (later Pope Nicholas III), and the Lateran Basilica." Folsom, "The Liturgical Books of the Roman Rite," 265. The liturgy of the papal court—including its "missal"—was revised and reorganized under the direction of the Franciscan minister general, Haymo of Faversham, in 1243–44. See ibid., 266.

76. *The First and Second Prayer Books of King Edward VI*, Everyman's Library no. 448 (New York: Dutton, 1910), 4.

77. In the same preface, Cranmer appeals to the ancient notion of episcopal authority over the liturgy: "And forsomuche as nothyng can, almoste, be so plainly set furth, but doutes maie rise in the use and practisying of the same: to appease all suche diuersitie (if any arise), and for the resolucion of all doubtes, concernyng the maner how to understande, do, and execute the thynges conteygned in this booke: the parties that so doubt, or diuersely take any thyng, shall always resorte to the Bishop of the Diocese, who by his discrecion shall take order for the quietying and appeasyng of the same: so that the same ordre be not contrary to any thng conteigned in this boke. " Ibid., 5.

book."[78] In 1474, the first printed version *(editio princeps)* of the *Missale Romanum (MR1474)* appeared at Milan.[79] Predictably, it contains an *"ordinarium Misse [sic]"* that begins with the "prayers at (the foot of) the altar" (*"Introibo ad altare dei,"* etc.) and concludes with the prayer *"Placeat tibi sancta trinitas,"* to be said after the presider has given the (final) blessing at the end of Mass.[80] In between are most of the texts and prayers for the *Ordo Missae* which anyone familiar with the later *MR1570* will find familiar, though some elements (e.g., the *Kyrie*) are missing. Prayers for the "offertory" (now replaced by the *praeparatio donorum,* "preparation of the gifts") are provided (e.g., *"Suscipe, sancte pater,"* which accompanies the priest's offering of the host; and *"Deus, qui humane substantie,"* which accompanies the act of mixing water into the wine, etc.). Also included is a text of the old Roman canon (the basis of today's Eucharistic Prayer I), with variable prefaces and, where applicable, proper *communicantes* (EP I: "In union with the whole church") and *hanc igitur* (EP I: "Father, accept this offering").[81] The Lord's Prayer and its embolism follow the doxology of the Eucharistic Prayer, and the *Agnus Dei* accompanies the fraction rite.[82]

Yet the printed *MR1474* provides few "how to" details or rubrics for the eucharistic liturgy. It contains neither a *ritus servandus* (included, a century later, as part of the "front matter" in *MR1570*), nor interpretive pastoral or catechetical notes on the *Ordo Missae,* in the manner, for instance, of the late-medieval *Lay Folk's Mass Book.*[83] This is somewhat surprising, since earlier medieval *ordines*—including Haymo of Faversham's mid-thirteenth-century *Indutus planeta* (an *Ordo Missae* that draws heavily upon the papal liturgies, though it was composed for the ordained Franciscans) contain a generous amount of ritual

78. As Cyrille Vogel (*Medieval Liturgy,* 105) remarks, "Even by the end of the IX century, the *Liber sacramentorum* was giving way before the *Missalis plenarius,* a new kind of volume made up of four previous types of liturgical books: sacramentary, epistolary, evangelary and antiphonary. By the second half of the IX century, the plenary missals were already beginning to be more numerous than the sacramentaries. In the first half of the XII century, the sacramentaries were a small minority, in the XIII they were exceptional and in the XIV, they were archaic leftovers." For a succinct summary of how the missal evolved as the principal book connected with celebration of the Roman Eucharist, see Palazzo, *A History of Liturgical Books,* 107–110. See also Folsom, "The Liturgical Books of the Roman Rite," 262–67.

79. See Robert Lippe, ed., *Missale Romanum Mediolani, 1474,* 2 vols., Henry Bradshaw Society, vols. 17 and 33 (London: Harrison and Sons, 1899). The text of the *Missale* is in Vol. 1 (HBS vol. 17). In the quotations from this printed missal, I follow the conventions of the text, even when this departs from more traditional Latin spellings. Note that in the second volume of this work (HBS 33), Lippe collates the text of *MR1474* with other printed editions of the *Missale Romanum* that appeared prior to the Pian Missal of 1570 (*MR1570*).

80. Ibid., Vol. 1, 198–211.

81. Ibid., Vol. 1, 200–201 ("offertory prayers"), 202–209 (Eucharistic Prayer, with proper prefaces and variables).

82. Ibid., Vol. 1, 209.

83. See Thomas F. Simmons, ed., *The Lay Folks Mass Book,* Early English Text Society, no. 71 (London: Oxford University Press, 1879; reprinted, 1968), 2–60.

and rubrical detail. Here, for example, is how the presider's initial approach to the altar is described in Haymo's *ordo*:

> *Indutus planeta sacerdos stet ante gradum altaris et, iunctis manibus mediocriter elevatis, dicit ant.* Introibo ad altare Dei . . .
>
> *Deinde facit confessionem absolute, inclinatus mediocriter. Et stat taliter inclinatus donec responsum fuerit* Misereatur tui, *etc., et tunc erigens, se facit absolutionem. Qua facta dicit* V. Deus tu conversus . . . [and the other versicles and responses up to the prayer] Aufer a nobis et cetera. *Et dicitur hec oratio aliquantulum alte, dum ascendit sacerdos ad altare . . .*
>
> *Postea inclinatus coram medio altaris, iunctis manibus, dicit sub silentio hanc orationem.* Oramus te domine . . . per merita omnium sanctorum tuorum *et cetera. Qua completa, erigit se et manus super altare deponens osculatur illud.*[84]

Indutus planeta gives us rather precise details about the presider's vesture, posture, hand positions, and movements as the Mass liturgy begins. But *MR1474,* while it follows the basic pattern of Haymo's *ordo,* omits many ritual specifics. Thus, while Haymo's text reads, *"Indutus planeta sacerdos stet ante gradum altaris et iunctis manibus mediocriter elevatis . . . ,"* *MR1474* says merely, *"Paratus sacerdos cum intrat ad altare, dicat . . ."*[85] and omits references to the presider's vesture, posture, or hand positions. Similarly, when it comes to the ritual acts that accompany that portion of the old Roman canon that contains the institution narrative, *Indutus planeta* reads:

> *Cum vero perventum est ad* Qui pridie, *ductis plane digitis super pallam altaris, accipit hostiam dicens* accepit panem *et parum elevans signat eam dicens* benedixit *et, dicto* Hoc est corpus meum *et adorato corpore domini cum mediocri inclinatione, elevat illud reverenter ita quod a circumstantibus possit videri. Postea deponit in loco suo.*[86]

Once again, the "how-to" directions in *MR1474* are quite spare. Just before the words *"Qui pridie,"* we find merely *"Hic accipiat hostiam in manibus dicendo."* Similarly, once the words *"Hoc est enim corpus meum"* have been spoken, we find only *"Hic deponat hostiam. et leuet calicem"* (followed by the *"Simili modo"* text that precedes the formula over the chalice).[87] One may note that neither of these texts includes the modern ritual gestures of genuflection following the words of institution; *Indutus planeta* says *"adorato corpore domini cum mediocri inclinatione,"* while *MR1474* says nothing at all about ritually reverencing the Lord's body and blood or about showing the consecrated species to the people. In this, *MR1474* follows the shorter and more sober rubrics of another medieval

84. Latin text in Stephen J.P. van Dijk, ed., *Sources of the Modern Roman Liturgy: The Ordinals by Haymo of Faversham (1243–1307)*, 2 vols. (Leiden: Brill, 1963), Vol. 2, 3–14; here, 3.

85. Lippe, ed., *MR1474*, no. 1198.

86. van Dijk, *Sources of the Modern Roman Liturgy*, Vol. 2, 11.

87. Lippe, ed., *MR1474*, Vol. 1, 207.

Ordo Missae, "Paratus," which likewise fails to mention either gestures of adoration or elevation of the species following the two consecratory formulas of the institution narrative.[88]

Paratus, Indutus, and *MR1474* were certainly among the liturgical forbears that influenced the *Ordo [*or *ritus] servandus* and *Rubricae generales* that accompanied *MR1570.* But a more important and immediate source for *MR1570* was John Burckard's *Ordo Missae* of 1501.[89] Burckard was a papal master of ceremonies whose *ordo* opens with a brief biographical note:

> Engaged from my youth in the sacred ceremonies, when I saw that not a few priests in the celebration of Mass frequently imitated many abuses, and diverse rites and unsuitable gestures, I thought it unworthy that there is no definite norm transmitted to the priests by the holy Roman Church, Mother and Teacher of all the churches, to be universally observed in the celebration of the Mass.[90]

Uniform practice and universal observance were the goals that prompted Burckard to produce his *Ordo Missae.* From its very beginning, indeed, Burckard's eye for completeness, precision, and ritual detail is evident. Here, for instance, is his description of how the presider should bless himself at the beginning of Mass:

> *Cum sibiipsi benedicit: vertit ad se palmam manus dextre: et omnibus illius digitis iunctis et extensis a fronte quam tangit ad pectus: ac ab humero sinistro ad humerum dextrum signum crucis format.*[91]

88. For the text of the *ordo* known as *"Paratus,"* see Iohannes Brinktrine, *"Ordo et Canon Missae* (Cod. Vat. Ottobon. lat. 356)," *Ephemerides Liturgicae* 51 (1937): 198–209. *Paratus* is a late-twelfth-century document, composed perhaps fifty years earlier than Haymo's *Indutus planeta.* See Cassian Folsom, "Gestures Accompanying the Words of Consecration in the History of the *Ordo Missae,"* in Centre International d'Études liturgiques, *The Veneration and Administration of the Eucharist: The Proceedings of the Second International Colloquium of historical, canonical and theological studies on the Roman Catholic Liturgy, Notre-Dame-Du-Laus, France, October 1996* (Southampton, UK: The Saint Austin Press, 1997), 75–94, here, 75–77. *Paratus* appears to reflect liturgical customs of the Roman curia that were in place by the end of the twelfth century. It does indicate that the presider should take the host into his hands *"reverenter"* and to lift it *"iunctis manibus"* just before he begins the text, *"Qui pridie quam pateretur."*

89. See J. Wickham Legg, ed., *Tracts on the Mass,* Henry Bradshaw Society, vol. 27 (London: Harrison and Sons, 1904), 119–74. See Folsom, "Gestures Accompanying the Words of Consecration," 78–81. There is some dispute among scholars about the exact date of Burckard's *ordo;* 1501 or 1507 are the usual dates given.

90. The English translation of the opening of Burckard's *ordo* is taken from Folsom, "Gestures Accompanying the Words of Consecration," 78–79. For the Latin text, see Legg, *Tracts on the Mass,* 121 (*"Versatus . . . universaliter obseruaretur"*).

91. Legg, *Tracts on the Mass,* 133–34. "When he blesses himself, he turns the palm of his right hand toward himself—[with] which hand, with all its fingers joined and extended, he touches from forehead to breast, and from left shoulder to right shoulder, making the sign of the cross" (author's translation).

Burckard's directions for how the presider should act during the institution narrative of the Eucharistic Prayer are similarly precise. After the words, *"Simili modo posteaquam [sic] cenatum est,"* he instructs the presider to take the chalice into both hands *(amabus manibus),* seizing its base with his left hand and its node with his right, just below the cup; and, with his elbows resting on the altar, standing with head bowed, he says over the chalice—quietly, distinctly, and reverently *(secrete, distincte, et reverenter)*—the words of consecration *(verbu consecrationis)*.[92] These directions are familiar to anyone who remembers the *Ordo Missae* of *MR1570,* as are the instructions Burckard gives to the presider after he has finished pronouncing the words, *"Hoc quotienscumque feceritis: in mei memoriam facietis:"*

> *Et genuflexus sanguinem reverenter adorat: tum se erigit: accipit calicem discoopertum cum sanguine ambabus manibus ut prius: eleuat eum quantum commode potest: illum populo ostendens adorandum.*[93]

Here, we find ritual gestures that have remained part of the Roman Mass from *MR1570* to the present.

Although its focus is the presider, Burckard's *ordo* does not utterly ignore others present at the celebration. Thus, he speaks of the role of the assisting acolyte *(minister),* of those who may be present *(interessentes)* at Mass, and of those who wish to make an offering at the preparation of the gifts *(qui volentes offerre).*[94] He notes that at a Mass which is "read," those present should kneel from the beginning until the celebrant gives the final blessing, except during the gospel, when all should stand attentively.[95] At a "sung Mass" on Sundays, feasts, or weekdays between Easter and Trinity Sunday, the people kneel only at the confession *(Confiteor),* genuflect to adore the sacrament "when the celebrant shows it to the people," then immediately stand once more until the end of Mass.[96]

Thus, although Burckard's *ordo* gives rubrics for various styles of celebration (e.g., sung Masses and "read" Masses), as well as for varying degrees of solemnity, the basic model seems to be that of the "read" or "low" Mass, with no singing and with minimal activity by the people present (who are to remain kneeling from start to finish, except for the gospel). In its length, precision, scope, and rubrical detail, moreover, Burckard's *ordo* goes well beyond medieval precedents, such as *Indutus planeta* and *Paratus,* documents that are relatively brief by comparison. The same is true of the rubrics and ritual directions contained in *MR1474.* Thus, while one might logically assume that the latter would

92. Ibid., 157.

93. Ibid.; "And genuflecting, he reverently adores the blood. He takes the uncovered chalice, containing the blood, into both hands, as before, and elevates it in as fitting a manner as possible, showing it to the people for adoration" (my translation).

94. Ibid., 134 and 149.

95. Ibid., 134.

96. Ibid.

serve as the immediate prototype for *MR1570* (in both its *ordo* and its texts), the provisions of *MR1474* were perceived as "too lean to respond to the pressing need . . . for precise and complete rubrical directives," and hence recourse was had to the work of John Burckard.[97]

Proximate Ancestors of IGMR

Now we are in a better position to understand how *IGMR2002* combines elements from all these sources to create a new species of liturgical document that is simultaneously liturgical/rubrical, legal/juridical, and theological/pastoral.

1. One should first note that by the time *MR1570* appeared, there was already a distinction of genre between the *"ritus servandus"* (modeled on Burckard's *ordo,* with precise and abundant detail about how the Roman Mass was to be celebrated) and the *Ordo Missae.* In printed editions of *MR1570,* the *ritus servandus* became a lengthy preface dealing with a full range of ritual and rubrical complexities related to the presider's role; in contrast, the *Ordo Missae* was a distilled outline of the ordinary, invariable parts of the Mass, printed within the body of the *Missale* itself.[98] The succinct rubrics found within the *Ordo Missae* were a mnemonic aimed at jogging the memory of the presider, who could then turn to the *ritus servandus* for a more detailed description of his own role and those of the other ministers. This distinction between genres endured; it still appears in *MR2002,* where the detailed, prefatory *IGMR2002* (replacing *MR1570*'s *ritus servandus* and *rubricae generales*) is followed by the *proprium de tempore,* then by texts for the liturgical season *per annum* (including "solemnities of the Lord" that occur in ordinary time), and then by the *Ordo Missae.*[99]

2. When *Sacrosanctum Concilium (SC)* undertook the renewal of the Roman rite in 1963, it proposed not a reform of the rubrics, but a substantial revision of the *Ordo Missae* itself. "The rite of the Mass is to be revised in such a way that the intrinsic nature and purpose of its several parts, as well as the connection between them, may be more clearly manifested, and that devout and active

97. Folsom, "Gestures Accompanying the Words of Consecration," 82.

98. In *MR1570* the *Ordo Missae* (called *ordinarium missae*) follows the liturgical texts and rubrics for the Easter Vigil ("*Sabbato sancto*"). See Manlio Sodi and Achille Maria Triacca, eds., *Missale Romanum Editio Princeps* (1570) (Città del Vaticano: Libreria Editrice Vaticana, 1998), 293–352 (includes the *Canon missae*). This edition of Sodi and Triacca is a facsimile of the printed *MR1570,* with editorial introduction; page numbers are those of the modern editors. Note that the *ritus servandus* was sometimes supplemented by a "*De defectibus in celebratione missae.*" On the genre distinction between *ritus servandus* and *Ordo Missae,* see Folsom, "Gestures Accompanying the Words of Consecration," 82.

99. See *Missale Romanum ex decreti sacrosancti oecumenici concilii Vatican II instauratum auctoritate Paul PP. VI promulgatum, Ioannis Pauli PP. II cura recognitum,* editio typica tertia (Città del Vaticano: Typis Vaticanis, 2002). The *Ordo Missae* occupies pp. 501–706 of this (altar) edition of *MR2002;* it is immediately followed by the *proprium de sanctis.*

participation by the faithful may be more easily achieved" (*SC*, no. 50). This is a clear indication that, in the minds of a majority of the bishops at Vatican II (1962–65), the *Ordo Missae* found in then-current editions of the Tridentine missals (including *MR1962*) was not well suited to "easily achieving" a "devout and active participation by the people." Since *SC* had already stated that "in the restoration and promotion of the sacred liturgy the full and active participation by all the people is the aim to be considered before all else" (no. 14), it was immediately clear that a revision of *MR1570's ritus servandus*—which limited itself primarily to the ritual activities of the presider and said virtually nothing about the role of the people—would need to be set aside or drastically altered.

Still, before such a far-reaching change could occur, *SC* itself had to be interpreted, and this process began under the direction of the Consilium (or Commission) "for the implementation of the Constitution on the Sacred Liturgy" created by Pope Paul VI (d. 1978) in January of 1964, with Annibale Bugnini as its secretary.[100] The Consilium immediately set to work, publishing on 26 September 1964 the first of what would become a series of "Instructions" on the "orderly carrying out of the Constitution on the Liturgy," *Inter Oecumenici (IntOec).*[101] Because the Consilium worked in tandem with what was then called the Congregation of Rites (now the Congregation for Worship and Discipline of the Sacraments), there was intense debate about how much latitude the Consilium had. Cardinal Antonelli, who was then prefect of the Congregation of Rites, believed that when it issued "Instructions," the Consilium could only rubber-stamp the text of *SC*; it could not propose anything "contrary to or go beyond the Constitution."[102] But members of the Consilium took the view that documents such as *IntOec* were by definition transitional, provisional preliminaries to the more substantial changes envisaged by *SC* but (for obvious reasons) not yet determined and legislated by *SC*. As history records, it was the Consilium's view that prevailed and decisively shaped both the reform of the *Ordo Missae* and the provisions of the "General Instruction" that eventually accompanied the revised *MR1970.*[103]

100. For historical details about the Consilium's creation, see Bugnini, *The Reform of the Liturgy*, 49–53.

101. To date, there have been five such "Instructions," the most recent of which is *Liturgiam Authenticam*, (*LitAuth*) "on the use of vernacular languages in the publication of the books of the Roman liturgy" (28 March 2001).

102. See Folsom, "Gestures Accompanying the Words of Consecration," 83.

103. On the history of how the Consilium, with papal support, gained the upper hand in directing the liturgical reform after the promulgation of *SC*, see Pietro Marini, "L'Istruzione *Inter Oecumenici*, una svolta decisiva (Iuglio-Ottobre 1964)," *Ephemerides Liturgicae* 108, no. 3 (May–July, 1994): 205–31; idem, "Il Consilium in piena attività in un clima faverevole (Ottobre 1964–Marzo 1965)," *Ephemerides Liturgicae* 109, no. 2 (1995): 97–158.

Reshaping the Ordo Missae

The first task facing the Consilium was a reform of the *Ordo Missae* itself, a process that began in 1965 and was completed with the appearance of *MR1970*.[104] Already, in the month that followed the promulgation of *SC*, Pope Paul VI had issued *Sacram liturgiam, motu proprio*, a document that initiated certain changes in the celebration of Mass, the Liturgy of the Hours, and the celebration of the sacraments.[105] Thus, for example, in line with *SC* (no. 52), the pope ordered the inclusion of a homily at Mass on Sundays and holy days of obligation. Paul VI followed this up with a forceful endorsement of preaching in his encyclical *Ecclesiam suam* (6 August 1964), noting that "our ministry before all else . . . is the ministry of the word."[106] The following month, as noted above, the Consilium issued *IntOec*, which launched the process of reshaping the *Ordo Missae*.[107]

We may thus identify stages by which, through documents of the Consilium endorsed by Pope Paul VI, the *Ordo Missae* with which we are familiar today was set in place:

1. **1964:** *IntOec*, which began the important movement toward recognizing both the essential role of the congregation and the diversity of roles required for a eucharistic celebration in which each minister does "all and only" those parts properly assigned to that office (see *SC*, no. 28). This instruction also set in place the procedures by which the "competent authority in liturgical matters" (*SC*, no. 22) was to be established (taking into account the rights of national conferences of bishops, local ordinaries, etc.).

2. **1965:** On 27 January 1965, the Consilium (working through the Congregation of Rites) issued the decree *Nuper edita instructione*, which confirmed the changes to the order of Mass outlined in *IntOec*, revised the 1570 *ritus servandus* to reflect those changes, and ordered that all these alterations be "published and incorporated into any new editions of the *Missale Romanum*, so that the rules contained are exactly observed by all."[108] In follow-up documents, the Consilium also confirmed new rituals, such as those for concelebration and communion in both kinds (*Ecclesia semper*, 7 March 1965),[109] and affirmed the appropriateness of new arrangements, such as altars facing the people (*Le renouveau liturgique*, 30 June 1965).[110] When the Second Vatican Council recon-

104. See Section 2, "The Ordo Missae Prior to 1969," in DOL, nos. 1338–1356.

105. See DOL, nos. 276–289. The document is dated 25 January 1964. The changes became effective on the First Sunday of Lent in 1964.

106. See DOL, no. 1338.

107. See the text of *IntOec* in DOL, nos. 293–391. The sections dealing with the *Ordo Missae* may be found at DOL, nos. 340–352.

108. See DOL, no. 1340. The precise changes in the *ritus servandus* were listed in the Congregation of Rite's letter (15 February 1965) to publishers of liturgical books. See the list in *Notitiae* 1 (1965): 215–19.

109. See DOL, nos. 1788–1793.

110. See DOL, nos. 407–418.

vened for its fourth and final session, the Consilium issued a booklet, *Masses for the Fourth Period of Vatican Council II* (14 September 1965), which included the sketch of a revised *Ordo Missae* that reiterated the provisions of *Nuper edita instructione.* Meanwhile, Pope Paul VI continued to express vigorous and vocal support for these unfolding reforms, noting that "for the good of the faithful," the church "has sacrificed its native tongue, Latin," calling for assemblies that are "alive and active," and closing the door on any "return to the former, undisturbed devotion or apathy."[111]

3. **1967:** By 1967, the Consilium was prepared for a further revision of the *Ordo Missae,* and this was reflected in its second "Instruction on the orderly carrying out of the Constitution on the Liturgy," *Tres abhinc annos* (4 May 1967, hereafter *TAA*).[112] The provisions of *TAA* affected primarily the ritual actions of the presider. They were confirmed and promulgated in a follow-up decree, *Per instructionem alteram* (18 May 1967), which further revised the *ritus servandus* that accompanied printed editions of the *Missale Romanum.* The changes promulgated by the decree *Per instructionem alteram* were published in a small booklet entitled *Variationes in Ordinem Missae inducendae ad normam Instructionis S.R.C. diei 4 maii 1967.*[113] Among the changes introduced were a reduction in repetitive ritual gestures (e.g., genuflections, signs of the cross), as well as repeal of the rubric requiring the presider to hold thumb and forefinger together after the consecration (see *TAA,* nos. 7–12).

4. **1969:** The stage was thus set for a more decisive, permanent reform of the *Ordo Missae,* which occurred, as will be seen in the section that follows, in April of 1969.

Replacing the ritus servandus

As Archbishop Pietro Marini has observed, after the documents *IntOec* (1964), *Nuper edita instructione* (1965), *TAA* (1967), and *Per instructionem alteram* (1967) had appeared, the *ritus servandus* of *MR1570* remained technically in effect, but was so altered by its newly emerging context that, while its letter survived, its spirit did not. Indeed, by the time Pope Paul VI approved a new Missal, with a new *Ordo Missae,* through his apostolic constitution *Missale Romanum* (3 April 1969), the liturgical landscape of the Roman Rite had already changed dramatically. Vernaculars were in use,[114] churches were being remodeled, altars were turned so that the presider faced the assembly, homilies at

111. See the texts of Paul VI in DOL, nos. 399–402.

112. See DOL, nos. 445–474.

113. The text of this booklet was printed in *Notitiae* 3 (1967): 195–211. The texts of the old order of celebration ("*vetus ordo*") are set side by side with the *novus ordo* for easy comparison.

114. On the shift from Latin to the vernaculars, see Bugnini, *The Reform of the Liturgy,* 99–113.

Sunday Mass were the norm, new liturgical ministries were emerging, communion in both kinds was becoming more common, the rites of Holy Week had been further revised, a rite for eucharistic concelebration was in place (see Ostdiek and Ciferni, pp. 281–282 below), and reforms of the Liturgy of the Hours and of other sacramental rites were well underway.

It had become increasingly clear, moreover, that the old *ritus servandus* of *MR1570* was becoming obsolete, that it would need not merely revision, but replacement by another kind of document, one that took into account not only differing "degrees" and "styles" of celebration, but the diverse roles of presider, congregation, deacons, readers, servers (acolytes), and musicians. A document was needed, in short, that not only legislated but instructed, that not only regulated rites but reflected on the mysteries being celebrated by God's "holy people united and arranged under their bishops" (*SC*, no. 26).

This document was the *IGMR*, which saw four editions during the period between 1969 and 1975, and was most recently revised in 2002 to accompany the publication of the third *editio typica* of *MR2002*.[115] The same decree that promulgated the Consilium's *editio typica* of a new *Ordo Missae* (*Ordine Missae*, 6 April 1969) also included, for the first time, an *IGMR* which "will replace the following preliminaries of the present Roman Missal: *Rubricae generales, Ritus servandus in celebratione et concelebratione Missae; De defectibus in celebratione Missae occurrentibus*."[116] In a subsequent declaration (18 November 1969), the Congregation of Rites clarified the fundamental purposes of the new *IGMR*:

> The Instruction [i.e., *IGMR*] is an accurate resumé and application of those doctrinal principles and practical norms on the eucharist that are contained in the conciliar Constitution *Sacrosanctum Concilium* (4 December 1963), Paul VI's Encyclical *Mysterium fidei* (3 September 1965), and the Congregation of Rites' Instruction *Eucharisticum mysterium* (25 May 1967).
>
> Nevertheless the Instruction should not be looked on as a doctrinal, that is to say, dogmatic document. Rather it is a pastoral and ritual instruction: it outlines the celebration and its parts in the light of the doctrinal principles contained in the documents noted. For the rites both have doctrine as their source and give to doctrine its outward expression.
>
> The Instruction thus seeks to provide guidelines for catechesis of the faithful and to offer the main criteria for eucharistic celebration to be used by those who take part in the celebration according to their different orders and ranks.[117]

This is a crucial text for understanding (a) the nature of an *IGMR*; (b) the intent of those who crafted the Instruction; and (c) *IGMR*'s difference from

115. The first edition of *IGMR* accompanied the Consilium's publication of the decree *Ordine Missae*, which promulgated the *editio typica* of the new *Ordo Missae* on 6 April 1969.

116. See DOL, no. 1367.

117. DOL, nos. 1368–69.

earlier documents aimed at the "good ordering" of the liturgy (e.g., the *Ritus servandus and Rubricae generales* of *MR1570* and subsequent editions of the Tridentine missal). Note that while *IGMR* faithfully reflects eucharistic doctrine, it "should not be looked on as a . . . dogmatic document." Its tone and intent are pastoral, practical, and catechetical rather than juridical or dogmatic. Instead of restricting itself to the ritual tasks of the presider alone, *IGMR* offers "criteria" for all those who "take part in the celebration according to their different orders and ranks." Moreover, it is not a "document for the ages," but a set of "guidelines" open to ongoing revision for the sake of "better pastoral and catechetical understanding and for improving rubrics."[118]

Indeed, over a period of just five years, *IGMR* went through four editions. The first of these (published 6 April 1969) was noted above. A second, emended edition appeared when the *Missale Romanum* was promulgated on 26 March 1970.[119] Almost immediately, this second edition was further amended, in May of 1970, by a document entitled *Edita instructione,* from the Congregation for Divine Worship (formerly the Congregation of Rites).[120] The Congregation noted that it was responding to a variety of legitimate "doctrinal and rubrical" comments, but also observed that "some complaints . . . were based on prejudice against anything new," and that "these were not deemed worth considering because they are groundless."[121] Once the ministry of subdeacon was suppressed by Paul VI in 1972 (see Morrill and Roll, p. 208), it became necessary to issue a third edition of *IGMR,* which the Congregation for Divine Worship issued on 23 December 1972.[122] Three years later, a fourth edition of *IGMR* appeared to accompany the second *editio typica* of the postconciliar *Missale Romanum* in 1975.[123]

Finally, with the publication of a third *editio typica* of the postconciliar missal *(MR2002),* still another, amended version of *IGMR* was necessary. It is this most recent edition *(IGMR2002)* that forms the basis for the commentary contained in this volume. We hope the foregoing historical sketch of how documents aimed at the "good ordering of the liturgy" in the Latin West evolved over two millennia will provide a fuller context for understanding how *IGMR* itself was proposed, promulgated, and subsequently revised in the years between 1969 and 2002.

118. Ibid.

119. The decree of the Congregation for Divine Worship which promulgated the new *Missale Romanum* as reformed after the Second Vatican Council was entitled *Celebrationes eucharisticae*. See DOL, no. 1765.

120. See DOL, no. 1371. The actual changes, most of them quite minor, may be found in *Notitiae* 6 (1970): 177.

121. See DOL, no. 1371.

122. See annotation between DOL, nos. 1371 and 1372.

123. See DOL, nos. 1374–1375 for the decree *Cum Missale Romanum* (27 March 1975), concerning the second *editio typica* of the Roman Missal as reformed after the Second Vatican Council. See also DOL, nos. 1376–1731, for the fourth edition of *IGMR*.

Liturgy and Ecclesiastical Law

R. Kevin Seasoltz

Post-Conciliar Liturgical Documents in Context

Sacrosanctum Concilium (*SC*) is a document that is evangelical, theological, juridical, and pastoral. It is evangelical in that it has been framed in the spirit of the New Testament, as the words of the Constitution are often the very words of the Gospel. It is theological in that it elaborates at length the theological foundations for the way in which the Church is sanctified and worships, for example, in Christ and through the power of the Holy Spirit. It is juridical in the sense that it proposes definite practical lines of action in matters of the liturgy. Finally, it is pastoral in that its objective is, as the first paragraph of the document states, "to impart an ever-increasing vigor to the Christian lives of the faithful; to adapt more closely to the needs of our age those institutions which are subject to change; to encourage whatever can promote the union of all who believe in Christ; to strengthen whatever serves to call all of humanity into the Church's fold" (*SC*, no. 1).

Most, but not all of the major liturgical documents issued since Vatican II (1962–65) have also been evangelical, theological, juridical, and pastoral. One of the greatest challenges confronting ministers in the Church is to keep these characteristics in a poised tension with one another.[1] Because of background and training, some people respond only to commands and ignore counsels. Such people tend to give little response to the theological values set forth in liturgical documents and often feel free to ignore liturgical reform and renewal unless they are subject to sanctions and commands. Other people, steeped in a legalistic mentality, give a strict juridical interpretation where it least belongs. Failing to understand the constructive nature of Church law, still others manifest only contempt for practical norms in an exaggerated effort to counteract legalism. They are often simply antinomian.

1. An example of a document that is primarily juridical rather than evangelical and theological would be the Instruction *Redemptionis Sacramentum* (*RedSac*). A recent document that is in fact evangelical, theological, juridical, and pastoral is the *Directory on Popular Piety and the Liturgy* (DPPL). For a commentary on this document, see *Directory on Popular Piety and the Liturgy: Principles and Guidelines*, ed. Peter C. Phan (Collegeville, MN: Liturgical Press, 2005).

If Christian theology is the science that is founded on the Word that God speaks to us and the tradition of living out that Word faithfully, canon law as a science is concerned with the practical life of the Church founded on God's Word and the living tradition. Although it has God's Word as a primary source, its formulation is the work of those human agents who are responsible for ordering the life of the Church. It is by reflecting on the Word of God and people's faithful living out of that Word that the Church concludes how people should act. As the history of the liturgy shows, in the early centuries of the Church the practical expression of the Church's worship was not separated from its inner spirit. The patristic writers, who were steeped in a theology of the Church and the Church's worship, were also responsible for the concrete expression of the liturgy in the life of the Christian people.

When the Sacred Congregation of Rites and Ceremonies was created in 1588, Pope Sixtus V (d. 1590) manifested a special concern for the interior transformation of the faithful through the Church's liturgy. He stressed that the congregation was established to put into effect and promote the theological and liturgical reforms that were an outgrowth of the Council of Trent (1545–63).[2] Due to the strong influence of nominalism, which prevailed among the fathers at Trent, the intelligent, meaningful celebration of the liturgy tended to give way to a concern mainly for the validity of the sacraments. In no way did the Council fathers intend to set out a fully developed theology of worship. They were primarily concerned with responding to what they considered the major errors of the Protestant Reformers, and clarifying the minimum requirements for the validity of the seven sacraments. However, in the centuries that followed Trent, the rubrics governing the liturgical rites came to be interpreted simply as rigid norms for mere ceremonial, often devoid of theological significance. As a result there was a widening rift between the theological meaning of the Church's worship and the norms that regulated the external organization and expression of that worship.

Certainly contemporary liturgical theologians have rediscovered the fundamental theological nature of the Church and the Church's worship; hence the emphasis in recent decades has not only been on the validity of the sacraments but also and above all on the meaningful celebration of the paschal mystery of Jesus Christ. The sacraments are not magical sources where people are automatically made holy and assured salvation; they are rather rich and often complex rituals through which women and men as body-persons are transformed and sanctified by Christ in the Spirit, and, in union with Christ and through the power of the Spirit, worship the Father and are transformed in their relations with one another.

If people understand the true nature of liturgical law as a complex system of practical norms ordering the rituals in and through which people are sanctified

2. *Bullarum diplomatum et privilegiorum Romanorum pontificum Taurensis Editio* (1857–67) VIII: 989–90.

and in turn worship God, surely they will admit that a canonical study of the liturgy is important; but ministers who blindly follow the ritual directives in the reformed liturgical books will run the risk of producing a new form of liturgical pageantry that might be externally correct and aesthetically interesting but interiorly dead.

To a great extent competent canonists must depend on the insights of liturgical theologians. Canonical actions should proceed from sound theology. The Church is the living Body of Christ, and its worship is the worship of Christ, who sanctifies the members of his Body and leads them back to the Father through the outpouring of the Spirit. It must be remembered, however, that the Spirit was not given once and for all on Pentecost but is continually being poured out on all of God's people. Hence, in order that the new inspirations of the Spirit might be put into practice, the legal requirements must be formulated in such a way that there is still room for growth and development. If the practical life of the Church is to reflect the ever-deepening understanding of the faith and the development of doctrine, it is imperative that the body of the Church's law should have an elastic quality so that new insights may be assimilated to what is already good in the Church's life.[3]

SC certainly established the principle of historical relevance; the document conceives of the people of God in a historical context. That history is constantly changing, revealing God to God's people in varying ways. The Constitution does not visualize a fully developed form of worship that the Church is to impose on all people for all time, but leaves open the possibility that new forms of worship may always be accepted if they are recommended as being the fruit of serious scholarship and experience and are felt to be beneficial to the Church as it exists in concrete situations.[4]

Furthermore, the Constitution is based on the principle of personal and communal consciousness and responsibility. Ritual forms can be controlled, but worship itself cannot be legislated, for it is the free and loving response of human persons and communities to a loving God. When good laws are internalized in personal and communal consciences, when people have an awareness of God's power to save them and of God's desire to save them through the liturgy of the Church, the written law of the Church does not have to address minute details.[5] Liturgical ministers should be aware of the canonical axiom derived from Roman law: *De minimis non curat praetor* ("the lawgiver is not concerned with minutiae"). That means that sometimes matters are of such

3. See Ladislas Örsy, "Theology and Canon Law," in *The New Commentary on the Code of Canon Law*, ed. John P. Beal, James A. Coriden, and Thomas J. Green (New York: Paulist Press, 2000), 1–9.

4. See Mark R. Francis, *Shape a Circle Ever Wider: Liturgical Inculturation in the United States* (Chicago: Liturgical Training Publications, 2000), 48–77.

5. David Granfield, *The Inner Experience of Law: A Jurisprudence of Subjectivity* (Washington, DC: Catholic University of America, 1988).

minimal significance that it is not appropriate to make them the object of a canonical norm. Likewise symbols and rituals not explicitly authorized are sometimes introduced into celebrations, but they are of such minor importance that they do not call for specific authorization. Examples would be the introduction of additional popular acclamations into the structure of the Eucharistic Prayer so as to provide more active participation on the part of the community, or the introduction of liturgical dance and gestures at various appropriate times during the liturgy.[6]

When consciences have been well formed and sound theological awareness has been deepened, it is best that Church laws emphasize only the basic norms and principles. In this way there is room for the free development and assimilation of wholesome customs and usages. This is the best way of promoting that unity in diversity that should characterize the Church of Jesus Christ.

Certainly *SC* and most of the liturgical documents issued in the decades immediately following Vatican II were formulated in that spirit. The norms were general and were concerned with major issues, not with picayune details. For example, in matters of liturgical music and liturgical architecture and art, only directives of a very general nature were issued, and rightly so, for the creation of art, like morality, is something that cannot be legislated. Artists, architects, and musicians who agree to work for the Church should acknowledge that they are ministers, servants of the Church; hence they should have a clear understanding of the theology of the liturgy and the role of their proper arts in the liturgy, but talent and genius should not be stifled by legislators who are not themselves conversant with the arts. It is above all in these areas that the law should not go into great detail once the role of the arts in the liturgy has been established. This seems to have been the attitude behind the formulation of chapters six and seven in *SC*.

In the years following Vatican II, provision was made for experimentation before final texts were promulgated. In many instances options were given in the celebration of the liturgy. Extensive power was transferred from the Holy See and placed in the hands of national episcopates, thus providing for more diversification in the Church's rites as determined by culture and need. In more recent times, however, much power has been transferred back into the hands of the Holy See; options have been limited; and cultural adaptation has been restricted.[7]

6. See Lucien Deiss, *Spirit and Song in the New Liturgy*, rev. ed. (Cincinnati: World Library Publications, 1976), 91–99.

7. See, for example, Congregatio de Cultu Divino et Disciplina Sacramentorum, "Instructio quinta ad exsecutionem Constitutionis Concilii Vaticani Secundi de Sacra Liturgia recte ordinandam: De Usu Linguarum Popularium in Libris Liturgicae Romanae Edendis" (28 March 2001) *AAS* 93 (2001): 685–726; idem, "Instructio de quibusdam observandis et vitandis circa sanctissimam Eucharistiam," (25 March 2004) *AAS* 96 (2004): 549–601.

The primary liturgical issues that continue to challenge Catholic communities are how to implement to best advantage the reform measures embodied in the revised service books; how to foster the growth of faith communities that can genuinely express their Christian life and deepen that life in the liturgical forms approved by the Church; how to carry out the liturgical catechesis that is always essential to liturgical renewal; and how to be liturgically creative and responsive to pastoral needs without being antinomian or frivolously iconoclastic.[8] These issues, however, must be confronted along with the complicated question of how one should maintain fidelity to clearly established norms while being pastorally responsible. The challenge is underlined in article 11 of *SC*: "Pastors . . . must realize that, when the liturgy is celebrated, their obligation goes further than simply ensuring that the laws governing valid and lawful celebrations are observed. They must also ensure that the faithful take part fully aware of what they are doing, actively engaged in the rite and enriched by it."

The text is clear that the responsibility of ministers is not only to the faithful observance of norms but also to the enrichment of the Christian lives of all those who take part in the celebrations. No longer may ministers feel that they have done their duty if they have carried out the norms in the liturgical books; they must go beyond the norms, in the sense that they must lead the people in bringing the liturgy to life. Consequently, they must develop a ministerial style that enables them to be aware of the pastoral needs of the people and to structure and execute the rites in such a way that they truly respond to people's needs. This presupposes an understanding of both the theological and aesthetic dimensions of the liturgy. Without undermining liturgical discipline, ministers may and should explore opportunities for creativity within the liturgical celebrations.[9]

A pastoral, responsible, and creative approach to the interpretation of liturgical law was taken by the Catholic Bishops' Conference of England and Wales in their 2005 response to the publication of the *Institutio Generalis Missalis Romani* 2002 (*IGMR2002*). The bishops did not issue an English translation of the *IGMR2002* until April 2005. At the same time that they issued the translation, they released a carefully nuanced pastoral introduction, *Celebrating the Mass*.[10] Sound theological observations are carefully woven throughout the commentary. It is, however, the bishops' pastoral interpretations of what otherwise might be interpreted as restrictive directives in *IGMR2002* that are especially

8. Frederick R. McManus, "Liturgical Law and Difficult Cases," *Worship* 48 (1974): 347.

9. E. Dekkers, "Créativité dans la liturgie d'aujourd'hui," *Notitiae* 8 (1972): 151–56; D. Hameline, "La créativité: Fortune d'un concept, ou concept de fortune?" *La Maison-Dieu* 111 (1972): 84–109.

10. Catholic Bishops' Conference of England and Wales, *Celebrating the Mass: A Pastoral Introduction* (London: Catholic Truth Society and Colloquium, 2005). There is no indication that this document was first of all submitted to the Congregation for Divine Worship and the Discipline of the Sacraments for approval before publication.

refreshing. For example, the movements and postures of the assembly are carefully regulated in *IGMR2002*, nos. 42–44. Rather than insisting on uniformity throughout the two countries, the English and Welsh bishops allow for a variety of possibilities and for local variations in their commentary: "Within the dioceses of England and Wales different communities will have preference for different posture" (no. 61). In the matter of vesture, the bishops do not insist that the chasuble be worn over the stole as indicated in *IGMR2002*, no. 337. The bishops are aware that many parishes and religious communities have, since the Second Vatican Council, purchased expensive vestments designed in such a way that the stole must be worn over the chasuble. So as not to insist that such vestments be discarded, the bishops simply state in their document: "The chasuble, worn with alb and stole, is the proper vestment of the presiding priest" (no. 111). They likewise take a sound pastoral approach in their commentary on *IGMR2002*, no. 308 which states: "There is also to be a cross, with the figure of Christ crucified upon it. . . ." In *Celebrating the Mass,* the bishops of England and Wales state: "It is usual for this Cross to bear a figure of Christ crucified. However, in the tradition of the Church the saving mystery of the Crucified One has been represented in different ways, sometimes by a figure of the suffering or dead Christ on the cross, sometimes by a figure showing the Resurrected Lord standing in triumph as King or High Priest at the cross, sometimes without representation of the person of the Lord but simply by a plain cross" (no. 104). *Celebrating the Mass* is an excellent example of liturgical law that is flexible, pastoral, and creative.

Legitimate Legislators

In the early centuries of the Church, the bishops were responsible for the liturgy in their dioceses, not the bishop of Rome. Consequently there were different liturgical practices in various dioceses even in the West; no centralized authority attempted to impose liturgical uniformity.[11] The local bishop was both a member of the local community and also one who had the distinctive roles of leader, teacher, and symbol of unity in the community. He was free to adapt the liturgy to the needs of the local community.[12] Gradually, however, ecumenical councils began to assert authority over local liturgies. Furthermore the gradual increase in papal authority was joined with an increase in the prestige of Roman practices, resulting in a more uniform practice of liturgy in the West.[13] In the eighth and ninth centuries, the Carolingian emperors tried to

11. See Paul F. Bradshaw, *The Search for the Origins of Christian Worship* (Oxford: Oxford University Press, 2002), 73–117; Marcel Metzger, *History of the Liturgy: The Major Stages* (Collegeville, MN: Liturgical Press, 1997), 16–112. Also, Mitchell and Baldovin, 11 above.

12. John R. Rotelle, "Liturgy and Authority," *Worship* 47 (1973): 515–24; J. Colson, "Le rôle du presbytérium et l'évéque dans le contrôle de la liturgie chez saint Ignace d'Antioche et le rôle de Rome au IIe siècle," *Pariosse et Liturgie* 47 (1965): 14–24.

13. Metzger, 116–19; also, Mitchell and Baldovin, 11 above.

impose the Roman practice of liturgy throughout their empires as an effective way to establish both political and ecclesial unity. Despite this trend, however, many bishops continued to take responsibility for the liturgy in their respective dioceses.[14]

Charlemagne (d. 814) asked Pope Hadrian I (d. 795) to send him a purely Roman sacramentary. The text was placed in the royal palace in Aachen and served as a model which was copied by many scribes and then diffused throughout the Carolingian Empire. This contributed to the demise of oral traditions in liturgical matters, since local oral traditions were gradually replaced by written directives, which were eventually codified and gained in prestige because the Roman liturgical texts were considered the work of the popes themselves, including the highly respected Gregory the Great (d. 604). Beginning in the tenth and eleventh centuries the texts for diverse liturgical ministries were brought together in complete books. These books, however, contained not only the liturgy as celebrated in Rome but also additions from the churches of the Carolingian Empire. Somewhat later, these same hybrid books were adopted by the Church in Rome, especially during the reform of Pope Gregory VII (1073–1085). After this the rites of the Roman Church did not change much but were stabilized in their principal forms.[15]

The Roman liturgy of the late Middle Ages, propagated very widely by the Franciscans and other mendicant orders of the thirteenth century, was essentially the rite that came down to the fathers at the Council of Trent and made its way into the post-Tridentine liturgical books.[16] These liturgical books generally replaced all other local rites in the West. As a result, the publication of the Tridentine liturgical books had the effect of suppressing the ancient notion that the bishop was the chief liturgical legislator for his diocese; the Apostolic See assumed that role for the whole Latin Church.

According to the 1917 Code of Canon Law (*CIC1917*), only the Apostolic See could enact liturgical laws (c. 1257). Diocesan bishops possessed only what might be called a "negative" legislative authority in liturgical matters, since they could pass laws only to enforce the observance of the canonical rules and decrees of the Apostolic See on divine worship.[17] Their primary role was one of supervision, to see that canon law was faithfully observed in their dioceses

14. Ibid., 114–16; also, Mitchell and Baldovin, 11 above.

15. See Cyrille Vogel, *Medieval Liturgy: An Introduction to the Sources*, trans. William Storey and Niels Rasmussen (Washington, DC: The Pastoral Press, 1986), 31–59; Eric Palazzo, *A History of Liturgical Books from the Beginning to the Thirteenth Century*, trans. Madeleine Beaumont (Collegeville, MN: The Liturgical Press, 1998), 19–56; also, Mitchell and Baldovin, 5–22 above.

16. See Stephen J. P. Van Dijk, *The Origins of the Modern Roman Liturgy: The Liturgy of the Papal Court and the Franciscan Order in the Thirteenth Century* (Westminster: Newman, 1960); also, Mitchell and Baldovin, 18–20 above.

17. Frederick R. McManus, "The Juridical Power of the Bishop in the Constitution on the Sacred Liturgy," *Concilium* 2 (New York: Paulist Press, 1964), 36–37.

and that abuses were prevented.[18] In his 1947 encyclical *Mediator Dei*, Pope Pius XII (d. 1958) accurately reflected the mind of *CIC1917* when he clearly stated that "the supreme pontiff alone has the right to permit or establish any liturgical practice, to introduce or approve new rites, or to make any changes in them he considers necessary." The bishops were "to enforce diligently the observance of the canonical rules on divine worship" (*Mediator Dei*, no. 58). *SC* altered the law in *CIC1917* by giving diocesan bishops real authority over the liturgy: "Regulation of the liturgy depends solely on the authority of the Church, that is, on the Apostolic See and, accordingly as the law determines, on the bishop" (no. 22). However, Vatican II did not fully restore to diocesan bishops the wide authority they had over the liturgy before the Council of Trent. *SC* gave limited authority to episcopal conferences, which was further defined in the Decree on the Pastoral Office of Bishops in the Church, *Christus Dominus*.[19]

Current Sources of Liturgical Law

Liturgical law is undoubtedly the largest body of Roman Catholic ecclesiastical law, with countless universal laws in the approved liturgical books, in Book IV of the 1983 Code of Canon Law (*CIC1983*) on "The Office of Sanctifying in the Church," in parts of Book III on "The Teaching Function of the Church," and in papal laws outside the code. There are also numerous laws regulating the liturgy that have been enacted by conferences of bishops and dioceses throughout the world. Additionally, the Roman dicasteries have issued various documents on the liturgy, some of which are legislative, others, administrative. These norms constitute part of a complex canonical system that requires skills in both interpreting and applying laws. It is, however, a system that often lies beyond the understanding and competence of most pastoral ministers who are nonetheless responsible for planning and celebrating liturgies. Liturgical laws are subject to the same principles of interpretation and dispensation as other ecclesiastical laws.[20]

Two principal sources of liturgical law are the *praenotandae* (introductions) and rubrics of the various approved liturgical books. The *praenotandae* provide theological background and the major disciplinary regulations affecting the preparation and celebration of rites. The rubrics, which are found throughout the liturgical books, usually provide more precise directions, specifying what the ministers or assembly should say or do at a specific time in the celebration. Liturgical manuals have traditionally described rubrics as preceptive, directive,

18. See 1917 *Codex Iuris Canonici* (*CIC1917*), cc. 336 and 1261.

19. *Christus Dominus*, nos. 37–38. See Frederick R. McManus, "The Scope of Authority of Episcopal Conferences," in *The Once and Future Church*, ed. James A. Coriden (New York: Alba House, 1971), 129–78; and Julio Manzanares Marijuan, *Liturgia y Descentralización en el Concilio Vaticano II*, Analecta Gregoriana 177 (Rome: Università Gregoriana Editrice, 1970).

20. See John M. Huels, "The Interpretation of Liturgical Law" (Washington, DC: Catholic University of America Canon Law Studies, 1981), 11–28.

or facultative. For example, the directive in *IGMR2002* which states that the presider "selects a Eucharistic Prayer from those found in the *Roman Missal* or approved by the Apostolic See" (no. 147) is a preceptive rubric; whereas that which states that "the priest may say the formulas of blessing aloud" (no. 142), is a facultative rubric. Preceptive rubrics are binding, while directive or non-preceptive rubrics are not strictly binding. Facultative rubrics provide some choice or option.

It is well known among canonists that Roman law has had major influence on the general norms that have been incorporated in both *CIC1917* and *CIC1983* and also on the canons that deal with canonical procedures.[21] There are, however, two major differences between Roman law and Anglo-Saxon law that have very important implications for the way English-speaking Catholics, especially in North America and the United Kingdom, interpret canon law in general and liturgical law in particular.

The first principle is that in Roman law there is clear allowance for the progressive evolution of its institutes and the consequent necessity of keeping the law in step with the development of the institutes. In a sense, then, theory and practice in Roman law are often out in front of the written law itself. Roman law would therefore allow for the development of doctrine and also for the development of customs, even those contrary to law. By contrast, Anglo-Saxon law does not make allowance for the progressive evolution of its institutes; if there is to be allowance for changed practice, the law itself must first of all be changed. Anglo-Saxon jurists would maintain that they should adhere to the precise words of a legal text, since the precise meaning of the words has been locked into place at the time the text was written. Roman jurists would argue that the genius of a law is that it rests not in any static meaning it might have had in a world that is dead and gone, but in the adaptability of juridic principles that enable governments and other administrators to cope with current problems.

The second principle is that in Roman law there seems to be a penchant for articulating universal laws, while at the same time making allowance for generous dispensations. In Anglo-Saxon law, however, the law itself must be changed if there is to be a legitimate change in practice. In other words, Roman law is more dynamic while Anglo-Saxon law is more static. Difficulty naturally arises for English-speaking North American Catholics, because they tend to use the rigid principles of Anglo-Saxon law to interpret canon law in general and liturgical law in particular, with the result that they are often much more rigorous than the law ever intended them to be. In other words, those influenced by an Anglo-Saxon worldview tend to give an overly literal interpretation to documents while those from the Mediterranean, whose national laws are clearly

21. See Barry Nichols, *An Introduction to Roman Law* (Oxford: Clarendon, 1962); Albert Gauthier, *Roman Law and Its Contribution to the Development of Canon Law* (Ottawa: Saint Paul University, 1996).

based on Roman law, have developed ways of interpreting canon law in general and liturgical law in particular that are much more relaxed and liberating. The major differences between Roman law and Anglo-Saxon law must be kept in mind when discussing the various current sources of liturgical law.

Vatican II's discipline regarding the competence of various authorities over the liturgy was largely incorporated in *CIC1983*. Diocesan bishops have limited authority over the liturgy, even though "they are high priests, principal dispensers of the mysteries of God and moderators, promoters and custodians of the whole liturgical life of the church committed to them" (c. 835). They do have general legislative power for their dioceses (c. 391) but can only make laws that are not contrary to universal law (c. 135, par. 2).

As for the liturgical competence of episcopal conferences, the code mentions only that these national bodies may prepare translations of the liturgical books into the vernacular and make adaptations in the liturgy permitted by the liturgical books themselves (c. 838, par. 3). The matter of translating liturgical texts, however, has been treated extensively in *Liturgiam Authenticam* (*LitAuth*).[22] The conferences of bishops must approve translations of liturgical texts. For English-speaking conferences the translations are prepared by the International Commission on English in the Liturgy (ICEL). Once the bishops have approved a translation, it requires confirmation (*recognitio)* by the Holy See before it may be used in the liturgy. An international group of bishops, the *Vox Clara* Committee, advises on questions of English translation (see no. 392 below). In cases where the universal law does not specify that episcopal conferences may legislate, a conference must obtain permission from the Holy See to do so. Whether the permission to legislate comes by way of the law itself or from the Holy See, a two-thirds vote of the total membership of the conference is always necessary for a decision to be binding in that conference's territory, and before the decision may be promulgated it must be reviewed and approved by the Apostolic See (c. 455).

One of the useful ways that subsidiarity is fostered in the Church is through the power of diocesan bishops to dispense from universal laws. Canon 85 states that a dispensation is the relaxation of a merely ecclesiastical law in a particular case. Whenever the diocesan bishop judges that it will benefit the spiritual good of the faithful, he may dispense from all disciplinary laws, whether universal or particular, except those laws whose dispensation is reserved to the Apostolic See (c. 870). For the validity of a dispensation, there must be a just and reasonable cause (c. 90). Not all laws, however, may be dispensed. By definition, only ecclesiastical laws may be dispensed, not divine laws, and even among merely ecclesiastical laws, there are three categories of law which cannot be dispensed: procedural laws, penal laws, and constitutive laws which define the essential elements necessary to constitute a juridical institute or act (c. 86). For example,

22. For a detailed commentary on this instruction, see Peter Jeffery, *Translating Tradition: A Chant Historian Reads* Liturgiam Authenticam (Collegeville, MN: Liturgical Press, 2005).

a bishop could not dispense from the matter and form of a sacrament because without them there would be no sacrament. He could, however, dispense from a regulation requiring that the wine to be consecrated during the Eucharist should be placed in chalices at the preparation of the gifts rather than consecrated in a decanter placed on the altar. Likewise, he could dispense from the liturgical law in the United States that directs that the faithful should kneel during the Eucharistic Prayer from the end of the *Sanctus* until after the Great Amen concluding the Eucharistic Prayer. For the most part, liturgical laws are disciplinary laws, not divine, constitutive, penal, or procedural; hence they are subject to dispensation.

Another way in which subsidiarity can be fostered is by the petition for and granting of indults. The term "indult" designates a special favor given for a determinate period of time; it is distinguished from a privilege which is a special favor granted in perpetuity. For example, a bishop might petition the Holy See and be given an indult to allow lay men and women to give a homily during the celebration of the Eucharist because the presider does not speak well the language in which the liturgy is being celebrated.

Closely related to the understanding of liturgical law is the role that custom plays in the interpretation of law. Canon 27 of *CIC1983* states that "custom is the best interpreter of the law."[23] Adapted from Roman law, this maxim has long been an accepted principle of canonical interpretation. It shows that the Church's legal system has great respect for the sound practices of a community. Hence, one of the best ways to learn how a law is to be understood and put into practice is to look at the ways a local Catholic community actually observes a law.

Throughout history local customs have exercised a far greater role in the development of the liturgy than has canon law. Local customs have varied from one diocese to another and often from one parish to another. The role of custom in the Church's worship, however, greatly diminished following the Council of Trent and the publication of the reformed liturgical books.

CIC1983 treats custom in cc. 23–28 and speaks of customs in accord with the law, apart from the law, and contrary to the law. Customs in accord with the law simply support and flesh out the spirit and letter of the written law; certainly there should be no objection to such customs. Customs apart from the law are those which the law does not regulate at all; they may be laudable or they may be abusive. Customs contrary to the law are those which are against the law and clearly violate the spirit and letter of the law. Customs apart from or contrary to the law do not readily become recognized as legitimate in terms of canon law. However, customs apart from or contrary to the law can play an important role in the local church's adaptation of the liturgy to its pastoral

23. See John M. Huels, "Back to the Future: The Role of Custom in a World Church," *Canon Law Society of America Proceedings* 59 (1997): 1–25.

needs. For example, in most parishes in this country, it has been the common practice for the presider at the Mass of the Lord's Supper on Holy Thursday to wash the feet of women as well as men even though this is in violation of the rubric in the Sacramentary that specifies men (*viri*). Such a practice reminds the assembly that all in the Church are called both to be served and to serve. Such a custom, even though it may be contrary to the letter of the law, actually upholds the law's basic spirit and Gospel purpose and therefore should be both tolerated and encouraged throughout the country.

It should be noted, however, that not all customs should be tolerated. Often they can be real abuses of the liturgy that result from negligence, ignorance, pastoral insensitivity, or indifference on the part of liturgical ministers. For example, it is a clear abuse for a presider to omit the homily on Sundays and holy days; likewise, it is an abuse for the presider never to offer the chalice to the assembly. It takes a well-informed interpreter to know the difference between an abuse and a legitimate custom that is contrary to the law. Such an interpreter knows not only what the law says but also discerns the pastoral context and has some understanding of the history, structure, and theology of the liturgy in general and a detailed knowledge of the pastoral context in question.

Interpretation of Liturgical Law

In the 1960s and 1970s canonists often tried to help their brothers and sisters understand the nature, role, and interpretation of official liturgical documents and laws, but they tended to approach the problem simply in terms of authority and obedience. That approach, however, overlooked a more fundamental question, that of hermeneutics that tends to cast the issue not in terms of authority and obedience but in terms of prudence: doing the right thing at the right time for the right reason. This approach leads to much more flexibility and also to a greater sense of personal and communal responsibility, creativity, and pastoral sensitivity. Sound interpretation is a complex task, but when it is properly understood both by the lawmakers and by those for whom laws are intended, then much of the tension between authority figures and the rest of the community is apt to be reduced or even eliminated.

The current interest in canonical hermeneutics has been inspired to a great extent by the writings of Ladislas Örsy, whose basic approach is set out in certain qualities of the interpreters and in specific rules of interpretation.[24] Interpreters should be aware that their interpretation is always a historical occurrence in two ways: they describe the law at a specific time in history and their capacity to understand occurs at a specific point of development. This principle does not relativize all knowledge, but it reminds us that our grasp of knowledge is always relative to what is absolute. There is an evolutionary character to laws;

24. Ladislas Örsy, *Theology and Canon Law: New Horizons for Legislation and Interpretation* (Collegeville, MN: The Liturgical Press, 1992), 53–82.

hence interpreters should know to what point in history the law has evolved. Likewise, the interpreters do not stand still but are always involved in history too; they are developing all the time. Consequently, an interpreter might give one interpretation to a law at one time and a different interpretation ten years later, because both the value that the law intends to uphold and the experience and horizon of the interpreter have developed over the years.

The second quality of the interpreter is that the broader the horizon of the interpreter, the closer the interpreter's interpretation is apt to be to the truth. Horizon means the extent of the field that the understanding of the interpreter can embrace. Canon lawyers who are *merely* lawyers cannot grasp the full meaning of ecclesiastical laws. Since the whole discipline of canon law is rooted in Christian doctrine and its systematic understanding, in order to grasp the correct legal meaning the interpreter must go back to the doctrinal roots. Furthermore, Christian faith cannot be properly understood apart from those auxiliary disciplines, such as philosophy, anthropology, psychology, and sociology, which affect the development of Christian doctrine. It is within that broad context that laws exist. To grasp the meaning of the laws, interpreters need to grasp the broad context.

It follows then that interpreters who can approach the law with broad and sophisticated categories are more likely to find the right meaning. If canon lawyers wish to understand and grasp the real meaning of laws, they need to look for help in the fields of other sciences. What has become increasingly clear since the Second Vatican Council is that liturgical studies is increasingly an interdisciplinary field of investigation. Canon lawyers who interpret liturgical laws need to recognize the interdisciplinary foundation on which liturgical laws are based and interpret the laws accordingly.

Against the background of his rules for interpreters, Örsy sets out his guiding principles for interpretation. He reminds us that every legal norm is a child of history. To grasp the meaning of a norm, one should know the history of the law. Furthermore, the meaning of every norm depends on its literary form. A commonly accepted hermeneutical principle in the study of Scripture has shown the need to identify the literary form of a text. Örsy has shown that literary forms also exist in canon law. The literary forms of canon law may be divided into proclamations of doctrine and norms of action. When the origin of a law lies in a theory, one must go back to the theory to understand the meaning of the law. Here theory means the basic doctrine that inspired the law in the first place. Likewise, the legislator cannot speak or write except within his own cultural context. Hence one must know something of the cultural background of the person who wrote the law and also the cultural background of the interpreter. Is the person inclined to be rigorous or flexible? Just as the mission of the Church is to be a light to the world, so the Church's laws should show forth the wisdom of the Church to all people. The interpretation of canon law must be faithful to sound ecclesiological principles. If the interpretation of church laws does not show them to be expressions of wisdom and responsibility for all people, they are not adequate interpretations—or perhaps the laws are simply unreasonable. If a law is clearly unjust, it certainly cannot be a reasonable law of the Church, for canon law is meant to uphold Christian values and the dignity of human persons.

The primary purpose of liturgical law is to protect the fundamental structures of the liturgy and thereby uphold the unity and catholicity of the liturgy itself in the interest of the good order of the whole Church. All laws should seek to promote unity, order, and the common good, but liturgical law is a unique kind of law, so its interpretation must be rather different in some respects from that of other disciplinary laws. The difference stems from the uniqueness of the liturgy itself. Liturgy speaks the language of symbol and mystery, a language involving dimensions that go beyond the proper realm of law. It is living and dynamic, and its fundamental elements require fresh and creative expressions according to the varying cultures and particular needs of local churches. Thus, not only must liturgical law seek to protect the foundational elements of the liturgy, it must also facilitate the fruitful experience and celebration of liturgical rites by the faithful. In short, liturgical law must be pastorally oriented. It must enhance the spiritual and pastoral good of the worshiping community by promoting effective celebrations of the paschal mystery.

Universal laws are meant for the universal Church. If a law cannot be readily observed in a third-world country, it is not then a universal law. What might be an ideal practice in theory is not always ideal in practice. In the Christian community, law is there to support values; when the observance of a law becomes a sheer formality, it collapses and ceases to exist. Furthermore, the meaning of a single norm must be understood in the context of a whole system. If an interpreter has a good grasp of the characteristics of canon law as a whole, this knowledge will provide a much broader basis for skillfully interpreting liturgical laws. Of course all interpreters must keep in mind the final canon of *CIC1983,* which asserts that the salvation of souls is the supreme law in the Church.[25]

Every rule has its own authority; hence church laws are weighted differently. Francis Morrisey, the distinguished Canadian canon lawyer, has identified numerous types of pronouncements made by various popes and curial dicasteries in recent decades.[26] It should be noted first of all that the constitutions promulgated by the Second Vatican Council, including *SC,* are most important. Hence *CIC1983* and other liturgical documents emanating from the Holy See should be interpreted in light of *SC,* not vice versa.

25. *servata aequitate canonica et prae oculis habita salute animarum, quae in Ecclesia suprema semper lex esse debet* (c. 1752).

26. Francis G. Morrisey, *Papal and Curial Pronouncements: Their Canonical Significance in Light of the Code of Canon Law* (Ottawa: Saint Paul University, 1995).

Major legislative texts and liturgical books, such as *CIC1983* and the Roman Missal (*MR2002*), were promulgated by the pope by means of an apostolic constitution, which is the highest kind of document issued by the pope. Such documents are both doctrinal and disciplinary in content and deal with matters of great importance. Another form for papal legislation is the apostolic letter *motu proprio*, so-called because the pope acts on his own initiative. Such documents address serious topics and are generally legislative in nature and so affect the whole Latin Church.

Encyclicals are papal acts in the form of letters; they are an expression of the pope's ordinary teaching authority; their contents are presumed to belong to the ordinary magisterium unless the opposite is clearly stated. Because of this, the teaching of an encyclical is capable of being changed on specific points of detail. They are usually addressed to the entire world and are not generally used for dogmatic definitions but rather to give counsel or to shed light on points of doctrine which must be made more precise or which must be taught in view of specific circumstances in various countries. They can in fact abrogate or derogate from earlier legislation. Pope John Paul II (d. 2005) issued many encyclicals, including letters such as *Ut Unum Sint* and *Ecclesia de Eucharistia*,[27] both of which addressed important liturgical issues.

The Roman curia, as an executive arm of the papacy and its various dicasteries, cannot enact laws except in particular cases when this power has been expressly granted to them by the pope (*CIC1983*, c. 30). Such curial documents fall into the category of "general decrees." Many documents pertaining to the liturgical reform have been issued by means of curial decrees, including the various sections of the revised liturgical books. Decrees have the same weight as the canons of *CIC1983*.

One of the more common forms of curial documents issued in recent years is the instruction (*instructio*), which is an act of executive power of lesser juridic weight than a legislative text such as *IGMR2002*. Instructions cannot alter either universal or particular laws. However, if an instruction concludes with the words "everything to the contrary notwithstanding" (*Contrariis omnibus quibuslibet non obstantibus*), it means that such a decree is legislative due to the papal mandate given to the congregation to promulgate the document. It is significant that the instruction *RedSac* was prepared by the Congregation for Divine Worship by mandate of the pope in collaboration with the Congregation for the Doctrine of the Faith and was approved by the pope.[28]

Although familiarity with the distinctions among various kinds of church documents is important for good interpretation, it is not among the most important factors. All the laws found in a liturgical book have the same extrinsic

27. *AAS* 87 (1995): 921–82, and *AAS* 95 (2003): 433–75.

28. See John M. Huels, "Canonical Observations on *Redemptionis Sacramentum*," *Worship* 78 (2004): 404–20.

force arising from the legislator who promulgated the book, yet the many individual norms within the book can have very different degrees of intrinsic binding force depending on other factors, such as their literary form or their perceived importance to the Christian community. For example, *MR2002* was promulgated by means of an apostolic constitution, and the norms of its *IGMR2002* as well as its rubrics all have the force of papal law. Yet anyone with even an elementary knowledge of the structure of the Eucharist would never equate in importance the rubric governing the presider's washing of hands with that concerning the transformation of the bread and wine through the Eucharistic Prayer. Obviously there is more to interpretation than learning a few rules pertinent to the text of the laws; the more difficult endeavor is to interpret the law properly according to its total context, including its historical and theological contexts.

There are two relatively new forms of documents emanating from the Holy See. One takes the form of a circular letter which outlines procedures and indicates new obligations. Since circular letters are never published in the *Acta Apostolicae Sedis* (*AAS*), they are not legislative documents in the strict sense but are simply effective means of expressing the policies and intentions of various congregations. The other type of document is the directory which contains guidelines for the application of accepted principles. Examples would include the Directory for Masses with Children and the various editions of the Directory for the Application of the Principles and Norms of Ecumenism.

A longstanding canonical axiom states that "favors are to be multiplied; burdens are to be restricted." In other words persons should interpret laws broadly when such an interpretation is favorable to them; they should give a strict interpretation when individual rights or other values are apt to be compromised or harmed. Broad interpretation stretches the meaning of a legal text in order to allow the most favorable interpretation without going beyond the actual meaning of the words of the law. Strict interpretation limits the application of the law to those situations and under the minimal conditions that are specified in the law. According to c. 18, strict interpretation is required of all laws that establish a penalty, restrict the free exercise of human rights, or contain an exception to the law. As a general rule, liturgical law is subject to broad interpretation rather than strict interpretation.

The Eastern Catholic Churches have long been comfortable with the assertion that acceptance by the community is a requisite for the reasonableness and hence the authority of a church law. A law may be so far removed from the goal it intends to achieve and so foreign to the experiences and cultural situations of a community that it can in no way function as an effective law for such a community. There are three long-standing canonical principles that should regularly be kept in mind when applying liturgical laws. The first is: observe economy. The principle of economy (from the Greek *oikonomia* meaning management or stewardship) implies that church administrators should imitate

God's stewardship over human salvation. In the tradition of the Eastern Churches, economy means both the prudent management of the Church and accommodation, adaptation, or compromise in certain matters. It flows from the contemplation of God's just and merciful purpose and presence in the Church, and it can sometimes lead beyond the limits of the Church's law. Economy is not so much an exception to the law as an obligation to decide individual issues in the general context of God's plan for the salvation of the world.[29]

The second principle is: remember *epikeia*. *Epikeia* is a virtue, a part of justice, that enables one to correct deficiencies in general rules when they are applied to particular situations. It enables one to take account of the inherent inadequacy of all human laws by applying them sensibly and wisely to individual cases. Hence the application of *epikeia* is morally superior to a merely verbal or rigid application of rules, and therefore is a better form of justice.[30]

The third principle is: do equity. In canon law equity is to govern the application of norms to concrete cases. It takes the form of mercy and pastoral charity, and seeks not a rigid application of the law but the true welfare of the faithful. Canonical equity is the fruit of kindness and charity. It understands that the ideal of justice is actually realized in fair decisions, that justice should be tempered by mercy, and the rigor of justice should be conditioned by charity.[31]

In the application of liturgical laws, these principles are in keeping with the medieval axiom that "sacraments are for people" (*sacramenta sunt propter homines);* people do not exist for the sacraments. The Church is likewise for people; people do not exist for the Church. For example, in communities that are seeking to be responsible and committed to efforts to assure justice for women and minorities in the Church, the use of sexist or exclusive language in the liturgy is often both irritating and alienating; in some instances it arouses deep hostility. Hence every responsible effort is made to avoid offensive language. Sometimes the bias against women is built into the vernacular translations of texts but is not found in the original language. That is what happened in the case of the English translation of the Catechism of the Catholic Church where the English text is much more exclusive than the French original.

Conclusion

Liturgical law is not simply the concern of canonists. On the contrary, the legislator intends the chief audience for his laws to be the people of God who put the laws into effect in their church life. Since the liturgy is so central and fundamental to the development and nurturing of the faith and life of the

29. James A. Coriden, *An Introduction to Canon Law,* rev. ed. (New York: Paulist Press, 2004), 205.

30. Ibid.

31. Ibid.

Catholic community, it is essential that the Church's discipline regulating the worship be familiar to and properly understood and implemented by the community, especially by all those entrusted with preparing for and ministering in the liturgical celebrations. Effective liturgical celebrations are the result of many factors. Even if the bishops, priests, deacons, parish liturgists, and members of liturgy committees know and understand liturgical laws, that in itself will not guarantee positive experience of worship by the community. However, it must be the starting point. Liturgical laws provide the skeletal directions from which the living liturgy is enfleshed by the diverse talents, creativity, and spirituality of the local Catholic communities. The study of liturgical law is foundational, but it only achieves its final purpose in the living, Spirit-filled worship of God's people, the Church.

Adequate formation must be given to leaders of prayer and other ministers so they may serve the community of faith well. A responsible approach to liturgy and law is never fostered by an anxious, suspicious, fearful, or rigid attitude that inhibits both a true and fruitful development of Christian faith. A mature attitude is dependent on excellence in liturgical leadership, planning, and celebration of the Catholic rites. It is never fostered by untrained amateurs whose inept and haphazard efforts tend to distort the Christian mysteries and endanger the honest renewal of the Christian faith. Efforts to initiate the faithful into the meaning of the Church's liturgy must be given priority so that their participation will be enlightened and the mystery of Christ interiorized in the lives of the people. The most profound change has to be that of the heart, which takes place through the power of the Spirit who comes to us in the celebration of the liturgy as well as in other ways. Both liturgy and law must promote fullness of life in preparation for the day when the Lord will come again to make all things new.[32]

32. Yves Congar, "Autorité, initiative, coresponsabilité: Elements de réflexion sur conditions dans lesquelles le problème se pose aujourd'hui dans l'Église," *La Maison-Dieu* 97 (1969): 34–57.

Theological and Pastoral Reflections

David N. Power and Catherine Vincie

This article offers a commentary on the theology of the 2002 *Institutio Generalis Missalis Romani* (*IGMR2002*). On the one hand it will attend to the modifications and new emphases given in this revised text, and on the other, it will offer some critique of the theological foundations of Eucharist that predate the current version.

IGMR is primarily about the liturgical law governing the celebration of the Eucharist (cf. Seasoltz, above). The section that is mainly theological is the Preamble (see nos. 1–15 below), though theological and pastoral elements are also scattered throughout the document. It has been thirty years since *IGMR1975*, and it is appropriate to take a fresh look at the theology of this introduction to the Roman Missal in its new configuration, *IGMR2002*. While remaining substantially the same as *IGMR1975*, the new Instruction takes into account thirty-five years of pastoral experience with the revised Order of Mass. Accordingly, it makes certain rubrical clarifications, expands some theological explanations, gives further specificity to gestures of both clergy and people, and includes some changes in practice as well. It also corrects the previous Instruction so that the new text is consistent with other liturgical books and instructions published since 1974.

This commentary is made in the light of certain assumptions about the place of the Eucharist in the life of the Church and the worship of God. As the Church's most central of sacraments, the Eucharist expresses in an exemplary way the community's self-understanding, its core beliefs, its relationship to the divine, its understanding of salvation, and the meaning given to sacramental expression. Not only a theological source and resource, the Eucharist also aims at continually forming the faith of those participating in it, playing a dynamic role in the ongoing life of the faith community. While granting the expressive and formative nature of liturgical celebration, it is also important to attend to the specific and historically limited nature of the Eucharist at any given moment in history. The eucharistic tradition of the Church is broader and more complex than is expressed in the liturgical celebration of any given era. Thus theological reflection plays an important role in evaluating the adequacy of eucharistic practice of a particular time in light of a rich and diverse tradition.

The concern of *IGMR2002* is the celebration or performance of the Eucharist. Whatever is given in ritual books remains to be brought to life in actual celebration with the visual, the aural, and the kinesthetic dimensions adding their own surplus of meaning. Yet in a tradition like Roman Catholicism, that values the universality of its liturgical practice even while accepting a certain local diversity, official ritual texts provide a great deal of material upon which to reflect. The commentary will first take a look at the principles for the interpretation and appropriation of the Roman tradition given in the Instruction itself. Attention will then be given to its theology of celebration, its theology of the liturgy of the Word, and finally its theology of eucharistic sacrifice.

Principles of Interpretation

It is valuable to start with an overview of the hermeneutical principles that the Instruction itself sets forth for the interpretation of the Roman Rite and its appropriation in contemporary circumstances.[1] While some of these might be applied to any eucharistic liturgy, it is clear that the Instruction is specifically concerned with the Roman tradition, as it began in the Church of Rome and then spread more widely, adapted to use in other local churches. While contemporary theologies draw on various liturgical traditions, and while the texts of the revision mandated by the Second Vatican Council drew on the liturgies of other Churches, a theological commentary on the Roman Rite needs to see it in the light of this particular tradition. To some extent it has to take a distance from the larger discourse in order to see the mystery of the Eucharist within the perspectives of this one tradition. Keeping faithful to this is the task the Instruction set itself.

The first principle concerns where the latest reforms fit within the longer tradition. While affirming an "unbroken tradition" (*Traditio non intermissa*) of faith (no. 6),[2] the document states that this may be expressed in a variety of prayers and texts, and allows for some change over the course of time. While showing the connection between the Second Vatican Council (1962–65) and the liturgical renewal of the *Ordo Missae*, it also makes appeal to the Decrees of the Council of Trent (1545–1563) and to the Missal (*MR1570*) promulgated under Pius V (d. 1572). By doing this, it situates Trent firmly in its own special historical setting, doctrinal, theological, and liturgical. It is noted that those who took part in the Council of Trent were much better acquainted with medieval commentaries on the Mass than they were with the "holy Fathers" (*sanctorum Patrum*) of the Church. The knowledge of liturgical tradition possessed by the

1. Even in the section dealing with adaptation and inculturation (nos. 397–398 below), the document makes it clear that it is not meant to envisage the development of new liturgical families, but only development within the tradition of the Roman Liturgy.

2. Quotations from the *IGMR2002* in this commentary are paired with the English translation found in GIRM2003.

reformers of *MR1570* was also limited, coming mainly from *MR1474* and the Missal used in Rome in the time of Innocent III (d. 1216) (*IGMR2002*, no. 7).

Hence, in relation to Trent and *MR1570*, the reform promulgated after the Second Vatican Council could, on the one hand, respect both the doctrinal teaching of Trent and the norms and texts of the Missal and, on the other hand, make its own revisions in the light of a more ancient tradition, both doctrinal and liturgical. Some of the consequences of this are spelled out. As far as doctrine is concerned, it is noted by the Instruction that at Vatican II there was no longer the need to defend the sacrificial nature of the Mass or the real presence of Christ in the Eucharist, as the Council of Trent was obliged to do. In the light of the present knowledge of earlier traditions, new insight arises today concerning what Trent itself affirmed about the commemorative or memorial character of the sacramental sacrifice.[3]

As far as rites and texts are concerned, the latest revision of the Missal drew more fully on the "norms of the holy Fathers" (*sanctorum Patrum norma,* no. 8) and on the "variety of prayers and rites" (*precum rituumque varietas*) that come from different liturgical traditions and from different epochs of the Roman tradition (no. 9). Indeed, even while the intention is to keep faithful to the Roman tradition, study is required of "the quite diverse human and social forms prevailing in the Semitic, Greek, and Latin areas" (*humani civilisque cultus formis tam inter se differentibus, quippe quae vigerent in regionibus semiticis, graecis, latinis,* no. 9). It is in light of this knowledge of the historical and contextual nature of the eucharistic tradition, that the work mandated by Vatican II could accommodate the pastoral principle of accommodation to the needs and orientations of the present time. This is to remain faithful to the spirit of the Council of Trent and *MR1570*, both of which had made accommodations to the needs of their own epoch. Today's accommodations include all that aids the active participation of the assembly (since *Sacrosanctum Concilium* [*SC*], no. 14 articulates this as a central principal of the reform), such as the use of the vernacular, the praying aloud of the Eucharistic Prayer, and the possibility of communion under two forms.

It is much further down in the Instruction that a scriptural principle is seen to lie behind the effort to be faithful both to the patristic and early liturgical tradition, and to the current times (no. 72). This principle teaches that in every era, the celebration of the Lord's Supper should follow the pattern of the Last Supper, as it is known from the texts of the New Testament. While this is not clearly said, what is implied is that liturgical reform and teaching look to the scriptural word as the ultimate norm, even though this is always, and has to be, appropriated and interpreted in context and by the reception of the believing community. Not only does the New Testament give the Church right belief about the Eucharist, it even gives us the pattern of the celebration to be followed. Quite naturally, the Instruction avoids the discussions of liturgical scholars about the exact pat-

3. In this respect, including an *epiclesis* as well as an *anamnesis* in new Eucharistic Prayers is consistent with the patristic and liturgical tradition of the apostolic faith.

tern or form of the Last Supper or the early Christian Eucharist or Supper,[4] but it does ask that the Church attend to the pattern of Jesus' own action: the Word remembered, the taking of elements of bread and wine, the thanksgiving whereby the "offerings" become the Body and Blood of Christ, and communion of the gathering in the blessed and sanctified offerings. Aspects of such a reading of the NT narratives may be discussed or disputed by scriptural and liturgical authors, but what is important is the reference to the total action or ritual as key to the meaning of what was and is now done, and as key to how churches celebrate in the memory of Christ in obedience to his memorial command. This is akin to what is known in semiotics and semantics as an interpretation of the whole in reference to units, and of units in the context of the whole.

A further principle is found in *IGMR2002*'s claim that good adaptation to cultures may be done within the Roman Rite, given that the Roman Rite in the course of history "has in a deep, organic, and harmonious way incorporated into itself certain other usages derived from the customs and cultures of different peoples and of various particular Churches of both East and West, so that in this way, the Roman Rite has acquired a certain supraregional character" (*profundo, organico et harmonico modo alios quosdam in se integravit, qui e consuetudinibus et ingenio diversorum populorum variarumque Ecclesiarum particularium sive Occidentis sive Orientis derivabantur, indolem quandam supraregionalem sic acquirens*, no. 397). How this claim to be supraregional is coupled with the process of mutual enrichment through the process of the inculturation of eucharistic liturgy is not further explained, nor the extent to which it can organically incorporate elements from Semitic, Greek, and other Latin liturgies.

Theology of Celebration

In looking at the underlying theology of *IGMR2002* and its influence on ritual prescriptions, we begin with the theology of celebration, inclusive of the notion of assembly. The authors of *SC* took great pains to stress the interrelationship between Christ, the Church, and the liturgy. Jesus Christ, anointed by the Holy Spirit, was sent by the Father to bring the saving work of God to fulfillment (*SC*, no. 5). The Church, born from his side, was sent to proclaim the paschal mystery. To accomplish this, Christ "willed that the work of salvation which [the apostles] preached, they should [also] enact through the sacrifice and sacraments around which the entire liturgical life revolves" (*SC*, no. 6). The liturgy, a work of Christ himself and the whole Church, is the means of human sanctification and of giving glory to God (*SC*, no. 7). Thus *SC* presents Christ, the Church, and the liturgy as inextricably bound together in continuing the work of salvation and of offering continual praise to God.

4. For a summary of this, see Paul F. Bradshaw, *The Search for the Origins of Christian Worship: Sources and Methods for the Study of the Early Liturgy*, 2nd ed. (London and New York: Oxford University Press, 2000), 118–143.

IGMR2002 continues to work with this triadic relationship. The Mass is the action of Christ and the People of God (nos. 16, 27, 35, 91). The eucharistic liturgy pertains to the whole Body of the Church, manifests it and has its effect upon it (no. 91). The meaning of the Eucharistic Prayer is that the entire congregation should join itself with Christ in confessing the great deeds of God and in the offering of sacrifice (no. 78). Christ, Church, and liturgy continue to be intertwined as the Church lives out its mandate to keep memorial of the crucified and risen One.

If there is one change in the Christ/Church/liturgy triad, it is the more deliberate inclusion of the role of the Holy Spirit in *IGMR2002* than we see in *SC* or in previous versions of *IGMR*. The priest and the assembly together offer the sacrifice through Christ *in the Holy Spirit* to God the Father (*IGMR2002*, nos. 16, 78, 93, emphasis added). The Holy Spirit aids in the appropriation of the Word (no. 56). The epiclesis is deliberately described as the power of the Holy Spirit, for it is especially by the Holy Spirit that the Church's prayer is efficacious (no. 79c). Although one might have hoped for even greater elaboration on the role of the Holy Spirit, these are not insignificant inclusions in that they provide a key marker of the gradual recovery of the Holy Spirit in the Latin West in both prayer and theology.

IGMR2002 stands in continuity with *SC* in another important respect: the liturgy is an *action* and one accomplished by the *whole gathered community*. In regard to the practice of centuries when the action of the liturgy was confined to the clergy, the Second Vatican Council recovered the vision whereby the liturgies of the Church are seen as the action of the entire congregation, "the holy people united and organized under their bishops" (*SC*, no. 26). Since that time our liturgical books, beginning with *Ordo Missae* of Paul VI in 1969, have been so revised as to make that statement a reality.

IGMR2002 continues to emphasize this point. It begins the very first chapter with the statement that "The celebration of Mass, as the *action* of Christ and the *People of God*. . ." (*Celebratio Missae, ut* actio *Christi et* populi Dei) is the center of Christian life (no. 16, emphasis added). The full expression of the local Church is the Sunday celebration of the Eucharist with its full complement of ministers inclusive of the bishop actively taking part (nos. 112 and 113). *IGMR2002* insists that the Mass has by its nature a communitarian character (no. 34). Acclamations and responses are important "so that the action of the entire community may be clearly expressed and fostered" (*ut actio totius communitatis clare exprimatur et foveatur,* no. 35). While the hierarchical nature of the assembly is also a foundational element of *IGMR2002,* it retains the emphasis on the nature of the Eucharist as an action of the whole People of God.

This has practical results in the emphasis placed on singing and on moments of silence. While previous *IGMR*s had noted this, *IGMR2002* is even more insistent on the integral place of singing in the celebration of the Eucharist (nos. 41, 61, 62, 393). Of particular interest is a new paragraph on the Alleluia before the gospel, describing it as something which "constitutes in itself a rite or act, by which the assembly of the faithful praises and welcomes and greets the Lord who is about to speak to them in the Gospel and professes its faith in liturgical song" (*ritum seu actum per se stantem constituit, quo fidelium coetus Dominum sibi in Evangelio locuturum excipit atque salutat fidemque suam cantu profitetur*, no. 62). Fresh attention is given to the singing of the appropriate elements in the Eucharistic Prayer as the association of the faithful with the prayer of the priest (no. 147). It is also noted that the communion song is meant to highlight the communitarian character of the communion procession (no. 86).

Alongside song, silence is highlighted as a mode of participation of all in the liturgy. It is presented as an appropriate way to grasp the Word of God (no. 56). Repeating what previous editions said of the importance of silence in the penitential rite, after the homily, and after communion, this edition adds a new paragraph commending silence throughout the whole building in preparation for the celebration of the Mass (no. 45).

The Liturgical Assembly

In light of these principles for active participation in eucharistic celebration, one can consider how *IGMR2002* envisages the liturgical assembly as such. In the decade before the Council, French-speaking scholars made significant efforts to retrieve the theological importance of the gathered assembly. In the minds of authors such as Thierry Maertens and Aimé-George Martimort, it was important to retrieve the biblical notion of the assembly to reclaim the communal nature of the Christian assembly and the corporate dimension of its work.[5] The Christian assembly is the new People of God gathered around Christ and sent to continue his mission and ministry. The assembly, presided over by the priest or bishop, together offers the sacrifice and is the active subject of the liturgical action.

SC made some strides in incorporating this material, but it did so only obliquely. The gathered assembly was not explicitly named as much as the generic word "Church" or the term "mystical Body" was used. At times it was difficult to know if the Church in general was meant as the subject of the liturgical action or the gathered assembly. In the years after the Council, Church documents became much clearer in this regard.

5. See Aimé-George Martimort, *The Church at Prayer,* vol. 1 (Collegeville, MN: The Liturgical Press, revised edition, 1984); idem, "L'assemblé liturgique," *La Maison-Dieu* 20 (1949): 153–175; idem, "L'assemblé liturgique, mystère du Christ," *La Maison-Dieu* 40 (1954): 5–29; idem, "Dimanche, assemblée et paroisse," *La Maison-Dieu* 57 (1959): 55–84; idem, "Précisions sur l'assemblée," *La Maison-Dieu* 60 (1959): 7–34; Thierry Maertens, *Assembly for Christ: From Biblical Theology to Pastoral Theology in the Twentieth Century* (London: Darton, Longman & Todd, 1970); idem, "L'assembleé festive du Dimanche," *Assemblée du Seigneur* 1 (1962): 28–42; idem, *L'Assemblée chrétienne* (Bruges: Biblica, 1964).

IGMR2002 is one of those documents that attend more carefully to the Church here and now gathered. All *IGMR*s note that the people of God called together to celebrate the Lord's memorial are a "local gathering together of the Church" (*sanctae Ecclesiae coadunatione locali, IGMR1975*, no. 7; *IGMR2002*, no. 27). It is most obvious in the reworking of *SC*'s paragraph on the multiple modes of Christ's presence in the Eucharist. In *SC* we read that "[Christ] is present when the Church prays and sings" (no. 7). In *IGMR*s we read that "Christ is really present in the very liturgical assembly gathered in his name. . ." (*Christus realiter praesens adest in ipso coetu in suo nomine congregato, IGMR1975*, no. 7; *IGMR2002*, no. 27). Other places continue this care to specify the Church here gathered in liturgical assembly. The priest exercises his office "over the gathered assembly" (*coetus congregati fungentem, IGMR1975*, no. 11; *IGMR2002*, no. 31), and the priest presides over the faithful people here and now gathered (*IGMR1975*, no. 60; *IGMR2002*, no. 93).

This emphasis on the gathered assembly and the insistence of Christ's presence in the assembly accomplishes several things. It focuses our attention on the assembly inclusive of its presider as a subject of the liturgical action. This realization paved the way for the Second Vatican Council to declare that "full, conscious, and active" participation is "demanded by the very nature of the liturgy" and is the assembly's right and duty by virtue of their baptism (*SC*, no. 14). Overturning centuries of passivity, the Council challenged the gathered Church to take full responsibility for the unfolding of the liturgy according to their proper roles. *IGMR2002* states that it is of the greatest importance that the celebration of the Mass be "so arranged that the sacred ministers and the faithful taking part in it" (*ita ordinetur, ut sacri ministri atque fideles . . . participantes*) might benefit more fittingly from it as was intended (no. 17). Reiterating what is said in *SC* (no. 14), *IGMR2002* insists "with due regard for the nature and the particular circumstances of each liturgical assembly" (*attentis natura aliisque adiunctis uniuscuiusque coetus liturgici*), the entire celebration is planned so that the full, conscious, and active participation may be promoted (no. 18). That participation is specified according to a distinction of roles, but all, whether ordained or lay, in fulfilling their office or their duty should carry out solely but completely that which pertains to them (no. 91). Rather than seeing this sentence as limiting participation of the assembly, this statement may be understood as a corrective to pre-Conciliar practice when the ordained minister duplicated what every other minister said. Now the distribution of roles without redundancy, inclusive of the assembly, is to prevail.

Perhaps the clearest expression of the unity of the gathered Body is given in that section devoted to the "Duties of the People of God" (*De Muneribus Populi Dei*). Here the assembly is invited to shun all appearances of individualism or division and to keep their unity in the forefront. *IGMR2002*, no. 96 reads that "Indeed, [the assembly] form[s] one body, whether by hearing the word of God, or by joining in the prayers and the singing, or above all by the common offering of Sacrifice and by a common partaking at the Lord's table" (*Unum autem corpus efficiant sive verbum Dei audiendo, sive in orationibus et in cantu partem habendo, sive praesertim in communi oblatione sacrificii et in communi participatione mensae Domini*).

The presentation of the active and conscious participation of all the baptized is not without a certain ambiguity in this document, however. There is a tendency in *IGMR2002* to treat it primarily in terms of the assembly's inner meditation on the Word (see nos. 56 and 61 below) or their inner consent to what the priest does in the liturgy of the Eucharist. While this configuration to Christ in mind and body is most basic and is the core of all good participation, there is a growing body of literature on active participation that helps to bring out the point that an externally manifested participation belongs to the sacramental structures of the celebration of the mystery of redemption in the Eucharist.[6]

To say that the liturgical assembly forms one body and is the subject of liturgy is not to say that there are no distinctions within it. All *IGMR*s have been firm in stating that the assembly is hierarchically ordered (*IGMR2002*, no. 16). The priest presides over the assembly and acts *in persona Christi* (nos. 27, 31, 33, 93). He also prays in the name of the Church and of the assembly community (no. 33). Other ministers such as deacons, acolytes, lectors, the schola and the assembly also have their distinct roles to play and offer true liturgical service (nos. 98–107).

IGMR2002 goes further than its predecessor in noting the distinction of roles within the liturgical assembly. It takes particular care to emphasize which actions are to be done by the ordained and not by the laity. One can assume that these new additions to *IGMR2002* were put in place to counter what had become common practice in many local churches and are meant to sharpen the distinction between the ordained and the lay. Some additions are only phrases inserted in paragraphs that stand substantially the same. For example, in the section on a eucharistic service without the presence and participation of the faithful, the phrase the priest "fulfills his own principal office" (*munus suum praecipuum adimplet*, no. 19) is added. In an entirely new section on the homily it is stated that the priest presider may entrust the homily to a concelebrating priest or to a deacon, but he may never entrust it to a lay person (no. 66). The fraction rite is described as a rite "reserved to the priest and deacon" (*sacerdoti et diacono reservatur*, no. 83), while the Eucharistic Prayer is reserved to the priest "by virtue of his ordination" (*vi ordinationis*, no. 147). In a new paragraph the laity are instructed not to approach the altar before the priest has received communion, and extraordinary ministers of the Eucharist should always wait for the priest to give them the vessels for distribution to the faithful (no. 162).

While distinctions within the community are made clear, one could have hoped for a more integrated treatment of the ministerial priesthood and the royal priesthood of all believers particularly regarding who offers the sacrifice.

6. See J. Lamberts, *The Active Participation Revisited. La participation active 100 ans après Pie X et 40 ans après Vatican II.* Textes et Études liturgiques. Studies in Liturgy XX (Leuven: Peeters, 2004); *La Maison-Dieu* 241 (2005/1), *La participation active.*

It is only by placing the role of all ministries and actions within a theology of Church as Body of Christ, People of God, and royal priesthood, that we can have a proper perspective of the Mass. It is the congregation, in its diversity of actions, role, and ministries, which embodies the mystery of salvation. It is in assembly, Word, sacrifice, and sacrament that the Church itself is the sacrament of the renewal of the mysteries of redemption, through which in Christ's name and the power of the Spirit, it renders true worship to the Father and is itself shown to be the Sacrament of reconciliation of humanity with God.

The reference in the Preamble to the preface for the Chrism Mass of Holy Thursday (no. 4) could have been used more fully. Within the one royal priesthood, says the preface, some are chosen for ministry through the laying-on of hands. It then lists the services exercised by this ministry, which include guidance of the community, preaching of the Word, and the celebration of the sacraments. This is a comprehensive vision of ministerial priesthood that echoes the documents of the Second Vatican Council and, in fact, brings us back to some patristic sources quite important to the understanding of the Roman liturgy.

To quote one of the most authoritative sources on the Roman tradition, Leo the Great (d. 461), in his sermons on the Passion, points to the one unique mediation and sacrifice of Christ, on which the existence of the priestly and kingly people of the Church is founded. Of this the Eucharist is the visible sacrament: "Lord, . . . you drew all things to yourself so that the devotion of all peoples everywhere might celebrate, in a sacrament made perfect and visible, what was carried out in the one temple of Judea under obscure foreshadowings."[7] This would allow the priestly service of the bishop and the kingly devotion and priesthood of the people to be seen in a more integrated way than is achieved in *IGMR2002*. Leo does not enunciate the distinction between the ministerial priesthood and the royal priesthood of the faithful that we find in *IGMR2002*, but speaks of the ordering of the one royal priesthood and of the service of the bishop within it. Seeing the Eucharist as the sacrament and the sacrifice of the one royal priesthood that shares in the one sacrifice, the one priesthood and the one kingship of Christ that the sacrament commemorates, is the principle on which eucharistic theology is founded in the Roman tradition. This is in keeping with what is found in the holy fathers cited by *IGMR2002* (no. 8), namely Irenaeus (d. ca. 200), Cyril of Jerusalem (d. 387), Ambrose (d. 397) and John Chrysostom (d. 407).

This said, with relief one can note that *IGMR2002* modifies *IGMR1975* not only by adding new material but by eliminating offensive material as well. *IGMR1975* contains a section that detailed the participation of women, saying that their ministries must be exercised outside the sanctuary at the discretion

7. On the one priesthood of Christ in which all Christians share by participation in its blessings and its offering, see *Sermo* 8.6–8 on the Passion (*PL* 54:340–342). Although the term is not frequently employed, the image of the Church as Body of Christ exists in the sermons of Leo alongside that of royal priesthood.

of the rector, while participation of women at the altar itself was completely denied (no. 70). The US adaptation of *IGMR1975* did not limit their participation to outside the sanctuary area, either as readers, cantors, musicians, etc.; however the participation of women at the altar continued to be denied until 1994. *IGMR2002* must be complimented on having left behind any gender-specific ministries except that of the ordained presider (e.g., no. 107).

Liturgy and Theology of the Word

SC recognizes the presence of Christ to the Church through the proclamation of the Scriptures (no. 7). The section of *IGMR2002* on the Liturgy of the Word (nos. 55–71) brings out the meditative, active, and participatory aspects of this part of the Mass. As the Second Vatican Council said, Word and Eucharist belong together in constituting the celebration of Christ's mysteries. Together they belong in the Church as expression and manifestation of what it is for the Church to live and celebrate the mystery of salvation, centered on Christ.

This is not simply giving attention to the Word of God in the Sacred Scriptures, but attending to an act of the Church, the Word presented and received within the faith of the Church as it relates the Scriptures to the mystery of Christ. It is for this reason that the Gospel is the "high point." In faith and in celebration of the Paschal Mystery, the Church reads the rest of the Scriptures in relation to Christ, as the Risen Christ himself did when he encountered the two disciples on the road to Emmaus. While the Church reads the Scriptures in different ways in different settings, in the liturgy they are heard in the context of faith proclaimed in the creed and ritualized in the solemnity attached to the proclamation of the gospel. Since the Liturgy of the Word is an act of the assembly, an act of Church, and an expression of the faith of the royal priesthood, it is good that *IGMR2002* underlines the active and conscious elements of the participation of all, not only by listening but also by silence and by song, and by the participation of readers who belong to the body of the baptized.

In presenting the role of the homily (nos. 65, 66) the Instruction attends most of all to its didactic or instructional character (see no. 28 below), and the need to relate the texts to the liturgical year and its feasts. This is indeed something that is indicated in the didactic principles of *SC*. Readers and interpreters of the Instruction will also be mindful of the place of the homily in bringing about what liturgical theology speaks of as the "actualization" of God's Word. This is to say that in its celebration of the mystery of Christ and Church, the homilist also guides the people of God as they learn to see how the mystery unfolded in the scriptures is brought to reality in the particular circumstances of their own lives and place in history. So will they continue to discover how, in the Holy Spirit, the Lord continues to be present to the Church in the Word.

IGMR2002 makes some mention of the role of the Spirit in the meditation of the Scriptures (no. 56), but it could have said more on the place of the Spirit in the Liturgy of the Word, since the Spirit is active there as well as in the Liturgy of the Eucharist. To see more fully the role of the Spirit in the Liturgy of the Word, one may refer to the *praenotanda* of the *Ordo Lectionum* (*OLM1981-Pr*) where mention is made several times of the action of the Spirit in the Liturgy of the Word.[8]

In *OLM1981-Pr* the role of the Spirit in the hearts of the faithful as they individually meditate the Scriptures is indeed mentioned (nos. 3, 9, 28). It goes forward, however, in recalling that the assembly gathers in the Spirit to hear the Word (no. 7) and that it is in the power of the Spirit that the Word is proclaimed and received in faith. *OLM1981-Pr* also relates the work of the Spirit in the Liturgy of the Word to the work of the Spirit in the economy of revelation and salvation. First it refers to the Sacred Scriptures as works inspired by the Spirit (no. 2). Then it recalls that, when read in the assembly, the proclamation of the work of salvation becomes a living and effective Word through the power of the Spirit (no. 4) and relates the response of the Church to the Amen pronounced by Christ when, as he shed his blood to seal God's covenant, he did so in the Holy Spirit (no. 6). Christ and Church are thus bound together in their response to God's initiative and grace through the Holy Spirit. Finally, it says that it is the Spirit who endows the Church with a diversity of gifts, for the building up of the Church in faith in God's Word (nos. 9 and 12).

To this relation between Word and Spirit affecting the Liturgy of the Word, one could add some further points. We know how throughout liturgical history, churches have made their selection of passages in faith, but the faith is what is bestowed when heeding the Spirit and reading the Scriptures in the light given by the Spirit. This is also the eschatological Spirit which is at work, and in this we know that all hearing of the Scripture, all appropriation of the Word of God, is done in anticipation of the Lord's coming, just as communion in his Body and Blood is a proclamation of the Lord's death, "until he comes." In this proclamation and expectation, there is in the power of the Spirit an even more intimate link between the Liturgy of the Word and the Liturgy of the Eucharist in the celebration of the Mass.

Theology and Liturgy of Eucharistic Sacrifice

In its Preamble, *IGMR2002* presents a theology of eucharistic sacrifice as fundamental to traditional Catholic understanding and celebration of the Mass. This needs some examination and discussion. The Preamble was added by Paul VI (d. 1978) to address some of the complaints that the new Order of Mass was not in continuity with tradition. It speaks insistently of the sacrificial nature of the Mass. It quotes selectively from *SC*, no. 47, stressing that "At the Last Supper our Savior instituted the Eucharistic Sacrifice of his Body and Blood, by which he would perpetuate the Sacrifice of the Cross throughout the centuries. . ." (*Salvator noster*

8. *OLM1981-Pr*, nos. 3, 6, 7, 9, 12 and 28.

in Cena novissima sacrificium eucharisticum Corporis et Sanguinis sui instituit, quo sacrificium crucis in saecula, IGMR2002, no. 2). Referencing the *Veronense* the text further states, "As often as the commemoration of this sacrifice is celebrated, the work of our redemption is carried out" (*quoties huius hostiae commemoratio celebratur, opus nostrae redemptionis exercetur,* no. 2). And again, the priest in the name of the whole people renders God thanks and offers the living and holy Sacrifice. Instituted at the Last Supper, the Mass is the sacramental renewal of the sacrifice of the cross, a sacrifice of praise and thanksgiving, of propitiation and satisfaction (no. 2). The ministerial priesthood and the royal priesthood of believers unite their spiritual sacrifice with the sacrifice of Christ and together give thanks for the mystery of salvation in Christ through the eucharistic sacrifice (no. 5).

The Eucharist is to be understood as a "commemorative sacrifice"; it is a memorial of Christ's death and resurrection, a sacrifice acceptable to the Father and salvific for the whole world (nos. 2 and 17). *IGMR2002* speaks further of memorial, stating that in the Mass the mysteries of redemption are recalled "so as in some way to be made present" (*ut quodammodo praesentia reddantur,* no. 16). Because of this the Eucharist serves as the high point of God's work to sanctify the world and of humanity's efforts to offer worship to God (no. 16).

What is surprising is the lack of stress on Eucharist as the expression and source of the communion of the Church, although there are some places that pick up this theme. One reference we do find to Eucharist as communion is in the section of the Eucharistic Prayer on the offering. There the assembly is invited to offer themselves to the Father so that through Christ the Mediator they may be united with God and with each other (no. 79f). While this sentence footnotes *Eucharisticum Mysterium* (no. 12), which is a passing reference to eucharistic communion, it ignores the extended section on the Eucharistic Mystery and the Unity of Christians in no. 8 of that document and a more limited section on communion with the local and universal church and even of all humanity in *Eucharisticum Mysterium,* no. 18. A second reference to communion in *IGMR2002* is made in the description of the fraction rite which states that "the many faithful are made one body (1 Cor 10:17) by receiving Communion from the one Bread of Life which is Christ" (*significat fideles multos in Communione ex uno pane vitae, qui est Christus . . . unum corpus effici,* no. 83, see also nos. 5 and 321), but there is no elaboration upon it.

IGMR2002 presents its theological understanding of the Eucharist starting in nos. 2 and 72. In no. 2 of the Preamble, *IGMR2002* quotes only what is said of the institution of the memorial sacrifice and omits the rest of *SC,* no. 47. On the other hand, no. 72 is more complete: "At the Last Supper Christ instituted the Paschal Sacrifice and banquet by which the Sacrifice of the Cross is continuously made present in the Church whenever the priest, representing Christ the Lord, carries out what the Lord himself did and handed over to his disciples to be done in his memory" (*In Cena novissima, Christus sacrificium et convivium paschale instituit, quo sacrificium crucis in Ecclesia continue praesens efficitur, cum sacerdos, Christum Dominum repraesentans, idem perficit quod ipse Dominus egit atque discipulis in sui memoriam faciendum tradidit*). This paragraph balances the Preamble's emphasis on the Mass as sacrifice by stating that the Mass is both Paschal Sacrifice and *banquet*. This addition of banquet imagery is suggestive of the eschatological banquet of the Lamb and at the same time places greater emphasis on the meal nature of the Eucharist (see no. 281). *IGMR2002* goes further than its predecessors in making normative the communion of both bread and cup first by repeating that Holy Communion has a fuller form as a sign when it is distributed under both kinds (no. 282), and then by making small but significant changes in phrases and in ritual action. In describing the Fraction Rite, *IGMR2002* spells out in a fuller way the reception from bread and cup. "The faithful, though they are many, receive from the one bread the Lord's Body and from the one chalice the Lord's Blood. . ." (*fideles, quamvis multi, ex uno pane accipiunt Corpus et ex uno calice Sanguinem Domini*, no. 72.3). Following the Lamb of God, the priest is now allowed to raise the host "above the chalice" (*super calicem*), showing more clearly the unity of the body and blood of the Lord (nos. 84 and 157). The number of occasions when communion under both forms may be received is significantly broadened (nos. 281–287). Several occasions are listed when it is expected, and then it is up to the discretion of bishop and priests to decide when it is pastorally more suitable.

The Eucharistic Prayer is introduced as the center and summit of the Mass and is described as that great prayer of thanksgiving and sanctification (no. 78). Whereas for a long time almost all attention was given to the institution narrative and its consecratory effect, current scholarship has spent enormous energy in considering the history and meaning of the whole Eucharistic Prayer as a unit and the function of the institution narrative within this great prayer.[9] The addition of nine other Eucharistic Prayers to the traditional Roman Canon has likewise broadened the discussion of what constitutes eucharistic praying.

Reiterating *IGMR1975* (no. 54), *IGMR2002* states that the meaning of the prayer is that the entire congregation "should join itself to Christ in confessing the great deeds of God and in the offering of Sacrifice" (*se cum Christo coniungat in confessione magnalium Dei et in oblatione sacrificii*, no. 78). It then briefly explains each part of the Eucharistic Prayer. The *thanksgiving* expresses thanksgiving for all the works of salvation, the *acclamation* is a joining with heavenly powers, the *epiclesis* is where the church implores the power of the Holy Spirit to consecrate the gifts and transform the community. The *institution narrative and consecration* is explained as the means by which the Sacrifice is carried out, while the *anamnesis* is where the Church keeps memorial of the Paschal Mystery.

9. On the parts of the prayer and the pertinent literature, see David N. Power, "A Prayer of Intersecting Parts: Elements of the Eucharistic Prayer," *Liturgical Ministry* 14 (Summer 2005): 120–131; also no. 43 below.

The *offering* is where the church offers in the Holy Spirit the spotless victim to the Father, and the *intercessions* plead for the whole church, living and dead, for the redemption purchased by Christ's Body and Blood. The *doxology* is the final act of glorification of God and concludes with the people's Amen (no. 79a-h). What is of special significance is the giving of consecratory power to the epiclesis, aligning the Latin West more closely with the Eastern Churches than it has been in a millennium.

Priest and Faithful

A problem with the Instruction's theology of sacrifice lies in the way in which it distinguishes between the role of the ordained priest and the role of the congregation of the faithful. In the didactic part of the document, *IGMR2002* puts the doctrinal focus on the nature of the Eucharist as sacramental and memorial sacrifice. The basic principle is enunciated in no. 2 of the Instruction, quoting the prayer over the offerings of the Mass of Holy Thursday: "as often as commemoration is kept of Christ's sacrifice, our redemption is renewed" (*quoties huius hostiae commemoratio celebratur, opus nostrae redemptionis exercetur)*. In line with theological and liturgical history, this makes it quite clear that the Eucharist may be called a sacrifice inasmuch as it is memorial and sacramental. The Instruction, however, immediately goes on to locate this offering in the Eucharistic Prayer as proclaimed by the ordained priest, who in performing the commemoration prays in the name of the whole people, offering the Church's offering. Later, in treating of the Eucharistic Prayer in its various parts (no. 79), *IGMR2002* locates the renewal of sacrifice in the words and actions of Christ himself in the institution narrative, now repeated by the priest, and the offering of this sacrifice in what follows in the Eucharistic Prayer. In reference to the epiclesis, the role of the Spirit in the consecration through the words of Jesus, and the role of the Spirit in the offering by the Church, is acknowledged (no. 79c).

It is repeated several times (nos. 2, 5, 16) that the eucharistic action and eucharistic offering is the work of the whole Church. This, however, is said to be achieved in virtue of its hierarchical ordering (no. 16) and depends on the exercise of the ministerial priesthood. The inclusion of the people in the sacrifice is treated in nos. 5 and 79: their role is to offer their spiritual sacrifice, to offer not only Christ but also themselves. This is their exercise of their royal priesthood, as distinct from the ministerial priesthood. The document makes a clear distinction therefore between the royal priesthood of the people and the ministerial priesthood of the ordained. Indeed, it claims that the former can be exercised only in virtue of the latter. Even more, the priesthood of the laity is fully comprehensible only by being related to the latter (no. 5).

Within the Roman tradition, Leo the Great certainly underlines the spiritual action of priesthood and kingship within the Body of Christ, but there is a better integration of the spiritual and the sacramental in the corpus of his sermons. Within Leo's vision of the work of redemption as mystery and sacrament, the visible and bodily are intertwined with the invisible and spiritual.[10] An offering that is *rationabilis*, as it is called by him and indeed later in the Roman Canon, is one made according to the Spirit, but it is both external and internal, or in other words truly sacramental. The liturgical roles of the bishop and the people differ, but together, acting as one, they constitute the mystery and sacrament of Christ's redemptive action and true sacrifice. It is through liturgy, externally expressed devotion, e.g., by the gifts brought, participation in liturgy, or Lenten penance, and through following the *exemplum* of Christ himself, that all may share in the offering of the one true *hostia*, which was offered not on the altar of the temple but on the altar of the world.[11]

The Roman Tradition: the Appeal to Doctrine

Fundamentally, the position taken by *IGMR2002* on the nature of eucharistic sacrifice dictates its positions on other matters. This affects the theology of eucharistic communion and the communion of all participants, the theology of assembly that underlies what is said of the Eucharist as manifestation of the Church and of active and conscious participation, and the theology of the Word that underlies what is said of the Liturgy of the Word. We need then to consider how true to the Roman liturgical and doctrinal tradition is *IGMR*'s theology of eucharistic sacrifice, which is given in the Preamble as the most fundamental theological principle for the celebration of the eucharistic liturgy.

In presenting its position, the current Roman Instruction refers to the doctrinal authority of both the Council of Trent and the Second Vatican Council. Leaving aside momentarily the claim to organic growth in liturgical celebration, one may ask whether in relation to these two magisterial sources the document represents an organic growth in doctrine. The difficulty is that the appeal to these past formulations of doctrine is incomplete.

Council of Trent

In citing Trent, the Instruction is not faithful to its own principle of seeing Trent in its context, when treatment of the sacrament, treatment of sacrifice and treatment of communion under one or two kinds were divided into three separate decrees, some years apart and each addressing some very specific controverted issues. In the course of these decrees, Trent actually uses the language of institution more than once to state what Christ did. The Decree on the Sacrament says clearly that in instituting it, Christ wished his Church in its consumption (*in sumptione*) to cultivate or cherish (*colere*) his memory and to proclaim

10. On Leo and the liturgy, see M. de Soos, *Le mystère liturgique d'après saint Léon le Grand* (Münster: Aschendorff, 1958).

11. . . . *nova hostia, novo imponeretur altari, et crux Christi non templi esset ara, sed mundi.* Sermon VIII on the Passion, no. 5 in *Léon le Grand, Sermons,* 2nd ed., ed. René Dolle, Sources Chrétiennes 74 (Paris: Éditions du Cerf, 1961), 112.

his death, here quoting 1 Corinthians 11:26.[12] That is to see the rite of communion as a sacramentally commemorative act. Alongside the Tridentine statement that Christ left the eucharistic sacrifice to his Church, to be offered by priests, to represent and commemorate his own sacrifice,[13] we have the assertion that this death is remembered and proclaimed in sacramental communion. This is not mentioned by *IGMR2002*.

As the Instruction says, the Church needs to place Trent and our dependence upon it in a larger historical context. The teachings of Trent, as well as the liturgical practices or texts that these teachings sanctioned, have to be seen in the light of the holy fathers and liturgical traditions. If in present theology and liturgy we are to refer back to Trent, a more complete and accurate treatment is surely required than is given by the Instruction. Trent, given the difference in time and concern, did not itself coordinate these statements into a harmonious doctrine, but doctrine and theology cannot eliminate the problem by preferring one set of conciliar statements and passing over others in silence.[14]

Sacrifice: The Liturgical Tradition

The initial description of the Eucharist as a sacrifice is accompanied in *IGMR2002* by a reference (no. 2) to the prayer over the gifts in the Mass of the Lord's Supper on Holy Thursday, a prayer whose origins can be traced back to *Veronense*. The Missal has in fact changed the original text, but that had indeed already been done in other sacramentaries and *MR1570*. The prayer from the present Liturgy of Holy Thursday mentioned in the Instruction and which is based on *Veronense* reads: *quoties hostiae commemoratio celebratur, opus nostrae redemptionis exercetur* ("as often as the commemoration of this sacrifice is celebrated, the work of our redemption is carried out").

The text given in *IGMR2002*, no. 2, dates to *MR1570*. In the old Roman Sacramentary it reads: *Da nobis haec, quaesumus, domine, frequentata mysteria: quia quotiens hostiae tibi placatae commemoratio celebrantur, opus nostrae redemptionis exeritur* (no. 93).[15] This is a prayer for the offerings of the gifts of the faithful. While the first part of the prayer asks that we may always be given the grace of frequenting the mysteries celebrated, the second and pertinent part could

12. Session 13, ch. 2, in Tanner, 2:693.

13. Session 22, chs. 1–2 in Tanner, 2:733–34.

14. In this regard, it is of no little interest to note how the various elements and images of the Eucharist are presented in the letter inviting the Church to the observance of a special eucharistic year, *Mane nobiscum* (2004). In no. 15 of this letter, John Paul II draws attention to the most obvious sacramental sign, that of eucharistic meal, eating and drinking the Body and Blood of Christ. He points out that the important and irreplaceable theologies of sacrifice and presence need to be related to this sign, and that it is also in this sign that we can ground the Eucharist's eschatological orientation.

15. The text is given as in the critical edition, complete with what look to us as grammatical errors.

be translated: "as often as the commemoration of the victim/offering pleasing to you is celebrated, the work of our redemption is carried out."

It is significant that the reference in the Instruction seems to assume that there is but one meaning to the word *hostia*, so that it avoids the complex usage of this and other cultic terms in the original forms of the Roman liturgy. The use of the word *hostia* in Christian Latin is rooted in the Latin translation of Ephesians 5:2, though in patristic writings it is not very broadly used. The liturgy, however, has appropriated several cultic uses of the term found in a wider Latin cultic literature.

One must then ask what meaning and significance is given to the word *hostia* in this early collection of Roman prayers known as *Veronense*.[16] Given the historical affinities between the Roman liturgy and that of Alexandria, it is not surprising to see that in Roman sources, the most prominent use of *hostia*, usually in the plural, is when it is used of the sacrifice of praise (*hostiae laudis*), which is offered in memorial of Christ and all God's wonderful deeds.[17] Indeed it is a well-regarded hypothesis that the language of sacrifice was introduced into the Roman Liturgy in reference to this, and under the influence of the Christian reading of Malachi 1:11.[18] To grasp fully the significance of this commemorative praise, however, one has to consider the multiplicity of meanings given to *hostia* in the Roman liturgy.

In *Veronense* there are only a few places where *hostia* is directly identified with Christ himself and his offering on the cross. In two cases it is said that the mystery or commemoration of Christ's sacrifice is kept. Number 93 says that it commemorates or keeps memorial of it, while no. 92 places this commemoration in the offering of praise, from which one cannot cease in the remembrance of God's wonderful acts. Number 253 is more complex, saying that the Church in its service brings forth (*deferimus*) this spiritual victim, which in this wonderful and ineffable mystery is both immolated and offered, being both the gift of those who come in devout service and the reward given by the one who recompenses. [19]

16. This essay focuses on the word *hostia*, given its use in the Instruction, but of course a complete study would have to look to the rest of the vocabulary of gift and offering found in liturgical Latin.

17. See the index to the *Sacramentarium Veronense*, ed. Leo Cunibert Mohlberg, Rerum Ecclesiasticarum Documenta, 2nd ed. (Rome: Herder, 1966), s.v. *hostia*; for other sacramentaries see the verbal concordance published by Jean Deshusses. Jean Deshusses-Benoit Darragon, *Concordances et tableaux pour l'étude des grands sacramentaires*, 6 vols., Spicilegii Friburgensis Subsidia, 9–14 (Fribourg: Éditions Universitaires, 1983) 3.2:268–72.

18. Enrico Mazza, *The Origins of the Eucharistic Prayer*, trans. Ronald A. Lane (Collegeville, MN: The Liturgical Press, 1995), 191–193.

19. *Remotis obumbrationibus carnalium victimarum spiritalem tibi, summe pater, hostiam supplici servitude deferimus, quae miro ineffabilique mysterio et immolater semper et eadem semper offertur, pariterque et devotorum munus et remunerantis est praemium.*

There is an unusual reference to the gifts as the body and blood of Christ in *Veronense*, no. 1246. This is a prayer for the offering of gifts and so occurs before the memorial prayer. The text identifies the gift (*munus*) of the people with the body and blood of Christ, but this is clearly in the sense that they are types, figures, or symbols of them, since the elements have not yet been blessed.[20] In other words, the prayer gives a sacramental meaning to the action of the people in making gifts, which relates it to the commemoration of Christ's own offering. This is not unlike what we find in the elements of the Canon found in both Ambrose of Milan and the Mozarabic *Liber Ordinum*. Ambrose refers to the oblations of the people as the figure (*figura*) of the body and blood of Christ,[21] while the Mozarabic book calls them the *imago* or image.[22]

Beyond the designation of praise as *hostia* and the direct reference to Christ as *hostia*, one has to be alert to the other interlocked meanings given to *hostia* in the context of the Roman Mass, which can be verified by looking at other prefaces and offertory prayers in *Veronense*. There we see that it includes the gifts offered by the faithful, their praise and their devout prayers (e.g., nos. 21, 29, 38, 72, 131, 142, 201, 202). In the act of commemoration, it is the entire complex of offerings, including those offered by the faithful who render their service to God, which is pleasing to God. These are easily verified in *Veronense* and indeed remain scattered throughout *MR1975*.[23] The action of the people, their prayers and devotion, and the Eucharistic Prayer offered with and for them by the bishop/priest, all together constitute the sacramental memorial of Christ's offering, whereby God is pleased and placated.

In the Roman Canon, for which we have evidence in the *Sacramentarium Gelasianum* (*Gelasianum*), the multiple references of the term *hostia* are retained. The various meanings of *hostia* come together in the *Unde et memores* or anamnesis. After the recital of the supper narrative and memorial command, the Church offers the pure, holy, and immaculate sacrifice (*hostia*) and then in the following prayer appeals to the memory of the sacrifices of Abel, Abraham, and Melchisedech, which God saw fit to accept. The meaning of this anamnesis is elucidated in a preface for Christmas found in *Veronense*[24] and included in *Gelasianum*. The Church unceasingly immolates the sacrifice of praise (*tuae*

20. An English translation of the prayer: "Look kindly, O Lord, on the gift of your people, by which it is not some alien fire that is placed on the altar, nor is it the blood shed of senseless animals, but by the working of the Holy Spirit it is already the body and blood of our priest (*pontifex*) himself."

21. *Ambroise de Milan, Des sacraments. Des mystères*, ed. Bernard Botte, Sources Chrétiennes 25bis (Paris: Éditions du Cerf, 1961), 108, 114–116.

22. *Le Liber Ordinum en usage dans l'église wisigothique et mozarabe d'Espagne du cinquième au onzième siècle*, ed. Marius Férotin, Monumenta Ecclesiae Liturgica 5 (Paris: Librairie de Firmin-Didot, 1904), 321.

23. See Winfried Haunerland, *Die Eucharistie und ihre Wirkungen im Spiegel der Euchologie des Missale Romanum* (Münster: Aschendorf, 1989), 77–84.

24. *Veronense*, no. 1250.

laudis hostiam iugiter immolantes), a sacrifice or offering prefigured in the offering of Abel, celebrated by Abraham and Melchisedech, instituted by the Lamb, prescribed by the Law, and fulfilled this day (Christmas) in the true Lamb and eternal High Priest. It is the Church's praise, which is said to be the sacrifice immolated, this however being a sacrifice in virtue of what was prefigured and is now fulfilled in Christ.

As Joseph Jungmann commented, the petition of the Canon is made in clear reference to the self-offering of Christ, which has been recalled in the Supper narrative and which is in the Eucharist commemorated and present in mystery.[25] It is, however, the Church which is making offering, in a way that incorporates into one its commemorative praise, the devotion of the faithful, and their gifts of bread and wine over which the prayer is prayed. In other words, the efficacious representation of the self-offering or sacrifice of Christ is made through the Church's sacramental action of a prayer of praise which takes up into itself the offerings of the people.

In short, in citing the liturgical tradition, *IGMR2002* attends to only one sense of the word, that namely of the unique sacrifice of Christ, ignoring any possible reference to other offerings. This reflects a problem with offering which is already present in the revisions of the *Ordo Missae* after the Second Vatican Council. The most obvious example of this is the replacement of Offertory Rites with what is called the preparation of gifts. The Missal, however, still has the Roman Canon and has yet to come to terms with the Roman tradition of making offerings, of talking clearly of these offerings, and yet not taking away from the once-and-for-all offering of the Paschal Victim.[26]

Holy Spirit and Offering

In the chapter of *SC* on the Eucharist and in its short doctrinal definition of the Eucharist, the Council failed to include the action of the Holy Spirit.[27] On the other hand, when the commission for the renewal of the eucharistic liturgy included new prayers in the *Ordo Missae*, these incorporated a twofold epiclesis, one before and one after the Supper narrative. *IGMR2002* includes no mention of the Holy Spirit in its Preamble or doctrinal introduction on eucharistic sacrifice. When presenting the Eucharistic Prayer, it defines the function of the

25. Joseph Jungmann, *The Mass of the Roman Rite*, trans. Francis Brunner, 2 vols. (Westminster: Christian Classics, 1986), II: 225–231. See also Haunerland, as cited above, n. 23.

26. There seems to have been some feeling of embarrassment in ecumenical dialogue over this profusion of offerings, but rather than suppress them we have to be attentive to their sacramental significance, within the commemoration of the Lord's Supper and Sacrifice.

27. For a discussion of the role of the Holy Spirit in the Eucharist, with particular reference to offering, see John McKenna, *Eucharist and the Holy Spirit* (London: Mayhew-McCrimmon, 1975); idem, "The Epiclesis Revisited: A Look at Modern Eucharistic Prayers," *Ephemerides Liturgicae* 99 (1985): 313–36; Edward Kilmartin, *The Eucharist in the West: History and Theology*, ed. Robert J. Daley (Collegeville, MN: The Liturgical Press, 1998); Patrick Regan, "Quenching the Spirit: The Epiclesis in Recent Roman Documents," *Worship* 79 (2005): 386–404.

invocation of the Spirit, saying that this invocation implores that by the power of the Spirit the gifts offered by human hands may be consecrated, and that the spotless Victim may be received in communion unto salvation (no. 79c).

The revised Order of Mass was intended to overcome the shortcoming of the Roman liturgical tradition, and particularly of the Canon, in its failure to include the invocation of the Spirit. How this may be done harmoniously needs examination. The Instruction's description of the epiclesis touches on this point and on its own emphasis on sacrifice when it mentions the invocation over the gifts offered by human hands. To pursue the matter further, however, we may find a point of departure in the affinity between the Alexandrian Liturgy of Mark and the Roman Canon.[28]

The liturgy of Alexandria, like that of Rome, includes much of the rich language of offering, inclusive of the gifts, the devotion of the people, and the sacrifice of praise, and it has the same mention of Abel, Abraham, and Melchisedech. It has, however, been influenced by Eastern traditions in its inclusion, at two moments of the prayer, of an invocation of the Spirit. This in fact harmonizes well with the imagery of sacrifice and offering and may be taken as an example for a similar inclusion in the Roman liturgy. The first epiclesis comes after the *Sanctus*. The *Sanctus* itself is the conclusion to the sacrifice of praise and to the prayers of petition for the acceptance of offerings that mark the Alexandrian anaphora. It is the final word of praise of the mystery of the suffusion of the world by the holiness of God, in creation and redemption, the final words of the hymn of the Church's offering. Following the *Sanctus*, the congregation in the person of its minister is moved to implore that by the descent of the Holy Spirit this fullness of divine glory may fill the offering which it has made. This leads to the recital of the Supper narrative, which is given as the motivation for this request.

The second invocation of the Spirit comes after the narrative and the anamnesis whereby the death of the Lord is proclaimed in expectation of his coming. It is then in remembering the mysteries of Christ's flesh that the Church prays for the sending of the Holy Spirit upon the loaves and cups offered, that they may be sanctified and perfected and become the body and the blood of the covenant. This is for the sake of those who, having brought them and praised God, will partake of them and through them participate in the praise of the divine name, or in God's holiness and glory. In making the petition, the Church remembers how the Spirit is present everywhere and fills everything, and how it worked through the Law and the prophets and the Apostles, and shares the throne of God's kingdom together with the Son. Rather than an epiclesis that

28. Mazza, *Origins*, 243–282. See also Louis Bouyer, *Eucharistie. Théologie et spiritualité de la prière eucharistique* (Paris: Desclée, 1966), 193–196, 207–212. An English translation of the prayer may be found in R. C. D. Jasper and G. J. Cuming, *Prayers of the Eucharist: Early and Reformed*, 3rd ed. (New York: Pueblo Publishing Company, 1987), 57–66.

has a different purpose than the first, it repeats its main elements and complements it.

What can be seen from this anaphora is how well the request for the presence and action of the Spirit harmonizes with its own sacrificial language and theology. The Church's offering of praise for God's deeds, and its prayers that its offering be acceptable, is perfected through the action of the Holy Spirit, whose action fills it with divine holiness and glory so that it may truly resound to the glory of God's name. It is also the sending of the Spirit which sanctifies the gifts of bread and wine so that they may become the body and blood of Christ and so that their consumption may bring them to a fuller share in God's holiness and in the praise of the divine name, a holiness and a praise which are to continue to be perfected until the coming of the Lord in the visible manifestation of his glory.

It is in fact in light of the singing of the Holy that the first epiclesis is introduced into Eucharistic Prayers II and III of the new *Ordo Missae*, even if it sounds muted in comparison with the Liturgy of Mark. However, the second epiclesis is purely a prayer for the grace of the Spirit on those who consume the body and blood of Christ. Whatever criticism may be made of the Roman liturgy's form of double epiclesis, there is nonetheless material in the revised Missal on which *IGMR2002* might have drawn in presenting the action of the Holy Spirit in the Church's commemorative prayer and in the sanctification of the gifts. Seeing how the Roman prayers draw on the Liturgy of Mark, and with this liturgy itself in mind, we can see how a harmonious and organic development of the Roman liturgy's sacrificial theology, open to the influences of the East, may integrate an invocation of the Holy Spirit.

Theology and Rite

There are some instances of rubrical directives where the influence of *IGMR*'s somewhat limited theology of eucharistic sacrifice is apparent. This pertains in particular to the preparation of gifts and the rite of communion.

Preparation of Gifts

Number 73 of the Instruction addresses the preparation of the gifts before the Eucharistic Prayer. In what it says, it is faced by the dilemma of how to relate its directives to the theology of sacrifice that it has already given. How may the gifts of the faithful be said to belong in the sacramental commemoration of the once-and-for-all sacrifice of Christ? The Instruction says that the "gifts" (*dona*), the "bread and wine," the "offerings" (*oblationes*) are brought forward as part of the preparation. Indeed, no. 74 even refers to this part of the Mass as the offertory, when it mentions the *cantus ad offertorium* (see no. 37 below).

Sense has to be attributed to these offerings made by the people, though the matter is made somewhat ambiguous when the Instruction notes that today the bread and wine do not come from the people themselves as in earlier times.

They do not bring offerings, yet they are said to make gifts and offerings. In light of this situation the Instruction states that, even though the people do not today offer of their own possessions, the rite "still retains its force and its spiritual significance." What this force and spiritual significance could be is unclear in light of three uncoordinated assertions. In the first place, this action is said to be a preparation of the gifts to be consecrated rather than an offering; in the second, the things brought are still said to be gifts and offerings; while in the third, it is said that the people do not offer of their own possessions. It is not clear what the significance is supposed to be, though no doubt the position taken is in line with the theology that allows a spiritual but not a material or sacramental offering to the royal priesthood. Talking of a spiritual significance which can remain, even though the corporeal and earthly significance has disappeared, undermines the sense of a rite that is rooted in human life and its vivid corporeality.

Sacramental Communion

Given its stress on offering sacrifice in commemoration of Christ's own, *IGMR2002* is jejune on the meaning of the Communion and the Communion rite. In the Preamble, it says only that the people who offer their spiritual sacrifice are "made one by sharing in the Communion of Christ's Body and Blood" (*qui per Communionem Corporis et Sanguinis Christi in unum coalescit,* no. 5). In no. 85 it does add that receiving from hosts consecrated at the Mass being celebrated, or receiving of the chalice, are signs whereby it stands out more clearly that the people "participate in the sacrifice actually being celebrated" (*participatio sacrificii, quod actu celebratur*). In no. 281 on communion under both kinds, the Instruction finds that this is a more evident sign of participation in the eucharistic banquet and the ratification of the New Covenant "in the Blood of the Lord" (*in Sanguine Domini*).

Something more would need to be said on how sharing at the communion table is integral to the sacramental sign of the commemoration of the Lord's sacrifice. Do the prayers of the Sacramentary shed any further light on this connection between sacrifice, proclamation and communion? Prayers after Communion in the old Roman sacramentaries do not use the word *hostia.* They do, however, continue to use cultic and sacrificial vocabulary, especially through the words *libamen* and *libatio,* which in sacrifice meant partaking of drink offerings. God is asked to give earthly and eternal benefits to those who partake of the gift (*munus*) and drink offering of the Lord's body and blood.[29]

How this is connected with the act of offering itself, being as it were its completion, is expressed in the following post-Communion prayer from *Veronense*: "Filled with the libation of the sacred body and precious blood, we ask you, Lord our God: grant that what we enact with faithful devotion, we may

29. *Veronense*, nos. 6, 69, 441, 561, 585 and 1202.

obtain by certain redemption."[30] In one of the prefaces of the *Hadrianum* in which thanksgiving has turned to petition, similar expression is given to this total sacramental action through using the figure of the offering of Melchisedech,[31] which as we know is also found in the Roman Canon. The preface recalls first the *oblatio* or offering which he made, then the gifts (*munera*) upon the altar, and finally the consumption *(libamen)* of what has been offered.

These prayers may serve as background to better understand the doctrinal positions of the Council of Trent, which in separate decrees state that the Lord's death and self-offering is represented in the sacrifice of the Eucharist and that it is proclaimed in the act of consumption. It is when these two assertions are brought together to speak of the sacramental action in its totality that we can appreciate the eucharistic action as the action of the whole congregation, priest and people. In their respective ways, they together celebrate the sacrament and memorial of the Lord's death. The people's action, the priest's prayers and the people's communion, together constitute the sacrament and memorial sacrifice of the Lord's Pasch.

Why the Church and its members can make offerings, either of praise, devotion, or gifts, through which the redemptive sacrifice of Christ is commemorated and celebrated, is made clear through the ways in which the assembly is designated. It is the people of God (*plebs, populus*)[32] and the Church (*aeclesia*)[33] of God, the body of the Church made up of many members (*corpus aeclesiae*),[34] which has been made one through the power of baptism and the sanctification of the Spirit. It is as such a people that they make their offerings, so that Christ and the Spirit are at work in them. It is not a random gathering, but the gathering of those who have been given the grace to partake of the exchange of natures brought about by the mysteries of Christ's flesh.

This leads us to take note that some other prayers from the old sacramentaries show how this conception of sacrifice is grounded in the image of commerce or exchange that is brought about through the incarnation. By taking on human

30. *Veronense*, no. 16: *Corporis sacri et praetiosi sanguinis repleti libamine quaesumus, Deus noster: quod pia devotione gerimus, certa redemptione capiamus.*

31. *Hadrianum*, no. 821: . . . *te supplices deprecamur, ut altare hoc sanctis usibus praeparatum, caelesti dedicatione sanctifices, et sicut Melchisedech sacerdotis praecipui oblationem dignatione mirabili suscepisti, ita imposito novo huic altari munera semper accepta ferre digneris, ut populus qui in hanc ecclesiae domum sanctam convenit, per haec libamina celesti sanctificatione salvatus animarum quoque suarum salutem perpetuam consequatur* (". . . with supplication we beseech you, that you may sanctify this altar prepared by holy usage, and as by wonderful condescension you accepted the oblation of the high priest Melchisedech, so may you always grant that the gifts placed on this new altar may be made acceptable, so that the people which has gathered in this holy house of the church, saved through these libations by heavenly sanctification, may attain the eternal salvation of their souls").

32. E.g., *Veronense*, nos. 3, 8, 17, 36, 87, 100, 168, 212 (where the reference is to the offerings of your people, *hostia populi tui)*, 241, 286 (*oblations populi*), 279, 581, 698, 1230.

33. E.g., *Veronense*, nos. 3, 303, 310, 316, 412, 425.

34. *Veronense*, no. 412.

nature, Christ gave humanity a share in his divine nature, so that rather than being a bartering between things of equal value the exchange is in fact a granting of the abundance which the divine gives to the nature taken up. The sacrament of the Eucharist becomes in turn the means for prolonging this exchange and is itself called a sacred exchange (*sancta commercia*) through which those who offer the sacrifice of praise receive the form of him whom they commemorate, the absolution of sins, or help in the present life and pledge of eternal joy.[35]

A knowledge of the old Roman liturgy, its actions of offering, its offertory prayers and the prayer of the Canon shows how inclusive is the ritual commemoration of the death and resurrection of Christ, even when it is designated by words of offering and sacrifice. Within the assembly of those come together in faith it runs from offering of gifts, through the Canon, to the communion in the gifts sanctified by the prayer of anamnestic thanksgiving. It is with devotion that the people are said to offer their gifts and their praise, or indeed that their devotion in its external expression is one of the things offered. This devotion is given its final sacramental expression in eating and drinking of the body and blood offered in sacrifice through the Church's commemorative thanksgiving. Therefore, the total sacrament of memorial sacrificial enactment includes: the offering of the earthly gifts of bread and wine, and along with this other gifts, acts of devotion, or devotion itself. In the commemorative sacrifice of praise offered over these gifts and all that they express, the Church is united with the once-and-for-all sacrifice of Christ. Finally, the Church assembled partakes of the sacrificial food and drink of Christ's body and blood, the people's own gifts transformed by his grace.

Attention to this liturgical tradition would have enabled the authors of the *IGMR2002* to avoid the implication that participation in offering sacrifice is one thing and communion another.[36] Communion of the assembly appears to be participation in the sacrifice enacted, and not integral to the very signification that this is by its sacramental nature communion in Christ's sacrifice and an act of memorial proclamation. In *IGMR2002*, what the priest is said to do and what the faithful are said to do may seem to be parallel actions rather than one total sacramental action.

Only in light of this separation, which is more than a distinction of roles, is it possible to treat of the issue of communion under one or under two kinds as the Instruction does. While saying that this mode of communion is more significant, the document quotes Trent's assertion that in receiving under only one kind nobody is deprived of the grace needed. There is no acknowledgment at this point that Trent dealt with this in a very particular historical situation, wishing to save itself from the political and ecclesiastical implications of meeting the demand from north European countries to give the chalice to the laity.

35. *Hadrianum*, nos. 37, 214, 421. On *commercium* in *Veronense*, see nos. 69, 90, 1249, 1260, 1256.

36. This distinction is very clear in *Mediator Dei*, no. 112.

Apart from a lapse in historical awareness, and apart from being in present circumstances a strange and stingy pastoral principle, it is also weak in the theological requirement of fidelity to ritual signs for the sake both of sacramental meaning and of bodily and spiritual participation in the sacrament.

The reference to the scriptural norm mentioned in the Instruction draws attention to the task of liturgical theology to interpret sacramental signs, words, and actions. A theology that is a presentation of the sacramental sign would be a theology of communion in bread and wine, with thanksgiving, in virtue of faith in the reality and mystery of the Word made flesh, to renew and recapitulate what God created by this same word.

Organic Growth

One of the accomplishments of focusing on the Church here and now gathered into a liturgical assembly is the importance of the particularity of each assembly. At the micro level, the presider is instructed to shape whatever instructions are necessary "in order that they respond to the understanding of those participating" (*ut participantium captui respondeant*, *IGMR2002*, no. 31). At the macro level it means taking into account the culture of a local church. *IGMR2002* adds five full paragraphs on the necessity of adaptation to the local culture (nos. 22–26).[37] Some adaptations are given over to the responsibility of the local bishop or the conference of bishops, while other adaptations are left to the presiding priest. These adaptations are made to "respond better to the needs, preparation, and culture of the participants" (*necessitatibus, praeparationi et ingenio participantium magis respondentes*, no. 24). *IGMR2002* leaves no doubt that the subject of the liturgical action is not the universal Church or even a generic local church, but a specific local church here and now gathered.

Given this view of the organic growth of the Roman Liturgy in its assimilation of cultural traditions, some questions need to be considered. The point of what has been said on sacrifice is that if the doctrinal principles about sacrifice are to follow in the tradition of the Roman liturgy, organic growth would require the inclusion of the offerings of the faithful in the sacrifice of praise and in the memorial communion with Christ in the sacrifice of Supper and Cross. However, it needs to be asked whether the revision of the Roman Missal has in fact been done in line with the principles of organic growth, and whether indeed given the current mutual interaction between Western and Eastern liturgical traditions a different liturgical growth may be in order.

37. It should be noted that *IGMR2002* speaks specifically of "adaptation" when it addresses the question of cultural accommodation; "inculturation" appears only in no. 398 and in very cautionary terms (see Francis and Neville, 465–466 below). This follows the tone and intent of *Varietates Legitimae* (*VarLeg*) or the Fourth Instruction on Inculturation where a general presentation on inculturation is given, but a preference for the more conservative adaptation is set forth.

As we know, the Roman Canon after the initial thanksgiving and the Holy, continues with the offering of the gifts of the faithful through the prayer of the priest. The new Eucharistic Prayers of the revised Missal make mention of the gifts of the people *(dona, munera*) in asking the descent of the Spirit through the first epiclesis. This is not, however, for their offering but for their transformation. Verbs of offering occur only after the Supper narrative and in strict conjunction with the anamnesis and second epiclesis. This is in line with Eastern liturgies, which do not neglect the offering of the bread and wine by the faithful but are more reticent about giving it the kind of prominence that it has in the Roman Liturgy. This serves to highlight the primacy of the offering of praise, the action of the Holy Spirit in the synaxis, and the anticipation of receiving the body and blood of Christ at the communion table.

In short, what the Roman liturgy of the Mass now offers us is a mixture of liturgical traditions, opening options to congregations as to what line to follow. The organic growth may be with the larger tradition with its emphasis on the memorial and epicletic sacrifice of praise rather than on the offering of gifts. Even in this case, however, some sacramental inclusion of the offering of the gifts is taken into account in the prayer, and the sanctifying prayer is one proclaimed with and for the congregation. In other words, even in these new developments there is no foundation for the theology of the *IGMR2002* that marks off priest's action and people's action so sharply.

When the principles of interpretation invoke the supraregional character of the Roman liturgy, this raises the issue of how it may be integrated into a variety of cultures. The liturgical historian[38] and the cultural anthropologist may well question this affirmation on the basis of an examination of texts and rites, as well as principle. For example, in revising *Hadrianum* for its use among Nordic peoples, there was simply an addition of material, something which does not amount to inculturation. Indeed, the well-known liturgical historian, Edmund Bishop,[39] in writing of the genius of the Roman Rite, saw these as simple accretions, not in organic keeping with what was the wont in Rome, as indeed he was also inclined to do for the collections known under the common name of Gelasian sacramentaries. However, putting aside questions of style, what a theological commentary may ask is whether the Instruction is in organic and harmonious continuity with the original Roman tradition when it enunciates its own theology.

This hermeneutical principle, which says that even inculturation has to be done in harmony with the Roman liturgy, is even more ambiguous as a result of the mingling of Eastern and Western traditions noted above. This may indeed be of advantage in allowing for peoples to take their own cultures and their own faith expression into account, if ever curial authorities show themselves

38. See David N. Power, "Inculturation, the Roman Rite, and Plurality of Liturgies," *Pastoral Music* 22 (June 1998): 26–29.

39. Edmund Bishop, *Liturgica Historica* (Oxford: Clarendon Press, 1918).

more ready to allow peoples to develop their own Eucharistic Prayers and their own liturgical action. Even as it is, a number of unofficial prayers from the continents of Africa and Asia could be studied for the way in which they relate on the one hand to a past inclusive of several eucharistic traditions and on the other the religious outlook of their own cultural and religious past.[40]

Conclusion

In this theological commentary, we have pointed to the relation of *IGMR2002* to earlier editions, and we have also addressed its more fundamental theological principles that guide rubrical directives and attempt to offer a pastoral understanding of liturgical celebration. While there is much that is positive, a revision of the theology of eucharistic sacrifice and a fuller integration of a theology of the Holy Spirit would have further consequences. It seems that there is still work to be done on the revision of the Roman liturgy in keeping with patristic and liturgical sources. One may conclude that in the light of the doctrinal and liturgical tradition of the Roman Church, the doctrinal part of *IGMR2002* needs a further elaboration, one that would have implications for the ceremonial directives.

40. For a brief survey of African ritual developments and texts, see F. Kabasele Lumbala, *Celebrating Jesus Christ in Africa. Liturgy and Inculturation* (Maryknoll, NY: Orbis Books, 1998), 19–57.

Preamble

(PROŒMIUM)

Margaret Mary Kelleher

Overview

The Preamble or introduction was not part of the first edition of the *Institutio Generalis Missalis Romani* (*IGMR1969*), but it did appear in the second edition of the Instruction (*IGMR1970*), which was issued with the first *editio typica* of the revised *Missale Romanum* (*MR1970*). The content of the Preamble has not undergone any substantial changes in succeeding editions, including the most recent version of *IGMR2002*.

The topics treated in the Preamble are gathered under three headings: "A Witness to Unchanged Faith" (*Testimonium fidei immutatae*), "A Witness to Unbroken Tradition" (*Traditio non intermissa declaratur*), and "Accommodation to New Conditions" (*Ad novas rerum condiciones accommodatio*). These headings illustrate a consistent concern in the Preamble to connect the content of the revised Missal with the Church's tradition even while recognizing that significant changes have been made in its liturgical practice. Statements made in the Preamble are supported by references to the documents of Vatican II (1962–1965), especially *Sacrosanctum Concilium* (*SC*) but also *Lumen Gentium* (*LG*) and *Presbyterorm Ordinis* (*PO*), the decrees of the Council of Trent (1545–1563), several papal documents, an instruction from the Sacred Congregation of Rites (*Eucharisticum Mysterium*), and several Eucharistic Prayers. The decrees of Trent are used in two ways. Most references to Trent are made to show that what is in the revised Missal is consistent with what was taught at Trent. At other times, the intent is to show that a practice being implemented in the revised Missal is not in contradiction with the intent of what was said at the Council of Trent.

The Preamble introduces a number of significant theological and pastoral topics that will reappear in various sections of *IGMR2002*. They are: the sacrificial nature of the Mass, the mystery of the Lord's real presence, the nature of the ministerial priesthood, the priesthood of the faithful, the Eucharist as action of the Church, the importance of fostering participation in the liturgy, the catechetical nature of the liturgy, the use of the vernacular, the significance of sacramental reception of the Eucharist, the possibility for Communion under both

Including Adaptations for the Dioceses of the United States of America*

PREAMBLE ***

1. When he was about to celebrate with his disciples the Passover meal in which he instituted the sacrifice of his Body and Blood, Christ the Lord gave instructions

Institutio Generalis Missalis Romani **

PROŒMIUM

1. Cenam paschalem cum discipulis celebraturus, in qua sacrificium sui Corporis et Sanguinis instituit, Christus Dominus cenaculum magnum, stratum (*Lc* 22, 12)

---

kinds, the importance of continuity in the tradition, the need for incorporating new elements into the liturgy and accommodating others because of contemporary needs and circumstances, and the recognition that participation in the Eucharist should promote holiness and a deeper Christian life.

In its recognition of the need for both continuity and change, the Preamble sets forth a dynamic notion of tradition. It envisages a living tradition, one that has roots in the origins and history of the Church, but one that is also organic and can grow and manifest itself in diverse situations. This notion of a living tradition appears in various ways in the Preamble, but is especially evident in the final section that treats "Accommodation to New Conditions" (*Ad Novas Rerum Condiciones Accommodatio*). Here we find the explication of a foundational principle—that changes can be made in the liturgy to accommodate contemporary needs and circumstances and that these changes can include elements that are new to the liturgy. This principle is developed in a number of other places in *IGMR2002*. For example, nos. 23–26 introduce the possibility of making accommodations and adaptations in the liturgy in order to make it pastorally more effective, and cultural diversity is one of the reasons given for such change. In addition, *IGMR2002* has a new chapter (Chapter IX) that treats the topic of "Adaptations Within the Competence of Bishops and Bishops' Conferences" (*De Aptationibus quae Episcopis eorumque Conferentiis Competunt*).

It is clear in the Preamble that the basis for any changes to be introduced in the Mass is a pastoral concern that the faithful might be able to participate in the liturgy and be nourished by such participation. Such concern was foundational for the Second Vatican Council's mandate for the revision of the liturgy (*SC*, no. 14) and, in particular, the rite of the Mass (*SC*, no. 50). It was repeated

* The English text of the *General Instruction of the Roman Missal* is that of the published version by the United States Conference of Catholic Bishops. *General Instruction of the Roman Missal* © 2002, ICEL. All rights reserved. Liturgy Documentary Series 2 (Washington, D.C.: USCCB, 2003).

** The Latin text of the *Institutio Generalis Missalis Romani* is that of the published version of this Instruction found in the *Missale Romanum, editio iuxta typica tertia* (2002).

*** In this and all subsequent chapters, footnotes to the text of GIRM2003 and *IGMR2002* are gathered at the end of each respective chapter in this volume.

that a large, furnished upper room should be prepared (Lk 22:12). The Church has always regarded this command as applying also to herself when she gives directions about the preparation of people's hearts and minds and of the places, rites, and texts for the celebration of the Most Holy Eucharist. The current norms, prescribed in keeping with the will of the Second Vatican Ecumenical Council, and the new Missal that the Church of the Roman Rite is to use from now on in the celebration of Mass are also evidence of the great concern of the Church, of her faith, and of her unchanged love for the great mystery of the Eucharist. They likewise bear witness to the Church's continuous and unbroken tradition, irrespective of the introduction of certain new features.

parari mandavit. Quod quidem iussum etiam ad se pertinere Ecclesia semper est arbitrata, cum de iis statuebat, quæ, in disponendis hominum animis, locis, ritibus, textibus, ad sanctissimæ Eucharistiæ celebrationem spectarent. Normæ quoque hodiernæ, quæ, voluntate Concilii Œcumenici Vaticani II innixæ, præscriptæ sunt, atque novum Missale, quo Ecclesia Ritus romani in Missa celebranda posthac utetur, iterum sunt argumentum huius sollicitudinis Ecclesiæ, eius fidei immutatique amoris erga summum mysterium eucharisticum, atque continuam contextamque eius traditionem, quamquam res novæ quædam inductæ sunt, testantur.

---

by Pope Paul VI (d. 1978) in his 1969 *Apostolic Constitution*,[1] in which he approved the new *MR1970*, and it appears in a number of places in this Preamble.[2] This guiding principle will reappear throughout *IGMR2002*.[3] Both the Preamble and the whole document illustrate fidelity to Vatican II's pastoral concern.

1. The Preamble begins with a claim that the Church's practice of giving directions for the celebration of the Eucharist is rooted in the instructions Jesus Christ gave to his disciples when he told them to prepare the Passover meal (Luke 22:12). Although questions of biblical interpretation and historical accuracy can be raised here, the statement that "the Church has always regarded this command as applying also to herself when she gives directions . . ." (*Quod quidem iussum etiam ad se pertinere Ecclesia semper est arbitrata, cum de iis statuebat*) is clearly an attempt to establish continuity in the tradition by suggesting that the Church has acted in the name of Christ whenever it has issued such instructions. In addition to making a connection between the norms governing the new Missal and Christ, this introductory paragraph also connects them with the Second Vatican Council and "the Church's continuous and unbroken tradition, irrespective of the introduction of certain new features" (*continuam contextamque eius traditionem, quamquam res novae quaedam inductae sunt, testantur*). Here we have the first indication of the notion of the liturgy as a living tradition, one constructed by weaving the old and new together.

1. *Missale Romanum*, *AAS* 61 (1969): 217–222.
2. E.g., nos. 5, 11, 12, 13, 14 and 15.
3. E.g., nos. 16, 20, 55, 95 and 289.

A Witness to Unchanged Faith

2. The sacrificial nature of the Mass, solemnly asserted by the Council of Trent in accordance with the Church's universal tradition,[1] was reaffirmed by the Second Vatican Council, which offered these significant words about the Mass: "At the Last Supper our Savior instituted the Eucharistic Sacrifice of his Body and Blood, by which he would perpetuate the Sacrifice of the Cross throughout the centuries until he should come again, thus entrusting to the Church, his beloved Bride, the memorial of his death and resurrection."[2]

Testimonium fidei immutatæ

2. Missæ natura sacrificalis, a Concilio Tridentino, quod universæ traditioni Ecclesiæ congruebat, sollemniter asserta,[1] rursus enuntiata est a Concilio Vaticano II, quod circa Missam hæc significantia protulit verba: « Salvator noster in Cena novissima sacrificium eucharisticum Corporis et Sanguinis sui instituit, quo sacrificium crucis in sæcula, donec veniret, perpetuaret, atque adeo Ecclesiæ dilectæ sponsæ memoriale concrederet mortis et resurrectionis suæ ».[2]

A Witness to Unchanged Faith

2. This article focuses on the sacrificial nature of the Mass. The intent here is not to engage in a full discussion of this complex topic, but to show that the *IGMR2002* is in continuity with Trent. The first paragraph begins by noting that the Second Vatican Council had reaffirmed what the Council of Trent had solemnly asserted about the sacrificial nature of the Mass. In support of this, the Preamble quotes *SC*: "At the last supper . . . our Savior instituted the eucharistic sacrifice of his body and blood. This he did in order to perpetuate the sacrifice of the cross throughout the ages until he should come again, and so to entrust to his beloved spouse, the church, a memorial of his death and resurrection" (no. 47). It is interesting that the rest of *SC*, no. 47, which elaborates on the eucharistic memorial as a "sacrament of love, a sign of unity, a bond of charity, a paschal banquet. . ." was not included in the quotation given here in the instruction. This choice may be due to the emphasis on continuity with Trent where the notions of the Eucharist as a sacrament of love and unity and as a paschal meal were not treated under the category of sacrifice. The image of paschal banquet does appear later in *IGMR2002*, no. 72 where *SC*, no. 47 is also given as a reference.

Working with the principle that there is a correspondence between the Church's prayer and its belief, the Preamble proceeds to use a prayer from an ancient sacramentary and Eucharistic Prayers III and IV, newly composed for *MR1970*, to show continuity in the Church's teaching regarding the sacrificial nature of the Mass. These sources are used to show the Church's belief that, in the eucharistic commemoration of Christ's sacrifice, his redemptive mission is actualized. In other words, the Eucharist is an effective sacrifice. The Council of Trent affirmed that the sacrifice of the Mass was a propitiatory sacrifice[4] and

4. Council of Trent, Session 22, ch. 2, in Tanner, 2:733.

What the Council thus teaches is expressed constantly in the formulas of the Mass. This teaching, which is concisely expressed in the statement already contained in the ancient Sacramentary commonly known as the Leonine—"As often as the commemoration of this sacrifice is celebrated, the work of our redemption is carried out"[3]—is aptly and accurately developed in the Eucharistic Prayers. For in these prayers the priest, while he performs the commemoration, turns towards God, even in the name of the whole people, renders him thanks, and offers the living and holy Sacrifice, namely, the Church's offering and the Victim by whose immolation God willed to be appeased;[4] and he prays that the Body and Blood of Christ may be a sacrifice acceptable to the Father and salvific for the whole world.[5]

Quod sic a Concilio docetur, id formulis Missæ continenter exprimitur. Etenim doctrina, quæ hac sententia, iam in antiquo Sacramentario, vulgo Leoniano nuncupato, exstante, presse significatur: « quoties huius hostiæ commemoratio celebratur, opus nostræ redemptionis exercetur »,[3] apte accurateque explicatur in Precibus eucharisticis; in his enim sacerdos, dum anamnesin peragit, ad Deum nomine etiam totius populi conversus, ei gratias persolvit et sacrificium offert vivum et sanctum, oblationem scilicet Ecclesiæ et hostiam, cuius immolatione ipse Deus voluit placari,[4] atque orat, ut Corpus et Sanguis Christi sint Patri sacrificium acceptabile et toti mundo salutare.[5]

IGMR2002 seems to be demonstrating continuity with this position in its references to the language used in the two Eucharistic Prayers. For example, in referring to Eucharistic Prayer III, the Preamble notes that the priest "offers the living and holy Sacrifice, namely, the Church's offering and the Victim by whose immolation God willed to be appeased" (*et sacrificium offert vivum et sanctum, oblationem scilicet Ecclesiae et hostiam, cuius immolatione ipse Deus voluit placari).* The translation of that part of the prayer in the present Sacramentary is "the Victim whose death has reconciled us to yourself." In his commentary on this prayer, Enrico Mazza calls attention to the problematic nature of "victim" language for an adequate understanding of the sacrificial nature of the Eucharist and suggests that it is possible to offer a translation that avoids that word while still remaining faithful to the Latin.[5] In his study of the Council of Trent's teaching on the sacrificial nature of the Mass, David Power notes that the primacy given to the language of propitiation meant that other types of sacrifice (e.g., thanksgiving) received a secondary status. He also points out that Trent's tendency to equate sacrifice with the offering of a victim led to a very limited understanding of the nature of the Eucharist as sacrifice.[6]

5. Enrico Mazza, *The Eucharistic Prayers of the Roman Rite*, trans. Matthew J. O'Connell (New York: Pueblo, 1986), 136–137.

6. David N. Power, *The Sacrifice We Offer: The Tridentine Dogma and Its Reinterpretation* (New York: Crossroad, 1987), 151–154; also, see the discussion of this topic by David Power and Catherine Vincie, 61–64 above.

In this new Missal, then, the Church's rule of prayer *(lex orandi)* corresponds to her perennial rule of belief *(lex credendi),* by which namely we are taught that the Sacrifice of the Cross and its sacramental renewal in the Mass, which Christ the Lord instituted at the Last Supper and commanded the Apostles to do in his memory, are one and the same, differing only in the manner of offering, and that consequently the Mass is at once a sacrifice of praise and thanksgiving, of propitiation and satisfaction.

3. Moreover, the wondrous mystery of the Lord's real presence under the Eucharistic species, reaffirmed by the Second Vatican Council[6] and other documents of the Church's Magisterium[7] in the same sense and with the same words that the Council of Trent had proposed as a matter of faith,[8] is proclaimed in the celebration

Ita in novo Missali lex orandi Ecclesiæ respondet perenni legi credendi, qua nempe monemur unum et idem esse, excepta diversa offerendi ratione, crucis sacrificium eiusque in Missa sacramentalem renovationem, quam in Cena novissima Christus Dominus instituit Apostolisque faciendam mandavit in sui memoriam, atque proinde Missam simul esse sacrificium laudis, gratiarum actionis, propitiatorium et satisfactorium.

3. Mirabile etiam mysterium præsentiæ realis Domini sub speciebus eucharisticis, a Concilio Vaticano II[6] aliisque Ecclesiæ Magisterii documentis[7] eodem sensu eademque sententia, quibus Concilium Tridentinum id credendum proposuerat,[8] confirmatum, in Missæ celebratione declaratur non solum ipsis verbis consecrationis, quibus Christus per trans-

---

This part of the Preamble comes to a conclusion by reaffirming that the prayers of the new Missal correspond with the Church's belief that "the Sacrifice of the Cross and its sacramental renewal in the Mass . . . are one and the same, differing only in the manner of offering, and that consequently the Mass is at once a sacrifice of praise and thanksgiving, of propitiation and satisfaction" (*crucis sacrificium eiusque in Missa sacramentalem renovationem . . . atque proinde Missam simul esse sacrificium laudis, gratiarum actionis, propitiatorium et satisfactorium*). This statement is in continuity with Trent because that council did not deny that the Eucharist is a sacrifice of thanksgiving. It condemned those who taught that the sacrifice of the Mass is only one of praise and thanksgiving.[7] The statement quoted above is also significant because it links the language of sacrifice and sacrament.[8]

While *IGMR2002* has used liturgical prayers to demonstrate the continuity of the Church's belief regarding the sacrificial nature of the Mass between the Council of Trent and the Missal revised in light of the Second Vatican Council, it has been selective in doing so. It would be a mistake to read the Instruction as claiming that the Church's whole tradition of eucharistic prayers supports a particular understanding of the sacrificial nature of the Eucharist. Those who have studied that tradition would suggest otherwise. For example, Edward

7. Council of Trent Session 22, c. 3 in Tanner, 2:735.

8. See Kevin W. Irwin, *Models of the Eucharist* (New York/Mahwah: Paulist Press, 2005), 231. See Power, *The Sacrifice We Offer,* 130–131 for his statement that the idea of the Eucharist as a sacramental sacrifice is in line with the teaching of Trent.

of Mass not only by means of the very words of consecration, by which Christ becomes present through transubstantiation, but also by that interior disposition and outward expression of supreme reverence and adoration in which the Eucharistic Liturgy is carried out. For the same reason the Christian people is drawn on Holy Thursday of the Lord's Supper, and on the solemnity of the Most Holy Body and Blood of Christ, to venerate this wonderful Sacrament by a special form of adoration.

substantiationem præsens redditur, sed etiam sensu et exhibitione summæ reverentiæ et adorationis, quæ in Liturgia eucharistica fieri contingit. Eadem de causa populus christianus adducitur, ut feria V Hebdomadæ sanctæ in Cena Domini, et in sollemnitate Ss.mi Corporis et Sanguinis Christi, hoc admirabile Sacramentum peculiarem in modum excolat adorando.

Kilmartin criticized the modern Catholic theology of eucharistic sacrifice as a synthesis that is weak on biblical grounds and in its integration of the role of the Holy Spirit and suggested that a study of classical eucharistic prayers would provide a more authentic theology of the Eucharist.[9]

3. This section of the Preamble focuses on "the wondrous mystery of the Lord's real presence under the Eucharistic species" (*Mirabile . . . mysterium praesentiae realis Domini sub speciebus eucharisticis*). The concern is to show that the teaching of the Council of Trent had been reaffirmed in the documents of the Second Vatican Council and in other magisterial documents. While the documents given in footnotes to support this claim certainly do reaffirm the Church's belief in the real presence of Christ in the eucharistic elements, several of them provide a significant context for that presence. *SC*, no. 7 introduces this context by identifying multiple ways in which Christ is present in the sacrifice of the Mass. He is present in the person of the minister, in the eucharistic elements, in the sacraments, in the Word of the Scriptures, and in the Church gathered in his name. In his encyclical *Mysterium Fidei*, Pope Paul VI elaborated on these diverse forms of the presence of Christ. In referring to the presence of Christ in the sacrament of the Eucharist he noted that "this presence is called the *real presence* not to exclude the other kinds as though they were not real, but because it is real par excellence, since it is substantial, in the sense that Christ whole and entire, God and man, becomes present."[10] Here he gave a note to the Council of Trent. It is unfortunate that this teaching of the multiple ways in which Christ is present in the Mass is not part of this section of the Preamble. However, it does appear later in no. 27 of *IGMR2002*.

As part of the attempt to show continuity with the faith expressed at the Council of Trent, this section refers to "the very words of consecration, by which

9. See Edward J. Kilmartin, *The Eucharist in the West: History and Theology*, ed. Robert J. Daly (Collegeville, MN: The Liturgical Press, 1998), 365–383.

10. No. 39, in DOL, no. 1183.

4. Further, the nature of the ministerial priesthood proper to a Bishop and a priest, who offer the Sacrifice in the person of Christ and who preside over the gathering of the holy people, is evident in the form of the rite itself, by reason of the more prominent place and office of the priest.

4. Natura vero sacerdotii ministerialis, quod episcopi et presbyteri proprium est, qui in persona Christi sacrificium offerunt cœtuique populi sancti præsident, in ipsius ritus forma, e præstantiore loco et munere eiusdem sacerdotis elucet. Huius vero muneris rationes edicuntur et perspicue ac

---

Christ becomes present through transubstantiation" (*ipsis verbis consecrationis, quibus Christus per transubstantiationem praesens redditur*). The Council of Trent, itself, was more nuanced in its use of language. It chose to use the term "*aptissime*" in reference to its choice of the language of "transubstantiation."[11] In doing so it was recognizing the suitability or appropriateness of the term. As Edward Kilmartin has noted, "Trent did not canonize the philosophical explanation underlying the scholastic theology of transubstantiation."[12] The final concern of this section of the Preamble is with the appropriate response to the Lord's real presence in the eucharistic species. It notes that the Church's belief in the real presence is also proclaimed "by that interior disposition and outward expression of supreme reverence and adoration in which the Eucharistic Liturgy is carried out" (*sensu et exhibitione summae reverentiae et adorationis, quae in Liturgia eucharistica fieri contingit*) and relates this to the practices of adoration that take place on Holy Thursday and on the solemnity of the Most Holy Body and Blood of Christ. Here we see continuity with the Council of Trent, which did defend the practice of the adoration of Christ in the sacrament of the Eucharist. However, that council also recognized that the sacrament had been instituted by Christ in order to be consumed.[13] It is interesting to note that "supreme reverence" was chosen to translate "*summae reverentiae*." There seems to be an intent to overstate the need for reverence while, in contrast, the word "*summae*" is not translated in GIRM1975. In fact, several instructions about showing reverence or adoration to Christ present in the sacrament have been added to this most recent version.[14]

4. This article is concerned with the nature of the ministerial priesthood while no. 5 will attend to the priesthood of the faithful. The order of these two sections is surprisingly inconsistent with that which was set out in *LG*. In that document, the mystery of the Church and the Church as the people of God are

11. Council of Trent, Session 13, c. 2 in Tanner, 2:697.

12. Kilmartin, 179; Karl Rahner, "The Presence of Christ in the Sacrament of the Lord's Supper," *Theological Investigations IV*, trans. Kevin Smyth (London: Darton, Longman & Todd, 1966), 287–311; Edward Schillebeeckx, *The Eucharist*, trans. N. D. Smith (New York: Sheed & Ward, 1968), 44–45.

13. Council of Trent, Session 13, ch. 5 in Tanner, 2:695. See Kilmartin, 170 for his commentary on this.

14. E.g., nos. 160, 179 and 274.

The meaning of this office is enunciated and explained clearly and at greater length, in the Preface for the Chrism Mass on Holy Thursday, the day commemorating the institution of the priesthood. The Preface brings to light the conferral of the priestly power accomplished through the laying on of hands; and, by listing the various duties, it describes that power, which is the continuation of the power of Christ the High Priest of the New Testament.

fusius explanantur in gratiarum actione Missæ chrismatis, feria V Hebdomadæ sanctæ; quo videlicet die institutio sacerdotii commemoratur. In illa enim collatio potestatis sacerdotalis per manuum impositionem facta illustratur; atque ipsa potestas, singulis officiis recensitis, describitur, quæ est continuatio potestatis Christi, Summi Pontificis Novi Testamenti.

---

presented before the hierarchical nature of the Church is treated, and the foundational nature of baptism for membership in Christ and participation in his priesthood is quite clear (*LG,* nos. 7 and 10).

The focus of no. 4 is "the nature of the ministerial priesthood proper to a Bishop and a priest, who offer the Sacrifice in the person of Christ and who preside over the gathering of the holy people. . ." (*Natura vero sacerdotii ministerialis, quod episcopi et presbyteri proprium est, qui in persona Christi sacrificium offerunt coetuique populi sancti praesident*). The word *episcopi* was added to *IGMR2002*. Previous versions of the Latin text had only *presbyteri*. GIRM1975 translates this term as "presbyter," but GIRM2003 uses the word "priest." This seems odd, given the emphasis placed on literal translation of terms in the most recent instruction on translation. The emphasis on the priest offering the sacrifice in the person of Christ is faithful to statements made by the Council of Trent, although there are no references to that council. There are also no references to the Second Vatican Council. The language of no. 4 does not reflect *SC,* no. 48, which makes it clear that members of the Church offer the sacrifice with the priest.

The theology of ministerial priesthood in this section is one that stresses priestly power. It calls attention to the more prominent place and office of the priest in the rite, identifies Holy Thursday as "the day commemorating the institution of the priesthood" (*quo videlicet die institutio sacerdotii commemoratur*) and sends the reader to the Preface for the Chrism Mass of Holy Thursday for an explanation of the meaning of the office of the ministerial priesthood. The association of Holy Thursday with the institution of the ministerial priesthood is not part of the Church's earlier traditions regarding this day. Rather, it was a day for reconciling public penitents, blessing oils, and commemorating the Lord's Supper and the institution of the Eucharist. The Preface for the Chrism Mass was composed for *MR1970* to support the innovative practice of having all ordained priests renew their commitment to priestly service.[15] Actually, the

15. See Kenneth Stevenson, *Jerusalem Revisited: The Liturgical Meaning of Holy Week* (Washington, DC: Pastoral Press, 1988), 42–43; also, J. Frank Henderson, "The Chrism Mass of Holy Thursday," *Worship* 51 (1977): 149–158.

5. In addition, the nature of the ministerial priesthood also puts into its proper light another reality, which must indeed be highly regarded, namely, the royal priesthood of the faithful, whose spiritual sacrifice is brought to completeness through the ministry of the Bishop and the priests in union with the sacrifice of Christ, the one

5. Sed hac sacerdotii ministerialis natura etiam aliud quiddam, magni sane faciendum, in sua luce collocatur, id est regale sacerdotium fidelium, quorum sacrificium spirituale per Episcopi et presbyterorum ministerium in unione cum sacrificio Christi, unici Mediatoris, consummatur.[9] Namque celebratio Eucharistiæ est actio

---

Preface puts the ordained priesthood within the context of the priesthood of Christ and the priesthood of the Church, but *IGMR2002* does not allude to this ecclesial context. Rather, in referring to the Preface, it focuses on the conferral of priestly power through the laying on of hands and notes that this power "is the continuation of the power of Christ the High Priest of the New Testament" (*est continuatio potestatis Christi, Summi Pontificis Novi Testamenti)*.

5. The narrowly construed theology of the ordained ministry in no. 4 continues at the beginning of this article, which focuses on "the royal priesthood of the faithful" (*regale sacerdotium fidelium)*, but says that this priesthood is put into its proper light by the nature of the ministerial priesthood. There is no mention of baptism as foundational for the Church's ministry in this section. *PO*, no. 2, is given in a footnote to support the statement that the spiritual sacrifice of the faithful is brought to completion through the ministry of the bishop and priests. That is an accurate reference but the first part of *PO*, no. 2, which sets a context for the rest, has been ignored. *PO*, no. 2, begins with a statement that all who are part of Christ's body share in his anointing and are made into a holy priesthood. Only then does the document move into a discussion of the ordained ministry. As in *IGMR2002*, no. 4, the ministry of the bishop has been added to that of the priests.

Although the starting point for this section on the priesthood of the faithful is clearly wanting, the document goes on to present the celebration of the Eucharist as the action of the whole Church. This principle is consistent with statements made in *SC*, nos. 7 and 26, but there are no references to this conciliar decree. This article presents the Church as "the People of God, purchased by Christ's Blood, gathered together by the Lord, nourished by his word" (*populus Dei, Sanguine Christi acquisitus, a Domino congregatus, eius verbo nutritus*), but there is no reference to *LG*, no. 9, where this image for the Church was introduced at Vatican II. The document here recognizes that the Church is a people who give thanks in Christ by offering his sacrifice, that "it is a people made one by sharing in the Communion of Christ's Body and Blood" (*populus denique, qui per Communionem Corporis et Sanguinis Christi in unum coalescit*). These statements provide the grounds for developing a rich eucharistic ecclesiology. The theme of holiness is associated with that of participation in the last sentence of this article, which suggests that this people "grows continually in holiness by its conscious, active, and fruitful participation in the mystery of the Eucharist"

and only Mediator.[9] For the celebration of the Eucharist is an action of the whole Church, and in it each one should carry out solely but completely that which pertains to him or her, in virtue of the rank of each within the People of God. In this way greater consideration will also be given to some aspects of the celebration that have sometimes been accorded less attention in the course of time. For this people is the People of God, purchased by Christ's Blood, gathered together by the Lord, nourished by his word. It is a people called to bring to God the prayers of the entire human family, a people giving thanks in Christ for the mystery of salvation by offering his Sacrifice. Finally, it is a people made one by sharing in the Communion of Christ's Body and Blood. Though holy in its origin, this people nevertheless grows continually in holiness by its conscious, active, and fruitful participation in the mystery of the Eucharist.[10]

Ecclesiæ universæ; in qua unusquisque solum et totum id agat, quod ad ipsum pertinet, respectu habito gradus eius in populo Dei. Quo efficitur, ut etiam rationes quædam celebrationis magis attendantur, quibus sæculorum decursu interdum est minor cura adhibita. Hic enim populus est populus Dei, Sanguine Christi acquisitus, a Domino congregatus, eius verbo nutritus, populus ad id vocatus, ut preces totius familiæ humanæ ad Deum admoveat, populus, qui pro mysterio salutis gratias in Christo agit eius sacrificium offerendo, populus denique, qui per Communionem Corporis et Sanguinis Christi in unum coalescit. Qui populus, licet origine sua sit sanctus, tamen per ipsam participationem consciam, actuosam et fructuosam mysterii eucharistici in sanctitate continenter crescit.[10]

A Witness to Unbroken Tradition

6. In setting forth its instructions for the revision of the Order of Mass, the Second Vatican Council, using the same words as did St. Pius V in the Apostolic Constitution *Quo primum,* by which the Missal of Trent

Traditio non intermissa declaratur

6. Cum præcepta enuntiaret, quibus Ordo Missæ recognosceretur, Concilium Vaticanum II præter alia mandavit quoque, ut ritus nonnulli restituerentur « ad pristinam sanctorum Patrum normam »,[11] iisdem

---

(*per ipsam participationem consciam, actuosam et fructuosam mysterii eucharistici in sanctitate continenter crescit*). It is odd that the footnote here is to *SC,* no. 11, rather than to *SC,* no. 14, which grounds liturgical participation in baptism or to *SC,* no. 10 which identifies liturgy as a source for sanctification.

The principle that the Eucharist is the action of the Church is a primary one that appears at the very beginning of Chapters I through V of *IGMR2002*. The significance of participation in the Eucharist will also permeate the document and the baptismal basis for this participation will be made clear (no. 18).

A Witness to Unbroken Tradition

6. The claim that the tradition has been unbroken can be misleading since *MR1969* incorporated significant changes from its predecessor. The tradition referenced in this section of the Preamble is that of the fathers of the Church. Number 6 creates a link between the Missal of 1570 (*MR1570*) and *MR1970* by

was promulgated in 1570, also ordered, among other things, that some rites be restored "to the original norm of the holy Fathers."[11] From the fact that the same words are used it can be seen how both *Roman Missals*, although separated by four centuries, embrace one and the same tradition. Furthermore, if the inner elements of this tradition are reflected upon, it also becomes clear how outstandingly and felicitously the older *Roman Missal* is brought to fulfillment in the new.

7. In a difficult period when the Catholic faith on the sacrificial nature of the Mass, the ministerial priesthood, and the real and permanent presence of Christ under the Eucharistic species were placed at risk, St. Pius V was especially concerned with preserving the more recent tradition then unjustly being assailed, introducing only very slight changes into the sacred rite. In fact, the Missal of 1570 differs very little from the very first printed edition of 1474, which in turn faithfully follows the Missal used at the time of Pope Innocent III. Moreover, even though manuscripts in the Vatican Library provided material for the emendation of some expressions, they by no means made it possible to inquire into "ancient and approved authors" farther back than

videlicet usum verbis ac S. Pius V in Constitutione Apostolica « Quo primum » inscriptis, qua anno 1570 Missale Tridentinum est promulgatum. Ob hanc vero ipsam verborum convenientiam notari potest, qua ratione ambo Missalia romana, quamvis intercesserint quattuor sæcula, æqualem et parem complectantur traditionem. Si autem huius traditionis ponderentur interiora elementa, intellegitur etiam, quam egregie ac feliciter prius perficiatur altero.

7. Temporibus sane difficilibus, quibus catholica fides de indole sacrificali Missæ, de ministeriali sacerdotio, de reali et perpetua Christi sub eucharisticis speciebus præsentia in discrimen fuerat adducta, id S. Pii V imprimis intererat, ut recentiorem traditionem, immerito oppugnatam, servaret, minimis tantummodo ritus sacri mutationibus inductis. Re quidem vera Missale illud anni 1570 paulum admodum distat a primo omnium anno 1474 typis edito Missali, quod vicissim fideliter quidem repetit Missale temporis Innocentii PP. III. Codices insuper Bibliothecæ Vaticanæ, quamquam aliquot intulerant locutionum emendationes, haud tamen permiserunt, ut in illa pervestigatione « veterum et probatorum auctorum » plus

---

saying that those who compiled both liturgical books had the same goal. It quotes *SC*, no. 50, which notes that the rites of the Mass are to be restored "to the original norm of the holy Fathers." This was the same intention that had been articulated by Pius V (d. 1572) when he promulgated *MR1570*. His desire was to reform the rites of the Mass by returning to the tradition of the early Church although insufficient time and resources kept this goal from being fulfilled.[16] This article suggests that this fulfillment can be found in *MR2002*.

7. This article provides a rationale for the fact that the goal of returning to the early traditions of the Church was not carried out in the *MR1570*. In addition to the lack of adequate sources in the Vatican Library, Pope Pius V was concerned with preserving the more recent tradition against attacks that were

16. See Robert Cabié, *History of the Mass*, trans. Lawrence J. Johnson (Beltsville: Pastoral Press, 1992) 88.

the liturgical commentaries of the Middle Ages.

8. Today, on the other hand, countless learned studies have shed light on the "norm of the holy Fathers" which the revisers of the Missal of St. Pius V followed. For following the publication first of the Sacramentary known as the Gregorian in 1571, critical editions of other ancient Roman and Ambrosian Sacramentaries were published, often in book form, as were ancient Hispanic and Gallican liturgical books which brought to light numerous prayers of no slight spiritual excellence that had previously been unknown.

In a similar fashion, traditions dating back to the first centuries, before the formation of the rites of East and West, are better known today because of the discovery of so many liturgical documents.

Moreover, continuing progress in the study of the holy Fathers has also shed light upon the theology of the mystery of the Eucharist through the teachings of such illustrious Fathers of Christian antiquity as St. Irenaeus, St. Ambrose, St. Cyril of Jerusalem, and St. John Chrysostom.

quam liturgici commentarii mediæ ætatis inquirerentur.

8. Hodie, contra, illa « sanctorum Patrum norma », quam sectabantur Missalis S. Pii V emendatores, locupletata est innumerabilibus eruditorum scriptis. Postquam enim Sacramentarium Gregorianum nuncupatum anno 1571 primum editum est, vetera Sacramentaria romana et ambrosiana critica arte sæpe typis sunt divulgata, perinde ac vetusti libri liturgici hispani et gallicani, qui plurimas preces non levis præstantiæ spiritualis, eo usque ignoratas, in conspectum produxerunt.

Traditiones pariter priscorum sæculorum, antequam ritus Orientis et Occidentis constituerentur, nunc idcirco melius cognoscuntur, quod tot reperta sunt documenta liturgica.

Præterea progredientia sanctorum Patrum studia theologiam mysterii eucharistici lumine perfuderunt doctrinæ Patrum in antiquitate christiana excellentissimorum, uti S. Irenæi, S. Ambrosii, S. Cyrilli Hierosolymitani, S. Ioannis Chrysostomi.

---

being made at the time. As a result, *MR1570* did not depart in any radical way from the *MR1474*.[17]

8. This article explains why those who worked on *MR1970* were able to be more faithful to the goal of restoring the rites of the Mass to the "norm of the holy Fathers" (*sanctorum Patrum norma*). It recognizes the scholarly work that has been done in studying the theology of the Eucharist in the writings of such people as Irenaeus (d. ca. 200), Cyril of Jerusalem (d. 387), Ambrose (d. 397), and John Chrysostom (d. 407). It notes the importance of the publication of critical editions of ancient sacramentaries and other liturgical books, which resulted in bringing to light "numerous prayers of no slight spiritual excellence that had previously been unknown" (*qui plurimas preces non levis praestantiae spiritualis, eo usque ignoratas, in conspectum produxerunt*). The Preamble calls attention to the fact that the discovery of ancient liturgical documents has given

17. For a summary of the kinds of changes that were made see Joseph A. Jungmann, *The Mass of the Roman Rite*, trans. Francis A. Brunner, 2 vols. (Westminster: Christian Classics, 1986) I:135–141; also, Mitchell and Baldovin, 18–22 above.

9. For this reason, the "norm of the holy Fathers" requires not only the preservation of what our immediate forebears have passed on to us, but also an understanding and a more profound study of the Church's entire past and of all the ways in which her one and only faith has been set forth in the quite diverse human and social forms prevailing in the Semitic, Greek, and Latin areas. Moreover, this broader view allows us to see how the Holy Spirit endows the People of God with a marvelous fidelity in preserving the unalterable deposit of faith, even amid a very great variety of prayers and rites.

9. Quapropter « sanctorum Patrum norma » non postulat solum, ut conserventur ea, quæ maiores nostri proximi tradiderint, sed ut comprehendantur altiusque perpendantur cuncta præterita Ecclesiæ tempora ac modi universi, quibus unica eius fides declarata est in humani civilisque cultus formis tam inter se differentibus, quippe quæ vigerent in regionibus semiticis, græcis, latinis. Amplior autem hic prospectus cernere nos sinit, quemadmodum Spiritus Sanctus præstet populo Dei mirandam fidelitatem in conservando immutabili fidei deposito, licet permagna sit precum rituumque varietas.

Accommodation to New Conditions

10. The new Missal, therefore, while bearing witness to the Roman Church's rule of prayer (*lex orandi*), also safeguards the deposit of faith handed down by the

Ad novas rerum condiciones accommodatio

10. Novum igitur Missale, dum testificatur legem orandi Ecclesiæ romanæ, fideique depositum a Conciliis recentioribus traditum tutatur, ipsum vicissim magni

---

us knowledge of "traditions dating back to the first centuries" (*Traditiones . . . priscorum saeculorum*). The use of the plural here is very significant. One of the richest consequences of the scholarly work done in the history of liturgy has been that of making available for the Church an awareness of the diversity of its traditions.

9. This article affirms our last point on no. 8 by making a very important statement about unity and diversity. It says that following the "norm of the holy Fathers" (*sanctorum Patrum norma*) includes the task of studying the diverse ways in which the faith of the Church has been set forth. This section of the Preamble ends by suggesting that an understanding of such diversity shows us "how the Holy Spirit endows the People of God with a marvelous fidelity in preserving the unalterable deposit of faith, even amid a very great variety of prayers and rites" (*quemadmodum Spiritus Sanctus praestet populo Dei mirandam fidelitatem in conservando immutabili fidei deposito, licet permagna sit precum rituumque varietas)*. A focus on the goal shared by the revisers of the *MR1570* and that of *MR1970* to return to the "norm of the holy Fathers" has opened the door to diversity and provides a basis for the next section of the Preamble.

Accommodation to New Conditions

10. This final section of the Preamble begins with the indirect articulation of two important principles that will be operative in the rest of the section.

more recent Councils, and marks in its own right a step of great importance in liturgical tradition.

Indeed, when the Fathers of the Second Vatican Council reaffirmed the dogmatic pronouncements of the Council of Trent, they spoke at a far different time in world history, so that they were able to bring forward proposals and measures of a pastoral nature that could not have even been foreseen four centuries earlier.

11. The Council of Trent already recognized the great catechetical value contained in the celebration of Mass but was unable to bring out all its consequences in regard to actual practice. In fact, many were press-

momenti gradum designat in liturgica traditione.

Cum enim Patres Concilii Vaticani II asseverationes dogmaticas Concilii Tridentini iterarunt, in longe alia mundi ætate sunt locuti; qua de causa in re pastorali valuerunt afferre proposita et consilia, quæ ante quattuor sæcula ne prævideri quidem potuerunt.

11. Agnoverat iam Tridentinum Concilium magnam utilitatem catecheticam, quæ in Missæ celebratione contineretur; unde tamen colligere omnia consectaria, ad vitæ usum quod attinet, nequibat. A

Paragraph one states that the new Missal, "while bearing witness to the Roman Church's rule of prayer, also safeguards the deposit of faith handed down by the more recent Councils, and marks in its own right a step of great importance in liturgical tradition" (*dum testificatur legem orandi Ecclesiae romanae, fideique depositum a Conciliis recentioribus traditum tutatur, ipsum vicissim magni momenti gradum designat in liturgica traditione*). The implication here is that the Church's liturgical tradition is a dynamic, living one, and that it can change. Although there are no footnotes to conciliar documents, this statement is in keeping with *SC*, no. 23, which recognizes the importance of both sound tradition and legitimate progress and notes that new forms should grow organically from already existing forms.

Paragraph 2 admits that when the bishops at Vatican II reaffirmed pronouncements of Trent, they were doing so at a very different time in history. As a result of this, they were able to make pastoral proposals that would not have been imagined in the sixteenth century. This is an implicit recognition of a significant principle of hermeneutics, namely, that the pronouncements of any council have to be understood within the historical, social, cultural, and theological context in which they are made (see Seasoltz, 39–40 and Power and Vincie, 93 above).

11. This and the following article address the topic of the vernacular. Number 11 illustrates the hermeneutical principle of contextualization in its explanation of why the Council of Trent did not give permission for the vernacular in celebrations of the Eucharist. The Preamble recognizes that many were requesting permission for the use of the vernacular but notes that the Council's decision on this matter was made within a consideration of "the conditions of that age" (*adiunctorum illa aetate*). The Council of Trent's statements regarding the use of the vernacular were made at Session 22 (1562). The main concern of the Council

ing for permission to use the vernacular in celebrating the Eucharistic Sacrifice; but the Council, weighing the conditions of that age, considered it a duty to answer this request with a reaffirmation of the Church's traditional teaching, according to which the Eucharistic Sacrifice is, first and foremost, the action of Christ himself, and therefore its proper efficacy is unaffected by the manner in which the faithful take part in it. The Council for this reason stated in firm but measured words, "Although the Mass contains much instruction for people of faith, nevertheless it did not seem expedient to the Fathers that it be celebrated everywhere in the vernacular."[12] The Council accordingly anathematized anyone maintaining that "the rite of the Roman Church, in which part of the Canon and the words of consecration are spoken in a low voice, is to be condemned, or that the Mass must be celebrated only in the

multis reapse flagitabatur, ut sermonem vulgarem in sacrificio eucharistico peragendo usurpari liceret. Ad talem quidem postulationem, Concilium, rationem ducens adiunctorum illa ætate obtinentium, sui officii esse arbitrabatur doctrinam Ecclesiæ tralaticiam denuo inculcare, secundum quam sacrificium eucharisticum imprimis Christi ipsius est actio, cuius proinde efficacitas propria eo modo non afficitur, quo fideles eiusdem fiunt participes. Idcirco firmis hisce simulque moderatis verbis edictum est: « Etsi Missa magnam contineat populi fidelis eruditionem, non tamen expedire visum est Patribus, ut vulgari passim lingua celebraretur ».[12] Atque condemnandum esse pronuntiavit eum, qui censeret « Ecclesiæ romanæ ritum, quo submissa voce pars canonis et verba consecrationis proferuntur, damnandum esse; aut lingua tantum vulgari Missam celebrari debere ».[13] Nihilominus, dum hinc vetuit

---

during this session was to confirm Church doctrine regarding the sacrificial nature of the Mass against those reformers who challenged it. These same reformers were promoting the use of the vernacular. Robert Cabié has suggested that the "use of the vernacular was rejected solely in order that the Council might not seem to be crediting the reasons put forward by the Reformers to justify the vernacular."[18]

Article 11 of the Preamble quotes the conciliar statement of Trent that "although the Mass contains much instruction for people of faith, nevertheless it did not seem expedient to the Fathers that it be celebrated everywhere in the vernacular." The language of this statement, especially the use of the phrase "seem expedient" (*expedire visum est*) is very important. In his book *Dynamic Equivalence*, Keith Pecklers quotes an earlier version of this statement which was much more negative on the use of the vernacular.[19] The Council of Trent did not condemn the use of the vernacular and this can be clearly seen in the

18. Robert Cabié, *The Eucharist*, trans. Matthew J. O'Connell, Vol. II: *The Church at Prayer*, ed. A. G. Martimort (Collegeville, MN: The Liturgical Press, 1986), 174.

19. "The Latin language, too, which is used for the celebration of Mass in the Western Church, is in the highest degree appropriate, seeing that it is common to many nations. It seems beyond doubt that, were Mass to be carried out in each people's vulgar tongue, the divine Mysteries would be celebrated with less reverence. There would even be grave danger of various errors arising in many translations, with the result that the mysteries of our religion would differ, instead of being, as they are, one and unchanging." In Keith F. Pecklers, *Dynamic*

vernacular."[13] Although on the one hand it prohibited the use of the vernacular in the Mass, nevertheless, on the other hand, the Council did direct pastors of souls to put appropriate catechesis in its place: "Lest Christ's flock go hungry . . . the Holy Synod commands pastors and all others having the care of souls to give frequent instructions during the celebration of Mass, either personally or through others, concerning what is read at Mass; among other things, they should include some explanation of the mystery of this most holy Sacrifice, especially on Sundays and holy days."[14]

in Missa linguæ vernaculæ usum, illinc animarum pastores eius in locum congruentem substituere catechesim iussit: « ne oves Christi esuriant . . . mandat sancta Synodus pastoribus et singulis curam animarum gerentibus, ut frequenter inter Missarum celebrationem vel per se vel per alios, ex his, quæ in Missa leguntur, exponant atque inter cetera sanctissimi huius sacrificii mysterium aliquod declarent, diebus præsertim Dominicis et festis ».[14]

12. Therefore, when the Second Vatican Council convened in order to accommodate the Church to the requirements of her proper apostolic office precisely in these times, it examined thoroughly, as had Trent, the instructive and pastoral character

12. Propterea congregatum, ut Ecclesiam aptaret ad proprii muneris apostolici necessitates hisce ipsis temporibus, Concilium Vaticanum II funditus perspexit, quemadmodum Tridentinum, didascalicam et pastoralem indolem sacræ Liturgiæ.[15]

---

canon quoted in the Preamble. The Council's anathema was directed to those who held that the "Mass should only be celebrated in the vernacular" (*lingua tantum vulgari Missam celebrari debere)*.[20] The inclusion of "only" (*tantum*) is very significant here. In light of the careful use of language in the statement of Trent, it is curious that the Preamble states that the Council "prohibited the use of the vernacular in the Mass" (*hinc vetuit in Missa linguae vernaculae usum*). The use of "prohibit" (*vetuit*) could easily be misunderstood and does not really convey what was actually said by the bishops at Trent.

The Preamble draws attention to the Council of Trent's recognition of the catechetical value of the Mass within the context of its statements about the use of the vernacular. Although the Council decided that the use of the vernacular was not expedient at the time, it did express a pastoral concern for the people and indicated that instructions should be given during the Mass about the readings and other aspects of the mystery of the eucharistic sacrifice.

12. This article moves into a new historical context, that of the Second Vatican Council, but it creates a link with the Council of Trent by saying that both councils examined "the instructive and pastoral character of the Sacred Liturgy" (*didascalicam et pastoralem indolem sacrae Liturgiae*). This is supported by a

---

Equivalence: The Living Language of Christian Worship (Collegeville, MN: The Liturgical Press, 2003), 10.

20. See Council of Trent, Session 22, c. 9 in Tanner, 2:736. Footnote 13 of the Preamble is incorrect in referring to ch. 9 rather than c. 9.

of the Sacred Liturgy.[15] Since no Catholic would now deny the lawfulness and efficacy of a sacred rite celebrated in Latin, the Council was also able to grant that "the use of the vernacular language may frequently be of great advantage to the people" and gave the faculty for its use.[16] The enthusiasm in response to this measure has been so great everywhere that it has led, under the leadership of the Bishops and the Apostolic See itself, to permission for all liturgical celebrations in which the people participate to be in the vernacular, for the sake of a better comprehension of the mystery being celebrated.

Et, cum nemo catholicorum esset, qui legitimum efficacemque ritum sacrum negaret lingua latina peractum, concedere etiam valuit: « Haud raro linguæ vernaculæ usurpatio valde utilis apud populum exsistere possit », eiusque adhibendæ facultatem dedit.[16] Flagrans illud studium, quo hoc consultum ubivis est susceptum, profecto effecit ut, ducibus Episcopis atque ipsa Apostolica Sede, universæ liturgicæ celebrationes quas populus participaret, exsequi liceret vulgari sermone, quo plenius intellegeretur mysterium, quod celebraretur.

---

footnote to *SC*, which states that "although the liturgy is above all things the worship of the divine majesty, it likewise contains rich instruction for the faithful" (no. 33). This conciliar statement is accompanied by a note to chapter 8 of Session 22 of the Council of Trent (1562), which made a similar statement about the instructive nature of the liturgy. The Preamble recognizes that, in this new context, people were not denying "the lawfulness and efficacy of a sacred rite celebrated in Latin" (*legitimum efficacemque ritum sacrum . . . lingua latina peractum*). This made it possible for Vatican II to grant a wider use of the vernacular. Article 12 goes on to note that the enthusiastic response to the use of the vernacular led "to permission for all liturgical celebrations in which the people participate to be in the vernacular, for the sake of a better comprehension of the mystery being celebrated" (*universae liturgicae celebrationes quas populus participaret, exsequi liceret vulgari sermone, quo plenius intellegeretur mysterium, quod celebraretur).*

Although the association made here between the vernacular and the people's instruction or comprehension creates a link with the Council of Trent, it does not adequately reflect the Second Vatican Council's understanding of the liturgy as ecclesial action (*SC*, nos. 26, 41 and 42) in which the faithful are called to "full, conscious, and active participation . . . by reason of their baptism" (*SC*, no. 14). In his 1965 remarks on the introduction of the vernacular into the liturgy, Pope Paul VI combined the goals of instruction and participation. He said that the use of the vernacular had been judged by the Church "to be necessary to make its prayer understandable and grasped by all. The good of the faithful calls for this kind of action, making possible their active share in the Church's worship." He went on to say to the people gathered in St. Peter's Square, "that means you, the faithful, so that you may be able to unite yourselves more closely to the Church's prayer, pass over from being simply spectators to becoming

13. Indeed, since the use of the vernacular in the Sacred Liturgy may certainly be considered an important means for presenting more clearly the catechesis regarding the mystery that is inherent in the celebration itself, the Second Vatican Council also ordered that certain prescriptions of the Council of Trent that had not been followed everywhere be brought to fruition, such as the homily to be given on Sundays and holy days[17] and the faculty to interject certain explanations during the sacred rites themselves.[18]

13. Verumtamen, cum linguæ vernaculæ usus in sacra Liturgia instrumentum sit, quamvis magni momenti, quo apertius exprimeretur catechesis mysterii, quæ in celebratione continetur, Concilium Vaticanum II admonuit præterea, ut aliqua Tridentini præscripta, quibus non omnibus locis erat obtemperatum, ad exitum deducerentur, veluti homilia diebus dominicis et festis habenda[17] et facultas inter ipsos sacros ritus quasdam monitiones intericiendi.[18]

---

active participants."[21] This combination of reasons—increased participation and better understanding—provided the rationale for the expansion of the use of the vernacular in the second instruction for implementing *SC* that was issued in 1967.[22] *IGMR2002* has several new references to the vernacular in Chapter IX which has been added to the document.[23]

13. Both paragraphs of this article place the prescriptions of the Second Vatican Council in continuity with the Council of Trent. Paragraph one returns to the concern for the catechetical nature of the liturgy, introduced in conjunction with the vernacular. It notes that the bishops at Vatican II realized that the prescriptions set out by the bishops at the Council of Trent regarding the giving of homilies and the offering of explanations had often not been followed. Therefore, Vatican II brought Trent "to fruition" (*ad exitum*) by instructing that a homily should be given on Sundays and holy days (*SC*, no. 52) and providing for the possibility of brief comments during the liturgy (*SC*, no. 35.3). The homily and explanations, obviously to be given in the vernacular, are intended as means "for presenting more clearly the catechesis regarding the mystery that is inherent in the celebration itself" (*quo apertius exprimeretur catechesis mysterii, quae in celebratione continetur*).

The understanding of catechesis suggested here is one that seems to go beyond the notion of mere instruction. *IGMR2002* would have been enriched by referencing the *Directorium generale pro catechesi* issued in 1997 which presents the catechesis associated with Christian initiation as a formation in the faith that "includes more than instruction: it is an apprenticeship of the entire Christian life" (no. 67). The Directory quotes *Catechesi Tradendae* in presenting the

21. Paul VI, "Remarks at the Angelus to the people in St. Peter's Square, on the beginning of the vernacular in the liturgy," 7 March 1965, in DOL, no. 399.

22. SC Rites (Consilium), "Instruction (second) *Tres abhinc annos*, on the orderly carrying out of the Constitution on the Liturgy," 4 May 1967, in DOL, nos. 445 and 474.

23. E.g., nos. 389, 391 and 392.

Above all, the Second Vatican Council, which urged "that more perfect form of participation in the Mass by which the faithful, after the priest's Communion, receive the Lord's Body from the same Sacrifice,"[19] called for another desire of the Fathers of Trent to be realized, namely that for the sake of a fuller participation in the holy Eucharist "the faithful present at each Mass should communicate not only by spiritual desire but also by sacramental reception of the Eucharist."[20]

Potissimum vero Concilium Vaticanum II, a quo suadebatur « illa perfectior Missæ participatio, qua fideles post Communionem sacerdotis ex eodem sacrificio Corpus dominicum sumunt »,[19] incitavit, ut aliud optatum Patrum Tridentinorum in rem transferretur, ut scilicet ad sacram Eucharistiam plenius participandam « in singulis Missis fideles adstantes non solum spirituali affectu, sed sacramentali etiam Eucharistiæ perceptione communicarent ».[20]

---

aim of catechesis as that of putting people "in communion and intimacy with Jesus Christ" (no. 80). The catechetical nature of the liturgy is treated explicitly or implicitly elsewhere in *IGMR2002*. For example, no. 28 recognizes that the faithful are instructed and refreshed at the table of God's Word and Christ's Body. Also, no. 65 identifies the homily as "part of the Liturgy" (*pars Liturgiae*) and as "necessary for the nurturing of the Christian life" (*ad nutrimentum vitae christianae necessaria*).

Paragraph two of no. 13 is concerned with participation in the Mass through sacramental reception of the Eucharist. Once again, the Second Vatican Council is presented as the fulfillment of something expressed at the Council of Trent. Chapter six of session 22 (1562) of that Council is quoted as indicating the desire that "the faithful present at each Mass should communicate not only by spiritual desire but also by sacramental reception of the Eucharist" (*in singulis Missis fideles adstantes non solum spirituali affectu, sed sacramentali etiam Eucharistiae perceptione communicarent*). While chapter six of session 22 begins with this affirmation, the concern of the chapter is not the promotion of sacramental reception of the Eucharist. Rather, it is a defense of Masses in which only the priest communicated over against those who wished such Masses to be condemned. In a new historical context, Vatican II could promote what is stated in *SC*, no. 55 and quoted here as "that more perfect form of participation in the Mass by which the faithful, after the priest's Communion, receive the Lord's Body from the same Sacrifice" (*illa perfectior Missae participatio, qua fideles post Communionem sacerdotis ex eodem sacrificio Corpus dominicum sumunt*).

In stating that the faithful should "receive the Lord's Body from the same Sacrifice," the bishops were not only reaffirming the importance of sacramental reception of the Eucharist. They were setting out a very important principle about the meaning of participation in the celebration of the Eucharist that went beyond what was articulated by the Council of Trent. That this principle has not been well received is evident in the many parishes where Holy Communion comes from the tabernacle rather than the table of the Lord. The principle will be repeated in *IGMR2002*, no. 85, and the reason given there is "that even by

14. Moved by the same desire and pastoral concern, the Second Vatican Council was able to give renewed consideration to what was established by Trent on Communion under both kinds. And indeed, since no one today calls into doubt in any way the doctrinal principles on the complete efficacy of Eucharistic Communion under the species of bread alone, the Council thus gave permission for the reception of Communion under both kinds on some occasions, because this clearer form of the sacramental sign offers a particular opportunity of deepening the understanding of the mystery in which the faithful take part.[21]

14. Eodem quidem animo ac studio pastorali permotum, Concilium Vaticanum II nova ratione expendere potuit institutum Tridentinum de Communione sub utraque specie. Etenim, quoniam hodie in dubium minime revocantur doctrinæ principia de plenissima vi Communionis, qua Eucharistia sub una specie panis suscipitur, permisit interdum Communionem sub utraque specie, cum scilicet, per dilucidiorem signi sacramentalis formam, opportunitas peculiaris offerretur altius intellegendi mysterii, quod fideles participarent.[21]

---

means of the signs Communion will stand out more clearly as a participation in the sacrifice actually being celebrated" (*quo etiam per signa Communio melius appareat participatio sacrificii, quod actu celebratur*). The theological significance of this principle is that it reconnects the two dimensions of sacrifice and meal in the celebration of the Eucharist.[24]

14. The focus of this article is Communion under both kinds. Once again, there is a concerted effort to make a link with the Council of Trent in order to show that the permission given by Vatican II for the reception of Communion under both kinds on some occasions was not in contradiction with the principles set out by Trent. The link is made by saying that both the bishops at Trent and those at Vatican II were "moved by the same desire and pastoral concern" (*Eodem quidem animo ac studio pastorali permotum*). The difference between the two councils is a difference, once again, of context. Whereas the bishops at Trent were in a defensive posture against persons who questioned the efficacy of reception of Communion under the species of bread alone, this was not part of the context for the bishops at Vatican II.

Article 14 notes that permission was given at Vatican II for Communion under both kinds on some occasions, "because this clearer form of the sacramental sign offers a particular opportunity of deepening the understanding of the mystery in which the faithful partake" (*per dilucidiorem signi sacramentalis formam, opportunitas peculiaris offerretur altius intellegendi mysterii, quod fideles participarent*). There is a footnote to *SC*, no. 55, which does allow for the possibility for Communion under both kinds after a clear statement about the dogmatic principles of Trent being intact. However, nothing is said about the sign value of the action. *Eucharisticum Mysterium*, no. 32, did state that "holy communion has a more complete form as a sign when it is received under both

24. See Irwin, 231–233.

15. In this manner the Church, while remaining faithful to her office as teacher of truth safeguarding "things old," that is, the deposit of tradition, fulfills at the same time another duty, that of examining and prudently bringing forth "things new" (cf. Mt 13:52).

Accordingly, a part of the new Missal directs the prayers of the Church in a more open way to the needs of our times, which is above all true of the Ritual Masses and the Masses for Various Needs, in which tradition and new elements are appropriately harmonized. Thus, while many expressions, drawn from the Church's most ancient tradition and familiar through the

15. Hoc pacto, dum fida permanet Ecclesia suo muneri ut magistræ veritatis, custodiens « vetera », id est depositum traditionis, officium quoque explet considerandi prudenterque adhibendi « nova » (cf. *Mt* 13, 52).

Pars enim quædam novi Missalis preces Ecclesiæ apertius ordinat ad temporis nostri necessitates; cuius generis sunt potissimum Missæ rituales et pro variis necessitatibus, in quibus traditio et novitas opportune inter se sociantur. Itaque, dum complures dictiones integræ manserunt ex antiquissima haustæ Ecclesiæ traditione, per ipsum sæpius editum Missale Romanum patefacta, aliæ plures ad hodierna

---

forms," and this document is referenced in no. 281 below, where there is an elaboration of the sign value of Communion under both kinds.

15. This article returns to the image of a living tradition that was introduced at the beginning of the Preamble. The first paragraph suggests that the Church has the twofold task of "safeguarding 'things old,' that is, the deposit of tradition" and "prudently bringing forth 'things new'" (*custodiens "vetera", id est depositum traditionis . . . prudenterque adhibendi "nova"*). This serves as background for paragraph two, which introduces the Ritual Masses and Masses for Various Needs that are part of the new Missal. The Preamble notes that, in the prayers of these Masses, the Church is responding to the needs of our times and bringing tradition and new elements into harmony. It indicates that this happens because the prayers of these Masses include ancient expressions that have not been changed as well as those that "have been accommodated to today's needs and circumstances" (*ad hodierna requisita et condiciones accommodatae sunt*). Here we have the link with tradition, but the Preamble goes on to note that some of the prayers have been newly composed, including those that are related to "certain needs proper to our era" (*necessitatibus quibusdam nostrae aetatis propriis*). Here *IGMR2002* recognizes the dynamic nature of liturgical prayer, because it is the prayer of a living Church. This continues in paragraph three, which notes that some phrases of the ancient texts have been changed "so that the style of language would be more in accord with the language of modern theology and would truly reflect the current discipline of the Church" (*quo convenientius sermo ipse cum hodiernae theologiae lingua concineret referretque ex veritate condicionem disciplinae Ecclesiae praesentem*).

Although there are no notes to conciliar documents, the Preamble indicates that the thoughts and even phrasing of recent documents of the Council have been influential in the composition of new prayers and the adaptations made

many editions of the *Roman Missal,* have remained unchanged, many other expressions have been accommodated to today's needs and circumstances. Still others, such as the prayers for the Church, the laity, the sanctification of human work, the community of all peoples, and certain needs proper to our era, have been newly composed, drawing on the thoughts and often the very phrasing of the recent documents of the Council.

Moreover, on account of the same attitude toward the new state of the present world, it seemed that in the use of texts from the most ancient tradition, so revered a treasure would in no way be harmed if some phrases were changed so that the style of language would be more in accord with the language of modern theology and would truly reflect the current discipline of the Church. Thus, not a few expressions bearing on the evaluation and use of goods of the earth have been changed, as have also not a few allusions to a certain form of outward penance belonging to past ages of the Church.

requisita et condiciones accommodatæ sunt, aliæ, contra, uti orationes pro Ecclesia, laicis, operis humani sanctificatione, omnium gentium communitate, necessitatibus quibusdam nostræ ætatis propriis, ex integro sunt contextæ, sumptis cogitationibus ac sæpe ipsis locutionibus ex recentibus Concilii documentis.

Ob eandem porro æstimationem novi status mundi, qui nunc est, in vetustissimæ traditionis textuum usu, nulla prorsus videbatur inferri iniuria tam venerando thesauro, si quædam sententiæ immutarentur, quo convenientius sermo ipse cum hodiernæ theologiæ lingua concineret referretque ex veritate condicionem disciplinæ Ecclesiæ præsentem. Hinc dicta nonnulla, ad existimationem et usum bonorum terrestrium attinentia, sunt mutata, haud secus ac nonnulla, quæ exterioris quandam pænitentiæ formam prodebant aliarum Ecclesiæ ætatum propriam.

Hoc denique modo normæ liturgicæ Concilii Tridentini pluribus sane in partibus completæ et perfectæ sunt normis Concilii Vaticani II, quod ad exitum per-

---

to the old. Several possible references come to mind. *SC,* no. 2, presents the liturgy as an action in which the Church is disclosed. *LG,* no. 48, provides us with the image of a pilgrim Church, a Church moving forward to the new heavens and the new earth, but belonging to the present age. Finally, *GS,* no. 1, begins with the memorable statement that "the joys and hopes, the struggle and grief and anguish of the people of our time, especially of those who are poor or afflicted, are the joys and hopes, the grief and anguish of the followers of Christ as well. Nothing that is genuinely human fails to find an echo in their hearts." Surely such passages provide a foundation for thinking of the liturgy as a living tradition that can repeat and modify the old as well as incorporate the new.

The Preamble comes to a close by emphasizing continuity with the Council of Trent by stating that its liturgical norms "have certainly been completed and perfected in many respects by those of the Second Vatican Council" (*sane in partibus completae et perfectae sunt normis Concilii Vaticani II*). The norms set out by Vatican II have realized the goal of bringing "the faithful closer to the Sacred Liturgy" (*ad sacram Liturgiam fideles propius*). Thus, the Preamble ends by highlighting the pastoral concern that has been evident in many of its statements and will reappear in numerous ways throughout the rest of *IGMR2002.*

Finally, in this manner the liturgical norms of the Council of Trent have certainly been completed and perfected in many respects by those of the Second Vatican Council, which has brought to realization the efforts of the last four hundred years to bring the faithful closer to the Sacred Liturgy especially in recent times, and above all the zeal for the Liturgy promoted by St. Pius X and his successors.

duxit conatus ad sacram Liturgiam fideles propius admovendi, qui per hæc quattuor sæcula sunt suscepti, præsertim vero recentiore ætate, maxime studio rei liturgicæ a S. Pio X eiusque Successoribus promoto.

GIRM—Notes (English)

1. Ecumenical Council of Trent, Session 22, *Doctrina de ss. Missae sacrificio*, 17 September 1562: *Enchiridion Symbolorum*, H. Denzinger and A. Schönmetzer, editors (editio XXXIII, Freiburg: Herder, 1965; hereafter, Denz-Schön), 1738–1759.

2. Second Vatican Ecumenical Council, Constitution on the Sacred Liturgy, *Sacrosanctum Concilium*, no. 47; cf. Dogmatic Constitution on the Church, *Lumen gentium*, nos. 3, 28; Decree on the Ministry and Life of Priests, *Presbyterorum ordinis*, nos. 2, 4, 5.

3. Evening Mass of the Lord's Supper, prayer over the offerings. Cf. *Sacramentarium Veronense*, L.C. Mohlberg et al., editors (3rd edition, Rome, 1978), section I, no. 93.

4. Cf. Eucharistic Prayer III.

5. Cf. Eucharistic Prayer IV.

6. Second Vatican Ecumenical Council, Constitution on the Sacred Liturgy, *Sacrosanctum Concilium*, nos. 7, 47; Decree on the Ministry and Life of Priests, *Presbyterorum ordinis*, nos. 5, 18.

7. Cf. Pius XII, Encyclical Letter *Humani generis*, 12 August 1950: *Acta Apostolicae Sedis*, Commentarium Officiale (Vatican City; hereafter, AAS), 42 (1950), pp. 570–571; Paul VI, Encyclical Letter *Mysterium fidei*, On the doctrine and worship of the Eucharist, 3 September 1965: AAS 57(1965), pp. 762–769; Paul VI, Solemn Profession of Faith, 30 June 1968, nos. 24–26: AAS 60 (1968), pp. 442–443; Sacred Congregation of Rites, Instruction *Eucharisticum mysterium*, On the worship of the Eucharist, 25 May 1967, nos. 3f, 9: AAS 59 (1967), pp. 543, 547.

IGMR—Notes (Latin)

1. Conc. Œcum. Trid., Sessio XXII, 17 septembris 1562: Denz.-Schönm. 1738–1759.

2. Conc. Œcum. Vat. II, Const. de sacra Liturgia, *Sacrosanctum Concilium*, n. 47; cf. Const. dogm. de Ecclesia, *Lumen gentium*, nn. 3, 28; Decr. de Presbyterorum ministerio et vita, *Presbyterorum ordinis*, nn. 2, 4, 5.

3. Missa vespertina in Cena Domini, oratio super oblata. Cf. *Sacramentarium Veronense*, ed. L.C. Mohlberg, n. 93.

4. Cf. Prex eucharistica III.

5. Cf. Prex eucharistica IV.

6. Conc. Œcum. Vat. II, Const. de sacra Liturgia, *Sacrosanctum Concilium*, nn. 7, 47; Decr. de Presbyterorum ministerio et vita, *Presbyterorum ordinis*, nn. 5, 18.

7. Cf. Pius XII, Litt. Enc. *Humani generis*, diei 12 augusti 1950: A.A.S. 42 (1950) pp. 570–571; Paulus VI, Litt. Enc. *Mysterium Fidei*, diei 3 septembris 1965: A.A.S. 57 (1965) pp. 762–769; *Sollemnis professio fidei*, diei 30 iunii 1968, nn. 24–26: A.A.S. 60 (1968) pp. 442–443; S. Congr. Rituum, Instr. *Eucharisticum mysterium*, diei 25 maii 1967, nn. 3 f, 9: A.A.S. 59 (1967) pp. 543, 547.

8. Cf. Council of Trent, session 13, *Decretum de ss. Eucharistia*, 11 October 1551: Denz-Schön, 1635–1661.

9. Cf. Second Vatican Ecumenical Council, Decree on the Ministry and Life of Priests, *Presbyterorum ordinis*, no. 2.

10. Cf. Second Vatican Ecumenical Council, Constitution on the Sacred Liturgy, *Sacrosanctum Concilium*, no. 11.

11. Ibid, no. 50.

12. Ecumenical Council of Trent, Session 22, *Doctrina de ss. Missae sacrificio*, 17 September 1562, chapter 8: Denz-Schön, 1749.

13. Ibid., chap. 9: Denz-Schön, 1759.

14. Ibid., chap. 8: Denz-Schön, 1749.

15. Cf. Second Vatican Ecumenical Council, Constitution on the Sacred Liturgy, *Sacrosanctum Concilium*, no. 33.

16. Ibid., no. 36.

17. Ibid., no. 52.

18. Ibid., no. 35:3.

19. Ibid., no. 55.

20. Ecumenical Council of Trent, Session 22, *Doctrina de ss. Missae sacrificio*, 17 September 1562, chapter 6: Denz-Schön, 1747.

21. Cf. Second Vatican Ecumenical Council, Constitution on the Sacred Liturgy, *Sacrosanctum Concilium*, no. 55.

8. Cf. Conc. Œcum. Trid., Sessio XIII, 11 octobris 1551: Denz.-Schönm. 1635–1661.

9. Cf. Conc. Œcum. Vat. II, Decr. de Presbyterorum ministerio et vita, *Presbyterorum ordinis*, n. 2.

10. Cf. Conc. Œcum. Vat. II, Const. de sacra Liturgia, *Sacrosanctum Concilium*, n. 11.

11. *Ibidem*, n. 50.

12. Conc. Œcum. Trid., Sessio XXII, Doctr. de ss. Missæ sacrificio, cap. 8: Denz.-Schönm. 1749.

13. *Ibidem*, can. 9: Denz.-Schönm. 1759.

14. *Ibidem*, cap. 8: Denz.-Schönm. 1749.

15. Cf. Conc. Œcum. Vat. II, Const. de sacra Liturgia, *Sacrosanctum Concilium*, n. 33.

16. *Ibidem*, n. 36.

17. *Ibidem*, n. 52.

18. *Ibidem*, n. 35, 3.

19. *Ibidem*, n. 55.

20. Conc. Œcum. Trid., Sessio XXII, Doctr. de ss. Missæ sacrificio, cap. 6: Denz.-Schönm. 1747.

21. Cf. Conc. Œcum Vat. II, Const. de sacra Liturgia, *Sacrosanctum Concilium*, n. 55.

CHAPTER I

Importance and Dignity of the Eucharistic Celebration

(*DE CELEBRATIONIS EUCHARISTICÆ MOMENTO ET DIGNITATE*)

Keith F. Pecklers

Introduction

Chapter I is an amplified version of what appears in the 1975 *Institutio Generalis Missalis Romani* (*IGMR1975*) and the first six articles (nos. 16–21) are essentially a repetition of what is found in the former Instruction. This introductory chapter discusses the eucharistic celebration in general terms, establishing the framework for particular aspects of the liturgical action that will be treated in subsequent chapters. While emphasizing the hierarchical nature of the Church's worship, active participation is strongly affirmed both as a right and duty of all Christians by virtue of their baptism. The eucharistic celebration is the heart of the Christian life and the source and summit of all its activity (*Sacrosanctum Concilium* [SC], no. 10; *Catholicae Ecclesiae Catechismus* [CEC], no. 1071). In *Ecclesia de Eucharistia* Pope John Paul II (d. 2005) called it "the most precious possession which the Church can have in her journey through history" (no. 9). Thus, the better the active participation of the liturgical assembly, the more is the ecclesial nature of that celebration revealed.

Articles 22–26 offer new material, which focuses largely on the diocesan bishop as the chief liturgist of the diocese (see no. 387 below; also cf. Mitchell and Baldovin, 11 and Seasoltz, 33 above). It is the bishop's role to promote and safeguard the dignity of proper celebration according to the local norms established by the conference of bishops. Eucharistic celebrations presided over by the bishop should be examples for the entire diocese of beauty in the arrangement of the liturgical space, tasteful use of art and sacred music. Here, particular aspects of adaptation and issues of translation are discussed, although those topics will be treated in much greater detail later in the Instruction.

Chapter I THE IMPORTANCE AND DIGNITY OF THE EUCHARISTIC CELEBRATION

16. The celebration of Mass, as the action of Christ and the People of God arrayed hierarchically, is the center of the whole Christian life for the Church both universal and local, as well as for each of the faithful individually.[22] In it is found the high point both of the action by which God sanctifies the world in Christ and of the worship that the human race offers to the Father, adoring him through Christ, the Son of God, in the Holy Spirit.[23] In it, moreover, during the course of the year, the mysteries of redemp-

Caput I DE CELEBRATIONIS EUCHARISTICÆ MOMENTO ET DIGNITATE

16. Celebratio Missæ, ut actio Christi et populi Dei hierarchice ordinati, centrum est totius vitæ christianæ pro Ecclesia tum universa tum locali, ac pro singulis fidelibus.[22] In ea enim culmen habetur et actionis qua Deus in Christo mundum sanctificat, et cultus quem homines exhibent Patri, eum per Christum Dei Filium in Spiritu Sancto adorantes.[23] In ea insuper mysteria redemptionis ita per anni circulum recoluntur, ut quodammodo præsentia reddantur.[24] Ceteræ autem actiones sacræ

---

16. Article 16 emphasizes the ecclesial nature of the eucharistic celebration as the action of Christ and the whole Church as it gathers liturgically in hierarchical order (*SC*, no. 41; *Lumen Gentium* [LG], no. 11; *Christus Dominus* [*ChrDom*], no. 30; *Eucharisticum Dominum*, no. 30; *CEC*, nos. 1136 and 1140). The entire Christian community functions as celebrants in the sacred liturgy, albeit with different roles and functions (*CEC*, no. 1142; also Power and Vincie, 51 above). The Mass is the culmination of the Christian life; the liturgical assembly worships God through Christ in the Holy Spirit; God sanctifies the Church through Christ's action and strengthens it for its mission within the world (*SC*, no. 10; *Ad Gentes [AG]*, nos. 6, 9, and 36; *CEC*, no. 1072). Throughout the liturgical year the Eucharist recalls the various mysteries of our redemption and those mysteries are made present in word and sacrament. In this way all of the other rites of the Church have their origins in the eucharistic celebration, as does the daily living out of the Gospel itself (*Presbyterorum Ordinis* [*PO*], no. 5).

In this first article one hears resonances of the two groundbreaking encyclicals of Pius XII (d. 1958): *Mystici Corporis* (1943) and *Mediator Dei* (1947). *Mystici Corporis* reawakened the Church to the fundamentally Pauline and Augustinian theology of the organic unity within Christ's body, which has the Eucharist at its heart. The doctrine of the Church as the mystical body of Christ was first recovered by nineteenth-century theologians at Tübingen and provided the theological foundations for the liturgical movement in the early twentieth century. In promoting a liturgical vision that linked together Christian worship with the Church's mission in the world, pioneers of that movement found a solid foundation for their efforts in the theology of the mystical body.

Mediator Dei was the first major encyclical on the subject of the liturgy, and the eccesiological dimension of worship found in no. 16 is clearly articulated in that preconciliar papal document. We read: "Christ acts each day to save us,

tion are recalled so as in some way to be made present.[24] Furthermore, the other sacred actions and all the activities of the Christian life are bound up with it, flow from it, and are ordered to it.[25]

et omnia opera christianæ vitæ cum ea cohærent, ex ea profluunt et ad eam ordinantur.[25]

17. It is therefore of the greatest importance that the celebration of the Mass—that is, the Lord's Supper—be so arranged that the sacred ministers and the faithful taking part in it, according to the proper state of each, may derive from it more abundantly[26] those fruits for the sake of which Christ the Lord instituted the Eucharistic Sacrifice of his Body and Blood and entrusted it to the Church, his beloved Bride, as the memorial of his Passion and Resurrection.[27]

17. Maxime proinde interest ut celebratio Missæ seu Cenæ dominicæ ita ordinetur, ut sacri ministri atque fideles, illam pro sua condicione participantes, eos fructus plenius exinde capiant,[26] ad quos obtinendos Christus Dominus sacrificium eucharisticum sui Corporis et sui Sanguinis instituit illudque, velut memoriale passionis et resurrectionis suæ, Ecclesiæ dilectæ sponsæ concredidit.[27]

---

in the sacraments and in His holy sacrifice. . . . Not from any ability of our own, but from the power of God, are they endowed with the capacity to unite the piety of members with that of the Head, and to make this, in a sense, the action of the whole community" (no. 29).

Article 16 cites *SC* to emphasize the important role that all members of the Church have as they are united together in Christ's action. Number 10 of that Constitution refers to the liturgy as "the summit toward which the activity of the Church is directed; it is also the source from which all its power flows." Consequently, those who have been baptized into Christ "should come together to praise God in the midst of his Church, to take part in the sacrifice, and to eat the Lord's supper."

Throughout the liturgical year, even as various aspects of the mysteries of Christ's life are recalled in different eucharistic celebrations (*CEC,* nos. 1163–1165 and 1168–1170), it is nonetheless the same paschal mystery of Jesus Christ that is celebrated (*CEC,* nos. 1171 and 1172–1174). Strengthened at the table of the Word and the table of Eucharist, Christians are sent forth to serve the Body of Christ beyond the confines of the church buildings (see *Mane Nobiscum Domine,* no. 13). And it is to that eucharistic assembly they will return, offering back to God their lives and the mission of the Church in which they have been engaged during the previous week.

17. The diversity of ministries within the liturgical assembly is highlighted here. In the Mass, each participant assumes his or her proper liturgical role for an effective celebration (*SC,* nos. 14, 19, 26, 28 and 30). The specifics of these roles will be presented and discussed later in the Instruction (e.g., see nos. 95–97 below), but their importance is affirmed here from the outset. This recovery of baptism as foundational for all liturgical ministry was a radical change from Tridentine worship, which left very little room for lay participation in the

18. This will best be accomplished if, with due regard for the nature and the particular circumstances of each liturgical assembly, the entire celebration is planned in such a way that it leads to a conscious, active, and full participation of the faithful both in body and in mind, a participation burning with faith, hope, and charity, of the sort which is desired by the Church and demanded by the very nature of the celebration, and to which the Christian people have a right and duty by reason of their Baptism.[28]

18. Quod apte fiet si, attentis natura aliisque adiunctis uniuscuiusque cœtus liturgici, universa celebratio ita disponatur, ut consciam illam, actuosam atque plenam participationem fidelium inducat, corporis nempe et animi, fide, spe et caritate ferventem, quæ ab Ecclesia exoptatur et ab ipsa celebrationis natura postulatur, et ad quam populus christianus vi baptismatis ius habet et officium.[28]

Eucharist. Such recovery was one of the greatest accomplishments at Vatican II. We read in *SC*, no. 14, "It is very much the wish of the church that all the faithful should be led to take that full, conscious and active part in liturgical celebration which is demanded by the nature of the liturgy, and to which the Christian people, 'a chosen race, a royal priesthood, a holy nation, a redeemed people' (1 Pet. 2:9, 4-5) have a right and to which they are bound by reason of their Baptism." *SC* further states that full and active participation of Christians gathered together in worship must be the goal to be pursued above all else. *SC* then quotes from Pius X's (d. 1914) 1903 *motu proprio, Tra le sollecitudini*, which some consider the *Magna Carta of* the liturgical movement, since it defined the liturgy as the "primary, indeed the indispensable source from which the faithful are to derive the true Christian spirit" (*SC*, no. 14). The Eucharist was instituted by Christ himself and entrusted by Christ himself to the Church as a memorial of his passion and death. Consequently, participation in that eucharistic sacrifice by the entire People of God is essential (*SC*, no. 47).

18. Here *IGMR2002* gives further attention to the importance of "conscious, active, and full participation" in the eucharistic celebration, suggesting how this participation will come about. First, careful attention will need to be given to the "nature and circumstances of each liturgical assembly." In other words, the context of the particular worshiping community is always significant since it should determine in what manner the liturgy is celebrated so that the faithful's participation is both facilitated and encouraged. This is especially true in liturgical preaching where the homily necessarily must address the problems and issues within that particular community in light of the biblical readings assigned to that day (see nos. 65–66 below). This theme will be further developed in Chapter IX as *IGMR2002* treats the subject of adaptation and liturgical inculturation (see Francis-Neville, 448 below). In the post–Vatican II Church it has become abundantly clear that pastoral situations around the world are quite diverse and the eucharistic celebration needs to be planned and celebrated in such a way that it manifests the particular community that celebrates.

19. Even if it is sometimes not possible to have the presence and active participation of the faithful, which bring out more plainly the ecclesial nature of the celebration,[29] the Eucharistic Celebration always retains its efficacy and dignity because it is the action of Christ and the Church, in which the priest fulfills his own principal office and always acts for the people's salvation.

19. Quamvis fidelium præsentia et actuosa participatio, quæ ecclesialem celebrationis naturam apertius manifestant,[29] aliquando non possint haberi, eucharistica celebratio sua efficacia et dignitate semper est prædita, quippe quæ sit actus Christi et Ecclesiæ, in quo sacerdos munus suum præcipuum adimplet et semper agit pro salute populi.

A second aspect mentioned is that of proper liturgical planning so as to bring about the participation desired by the Council. This planning necessarily includes attention to liturgical catechesis so that communities are taught the importance of participating both "in body and spirit." This goes beyond emphasizing the importance of singing the hymns and responses, praying aloud the spoken prayer texts along with the rest of the assembly. It also includes attention to the link between eucharistic participation and daily life, and what the assembly's eucharistic "Amen" signifies as it lives out its liturgical participation during the week. Many Roman Catholics do not understand the mutuality between *lex orandi* and *lex credendi* and hence do not recognize the formative character of the eucharistic liturgy (*CEC*, no. 1124). Greater attention to liturgical preaching and liturgical catechesis will assist the faithful to enter more deeply into the mystery of the Eucharist and live the liturgy more intentionally in daily life (*CEC*, nos. 1074 and 1075).

Full and active eucharistic participation is motivated by the evangelical virtues of faith, hope, and charity. Catholics do not worship in a vacuum but are bound together with others both in their particular local community and with the Church throughout the world. *CEC* clearly states, "In the New Testament the word 'liturgy' refers not only to the celebration of divine worship but also to the proclamation of the Gospel and to active charity" (no. 1070). The third century *Didascalia Apostolorum* admonished bishops to give careful attention to the way in which they showed hospitality within the liturgical assembly—how they welcomed the poor and needy, the elderly and foreigners.[1] Today it is more important than ever that our liturgical participation be motivated not only by faith and hope but also by charity, expressed most immediately in the way we welcome those on our left and right in the liturgical assembly and how that eucharistic charity is lived beyond the walls of the church building (*SC*, no. 14; *AG*, no. 36).

19. *IGMR2002* asserts that the combination of the liturgical assembly's presence and its active participation most fully highlights the ecclesial nature of the

1. 12 (2.57) in F.X. Funk, ed., *Didascalia et Constitutiones Apostolorum I* (Paderborn, 1905), 158–167.

It is therefore recommended that the priest celebrate the Eucharistic Sacrifice even daily, if possible.[30]

Ipsi ergo commendatur ut sacrificium eucharisticum etiam cotidie, pro posse, celebret.[30]

20. Because, however, the celebration of the Eucharist, like the entire Liturgy, is carried out through perceptible signs that nourish, strengthen, and express faith,[31] the utmost care must be taken to choose and to arrange those forms and elements set forth by the Church that, in view of the circumstances of the people and the place, will more effectively foster active and full

20. Cum autem Eucharistiæ celebratio, sicut et universa Liturgia, fiat per signa sensibilia, quibus fides alitur, roboratur et exprimitur,[31] maxime curandum est eas formas et elementa ab Ecclesia proposita seligi et ordinari, quæ, attentis personarum et locorum adiunctis, actuosam et plenam participationem intensius foveant et fidelium utilitati spirituali aptius respondeant.

Church. As the community gathers together to hear God's Word and be nourished by the Eucharist, the Eucharist should be at the heart of the Christian life (cf. *Mane Nobiscum Domini,* no. 17). While the celebration of Mass with the presence of the liturgical assembly is always normative (*SC,* no. 41; *Codex Iuris Canonici* 1983 [*CIC1983*], c. 837, par. 1; *CEC,* no. 1140), the eucharistic celebration is never diminished even when it is not possible for the lay faithful to be present. This is so because the liturgical action itself belongs to Christ and the Church, and the priest carries out his office in the name of Christ and the Church even in those exceptional situations when the faithful are not present. What is new in this section is the recommendation that the priest should celebrate the Eucharist "even daily whenever possible" (*PO,* no. 13). This is a repetition of what is stated in *CIC1983* (c. 904). *Codex Iuris Canonici* 1917 *(CIC1917)* required priests to celebrate Mass several times a year but also directed bishops and religious superiors to encourage their priests in celebrating the Eucharist at least on Sundays (*CIC1917,* c. 805). Canon 904 does not retain the obligatory language of the *CIC1917* where priests are required to celebrate Mass but rather states that priests should "celebrate frequently" and that daily celebration is "strongly recommended." Thus, while there is no legal obligation for priests to celebrate daily Mass, it is nonetheless strongly recommended.[2]

20. *IGMR2002* points to the "outward signs" within the eucharistic celebration that "foster, strengthen, and express faith." The purpose of the Eucharist,

2. Foundations for this perspective can be traced back to the early seventeenth century and the Oratory of French Cardinal Pierre de Bérulle (d. 1629)—what came to be known as the "Bérulle School." There, the Eucharistic celebration was established as the center of Catholic piety giving greater prominence to the sacrificial nature of the Mass and the action of the priest within the sacrifice. Thanks to the efforts of the Bérulle School, along with the approaches to piety represented by two of his contemporaries: Condren (d. 1641) and Olier (d. 1657), personal piety and private devotion came to be linked to the celebration of Mass—both for the laity as well as the clergy—albeit in different forms. Consequently, the emphasis on the priest's daily celebration of the Mass found fertile ground there. See Joseph A. Jungmann, *The Mass of the Roman Rite,* trans. Francis Brunner, 2 vols. (Westminster: Christian Classics, 1986), I:143.

participation and more properly respond to the spiritual needs of the faithful.

21. This Instruction aims both to offer general guidelines for properly arranging the Celebration of the Eucharist and to set forth rules for ordering the various forms of celebration.[32]

21. Hæc itaque Institutio eo spectat ut tum lineamenta generalia præbeat, quibus Eucharistiæ celebratio apte ordinetur, tum regulas exponat, quibus singulæ celebrationis formæ disponantur.[32]

---

as with all the sacraments, is the sanctification of the People of God, the spiritual upbuilding of the Body of Christ, and the worship of God "in spirit and in truth" (*CIC1983*, c. 834, par. 1). The sacraments as events are themselves signs that teach and communicate meaning. They nourish the faith of the liturgical assembly and impart grace so that Christians are able to live faithful lives in service of the gospel through their practice of charity (*SC*, no. 59). Already in the fifth century, St. Augustine (d. 430) suggested that we call the Eucharist a "sacrifice" because it is a sacrament or a "sacred sign" (*De civitate Dei*, 10, 5). In his classic *Sacred Signs*, Romano Guardini reminded the Church of how simple, common objects and actions can be bearers of great mystery.[3] The liturgy itself is replete with signs whose meanings are only appropriately interpreted by believers within particular cultures (*CEC*, nos. 1145–1148). But these signs will only be able to foster, strengthen, and express faith to the extent that they are understood and appropriated by the celebrating community gathered together by God in a particular time and place.

Soon after the Council, some pastors believed that the most effective way to assist their assemblies in understanding these signs was to explain, even at times to overexplain them. The postconciliar experience along with the rich contribution made by the social sciences, has helped the Church to recognize a fundamental truth: when sacramental signs are properly enacted they communicate on their own behalf. They convey a depth of meaning that transcends verbal expression, and they foster the active and full participation of the whole body of Christ desired by the Church. Thus, pastoral agents are encouraged to make wise use of the forms and elements which the Church provides.

21. This article provides the rationale for why *IGMR2002* is needed in the first place: both to assist proper liturgical planning for celebrations of the Eucharist and also to offer direction for individual celebrations of Mass without a congregation. Liturgy is more than words; it is action whose unity is essential for the effective performance of the ritual. The concept of choreography is quite helpful in discussing ritual. The *Anaphora of Serapion* used the term *choregos*[4]—a term borrowed from Greek theatre—to speak of God as the "choreographer of

3. Romano Guardini, *Sacred Signs*, rev. ed. (Wilmington DE: Michael Glazier, Inc., 1979).

4. 1.5, see Johannes Quasten, *Monumenta eucharistica et liturgica vetustissima*, Florilegium Patristicum 7, ed. Bernhard Geyer and Johannes Zellinger (Bonn: Peter Hanstein, 1935), 60.

22. The celebration of the Eucharist in a particular Church is of utmost importance.

For the diocesan Bishop, the chief steward of the mysteries of God in the particular Church entrusted to his care, is the moderator, promoter, and guardian of the whole of its liturgical life.[33] In celebrations at which the Bishop presides, and especially in the celebration of the Eucharist led by the Bishop himself with the presbyter-

22. Summi autem momenti est Eucharistiæ celebratio in Ecclesia particulari.

Episcopus enim diœcesanus, primus mysteriorum Dei dispensator in Ecclesia particulari sibi commissa, moderator est, promotor et custos totius vitæ liturgicæ.[33] In celebrationibus quæ, ipso præsidente, aguntur, præsertim vero in celebratione eucharistica, quæ ab ipso agitur, presbyterio, diaconis et populo participantibus,

---

immortality" who essentially leads all of creation in the dance. Analogously, Ignatius of Antioch spoke of the Church as a choir and God as the choir director.[5] *IGMR2002* suggests a sort of liturgical choreography by which the assembly is able to move together as one body—the mystical body of Christ. It also protects against the idiosyncratic behavior of some presiders evident in the years immediately after the Council. Moving together creates greater harmony and unity within the eucharistic celebration. The Instruction offers ample room for adaptation and flexibility in the celebration, but presidential improvisation beyond what is called for in *IGMR2002* can overburden the ritual and texts and weaken the nonverbal symbolic communication within the action.

In the second century, Justin Martyr's *First Apology* noted that the president of the Sunday eucharistic assembly should pray the Eucharistic Prayer "according to his ability,"[6] i.e., to improvise—a necessity in the era preceding the development of liturgical books. By contrast, the sixteenth-century Tridentine liturgical reforms fixed liturgical texts in uniformly printed books, often leading to a slavish preoccupation with rubrics, a preoccupation that lasted four centuries. Happily the liturgical reforms of Vatican II have restored a helpful balance: the rubrics within the *Missale Romanum* maintain the unity of the Roman Rite and help the liturgical ministers in properly fulfilling their tasks, but they are not ends in themselves. When bishops and priests take the time to study carefully *IGMR2002* and become familiar with it, their presidency at the Eucharist has greater potential for being more prayerful and transparent, calling less attention to the presider and more attention to Jesus Christ whose paschal mystery lies at the heart of the celebration.

22. Articles 22 through 26 contain material not in earlier editions of *IGMR*. Article 22 addresses the importance of the eucharistic celebration within the local Church. As shepherd of the flock in that particular church, the diocesan bishop is the "moderator, promoter, and guardian" of the liturgical life within

5. *Phil.*, no. 4, see *Ignace d'Antioche: Lettres. Martyre de Polycarpe*, ed. Pierre Camelot, Sources Chrétiennes 10 (Paris: Éditions du Cerf, 1969), 122.

6. 67.5, see Quasten, *Monumenta eucharistica et liturgica vetustissima*, 20.

ate, the deacons, and the people taking part, the mystery of the Church is revealed. For this reason, the solemn celebration of Masses of this sort must be an example for the entire diocese.

The Bishop should therefore be determined that the priests, the deacons, and the lay Christian faithful grasp ever more deeply the genuine meaning of the rites and liturgical texts and thereby be led to an active and fruitful celebration of the Eucharist. To the same end, he should also be vigilant that the dignity of these celebrations be enhanced. In promoting this dignity, the beauty of the sacred place, of music, and of art should contribute as greatly as possible.

mysterium Ecclesiæ manifestatur. Quare huiusmodi Missarum sollemnia exemplo esse debent universæ diœcesi.

Eius ergo est animum intendere ut presbyteri, diaconi et christifideles laici, genuinum sensum rituum et textuum liturgicorum penitius semper comprehendant et ita ad actuosam et fructuosam Eucharistiæ celebrationem ducantur. Eundem in finem invigilet ut ipsarum celebrationum dignitas augeatur, ad quam promovendam loci sacri, musicæ et artis pulchritudo quamplurimum conferat.

---

the diocese (*ChrDom*, no.15; *CIC1983* cc. 835, par. 1; 838, par. 1). *SC*, no. 41 quotes Ignatius of Antioch in speaking of the local church gathered together with its bishop in the "same Eucharist, in one prayer, at one altar."[7] By implication, the cathedral should be the liturgical model for the diocese, especially in those solemn celebrations at which the bishop himself presides (*CEC*, no. 1561). In the years since the Council increasing numbers of residential bishops have been restoring the ancient tradition of presiding and preaching at the principal Eucharist in their own cathedrals each Sunday morning.

The diocesan bishop should also assist his clergy and the lay faithful to grow in their appreciation of the genuine sense of the liturgical rites themselves, which will then lead them to a more fruitful participation in the eucharistic celebration. *LG* states that "every lawful celebration of the Eucharist is regulated by the bishop" (no. 26). The bishop's role and responsibility as chief guardian of the diocese's liturgical life is given even greater emphasis in *Redemptionis Sacramentum* (*RedSac*). In presenting *RedSac*, Cardinal Francis Arinze, the Prefect of the Congregation for Divine Worship and the Discipline of the Sacraments, noted:

> I single out the role of the Diocesan Bishop. He is the high priest of his flock. He directs, encourages, promotes, and organizes. He looks into sacred music and art. He sets up needed commissions for liturgy, music and sacred art (*RedSac*, nos. 22, 25). He seeks remedies for abuses and it is to him or his assistants that recourse should first be made rather than to the Apostolic See (*RedSac*., nos. 176–182, 184).[8]

7. *Smyrn*., no. 8; *Magn*., no. 8; *Phil*., no. 4, see *Ignace d'Antioche: Lettres. Martyre de Polycarpe*, ed. Pierre Camelot, Sources Chrétiennes 10 (Paris: Éditions du Cerf, 1969), 138, 84 and 122.

8. "Introducing *Redemptionis Sacramentum*," Press Conference, 23 April 2004.

23. Moreover, in order that such a celebration may correspond more fully to the prescriptions and spirit of the sacred Liturgy, and also in order to increase its pastoral effectiveness, certain accommodations and adaptations are specified in this General Instruction and in the Order of Mass.

24. These adaptations consist for the most part in the choice of certain rites or texts, that is, of the chants, readings, prayers, explanations, and gestures which may respond better to the needs, preparation, and culture of the participants and which are entrusted to the priest celebrant. Nevertheless, the priest must remember that he is the servant of the sacred Liturgy and that he

23. Quo insuper celebratio præscriptis et spiritui sacræ Liturgiæ plenius respondeat, eiusque efficacitas pastoralis augeatur, in hac Institutione generali et in Ordine Missæ, aliquæ accommodationes et aptationes exponuntur.

24. Hæ aptationes, ut plurimum, in electione consistunt quorundam rituum aut textuum, id est cantuum, lectionum, orationum, monitionum et gestuum, qui sint necessitatibus, præparationi et ingenio participantium magis respondentes quique sacerdoti celebranti committuntur. Attamen meminerit sacerdos se servitorem esse sacræ Liturgiæ, sibique quidquam proprio

---

The Cardinal's comments, as *RedSac* itself, suggest that greater emphasis is to be placed on the role of the diocesan bishop, as evidenced in nos. 22–26, perhaps in an attempt to remedy what was considered lacking in the earlier editions of the *IGMR*. Indeed, many who have criticized implementation of the conciliar liturgical reforms have faulted residential bishops who failed to give adequate liturgical guidance and direction to their local churches when they returned home from the Vatican Council. The experience of forty years with the conciliar liturgy and an increased concern over liturgical abuses might offer some explanation for this expanded section on the role of the bishop in the implementation of liturgical norms.

23. This article simply introduces the last four articles of this first chapter, which deal with adaptations. It notes that *IGMR2002* and the *Ordo Missae* establish exactly where pastoral "accommodation or adaptation" is possible within eucharistic celebrations. Such guidelines help to facilitate celebrations that are more pastorally effective while corresponding both to the prescriptions and spirit of the sacred liturgy.

24. In noting where pastoral adaptations are possible in the choice of liturgical music, readings, prayers, introductory comments and gestures, this article recognizes that these choices are left to the presider, commonly in consultation with other parish ministers and musicians who assist him (no. 352 below). The purpose of such adaptations is to align these elements of the Mass to the cultural genius and pastoral needs of the particular celebrating community. The eucharistic celebration is not the personal domain of the priest; rather, he is the servant of the worship and of the people of God assembled for the Church's liturgy. Consequently, it is not within his competence to "add, remove, or change anything in the liturgy" (*SC*, no. 22).

himself is not permitted, on his own initiative, to add, to remove, or to change anything in the celebration of Mass.[34]

25. In addition, certain adaptations are indicated in the proper place in the Missal and pertain respectively to the diocesan Bishop or to the Conference of Bishops, in accord with the *Constitution on the Sacred Liturgy*[35] (cf. nos. 387, 388–393).

marte in Missæ celebratione addere, demere aut mutare non licere.[34]

25. Insuper in Missali suo loco aptationes quædam innuuntur quæ, iuxta Constitutionem de sacra Liturgia, respective competunt aut Episcopo diœcesano aut Conferentiæ Episcoporum[35] (*cf.* infra, *nn. 387, 388–393*).

---

25. Aside from the adaptations mentioned in the previous article, any additional adaptations are entrusted either to the residential bishop himself or to the Episcopal Conference (cf. nos. 387 and 388–393 below). The diocesan bishop regulates the manner of concelebration and is to establish norms regarding the function of altar servers and other liturgical ministries, the distribution of Communion under both kinds, and the construction and renovation of churches. This latter task is often delegated to a diocesan liturgical commission if there is one, or an art and environment commission within the diocese entrusted with overseeing the proper implementation of liturgical guidelines in the arrangement of liturgical space.

Other liturgical adaptations requiring a greater level of collaboration on national or regional levels are decided by the episcopal conference. One of their most important tasks is to prepare and approve an edition of the *Missale Romanum* in the vernacular and then submit the proposed text to the Holy See for confirmation (*recognitio, CIC1983,* c. 838, par. 3; also Seasoltz, 37 above). Episcopal conferences within the English-speaking world joined together in 1963 to form the International Commission on English in the Liturgy (ICEL), where vernacular translations of the liturgical books are prepared by an international commission of experts. Nonetheless, each particular bishops' conference must independently submit its own liturgical texts for confirmation by the Congregation for Divine Worship and the Discipline of the Sacraments.

Along with the important task of preparing vernacular translations of the liturgical books, episcopal conferences decide on the adaptations indicated within *IGMR2002* and the *Ordo Missae*. Those decisions must also be submitted to the Holy See for the normal *recognitio* and once approval has been granted, the episcopal conference is then charged with the task of implementation on the national or regional level. These adaptations include the chant texts in the entrance rite, at the preparation of the gifts, and the Communion; gestures and postures of the faithful (e.g. during the Eucharistic Prayer); the gestures of veneration before the altar and the Book of the Gospels; scriptural readings to be used on special occasions; the manner of exchanging the greeting of peace and Holy Communion; materials used for the altar and liturgical furnishings and sacred vessels; and both the color and form used for liturgical vesture.

26. As for variations and the more substantial adaptations in view of the traditions and culture of peoples and regions, to be introduced in accordance with article 40 of the *Constitution on the Sacred Liturgy* because of benefit or need, the norms set forth in the Instruction *On the Roman Liturgy and Inculturation*[36] and in nos. 395–399 are to be observed.

26. Quod autem ad varietates et aptationes profundiores attinet, quæ ad traditiones et ingenium populorum et regionum attendant, ad mentem art. 40 Constitutionis de sacra Liturgia pro utilitate vel necessitate introducendas, ea serventur quæ in Instructione « De Liturgia romana et inculturatione »[36] et infra, *(nn. 395–399)* exponuntur.

---

26. This final article notes that certain pastoral situations will need more substantial cultural adaptation than what has been mentioned above. Such adaptation must take into account "the traditions and culture of peoples and regions." The article references *SC*, no. 40 which states: "In some places and circumstances, however, an even more radical adaptation of the liturgy is needed." An example of "radical adaptation" can be found in the *Roman Missal for the Dioceses of Zaire* approved by the Holy See in 1987. Popularly called the "Zairean (or Congolese) Rite" (cf. no. 78 below), this inculturated form of the Roman Rite includes distinctly Zairean/Congolese ritual elements that reflect the African genius and yet would be out of place in another part of the world. Such adaptations should follow the guidelines as established in *SC*, no. 40, which begins with the important role played by the episcopal conference in the process.

Article 26 also refers in a footnote to *Varietates Legitimae.* That 1994 document reflects thirty years of postconciliar experience in the area of liturgical inculturation. As a help to bishops and episcopal conferences, it attempts to respond to problems and situations not envisaged at the time of the Council. Specifically, the document aims to help bishops "to consider or put into effect, according to the law, such adaptations already foreseen in the liturgical books; to re-examine critically arrangements that have already been made; and if, in certain cultures, pastoral need requires that form of adaptation of the liturgy which the Constitution calls 'more profound' and at the same time considers 'more difficult,' to make arrangements for putting it into effect in accordance with the law" (no. 3).

Finally, the article notes that more profound cultural adaptations to the liturgy will also need to follow guidelines established in *IGMR2002*, nos. 395–399. Among other things, those articles note that the goal of liturgical inculturation is not to create new families of rites but rather to adapt the Roman Rite so that it responds to various cultural needs while maintaining its substantial unity. It cautions against any hasty and incautious manner of liturgical inculturation lest "the authentic liturgical tradition suffer contamination" (*authentica traditio liturgica contaminetur,* no. 398).

Conclusion

Chapter I establishes a framework for *IGMR2002* and lays out basic theological and functional principles, each of which will receive greater attention later in the document. There is little new information here, despite the addition of nos. 22–26 which were not in *IGMR1975*. Perhaps the most significant addition is the emphasis given to the bishop as "moderator, promoter, and guardian" of the diocese's liturgical life (no. 22) which amplifies c. 835 of *CIC1983*. Concretely, this means that the bishop himself, far from being simply a liturgical disciplinarian, should be an effective model of how to preside at worship, making it his aim to lead the people of his diocese to a deeper appreciation of the liturgy's riches through beautiful, prayerful, and dignified celebrations.

GIRM—Notes (English)

22. Cf. Second Vatican Ecumenical Council, Constitution on the Sacred Liturgy, *Sacrosanctum Concilium*, no. 41; Dogmatic Constitution on the Church, *Lumen gentium*, no. 11; Decree on the Ministry and Life of Priests, *Presbyterorum ordinis*, nos. 2, 5, 6; Decree on the Pastoral Office of Bishops, *Christus Dominus*, 28 October 1965, no. 30; Second Vatican Ecumenical Council, Decree on Ecumenism, *Unitatis redintegratio*, 21 November 1964, no. 15; Sacred Congregation of Rites, Instruction *Eucharisticum mysterium*, On the worship of the Eucharist, 25 May 1967, nos. 3e, 6: AAS 59 (1967), pp. 542, 544–545.

23. Cf. Second Vatican Ecumenical Council, Constitution on the Sacred Liturgy, *Sacrosanctum Concilium*, no. 10.

24. Cf. ibid., no. 102.

25. Cf. Second Vatican Ecumenical Council, Constitution on the Sacred Liturgy, *Sacrosanctum Concilium*, no. 10; cf. Decree on the Ministry and Life of Priests, *Presbyterorum ordinis*, no. 5.

26. Cf. Second Vatican Ecumenical Council, Constitution on the Sacred Liturgy, *Sacrosanctum Concilium*, nos. 14, 19, 26, 28, 30.

27. Cf. ibid., no. 47.

28. Cf. ibid., no. 14.

29. Cf. ibid., no. 41.

30. Cf. Second Vatican Ecumenical Council, Decree on the Ministry and Life of Priests, *Presbyterorum ordinis*, no. 13; *Codex Iuris Canonici*, can. 904.

IGMR—Notes (Latin)

22. Cf. Conc. Œcum. Vat. II, Const. de sacra Liturgia, *Sacrosanctum Concilium*, n. 41; Const. dogm. de Ecclesia, *Lumen gentium*, n. 11; Decr. de Presbyterorum ministerio et vita, *Presbyterorum ordinis*, nn. 2, 5, 6; Decr. de pastorali Episcoporum munere, *Christus Dominus*, n. 30; Decr. de Œcumenismo, *Unitatis redintegratio*, n. 15; S. Congr. Rituum, Instr. *Eucharisticum mysterium*, diei 25 maii 1967, nn. 3 e, 6: A.A.S. 59 (1967) pp. 542, 544–545.

23. Cf. Conc. Œcum. Vat. II, Const. de sacra Liturgia, *Sacrosanctum Concilium*, n. 10.

24. Cf. *ibidem*, n. 102.

25. Cf. Conc. Œcum. Vat. II. Const. de sacra Liturgia, *Sacrosanctum Concilium*, n. 10; Decr. de Presbyterorum ministerio et vita, *Presbyterorum ordinis*, n. 5.

26. Cf. Conc. Œcum. Vat. II, Const. de sacra Liturgia, *Sacrosanctum Concilium*, nn. 14, 19, 26, 28, 30.

27. Cf. *ibidem*, n. 47.

28. Cf. *ibidem*, n. 14.

29. Cf. *ibidem*, n. 41.

30. Cf. Conc. Œcum. Vat. II, Decr. de Presbyterorum ministerio et vita, *Presbyterorum ordinis*, n. 13; *Codex Iuris Canonici*, can. 904.

31. Cf. Second Vatican Ecumenical Council, Constitution on the Sacred Liturgy, *Sacrosanctum Concilium*, no. 59.

32. Special celebrations of Mass should observe the guidelines established for them: For Masses with special groups, cf. Sacred Congregation for Divine Worship, Instruction *Actio pastoralis*, On Masses with special groups, 15 May 1969: AAS 61 (1969), pp. 806–811; for Masses with children, cf. Sacred Congregation for Divine Worship, *Directory for Masses with Children*, 1 November 1973: AAS 66 (1974), pp. 30–46; for the manner of joining the Hours of the Office with the Mass, cf. Sacred Congregation for Divine Worship, *General Instruction of the Liturgy of the Hours, editio typica*, 11 April 1971, *editio typica altera*, 7 April 1985, nos. 93–98; for the manner of joining certain blessings and the crowning of an image of the Blessed Virgin Mary with the Mass, cf. The Roman Ritual, *Book of Blessings*, *editio typica*, 1984, Introduction, no. 28; *Order of Crowning an Image of the Blessed Virgin Mary*, *editio typica*, 1981, nos. 10 and 14.

33. Cf. Second Vatican Ecumenical Council, Decree on the Pastoral Office of Bishops, *Christus Dominus*, no. 15; cf. also Constitution on the Sacred Liturgy, *Sacrosanctum Concilium*, no. 41.

34. Cf. Second Vatican Ecumenical Council, Constitution on the Sacred Liturgy, *Sacrosanctum Concilium*, no. 22.

35. Cf. also Second Vatican Ecumenical Council, Constitution on the Sacred Liturgy, *Sacrosanctum Concilium*, nos. 38, 40; Paul VI, Apostolic Constitution *Missale Romanum*.

36. Congregation for Divine Worship and the Discipline of the Sacraments, Instruction *Varietates legitimae*, 25 January 1994: AAS 87 (1995), pp. 288–314.

31. Cf. Conc. Œcum. Vat. II, Const. de sacra Liturgia, *Sacrosanctum Concilium*, n. 59.

32. Quoad peculiares Missæ celebrationes servetur quod statutum est: cf. pro Missis in cœtibus particularibus: S. Congr. pro Cultu Divino, Instr. *Actio pastoralis*, diei 15 maii 1969: A.A.S. 61 (1969) pp. 806–811; pro Missis cum pueris: *Directorium de Missis cum pueris*, diei 1 novembris 1973: A.A.S. 66 (1974) pp. 30–46; de modo uniendi Horas Officii cum Missa: *Institutio generalis de Liturgia Horarum*, nn. 93–98; de modo uniendi quasdam benedictiones et coronationem imaginis beatæ Mariæ Virginis cum Missa: Rituale Romanum, *De Benedictionibus*, Prænotanda, n. 28; *Ordo coronandi imaginem beatæ Mariæ Virginis*, nn. 10 et 14.

33. Cf. Conc. Œcum. Vat. II, Decr. de pastorali Episcoporum munere, *Christus Dominus*, n. 15; cf. etiam Const. de sacra Liturgia, *Sacrosanctum Concilium*, n. 41.

34. Cf. Conc. Œcum. Vat. II, Const. de sacra Liturgia, *Sacrosanctum Concilium*, n. 22.

35. Cf. etiam Conc. Œcum. Vat. II, Const. de sacra Liturgia, *Sacrosanctum Concilium*, nn. 38, 40; Paulus VI, Const. Ap. *Missale Romanum*, supra.

36. Congr. de Cultu Divino et Disciplina Sacramentorum, Instr. *Varietates legitimæ*, diei 25 ianuarii 1994: A.A.S. 87 (1995) pp. 288–314.

CHAPTER II

The Structure of the Mass, Its Elements and Its Parts

(*DE STRUCTURA MISSÆ EIUSQUE ELEMENTIS ET PARTIBUS*)

Edward Foley

This chapter provides an overview of the major structural elements of the eucharistic liturgy, its liturgical subdivisions, and the individual elements of those. Like its predecessors, it provides both rubrical description as well as theological commentary, exhortation, and clear prescriptions. This overview provides the general framework for considering the three different forms of celebrating Mass, outlined below in Chapter IV.

In general, the new *Institutio Generalis Missalis Romani* (*IGMR2002*) is more precise than previous Instructions, and offers more detail in this chapter about the various elements of the Mass. Many times this means including information in this Instruction that has been part of the revised *Missale Romanum* but never mentioned in an *IGMR* (e.g., the sprinkling rite). As in other chapters, it has also rearranged materials from previous editions, in some cases provided new divisions of that material, and generally offers an improved overview of and introduction to the structure of the Mass. It also has provided richer introductions in section II on the Word of God, vocal expression, the importance of singing, movement and posture, and silence.

There is a clear emphasis on the active participation of the assembly, and their central role as one of the subjects of the eucharistic action. As has been noted above and will be specified below (see Power and Vincie, 59–60 above, and no. 91 below), however, *IGMR2002* is also stronger than any of its predecessors in emphasizing distinctions between the ministerial priesthood and the common priesthood of the baptized. This is sometimes done through emphasizing silence, meditation, and the use of more passive verbs regarding the assembly than previous *IGMR*s.

There are some inconsistencies that will need attention in future editions of this Instruction. Some of these concern the naming of various elements (e.g.,

Chapter II
THE STRUCTURE OF THE MASS, ITS ELEMENTS AND ITS PARTS

I. The General Structure of the Mass

27. At Mass—that is, the Lord's Supper—the People of God is called together, with a priest presiding and acting in the person of Christ, to celebrate the memorial of the Lord, the Eucharistic Sacrifice.[37] For this reason Christ's promise applies in an outstanding way to such a local gathering of the holy Church: "Where two or three are gathered in my name, there am I in their midst" (Mt 18:20). For in the celebration of Mass, in which the Sacrifice of the Cross is perpetuated,[38] Christ is really present in the very liturgical assembly gathered in his name, in the person of the minister, in his word, and indeed substantially and continuously under the Eucharistic species.[39]

Caput II
DE STRUCTURA MISSÆ EIUSQUE ELEMENTS ET PARTIBUS

I. De Generali Structura Missæ

27. In Missa seu Cena dominica populus Dei in unum convocatur, sacerdote præside personamque Christi gerente, ad memoriale Domini seu sacrificium eucharisticum celebrandum.[37] Quare de huiusmodi sanctæ Ecclesiæ coadunatione locali eminenter valet promissio Christi: « Ubi sunt duo vel tres congregati in nomine meo, ibi sum in medio eorum » (*Mt* 18, 20). In Missæ enim celebratione, in qua sacrificium crucis perpetuatur,[38] Christus realiter præsens adest in ipso cœtu in suo nomine congregato, in persona ministri, in verbo suo, et quidem substantialiter et continenter sub speciebus eucharisticis.[39]

---

the problematic *cantus ad offertorium*), while others concern the very nature of an element (e.g., the mixed message about the nature of the homily). Overall, this chapter offers an improved structural overview, with richer theological commentary, while exhibiting clear tendencies toward a more hierarchical and sacralized vision of eucharistic worship than its predecessors.

The General Structure of the Mass

27. Notable in this opening paragraph of this chapter is the stress on the assembly, and how Christ is present therein. While acknowledging the priest presider as one acting in the person of Christ, it is the whole gathering which celebrates and offers the sacrifice with Christ (no. 78 below). This recovering of a biblical understanding of the subject of the liturgical action was an important work of *Sacrosanctum Concilium* (*SC*), no. 7, and reversed the theology embedded in *Missale Romanum* 1570 (*MR1570*) in which, according to the prayers at the "offertory," the priest offered the Mass.[1] As noted above (Power and Vincie, 51–52), the identity of the liturgical subjects has been greatly clarified by the various versions of the *IGMR*, which make it clear that it is not simply the Church in general, but it is a specific gathered assembly, along with Christ, who is the subject of the liturgy. The stress on the assembly as a mediator of Christ's presence in *IGMR2002* is further enhanced by the Instruction's

1. *Suscipe, sancte Pater, omnipotens aeterne Deus, hanc immaculatam hostiam, quam* ego *indignus famulus tuus* offero *tibi* (emphasis added).

28. The Mass is made up, as it were, of two parts: the Liturgy of the Word and the Liturgy of the Eucharist. These, however, are so closely interconnected that they form but one single act of worship.[40] For in the Mass the table both of God's word and of Christ's Body is prepared, from which the faithful may be instructed and refreshed.[41] There are also certain rites that open and conclude the celebration.

28. Missa duabus partibus quodammodo constat, liturgia nempe verbi et liturgia eucharistica, quæ tam arcte inter se coniunguntur, ut unum actum cultus efficiant.[40] Siquidem in Missa mensa tam verbi Dei quam Corporis Christi paratur e qua fideles instituantur et reficiantur.[41] Quidam autem ritus celebrationem aperiunt et concludunt.

---

inversion of the various modes of Christ's presence, here beginning with Christ's presence "in the very liturgical assembly gathered in his name" (*in ipso coetu in suo nomine congregato),*[2] despite the fact that *SC,* no. 7 considers this mode only after mentioning all others. Finally, the introduction of the adjective "holy" (*sanctae*), while possibly indicative of a pervasive trend in *IGMR2002* to enhance the sacrality of actions, objects, and people (see no. 91 below) seems a fitting addition given the context of this paragraph. An appropriate interpretation is not only that the Church is holy, but that every local gathering is a distinctive reflection of this mark of the Church.

Previous commentaries have noted some of the narrowness of *IGMR2002* with regards to its focus on the sacrificial nature of the Mass (Power and Vincie, 56–66, and no. 2 above). That trend is apparent with this paragraph, which twice references the Mass as sacrifice, while invoking no other eucharistic images. Given the emphasis on the people of God, assembly, and gathering, some reference to *communio* would have been appropriate.[3]

28. *SC,* no. 56 shifted significantly the official Western understanding of the structure of the Mass in its abandonment of previous divisions and terminology (e.g., *Missa catechumenorum, Missa fidelium*). According to *SC,* there are two "tables" in the celebration of the Eucharist: the table of the Word (no. 51) and that of the Lord's Body (no. 48). Each succeeding version of the *IGMR* has respected and clarified this understanding. In more felicitous language, the *IGMR*s have spoken of the Liturgy of the Word and the Liturgy of the Eucharist that are distinctive but not separate, and together constitute a singular act of worship. By noting the existence of other opening and concluding rites, the *IGMR*s implicitly acknowledge that every moment of the Mass is not of equal significance, an important pastoral awareness both for planning and celebration of the Eucharist.

A minor difficulty apparent in this paragraph and others (see no. 29) is the consistent pattern of *IGMR*s to consider the Liturgy of the Word in general, and

2. *Eucharisticum mysterium* (1967) offers a similar inversion in no. 55, in DOL 1284.

3. E.g., *Catholicae Ecclesiae Catechismus (CEC),* no. 1382 notes that the Mass is "inseparably" the sacrificial memorial and the sacred banquet of Communion.

II. The Different Elements of the Mass

Reading and Explaining the Word of God

29. When the Sacred Scriptures are read in the Church, God himself speaks to his people, and Christ, present in his own word, proclaims the Gospel.

Therefore, all must listen with reverence to the readings from God's word, for they make up an element of greatest importance in the Liturgy. Although in the readings

II. De Diversis Elementis Missæ

De lectione verbi Dei eiusque explanatione

29. Cum sacræ Scripturæ in Ecclesia leguntur, Deus ipse ad populum suum loquitur et Christus, præsens in verbo suo, Evangelium annuntiat.

Ideoque lectiones verbi Dei, quæ elementum maximi momenti Liturgiæ præbent, cum veneratione ab omnibus sunt audiendæ. Quamvis autem verbum

---

the homily in particular, in didactic terms (see no. 13 above). This is one of the shortcomings of *SC*, which describes the Liturgy of the Word as the moment in which the readings are proclaimed and "explained in the homily" (*in homilia explicantur*, no. 24; an image repeated in the *praenotanda* of the revised *Ordo Lectionum Missae* [*OLM1981-Pr*], no. 10). While the Latin *instituo* in this paragraph has many nuances (e.g., to establish, found, or organize), GIRM2003 leans toward its ternary meaning, "to instruct." Conversely, while *SC* begins a new division at no. 33 with the subtitle "Norms based on the Educative and Pastoral Nature of the Liturgy," that same paragraph makes it clear that while the liturgy "contains much instruction for the faithful," the liturgy is not understood as fundamentally a didactic event. Thus, it is ill-conceived to characterize one of the two great tables of the Eucharist as essentially a moment of instruction while, conversely, the eucharistic table is the time when the faithful are "refreshed" (*reficiantur*). If *SC*'s understanding of the multiple modes of Christ's presence affirms that Christ is present in his Word (no. 7), then the Liturgy of the Word is also a time when the faithful are refreshed. Thus *Dei Verbum* (*DV*) teaches that the Scriptures are venerated like the Lord's body, and in the liturgy the Church offers to the faithful the bread of life from both the table of the Word and that of the Eucharist (no. 21).

The Different Elements of the Mass

This greatly improved section positions the reader to understand specific elements in the eucharistic liturgy by offering useful reflections on overarching liturgical dynamics. The particulars that follow in section III of this chapter need to be interpreted in view of these preliminary principles.

Reading and Explaining the Word of God

29. This first paragraph of the second subdivision on "The Different Elements of the Mass" focuses on the first "table" of the Word. A concern about the title, with its focus on "explaining," was noted above (no. 28). Echoing *SC*, no. 33, the Instruction advances the perspective that scriptural proclamation

from Sacred Scripture God's word is addressed to all people of every era and is understandable to them, nevertheless, a fuller understanding and a greater effectiveness of the word is fostered by a living commentary on the word, that is, the homily, as part of the liturgical action.[42]

divinum in lectionibus sacræ Scripturæ ad omnes homines cuiusque temporis dirigatur iisque intellegibile sit, eius tamen plenior intellegentia et efficacitas expositione viva, id est homilia, utpote parte actionis liturgicæ, fovetur.[42]

The Prayers and Other Parts Pertaining to the Priest

30. Among the parts assigned to the priest, the foremost is the Eucharistic Prayer, which is the high point of the entire

De orationibus aliisque partibus ad sacerdotem pertinentibus

30. Inter ea quæ sacerdoti tribuuntur, primum locum obtinet Prex eucharistica, quæ culmen est totius celebrationis.

---

in the liturgy is a God act, and the proclamation of the gospel is a particularly Christological event. Teaching that the Word is addressed to all people and is understandable to them underscores the importance of vernacular proclamation in suitable and accessible translations (cf. *DV*, no. 22).

While previous *IGMR*s have noted that through the homily the Word's effectiveness is increased (*efficacitas . . . augetur*), *IGMR2002* adds that it also fosters a "fuller understanding" (*plenior intellegentia*) of the Word. Presenting the homily as a "living commentary" (*expositione viva*) well explicates the dynamic nature of the liturgical homily. It also provides an important internal hermeneutic for conceiving the call for greater understanding as more than simply advocating advanced biblical knowledge. Rather, in the words of Paul VI, preaching is meant to bring hearers "to the knowledge of the relevance of God's word to human existence."[4]

The scope of the homily in this paragraph as a "living commentary on the word," is much more narrowly drawn than *SC*, no. 52, which does not limit the homily to a commentary on the Scriptures, but rather locates its source in the "sacred text" (*textu sacro*).[5] This broader view of homiletic sources, noted in *OLM1981-Pr* 24, is acknowledged below in no. 65. Finally, this article recognizes that the homily is not only *in* the liturgy but, at its core, is *of* the liturgy and is itself a liturgical act.

The Prayers and Other Parts Pertaining to the Priest

30. This reflection on the presidential prayers gives appropriate pride of place to the Eucharistic Prayer, which the Instruction acknowledges as the high

4. *Ecclesiam Suam*, no. 91, in DOL, no. 1339.

5. An official interpretation of this phrase is found in *Inter Oecumenici* (1964): "A homily on the sacred text means an explanation, pertinent to the mystery celebrated and the special needs of the listeners, of some point in either the readings from sacred Scripture or in another text from the Ordinary or Prayer of the day's Mass" (no. 54; in DOL, no. 346).

celebration. Next are the orations: that is to say, the collect, the prayer over the offerings, and the prayer after Communion. These prayers are addressed to God in the name of the entire holy people and all present, by the priest who presides over the assembly in the person of Christ.[43] It is with good reason, therefore, that they are called the "presidential prayers."

Accedunt deinde orationes, idest collecta, oratio super oblata et oratio post Communionem. Hæ preces a sacerdote, qui cœtui personam Christi gerens præest, ad Deum diriguntur nomine totius plebis sanctæ et omnium circumstantium.[43] Merito igitur « orationes præsidentiales » nominantur.

---

point of the celebration. While this is true theologically, it is not always true ritually. The US bishops implicitly admit this when they call Communion the "climax" of the eucharistic celebration (*Music in Catholic Worship* [MCW], no. 48). In order for the Eucharistic Prayer to be perceived pastorally as the true high point, presiders need to pay particular attention to their vocal expression (see no. 38 below) when proclaiming this most complex of prayer texts. Singing the prayer, and not simply the preface, is a particularly appropriate way to stress the importance of this prayer and to engage the faithful in whose name the priest proclaims this prayer.[6] *IGMR2002*, no. 78, provides an even richer theological foundation for actively engaging the assembly, noting that it is the entire congregation that Christ joins to himself in acknowledging God's great works and in offering the sacrifice.

Besides the central role of the assembly in these prayers, *IGMR*s have consistently noted that presidential prayers are also addressed to God "in the name of the entire holy people" (*nomine totius plebis sanctae*). Echoing the theology of *SC*, no. 10, this situates each local celebration of the Eucharist within a broad ecclesiological vision. The Eucharist is never solely the action of an individual community or presider, but an act of Christ united with the whole people of God, mediated through a particular community, gathered in a specific time and place.

This is the only occurrence of *circumstantes/circumstantium* in *IGMR2002*, an ancient designation of the faithful gathered around the table imbedded in the old Roman Canon.[7] The rich architectural, embodied, and theological symbolism of this term has much to contribute to both a theology of the assembly and eucharistic practice. This is not well captured in GIRM2003's rendering as "all present."

6. *IGMR2002*, no. 40, implicitly recognizes this; the US bishops' *Introduction to the Order of Mass* (ITTOM, originally developed and copyrighted by the International Commission on English in the Liturgy [ICEL]) is stronger, noting "Since the Eucharistic Prayer is the central prayer and high point of the Mass, the singing of this prayer expresses the solemn nature of the day or occasion being celebrated" (no. 37).

7. The original may have been *circum adstantium* rather than the current *circumstantium* which appears in *Missale Romanum* 2002 *(MR2002)*. See Anton Hänggi and Irmgard Pahl, *Prex Eucharistica: Textus e Variis Liturgiis Antiquioribus Selecti*, Spicilegium Friburgense 12 (Fribourg: Éditions Universitaires, 1968), 429.

31. It is also up to the priest, in the exercise of his office of presiding over the gathered assembly, to offer certain explanations that are foreseen in the rite itself. Where it is indicated in the rubrics, the celebrant is permitted to adapt them somewhat in order that they respond to the understanding of those participating. However, he should always take care to keep to the sense of the text given in the Missal and to express it succinctly. The presiding priest is also to direct the word of God and to

31. Item ad sacerdotem, munere præsidis cœtus congregati fungentem, spectat proferre quasdam monitiones in ipso ritu prævisas. Ubi a rubricis statuitur, celebranti licet eas aliquatenus aptare ut participantium captui respondeant; curet tamen sacerdos ut sensum monitionis quæ in Missali proponitur ipse semper servet eamque paucis verbis exprimat. Sacerdoti præsidi etiam spectat verbum Dei moderari, necnon benedictionem finalem impertire. Ipsi insuper licet, brevissimis verbis,

---

31. As in previous editions, *IGMR2002* acknowledges the appropriateness of the priest-presider offering explanations (*monitiones*) during Mass where such are foreseen by the rite itself. *IGMR2002* makes a number of minor changes here from *IGMR1975*. Most telling is the removal of the previous note (*IGMR1975*, no. 11) that the very nature of these instructions indicated that they did not need to be repeated verbatim as found in the Missal. The current text recognizes that these explanations may be adapted somewhat (*aliquantenus aptare*), but adds an extra caution that the presider should "keep to the sense of the text" (*sensum monitionis*) found in the Missal.[8] The instruction that these should be expressed "succinctly" (*paucis verbis*) is an appropriate presidential caution, though the meaning of "a few words" varies widely in different cultures. Essentially this is a matter of balance and proportionality, so that the instruction does not overshadow the ritual action or eclipse the liturgical texts. The 1973 instruction by the Congregation for Divine Worship is still useful here, noting that the purpose of such *monitiones* is to lead "the faithful to a more thorough grasp of the meaning of the sacred rites . . . and to an inner participation in them. . . . [T]he way any of these introductions is presented must respect the character proper to each and not turn into a sermon or homily. There must be a concern for brevity and the avoidance of a wordiness that would bore the participants."[9] It is unfortunate that *IGMR2002* eliminates the directive of *IGMR1975* regarding the advisability of adapting these introductions to the "concrete situation of the community" (*veris communitatis condictionibus*, no. 11), an important recognition of the particularity of every eucharistic celebration.[10] Overall, this paragraph is somewhat more restrictive regarding *monitiones* than *IGMR1975*.

8. *IGMR2000* reads *in libro liturgico* rather than the current *in Missali*.

9. Congregation for Divine Worship, Circular Letter *Eucharistiae participationem*, 27 April 1973, *Notitiae* 9 (1973) no. 14, in DOL, no. 1988.

10. Cf. the discussion of Power and Vincie on the hermeneutical importance of the historical context of each eucharistic celebration, 46 above.

impart the final blessing. In addition, he may give the faithful a very brief introduction to the Mass of the day (after the initial Greeting and before the Act of Penitence), to the Liturgy of the Word (before the readings), and to the Eucharistic Prayer (before the Preface), though never during the Eucharistic Prayer itself; he may also make concluding comments to the entire sacred action before the dismissal.

introducere fideles in Missam diei, post salutationem initialem et ante actum pænitentialem; in liturgiam verbi, ante lectiones; in Precem eucharisticam, ante Præfationem, numquam vero intra Precem ipsam; necnon universam actionem sacram, ante dimissionem, concludere.

32. The nature of the "presidential" texts demands that they be spoken in a loud and

32. Natura partium « præsidentialium » exigit ut clara et elata voce proferantur et

---

This article notes the other moments during the Eucharist when the priest may offer introductions. Much of this repeats what is found in *IGMR1975* with a few changes. Whereas the previous version spoke about the priest's responsibility to proclaim (*nuntiare*) the Word of God, *IGMR2002* more properly presents the priest as directing (*moderari*) the Word of God. *IGMR2002* appropriately adds that while it is permissible to introduce the Eucharistic Prayer, it is never permissible to offer instruction during the prayer itself, underscoring the unity of this central euchological act.

32. *IGMR*s offer a few directives about the vocal performance of the rite. This paragraph concerns volume and clarity. While these are two important elements when leading prayer, in and of themselves they are insufficient for engaging the faithful, who are called to listen with attention because these prayers are being addressed to God in their name (no. 30). Thus, these directives need to be read in conjunction with the broader directives provided below in no. 38.

Despite the fact that this paragraph footnotes *Musicam Sacram (MusSac)*, there is no recommendation about singing such texts until the broad reference to singing "texts that are of themselves meant to be sung" (*qui per se cantui destinantur*, no. 40). There may be some tension between this article's directive that musical instruments should be silent during presidential prayers, and the insight in no. 38 that in matters musical one should give due consideration to the culture of the people, e.g., to African-American worship in which it is common to provide an instrumental underlay for such texts. *Redemptionis Sacramentum* (*RedSac*, no. 53) cites this paragraph to underscore what it considers the inappropriateness of the use of musical accompaniment during the Eucharistic Prayer (except for the people's acclamations), contrary to the widespread and pastorally effective practice of such throughout the US.[11]

11. At the time of this writing, for example, Marty Haugen's setting of Eucharistic Prayer III entitled *Mass of Creation* (Chicago: GIA Publishing, 1984) is so well known and broadly accepted in the US that it could be considered a standard in our national repertoire of liturgical music.

clear voice and that everyone listen with attention.[44] Thus, while the priest is speaking these texts, there should be no other prayers or singing, and the organ or other musical instruments should be silent.

33. The priest, in fact, as the one who presides, prays in the name of the Church and of the assembled community; but at times he prays only in his own name, asking that he may exercise his ministry with greater attention and devotion. Prayers of this kind, which occur before the reading of the Gospel, at the Preparation of the Gifts, and also before and after the Communion of the priest, are said quietly.

The Other Formulas in the Celebration

34. Since the celebration of Mass by its nature has a "communitarian" character,[45] both the dialogues between the priest and the faithful gathered together and the

ab omnibus cum attentione auscultentur.[44] Proinde dum sacerdos eas profert aliæ orationes vel cantus non habeantur, atque organum vel alia instrumenta musica sileant.

33. Sacerdos etenim, tamquam præses, nomine Ecclesiæ et congregatæ communitatis preces effundit, aliquando autem nomine dumtaxat suo, ut ministerium suum maiore cum animi attentione et pietate adimpleat. Huiusmodi preces, quæ ante lectionem Evangelii, in præparatione donorum, necnon ante et post sacerdotis Communionem proponuntur, secreto dicuntur.

De aliis formulis in celebratione occurrentibus

34. Cum Missæ celebratio natura sua indolem « communitariam » habeat,[45] dialogis inter sacerdotem et fideles congregatos necnon acclamationibus magna vis

---

33. Sacerdotal *apologiae* were a Gallican introduction to the Latin rite.[12] More numerous in previous versions of the *Missale Romanum*, only a few remain in the current *Ordo Missae*. This paragraph properly situates such *apologiae* in a ternary place, noting first that the priest prays in the name of the Church and assembly. The pastoral goal of such prayers, i.e., that the priest may preside with greater attention and devotion, is laudable. *IGMR2002* adds a new sentence, clarifying when such prayers occur. GIRM2003's translation of *secreto* as "quietly" is unfortunate (GIRM1975, no. 13 used "inaudibly"), and could give the impression that such prayers need to be verbally articulated by the presider; better is their translation of the same word in no. 88 as "privately." The US bishops seem to confirm this latter translation when they note that *apologiae* are "by nature private and are recited inaudibly" (ITTOM, no. 39).

The Other Formulas in the Celebration

34. This is the first of four articles which consider the "other formulas" (*aliis formulis*) at Mass. It is notable that after presidential prayers, dialogues between priest and the faithful (*IGMR2002* has *fideles congregatos*, whereas previous *IGMR*s have *coetum fidelium*) are given pride of place. The theological rationale

12. *Missale Gothicum* (c. 700) contains an entry as part of the first Mass for Easter entitled *Apologia sacerdotes*. Leo Mohlberg, ed., *Missale Gothicum*, Rerum Ecclesiasticarum Documenta, Feries Maior, Fontes V (Roma: Herder, 1961), no. 275.

acclamations are of great significance;[46] in fact, they are not simply outward signs of communal celebration but foster and bring about communion between priest and people.

35. The acclamations and the responses of the faithful to the priest's greetings and prayers constitute that level of active participation that the gathered faithful are to contribute in every form of the Mass, so that the action of the entire community may be clearly expressed and fostered.[47]

36. Other parts, very useful for expressing and fostering the faithful's active par-

inhæret: [46] etenim non sunt tantum signa externa celebrationis communis, sed communionem inter sacerdotem et populum fovent et efficiunt.

35. Acclamationes et responsiones fidelium salutationibus sacerdotis et orationibus illum participationis actuosæ gradum constituunt, qui in omni Missæ forma a fidelibus congregatis præstandus est, ut actio totius communitatis clare exprimatur et foveatur.[47]

36. Aliæ partes, ad actuosam fidelium participationem manifestandam et foven-

---

for this sequencing is provided by the communitarian character of the liturgy itself. Furthermore, recognizing the effective nature of sacramental action in general and the eucharistic action in particular, the Instruction acknowledges that these shared actions not only express some level of communion but actually foster and create that unity, an idea repeated in nos. 35 and 36. A further theological foundation for the importance of liturgical dialogues and a broader understanding of all of worship as a dialogue is provided by *Ecclesiam Suam*. In the course of this encyclical, Paul VI (d. 1978) admits that all prayer is a divinely initiated dialogue, and that even the whole of revelation is well considered in dialogue terms (no. 70). Keeping with the earlier theologizing of *IGMR2002*, which noted that Eucharist is both the action of a particular assembly and that of the whole Church, these dialogic interchanges between presider and the faithful also speak to the dialogic character of the Church itself.

35. The model of active participation, made explicit in acclamations and dialogues, is held up as a standard of congregational participation in every form of eucharistic celebration outlined below in Chapter IV. This means that, as the US bishops have rightly suggested, the participation of the faithful in responses and acclamations is the "very minimum form of communal participation" (ITTOM, no. 36), whether that be a concelebration or a Mass with only one minister participating. Not simply serving as a lowest common denominator in assessing the active participation, however, such acclamations and responses can also be understood as models for every moment of a congregation's participation at Mass, i.e., symbols of total engagement whether or not the faithful have any explicit liturgical text to speak. Both the acclamatory and dialogic nature of the whole of eucharistic worship is thus made explicit without being confined to the limited number of responses and acclamations which the *Missale Romanum* specifically assigns to the faithful.

36. In its treatment of "other parts" (*Aliae partes*) of the Mass, *IGMR2002* emphasizes how these elements express and foster active participation among

ticipation, that are assigned to the whole assembly that is called together include especially the Act of Penitence, the Profession of Faith, the Prayer of the Faithful, and the Lord's Prayer.

dam valde utiles, quæ universo cœtui convocato tribuuntur, sunt præsertim actus pænitentialis, professio fidei, oratio universalis et Oratio dominica.

37. Finally, concerning the other formulas:

a. Some constitute an independent rite or act, such as the *Gloria*, the responsorial Psalm, the *Alleluia* and verse before the Gospel, the *Sanctus*, the Memorial Acclamation, and the *cantus post communionem* (song after communion);

b. Others accompany another rite, such as the chants at the Entrance, at the Offertory, at the fraction (*Agnus Dei*), and at Communion.

37. Demum ex aliis formulis:

a) nonnullæ ritum seu actum per se stantem, uti hymnus Glória, psalmus responsorius, Allelúia et versus ante Evangelium, Sanctus, acclamatio anamneseos, cantus post Communionem, constituunt;

b) nonnullæ vero, uti cantus ad introitum, ad offertorium, ad fractionem (Agnus Dei) et ad Communionem, ritum aliquem comitantur.

---

the faithful. While it is true that such elements are "assigned to the whole assembly" (*quae universo coetui . . . tribuuntur*), in their own way they yet embody something of the dialogic dynamic of the Roman liturgy, noted in the previous paragraph. The prayer of the faithful, comprising one of the more important litanies of the eucharistic liturgy, whose various components are shared between presider, assembly, and another assigned to articulate the intentions, well exemplifies this dialogic dynamic. Similar are the litanic forms that mark most penitential rites, shared between presiders, assembly, and sometimes a deacon (cf. no. 51 below). The profession of faith is also listed as one of those parts considered very useful for expressing and fostering active participation. Such may be best achieved by alternating the Creed between assembly and choir, or two parts of the assembly (no. 68), reflecting something of the dynamic interchange that marks baptismal creeds. Even the Our Father, with its introduction, embolism, and doxology reflects the dialogic dynamic of the Roman liturgy, somewhat overlooked in this paragraph.

37. In the final paragraph of this section, the other formulas under consideration are, in fact, lyrical elements of the Eucharist that presumably are to be sung.[13] The paragraph makes a useful ritual distinction between elements that constitute an "independent rite" and others that "accompany another rite." Because of the cryptic nature of an *IGMR*, however, such distinctions can be misunderstood. Considering the *Sanctus* or memorial acclamation as an independent rite, for example, could give the impression that these merely occur "during" the Eucharistic Prayer, rather than constituting essential parts of this prayer (cf. no. 79b below). Similar thinking about the responsorial psalm and

13. See, for example, the way the US bishops musically prioritize these elements in MCW, nos. 53–74; more recently, ITTOM, no. 46.

The Vocal Expression of the Different Texts

38. In texts that are to be spoken in a loud and clear voice, whether by the priest or the deacon, or by the lector, or by all, the

De modis proferendi varios textus

38. In textibus clara et elata voce proferendis sive a sacerdote vel diacono sive a lectore sive ab omnibus, vox respondeat

---

Alleluia could overlook the fact that the chants between the readings constitute one of the main parts of the Liturgy of the Word (no. 55).

More problematic is the placement of the Alleluia in 37a with the other "independent rites" rather than in 37b, in which music and text accompany another ritual action. *IGMR2002*, like its predecessors (as well as *OLM1981-Pr*, no. 23), gives the impression that the Alleluia, properly enacted, has little to do with the gospel procession.[14] A gospel procession in the Roman Rite is in evidence by about 700.[15] As ITTOM notes, the traditional music for accompanying the gospel procession is the Alleluia or other gospel acclamation (no. 89). The *Caeremoniale Episcoporum* (*CaerEp*, no. 140) gives ample testimony for grasping the intimate connection between the gospel acclamation and an accompanying gospel procession.[16] Even when no such procession of the book takes place, it is appropriate to raise the book so that the faithful may perceive the role of the gospel acclamation as the assembly's greeting to the Lord about to speak to them (*OLM1981-Pr*, no. 23) and the importance of the Book of the Gospels in symbolizing that mode of Christ's presence.

Finally, the use of the medieval designation "chant . . . at the Offertory" (*cantus ad offertorium*) for music sung during what *IGMR2002* and its predecessors call the "preparation of the gifts" (*praeparatio donorum*, no. 72.1) is confusing. *IGMR2002* and the ritual texts of *MR2002* (e.g., no. 105) make it clear that the offering, properly speaking, takes place during the Eucharistic Prayer (*IGMR2002*, no. 79f). Designating said chant as one that takes place "at the Offertory" (GIRM2003, no. 37b; cf. *MR2002*, nos. 21, 23, 25) inappropriately reintroduces the Tridentine title for the analogous liturgical unit (which clearly was an offering) as an acceptable alternative and contributes to pastoral confusion about when the offering actually takes place in the rite of Paul VI.

The Vocal Expression of the Different Texts

38. While reflecting some of the concerns raised above in no. 32, this paragraph goes further in underscoring the performative nature of worship and the subsequent responsibility of prayer leaders to interpret intelligently the

14. One slight exception is the implicit acknowledgment in no. 44 below.

15. *Ordo Romanus Primus (OR I)*, no. 58.

16. Hints about the relationship between the gospel procession and accompanying acclamation can be found in *IGMR2002*, nos. 44; 60 (a procession is one of the "special marks of honor"); 117, 122, 173, 195, 276c and 306; placing the Book of the Gospels on the altar at the beginning of Mass necessitates it being carried in procession to the ambo for its proclamation, as made explicit in nos. 133 and 175.

tone of voice should correspond to the genre of the text itself, that is, depending upon whether it is a reading, a prayer, a commentary, an acclamation, or a sung text; the tone should also be suited to the form of celebration and to the solemnity of the gathering. Consideration should also be given to the idiom of different languages and the culture of different peoples.

In the rubrics and in the norms that follow, words such as "say" and "proclaim" are to be understood of both singing and reciting, according to the principles just stated above.

generi ipsius textus, prouti hic est lectio, oratio, admonitio, acclamatio, cantus; necnon formæ celebrationis et sollemnitati cœtus. Ratio insuper habeatur indolis diversarum linguarum et ingenii populorum.

In rubricis ergo et in normis quæ sequuntur, verba « dicere » vel « proferre » intellegi debent sive de cantu sive de recitatione, servatis principiis supra propositis.

The Importance of Singing

39. The Christian faithful who gather together as one to await the Lord's coming

De momento cantus

39. Ab Apostolo monentur christifideles qui in unum conveniunt exspectantes

---

texts for which they are responsible. While previous *IGMR*s have noted this responsibility for the priest or "the ministers," *IGMR2002* explicates it for deacons and lectors as well. Beyond discerning the particular genre of the text being declaimed, basic skills in literary analysis can also help the minister interpret the differing motives within a single text, e.g., the move from praise to intercession during the opening prayer. Such textual analysis is especially important for effective rendering of some of the longer, more complex prayers such as the Eucharistic Prayer.

Besides the genre of the text, *IGMR* rightly recognizes that pastoral realities such as the form of the celebration and degree of solemnity[17] should have an impact on how texts are publicly declaimed. Even more notable here is *IGMR*'s recognition that the language and culture of the people provide an important hermeneutic for discerning how texts should be interpreted in worship. This is one of fourteen places that *IGMR2002* notes the importance of cultural and linguistic lenses for fashioning appropriate worship.[18] While significant for interpreting texts, the contextual lens is essential for interpreting every aspect of the eucharistic celebration.

The Importance of Singing

39. Three paragraphs are devoted to singing and its importance in the liturgy. They need to be read in light of *SC*, especially nos. 112–13, which provide

17. Cf. the principle of "progressive solemnity" in the 1971 *Institutio Generalis de Liturgia Horarum (IGLH1971)*, no. 273.

18. *ingenium* in nos. 24, 26, 38, 40, 43, 52, 82, 273, 325, 346, 352, 395, 397; *cultura* in no. 398.

are instructed by the Apostle Paul to sing together psalms, hymns, and spiritual songs (cf. Col 3:16). Singing is the sign of the heart's joy (cf. Acts 2:46). Thus Saint Augustine says rightly, "Singing is for one who loves."[48] There is also the ancient proverb: "One who sings well prays twice."

40. Great importance should therefore be attached to the use of singing in the celebration of the Mass, with due consideration for the culture of the people and abilities of each liturgical assembly. Although it is not always necessary (e.g., in weekday Masses) to sing all the texts that are of themselves meant to be sung, every

adventum Domini sui, ut una simul cantent psalmis, hymnis et canticis spiritualibus (cf. *Col* 3, 16). Cantus enim est signum exsultationis cordis (cf. *Act* 2, 46). Unde S. Augustinus recte dicit: « cantare amantis est »,[48] et iam antiquitus in proverbium venit: « bis orat qui bene cantat ».

40. Magni ergo fiat usus cantus in Missæ celebratione, attentis ingenio populorum et facultatibus cuiuslibet cœtus liturgici. Quamvis non semper necessarium sit, v. gr. in Missis ferialibus, omnes textus cantu proferre qui per se cantui destinantur, curandum omnino est ne desit cantus ministrorum et populi in celebrationibus, quæ

---

a richer theological foundation for liturgical singing than what is here. Three quotations in this opening paragraph emphasize song's connection to joy, love, and a spirit of prayer. *SC* also stresses the unitive power of liturgical song (also see ITTOM, no. 40) and the contribution it makes to the active participation of the faithful.[19] Note that the emphasis in these paragraphs is not on music, but more specifically on liturgical song. This is appropriate given *SC*'s assertion that the preeminence of the musical art in worship is precisely because of its ability to wed with liturgical texts, thus rendering it an integral part of the liturgy (no. 112).

40. This paragraph again raises the concern of cultural appropriateness when making determinations about liturgical singing. In attending to the "abilities" (*facultatibus*) of each liturgical assembly, *IGMR2002* recognizes that more than cultural questions are at work in shaping the lyrical life of a community. Singing ability, for example, is sometimes affected by the age or gender balance of the members of the assembly. It is also influenced by many other factors, such as the availability of musical resources to support the singing of the assembly. Supporting the lyrical gifts of a community takes leadership, commitment, time, and resources.

Implicitly interpreting *SC*'s affirmation of music as integral to the liturgy, *IGMR2002* goes beyond previous editions in recognizing that, while it is not necessary to sing all the texts that are meant to be sung[20] (for example, on a weekday), the lyrical nature of the Sunday Eucharist means that Sunday (and

19. This is reiterated and expanded in *MusSac,* nos. 15–16; no. 41 below will eventually raise the standard of the active participation of the faithful, but only in terms of Gregorian chant.

20. Neither this nor previous editions of *IGMR* either note which texts these are, or give any reference to previous documents, such as *MusSac* no. 16 which explicates these texts. ITTOM, no. 46 offers a useful summary here.

care should be taken that singing by the ministers and the people is not absent in celebrations that occur on Sundays and on holy days of obligation.

In the choosing of the parts actually to be sung, however, preference should be given to those that are of greater importance and especially to those to be sung by the priest or the deacon or the lector, with the people responding, or by the priest and people together.[49]

41. All other things being equal, Gregorian chant holds pride of place because it

diebus dominicis et festis de præcepto peraguntur.

In seligendis tamen partibus quæ revera canantur, eæ præferendæ sunt quæ maioris sunt momenti, et præsertim, quæ a sacerdote vel a diacono aut lectore, populo respondente, canendæ sunt, aut a sacerdote et populo simul proferendæ.[49]

41. Principem locum obtineat, ceteris paribus, cantus gregorianus, utpote Litur

---

by extension holy days) should not be devoid of music. This paragraph thus suggests an implicit normative pattern for liturgical singing that includes both when it should occur (particularly on Sunday) and where in the liturgy it should occur (in texts which are by their nature songs, acclamations, or are otherwise inherently lyrical). In a newly added paragraph, there is also an implicit normative pattern regarding who should be doing the singing. In giving great preference to parts sung dialogically between certain lead ministers[21] and the people, or by the priest and people together, *IGMR2002* has implicitly put the choir in a secondary position, and stressed the voice of the assembly as the *cantus firmus* of the eucharistic liturgy.

41. The first paragraph of this article is a new addition, paraphrasing *SC*, no. 116. In some respects, the text is more understandable in the context of the 1960s, given the state of chant research as well as the limited experience with musical inculturation in that era. Recent scholarship has raised multiple questions about both the nature and origin of Gregorian chant. While foundational strands of this chant were probably developed for the Roman liturgy, Gregorian chant was codified and modified north of the Alps where it became proper to the "Franco-Roman" liturgy.[22] The body of chant identified today as "Gregorian" was, thus, never proper to the papal liturgies of the fourth to eighth centuries. Besides historical questions, this paragraph offers little guidance in discerning when "all things [are] equal" (*ceteris paribus*) when it comes to making musical decisions in the liturgy.

The second paragraph of this article, which did appear in previous *IGMR*s, offers some guidance on this last point. A common and increasingly frequent

21. It is unfortunate that the psalmist or cantor, noted in such dialogic leadership with the assembly in no. 61 below, is not included in this list.

22. See, for example, James McKinnon, *The Advent Project: The Later-Seventh-Century Creation of the Roman Mass Proper* (Berkeley-Los Angeles: University of California Press, 2000), esp. 402–403.

is proper to the Roman Liturgy. Other types of sacred music, in particular polyphony, are in no way excluded, provided that they correspond to the spirit of the liturgical action and that they foster the participation of all the faithful.[50]

Since faithful from different countries come together ever more frequently, it is fitting that they know how to sing together at least some parts of the Ordinary of the Mass in Latin, especially the Creed and the Lord's Prayer, set to the simpler melodies.[51]

giæ romanæ proprius. Alia genera musicæ sacræ, præsertim vero polyphonia, minime excluduntur, dummodo spiritui actionis liturgicæ respondeant et participationem omnium fidelium foveant.[50]

Cum frequentius in dies fideles ex diversis nationibus inter se conveniant, expedit ut iidem fideles aliquas saltem partes Ordinarii Missæ, præsertim vero symbolum fidei et Orationem dominicam, modulis adhibitis facilioribus, lingua latina simul cantare sciant.[51]

---

experience for contemporary Roman Catholics is multilingual and multicultural Eucharist. In some countries, like the US, many urban and some rural parishes are comprised of parishioners from multiple language groups.[23] Previously, the Latin language and Gregorian chant were privileged vernaculars that allowed people of different cultures and language to "sing together" (*simul cantare*). While many multilingual settings of liturgical chants are available, there is much to recommend the simpler Gregorian chant melodies with their accompanying Latin texts for enabling *una voce dicentes*[24] and testifying to the unitive power of liturgical song (cf. no. 39 above). Also laudable are contemporary compositions that employ ancient Latin texts in multilingual settings,[25] which both enable musical *koinonia* while respecting the languages and different cultural heritages of the faithful.

Movements and Posture

42. In this first of three articles considering ritual embodiment, *IGMR2002* inserts a new paragraph proffering three general principles about gestures[26] and posture. Referencing *SC*, no. 34, it first instructs that such embodiment should

23. A recent pastoral response to this US phenomenon was Mark Francis' *Guidelines for Multicultural Celebrations,* published under the auspices of the Federation of Diocesan Liturgical Commissions (Washington, DC, 1998).

24. The image of *una voce dicentes* is widespread in patristic writings (e.g., Ignatius of Antioch [d. ca. 117], *Letter to the Ephesians* 4:1-3). While not a literal directive for unison singing, such texts did underscore both a proper spirit of ecclesial unity and the symbolization of such unity in the lyrical worship of a community. See Robert Skeris, *Chroma Theou* (Altötting: Alfred Coppenrath, 1976), esp. 121–22; also, Johannes Quasten, *Music and Worship in Pagan and Christian Antiquity,* trans. Boniface Ramsey (Washington, DC: National Association of Pastoral Musicians, 1983), 66–72.

25. E.g., the celebrated works composed for Taizé by Jacques Berthier, published in multiple volumes as *Music from Taizé* by Chicago's GIA Publications.

26. While both the title of this section and the text both employ the word *gestus,* GIRM2003 inexplicably translates one as "movements" and the second as "gestures."

Movements and Posture

42. The gestures and posture of the priest, the deacon, and the ministers, as well as those of the people, ought to contribute to making the entire celebration resplendent with beauty and noble simplicity, so that the true and full meaning of the different parts of the celebration is evident and that the participation of all is fostered.[52] Therefore, attention should be paid to what is determined by this General Instruction and the traditional practice of the Roman Rite and to what serves the common spiritual good of the People of God, rather than private inclination or arbitrary choice.

De gestibus et corporis habitibus

42. Gestus et corporis habitus tum sacerdotis, diaconi, et ministrorum, tum populi eo contendere debent ut tota celebratio decore nobilique simplicitate fulgeat, diversarum eius partium vera plenaque significatio percipiatur et omnium participatio foveatur.[52] Attendendum igitur erit ad ea quæ ab hac Institutione generali et tradita praxi Ritus romani definiuntur, et quæ ad commune bonum spirituale populi Dei conferant, potius quam ad privatam propensionem aut arbitrium.

Communis corporis habitus, ab omnibus participantibus servandus, signum est unitatis membrorum communitatis christianæ

---

illuminate the various parts of the Mass. Second, it notes that gesture and posture should contribute to the fundamental principle of active participation. Third, it asserts that observing *IGMR2002*'s directives on such matters will contribute to the common spiritual good. Cumulatively, there is a serious caution here, especially for priests and deacons, that the eucharistic liturgy is not the place for idiosyncratic or personalized ritual enactment that draws attention to the individual, but rather everything should elucidate the proper meaning of the liturgy. *SC*, no. 7, offers a stronger theological foundation for this position when it teaches that "perceptible symbols" like movement and gesture are tied to the participant's very sanctification. Consequently, this is not simply a matter of decorum or public order, but is the realization of a basic sacramental principle that the liturgy and its constitutive components such as words, music, environment, etc., effect what they signify, even apart from the intentions of ministers or participants.

Because human sanctification takes place concretely within specific cultures, and cultural context affects the interpretation of symbols, there is no universal standard for a principle such as "noble simplicity," whose meaning changes not only across cultures but also within the diversity of a single culture (e.g., between Masses with adults, and those primarily attended by children of catechetical age). A parallel caution concerns the call for attentiveness to *IGMR2002* and the traditional practice of the Roman Rite, where the use of the Latin singular *(tradita praxi)* gives the impression there has been a uniform practice defining noble simplicity. This is an historically untenable position given the enormous pluriformity of the eucharistic rite practiced in the Roman Church (see Mitchell and Baldovin, 11–17 above).

The second paragraph in no. 42 proposes that uniformity in posture effects and signifies unity. What is new in *IGMR2002* is that this signification is now

A common posture, to be observed by all participants, is a sign of the unity of the members of the Christian community gathered for the sacred Liturgy: it both expresses and fosters the intention and spiritual attitude of the participants.

ad sacram Liturgiam congregatorum: mentem enim et sensus animi participantium exprimit eosdemque fovet.

43. The faithful should stand from the beginning of the Entrance chant, or while the priest approaches the altar, until the end of the Collect; for the *Alleluia* chant before the Gospel; while the Gospel itself is proclaimed; during the Profession of Faith and the Prayer of the Faithful; from the invitation, *Orate, fratres (Pray, brethren)*, before the prayer over the offerings until the end of Mass, except at the places indicated below.

43. Fideles stent ab initio cantus ad introitum, vel dum sacerdos accedit ad altare, usque ad collectam inclusive; ad cantum Allelúia ante Evangelium; dum ipsum Evangelium proclamatur; dum professio fidei et oratio universalis fiunt; necnon ab invitatione Oráte fratres ante orationem super oblata usque ad finem Missæ, præter ea quæ infra dicuntur.

---

specified for "members of the Christian community gathered for sacred Liturgy" (*membrorum communitatis christianae ad sacram Liturgiam congregatorum*). *IGMR2002* has previously distinguished between the faithful and the priest (e.g., no. 30), but here instead speaks of the whole gathered assembly. Because of this language, this paragraph seems to raise questions about those times when the faithful and the priest do not share a common posture (e.g., the Eucharistic Prayer). If the above-noted sacramental principle is always operative in postures, a differentiated stance between priest and faithful also effects what it signifies regarding the unity of the community.

43. This second paragraph in the posture/movement section is mostly programmatic, giving an overview of the postures of the faithful during the Eucharist. Virtually no attention is here given to the postures of the priest or deacon, which are addressed at other places in *IGMR2002*. At the same time, this exclusive attention to the postures of the faithful confirms that their embodiment is one of those important "perceptible symbols" intimately wed to the participants' very sanctification (cf. no. 42 above).

We previously noted (no. 37 above) the potential confusion for introducing the term *offertorium* into what *IGMR2002* properly calls a *praeparatio donorum* (no. 72.1). Here the phrase *praeparatio donorum ad offertorium,* found in previous

They should, however, sit while the readings before the Gospel and the responsorial Psalm are proclaimed and for the homily and while the Preparation of the Gifts at the Offertory is taking place; and, as circumstances allow, they may sit or kneel while the period of sacred silence after Communion is observed.

In the dioceses of the United States of America, they should kneel beginning after the singing or recitation of the *Sanctus* until after the *Amen* of the Eucharistic Prayer, except when prevented on occasion

Sedeant autem dum proferuntur lectiones ante Evangelium et psalmus responsorius; ad homiliam et dum fit præparatio donorum ad offertorium; atque, pro opportunitate, dum sacrum silentium post Communionem servatur.

Genuflectant vero, nisi valetudinis causa, vel ob angustiam loci vel frequentiorem numerum adstantium aliasve rationabiles causas impediantur, ad consecrationem. Hi vero qui non genuflectunt ad consecrationem, inclinationem profundam peragant dum sacerdos genuflectit post consecrationem.

---

*IGMR*s, seems to compound the confusion as it conflates the Tridentine designation of the analogous "offertory" unit with the reformed terminology of "preparation of the gifts" found in every edition of the *Ordo Missae* since 1969. Another noteworthy language turn is the way this article fails to use the proper designation of "institution narrative and consecration" (*Narratio institutionis et consecratio*) found in no. 79d, but mentions only "at" or "after the consecration" *(ad* or *post consecrationem).* While this could be explained as a simple abbreviation, it also could be interpreted as a theological stress which affirms a Tridentine perspective, delimiting the consecration to a particular moment and text in the Eucharistic Prayer,[27] rather than the more ancient view that the whole of the Eucharistic Prayer is consecratory (cf. Power and Vincie, 58 above), and the more recent recovery of the role of the Holy Spirit and the epiclesis in the consecration (*Catholicae Ecclesiae Catechismus* [*CEC*], no. 1375; also Power and Vincie, 58 and 64–66 above). The view that the whole of the Eucharistic Prayer is consecratory is reiterated by contemporary theologians from Eastern and Western Catholicism as well as current strands in the Church's magisterium.[28]

GIRM2003 contains the approved adaptation that in dioceses of the US the faithful kneel after the *Sanctus* until after the great *Amen*. Here, as in the parallel section of *IGMR2002*, exceptions are made for various reasons. The continuation of this US pattern of kneeling after the *Sanctus* requires serious catechesis since

27. Cf. Denzinger, nos. 1640, 1642 and 1654.

28. Most striking here is the 26 October 2001 decree of the Holy See which recognized the validity of the Eucharist celebrated with the traditional Anaphora of Addai and Mari which has no institution narrative. This text as well as the historical and theological evidence for affirming the whole of the Eucharistic Prayer as consecratory is well rehearsed in Robert Taft, "Mass without the Consecration?" *Worship* 77 (2003): 482–509.

by reasons of health, lack of space, the large number of people present, or some other good reason. Those who do not kneel ought to make a profound bow when the priest genuflects after the consecration. The faithful kneel after the *Agnus Dei* unless the Diocesan Bishop determines otherwise.[53]

With a view to a uniformity in gestures and postures during one and the same celebration, the faithful should follow the directions which the deacon, lay minister, or priest gives according to whatever is indicated in the Missal.

Est tamen Conferentiæ Episcoporum, gestus et corporis habitus in Ordine Missæ descriptos ingenio et rationabilibus populorum traditionibus ad normam iuris aptare.[53] Attendendum tamen erit, ut sensui et indoli cuiusque partis celebrationis respondeant. Ubi mos est, populum ab acclamatione Sanctus expleta usque ad finem Precis eucharisticæ et ante Communionem quando sacerdos dicit Ecce Agnus Dei genuflexum manere, hic laudabiliter retinetur.

Ad uniformitatem in gestibus et corporis habitibus in una eademque celebratione obtinendam, fideles monitionibus obtemperent, quas diaconus, vel minister laicus, vel sacerdos proferunt, iuxta ea quæ in Missali statuuntur.

44. Among gestures included are also actions and processions: of the priest going with the deacon and ministers to the altar;

44. In gestibus numerantur etiam actiones et processiones, quibus sacerdos cum diacono, et ministris, ad altare adit; diaco-

---

in the reformed *Ordo Missae* the faithful actually change posture *during* the Eucharistic Prayer; as the Tridentine rite did not consider the preface a proper part of the Roman Canon, the faithful changed posture *before* the beginning of the "canon" in that rite. Without proper catechesis, this continuation of an old pattern in a new rite could contribute to confusion about when exactly the Eucharistic Prayer begins, and lead some to continue thinking that the preface and *Sanctus* are preliminary to, rather than integral elements of the Eucharistic Prayer.[29]

Finally, a paragraph about adaptations which belong to conferences of bishops, present in previous editions, has been removed and subsumed into the new Chapter IX of *IGMR2002*.

44. The last paragraph of this section expands the understanding of gestures and actions by including processions. Since *IGMR2002* includes the gospel procession here (not in *IGMR1975*) and indicates that such takes place while the proper liturgical song (i.e., acclamation) is sung, this is the one place *IGMR* implicitly recognizes the gospel acclamation as a processional song. The section closes with the directive that these be carried out with "decorum" (*decore*), a

29. Such a perspective was announced in the official newsletter of the Bishops' Committee on the Liturgy of the USCCB which reported, "The only licit posture during the Eucharistic Prayer is kneeling, unless they are prevented on occasion from kneeling due to 'health, lack of space, the large number of people present, or some other good reason.'" *BCL Newsletter* (September 2002): 1. In fact, however, it is licit and a requirement to change from standing to kneeling during the Eucharistic Prayer in the US.

of the deacon carrying the Evangeliary or *Book of the Gospels* to the ambo before the proclamation of the Gospel; of the faithful presenting the gifts and coming forward to receive Communion. It is appropriate that actions and processions of this sort be carried out with decorum while the chants proper to them occur, in keeping with the norms prescribed for each.

nus ante Evangelii proclamationem Evangeliarium seu Librum evangeliorum ad ambonem defert; fideles dona afferunt et ad Communionem accedunt. Convenit ut huiusmodi actiones et processions decore peragantur, dum cantus ipsis proprii fiunt, iuxta normas pro singulis statutas.

Silence

45. Sacred silence also, as part of the celebration, is to be observed at the designated times.[54] Its purpose, however, depends on

De silentio

45. Sacrum quoque silentium, tamquam pars celebrationis, suo tempore est servandum.[54] Eius autem natura a tempore pendet,

---

word that has different meanings across cultures and age groups. There is also a new affirmation of the intrinsically musical nature of processions, wed to a somewhat redundant directive that movements and processions should be carried out according to prescribed norms. There are a number of ancient gestures that are not mentioned throughout this section, e.g., people assuming the *orans* position during the Our Father, the sign of peace (cf. no. 82 below), and acts of reverence at the time of Communion (cf. no. 160 below; also ITTOM, no. 136).

Silence

45. The treatment of silence, as with other elements in this section, is more programmatic than overtly theological. Recognizing that silence serves different purposes within the liturgy, *IGMR2002* like its predecessors notes a few of silence's functions in the Eucharist. *IGLH1971* provides a richer theological rationale for silence, noting that silence both disposes worshipers to receive "the full sound of the voice of the Holy Spirit" and enables them to unite personal prayer "more closely with the word of God and the public voice of the Church" (no. 202). Drawing on this instruction, the US bishops recognize that rather than simply an absence of words, liturgical silence is a quieting of spirit and an antidote to haste (ITTOM, no. 48). *IGMR2002* adds a new paragraph at the end of this article, commending the value of silence before Eucharist as a way to help dispose the community for a devout celebration; a similar proposal will be the new paragraph on silence during the Liturgy of the Word (no. 56 below). The value of silence here and throughout the celebration always needs to be assessed in terms of the culture and context of the assembly. *IGLH1971* raises one important litmus test for the use of silence in worship, i.e., that it does not "disturb the structure of the [liturgy] or annoy and weary those taking part."[30]

30. *IGLH1971*, no. 202.

the time it occurs in each part of the celebration. Thus within the Act of Penitence and again after the invitation to pray, all recollect themselves; but at the conclusion of a reading or the homily, all meditate briefly on what they have heard; then after Communion, they praise and pray to God in their hearts.

Even before the celebration itself, it is commendable that silence [is] to be observed in the church, in the sacristy, in the vesting room, and in adjacent areas, so that all may dispose themselves to carry out the sacred action in a devout and fitting manner.

quo in singulis celebrationibus occurrit. In actu enim pænitentiali et post invitationem ad orandum singuli ad seipsos convertuntur; lectione autem vel homilia peracta, ea quæ audierunt breviter meditantur; post Communionem vero in corde suo Deum laudant et orant.

Iam ante ipsam celebrationem silentium laudabiliter servatur in ecclesia, in sacristia, in secretario et in locis ipsis propinquioribus, ut omnes se ad sacra peragenda devote et rite disponantur.

III. The Individual Parts of the Mass

A. The Introductory Rites

46. The rites preceding the Liturgy of the Word, namely the Entrance, Greeting, Act of Penitence, *Kyrie*, *Gloria*, and collect, have the character of a beginning, introduction, and preparation.

III. De Singulis Missæ Partibus

A) Ritus initiales

46. Ritus qui liturgiam verbi præcedunt, scilicet introitus, salutatio, actus pænitentialis, Kýrie, Glória et collecta, characterem habent exordii, introductionis et præparationis.

The Individual Parts of the Mass

The Introductory Rites[31]

IGMR2002 devotes nine articles to the "introductory rites" (*ritus initiales*). Number 46 makes it clear that, while these rites are initially defined as taking place before the Liturgy of the Word, they are not simply a prelude to the liturgy as they not only have the character of a "beginning" (*exordii*) but also of an "introduction and preparation" (*introductionis et praeparationis*). In a sense, they are key to all that follows, and the effectiveness of these opening rites sets the tone for the whole of the eucharistic liturgy. The first and most fundamental purpose of these rites is to ensure that the faithful establish authentic communion with one another, the wider Church, and God. *IGMR2002* admits that this first stage in *koinonia* prepares the assembly for "properly" (*recte*) listening to God's Word, though authentic celebration of the Liturgy of the Word also involves not only active listening but also responses in psalmody, profession of faith, and prayer. This engagement with the table of the Word in turn disposes the faithful for "worthily" (*digne*) celebrating the table of the Eucharist.

31. This commentary on nos. 46–54 is indebted to a preliminary draft by our colleague Michael Joncas. We are grateful for his help and collaboration.

Their purpose is to ensure that the faithful who come together as one establish communion and dispose themselves to listen properly to God's word and to celebrate the Eucharist worthily.

In certain celebrations that are combined with Mass according to the norms of the liturgical books, the Introductory Rites are omitted or performed in a particular way.

Finis eorum est, ut fideles in unum convenientes communionem constituant et recte ad verbum Dei audiendum digneque Eucharistiam celebrandam sese disponant.

In quibusdam celebrationibus, quæ cum Missa ad normam librorum liturgicorum conectuntur, ritus initiales omittuntur aut modo peculiari peraguntur.

The Entrance

47. After the people have gathered, the Entrance chant begins as the priest enters

Introitus

47. Populo congregato, dum ingreditur sacerdos cum diacono et ministris, cantus

---

IGMR2002 presents these introductory rites as of lesser import and oriented toward the liturgies of Word and table which follow. An implicit recognition of the secondary nature of these rites is the acknowledgment that they can be omitted or altered when, according to the norms, they are combined with other liturgical events, such as a funeral, the installation of a pastor, or the Liturgy of the Hours. The preparatory nature of these rites alerts pastoral ministers to be concerned with a sense of proportion in celebrating them, particularly when combined with other liturgical events. The introductory rites should not be so elaborate in ceremony or time that the primacy of God's Word and the celebration of the Lord's Supper are diminished.

The introductory rites as presented in *MR2002* do not always disclose a clear underlying logic.[32] The individual subunits of the introductory rites arose for different purposes at different points in the historical development of Roman Rite Eucharist. *SC* directs that the "rites are to be simplified. . . . Duplications made with the passage of time are to be omitted, as are less useful additions" (no. 50). Thus the Consilium proposed a much sparer set of introductory rites in 1967 for its so-called "*Missa normativa*," consisting of a chant to accompany the procession of the liturgical ministers, a greeting, and an opening presidential prayer. Such pruning was considered too radical, and there was concern that the piety of the faithful would be disturbed by such restructuring. The Consilium thus restored some elements it had eliminated and the present form of the introductory rites has remained substantially unchanged since the *Ordo Missae of* 1969.[33]

The Entrance

47. This article contributes to *IGMR2002*'s emphasis on the foundational role of the faithful in the eucharistic celebration with its opening phrase "After

32. Ralph Keifer, "Our Cluttered Vestibule: The Unreformed Entrance Rite," *Worship* 48 (1974): 270–77.

33. Annibale Bugnini, *The Reform of the Liturgy 1948–1975,* trans. Matthew O'Connell (Collegeville, MN: The Liturgical Press, 1990), 346–92.

with the deacon and ministers. The purpose of this chant is to open the celebration, foster the unity of those who have been gathered, introduce their thoughts to the mystery of the liturgical season or festivity, and accompany the procession of the priest and ministers.

48. The singing at this time is done either alternately by the choir and the people or in a similar way by the cantor and the

ad introitum incipitur. Finis huius cantus est celebrationem aperire, unionem congregatorum fovere, eorumque mentem in mysterium temporis liturgici vel festivitatis introducere atque processionem sacerdotis ministrorumque comitari.

48. Peragitur autem a schola et populo alternatim, vel simili modo a cantore et populo, vel totus a populo vel a schola

---

the people have gathered" (*Populo congregato*). Unlike the parallel passage in the *ritus servandus* of *MR1570*, where there are only directives for liturgical ministers, *IGMR2002* directs that the liturgical ministers can only begin their ritual functions (in a Mass celebrated with a congregation) after the faithful have assembled.

The chant that accompanies the entrance in many ways epitomizes the whole of the introductory rites in its fourfold function articulated in this article: 1) opening the celebration, much as the introductory rites themselves are an opening for the rest of the liturgy; 2) fostering unity, resonant with the overarching image of communion which is to mark these rites; 3) introducing the faithful to the mystery being celebrated; and, 4) accompanying the opening procession. Although these four elements are presented by *IGMR2002* as a single "purpose" (*finis*), they could also be considered distinctive but not necessarily separate goals that could possibly come into conflict with each other. For example, generic sung texts that serve to open the celebration may not introduce the assembly to the particular mystery of a given feast or season. Similarly, taking the time necessary for fostering a sense of unity in song may require much longer than the actual time needed to accompany the procession of the ministers. These different facets of an opening song need to be maintained in a dynamic tension, so that in the regular pattern of eucharistic gatherings, each is properly respected.

48. This article considers both how the entrance chant may be performed, as well as what texts are considered appropriate for it. First, *IGMR2002* outlines four possible patterns for singing the entrance chant. Two allow for alternation of the chant (between choir and people, or between cantor and people), and two are without alternation (people alone, or choir alone). The sequence of these four possible patterns in *IGMR2002* demonstrates the centrality of the assembly's voice in this musical ritual, since the possibility of the choir singing alone is given as the last option.[34] Furthermore, there is no allowance here for

34. Analogous is the MCW's pattern of giving primary attention to the congregation both in the planning of pastoral celebrations (nos. 15–18), as well as the role differentiation within sung worship (nos. 33–34).

people, or entirely by the people, or by the choir alone. In the dioceses of the United States of America there are four options for the Entrance Chant: (1) the antiphon from the *Roman Missal* or the Psalm from the *Roman Gradual* as set to music there or in another musical setting; (2) the seasonal antiphon and Psalm of the *Simple Gradual*; (3) a song from another collection of psalms and antiphons, approved by the Conference of Bishops or the diocesan Bishop, including psalms arranged in responsorial or metrical forms; (4) a suitable liturgical song similarly approved by the Conference of Bishops or the diocesan Bishop.[55]

If there is no singing at the entrance, the antiphon in the Missal is recited either by the faithful, or by some of them, or by a lector; otherwise, it is recited by the priest himself, who may even adapt it as an introductory explanation (cf. no. 31).

sola. Adhiberi potest sive antiphona cum suo psalmo in Graduali romano vel in Graduali simplici exstans, sive alius cantus, actioni sacræ, diei vel temporis indoli congruus,[55] cuius textus a Conferentia Episcoporum sit approbatus.

Si ad introitum non habetur cantus, antiphona in Missali proposita recitatur sive a fidelibus, sive ab aliquibus ex ipsis, sive a lectore, sin aliter ab ipso sacerdote, qui potest etiam in modum monitionis initialis *(cf. n. 31)* eam aptare.

---

solo singing or purely instrumental music. Resonant with its previous discussions of liturgical music, *IGMR2002* posits the voice of the assembly as the *cantus firmus* of the eucharistic liturgy (see no. 40 above).

IGMR2002 next outlines the possible sources for the entrance chant: the first option is the proper antiphon with its psalm verse from the Roman Gradual (*Graduale Romanum*); next the simpler antiphon and psalm from the Simple Gradual (*Graduale Simplex*), which are seasonal rather than proper to each Eucharist; and finally some other song (*alius cantus*), appropriate to the ritual action of the entrance rite and to the liturgical day or season being celebrated.

GIRM2003 offers an approved adaptation for the US which notes four options for the sources of the entrance chant. First is the antiphon from the Roman Missal or the psalm from the Roman Gradual. Notable is that GIRM2003 allows these to be used "in another musical setting," which presumably includes vernacular settings as well as those in which the antiphon could be repeated more often than is found in the Roman Gradual. Such adaptations of music and texts from the Roman Gradual would seem necessary if the entrance chant was to fulfill the previously stated goal of fostering the unity of the faithful. The second option is the seasonal antiphon and psalm of the Simple Gradual. Presumably the same permissions granted to the use of the Roman Gradual (using other musical settings and employing vernacular translations) would apply to the Simple Gradual. The third option offers the wide-ranging possibility of employing a song from another collection of approved psalms and antiphons. Here GIRM2003 gives explicit permission for "responsorial" arrangements of psalms

Greeting of the Altar and of the People Gathered Together

49. When they reach the sanctuary, the priest, the deacon, and the ministers reverence the altar with a profound bow.

Salutatio altaris et populi congregati

49. Cum ad presbyterium pervenerint, sacerdos, diaconus, et ministri altare salutant profunda inclinatione.

(i.e., the repetition of the antiphon throughout) which, however, seems to be implicit in the first option noted above. Metrical psalms, a tradition with roots in the Protestant Reformation, are also permitted. The fourth option is any "suitable liturgical song." This and the previous option require episcopal approval (either by the conference of bishops or the diocesan bishop). In establishing the criteria for such approval, it is necessary to respect the basic principles set out in *SC*, especially regarding the active participation of the faithful (no. 14), as well as *IGMR2002*'s own concern for the fostering of the unity of the faithful (no. 47 above) and the need to give due consideration to the culture of the people in liturgical music (no. 38 above). Also helpful is *MusSac's* admonition that, when selecting music for worship—which would also suggest when approving musical settings for worship—the "capacities of those who are to sing the music must [also] be taken into account" (no. 9).

This article concludes by prescribing how the antiphon from the Roman Missal is to be performed if there is no singing at the entrance. The options include its recitation by all of the faithful, by some of them, by the lector, by the priest, or the adaptation of the antiphon into the priest's introduction to the Mass of the day. The latter is clearly preferable, for as the foreword to GIRM1975 noted, "these antiphons are too abrupt for communal recitation." While there is historical evidence since the eighth century that the introit was recited by the priest in the absence of a choir (and legislation since the thirteenth century requiring this[35]), such practice was part of the gradual privatization of the Eucharist, culminating in Burckard's *Ordo Missae* of 1501, where private Mass was the underlying eucharistic model (see Mitchell and Baldovin, 20 above). Unlike Burckard's *Ordo Missae* or *MR1570*, however, the 1969 *Ordo Missae* prescribes a eucharistic model that presumes the active engagement of the assembly in a ritual that is intelligible to them (cf. *SC*, no. 34). *SC*'s directives about the elimination of duplication in the reformed rites and the dropping of "less useful additions" (no. 50) suggest that this liturgical remnant is no longer contributory to the eucharistic liturgy.

Greeting of the Altar and of the People Gathered Together

While the GIRM2003 translation of this title (*Salutatio altaris et populi congregati*) may sound awkward (GIRM1975 rendered it, "Veneration of the Altar and

35. *Tunc omnes* [Diaconus et Subdiaconus] *convenientes ad librum et stantes a dextris Sacerdotis ordinate secundum gradus suos, dicant Introitum et Kyrie eleison. Missale Conventuale,* in *Ordinarium juxta ritum Sacri Ordinis Fratrum Praedicatorum,* ed. Francis Guerrini (Rome: Collegium Angelicum, 1921), no. 47, 235.

As an expression of veneration, moreover, the priest and deacon then kiss the altar itself; as the occasion suggests, the priest also incenses the cross and the altar.

50. When the Entrance chant is concluded, the priest stands at the chair and,

Venerationis autem significandæ causa, sacerdos et diaconus ipsum altare deinde osculantur; et sacerdos, pro opportunitate, crucem et altare incensat.

50. Expleto cantu ad introitum, sacerdos, stans ad sedem, una cum universo

---

Greeting the Congregation") the use of the same word (*salutatio*) for greeting both altar and people is Christologically appropriate. There is a long tradition for regarding the altar as a symbol of Christ (cf. no. 298 below), and the gathered community is honored as a celebrated mode of Christ's presence (*SC*, no. 7).

49. There are minor differences between this article and its parallel in *IGMR1975* (no. 27). First is the explicit mention of the deacon who joins the priest and other ministers in reverencing the altar. The form of reverence is also newly described as a "profound bow" (*profunda inclinatione*). *IGMR2002* will later note that "If . . . the tabernacle with the Most Blessed Sacrament is present in the sanctuary, the priest, the deacon, and the other ministers genuflect when they approach the altar . . . " (*Si vero tabernaculum cum SS.mo Sacramento sit in presbyterio, sacerdos, diaconus et alii ministri genuflectunt, cum ad altare perveniunt*, no. 274). The conditional nature of this later instruction as well as the absence of any mention of genuflection in article 49 underscores that the altar itself is deserving of reverence. Long before tabernacles were linked with altars, the latter were even venerated outside of the liturgy.[36]

As in previous *IGMR*s, it is only the priest and deacon who kiss the altar, reserving this special act of veneration to the ordained. While the hieratic role of the deacon is here respected, *IGMR2002* makes it clear that his role is secondary to that of the priest (see nos. 66 and 94 below). Finally, this article notes that "as the occasion suggests" (*pro opportunitate*) the cross and altar may be incensed. Previous *IGMR*s did not mention the cross in the parallel article (no. 27), but later noted that if there was a cross on or beside the altar, that was incensed before the altar; if there was a cross behind the altar, the priest incensed it when he passes in front of it (*IGMR1975*, no. 236), an instruction repeated in *IGMR2002*, no. 277. The previously-mentioned principle of proportionality (see 135 above) needs to be kept in mind when introducing incensation in these introductory rites, so that the ritual elaboration in these beginning moments is commensurate with that which occurs during the rest of the Eucharist.

50. After the conclusion of the entrance chant, the Eucharist proceeds with the first invariable text of the liturgy, the sign of the cross. Made by the priest

36. Benedict of Aniane (d. 821) codified this practice, requiring the monks in his monastery at Inde to visit each altar three times a day. Edmund Bishop, *Liturgica Historica* (Oxford: Clarendon Press, 1918), 214.

together with the whole gathering, makes the Sign of the Cross. Then he signifies the presence of the Lord to the community gathered there by means of the Greeting. By this Greeting and the people's response, the mystery of the Church gathered together is made manifest.

After the greeting of the people, the priest, the deacon, or a lay minister may very briefly introduce the faithful to the Mass of the day.

cœtu signat se signo crucis; deinde communitati congregatæ præsentiam Domini per salutationem significat. Qua salutatione et populi responsione manifestatur Ecclesiæ congregatæ mysterium.

Salutatione populi facta, sacerdos, vel diaconus, vel minister laicus potest brevissimis verbis introducere fideles in Missam diei.

The Act of Penitence

51. Then the priest invites those present to take part in the Act of Penitence, which,

Actus pænitentialis

51. Postea sacerdos invitat ad actum pænitentialem, qui, post brevem pausam

---

and the "whole gathering" (*universo coetu),* this sign of contradiction that has become the Christian boast (Gal 6:14) looms large over the eucharistic liturgy, the sacrament of Christ's once-and-for-all sacrifice on the cross. Then follows the opening dialogue, which "signifies the presence of the Lord to the community" (*congregatae praesentiam Domini . . . significat*). As with previous editions of *IGMR*s, this article goes on to note that through the dialogue of greeting and response "the mystery of the Church gathered together is made manifest" (*manifestatur Ecclesiae congregatae mysterium*), further attesting to the significance of dialogue in Christian revelation and the model it offers for ecclesial identity (cf. no. 34 above). *IGMR2002* newly stipulates that these rites are to take place at the chair, possibly as a corrective to the practice of some presiders conducting these opening rites from the altar which is not to become the focus of liturgical action until the preparation of the gifts and table (cf. no. 124 below).

The next paragraph, indicating that the Mass of the day may be briefly introduced, appeared in *IGMR1975* but under the next heading (The Act of Penance), and here has been more appropriately subsumed under this heading on greeting and gathering. "Briefly" (the Latin *brevissimis* is more accurately rendered as "most briefly") will need to be interpreted in the context of the particular circumstances, cultural context, and the nature of the eucharistic celebration. Proportionality is once again key to this interpretation. The directive that such an introduction should not be turned into a mini-sermon (see no. 31 above) is most appropriate here. To the list of those allowed to offer this introduction, *IGMR2002* adds the deacon. The current text also recognizes that the nonordained may offer this introduction, but changes the text of *IGMR1975* from "other qualified minister" (*alius minister idoneus*) to "a lay minister" (*minister laicus*), continuing the pattern of drawing clear distinctions between the ordained and the laity.

after a brief pause for silence, the entire community carries out through a formula of general confession. The rite concludes with the priest's absolution, which, however, lacks the efficacy of the Sacrament of Penance.

On Sundays, especially in the Season of Easter, in place of the customary Act of Penitence, from time to time the blessing and sprinkling of water to recall Baptism may take place.[56]

silentii, a tota communitate formula confessionis generalis perficitur, et sacerdotis absolutione concluditur, quæ tamen efficacia sacramenti Pænitentiæ caret.

Die dominica, præsertim tempore paschali, loco consueti actus pænitentialis, quandoque fieri potest benedictio et aspersio aquæ in memoriam baptismi.[56]

The Act of Penitence

51. This article has been considerably expanded from that found in *IGMR1975*. Both versions indicate that the priest alone invites the community to participate in the "act of penitence" (*actum paenitentialem*). Because this invitation is different from the introduction to the Mass of the day (see no. 50 above), it requires some transition on the part of the presider, particularly if the introduction to the Mass of the day has been offered by some other minister. *IGMR2002* adds the detail, in the rubrics of *MR1970* but not in *IGMR1975*, that "a brief pause for silence" (*brevem pausam silentii*) takes place before the community joins in the act of penitence (cf. no. 45 above).

IGMR2002, like its predecessors, then notes that the entire community takes part in a "formula of general confession" (*formula confessionis generalis*), which is not entirely accurate. While form A (*Confiteor Deo*) in *MR2002* and its predecessors is rightly described as a formula of general confession, and the opening versicle of form B (*Miserere nostri*) could also be understood this way, form C (*Qui missus es*) is much more clearly a litany (cf. MCW, no. 75) of praise to God for the mercy revealed in Jesus Christ. This interpretation is verified by the seven seasonal forms of this litany of praise included in English versions of the Sacramentary approved for use in the US which do not focus on the confession of sin, but on praise for God's mercy. Form C includes the *Kyrie*, which *IGMR2002* itself considers an acclamatory act (cf. no. 52 below). The US bishops in their commentary acknowledge the differences here when they note that only the first form of the penitential rite is a general confession (ITTOM, no. 72.1). While all of these forms have strong penitential overtones, it is inaccurate to categorize all of them as formulas of general confession.

This first paragraph of article 51 ends by noting that the penitential rite concludes with the priest's absolution. *IGMR2002* adds the caution that this absolution "lacks the efficacy of the Sacrament of Penance" (*efficacia sacramenti Paenitentiae caret*). This caution is understandable, given the general decline of the faithful's participation in the Sacrament of Penance. This caution needs to be balanced with the Church's ancient tradition that the Lord's invitation of

The Kyrie Eleison

52. After the Act of Penitence, the *Kyrie* is always begun, unless it has already been included as part of the Act of Penitence. Since it is a chant by which the faithful acclaim the Lord and implore his mercy, it is ordinarily done by all, that is, by the people and with the choir or cantor having a part in it.

As a rule, each acclamation is sung or said twice, though it may be repeated several times, by reason of the character of the various languages, as well as of the artistry of the music or of other circumstances.

Kyrie, eleison

52. Post actum pænitentialem incipitur semper Kýrie eléison, nisi forte locum iam habuerit in ipso actu pænitentiali. Cum sit cantus quo fideles Dominum acclamant eiusque misericordiam implorant, peragitur de more ab omnibus, partem nempe in eo habentibus populo atque schola vel cantore.

Acclamatio quæque de more bis repetitur, maiore tamen numero non excluso, ratione ingenii diversarum linguarum necnon musicæ artis vel rerum adiunctorum. Quando Kýrie cantatur ut pars actus

---

forgiveness to sinners radiated from the table, evidenced by the charge leveled against Jesus across the gospels that he ate and drank with sinners (e.g., Luke 15:4-10). Furthermore, as noted in the *Praenotanda* of the Rite of Penance, "The people of God accomplishes and perfects [their] continual repentance in many ways" (no. 4), notably "baptism for the forgiveness of sins" and "the Mass [where] the passion of Christ is made present" (no. 2).

Finally, *IGMR2002* adds a new paragraph to this article, noting that on Sundays, "especially in the Season of Easter" (*praesertim tempore paschali*), the blessing and sprinkling of water may take place. It is good that the current Instruction has remedied this lacuna, not mentioned in previous *IGMR*s even though the blessing and sprinkling of holy water has been an option in the *Ordo Missae* since *MR1970*. It is notable, however, that this rite which recalls baptism and thus highlights the "common priesthood of the faithful" (*Lumen Gentium* [*LG*], no. 10), is put in a secondary place in this Instruction, since it only appears in an appendix in *MR2002*. The US bishops note that if the greeting and blessing take place at the door, the priest may sprinkle the people during the entrance procession (ITTOM, no. 74). They also requested an adaptation to move the rite of sprinkling out of an appendix, to no. 7b (just after the Act of Penitence and before the Gloria) in the *Ordo Missae* approved for use in the US.

The Kyrie Eleison

52. This article, virtually the same as that which appeared in *IGMR1975*, speaks to the nature, design, and performance of the *Kyrie*. As noted previously (cf. no. 51), the *Kyrie* is more than a penitential chant, and thus is not included as part of the "Act of Penitence" in the Instruction (although the US bishops subsume it under the heading "Act of Penance" in ITTOM, no. 73). Rather, it is done *after* the Act of Penitence (*IGMR2002* adds "always," *semper*). In its origins, the *Kyrie* was an acclamation which eventually acquired an important

When the *Kyrie* is sung as a part of the Act of Penitence, a trope may precede each acclamation.

pænitentialis, singulis acclamationibus « tropus » præponitur.

The Gloria

53. The *Gloria* is a very ancient and venerable hymn in which the Church, gathered together in the Holy Spirit, glorifies and entreats God the Father and the Lamb. The text of this hymn may not be replaced by any other text. The *Gloria* is intoned by the priest or, if appropriate, by a cantor or by the choir; but it is sung either by

Gloria in excelsis

53. Glória est antiquissimus et venerabilis hymnus, quo Ecclesia, in Spiritu Sancto congregata, Deum Patrem atque Agnum glorificat eique supplicat. Huius hymni textus cum alio commutari nequit. Inchoatur a sacerdote vel, pro opportunitate, a cantore, aut a schola, cantatur autem vel ab omnibus simul, vel a populo alternatim cum schola,

---

responsorial role in early Christian litanies in the East and West.[37] *IGMR2002* explicitly recognizes the *Kyrie* as an acclamation. Its essentially lyrical nature is underscored by this definition of the *Kyrie* here as a "chant" (*cantus*) that belongs to the community, with the choir or cantor taking part in it as well. Settings of the *Kyrie* that belong to the choir alone, therefore, do not fulfill the vision of this Instruction.

In the second paragraph of this article, the Instruction allows each acclamation—sung or said twice "as a rule" (*de more*, better translated "customarily")—to be repeated. The variables which need to be taken into consideration in determining these repetitions are noteworthy: language (necessarily understood in the context of particular cultures), musical artistry and "other circumstances" (*rerum adiunctorum*). While *IGMR2002* does not use the language of "litany" when discussing the *Kyrie*, permission to add tropes to the *Kyrie* when sung as part of the Act of Penitence can effectively transform the *Kyrie* into a litany. The models for doing this, provided by ICEL for the 1974 and subsequent sacramentaries, illustrate that such tropes (addressed to the second person of the Trinity) do not so much elaborate on the sinfulness of the faithful, as much as emphasize the gracious mercy of God in Jesus Christ.

If the *Kyrie* is employed as part of the Act of Penitence (i.e., if either form B or C of the Act of Penitence is employed), it is not repeated. Similarly, if the Sprinkling Rite is employed, the *Kyrie* is not used.

The Gloria

53. The *Gloria* is classified by *IGMR2002* as a hymn (*hymnus*). Sometimes known as the "greater doxology," it is one of many early Christian compositions called *psalmi idiotici*, written in imitation of the psalms of David and biblical

37. See John Baldovin, "Kyrie Eleison and the Entrance Rite of the Roman Eucharist," *Worship* 60, no. 4 (1986): 334–47.

everyone together, or by the people alternately with the choir, or by the choir alone. If not sung, it is to be recited either by all together or by two parts of the congregation responding one to the other.

It is sung or said on Sundays outside the Seasons of Advent and Lent, on solemnities and feasts, and at special celebrations of a more solemn character.

vel ab ipsa schola. Si non cantatur, recitandum est ab omnibus simul aut a duobus choris sibi invicem respondentibus.

Cantatur autem vel dicitur diebus dominicis extra tempus Adventus et Quadragesimæ, necnon in sollemnitatibus et festis, et in peculiaribus celebrationibus sollemnioribus.

---

canticles. An early version of the *Gloria* appeared in the *Apostolic Constitutions,*[38] and it became a standard element in Eastern matins.[39] While it is "very ancient" (*antiquissimus*), it did not become a common part of Sunday Eucharist in the West at which a priest presided until the eighth century. It is still an occasional element, employed on Sundays outside of Advent and Lent, and on solemnities and feasts. *IGMR2002* adds the prescription that the text of this "venerable" (*venerabilis)* hymn "may not be replaced by any other text" (*cum alio commutari nequit*).

Much of this article concerns the performance of the *Gloria*. New in *IGMR2002* is the explicit permission for it to be intoned by the cantor or choir (something previously allowed by MCW, no. 66), rather than the priest, "if appropriate" (*pro opportunitate*). The appropriateness of the cantor or choir intoning the *Gloria* is a determination often based on musical factors; at the same time, presiders need to be trained not to neglect their responsibility for musical leadership in the Eucharist, which is an inherently lyrical act. Performance of the *Gloria* is first ceded to "everyone together" (*ab omnibus simul*), which allows the possibility of choirs or cantors to add embellishment to the hymn around the *cantus firmus* of the assembly. The next preference is in alternatim between people and the choir; although not explicitly mentioned, by extension it might also be appropriate for the *Gloria* to be alternated between people and cantor. *IGMR2002* does permit the *Gloria* to be sung by the choir alone, and the US bishops recognized that this can provide an opportunity for the choir to sing alone on festive occasions (MCW, no. 66). Such is clearly not the preferred pattern for singing this hymn. The final alternative is recitation by everyone. A useful option here is the possibility of alternation between two parts of the congregation, which could preempt some of the monotony of communal recitation of this relatively long text.

38. No. 7.47–49 in *Didaskalia et Constitutiones Apostolorum,* ed. F.X. Funk, 2 vols. (Torino: Bottega d'Erasmo, 1964), II:454–458.

39. Robert Taft, *The Liturgy of the Hours in East and West* (Collegeville, MN: The Liturgical Press, 1986), 45.

The Collect

54. Next the priest invites the people to pray. All, together with the priest, observe a brief silence so that they may be conscious of the fact that they are in God's presence and may formulate their petitions mentally. Then the priest says the prayer which is customarily known as the collect and through which the character of the celebration is expressed. In accordance with the ancient tradition of the Church, the collect prayer is usually addressed to God the Father, through Christ, in the Holy Spirit,[57] and is concluded with a trinitarian ending, that is to say the longer ending, in the following manner:

Collecta

54. Deinde sacerdos populum ad orandum invitat; et omnes una cum sacerdote parumper silent, ut conscii fiant se in conspectu Dei stare, et vota sua in animo possint nuncupare. Tunc sacerdos profert orationem, quæ solet « collecta » nominari, et per quam indoles celebrationis exprimitur. Ex antiqua traditione Ecclesiæ, oratio collecta de more ad Deum Patrem, per Christum in Spiritu Sancto, dirigitur[57] et conclusione trinitaria, idest longiore, concluditur, hoc modo:

The Collect

54. The introductory rites are concluded by the collect (*collecta*, which GIRM1975 translates as "opening prayer," no. 32), a term of Gallican origins which underscores the movement of this prayer as a gathering up of the prayers of the community by the presider. While labeled an *oratio* in *MR1570*, all recent *MR*s have recovered the Gallican term, emphasizing the collecting of the assembly's prayers into what can be considered the climactic moment of the entrance rites.[40] The preeminence of this moment in these beginning rites is underscored by the fact that, while every other beginning element previously considered (nos. 47–53) can be omitted on some occasions (cf. no. 46 above), the opening collect is virtually never omitted. The limitation of a single collect in the reformed eucharistic liturgy (contrary to the possibility for multiple orations in *MR1570*) ritually contributes to the climactic potential of this prayer in bringing the introductory rites to a close.

This first of the presidential prayers is comprised of four elements. First is the priest's invitation to pray. This is followed by a silence that is to be "brief" (*parumper*), yet long enough to help the community to be conscious of being in God's presence and to formulate their own prayer. Then follows the body of the prayer, which expresses "the character of the celebration" (*indoles celebrationis*). This occurs more clearly in collects of feasts and proper seasons than ordinary time, as many of the latter have a rather generic content. Following the body of the prayer comes the people's Amen, which *IGMR2002* calls an acclamation, uniting them to the prayer and enabling them to make it their own.

40. See Josef Jungmann, *The Mass of the Roman Rite,* trans. Francis Brunner, 2 vols. (Westminster: Christian Classics, 1986), I:359–61.

- If the prayer is directed to the Father: *Per Dominum nostrum Iesum Christum Filium tuum, qui tecum vivit et regnat in unitate Spiritus Sancti, Deus, per omnia saecula saeculorum (Through our Lord, Jesus Christ, your Son, who lives ad reigns with you and the Holy Spirit, one God, forever and ever);*
- If it is directed to the Father, but the Son is mentioned at the end: *Qui tecum vivit et regnat in unitate Spiritus Sancti, Deus, per omnia saecula saeculorum (Who lives and reigns with you and the Holy Spirit, one God, forever and ever);*
- If it is directed to the Son: *Qui vivis et regnas cum Deo Patre in unitate Spiritus Sancti, Deus, per omnia saecula saeculorum (You live and reign with God the Father in the unity of the Holy Spirit, one God, forever and ever).*

– si dirigitur ad Patrem: Per Dóminum nostrum Iesum Christum Fílium tuum, qui tecum vivit et regnat in unitáte Spíritus Sancti, Deus, per ómnia sǽcula sæculórum;
– si dirigitur ad Patrem, sed in fine ipsius fit mentio Filii: Qui tecum vivit et regnat in unitáte Spíritus Sancti, Deus, per ómnia sǽcula sæculórum;
– si dirigitur ad Filium: Qui vivis et regnas cum Deo Patre in unitáte Spíritus Sancti, Deus, per ómnia sǽcula sæculórum.

The current instruction does, however, eliminate the phrase that in the Amen the people are "assenting" (*assentiens, IGMR1975*, no. 32) to the prayer, perhaps to remove any claim that the faithful might be able to withhold assent to a prayer text proposed by the Church and proclaimed by the presider. The *Directory for Mass with Children* (DMC, no. 51) allows the presider to choose a collect other than that appointed for the day, and even to paraphrase the collect so that it might be more accessible to children. In doing so, the presider should maintain this basic fourfold pattern of prayer.

The Instruction notes that, like much of classic Western euchology, the collect is ordinarily addressed to the Father, through Christ, in the Holy Spirit. At the same time, this article admits that some collects are addressed to Christ, by including a Trinitarian ending "if it is directed to the Son" (*si dirigitur ad Filium*). The result of a long rhetorical tradition, these prayers can be characterized as highly petitionary, with a preponderant appeal to the intellect rather than the emotions, with a dense and elevated prose style, a relative lack of direct scriptural citations, and rather generic content. The study of these texts could help in catechesis, preaching, and mystagogy.

The Liturgy of the Word

55. As is the pattern in section III of Chapter II of *IGMR2002*, the opening paragraph introducing the major subdivisions of the *Ordo Missae* provides both an overview of what is to come and highlights fundamental perspectives about this structural unit and its ritual performance.

The people, uniting themselves to this entreaty, make the prayer their own with the acclamation, *Amen*.

There is always only one collect used in a Mass.

Populus, precationi se coniungens, acclamatione Amen orationem facit suam.

In Missa semper unica dicitur collecta.

B. The Liturgy of the Word

55. The main part of the Liturgy of the Word is made up of the readings from Sacred Scripture together with the chants occurring between them. The homily, Profession of Faith, and Prayer of the Faithful, however, develop and conclude this part of the Mass. For in the readings, as explained by the homily, God speaks to his

B) Liturgia verbi

55. Partem præcipuam liturgiæ verbi constituunt lectiones e sacra Scriptura desumptæ cum cantibus inter eas occurrentibus; homilia autem, professio fidei et oratio universalis seu oratio fidelium illam evolvunt et concludunt. Nam in lectionibus, quas homilia exponit, Deus populum suum alloquitur,[58] mysterium redemptionis et

---

First is a more differentiated presentation of the Liturgy of the Word (largely reliant on *OLM1981-Pr*) than presented earlier in this chapter. Previously the Liturgy of the Word was defined as one of the two main parts of the Mass (no. 28 above). Here there is a further recognition that the Liturgy of the Word itself admits a natural subdivision between 1) the readings and chants, constituting the central part of this section where "God speaks," and 2) the homily, profession of faith, and prayer of the faithful which "develop and conclude" this section. This subdivision is twice articulated in this paragraph, but the second time the homily—in its role of explaining the readings—is more closely tied to the first than the second subdivision of this liturgical unit. This raises certain questions.

The first concerns the chants between the readings. Initially this paragraph recognizes these chants as the very Word of God, yet *IGMR2002* seems to limit God's speaking to the readings, and footnotes *SC*, no. 33, to this effect. However, this article in *SC* is not about the readings, but is a much more sweeping statement about how God speaks and people respond throughout the whole of the liturgy. Later this paragraph notes how people make God's Word their own, first through silence (a new addition, not found in previous *IGMR*s) and then through singing. What is missing is a recognition of the paradox that people respond to the Word of God *with* the Word of God, and so in their singing exhibit two of the modes of Christ's presence articulated in *SC*, no. 7: both the very Word of God as well as the communal act of the baptized praying and singing. Inserting *silentio* into this article, on the other hand, seems to mute the foundational insight that it is the performance of these chants that is both a mode of Christ's presence and an act of *communio* with that presence.

A second question raised by this article concerns the role of the homily. As previously noted (no. 28 above), there is some concern that *IGMR2002* considers the Liturgy of the Word and the homily in overly didactic terms. While there

people,[58] opening up to them the mystery of redemption and salvation and offering them spiritual nourishment; and Christ himself is present in the midst of the faithful through his word.[59] By their silence and singing the people make God's word their own, and they also affirm their adherence to it by means of the Profession of Faith. Finally, having been nourished by it, they pour out their petitions in the Prayer of the Faithful for the needs of the entire Church and for the salvation of the whole world.

salutis patefacit, atque nutrimentum spirituale offert; et ipse Christus per verbum suum in medio fidelium præsens adest.[59] Hoc verbum divinum populus suum facit silentio et cantibus, atque ipsi adhæret professione fidei; eo autem nutritus, oratione universali pro necessitatibus totius Ecclesiæ et pro totius mundi salute preces fundit.

Silence

56. The Liturgy of the Word is to be celebrated in such a way as to promote meditation, and so any sort of haste that hinders recollection must clearly be avoided. During

Silentium

56. Liturgia verbi ita celebranda est ut faveat meditationi, ideo plane vitanda est omnis forma festinationis quæ recollectionem impediat. In ea conveniunt etiam bre-

---

is a basis for this in *SC,* no. 24, the broader lens of *SC,* no. 52, requires that we think of the homily as an essentially liturgical act. Since *SC* has five times reiterated that the purpose of liturgical action is the glorification of God and the sanctification of people,[41] then by extension preaching must be a doxological act. Furthermore, the homily itself is an event of divine presence, since in liturgical preaching the priest-presider is acting *in persona Christi* (cf. no. 29 above). Thus *Ad Gentes* (*AG*) teaches that preaching "brings about the presence of Christ" (no. 9)[42] and *Codex Iuris Canonici* (*CIC1983,* c. 762) admonishes that the "word of the living God . . . is altogether proper to require from the mouth of priests." Thus, it is theologically appropriate to consider the homily more "encounter" of the living Word of God than instruction about that Word.

Silence

56. This new paragraph on silence is longer and theologically richer than the introductory paragraph on the topic in section II of this chapter (no. 45). Much of it repeats *OLM1981-Pr,* no. 28. In considering the contribution of silence, *IGMR2002* underscores the value of recollection and meditation. A focus on the interior disposition of worshipers is further stressed in the phrase "grasped by the heart" (*corde percipiatur*) and by envisioning the response to the Word through prayer. This particular paragraph, and *IGMR2002* in general, are strong in noting the importance of the interior disposition for the effective-

41. Nos. 5, 7, 10, 61 and12.
42. Reiterated in *OLM1981-Pr,* no. 24.

the Liturgy of the Word, it is also appropriate to include brief periods of silence, accommodated to the gathered assembly, in which, at the prompting of the Holy Spirit, the word of God may be grasped by the heart and a response through prayer may be prepared. It may be appropriate to observe such periods of silence, for example, before the Liturgy of the Word itself begins, after the first and second reading, and lastly at the conclusion of the homily.[60]

via momenta silentii, cœtui congregato accommodata, quibus, Spiritu Sancto fovente, Dei verbum corde percipiatur, ac responsio per orationem præparetur. Quæ momenta silentii opportune servari possunt, ex. gr., antequam inchoetur ipsa liturgia verbi, post primam et secundam lectionem, peracta denique homilia.[60]

The Biblical Readings

57. In the readings, the table of God's word is prepared for the faithful, and the riches of the Bible are opened to them.[61] Hence, it is preferable to maintain the arrangement of the biblical readings, by which

Lectiones biblicæ

57. In lectionibus mensa verbi Dei paratur fidelibus et thesauri biblici eis aperiuntur.[61] Præstat proinde lectionum biblicarum dispositionem servari, qua unitas utriusque Testamenti et historiæ salutis illustratur;

---

ness of the liturgy (cf. *SC*, no. 11). There is not always a parallel recognition that the visible stance and engagement of the faithful during the Liturgy of the Word is also essential to the dialogue (*OLM1981-Pr*, no. 28) that not only prepares us for prayer but for eucharistic action and living in continuity with this eucharistic renewal which "draws the faithful into the compelling love of Christ and sets them on fire" (*SC*, no. 10). Thus *OLM1981-Pr* recognizes that the proper response to the Word of God is an active one, "not only during Mass but in [our] entire Christian life" (no. 48). While not specifically concerned with the readings, no. 392 of *IGMR2002* offers a useful hermeneutic when, speaking of translation, it distinguishes between employing texts for meditation and for liturgical proclamation. Analogously, it is important to maintain a reflective spirit during the Liturgy of the Word without turning it into *lectio divina*.

The Biblical Readings

57. This article only has the first sentence in common with previous *IGMRs* (e.g., *IGMR1975*, no. 34), reiterating *SC*'s vision that more of the Scriptures be read in the reformed Order of Mass. New to *IGMR2002* are the emphases on maintaining the arrangement of readings found in the lectionary, and the prescription against substituting nonbiblical text for the readings and responsorial psalm. In support of this position, *IGMR* cites an apostolic letter from John Paul II (d. 2005), which prohibits substituting "profane readings for texts from Sacred Scripture." What is unusual here is the language at the end of paragraph which notes that the readings and responsorial psalm "contain the word of God" (*verbum Dei continent*), rather than the simpler and more theologically correct

light is shed on the unity of both Testaments and of salvation history. Moreover, it is unlawful to substitute other, non-biblical texts for the readings and responsorial Psalm, which contain the word of God.[62]

neque fas est lectiones et psalmum responsorium, quæ verbum Dei continent, cum aliis textibus non biblicis commutari.[62]

58. In the celebration of the Mass with a congregation, the readings are always proclaimed from the ambo.

58. In celebratione Missæ cum populo, lectiones semper ex ambone proferuntur.

59. By tradition, the function of proclaiming the readings is ministerial, not presidential. The readings, therefore,

59. Munus lectiones proferendi ex traditione non est præsidentiale sed ministeriale. Lectiones ergo a lectore proferantur,

---

assertion that these are the Word of God.[43] This and other segments of *IGMR2002* could give the impression that Christ's presence in the gospel is distinguishable from his presence in other readings or the psalm. *SC* makes no such distinction, but broadly asserts that Christ is present in the Word, and is present "when the holy Scriptures are read in the Church" (no. 7).

58. The theological rationale for this newly inserted paragraph on the ambo is found in no. 309 below. Reverence for the Word as one of the privileged modes of Christ's presence (*SC*, no. 7) makes this emphasis on the ambo appropriate. Given the pastoral reality of the diverse settings for celebrating the Eucharist, some of which do not allow for an ambo, it is the underlying concern for due reverence (no. 309) for the Word—however that is symbolized and negotiated—that is foundational.

59. The first part of this paragraph has been slightly adjusted from previous *IGMR*s. Particularly noteworthy is the change in language from "[duty] of reading the readings" (*officium legendi lectiones, IGMR1975,* no. 34) to "function of proclaiming the readings" (*munus lectiones proferendi*). This change is consistent with the overall tendency in *IGMR2002* to distinguish liturgical ministries of the ordained or instituted from those functions carried out by the laity (see no. 97 below). An evolution in language is also notable in the discussion of who should read the gospel. In the absence of a deacon, *IGMR1971* assigns the reading of the gospel to "another presbyter" (*alter presbyter*), who is distinguished from "the celebrant" (*celebrante,* no. 34); *IGMR1975* says "another priest" (*alius sacerdos*), who is distinguished from "the priest celebrant" (*sacerdote celebrante,* no. 34); this is virtually identical to *IGMR2002,* which also has "[another] priest" (*alius sacerdos*) distinguished from "the [priest] celebrant" (*sacerdos celebrans,* no. 59). New here is the additional sentence indicating that the latter should also read the other readings if a "suitable lector" (*idoneus lector*) is not present; no. 176 appropriately modifies this, noting that if a deacon is present but no suitable lector, the deacon reads. *IGMR2002* does not specify what renders a

43. Cf. *SC,* no. 7; also, *OLM1981-Pr,* nos. 45–47.

should be proclaimed by a lector, and the Gospel by a deacon or, in his absence, a priest other than the celebrant. If, however, a deacon or another priest is not present, the priest celebrant himself should read the Gospel. Further, if another suitable lector is also not present, then the priest celebrant should also proclaim the other readings.

After each reading, whoever reads gives the acclamation, to which the gathered people reply, honoring the word of God that they have received in faith and with grateful hearts.

60. The reading of the Gospel is the high point of the Liturgy of the Word. The Liturgy itself teaches that great reverence is to be shown to it by setting it off from the other readings with special marks of honor: whether on the part of the minister appointed to proclaim it, who prepares himself

Evangelium autem a diacono vel, eo absente, ab alio sacerdote annuntietur. Si tamen diaconus vel alius sacerdos præsto non sit, ipse sacerdos celebrans Evangelium legat; et si alius quoque idoneus lector absit, sacerdos celebrans etiam alias lectiones proferat.

Post singulas lectiones qui legit profert acclamationem, cui respondens, populus congregatus honorem tribuit verbo Dei fide et grato animo recepto.

60. Lectio Evangelii culmen constituit liturgiæ verbi. Maximam venerationem illi esse tribuendam, ipsa Liturgia docet, cum eam præ ceteris lectionibus speciali honore insigniat, sive ex parte ministri ad eam annuntiandam deputati et per benedictionem vel orationem sese præparantis; sive ex

---

lector "suitable," though later notes that they should receive careful training (no. 101).[44]

Also new is the second paragraph, which stipulates the role of the reader in announcing the acclamation after the reading. The people's response to this acclamation derives from having actively received the Word in faith and gratitude. Their response, as intimated in a parallel passage in no. 60, is itself an acclamation.

60. In the opening sentence of this paragraph, *IGMR2002* goes further than its predecessors in explicating that the gospel proclamation is the high point of the Liturgy of the Word, and a celebrated moment of Christ's presence. The rest of the paragraph is a model of *lex orandi, lex credendi* as *IGMR* offers a theological reflection on four distinctive ritual actions, particular to the proclamation of the gospel, i.e., 1) ministerial preparation by blessing or prayer, 2) change of stance by the faithful, 3) gospel acclamation, and 4) marks of reverence to the Book of the Gospels. While the marks of reverence are not elaborated, they traditionally include a gospel procession (cf. no. 37 above) with lighted candles, the use of incense, as well as signing the book before and kissing the book after the proclamation. Missing here is any reference to the unique action of the signing of the forehead, mouth, and breast with the cross during the text "A

44. Partial definitions of what may be suitable, or clarifications for what kind of instruction is required are found elsewhere. Valuable here is *OLM1981-Pr*, no. 55; also helpful are Consilium's letter (2 February 1968 in *Notitiae* 4 [1968]), nos. 5 and 7, in DOL, nos. 4203 and 4205; Paul VI's *Ministeria quaedam* (1972) no. 5, in DOL, no. 2930; and, ITTOM (2003), nos. 7–8 and 14–15.

by a blessing or prayer; or on the part of the faithful, who stand as they listen to it being read and through their acclamations acknowledge and confess Christ present and speaking to them; or by the very marks of reverence that are given to the *Book of the Gospels*.

The Responsorial Psalm

61. After the first reading comes the responsorial Psalm, which is an integral part of the Liturgy of the Word and holds great liturgical and pastoral importance, because it fosters meditation on the word of God.

The responsorial Psalm should correspond to each reading and should, as a rule, be taken from the Lectionary.

parte fidelium, qui per acclamationes Christum præsentem sibique loquentem agnoscunt et profitentur, et lectionem ipsam stantes auscultant; sive ex ipsis signis venerationis Evangeliario tributis.

Psalmus responsorius

61. Post primam lectionem sequitur psalmus responsorius, qui est pars integralis liturgiæ verbi et magnum momentum liturgicum et pastorale præ se fert, cum verbi Dei meditationem foveat.

Psalmus responsorius unicuique lectioni respondeat et e lectionario de more sumatur.

---

reading from the Holy Gospel" (*Sequentia sancti evangelii*), a practice dating from at least the eleventh century.[45]

Responsorial Psalm

61. While previous recensions of *IGMR*s recognized the important and integral role of the responsorial psalm in the Liturgy of the Word, *IGMR2002* seems to go further. First, it introduces the specific subtitle "responsorial psalm" in imitation of *OLM1981-Pr* (*Psalmus responsorius*), rather than the previously employed generic subtitle "chants between the readings" (*Cantus inter lectiones occurentes, IGMR1971* and *IGMR1975*, no. 36). Second, it adds the phrase "great liturgical and pastoral importance" *(magnum momentum liturgicum et pastorale)*[46] in the opening sentence of this section. As in previous versions, *IGMR2002* notes the correspondence between the psalm and the lections, and thus prescribes that either the designated psalm of the day, a seasonal psalm, or one from the common of the saints should be employed to maintain this linkage.

The lyrical nature of this liturgical moment is underscored with a new sentence stressing the preference that the psalm, or at least the people's response, should be sung (cf. *OLM1981-Pr,* no. 20). While singing the psalm directly through without an intervening response is an option, it is clearly not preferable and "as a rule" (*de more*) the faithful sing the response.

45. Amalarius of Metz (d. 850/1) already knows the custom of the faithful signing themselves on the forehead with a cross; William of Hirsau (d. 1091) attests to the fuller practice. See Jungmann, I:452–53.

46. Both of these changes were anticipated in *OLM1981-Pr,* no. 19.

It is preferable that the responsorial Psalm be sung, at least as far as the people's response is concerned. Hence, the psalmist, or the cantor of the Psalm, sings the verses of the Psalm from the ambo or another suitable place. The entire congregation remains seated and listens but, as a rule, takes part by singing the response, except when the Psalm is sung straight through without a response. In order, however, that the people may be able to sing the Psalm response more readily, texts of some responses and Psalms have been chosen for the various seasons of the year or for the various categories of Saints. These may be used in place of the text corresponding to the reading whenever the Psalm is sung. If the Psalm cannot be sung, then it should be recited in such a way that it is particularly suited to fostering meditation on the word of God.

In the dioceses of the United States of America, the following may also be sung in place of the Psalm assigned in the *Lectionary for Mass*: either the proper or

Præstat psalmum responsorium cantu proferri, saltem ad populi responsum quod attinet. Psalmista proinde, seu cantor psalmi, in ambone vel alio loco apto profert versus psalmi, tota congregatione sedente et auscultante, immo de more per responsum participante, nisi psalmus modo directo, idest sine responso, proferatur. Ut autem populus responsum psalmodicum facilius proferre valeat, textus aliqui responsorum et psalmorum pro diversis temporibus anni aut pro diversis ordinibus Sanctorum selecti sunt, qui adhiberi valent, loco textus lectioni respondentis, quoties psalmus cantu profertur. Si psalmus cani non potest, recitatur modo aptiore ad meditationem verbi Dei fovendam.

Loco psalmi in lectionario assignati cani potest etiam vel responsorium graduale e Graduali romano, vel psalmus responsorius aut alleluiaticus e Graduali simplici, sicut in his libris describuntur.

As noted previously (see no. 50 above), new in *IGMR2002* regarding the Liturgy of the Word in general, and the responsorial psalm in particular, is attention to "meditation" (*meditatio*). Twice this paragraph notes that the responsorial psalm "fosters meditation on the word of God" (*cum verbi Dei meditationem foveat*). This is the second time (cf. no. 57 above) that *IGMR2002* suggests, albeit in an indirect way, that the psalm is something less than the actual Word of God but is rather preparatory or in service to it. On the other hand, positioning the psalmist during the proclamation of the psalm in the ambo gives a different message, given that *IGMR2002* has chosen to insert a new paragraph closely connecting the ambo with the proclamation of the Word (no. 58). The responsorial Psalm is not simply related to the Word of God, but is the Word of God. *OLM1981-Pr* is clearer, when it speaks of "the word of God speaking in the psalms" (no. 19).

Besides those substitutions for the responsorial psalm allowed in *IGMR2002*, GIRM2003 includes an approved adaptation for dioceses of the US, allowing for the use of psalms and antiphons not included in the lectionary, including metrical arrangements, provided they have episcopal approval. The prohibition against the use of other songs or hymns underscores the centrality of the Word of God here.

seasonal antiphon and Psalm from the *Lectionary*, as found either in the *Roman Gradual* or *Simple Gradual* or in another musical setting; or an antiphon and Psalm from another collection of the psalms and antiphons, including psalms arranged in metrical form, providing that they have been approved by the United States Conference of Catholic Bishops or the diocesan Bishop. Songs or hymns may not be used in place of the responsorial Psalm.

The Acclamation Before the Gospel

62. After the reading that immediately precedes the Gospel, the *Alleluia* or another chant indicated by the rubrics is sung, as required by the liturgical season. An acclamation of this kind constitutes a rite or act in itself, by which the assembly of the

Acclamatio ante lectionem Evangelii

62. Post lectionem, quæ immediate Evangelium præcedit, canitur Allelúia vel alius cantus a rubricis statutus, prouti tempus liturgicum postulat. Huiusmodi acclamatio ritum seu actum per se stantem constituit, quo fidelium cœtus Dominum

---

The Acclamation Before the Gospel

62. Most of the material in this opening paragraph is new to *IGMR2002*, largely drawn from *OLM1981-Pr*, no. 23. Valuable here is the insight that the gospel acclamation functions as the community's profession of faith in the gospel proclamation, which is a Christological act of true presence (*SC*, no. 7). From this theological vantage point, the attention here to the ritual acts of standing and singing is very appropriate. As noted above (no. 37), it is problematic that *IGMR2002* does not articulate a relationship between this acclamation and the procession of the gospel book. When the gospel book is not processed or at least raised by the deacon or priest during the acclamation, the community's ability to grasp the acclamation as a profession of faith in Christ mediated through book and proclamation is diminished. The pastoral consequence is that many assemblies interpret the gospel acclamation as mere musical accompaniment as the deacon or priest moves to the ambo.

Similar to no. 61, the legitimate options for acclamations from the Lectionary or Roman Gradual are noted. However, GIRM2003 includes no parallel adaptation for employing acclamations not found in these two sources. The 1969 *Appendix to the General Instruction for the Dioceses of the United States* lists four texts which may be employed as gospel acclamations during Lent,[47] but also notes that "similar" acclamations may be employed. This is particular law for the US which has not been revoked to date.

47. Originally found in *OLM1969-Pr*, no. 9.

faithful welcomes and greets the Lord who is about to speak to it in the Gospel and professes its faith by means of the chant. It is sung by all while standing and is led by the choir or a cantor, being repeated if this is appropriate. The verse, however, is sung either by the choir or by the cantor.

a. The *Alleluia* is sung in every season other than Lent. The verses are taken from the Lectionary or the *Gradual*.
b. During Lent, in place of the *Alleluia*, the verse before the Gospel is sung, as indicated in the Lectionary. It is also permissible to sing another psalm or tract, as found in the *Gradual*.

sibi in Evangelio locuturum excipit atque salutat fidemque suam cantu profitetur. Cantatur ab omnibus stantibus, schola vel cantore præeunte, et si casus fert, repetitur; versus vero a schola vel a cantore canitur.

a) Allelúia cantatur omni tempore extra Quadragesimam. Versus sumuntur e lectionario vel e Graduali.
b) Tempore Quadragesimæ, loco Allelúia cantatur versus ante Evangelium in lectionario exhibitus. Cani etiam potest alius psalmus seu tractus, prout invenitur in Graduali.

63. When there is only one reading before the Gospel,

a. During a season when the *Alleluia* is to be said, either the *Alleluia* Psalm or the responsorial Psalm followed by the *Alleluia* with its verse may be used;
b. During the season when the *Alleluia* is not to be said, either the psalm and the verse before the Gospel or the psalm alone may be used;
c. The *Alleluia* or verse before the Gospel may be omitted if they are not sung.

63. Quando una tantum habetur lectio ante Evangelium:

a) tempore quo dicendum est Allelúia, haberi potest aut psalmus alleluiaticus, aut psalmus et Allelúia cum suo versu;
b) tempore quo Allelúia non est dicendum, haberi potest aut psalmus et versus ante Evangelium aut psalmus tantum;
c) Allelúia vel versus ante Evangelium, si non cantantur, omitti possunt.

---

63. In listing the options when there is only one reading before the gospel, *IGMR2002* seems to restrict what was found in previous *IGMR*s. First, in seasons calling for the Alleluia, it no longer permits the use of "just the psalm, or just the Alleluia" (*tantum psalmus vel [tantum] Alleluia*, *IGMR1975*, no. 38a) but requires both in some combination. Second, in seasons when the Alleluia is not sung there is no longer the option of using simply the gospel acclamation alone; rather the psalm, either with or without the gospel acclamation, must always be used. Two important principles undergird these prescriptions: 1) the responsorial Psalm is integral to the Liturgy of the Word (no. 61), and 2) the psalm or acclamation are essentially lyrical and are to be sung (nos. 61 and 62). Thus, according to the first of these principles, it seems appropriate that this integral element should never be omitted from the Liturgy of the Word. Second, because of the essentially lyrical nature of the gospel acclamations, *IGMR2002*, like its predecessors, recognizes the incongruity of merely reciting them, and allows them to be omitted when not sung (thus correcting *OLM1981-Pr*, no. 23).

64. The Sequence, which is optional except on Easter Sunday and on Pentecost Day, is sung before the *Alleluia*.

64. Sequentia, quæ præter quam diebus Paschæ et Pentecostes, est ad libitum, cantatur ante Allelúia.

The Homily

65. The homily is part of the Liturgy and is strongly recommended,[63] for it is necessary for the nurturing of the Christian life. It should be an exposition of some aspect of the readings from Sacred Scripture or of another text from the Ordinary or from the

Homilia

65. Homilia est pars Liturgiæ et valde commendatur:[63] est enim ad nutrimentum vitæ christianæ necessaria. Sit oportet explicatio aut alicuius aspectus lectionum sacræ Scripturæ aut alterius textus ex Ordinario vel Proprio Missæ diei, ratione

---

64. In keeping with the precedent in *MR1970*, *IGMR2002* prescribes the use of only two sequences: *Victimae Paschali* for Easter and *Veni Sancte Spiritus* for Pentecost. The two other sequences in *MR2002* (*Lauda Sion* for Corpus Christi and *Stabat Mater* for the Seven Sorrows of Mary), as well as any others (e.g., *Laeta dies* for St. Benedict in the *Graduale Romanum*) are optional. *IGMR2002* directs that these are to be sung before the Alleluia. Important here is the emphasis on singing. The essential poetics of these texts can only be realized musically. Pastorally to insert the recitation of such a text before the sung Alleluia diminishes the momentum the sequence is supposed to build toward the gospel proclamation.

The Homily

65. This central paragraph on the homily draws together and clarifies some of the earlier instructions about the homily in *IGMR2002* (nos. 29 and 55). First is the strong recommendation that the homily be an ordinary part of the Eucharist; no. 66, on the other hand, makes this an obligation, not a recommendation. Next the homily is here better presented in terms of nurturing Christian life, rather than previously used more cognitive language framing the homily in terms of "explanation" (e.g., the heading before nos. 29, 55 and 67). The homily is not so much about clarifying ideas as it is about inviting the faithful and even inquirers into a deeper relationship with God through Christ; thus, it is rightly understood as an act of first evangelization[48] and re-evangelization.[49] Third, this paragraph notes the intrinsically broad scope of the homily. While there is a normative presumption that liturgical preaching engages the lectionary readings (*DV*, no. 24), *SC*, no. 52, is referenced for its recognition that it is proper to preach on other texts of the Mass and important to engage the mystery (i.e., feast or season) being celebrated. Implicit here is the historical and doctrinal reality that it is the season, feast, or ritual event that sets the lectionary in the

48. Paul VI, *Evangelii Nuntiandi,* no. 36.

49. John Paul II, *Redemtoris Missio,* no. 34 *et passim.*

Proper of the Mass of the day and should take into account both the mystery being celebrated and the particular needs of the listeners.[64]

66. The Homily should ordinarily be given by the priest celebrant himself. He may entrust it to a concelebrating priest or occasionally, according to circumstances, to the deacon, but never to a lay person.[65] In particular cases and for a just cause, the homily may even be given by a Bishop or a priest who is present at the celebration but cannot concelebrate.

There is to be a homily on Sundays and holy days of obligation at all Masses that are celebrated with the participation of a congregation; it may not be omitted without a serious reason. It is recommended on other days, especially on the weekdays of Advent, Lent, and the Easter Season, as well as on other festive days and occasions

habita sive mysterii, quod celebratur, sive peculiarium necessitatum auditorum.[64]

66. Homilia de more ab ipso sacerdote celebrante habeatur vel ab eo committatur sacerdoti concelebranti, vel quandoque, pro opportunitate, etiam diacono, numquam vero laico.[65] In casibus peculiaribus iustaque de causa homilia haberi potest etiam ab Episcopo vel presbytero qui celebrationi interest quin concelebrare possit.

Diebus dominicis et festis de præcepto homilia habenda est nec omitti potest nisi gravi de causa, in omnibus Missis, quæ concurrente populo celebrantur; ceteris vero diebus commendatur, præsertim in feriis Adventus, Quadragesimæ et temporis paschalis, necnon in aliis festis et occasionibus, in quibus populus frequentior ad ecclesiam convenit.[66]

Catholic tradition.[50] The US bishops actually go further in noting the appropriateness of preaching not only on the "sacred texts"[51] but the liturgical rites themselves (ITTOM, no. 92.). Finally, in reiterating the claim that the homily should take into account the particular needs of the listeners, *IGMR2002* recognizes the homily as a local act of contextual theology, a principle that has broad ramifications for the whole of the eucharistic celebration. The implicit pastoral standard is that any pattern of preaching which does not explicitly engage the actual situation of a local faith community is not fulfilling the fundamental requirements of liturgical preaching.

66. The first paragraph of this article is new. *DV* notes that the homily is reserved to a priest or deacon (no. 24), a prescription repeated in *CIC1983*, c. 767. *IGMR2002* goes further in giving homiletic priority first to the presider, then to another concelebrant, and only by exception to the deacon. The latter seems to downplay the central role of preaching in diaconal ministry, made clear in the ordination rite when they are handed the gospel book and called heralds of Christ's Gospel.[52] The US bishops give more prominence to the deacon as

50. For example, RCIA, no. 146, which notes that the gospels assigned in Cycle A for the third, fourth and fifth Sundays of Lent must be used no matter when the scrutinies occur in the cycle of the Church year. See Fritz West, *Scripture and Memory: The Ecumenical Hermeneutic of the Three-Year Lectionaries* (Collegeville, MN: The Liturgical Press, 1997).

51. See n. 5 above.

52. *Rites of Ordination*, second typical edition (Washington, DC: USCCB, 2003), no. 208.

when the people come to church in greater numbers.[66]

After the homily a brief period of silence is appropriately observed.

Opportune post homiliam breve spatium silentii servatur.

The Profession of Faith

67. The purpose of the *Symbolum* or Profession of Faith, or Creed, is that the whole gathered people may respond to the word of God proclaimed in the readings taken from Sacred Scripture and explained in the

Professio fidei

67. Symbolum seu professio fidei eo tendit ut universus populus congregatus verbo Dei in lectionibus e sacra Scriptura nuntiato et per homiliam exposito respondeat, et ut, regulam fidei proferendo, formula pro usu

---

preacher, and list him before any concelebrating priest (ITTOM, no. 94). While laypeople can be permitted to preach (*CIC1983*, c. 766), even after the gospel during a eucharistic liturgy,[53] such preaching does not fulfill the legal definition of a homily.[54]

This second paragraph, found in previous *IGMR*s, notes what could be considered the normative role of the homily on Sundays and holy days (in stronger terms than no. 65 above), and its recommended nature on weekdays, during high holy seasons (e.g., Advent and Lent), and on other festivals. Pastoral sensitivity suggests that communities should be able to perceive the normative nature of Sunday and holy day preaching, ordinarily distinguished from weekday preaching, for example, in its length. A final new sentence reiterates the call for silence after the homily, noted in no. 56 above.

The Profession of Faith

67. While repeating much of what appeared in previous *IGMR*s, this paragraph in *IGMR2002* introduces some subtle changes. First, the expansion of "people" (*populus, IGMR1975*, no. 43) to "whole gathered people" (*universus populus congregatus*), emphasizes that the Creed is a joint response of faith to the Word of God made by everyone gathered, ministry and assembly, and not just the faithful. The nature of this response is also more richly explained as both calling to mind and confirming the great mysteries of faith. The rewritten phrase "before these mysteries are celebrated in the Eucharist" (*antequam eorum celebratio in Eucharistia incipiatur*)[55] needs to be understood in a way that it does

53. *Directory for Masses with Children*, no. 24.

54. Cf. James Coriden, "The Teaching Office of the Church," *The Code of Canon Law: A Text and Commentary*, ed., James Coriden et al. (New York: Paulist Press, 1985), 553; John Huels, "Lay Preaching at Liturgy," *More Disputed Questions in the Liturgy* (Chicago: Liturgy Training Publications, 1996), 182; James Provost, "Brought together by the Word of the Living God," *Studia canonica* 23 (1989): 361.

55. *IGMR1971* and *IGMR1975* have "before they begin to celebrate the Eucharist" (*antequam [populus] Eucharistiam celebrare incipiat*, no. 43).

homily and that they may also call to mind and confess the great mysteries of the faith by reciting the rule of faith in a formula approved for liturgical use, before these mysteries are celebrated in the Eucharist.

68. The Creed is to be sung or said by the priest together with the people on Sundays and Solemnities. It may be said also at particular celebrations of a more solemn character.

If it is sung, it is begun by the priest or, if this is appropriate, by a cantor or by the choir. It is sung, however, either by all together or by the people alternating with the choir.

If not sung, it is to be recited by all together or by two parts of the assembly responding one to the other.

liturgico probata, magna fidei mysteria recolat et confiteatur, antequam eorum celebratio in Eucharistia incipiatur.

68. Symbolum cantandum vel dicendum est a sacerdote cum populo diebus dominicis et in sollemnitatibus; dici potest etiam in peculiaribus celebrationibus sollemnioribus.

Si in cantu profertur, inchoatur a sacerdote vel, pro opportunitate, a cantore, aut a schola, cantatur autem vel ab omnibus simul, vel a populo alternatim cum schola.

Si non cantatur, recitandum est ab omnibus simul aut a duobus choris sibi invicem respondentibus.

---

not appear to limit the celebration of the great mysteries of faith to the second part of the Mass, i.e., the Liturgy of the Eucharist. For example, while the Eucharistic Prayer is a privileged moment for celebrating the paschal mystery, that mystery permeates the whole of the Eucharist and also Sunday itself, which *SC* teaches to be a special paschal feast (no. 106). Finally, as previously noted, the unfortunate characterization of the homily as an *exposito* of the Scriptures does not respect the scope of the homily outlined in *SC*, no. 54 (cf. no. 65 above).[56]

68. The underlying principle for the performance of the Creed is that this faith response belongs to the whole people gathered (cf. no. 67 above). Thus, while *IGMR2002* newly notes that, if it is sung it can be begun by priest, cantor, or choir, the people are yet to be centrally engaged in this profession; it is never to be performed by liturgical musicians apart from the assembly. While previous editions of *IGMR* note that the Creed could be sung alternately with the choir, *IGMR2002* also adds that if recited it is possible for two parts of the assembly to perform it responsorially. This ritual direction seems to recognize the pastoral problems that sometimes plague this liturgical element so often marked by lifeless repetition. If the text is so divided, care must be taken so that the literary division respects the integrity of the various mysteries and doctrine embedded in the Creed. Though not referenced here, the permission in DMC for the use of the Apostles' Creed in Masses with children (no. 49) is still in force.

56. ITTOM is better here when it notes that in the creed "people respond and assent to the word of God heard in the readings and the homily," no. 95.

The Prayer of the Faithful

69. In the Prayer of the Faithful, the people respond in a certain way to the word of God which they have welcomed in faith and, exercising the office of their baptismal priesthood, offer prayers to God for the salvation of all. It is fitting that such a prayer be included, as a rule, in Masses celebrated with a congregation, so that petitions will be offered for the holy Church, for civil authorities, for those weighed down by various needs, for all men and women, and for the salvation of the whole world.[67]

70. As a rule, the series of intentions is to be

a. For the needs of the Church;
b. For public authorities and the salvation of the whole world;

Oratio universalis

69. In oratione universali, seu oratione fidelium, populus, verbo Dei in fide suscepto quodammodo respondet et, sui sacerdotii baptismalis munus exercens, preces Deo offert pro salute omnium. Expedit ut huiusmodi oratio in Missis cum populo de more habeatur, ita ut obsecrationes fiant pro sancta Ecclesia, pro iis qui in potestate nos regunt, pro iis qui variis premuntur necessitatibus, ac pro omnibus hominibus totiusque mundi salute.[67]

70. Intentionum series de more sint:
a) pro necessitatibus Ecclesiæ,
b) pro rem publicam moderantibus et salute totius mundi,
c) pro oppressis quacumque difficultate,

The Prayer of the Faithful

69. This central paragraph on the prayer of the faithful offers one of the broadest missionary perspectives to be found in *IGMR2002*. Intimately connected with "the office of their baptismal priesthood" (*sui sacerdotii baptismalis munus*),[57] this prayer is not presented simply as an act of Christian charity, but as a ritual confirmation of what *AG* recognizes is the duty of the faithful: to cooperate in the missionary activity of the church and to "have a lively awareness of their responsibility to the world" (no. 36). Both the inclusion of this prayer within the Eucharist and the breadth of the petitions of this prayer beyond local need (outlined both in nos. 69 and 70) are normative, as they rehearse liturgically the assembly's individual and collective responsibilities to those in need. Thus the US bishops wisely note that the intentions "should look beyond the concerns of the local congregation to the needs of the whole Church and of the wider world" (ITTOM, no. 97). Such a response to the Word of God enables the community to pray more effectively the Liturgy of the Eucharist, and to live more effectively the "liturgy of the world."[58]

70. Two things need be noted about the series of intentions outlined here. First is the expansive nature of each of the four areas. For example, "needs of the church" (*necessitatibus Ecclesiae*) is much broader than the hierarchy, and

57. *IGMR1975* has *sui sacerdotii munus*, no. 45.

58. Karl Rahner, "Considerations on the Active Role of the Person in the Sacramental Event," in *Theological Investigations XIV: Ecclesiology, Questions in the Church, The Church in the World*, trans. David Bourke (New York: Seabury Press, 1976), 169.

c. For those burdened by any kind of difficulty;

d. For the local community.

Nevertheless, in a particular celebration, such as Confirmation, Marriage, or a Funeral, the series of intentions may reflect more closely the particular occasion.

d) pro communitate locali.

Attamen in celebratione aliqua particulari, uti Confirmatione, Matrimonio, Exsequiis, ordo intentionum pressius respicere potest particularem occasionem.

71. It is for the priest celebrant to direct this prayer from the chair. He himself begins it with a brief introduction, by which he invites the faithful to pray, and likewise he concludes it with a prayer. The intentions announced should be sober, be composed freely but prudently, and be succinct, and they should express the prayer of the entire community.

The intentions are announced from the ambo or from another suitable place, by the deacon or by a cantor, a lector, or one of the lay faithful.[68]

71. Est sacerdotis celebrantis precationem a sede moderari. Ipse eam brevi monitione introducit, qua fideles ad orandum invitat, ipsamque oratione concludit. Intentiones quæ proponuntur sint sobriæ, sapienti libertate et paucis verbis compositæ et precationem universæ communitatis exprimant.

Proferuntur ex ambone aut ex alio loco convenienti, a diacono vel a cantore vel a lectore, vel a fideli laico.[68]

"public authorities" (*rem republicam*) encompasses more than elected officials. Thus, the pastoral crafting of these intentions requires both imagination and attentiveness to larger ecclesial and societal needs. Prefabricated, published models are ordinarily insufficient. Second, while *IGMR*s have always recognized the need to shape some intentions for the needs of a particular celebration, *IGMR2002* and its predecessors neither suggest nor allow for every intention to be so designed. All the examples listed in this article as particular celebrations, while intensely personal, are also ecclesial events and the phrasing of the petitions must demonstrate some awareness of and commitment in prayer to those beyond the local assembly. Fostering such awareness should mark the catechesis for celebrations such as marriages and confirmations.

71. There are some textual implications in this article that could suggest that the priest-presider does not have an active role throughout this prayer.[59] Since it is clear that he is not the one who announces the intentions (cf. no. 264 below), it is presumed that he responds to each intention with the chosen invocation along with the faithful. The people's response in silence to the announcement of the invocations when employing the classic Roman form of this prayer (only employed in the Good Friday liturgy) is appropriate both because of the structure

59. E.g., 1) the emphasis on this prayer as an exercise of the *sacerdoti baptismalis munus* (no. 69); 2) this number which only indicates the priest presider introducing and concluding the prayer; 3) this number which only speaks of the people offering an invocation after each intention; and 4) the problematic translation of *oratio universalis* as "Prayer of the Faithful" in GIRM2003.

The people, however, stand and give expression to their prayer either by an invocation said together after each intention or by praying in silence.

Populus vero stans precationem suam exprimit sive invocatione communi post singulas intentiones prolatas, sive orando sub silentio.

C. The Liturgy of the Eucharist

72. At the Last Supper Christ instituted the Paschal Sacrifice and banquet, by which the Sacrifice of the Cross is continuously made present in the Church whenever the priest, representing Christ the Lord, carries out what the Lord himself did and handed over to his disciples to be done in his memory.[69]

C) Liturgia eucharistica

72. In Cena novissima, Christus sacrificium et convivium paschale instituit, quo sacrificium crucis in Ecclesia continue præsens efficitur, cum sacerdos, Christum Dominum repræsentans, idem perficit quod ipse Dominus egit atque discipulis in sui memoriam faciendum tradidit.[69]

---

and also the traditional performance of that prayer, which included the people's "Amen" at the close of every oration which concluded each intention. Otherwise, silence is a less-than-appropriate response to the prayer of the faithful in light of *SC*, no. 14, and the people should join with the ministry in speaking an invocation after each intention as well as their "Amen" after the concluding oration.

The Liturgy of the Eucharist[60]

72. This largely unchanged article corresponds to nos. 46, 55 and 90, providing an overview of the underlying purpose and function of a major ritual unit in the eucharistic liturgy. Here the focus is on the Liturgy of the Eucharist proper. It begins by affirming that during the Last Supper Christ instituted a "Paschal Sacrifice and banquet" (*sacrificium et convivium paschale instituit*). While respecting the once-and-for-all sacrifice on the cross, all *IGMR*s uphold the belief that this sacrifice is yet "continually made present to the church" (*in Ecclesia continue praesens efficitur*) as a sacrament of this sacrifice. According to *IGMR*, this occurs "whenever the priest, representing Christ the Lord, carries out what the Lord himself did and handed over to his disciples to be done in his memory" (*cum sacerdos, Christum Dominum repraesentans, idem perficit quod ipse Dominus egit atque discipulis in sui memoriam faciendum tradidit*). This assertion, present in previous *IGMR*s, needs to be placed in the larger theological framework set out in *SC* that "every liturgical celebration . . . is an action of Christ the priest and of his body, which is the church" (no. 7). All *IGMR*s have been clear that at the heart of the eucharistic action the whole assembly joins with Christ "in the offering of Sacrifice" (*in oblatione sacrificii*, no. 78 below; also Power-Vincie, 51 above). Indeed, neither of the two documents footnoted at the end of this paragraph make mention of the priest representing Christ in this action. Rather,

60. The commentary on nos. 72–90 is indebted to a preliminary draft by our colleague Michael Joncas. We are grateful for his help and collaboration.

For Christ took the bread and the chalice and gave thanks; he broke the bread and gave it to his disciples, saying, "Take, eat, and drink: this is my Body; this is the cup of my Blood. Do this in memory of me." Accordingly, the Church has arranged the entire celebration of the Liturgy of the Eu-

Christus enim accepit panem et calicem, gratias egit, fregit deditque discipulis suis, dicens: Accipite, manducate, bibite; hoc est Corpus meum; hic est calix Sanguinis mei. Hoc facite in meam commemorationem. Proinde Ecclesia totam celebrationem Liturgiæ eucharisticæ partibus hisce Christi

---

SC speaks of Christ perpetuating the sacrifice of the cross by entrusting it "to his beloved spouse, the church" (no. 47), a theological position reiterated in *Eucharisticum mysterium* (no. 3a). The tendency to focus on the priest as the apparent lone subject of the eucharistic action is indicative of the previously noted underdeveloped linkage between the ministerial priesthood and the common priesthood of the baptized in this document (Power-Vincie, 59–60 above). Finally, it should be noted that GIRM2003 inexplicably capitalizes "Paschal Sacrifice" and "Sacrifice of the Cross," though such capitalizations do not occur in the Latin. This could appear to stress "Sacrifice" over "banquet" (which is not capitalized) though *Eucharisticum mysterium* itself is clear that "In the Mass . . . the sacrifice and sacred meal belong to the same mystery—so much so that they are linked by the closest bond" (no. 3b).

The second paragraph conflates the multiple New Testament accounts of the Last Supper and the words of Jesus into a single narrative. This is understandable in an Instruction, although the readers need be aware of the historical-critical issues here. Four are particularly important: 1) like the sacrifice on Calvary, the Last Supper was a once-and-for-all event that cannot be repeated; 2) since it was an event, there is no *Urtext* of the Last Supper,[61] no agreement in the New Testament on the exact words spoken by Jesus, and no scholarly consensus on the same; 3) structurally the Church's Eucharist is significantly different from the rite of the Last Supper which included a full meal and two separate "sacramental" acts with a blessing of God over the bread before the meal and the blessing of God over the cup of wine following the meal,[62] and 4) it was not only the Last Supper but also the multitude of table experiences, the multiplication events, the post-resurrectional meals, and the table experiences of the early community which shaped Christian Eucharist.[63] These provide an indispensable hermeneutic for understanding the assertion in *IGMR* about the Church arranging the Eucharist to correspond to the words and actions of Christ. Furthermore, GIRM2003's translation of "precisely these words and

61. Despite attempts to establish one by scholars such as Joachim Jeremias in his *The Eucharistic Words of Jesus,* trans. Norman Perrin (Philadelphia: Fortress Press, 1966).

62. See Enrico Mazza, *The Celebration of the Eucharist,* trans. Matthew J. O'Connell (Collegeville, MN: The Liturgical Press, 1999), 21.

63. See, for example, Eugene LaVerdiere's treatment of the ten meals in the Gospel of Luke in his *Dining in the Kingdom of God* (Chicago: Liturgy Training Publications, 1994).

charist in parts corresponding to precisely these words and actions of Christ:

1. At the Preparation of the Gifts, the bread and the wine with water are brought to the altar, the same elements that Christ took into his hands.
2. In the Eucharistic Prayer, thanks is given to God for the whole work of salvation, and the offerings become the Body and Blood of Christ.

verbis et actibus respondentibus ordinavit. Siquidem:

1) In præparatione donorum, ad altare afferuntur panis et vinum cum aqua, ea nempe elementa, quæ Christus in manus suas accepit.
2) In Prece eucharistica Deo pro toto opere salutis gratiæ aguntur, et oblata Christi Corpus et Sanguis fiunt.

---

actions" (*hisce Christi verbis et actibus*) is misleading, both because it is an exaggerated translation (better would have been "these very words and actions") as well as because of the previously noted fact that we do not know precisely what Jesus said or did at the Last Supper.

IGMR2002 accepts the commonly held position, outlined by Gregory Dix, that the "seven-action scheme" of the Last Supper[64] is mirrored in the current structure of the eucharistic liturgy in a modified "four-action scheme": 1) taking bread and wine, 2) blessing God over bread and wine, 3) breaking bread, and 4) giving broken bread and a cup of wine. *IGMR* presents these four actions under three headings, since both the breaking and the giving occur during a single structural unit of the Eucharist, i.e., the Communion rite. This is a very useful analogy and quite helpful, for example, as the basis for mystagogical reflection on the Eucharist. The previously noted historical-critical issues, however, also need to be operative for understanding properly this paragraph. For example, while the bread and wine we employ in Eucharist are analogous to "the same elements that Christ took into his hands" (*ea nempe elementa, quae Christus in manus suas accepit*), they are also different. For example, since we do not know whether the Last Supper was a Passover meal, we do not know if the bread employed was leavened or unleavened. Furthermore, it is probable (though also not precisely known) that the bread employed at the Last Supper was barley not wheat bread, since that supper occurred in a Passover context which coincided with the first (barley) harvest of the spring in Israel. A similar caution applies to *IGMR*'s description of Communion in which the faithful receive the bread and chalice "in the same way the Apostles received them from Christ's own hands" (*eodem modo ac Apostoli de manibus ipsius Christi).* Christ seems to have passed his own cup, which moved from one disciple to another—something expressly forbidden to the faithful by *IGMR2002*, no. 160 (cf. *RedSac*, no. 94).

64. Jesus 1) took bread, 2) gave thanks over it, 3) broke it, 4) distributed it saying certain words, 5) took a cup, 6) gave thanks over it, and 7) handed it to his disciples saying certain words. In Gregory Dix, *The Shape of the Liturgy* (London: Dacre Press, 1945), 48.

3. Through the fraction and through Communion, the faithful, though they are many, receive from the one bread the Lord's Body and from the one chalice the Lord's Blood in the same way the Apostles received them from Christ's own hands.

3) Per fractionem panis et per Communionem fideles, quamvis multi, ex uno pane accipiunt Corpus et ex uno calice Sanguinem Domini eodem modo ac Apostoli de manibus ipsius Christi.

The Preparation of the Gifts

73. At the beginning of the Liturgy of the Eucharist the gifts, which will become Christ's Body and Blood, are brought to the altar.

First, the altar, the Lord's table, which is the center of the whole Liturgy of the Eucharist,[70] is prepared by placing on it the corporal, purificator, Missal, and chalice

Præparatio donorum

73. Initio Liturgiæ eucharisticæ dona, quæ Corpus et Sanguis Christi efficientur, ad altare afferuntur.

Imprimis altare, seu mensa dominica, quæ centrum est totius liturgiæ eucharisticæ,[70] præparatur, cum corporale, purificatorium, missale et calix, nisi ad abacum paratur, in eo collocantur.

Valuable is *IGMR*'s continued affirmation of the importance of sharing both the bread and the chalice as a presumed, even normative vision of Communion for the faithful (see nos. 281–84 below). *IGMR2002* even inserts a specific reference to the faithful receiving from "one chalice" (*ex uno calice*) not found in previous *IGMR*s. However, it also eliminates the rich theological comment found in previous *IGMR*s that through the breaking of the one bread "the unity of the faithful is expressed" (*unitas fidelium manifestatur, IGMR1975*, no. 48.3).

The Preparation of the Gifts

73. Largely unchanged from previous editions, this first of five articles on the preparation of the gifts elaborates how the gifts are to be brought to the altar. *IGMR2002* employs both the terms "altar" (*altare*) and "Lord's table" (*mensa dominica*), reiterating the essential and intimate relationship between the Paschal Sacrifice and banquet (see no. 72 above) which take place there. In this preparatory moment, corporal, purificator, missal, and chalice are brought to the altar (no. 139 below will add "pall"), indicating that before this none of these elements were to have been there; until this moment, the only element permitted on the table had been the gospel book (see no. 117 below) which was moved to the ambo during the gospel procession. The US bishops offer the useful comment that these items should be brought reverently but without ceremony from a side table (ITTOM, no. 103). *IGMR2002* notes the exception that the chalice may be left at the "credence table" (*abacum*) if the deacon chooses to prepare the chalice there (see no. 178 below). *IGMR2002* does not prescribe the use of any stand for the altar missal; these have become customary in some places and are not explicitly forbidden.

(unless the chalice is prepared at the credence table).

The offerings are then brought forward. It is praiseworthy for the bread and wine to be presented by the faithful. They are then accepted at an appropriate place by the priest or the deacon and carried to the altar. Even though the faithful no longer bring from their own possessions the bread and wine intended for the liturgy as in the past, nevertheless the rite of carrying up the offerings still retains its force and its spiritual significance.

It is well also that money or other gifts for the poor or for the Church, brought by the faithful or collected in the church, should be received. These are to be put in a suitable place but away from the Eucharistic table.

Oblationes deinde afferuntur: panis et vinum laudabiliter a fidelibus præsentantur, a sacerdote autem vel a diacono loco opportuno accipiuntur ad altare deferenda. Quamvis fideles panem et vinum ad liturgiam destinata non iam de suis proferant sicut olim, ritus tamen illa deferendi vim et significationem spiritualem servat.

Etiam pecunia vel alia dona pro pauperibus vel pro ecclesia a fidelibus allata vel in ecclesia collecta accepta habentur; quapropter loco apto extra mensam eucharisticam collocantur.

Like its predecessors, *IGMR2002* considers it "praiseworthy" (*laudabiliter*) that the bread and wine are presented by the faithful. On the change in the language here from "gifts" (*dona*) to "offerings" (*oblationes*), see no. 178 below. The Instruction also approves the custom that money or other gifts collected in the church be brought up by the faithful. Notable is the comment that these gifts are first designated "for the poor" (*pauperibus*) and then "for the church" (*pro ecclesia*). A mission trajectory is implicit here, both in the elements of bread and wine and in the monetary or other gifts brought forth at this time. Thus the US bishops speak about this whole procession of gifts as "a powerful expression of the participation of all present in the Eucharist and in the social mission of the church" (ITTOM, no. 105).[65] For this ritual to achieve such power, it is necessary for a worshiping community to have a sustained and recognizable commitment to the poor and oppressed that both extends outside of worship and also has explicitly been brought to prayer in the liturgy (see no. 69 above). It is only then that *IGMR*'s vision of this procession of gifts as a ritual action that still retains "its force and its spiritual significance" (*vim et significationem spiritualem*) can be realized.

65. In their pastoral letter, *Economic Justice for All* (1986), the US bishops elaborated on the intimate connection between Eucharist and care for the poor, noting "The unity of work and worship finds expression in a unique way in the Eucharist. As people of a new covenant, the faithful hear God's challenging word proclaimed to them—a message of hope to the poor and oppressed—and they call upon the Holy Spirit to unite all into one body of Christ. For the Eucharist to be a living promise of the fullness of God's Kingdom, the faithful must commit themselves to living as redeemed people with the same care and love for all people that Jesus showed" (no. 330).

74. The procession bringing the gifts is accompanied by the Offertory chant (cf. no. 37b), which continues at least until the gifts have been placed on the altar. The norms on the manner of singing are the same as for the Entrance chant (cf. no. 48). Singing may always accompany the rite at the offertory, even when there is no procession with the gifts.

74. Processionem, qua dona afferuntur, cantus ad offertorium comitatur *(cf. n. 37, b)*, qui protrahitur saltem usquedum dona super altare deposita sunt. Normæ de modo cantandi eædem sunt ac pro cantu ad introitum *(cf. n. 48)*. Cantus potest semper ritus ad offertorium sociare, etiam sine processione cum donis.

On one other point, *IGMR2002* makes a slight change from previous editions. *IGMR1975* indicates that the gifts of bread and wine, brought up by the faithful, are to be "accepted by the priest or deacon at a convenient place. The gifts are placed on the altar to the accompaniment of the prescribed texts" (*sacerdote autem vel a diacono loco opportuno accipiuntur et super altare deponuntur commitantibus formulis statuti*, no. 49). *IGMR2002* is no more specific about the place where the gifts are to be accepted by the priest or deacon, merely indicating that this is to be "an appropriate place" (*loco opportuno*). The addition of the phrase "and carried to the altar" (*ad altare deferenda*), however, makes it clear that the only ones allowed to place the elements on the altar are the priest and deacon. This prescription finds parallels in the Communion rite, where *IGMR2002* newly prescribes that the faithful never take the consecrated elements by themselves at Communion (see no. 160 below) and that extraordinary ministers of Communion never take consecrated elements from the altar, but only receive them from the hands of the priest (see no. 162 below). This is another place where *IGMR2002* seems concerned to make a clear distinction between the ministerial priesthood and the common priesthood of the baptized.

The monetary offerings or other gifts for the poor are "to be put in a suitable place but away from the Eucharistic table" (*quapropter loco apto extra mensam eucharisticam collocantur*), signifying that these do not have the same ritual status as the bread and wine.

74. This article provides principles for the music that is to accompany the procession and preparation of the gifts. We have previously noted the problem with the term "chant at Offertory" (*cantus ad offertorium*) for the song that accompanies these preparation rites (see no. 37 above). *IGMR2002* notes that the music continues "at least" (*saltem*) until the gifts have been placed on the table, but it is not limited to the accompaniment of the procession. Thus, in a new addition to this article, *IGMR2002* instructs that singing (*cantus*) may always accompany these rites, "even when there is no procession with the gifts" (*etiam sine processione cum donis*). As to how the music is to be performed, this article references no. 48, and indicates that "the norms on the manner of singing" (*normae de modo cantandi*) are identical to those outlined for the entrance chant. This would mean that, for dioceses in the US, the approved adaptations for the

75. The bread and wine are placed on the altar by the priest to the accompaniment of the prescribed formulas. The priest may incense the gifts placed upon the altar and then incense the cross and the altar itself, so as to signify the Church's offering and prayer rising like incense in the sight of God. Next, the priest, because of his sacred ministry, and the people, by reason of their baptismal dignity, may be incensed by the deacon or another minister.

75. Panis et vinum super altare a sacerdote deponuntur comitantibus formulis statutis; sacerdos dona super altare collocata incensare potest, dein crucem et ipsum altare, ut oblatio Ecclesiæ eiusque oratio sicut incensum in conspectum Dei ascendere significentur. Deinde sacerdos, propter sacrum ministerium, et populus, ratione baptismalis dignitatis, incensari possunt a diacono vel ab alio ministro.

---

entrance chant would also apply. However, this does not resolve the quandary of what to do with the *antiphona ad offertorium* if there is no singing. Number 48, implicitly recognizing that such an antiphon is "too abrupt for communal recitation" (Foreword, GIRM1975), allows the entrance antiphon to be adapted into the priest's introductory comments. Since the priest-presider makes no such comments at the preparation of the gifts, this option is not available here. Furthermore, *IGMR2002* eliminates the resolution found in *IGMR1975* that "if it is not sung, the presentation antiphon is omitted" (*Si non cantatur, antiphona ad offertorium omittitur*, no. 50).

This article gives no direction concerning what may be a suitable text (see no. 48 above) outside of those provided in the *Roman* or *Simple Gradual*. The US bishops provide some direction here when they suggest that texts "not speak of bread and wine, nor of offering" but express "joy, praise, community, as well as the spirit of the season" (ITTOM, no. 105). They also permit instrumental music, which *IGMR2002* does not mention here, although in a parallel passage it speaks of organ music (no. 142 below). Finally, the US bishops note that "silence may also be effective" (ITTOM, no. 105). This suggestion recalls the note in the 1969 *Appendix to the General Instruction* for the US which recognized that during the preparation of the gifts "it is good to give the assembly a period of quiet . . . before demanding at the preface, their full attention to the eucharistic prayer" (no. 50).

75. This article, like its parallel in *IGMR1975* (no. 51), is largely concerned with the optional act of incensation. The current Instruction introduces the article with the new and somewhat confusing sentence, "the bread and wine are placed on the altar by the priest to the accompaniment of the prescribed formulas" (*Panis et vinum super altare a sacerdote deponuntur comitantibus formulis statutis*). Since there are no prescribed texts for placing the elements on the altar (which no. 73 indicates can be done by a priest or deacon), this text must refer to the *berakoth* prayers recited (quietly or aloud, cf. nos. 141 and 142 below) after the elements have been placed on the altar.

76. The priest then washes his hands at the side of the altar, a rite that is an expression of his desire for interior purification.

76. Deinde sacerdos manus lavat ad latus altaris, quo ritu desiderium internæ purificationis exprimitur.

The Prayer over the Offerings

77. Once the offerings have been placed on the altar and the accompanying rites completed, the invitation to pray with the priest and the prayer over the offerings conclude the preparation of the gifts and prepare for the Eucharistic Prayer.

In the Mass, only one Prayer over the Offerings is said, and it ends with the shorter conclusion: *Per Christum Dominum nostrum (Through Christ our Lord)*. If, however, the Son is mentioned at the end of this prayer, the conclusion is, *Qui vivit et regnat in saecula saeculorum (Who lives and reigns forever and ever)*.

Oratio super oblata

77. Depositione oblatorum facta et ritibus qui eam comitantur perfectis, per invitationem ad orandum una cum sacerdote et per orationem super oblata præparatio donorum concluditur et Prex eucharistica præparatur.

In Missa unica dicitur oratio super oblata, quæ concluditur conclusione breviore, idest: Per Christum Dóminum nostrum; si vero in fine ipsius fit mentio Filii: Qui vivit et regnat in sǽcula sæculórum.

Regarding the optional incensation, *IGMR2002* reiterates the fundamental meaning of this act, derived from Psalm 141, which signifies the offering and the prayer of the community rising in the sight of God. In addition to what is found in *IGMR1975* (no. 51), the current Instruction adds that the cross is incensed after the gifts; this addition is parallel to that in no. 49 above. As in previous *IGMR*s, the current Instruction then notes that the priest and people may be incensed by a deacon or other minister. What is new here are the theological rationales for this incensation: the priest is incensed "because of his sacred ministry" (*propter sacrum ministerium*) while the people are incensed "by reason of their baptismal dignity" (*ratione baptismalis dignitatis*). Here is another example of *IGMR2002* drawing clear distinctions between the ministerial priesthood and the common priesthood of the baptized.

76. A very brief sentence notes that the priest then washes his hands "as an expression of his desire for interior purification" (*desiderium internae purificationis exprimitur*), correcting the theory that this act was originally only a functional necessity after the celebrating priest had received the various offerings of the faithful. This emphasis on personal purification also reveals the secondary nature of this deprecatory act (see no. 33 above), which *IGMR2002* acknowledges by adding that this personal ritual should take place "at the side of the altar" (*ad latus altaris*).

The Prayer over the Offerings

77. This presidential prayer brings the liturgical unit of the preparation of the gifts to a close. Its role as the apex of these preparatory rites is underscored

The people, uniting themselves to this entreaty, make the prayer their own with the acclamation, *Amen*.

Populus, precationi se coniungens, acclamatione Amen orationem facit suam.

The Eucharistic Prayer

78. Now the center and summit of the entire celebration begins: namely, the Eucharistic Prayer, that is, the prayer of

Prex eucharistica

78. Nunc centrum et culmen totius celebrationis initium habet, ipsa nempe Prex eucharistica, prex scilicet gratiarum actio-

---

by the fact that it is the only prayer during the preparation of the gifts that is required to be proclaimed aloud,[66] and it is the only prayer during this ritual unit that requires a response from the assembly (unless the presider exercises the option to speak the *berakoth* aloud) and to which they affix their "Amen." For this reason, it seems appropriate that *IGMR2002* provides a separate subheading for this article ("The Prayer over the Offerings," *Oratio super oblata*), although this should not be interpreted as removing this prayer from the preparation rites, but rather as acknowledging it to be the climax of these rites.

Besides concluding these rites, this prayer also serves to "prepare for the Eucharistic Prayer" (*Prex eucharistica praeparatur*). Here *IGMR2002*, like its predecessors, notes the transitional role of this prayer and, by extension, of the whole preparatory unit which serves as a prelude to the central act of thanksgiving.

This article twice emphasizes that this presidential prayer is offered by the priest in the name of the whole assembly (cf. no. 30 above): first, by describing the *Orate fratres* as "the invitation to pray with the priest" (*per invitationem ad orandum una cum sacerdote*), and second by noting that with their acclamatory Amen, "the people . . . make the prayer their own" (*Populus . . . orationem facit suam*). The latter is an addition not found in *IGMR1975*. A further addition here is a paragraph which prescribes that only one prayer over the offering is said, and notes that only two brief conclusions are used with this prayer, distinguishing these from the concluding formulae for the opening prayer (see no. 54 above).

The Eucharistic Prayer

78. In three key sentences, repeated verbatim from previous versions of *IGMRs*, this focal article provides an overview of the nature of the Eucharistic Prayer, speaks to the dynamics of its performance, and offers a pivotal inter-

66. *MR2002* (nos. 23 and 25) instructs that the *berakoth* over the gifts are said "in a low voice" (*submissa voce dicens*), and that if there is no singing the priest "may speak these words aloud" (*licet haec verba elata voce proferre*), but this is neither required nor is the first option. Similarly that book notes that all other prayers at the preparation by priest or deacon are said *secreto* (nos. 24 and 26).

thanksgiving and sanctification. The priest invites the people to lift up their hearts to the Lord in prayer and thanksgiving; he unites the congregation with himself in the

nis et sanctificationis. Sacerdos populum ad corda versus Dominum in oratione et gratiarum actione elevanda invitat eumque sibi sociat in oratione, quam nomine totius

---

pretation of the liturgical significance of this prayer. First, regarding the nature of the prayer, this article declares that the Eucharistic Prayer is the "center and summit of the entire celebration" (*centrum et culmen totius celebrationis*). Such language appears to be a clear evocation of *SC* which, although not footnoted here, similarly refers to the liturgy (especially the Eucharist) as the "summit toward which the activity of the church is directed" (*culmen ad quod actio Ecclesiae tendit*). Analogously, the Eucharistic Prayer is to the eucharistic liturgy as the liturgy itself is to the church: its center and summit. For this theological assertion to be realized in praxis demands clear pastoral planning as well as mature performative skills on the part of the presider, particularly regarding the ritual embodiment (see no. 42 above) and proclamation of this prayer in a dynamic and engaging manner (see no. 38 above). Otherwise, this theological vision will remain unrealized.[67]

Regarding the nature of the prayer, *IGMR* further defines the prayer as one of "thanksgiving and sanctification" (*gratiarum actionis et sanctificationis*). Different from the old Roman Canon (revised as Eucharistic Prayer I in *MR1970* and subsequent *MR*s) in which intercession is dominant, the recovery here of the ancient understanding of the Eucharistic Prayer as the great thanksgiving reflects the influence of sustained scholarship exploring this pivotal eucharistic moment.[68]

Concerning its performance, all *IGMR*s stress that the presider is the ritual initiator of the Eucharistic Prayer which begins with the preface dialogue. Through this dialogic beginning (cf. no. 34 above) the people are expressly invited into this great act of thanksgiving. The presider is charged with uniting the congregation with himself in this prayer, which is both an attitudinal and performative responsibility; intention is necessary here, but it is insufficient without the accompanying embodiment which is essential for an authentic and effective invitation into this prayer. While the presider leads the ritual, and

67. There is much anecdotal and some social-scientific data to suggest that the Eucharistic Prayer is experienced by many in the US as the "dullest" part of the eucharistic liturgy. See John Baldovin, "Pastoral Liturgical Reflections on the (Georgetown) Study," *The Awakening Church*, ed. Lawrence Madden (Collegeville, MN: The Liturgical Press, 1992), 107–109.

68. E.g., Louis Finkelstein, "The Birkat Ha-Mazon," *Jewish Quarterly Review* 19 (1929): 236–262; Jean Paul Audet, "Literary Forms and Contents of a Normal ευχαριστια in the First Century," *Studia Evangelica* I, ed. Kurt Aland (1959), 643–62; Louis Bouyer, *Eucharistie* (Paris: Desclée, 1966); Robert J. Ledogar, "The Eucharistic Prayer and the Gifts Over Which it Is Spoken," *Worship* 41 (1967): 578–596; Thomas J. Talley, "From Berakah to Eucharistia: A Reopening Question," *Worship* 50 (1976): 115–137.

prayer that he addresses in the name of the entire community to God the Father through Jesus Christ in the Holy Spirit. Furthermore, the meaning of the Prayer is that the entire congregation of the faithful should join itself with Christ in confessing the great deeds of God and in the offering of Sacrifice. The Eucharistic Prayer demands that all listen to it with reverence and in silence.

communitatis per Iesum Christum in Spiritu Sancto ad Deum Patrem dirigit. Sensus autem huius orationis est, ut tota congregatio fidelium se cum Christo coniungat in confessione magnalium Dei et in oblatione sacrificii. Prex eucharistica exigit ut omnes reverentia et silentio eam auscultent.

---

addresses the prayer in the name of the community to God, theologically this article emphasizes that Christ, who acts in the Holy Spirit, is the central protagonist here. This assertion is grounded in *SC*, no. 7, which stresses that every liturgical action is first an action of Christ (cf. no. 74 above). Thus, when explicating the meaning of the prayer, all *IGMR*s note that such meaning is found in the fact that the "entire congregation should join itself with Christ in confessing the great deeds of God and in the offering of Sacrifice" (*tota congregatio fidelium se cum Christo coniungat in confessione magnalium Dei et in oblatione sacrificii*). Grammatically and theologically this statement makes it clear that the assembly is an active subject (thus the active *coniungat* rather than the passive *coniungatur*) in this action. Even though the priest initiates the ritual invitation, and "unites the congregation with himself" (*eumque sibi sociat*) in this prayer, the presider is not the one who alone offers the great thanksgiving or the sacrifice, as was true in *MR1570* (see Power and Vincie, 51–52 above; also, no. 27 above).

Given this emphasis on the active role of the assembly, it is surprising that *IGMR2002* has transferred and notably altered a comment that, in previous *IGMR*s, follows the subsequent paragraph (no. 79). *IGMR1975*, no. 55 (parallel to *IGMR2002*, no. 79), ends with "The eucharistic prayer calls for all to listen in silent reverence, but also to take part through the acclamation for which the rite makes provision" (*Prex eucharistica exigit, ut omnes reverentia et silentio eam auscultent, eandem vero participent per acclamationes in ipso ritu praevisas). IGMR2002* here repeats that comment, though it excises the phrase "but also to take part through the acclamation for which the rite makes provision." In so doing, the text gives the impression that the essence of active participation is reverent silence, and overlooks its own previous comments about the importance of posture and gesture during this ritual unit (no. 43 above), as well as the opening dialogue and particularly the eucharistic acclamations which are essential vocalizations by the assembly (e.g., *MR2002*, nos. 83, 91 and 98). In some Eucharistic Prayers for children there are as many as twelve such acclamations. More recently, a Eucharistic Prayer approved for the Roman Missal in use in the dioceses of Zaire has an option for ten "Amens" during the final

79. The chief elements making up the Eucharistic Prayer may be distinguished in this way:

a. *Thanksgiving* (expressed especially in the Preface): In which the priest, in the name of the entire holy people, glorifies God the Father and gives thanks for the

79. Præcipua elementa e quibus Prex eucharistica constat, hoc modo distingui possunt:

a) Gratiarum actio (quæ præsertim in Præfatione exprimitur), in qua sacerdos nomine totius populi sancti Deum Patrem glorificat et ei gratias agit pro

---

doxology alone, with multiple options for as many as eleven other acclamations throughout the rest of the Eucharistic Prayer.[69]

79. This article, virtually unchanged from previous *IGMRs*, provides an overview of the "chief elements" (*praecipua elementa*) which comprise a Eucharistic Prayer. The focus here is on textual elements and their theological import, rather than any of the gestures or manual acts which accompany such texts. While these elements are clearly presented in chronological order, not all presently-approved Eucharistic Prayers in the Roman Rite strictly follow the outline presented in this theological introduction. Other liturgical traditions, some of which are historically older than that expressed by the current Roman Rite, also provide sometimes strikingly different configurations of these elements.[70] *IGMR2002* seems to acknowledge implicitly these differences when it notes that these elements "may [not "must"] be distinguished in this way" (*hoc modo distingui possunt*).

a. *Thanksgiving:* Reiterating the emphasis of no. 78, the first chief element mentioned is thanksgiving. *IGMR2002* parenthetically remarks that this element is "expressed especially in the Preface" (*quae praesertim in Praefatione exprimitur*). This formulation suggests that thanksgiving not only has a chronological but also a theological priority here. Thus, thanksgiving is not an isolated or discreet moment in the Eucharistic Prayer, but a fundamental mode of this praying, as signaled in the third and final interchange in the preface dialogue which proclaims that it is "right and just" (*dignum et iustum*) to give God thanks and praise. At the same time, by giving specific attention to the preface, *IGMR2002* clearly signals that the preface is part of the Eucharistic Prayer, and not a prelude to it as it was in the Old Roman Canon (cf. no. 43 above).

Particular attention is given to the prefaces, which are rich in thanksgiving. *IGMR2002* admits two different trajectories within prefaces, i.e., those which give thanks "for the whole work of salvation" (*pro toto opere salutis*) and those whose mode of thanksgiving is focused on "some special aspect of it" (*aliqua eius ratione particulari*). Eastern anaphoras, which virtually never have variable prefaces, illustrate the first type, while the many variable prefaces in the Roman

69. *Missel Romain pour les dioceses du Zaire* (Kinshasha, 1969), nos. 37–50 (pp. 101–108).
70. For example, cf. n. 29 above (Taft, "Mass without a consecration").

whole work of salvation or for some special aspect of it that corresponds to the day, festivity, or season.

b. *Acclamation*: In which the whole congregation, joining with the heavenly powers, sings the *Sanctus*. This acclamation, which is part of the Eucharistic Prayer itself, is sung or said by all the people with the priest.

c. *Epiclesis*: In which, by means of particular invocations, the Church implores the power of the Holy Spirit that the gifts offered by human hands

toto opere salutis vel aliqua eius ratione particulari, secundum diversitatem diei, festivitatis vel temporis.

b) Acclamatio: qua tota congregatio, cælestibus virtutibus se iungens, cantat Sanctus. Hæc acclamatio, quæ partem ipsius Precis eucharisticæ constituit, ab omni populo cum sacerdote profertur.

c) Epiclesis: qua per invocationes peculiares Ecclesia Spiritus Sancti virtutem implorat, ut dona ab hominibus oblata consecrentur, seu Corpus et

---

tradition illustrate the second.[71] In *MR2002* Eucharistic Prayer IV and Eucharistic Prayer III illustrate these two respective types.

While not considered a major element of the Eucharistic Prayer, and therefore not explicitly mentioned here, the post-*Sanctus* is often rich in thanksgiving motifs, and offers thanks for the work of creation and the continued unfolding of salvation history.

b. *Acclamation:* Regarding the *Sanctus*, *IGMR2002* offers brief but important theological insights about this eucharistic element and also indicates how this first eucharistic "Acclamation" (*acclamatio*) is to be performed. Reflecting the previous stress on singing (no. 39 above), the Instruction first notes that the whole congregation sings this acclamation. While choirs or cantors may have a role in enhancing the assembly's song (ITTOM, no. 117), there is no accommodation here for these or any others to substitute for the congregation's voice in the *Sanctus*. *IGMR2002* has dropped *IGMR1975*'s option that the *Sanctus* is to be sung "or recited" (*vel recitat*, no. 54b), though GIRM2003 has included "or said" in its translation. While previously the Instruction has noted that words for "say" and "proclaim" are to be understood of both singing and reciting (no. 38 above), the Instruction never suggests that a direction "to sing" can be interpreted as "to recite." Whereas *IGMR2002* explicitly allows recitation as an alternative to singing the *Gloria* (no. 53 above), there is no such option here. As the US bishops note "By its very nature [the *Sanctus*] is meant to be sung" (ITTOM, no. 117).

While previously *IGMR2002* has noted that every eucharistic celebration is an act of the whole church (Power-Vincie, 51–52 above), here the Instruction expands that vision to include "the heavenly powers" (*caelestibus virtutibus*) in one of its more explicit eschatological comments.

71. See Edmond Eugène Moeller, *Corpus praefationum*, 5 vols., Corpus Christianorum, Series Latina 161, 161A, 161B, 161C, 161D (Turnhout: Brepols, 1980–81), esp. "Étude préliminaire" in vol. I (161), cliv–cxci.

be consecrated, that is, become Christ's Body and Blood, and that the spotless Victim to be received in Communion be for the salvation of those who will partake of it.

Sanguis Christi fiant, et ut hostia immaculata, in Communione sumenda, sit in salutem eorum qui illam participaturi sunt.

The Instruction also makes clear that this (and by inference other eucharistic acclamations) are not simply "in" the Eucharistic Prayer, but are constitutive "of" the prayer, declaring that this acclamation "is part of the Eucharistic Prayer itself" (*quae partem ipsius Precis eucharisticae constituit*). The priest, whose action is integral to the whole of the eucharistic action, is thus instructed to sing this acclamation along with the people.

c. *Epiclesis:* Vatican II was concerned that the role of the Holy Spirit be more clearly recognized and celebrated in the life of the Church.[72] That concern was liturgically realized in the reformed eucharistic rites, which place the Holy Spirit at the center of the eucharistic action (see Power and Vincie, 50, 55–56, and 64–66 above). All *IGMR*s affirm the centrality of the Holy Spirit in the consecration of the gifts. *CEC* echoes this ritual reality by noting that Christ is made sacramentally present by "the power of the words *and* the action of Christ, and the power of the Holy Spirit" (no. 1353, emphasis added). This action, one of the two "particular invocations" (*invocationes peculiares*) in the Eucharistic Prayer, is traditionally identified with the prayer for the Holy Spirit before the institution narrative or the "consecratory epiclesis."

The power of the Holy Spirit in transforming the community is also recognized here. *IGMR2002* underscores this role when it speaks of the power of the Holy Spirit in enabling the act of receiving Communion "for the salvation of those who will partake of it" (*in Communione sumenda, sit in salutem eorum qui illam participaturi sunt*). This particular invocation in the Eucharistic Prayer is the "communion epiclesis" which usually occurs after the anamnesis and offering in Roman Rite prayers. Current Eucharistic Prayer texts provide a somewhat richer or at least more broadening interpretation than *IGMR2002* in this regard, as they not only look forward to the act of receiving Communion, but reveal the Eucharistic Prayer as itself an act of communion in the Holy Spirit that enables unity and, in particular, reconciliation.[73] This tradition of a "split-epiclesis" (with ritually distinctive "consecratory" and "communion" epicleses), present in Eucharistic Prayers influenced by an Antiochene tradition, has structurally influenced the shape of current prayers in the Roman Rite. At

72. The Holy Spirit is mentioned 46 times alone in *LG;* see, for example, Sally Vance-Trembath, "The Pneumatology of Vatican II with Particular Reference to *Lumen gentium* and *Gaudium et spes*" (University of Notre Dame: Unpublished Ph.D. dissertation, 2003).

73. See, for example, the communion epiclesis in "Eucharistic Prayer for Masses of Reconciliation I" which prays that by the power of the Holy Spirit those who share in the one sacrifice of Christ are made into "one body, healed of all division."

d. *Institution narrative and consecration*: In which, by means of words and actions of Christ, the Sacrifice is carried out which Christ himself instituted at the Last Supper, when he offered his Body and Blood under the species of bread and wine, gave them to his Apostles to eat and drink, and left them the command to perpetuate this same mystery.

d) Narratio institutionis et consecratio: verbis et actionibus Christi sacrificium peragitur, quod ipse Christus in Cena novissima instituit, cum suum Corpus et Sanguinem sub speciebus panis et vini obtulit, Apostolisque manducandum et bibendum dedit et iis mandatum reliquit idem mysterium perpetuandi.

---

the same time, *IGMR*s speak only of a single epiclesis and the singular "power of the Holy Spirit" (*Spiritus Sancti virtutem*) that has multiple effects. In so doing, there is resonance here with the ancient Alexandrian tradition which structurally wed consecratory and communion invocations into a single prayer.[74]

IGMR2002 also amends previous *IGMR*s here, which only spoke of "God's power" (*virtutem divinam*) rather than the "power of the Holy Spirit," thus providing another example of a more deliberate explication of the role of the Holy Spirit in *IGMR2002* than in *SC* or in previous versions of *IGMR*.

d. *Institution narrative and consecration:* It is traditional to speak generally of the "institution" of the sacraments and particularly of the institution of the Eucharist.[75] Largely under the influence of biblical studies, Jesus' words of institution recorded in the New Testament were frequently presented as "institution narratives" in twentieth-century biblical and liturgical studies. *IGMR1969* employs this term alone (*Narratio institutionis*, no. 55c) to designate this key element in the Eucharistic Prayer. Because of several objections,[76] subsequent *IGMR*s add the phrase "and consecration" (*et consecratio*) to the subtitle of this section.

The use of these two designations for this subunit of the Eucharistic Prayer speaks to the dynamic importance of this ritual moment in the Church's tradition and in the religious imagination of the faithful. *IGMR*s have not addressed the issue of the consecratory nature of the entire prayer, a topic of some significance, especially given the Vatican's recent affirmation of the validity of the Anaphora of Addai and Mari even though it is lacking an explicit institution narrative.[77] At the same time, *IGMR*s have been cautious about prescribing a single moment of the text as consecratory, which is particularly important in

74. See Cabié, 119–120.

75. For example, regarding the former see Thomas Aquinas, ST, III, q. 65, art 1; for the latter, see the Council of Trent, Session 13, ch. 2 *"De ratione institutionis santissimi hujus sacramenti"* in Tanner I:694.

76. Including the letter from Cardinals Alfredo Ottaviani and Antonio Bacci on 25 September 1969 published as *Breve esame critico del "Novus Ordo Missae"* (Rome: Fondazione "Lumen gentium," n.d.).

77. See n. 29 above; the US bishops do make a note of placing this narrative as "an integral part of the one continuous prayer of thanksgiving and blessing" and thus conclude that "it

e. *Anamnesis*: In which the Church, fulfilling the command that she received from Christ the Lord through the Apostles, keeps the memorial of Christ, recalling especially his blessed Passion, glorious Resurrection, and Ascension into heaven.

f. *Offering*: By which, in this very memorial, the Church—and in particular the Church here and now gathered—offers in the Holy Spirit the spotless Victim to the Father. The Church's

e) Anamnesis: per quam, mandatum adimplens, quod a Christo Domino per Apostolos accepit, Ecclesia memoriam ipsius Christi agit, recolens præcipue eius beatam passionem, gloriosam resurrectionem et ad cælos ascensionem.

f) Oblatio: per quam in ipsa hac memoria Ecclesia, eaque præsertim hic et nunc congregata, in Spiritu Sancto hostiam immaculatam Patri offert. Intendit vero Ecclesia ut fideles non

---

light of the renewed appreciation of the role of the Holy Spirit in this event (cf. no. 79c above). Here *IGMR2002* focuses on the sacramental renewal (see Power and Vincie, 57) of the once-and-for-all sacrifice of Christ which is here "carried out" (*sacrificium peragitur*). Notably, the Instruction recalls that Christ's institution of this sacrifice at the Last Supper was not confined to the institution narrative, but was constituted by the offering of his Body and Blood under the species of bread and wine, the giving of these to the Apostles to eat and drink, and the command to perpetuate this same mystery.

e. *Anamnesis*: *IGMR2002*'s introductory comment to this article, indicating that these various elements "may be distinguished in this way" (*hoc modo distingui possunt*), is helpful when considering the eucharistic anamnesis. There is a discreet moment of heightened memorial here in the Eucharistic Prayer, when the Church recalls Christ's passion, resurrection, and ascension. *IGMR* is quite nuanced, however, in noting that this is a way of "especially" (*praecipue*) keeping "the memorial of Christ" (*memoriam ipsius Christi*). This living memorial is also expressed in other ways: in the command "to perpetuate this same mystery" (*idem mysterium perpetuandi*, no. 79d above); in the institution narrative itself which recalls the words and actions of Jesus at the Last Supper; and in the proclamation of the mystery of faith which ordinarily follows the institution narrative, but which is not mentioned here. Even the post-*Sanctus* can be explicit in recalling Christ's saving work.[78] Thus this "chief element" of the Eucharistic Prayer, like others, is as much a pervasive aspect as it is a discreet moment in the prayer.

f. *Offering*: One of the more dramatic reforms of the *Novus Ordo Missae* was the elimination of an "offertory" before the Canon, and the reshaping of

---

should be proclaimed in a manner that does not separate it from its context of praise and thanksgiving" (ITTOM, no. 119).

78. Thus in the Eucharistic Prayer for Masses of Reconciliation II the post-*Sanctus* recalls Christ's death "so that we might turn again to you and find our way to one another."

intention, however, is that the faithful not only offer this spotless Victim but also learn to offer themselves,[71] and so day by day to be consummated, through Christ the Mediator, into unity with God and with each other, so that at last God may be all in all.[72]

g. *Intercessions*: By which expression is given to the fact that the Eucharist is celebrated in communion with the entire Church, of heaven as well as of

solummodo immaculatam hostiam offerant sed etiam seipsos offerre discant,[71] et de die in diem consummentur, Christo mediatore, in unitatem cum Deo et inter se, ut sit tandem Deus omnia in omnibus.[72]

g) Intercessiones: per quas exprimitur Eucharistiam celebrari in communione cum tota Ecclesia tam cælesti quam terrestri, oblationemque fieri pro ipsa et omnibus eius membris

---

Eucharistic Prayers and their theology, so that the central act of offering occurs within the Eucharistic Prayer. In this restructuring, offering is intimately tied to eucharistic memorial and, therefore, to the once-and-for-all self-offering of Christ. This respects the role of Christ as the initiator of every liturgical action (*SC*, no. 7), and theologically disallows any sense that the community is making some offering on their own initiative. Such an understanding is further strengthened when *IGMR2002* notes that the church offers "in the Holy Spirit" (*in Spiritu Sancto*). The language in this article that "the faithful . . . offer this spotless victim" (*fideles . . . immaculatam hostiam offerant*), when isolated from the wider context of memorial and thanksgiving, can be problematic, especially in ecumenical dialogues with other Christian churches.[79] The US bishops offer a useful interpretation that weds offering and memorial with thanksgiving when, commenting on this element in the Eucharistic Prayer, they teach that "In this memorial re-presentation, the Church offers the one sacrifice of praise and thanksgiving a sacramental offering of the sacrifice made 'once and for all' by Christ" (ITTOM, no. 121).

*IGMR*s have enriched the concept of offering by stressing that the faithful "also learn to offer themselves" (*etiam seipsos offerre discant*). This offering is not confined to the Eucharistic Prayer, but is realized throughout the lives of the baptized, "so day by day to be consummated, through Christ the Mediator, into unity with God and with each other" (*et de die in diem consummentur, Christo mediatore, in unitatem cum Deo et inter se*, quoted from *SC*, no. 48). This trajectory of self-sacrifice in Christian mission (*AG*, no. 5) will only reach fulfillment at the end of history when, "at last God may be all in all" (*sit tandem Deus omnia in omnibus*).

g. *Intercession.* As important as *IGMR*'s comments on intercession, is the placement of the intercessory element in contemporary Roman Catholic Eucharistic Prayers and in the *IGMR*s that introduce them. As noted above, contemporary Eucharistic Prayers and theology emphasize thanksgiving over

79. See David Power, "Eucharistic Sacrifice in Ecumenical Dialogue," in his *The Sacrifice We Offer* (New York: Crossroad, 1987), 1–26.

earth, and that the offering is made for her and for all her members, living and dead, who have been called to participate in the redemption and the salvation purchased by Christ's Body and Blood.

h. *Final doxology*: By which the glorification of God is expressed and which is confirmed and concluded by the people's acclamation, *Amen*.

vivis atque defunctis, quæ ad participandam redemptionem et salutem per Christi Corpus et Sanguinem acquisitam vocata sunt.

(h) Doxologia finalis: qua glorificatio Dei exprimitur, quæque acclamatione Amen populi confirmatur et concluditur.

---

intercession, which dominated the Old Roman Canon (see nos. 78 and 79a above). Partially under the influence of twentieth-century scholarship, which asserted that in their early development Eucharistic Prayers were influenced by the so-called "long form" of the Jewish *berakah* in which intercession was in the third place,[80] contemporary Eucharistic Prayers were designed so that intercession for the living and the dead was the penultimate ritual move in this euchology.

*IGMR*s acknowledge such intercession as symbolic of the communion that is celebrated in the Eucharist. This is an act of communion "with the entire church, of heaven as well as of earth" (*in communione cum tota Ecclesia tam caelesti quam terrestri*). This assertion continues a theological strand evident within *IGMR2002* (cf. nos. 30, 60 and 70) that recognizes the very local nature of each eucharistic gathering, while at the same time admits that Eucharist is by its very nature an ecclesial, even cosmic event. On the other hand, the assertion in this and previous editions of *IGMR*s that the Church's offering "is made for her and for all of her members" provides a more narrow vision than the enacted euchology of the Church,[81] whose Eucharistic Prayer texts offer a more Johannine vision of love not just for the Church but for the world (John 3:16), a vision reiterated in *Gaudium et Spes*, no. 1.

h. *Final Doxology.* The last of the chief elements to be considered is the doxology. *IGMR2002*, like its predecessors, describes a dual activity here: the expression of God's glorification by the priest, and the confirmation and conclusion of that doxological act by the people's *Amen,* which is the final and climactic eucharistic acclamation. The glorification of God, which *SC* consistently

80. See Talley, "From Berakah to Eucharistia."

81. E.g., EP II prays not only for "our brothers and sisters who have gone to their rest" but "all the departed"; EP III prayers that "this sacrifice which has made our peace with you advance the peace and salvation of all the world" and then prayers for "all who have left this world in your friendship"; EP IV prayers for "all who seek you with a sincere heart"; EP Reconciliation II prayers for the gathering of "people of every race, language and way of life to share in the one eternal banquet."

The Communion Rite

80. Since the Eucharistic Celebration is the Paschal Banquet, it is desirable that in keeping with the Lord's command, his Body and Blood should be received as spiritual food by the faithful who are properly disposed. This is the sense of the fraction and the other preparatory rites by which the faithful are led directly to Communion.

Ritus Communionis

80. Cum celebratio eucharistica convivium paschale sit, expedit ut, iuxta mandatum Domini, Corpus et Sanguis eius a fidelibus rite dispositis ut cibus spiritualis accipiantur. Ad hoc tendunt fractio aliique ritus præparatorii, quibus fideles ad Communionem immediate adducuntur.

---

recognizes as one of the two essential purposes of liturgy,[82] is a fundamental motif of the Eucharistic Prayer, which begins in grateful praise with the opening dialogue, preface, and *Sanctus* and—in what could be considered an act of Semitic enclosure—reiterates that praise at the end. The people's Amen not only confirms their engagement in this final act of praise, but also their engagement in the whole of this prayer. As the US bishops remark, this ratification on the part of the congregation was considered by St. Paul to be essential to the prayers of thanksgiving, and later theologians stressed this Amen "as the people's confirmation of all that has been proclaimed on their behalf by the priest" (ITTOM, no. 79).

The Communion Rite

80. This paragraph introduces ten articles detailing the actions, meanings, and purposes of the third ritual subunit of the Liturgy of the Eucharist: the Communion Rite. This subunit comprises four fundamental elements: 1) the Lord's Prayer, 2) the Rite of Peace, 3) the Fraction Rite, and 4) the Rites of Communion. Among these elements, the US bishops have observed that the principal texts in these rites are the Lord's Prayer, the Communion song and prayer after Communion (MCW, no. 48).

Unchanged from previous *IGMR*s, no. 80 focuses on the culminating act (cf. ITTOM, no. 125) of Communion. *IGMR* appropriately shifts the imagery here from sacrifice to "Paschal Banquet" (*convivium paschale*). This does not suggest that the act of Communion is lacking in a sacrificial character, and St. Paul is particularly strong in making this linkage (cf. 1 Cor 11:26). While intimately linked to sacrificial metaphors (see no. 72 above), banquet and food imagery predominate in this article and throughout this section of *IGMR2002*. This Instruction is consistent in urging that, "in keeping with the Lord's command" (*iuxta mandatum Domini*), all the faithful "who are properly disposed" (*rite dispositis*) should receive Communion under both forms (cf. nos. 85 and 281–84 below).

82. See n. 42 above.

The Lord's Prayer

81. In the Lord's Prayer a petition is made for daily food, which for Christians means preeminently the Eucharistic bread, and also for purification from sin, so that what is holy may, in fact, be given to those who are holy. The priest says the invitation to the prayer, and all the faithful say it with him; the priest alone adds the embolism, which the people conclude with a doxology. The embolism, enlarging upon the last petition of the Lord's Prayer itself, begs deliverance from the power of evil for the entire community of the faithful.

Oratio dominica

81. In Oratione dominica panis cotidianus petitur, quo christianis præcipue panis eucharisticus innuitur, atque purificatio a peccatis imploratur, ita ut sancta revera sanctis dentur. Sacerdos invitationem ad orationem profert, omnes vero fideles orationem una cum sacerdote dicunt, et sacerdos solus embolismum adiungit, quem populus doxologia concludit. Embolismus, ultimam petitionem ipsius Orationis dominicæ evolvens, liberationem a potestate mali pro tota communitate fidelium expetit.

IGMR2002 is explicit that the prayers and rituals in the Communion rite are "preparatory rites" (*ritus praeparatorii*) for the climactic event of Communion, thus countering any suggestion that the purpose of transforming elements into Christ's Body and Blood is primarily for adoration. While previous *IGMR*s also note that the fraction is one of these preparatory rites (*IGMR1975*, no. 56), *IGMR2002* seems to emphasize more than previous Instructions its secondary nature (see no. 83 below).

The Lord's Prayer

81. Virtually unchanged from the previous *IGMR*, this article begins by providing theological comment on two of the petitions found in this statutory Christian prayer. Although rich in eschatological images[83] and indebted to a Jewish spirituality that tends to place praise before petition (cf. no. 79g above), the Instruction highlights that this Dominical prayer is a biblical *tephillah*,[84] in which petition dominates. The article's first comment concerns the petition for "daily food" (*panis cotidianus*) which *IGMR* states has a preeminent meaning of eucharistic bread, though in the New Testament the eucharistic bread was not an isolated element but always connected to a meal.[85] This article also rightly connects Eucharist with the forgiveness of sins. In an implicit reference to the liturgy of St. John Chrysostom,[86] the "purification from sin" (*purificatio a peccatis*)

83. Raymond Brown, "The Pater Noster as an Eschatological Prayer," *Theological Studies* 22 (1961): 175–208.

84. Jakob Petuchowski and Michael Brocke, eds., *The Lord's Prayer and Jewish Prayer* (New York: Seabury Press, 1978), 4 *et passim*.

85. Eugene LaVerdiere suggests that "our daily bread" was the way early Christians referred to the whole of the Eucharist, in *The Eucharist in the New Testament and the Early Church* (Collegeville, MN: The Liturgical Press, 1996), 7.

86. "Holy things to the holy!" proclaimed by the priest to the people before Communion.

The invitation, the Prayer itself, the embolism, and the doxology by which the people conclude these things are sung or said aloud.

Invitatio, oratio ipsa, embolismus et doxologia qua populus hæc concludit, cantu vel clara voce proferuntur.

The Rite of Peace

82. The Rite of Peace follows, by which the Church asks for peace and unity for herself and for the whole human family, and the faithful express to each other their ecclesial communion and mutual charity before communicating in the Sacrament.

As for the sign of peace to be given, the manner is to be established by Conferences of Bishops in accordance with the culture and customs of the peoples. It is, however, appropriate that each person offer the sign of peace only to those who are nearest and in a sober manner.

Ritus pacis

82. Sequitur ritus pacis, quo Ecclesia pacem et unitatem pro se ipsa et universa hominum familia implorat et fideles ecclesialem communionem mutuamque caritatem sibi exprimunt, priusquam Sacramento communicent.

Ad ipsum signum pacis tradendæ quod attinet, modus a Conferentiis Episcoporum, secundum ingenium et mores populorum, statuatur. Convenit tamen ut unusquisque solummodo sibi propinquioribus sobrie pacem significet.

---

is accomplished so that "what is holy may . . . be given to those who are holy" (*sancta revera sanctis dentur*). Such purification does not only occur before the act of communion, however, for as the US bishops note, "mutual love and reconciliation . . . are both the condition and the fruit of worthy communion" (ITTOM, no. 125).

The article goes on to detail the fourfold ritual structure of proclaiming this prayer: 1) an invitation to the prayer by the priest; 2) the text of the prayer recited by priest and all the faithful; 3) the embolism, recited by the priest presider, enlarging upon the final petition of the prayer; and 4) a concluding doxology, recited by the people. All of these elements are to be sung or said aloud. If the text of the prayer is sung, the US bishops note that it is desirable that the priest sing the embolism as well, so that the priest and people can together sing the doxology (ITTOM, no. 126). Singing these three critical parts contributes to a unified performance and sense of the prayer, rather than a performance of disparate parts alternately said or sung.

The Rite of Peace

82. *IGMR2002* alters this text from previous *IGMR*s. Where previously "the faithful implore peace and unity for the Church and for the whole human family and offer some sign of their love for one another" (*Sequitur deinde ritus pacis, quo fideles pacem et unitatem pro Ecclesia et universa hominum familia implorant et mutuam caritatem sibi exprimunt*, *IGMR1975*, no. 56b), now it is the Church that prays for itself and the human family, and the faithful who not only express their mutual charity to each other, but also their "ecclesial communion" (*eccle-*

The Fraction

83. The priest breaks the Eucharistic Bread, assisted, if the case calls for it, by the deacon or a concelebrant. Christ's gesture of breaking bread at the Last Supper, which gave the entire Eucharistic Action its name in apostolic times, signifies that the many faithful are made one body (1 Cor 10:17) by receiving Communion from the one Bread of Life which is Christ, who died and rose for the salvation of the world. The fraction or breaking of bread is

Fractio panis

83. Sacerdos panem eucharisticum frangit, adiuvante, si casus fert, diacono vel concelebrante. Gestus fractionis a Christo in ultima cena peractus, qui tempore apostolico toti actioni eucharisticæ nomen dedit, significat fideles multos in Communione ex uno pane vitæ, qui est Christus pro mundi salute mortuus et resurgens, unum corpus effici (*1 Cor* 10, 17). Fractio inchoatur post pacem traditam, et debita cum reverentia peragitur, ne tamen innec-

---

sialem communionem). This phrase implicitly values a communion ecclesiology, although that term is far from univocal.[87] Since sacraments effect what they signify, this exchange of peace not only expresses charity and communion, but also contributes to its creation. Thus the US bishops recognize this ritual exchange as an "opening of ourselves and our neighbors to a challenge and a gift from beyond ourselves" (ITTOM, no. 127).

Moving from theology to performance, *IGMR2002* notes, like its predecessors, that the manner for offering the sign of peace is determined by conferences of bishops "in accordance with the culture and customs of the people" (*secundum ingenium et mores populorum*). New is the Instruction's addition on the appropriateness "that each person offer the sign of peace only to those who are nearest and in a sober manner" (*unusquisque solummodo sibi propinquioribus sobrie pacem significet*). Since the interpretation of "nearest" and "sober" are culturally determined, this new text cannot discount the need to respect local culture and customs. Concerning the new restrictions on the presider during the sign of peace, see no. 154 below. Unlike *MR2002*, this Instruction gives no suggestion that the rite of peace is optional, and sharing the sign of peace among the faithful is properly understood as one of the preparatory rites leading to Communion (cf. no. 266 below).

The Fraction

83. Under this article, *IGMR2002* brings together materials found in three different subsections of *IGMR1975* (nos. 56c, d, and e). It begins with a new sentence describing how the breaking of the bread is to proceed, with reference first to the possible assistance by a deacon, and then by a concelebrant. On the one hand, the specific reference to the deacon and his precedence over concelebrants in the fraction rite could indicate *IGMR2002*'s new emphasis on the importance of this ministry in the Eucharist (see no. 94 below). On the other

87. On the diversity of views expressed under the umbrella of "communion ecclesiology" see Dennis Doyle, *Communion Ecclesiology: Vision and Versions* (Maryknoll, NY: Orbis, 2000).

begun after the sign of peace and is carried out with proper reverence, though it should not be unnecessarily prolonged, nor should it be accorded undue importance. This rite is reserved to the priest and the deacon.

The priest breaks the Bread and puts a piece of the host into the chalice to signify

essarie protrahatur nec immoderato momento æstimetur. Ritus iste sacerdoti et diacono reservatur.

Sacerdos panem frangit et partem hostiæ in calicem immittit, ad significandam unitatem Corporis et Sanguinis Domini, in opere salutis, scilicet Corporis Christi Iesu viventis et gloriosi. Supplicatio Agnus Dei

---

hand, the explicit restriction of this action to the ordained could be another indicator of *IGMR2002*'s intention to draw clearer distinctions between the ministerial priesthood and the common priesthood of the faithful (see no. 91 below). *RedSac* is explicit in noting that the participation of the laity in this action is an abuse (no. 73), and at the end of this first paragraph, *IGMR2002* reiterates that participation in the fraction rite "is reserved to the priest and the deacon" (*sacerdoti et diacono reservatur*).

The Instruction then repeats the theological interpretation of previous *IGMR*s, noting the importance of Christ's action at the Last Supper in the very naming of the Eucharist in apostolic times, and the strong symbolism that "the many faithful are made one body by receiving Communion from the One Bread of Life" (*significat fideles multos in Communione ex uno pane vitae*). *IGMR2002* omits an insightful sentence from previous Instructions that "This rite is not simply functional" (*Hic ritus non habet tantum rationem effectivam, IGMR1975,* no. 56c). The US bishops comment that in this ritual "the natural, the practical, the symbolic, and the spiritual are all inextricably linked" (ITTOM, no. 130).

After a new exhortation that this rite should be carried out "with *proper* reverence" (the Latin only says, *cum reverentia*), *IGMR2002* expresses a new and unusual concern that "it should not be unnecessarily prolonged, nor should it be accorded undue importance" (*ne tamen innecessarie protrahatur nec immoderato momento aestimetur*).[88] Considering the importance the fraction rite plays in Gregory Dix's theory of the "shape of the liturgy," which seems foundational for no. 72 above, as well as commentaries like that of the US bishops who call it a "most powerful symbol" (ITTOM, no. 130), this downplaying of the ritual weight of the fraction rite seems surprising. On the other hand, the requirement to fill all cups with wine at the preparation of the gifts—effectively turning that preparation moment into a kind of "fraction rite"—renders this comment congruent with *IGMR2002*'s own changes. All wine is to be poured at the preparation of the gifts and the pouring of consecrated wine is to be completely avoided, according to *RedSac*, in case something detrimental to the sacrament should occur (no. 106). This ends a recently recovered practice, common in the US, of

88. *RedSac*, no. 83, considers the unnecessary prolonging and "undue emphasis" on this rite an abuse.

the unity of the Body and Blood of the Lord in the work of salvation, namely, of the living and glorious Body of Jesus Christ. The supplication *Agnus Dei*, is, as a rule, sung by the choir or cantor with the congregation responding; or it is, at least, recited aloud. This invocation accompanies the fraction and, for this reason, may be repeated as many times as necessary until the rite has reached its conclusion, the last time ending with the words *dona nobis pacem (grant us peace)*.

a schola vel a cantore, populo respondente, de more cantatur, vel saltem elata voce dicitur. Invocatio fractionem panis comitatur, quare repeti potest quoties necesse est adusque ritum peractum. Ultima vice concluditur verbis dona nobis pacem.

---

pouring consecrated wine from flagons during the fraction rite. The practice of pouring wine after it was consecrated was also a common practice in early medieval Roman stational liturgies with the pope.[89] Given the emphasis in *IGMR2002* on receiving "from the one bread the Lord's Body and from the one chalice the Lord's Blood" (*ex uno pane accipiunt Corpus et ex uno calice Sanguinem Domini*, no. 72 above), as well as our recent practice and ancient tradition, there appears to be some inconsistency here.

The second paragraph of this article treats the *commixtio*, amplifying the text of *IGMR1975* by offering the interpretation that this action signifies "the unity of the Body and Blood of the Lord in the work of salvation, namely, of the living and glorious Body of Jesus Christ" (*ad significandam unitatem Corporis et Sanguinis Domini, in opere salutis, scilicet Corporis Christi Iesu viventis et gloriosi*).

The concluding sentences explain the *Agnus Dei* as an invocation that "accompanies the fraction rite" (*fractionem panis comitatur*). Dropped is the reference in *IGMR1975* to the *Agnus Dei* being sung also during the commingling (no. 56e), ostensibly because the current Instruction treats the commingling as part of the Fraction and so eliminates this redundancy. This chant is preferably performed with choir or cantor chanting the invocations and the congregation responding. *IGMR*s stress that chant is to accompany the ritual action, and thus can be repeated until the Fraction is finished. It is surprising the *IGMR2002* does not explicitly allow troping of the *Agnus Dei*, given that it grants permission for doing so during the *Kyrie* (no. 52 above), and the ancient tradition[90] as

89. *Expleta confractione, diaconus minor, levata de subdiacono patena, defert ad sedem, ut communicet pontifex. Qui, dum communicaverit, [G], ipsam particulam de qua momorderat, consignando tribus vicibus, mittit in calicem in manus archidiaconi. Et ita confirmatur ab archidiacono. Deinde venit archidiaconus cum calice ad cornu altaris et adnuntiat stationem et* refuo parum de calice in sciffo *inter manus acolyti, accedunt primum episcopi ad sedem, ut communicent de manu pontificis secundum ordinem.* OR I, nos. 106–108, in Andrieu II:101–102 (emphasis added).

90. See, for example, Gunilla Iversen, ed., *Tropes de l'Agnus Dei,* Corpus Troporum 4 (Stockholm: Almqvist & Wiksell, 1980).

Communion

84. The priest prepares himself by a prayer, said quietly, that he may fruitfully receive Christ's Body and Blood. The faithful do the same, praying silently.

The priest next shows the faithful the Eucharistic Bread, holding it above the paten or above the chalice, and invites them to the banquet of Christ. Along with the faithful, he then makes an act of humility using the prescribed words taken from the Gospels.

85. It is most desirable that the faithful, just as the priest himself is bound to do, receive the Lord's Body from hosts consecrated at the same Mass and that, in the

Communio

84. Sacerdos oratione secreta se præparat, ut Corpus et Sanguinem Christi fructuose accipiat. Fideles idem faciunt silentio orantes.

Deinde sacerdos panem eucharisticum super patenam vel super calicem fidelibus ostendit eosque ad Christi convivium invitat; simul autem cum fidelibus actum humilitatis, verbis utens evangelicis præscriptis, elicit.

85. Valde optandum est, ut fideles, sicut et ipse sacerdos facere tenetur, ex hostiis, in eadem Missa consecratis, Corpus dominicum accipiant et in casibus prævisis cali-

---

well as contemporary practice of troping this litany. There is a clear preference that this litany should be sung, noting that "at the least" (*saltem*) it would be recited.

Communion

84. This is the first of five articles detailing the actions, functions, and meanings of the various elements of the Communion rite. Virtually identical in content to its predecessors, in this article *IGMR2002* draws together elements found in *IGMR1975*, nos. 56f–g. It begins by highlighting the importance of silent prayer in preparing for Communion. The priest is to do so "quietly" (*secreta*) and the people "silently" (*silentio*). Since the texts considers these "the same" (*idem*), the instruction of the US bishops that "the prayer for the private preparation of the priest is recited inaudibly" (ITTOM, no. 132) is apt.

The next paragraph, concerned with the invitation to Communion, instructs that the priest "shows" (*ostendit*) the eucharistic bread to the people; this is the same verb employed after the institution narrative in *MR2002*, distinguished from "elevating" bread and chalice at the doxology. *IGMR2002* adds that the eucharistic bread can be raised "above the paten or above the chalice" (*super patenam vel super calicem,* cf. nos. 157 and 268 below which add that it is to be raised "slightly" or "a little" [*aliquantulum*]*)*. The latter seems more appropriate in light of the document's preference for Communion under both forms (e.g., nos. 72, 85, 281). Finally, the Instruction notes that priest and people together make an "act of humility" (*actum humilitatis*), i.e., the ritual formula based on Luke 7:6. *IGMR2002* indicates that all are to use the "prescribed" (*praescriptis*) words taken from the gospel. Since the liturgical text is an adaptation of the

instances when it is permitted, they partake of the chalice (cf. no. 283), so that even by means of the signs Communion will stand out more clearly as a participation in the sacrifice actually being celebrated.[73]

cem *(cf. n. 283)* participent, quo etiam per signa Communio melius appareat participatio sacrificii, quod actu celebratur.[73]

---

biblical text, this addition seems to stress that the liturgical (not the biblical) formula is prescriptive, allowing no variance.

85. Repeating what is found in *IGMR1975* (no. 56g), this article stresses that two things are "most desirable" (*Valde optandum est*) regarding the Communion of the faithful. The first is that they "receive" (*accipiant*, while *IGMR1975*, no. 56h has *sumant*, which could suggest a more active stance on the part of the communicant) the Eucharistized bread from hosts consecrated at the same Mass.[91] *IGMR2002* provides new emphasis by adding the phrase "just as the priest himself is bound to do" (*sicut et ipse sacerdos facere tenetur*). Here the juridical requirement that the presider (see nos. 157 and 243 below; also *RedSac*, no. 98) must receive Communion from elements consecrated at the Mass at which he presides is offered as an image for the Communion of the faithful, stressing its importance. While exceptions can occur because of unforeseen pastoral need, the presumption here is that Communion from the tabernacle as a pastoral pattern is not allowed (cf. ITTOM, no. 134).

A second "most desirable" aspect of Communion is that the faithful drink from the chalice "when it is permitted" (*in casibus praevisis*). On the one hand, the inclusion of a conditional statement here could appear to diminish the emphasis on Communion under both forms. On the other hand, since the practice of extending the cup to the people was only authorized in 1963, and since *SC* is relatively restricted in its vision of when this might occur (no. 55), this statement is more properly understood as recognizing the recent history of its practice, which is still not the general practice in the universal church. *IGMR2002*, which expands the cases for Communion under both forms beyond that foreseen by *SC* (see the introduction to no. 281, and no. 283 below), leaves no doubt that Communion under both forms is highly desired and the pastoral norm (cf. nos. 72 and 85). The USCCB as well as other conferences of bishops have gone further, and Communion under both forms is allowed at virtually every Sunday Eucharist.[92]

In providing theological commentary, *IGMR2002* commends these two "most desirable" aspects of Communion so that Communion will more clearly signify

91. This is a stronger statement than that found in *SC*, no. 55, which spoke of this practice as "warmly recommended" *(valde commendatur)*.

92. The NCCB approved communion under both forms for Sundays and Holy Days in December, 1978 (the *recognitio* was obtained in 1984). See John Huels, *The Interpretation of the Law on Communion under Both Kinds*, CUA Canon Law Studies, no. 505 (Washington, DC: Catholic University of America, 1982), 304.

86. While the priest is receiving the Sacrament, the Communion chant is begun. Its purpose is to express the communicants' union in spirit by means of the unity of their voices, to show joy of heart, and to highlight more clearly the "communitarian" nature of the procession to receive Communion. The singing is continued for as long as the Sacrament is being administered to the

86. Dum sacerdos sumit Sacramentum, inchoatur cantus ad Communionem, cuius est spiritualem unionem communicantium per unitatem vocum exprimere, gaudium cordis demonstrare et indolem « communitariam » processionis ad Eucharistiam suscipiendam magis in lucem ponere. Cantus protrahitur, dum fidelibus Sacramentum ministratur.[74] Si tamen hymnus post

---

"participation in the sacrifice actually being celebrated" (*participatio sacrificii, quod actu celebratur*). In their commentary, the US bishops give special attention to drinking from the cup as symbolizing participation in the suffering of Christ,[93] but first provide an eschatological interpretation, noting that "drinking at the Eucharist is a sharing in the sign of the new covenant (and) a foretaste of the heavenly banquet" (ITTOM, no. 134).

86. This article is focused on the Communion chant, and largely repeats what was found in *IGMR1975*, no. 56i. The material has been rearranged, however, and instead of beginning with a statement that the Communion song is sung "during the priest's and the faithful's reception of the sacrament" (*dum sacramentum a sacerdote et fidelibus sumitur*), it begins by noting that the chant begins "while the priest is receiving communion" (*dum sacerdos sumit Sacramentum*). While *IGMR1975* goes on to note that, in fact, "The song begins when the priest takes communion" (*cantus inchoatur cum sacerdos se communicat*), the rearrangement in *IGMR2002* is symptomatic of the concern in this Instruction to distinguish between the ministerial priesthood and that of the baptized (see nos. 72, 73, 75, 83, 86 above), and could weaken the sense that priest and faithful receive sacramental Communion together.

All *IGMR*s generally agree that there is a threefold purpose for the Communion chant, expressing unity, joy, and emphasizing the communitarian nature of the Communion procession. *IGMR2002* adjusts the language of this third purpose and happily changes a gender-specific reference in the Latin (*fraternam*) to a neutral term (*communitariam*). In an unusually rich commentary, the US bishops invoke images of justice, pilgrimage, and eschatology when they note that the Communion procession "expresses the humble patience of the poor moving forward to be fed, the alert expectancy of God's people sharing the paschal meal in readiness for their journey, (and) the joyful confidence of God's people on the march towards the promised land" (ITTOM, no. 135).

*IGMR*s recognize that the Communion chant is song intimately wed to a ritual action, and thus it is to continue "for as long as the Sacrament is being

93. Useful in this regard is Xavier Léon-Dufour, *Sharing the Eucharistic Bread*, trans. Mathew O'Connell (New York: Paulist Press, 1987), 63–65.

faithful.[74] If, however, there is to be a hymn after Communion, the Communion chant should be ended in a timely manner.

Care should be taken that singers, too, can receive Communion with ease.

87. In the dioceses of the United States of America there are four options for the Communion chant: (1) the antiphon from the *Roman Missal* or the Psalm from the *Roman Gradual* as set to music there or in another musical setting; (2) the seasonal antiphon and Psalm of the *Simple Gradual*; (3) a song from another collection of psalms and antiphons, approved by the United States Conference of Catholic Bishops or the diocesan Bishop, including psalms

Communionem habetur, cantus ad Communionem tempestive claudatur.

Curetur ut etiam cantores commode communicare possint.

87. Pro cantu ad Communionem adhiberi potest aut antiphona ex Graduali romano sive cum psalmo sive sola, aut antiphona cum psalmo e Graduali simplici, aut alius cantus congruus a Conferentia Episcoporum approbatus. Cantatur sive a schola sola, sive a schola vel cantore cum populo.

Si autem non habetur cantus, antiphona in Missali proposita recitari potest sive a fidelibus, sive ab aliquibus ex ipsis, sive a

---

administered to the faithful" (*dum fidelibus Sacramentum ministratur).* Here, *IGMR2002* changes the language from the active voice found in *IGMR1975* (*dum fideles Corpus Christi sumunt*, no. 56i) to the passive voice (*ministratur*). This change is analogous to that from *sumant* to *accipiant* in no. 85 above. In so doing, *IGMR2002* seems not only to be distinguishing between actions of the priest and those of the faithful, but also hints that the priest is a doer, while the faithful are receivers. This contradicts the underlying presumption of this document and *SC*, no. 7, that the community is one of the subjects of the liturgy with Christ (see Power and Vincie, 51; also nos. 27, 78 above).

IGMR is ritually sensitive in noting that the Communion chant and any hymn after Communion cannot be performed contiguously, and for each to be effective it is necessary to have a reasonable time lapse between them. *IGMR2002* demonstrates pastoral sensitivity by adding a concern to care for the "singers" (*cantores*), and by extension all musicians ministering during the Communion procession, so that they too can receive Communion "with ease" (*commodo).*

87. In outlining the options for the Communion chant, as well as the approved US adaptations of GIRM2003, this article mirrors the directives of no. 48 above. While neither this nor previous *IGMR*s give further directions concerning the texts, the US bishops recognize that hymns that "concentrate on adoration rather than on the action of communion may not be appropriate" (ITTOM, no. 137).

What is different here is the stated preference for who sings this chant. The entrance chant, and by extension the chant at the preparation of the gifts (cf. no. 74 above), are to be sung by the choir and people, cantor and people, people alone or, lastly, by the choir alone. Number 87 inverts this order, and gives the first option to the "choir alone" (*a schola sola*), only then to choir or cantor with the people, and never to the people alone. Implicit here may be a recognition

arranged in responsorial or metrical forms; (4) a suitable liturgical song chosen in accordance with no. 86 above. This is sung either by the choir alone or by the choir or cantor with the people.

If there is no singing, however, the Communion antiphon found in the Missal may be recited either by the faithful, or by some of them, or by a lector. Otherwise the priest himself says it after he has received Communion and before he distributes Communion to the faithful.

lectore, sin aliter ab ipso sacerdote post quam ipse communicavit, antequam Communionem distribuat fidelibus.

88. When the distribution of Communion is finished, as circumstances suggest,

88. Distributione Communionis expleta, pro opportunitate, sacerdos et fideles per

---

that what makes this procession different from those at the entrance and the preparation of the gifts, is that at Communion the whole assembly processes. This would certainly make certain types of singing, such as metrical hymns, difficult (cf. *Liturgical Music Today* [LMT], nos. 18–19). Responsorial psalmody or liturgical songs with a refrain, however, are most appropriate for this ritual action (cf. ITTOM, no. 137), and would more properly fulfill the first purpose of the Communion chant, that of expressing the communicants' union "by means of the unity of their voices" (*per unitatem vocum exprimere*, no. 86 above). This is much less effectively achieved if the choir substitutes for the song of the assembly during this climactic ritual moment (see nos. 30 and 80 above).

The role of the Communion antiphon here is as problematic as that of the antiphon at the preparation of the gifts. *IGMR2002* at least allows the entrance antiphon to be subsumed into the priest's introduction (no. 48 above). No such option is offered for the antiphon at the preparation of the gifts or here at Communion. Even *IGMR1975* is inconsistent on this issue, however, for it allows the antiphon at the preparation of the gifts to be dropped if it is not recited (see no. 74 above). For unexplained reasons, that option never exists for the antiphon at Communion, which is the only one of the three that has to be recited if there is no singing. Reciting a remnant of a musical piece makes little ritual sense here. Future *IGMR*s will have to address this issue as part of the ongoing work of eliminating duplications and "less useful additions" to the rite (*SC*, no. 50).

88. Similar to its predecessors, *IGMR2002* directs that, "as circumstances suggest" (*pro opportunitate*), all may spend some time praying "privately" (*secreto; IGMR1975* has *in corde suo*, no. 56j). No directives are given for the length of time of this optional silence. The previously mentioned principle of proportionality is important here, and this "period of deep and tranquil communion" (ITTOM, no. 139) will be longer or shorter depending on the level of festivity, the priest and faithful spend some time praying privately. If desired, a psalm or other canticle of praise or a hymn may also be sung by the entire congregation.

89. To bring to completion the prayer of the People of God, and also to conclude the entire Communion Rite, the priest says the Prayer after Communion, in which he prays for the fruits of the mystery just celebrated.

In the Mass only one prayer after Communion is said, which ends with a shorter conclusion; that is,

- If the prayer is directed to the Father: *Per Christum Dominum nostrum (Through Christ our Lord)*;
- If it is directed to the Father, but the Son is mentioned at the end: *Qui vivit et regnat in saecula saeculorum (Who lives and reigns forever and ever)*;
- If it is directed to the Son: *Qui vivis et regnas in saecula saeculorum (You live and reign forever and ever)*.

The people make the prayer their own by the acclamation, *Amen*.

aliquod temporis spatium secreto orant. Si placet, etiam psalmus vel aliud laudis canticum vel hymnus a tota congregatione persolvi potest.

89. Ad precationem populi Dei complendam, necnon totum ritum Communionis concludendum, sacerdos orationem post Communionem profert, in qua pro fructibus mysterii celebrati deprecatur.

In Missa unica dicitur oratio post Communionem, quæ terminatur conclusione breviore, idest:

- si dirigitur ad Patrem: Per Christum Dóminum nostrum;
- si dirigitur ad Patrem, sed in fine ipsius fit mentio Filii: Qui vivit et regnat in sǽcula sæculórum;
- si dirigitur ad Filium: Qui vivis et regnas in sǽcula sæculórum.

Populus acclamatione Amen orationem facit suam.

---

the length of the worship, and particularly the extent of the Communion rites and procession. Thus, the silence here needs to blend with the "rhythm" (ITTOM, no. 139) of the rest of the rite and not interrupt that rhythm or bring it to a halt. The other option at this point in the rite is for the entire congregation to sing some psalm, canticle of praise, or hymn. While these elements were mentioned in previous *IGMR*s, this instruction rearranges them so that a priority is given first to psalmody, then to another canticle of praise, and finally to hymnody. MCW indicates that this is a particularly appropriate option if there was instrumental music or if the choir sang during Communion (no. 72). Even if such is done, some quiet should intervene between the Communion song and this hymn of praise and thanksgiving (no. 87 above). This will contribute to rendering each musical moment in this Communion rite more effective.

89. This article significantly expands on what is found in previous *IGMR*s and is more explicit about the twofold function of the prayer after Communion. First, it brings "to completion the prayer of the People of God" (*Ad precationem populi Dei complendam*), which points in a particular way to its role in gathering the private prayers of the faithful and presider (cf. nos. 84 and 88 above). Thus it functions as a true *collecta* at this ritual moment (see no. 127 below). Ecclesiologically rich, this comment emphasizes that, although the assembly is composed of individuals with particular needs and prayers, the eucharistic liturgy

D. The Concluding Rites

90. The concluding rites consist of

a. Brief announcements, if they are necessary;

b. The priest's greeting and blessing, which on certain days and occasions is enriched and expressed in the prayer over the People or another more solemn formula;

D) Ritus conclusionis

90. Ad ritus conclusionis pertinent:

a) breves notitiæ, si necessariæ sint;

b) salutatio et benedictio sacerdotis, quæ quibusdam diebus et occasionibus oratione super populum vel alia sollemniore formula ditatur et exprimitur;

---

is fundamentally communal. Thus individual prayer is incomplete eucharistically if it is not publicly united with the prayers and needs of a local assembly in communion with a universal Church (cf. no. 30 above). Second, *IGMR2002* explicates that this prayer brings the ritual unit of the Communion Rite to a close.

This twofold function of completing the prayer of the people and concluding this ritual unit is accomplished by the priest praying "for the fruits of the mystery just celebrated" (*in qua pro fructibus mysterii celebrati deprecatur*). Scholastic teaching held that the fruits of Christ's death were applied to Christians through the Mass in three ways: "general fruits for the entire Church, special fruits for those for whom the Mass is offered, and most special fruits for the celebrant."[94] Given the emphasis on the essentially communal nature of the Eucharist in *SC* (cf. nos. 7 and 14) and *IGMR2002*, the "fruits of the mystery" need to be understood less individualistically and less hierarchically. *AG* appropriately considers the eucharistic liturgy as a culminating act of mission (nos. 6, 9 and 36). Speaking of how the Christian community becomes "a sign of God's presence in the world," *AG* reminds us that "through the eucharistic sacrifice [the Christian community] . . . bears witness to Christ . . . walks in charity and is enlivened by an apostolic spirit" (no. 15). Thus, this closing prayer ultimately has a centrifugal trajectory. The people, who according to all *IGMR*s make this prayer their own by acclaiming "Amen," consequently make the commitment to charity and mission their own as well, as they are sent out "to do good works" (no. 90 below).

IGMR2002 conveniently lists the stereotyped endings for the prayer after Communion that in previous *IGMR*s had been consolidated with general guidelines for the opening prayer and prayer over the gifts (*IGMR1975*, no. 32).

The Concluding Rites

90. *IGMR2002* expands the list of the elements comprising the concluding rites found in earlier editions (cf. *IGMR1975*, no. 57) from two to four. New is

94. Gilbert Ostdiek, "The Threefold Fruits of the Mass: Notes and Reflections on Scotus' Quodlibetal Questions, q. 20," *Essays Honoring Allan B. Wolter,* ed. William A. Frank and Girard Etzkorn (St. Bonaventure NY: Franciscan Institute, 1985), 203.

c. The dismissal of the people by the deacon or the priest, so that each may go out to do good works, praising and blessing God;

d. The kissing of the altar by the priest and the deacon, followed by a profound bow to the altar by the priest, the deacon, and the other ministers.

c) dimissio populi ex parte diaconi vel sacerdotis, ut unusquisque ad opera sua bona revertatur, collaudans et benedicens Deum;

d) osculatio altaris ex parte sacerdotis et diaconi et deinde inclinatio profunda ad altare ex parte sacerdotis, diaconi, aliorumque ministrorum.

---

the recognition that this is the appropriate time for announcements "if they are necessary" (*si necessariae sint*). These are to be "brief" (*breves*), so as not to impede the concluding dynamics of this ritual moment. As in previous *IGMRs*, this article next prescribes the priest's greeting and blessing. Given the principles of progressive solemnity (see n. 17 above) and proportionality (cf. nos. 49, 50 and 88), these are appropriately "enriched" (*ditatur*) on more festive days or during more solemn seasons. Next is the dismissal of the people,[95] accomplished "so that each may go out to do good works, praising and blessing God" (*unusquisque ad opera sua bona revertatur, collaudans et benedicens Deum*). This provides a key interpretation of the exact nature of the "fruits of the mystery" prayed for in the prayer after Communion (cf. no. 89 above). The deacon is specifically mentioned as one who offers this dismissal when present (see no. 185 below). Finally, *IGMR2002* newly explicates the kissing of the altar by priest and deacon (and concelebrants, see nos. 251 and 272 below), followed by a profound bow by all (see no. 49 above).

While not forbidding the singing of a post-dismissal hymn or playing of recessional music, the document does not prescribe liturgical singing for the exit of the ministers as it does for the entrance rites. MCW notes that these are optional, and wisely notes that "the greeting, blessing, dismissal and recessional song or instrumental music ideally form one continuous action" (no. 49).

95. This rite is omitted in a Mass with only one minister, see no. 272 below.

GIRM—Notes (English)

37. Cf. Second Vatican Ecumenical Council, Decree on the Ministry and Life of Priests, *Presbyterorum ordinis*, no. 5; Constitution on the Sacred Liturgy, *Sacrosanctum Concilium*, no. 33.

38. Cf. Ecumenical Council of Trent, Session 22, *Doctrina de ss. Missae sacrificio*, 17 September 1562, chapter 1: Denz-Schön, 1740; Paul VI, Solemn Profession of Faith, 30 June 1968, no. 24: AAS 60 (1968), p. 442.

IGMR—Notes (Latin)

37. Cf. Conc. Œcum. Vat. II, Decr. de Presbyterorum ministerio et vita, *Presbyterorum ordinis*, n. 5; Const. de sacra Liturgia, *Sacrosanctum Concilium*, n. 33.

38. Cf. Conc. Œcum. Trid., Sessio XXII, Doctr. de ss. Missæ sacrificio, cap. 1: Denz.-Schönm. 1740; cf. Paulus VI, *Sollemnis professio fidei*, diei 30 iunii 1968, n. 24: A.A.S. 60 (1968) p. 442.

39. Cf. Second Vatican Ecumenical Council, Constitution on the Sacred Liturgy, *Sacrosanctum Concilium,* no. 7; Paul VI, Encyclical Letter *Mysterium fidei,* On the doctrine and worship of the Eucharist, 3 September 1965: AAS 57 (1965), p. 764; Sacred Congregation of Rites, Instruction *Eucharisticum mysterium,* On the worship of the Eucharist, 25 May 1967, no. 9: AAS 59 (1967), p. 547.

40. Cf. Second Vatican Ecumenical Council, Constitution on the Sacred Liturgy, *Sacrosanctum Concilium,* no. 56; Sacred Congregation of Rites, Instruction *Eucharisticum mysterium,* On the worship of the Eucharist, 25 May 1967, no. 3: AAS 59 (1967), p. 542.

41. Cf. Second Vatican Ecumenical Council, Constitution on the Sacred Liturgy, *Sacrosanctum Concilium,* nos. 48, 51; Dogmatic Constitution on Divine Revelation, *Dei Verbum,* 18 November 1965, no. 21; Decree on the Ministry and Life of Priests, *Presbyterorum ordinis,* no. 4.

42. Cf. Second Vatican Ecumenical Council, Constitution on the Sacred Liturgy, *Sacrosanctum Concilium,* nos. 7, 33, 52.

43. Cf. ibid., no. 33.

44. Cf. Sacred Congregation of Rites, Instruction *Musicam sacram,* On music in the Liturgy, 5 March 1967, no. 14: AAS 59 (1967), p. 304.

45. Cf. Second Vatican Ecumenical Council, Constitution on the Sacred Liturgy, *Sacrosanctum Concilium,* nos. 26–27; Sacred Congregation of Rites, Instruction *Eucharisticum mysterium,* On the worship of the Eucharist, 25 May 1967, no. 3d: AAS 59 (1967), p. 542.

46. Cf. Second Vatican Ecumenical Council, Constitution on the Sacred Liturgy, *Sacrosanctum Concilium,* no. 30.

47. Cf. Sacred Congregation of Rites, Instruction *Musicam sacram,* On music in the Liturgy, 5 March 1967, no. 16a: AAS 59 (1967), p. 305.

48. Saint Augustine of Hippo, *Sermo* 336, 1: *Patrologiae cursus completus: Series latina,* J. P. Migne, editor, Paris, 1844–1855 (hereafter PL), 38, 1472.

49. Cf. Sacred Congregation of Rites, Instruction *Musicam sacram,* On music in the Liturgy, 5 March 1967, nos. 7, 16: AAS 59 (1967), pp. 302, 305.

39. Cf. Conc. Œcum. Vat. II, Const. de sacra Liturgia, *Sacrosanctum Concilium,* n. 7; Paulus VI, Litt. Enc. *Mysterium Fidei,* diei 3 septembris 1965: A.A.S. 57 (1965) p. 764; S. Congr. Rituum, Instr. *Eucharisticum mysterium,* diei 25 maii 1967, n. 9: A.A.S. 59 (1967) p. 547.

40. Cf. Conc. Œcum. Vat. II, Const. de sacra Liturgia, *Sacrosanctum Concilium,* n. 56; S. Congr. Rituum, Instr. *Eucharisticum mysterium,* diei 25 maii 1967, n. 3: A.A.S. 59 (1967) p. 542.

41. Cf. Conc. Œcum. Vat. II, Const. de sacra Liturgia, *Sacrosanctum Concilium,* nn. 48, 51; Const. dogm. de divina Revelatione, *Dei Verbum,* n. 21; Decr. de Presbyterorum ministerio et vita, *Presbyterorum ordinis,* n. 4.

42. Cf. Conc. Œcum. Vat. II, Const. de sacra Liturgia, *Sacrosanctum Concilium,* nn. 7, 33, 52.

43. Cf. *ibidem,* n. 33.

44. Cf. S. Congr. Rituum, Instr. *Musicam sacram,* diei 5 martii 1967, n. 14: A.A.S. 59 (1967) p. 304.

45. Cf. Conc. Œcum. Vat. II, Const. de sacra Liturgia, *Sacrosanctum Concilium,* nn. 26–27; S. Congr. Rituum, Instr. *Eucharisticum mysterium,* diei 25 maii 1967, n. 3 d: A.A.S. 59 (1967) p. 542.

46. Cf. Conc. Œcum. Vat. II, Const. de sacra Liturgia, *Sacrosanctum Concilium,* n. 30.

47. Cf. S. Congr. Rituum, Instr. *Musicam sacram,* diei 5 martii 1967, n. 16 a: A.A.S. 59 (1967) p. 305.

48. S. Augustinus Hipponensis, *Sermo* 336, 1: PL 38, 1472.

49. Cf. S. Congr. Rituum, Instr. *Musicam sacram,* diei 5 martii 1967, nn. 7, 16: A.A.S. 59 (1967) pp. 302, 305.

50. Cf. Second Vatican Ecumenical Council, Constitution on the Sacred Liturgy, *Sacrosanctum Concilium*, no. 116; cf. also Sacred Congregation of Rites, Instruction *Musicam sacram*, On music in the Liturgy, 5 March 1967, no. 30.

51. Cf. Second Vatican Ecumenical Council, Constitution on the Sacred Liturgy, *Sacrosanctum Concilium*, no. 54; Sacred Congregation of Rites, Instruction *Inter Oecumenici*, on the orderly carrying out of the Constitution on the Sacred Liturgy, 26 September 1964, no. 59: AAS 56 (1964), p. 891; Sacred Congregation of Rites, Instruction *Musicam sacram*, On music in the Liturgy, 5 March 1967, no. 47: AAS 59 (1967), p. 314.

52. Cf. Second Vatican Ecumenical Council, Constitution on the Sacred Liturgy, *Sacrosanctum Concilium*, nos. 30, 34; cf. also Sacred Congregation of Rites, Instruction *Musicam sacram*, On music in the Liturgy, 5 March 1967, no. 21.

53. Cf. ibid., no. 40; Congregation for Divine Worship and the Discipline of the Sacraments, Instruction *Varietates legitimae*, 25 January 1994, no. 41: AAS 87 (1995), p. 304.

54. Cf. Second Vatican Ecumenical Council, Constitution on the Sacred Liturgy, *Sacrosanctum Concilium*, no. 30; Sacred Congregation of Rites, Instruction *Musicam sacram*, On music in the Liturgy, 5 March 1967, no. 17: AAS 59 (1967), p. 305.

55. Cf. John Paul II, Apostolic Letter *Dies Domini*, 31 May 1998, no. 50: AAS 90 (1998), p. 745.

56. Cf. *The Roman Missale*, Appendix II.

57. Cf. Tertullian, *Adversus Marcionem*, IV, 9: *Corpus Christianorum, Series latina*, Turnhout, Belgium, 1953– (hereafter, CCSL), 1, p. 560. PL 2, 376A; Origen, *Disputatio cum Heracleida*, no. 4, 24: Sources chrétiennes, H. deLubac et al., ed. (Paris, 1941–), p. 62; *Statuta Concilii Hipponensis Breviata*, 21: CCSL 149, p. 39.

58. Cf. Second Vatican Ecumenical Council, Constitution on the Sacred Liturgy, *Sacrosanctum Concilium*, no. 33.

59. Cf. ibid., no. 7.

60. Cf. *The Roman Missal, Lectionary for Mass, editio typica altera*, 1981, Introduction, no. 28.

50. Cf. CONC. ŒCUM. VAT. II, Const. de sacra Liturgia, *Sacrosanctum Concilium*, n. 116; etiam *ibidem*, n. 30.

51. Cf. CONC. ŒCUM. VAT. II, Const. de sacra Liturgia, *Sacrosanctum Concilium*, n. 54; S. CONGR. RITUUM, Instr. *Inter Œcumenici*, diei 26 septembris 1964, n. 59: A.A.S. 56 (1964) p. 891; Instr. *Musicam sacram*, diei 5 martii 1967, n. 47: A.A.S. 59 (1967) p. 314.

52. Cf. CONC. ŒCUM. VAT. II, Const. de sacra Liturgia, *Sacrosanctum Concilium*, nn. 30, 34; cf. *ibidem* etiam n. 21.

53. Cf. *ibidem*, n. 40; CONGR. DE CULTU DIVINO ET DISCIPLINA SACRAMENTORUM, Instr. *Varietates legitimæ*, diei 25 ianuarii 1994, n. 41: A.A.S. 87 (1995) p. 304.

54. Cf. CONC. ŒCUM. VAT. II, Const. de sacra Liturgia, *Sacrosanctum Concilium*, n. 30; S. CONGR. RITUUM, Instr. *Musicam sacram*, diei 5 martii 1967, n. 17: A.A.S. 59 (1967) p. 305.

55. Cf. IOANNES PAULUS II, Litt. Ap. *Dies Domini*, diei 31 maii 1998, n. 50: A.A.S. 90 (1998) p. 745.

56. Cf. *infra*, pp. 1157–1160.

57. Cf. TERTULLIANUS, *Adversus Marcionem*, IV, 9: CCSL 1, p. 560; ORIGENES, *Disputatio cum Heracleida*, n. 4, 24: SCh 67, p. 62; *Statuta Concilii Hipponensis Breviata*, 21: CCSL 149, p. 39.

58. Cf. CONC. ŒCUM. VAT. II, Const. de sacra Liturgia, *Sacrosanctum Concilium*, n. 33.

59. Cf. *ibidem*, n. 7.

60. Cf. MISSALE ROMANUM, *Ordo lectionum Missæ*, editio typica altera, n. 28.

61. Cf. Second Vatican Ecumenical Council, Constitution on the Sacred Liturgy, *Sacrosanctum Concilium*, no. 51.

62. Cf. John Paul II, Apostolic Letter *Vicesimus quintus annus*, 4 December 1988, no. 13: AAS 81 (1989), p. 910.

63. Cf. Second Vatican Ecumenical Council, Constitution on the Sacred Liturgy, *Sacrosanctum Concilium*, no. 52; *Codex Iuris Canonici*, can. 767 § 1.

64. Cf. Sacred Congregation of Rites, Instruction *Inter Oecumenici*, On the orderly carrying out of the Constitution on the Sacred Liturgy, 26 September 1964, no. 54: AAS 56 (1964), p. 890.

65. Cf. *Codex Iuris Canonici*, can. 767 § 1; Pontifical Commission for the Authentic Interpretation of the Code of Canon Law, response to *dubium* regarding can. 767 § 1: AAS 79 (1987), p. 1249; Interdicasterial Instruction on certain questions regarding the collaboration of the non-ordained faithful in the sacred ministry of priests, *Ecclesiae de mysterio*, 15 August 1997, art. 3: AAS 89 (1997), p. 864.

66. Cf. Sacred Congregation of Rites, Instruction *Inter Oecumenici*, On the orderly carrying out of the Constitution on the Sacred Liturgy, 26 September 1964, no. 53: AAS 56 (1964), p. 890.

67. Cf. Second Vatican Ecumenical Council, Constitution on the Sacred Liturgy, *Sacrosanctum Concilium*, no. 53.

68. Cf. Sacred Congregation of Rites, Instruction *Inter Oecumenici*, On the orderly carrying out of the Constitution on the Sacred Liturgy, 26 September 1964, no. 56: AAS 56 (1964), p. 890.

69. Cf. Second Vatican Ecumenical Council, Constitution on the Sacred Liturgy, *Sacrosanctum Concilium*, no. 47; Sacred Congregation of Rites, Instruction *Eucharisticum mysterium*, On the worship of the Eucharist, 25 May 1967, no. 3a, b: AAS 59 (1967), pp. 540–541.

70. Cf. Sacred Congregation of Rites, Instruction *Inter Oecumenici*, On the orderly carrying out of the Constitution on the Sacred Liturgy, 26 September 1964, no. 91: AAS 56 (1964), p. 898; Sacred Congregation of Rites, Instruction *Eucharisticum mysterium*, On the worship of the Eucharist, 25 May 1967, no. 24: AAS 59 (1967), p. 554.

61. Cf. CONC. ŒCUM. VAT. II, Const. de sacra Liturgia, *Sacrosanctum Concilium*, n. 51.

62. Cf. IOANNES PAULUS II, Litt. Ap. *Vicesimus quintus annus*, diei 4 decembris 1988, n. 13: A.A.S. 81 (1989) p. 910.

63. Cf. CONC. ŒCUM. VAT. II, Const. de sacra Liturgia, *Sacrosanctum Concilium*, n. 52; cf. *Codex Iuris Canonici*, can. 767 § 1.

64. Cf. S. CONGR. RITUUM, Instr. *Inter Œcumenici*, diei 26 septembris 1964, n. 54: A.A.S. 56 (1964) p. 890.

65. Cf. *Codex Iuris Canonici*, can 767 § 1; PONT. COMM. CODICI IURIS CANONICI AUTHENTICE INTERPRETANDO, respons. ad dubium circa can. 767 § 1: A.A.S. 79 (1987), p. 1249; Instructio interdicasterialis de quibusdam quæstionibus circa fidelium laicorum cooperationem sacerdotum ministerium spectantem, *Ecclesiæ de mysterio*, diei 15 augusti 1997, art. 3: A.A.S. 89 (1997) p. 864.

66. Cf. S. CONGR. RITUUM, Instr. *Inter Œcumenici*, diei 26 septembris 1964, n. 53: A.A.S. 56 (1964) p. 890.

67. Cf. CONC. ŒCUM. VAT. II, Const. de sacra Liturgia, *Sacrosanctum Concilium*, n. 53.

68. Cf. S. CONGR. RITUUM, Instr. *Inter Œcumenici*, diei 26 septembris 1964, n. 56: A.A.S. 56 (1964) p. 890.

69. Cf. CONC. ŒCUM. VAT. II, Const. de sacra Liturgia, *Sacrosanctum Concilium*, n. 47; S. CONGR. RITUUM, Instr. *Eucharisticum mysterium*, diei 25 maii 1967, nn. 3 a, b: A.A.S. 59 (1967) pp. 540–541.

70. Cf. S. CONGR. RITUUM, Instr. *Inter Œcumenici*, diei 26 septembris 1964, n. 91: A.A.S. 56 (1964) p. 898; Instr. *Eucharisticum mysterium*, diei 25 maii 1967, n. 24: A.A.S. 59 (1967) p. 554.

71. Cf. Second Vatican Ecumenical Council, Constitution on the Sacred Liturgy, *Sacrosanctum Concilium*, no. 48; Sacred Congregation of Rites, Instruction *Eucharisticum mysterium*, On the worship of the Eucharist, 25 May 1967, no. 12: AAS 59 (1967), pp. 548–549.

72. Cf. Second Vatican Ecumenical Council, Constitution on the Sacred Liturgy, *Sacrosanctum Concilium*, no. 48; Decree on the Ministry and Life of Priests, *Presbyterorum ordinis*, no. 5; Sacred Congregation of Rites, Instruction *Eucharisticum mysterium*, On the worship of the Eucharist, 25 May 1967, no. 12: AAS 59 (1967), pp. 548–549.

73. Cf. Sacred Congregation of Rites, Instruction *Eucharisticum mysterium*, On the worship of the Eucharist, 25 May 1967, nos. 31, 32; Sacred Congregation for the Discipline of the Sacraments, Instruction *Immensae caritatis*, 29 January 1973, no. 2: AAS 65 (1973), pp. 267–268.

74. Cf. Sacred Congregation for the Sacraments and Divine Worship, Instruction *Inaestimabile donum*, 3 April 1980, no. 17: AAS 72 (1980), p. 338.

71. Conc. Œcum. Vat. II, Const. de sacra Liturgia, *Sacrosanctum Concilium*, n. 48; S. Congr. Rituum, Instr. *Eucharisticum mysterium*, diei 25 maii 1967, n. 12: A.A.S. 59 (1967) pp. 548–549.

72. Cf. Conc. Œcum. Vat. II, Const. de sacra Liturgia, *Sacrosanctum Concilium*, n. 48; Decr. de Presbyterorum ministerio et vita, *Presbyterorum ordinis*, n. 5; S. Congr. Rituum, Instr. *Eucharisticum mysterium*, diei 25 maii 1967, n. 12: A.A.S. 59 (1967) pp. 548–549.

73. Cf. S. Congr. Rituum, Instr. *Eucharisticum mysterium*, diei 25 maii 1967, nn. 31, 32: A.A.S. 59 (1967) pp. 558–559; S. Congr. de Disciplina Sacramentorum, Instr. *Immensæ caritatis*, diei 29 ianuarii 1973, n. 2: A.A.S. 65 (1973) pp. 267–268.

74. Cf. S. Congr. pro Sacramentis et Cultu Divino, Instr. *Inæstimabile donum*, diei 3 aprilis 1980, n. 17: A.A.S. 72 (1980) p. 338.

CHAPTER III

The Duties and Ministries in the Mass

(DE OFFICIIS ET MINISTERIIS IN MISSA)

Bruce T. Morrill and Susan K. Roll

Chapter III
THE DUTIES AND MINISTRIES IN THE MASS

91. The Eucharistic celebration is an action of Christ and the Church, namely, the holy people united and ordered under the Bishop. It therefore pertains to the whole Body of the Church, manifests it, and has its effect upon it. It also affects the individual members of the Church in different ways, according to their different orders, offices, and actual participation.[75] In this

Caput III
DE OFFICIIS ET MINISTERIIS IN MISSA

91. Celebratio eucharistica est actio Christi et Ecclesiæ, scilicet plebis sanctæ sub Episcopo adunatæ et ordinatæ. Quare ad universum Corpus Ecclesiæ pertinet illudque manifestat et afficit; singula vero membra ipsius diverso modo, pro diversitate ordinum, munerum, et actualis participationis attingit.[75] Hoc modo populus christianus, « genus electum, regale

---

91. This initial article sets both the agenda and tone for Chapter III. Commenting upon it can serve as an introductory overview of the entire twenty-one articles of the chapter.

Celebrating the Eucharist is a work of the people (*leitourgia*) that at once unites the members of the Church in the action of corporate, communal, public service of God and "affects" (*attingit*) each individual participant's mystical bond with God, Christ, and the Church through each one's particular role in the act of worship. Identifying the action with both Christ and the Church evokes the supernatural dimension of the liturgy that Pius XII (d. 1958) advanced in *Mediator Dei*, no. 22, framing the celebration within the mystical body of Christ and as a priestly function of Christ the head through the members of the body. The members of that body, nonetheless, are distinctive, and the complexity of this body necessitates a variety of ministries proper to specific "orders" (*ordinum*) and "functions" (*munerum*). On this point the article reiterates, almost verbatim, *Sacrosanctum Concilium* (*SC*, no. 26). There the Constitution explicitly states what remains tacit in the present text, namely, that liturgical services are not private functions. If participants in a eucharistic celebration are to expect their participation in the ritual action to affect their lives in Christ, this depends not on whatever individual devotional interpretations they might bring to their particular service but, rather, on their knowledgeable engagement

way, the Christian people, "a chosen race, a royal priesthood, a holy nation, God's own people," expresses its cohesion and its hierarchical ordering.[76] All, therefore, whether they are ordained ministers or lay Christian faithful, in fulfilling their office or their duty should carry out solely but completely that which pertains to them.[77]

sacerdotium, gens sancta, populus acquisitionis », suam cohærentem et hierarchicam ordinationem manifestat.[76] Omnes ergo sive ministri ordinati sive christifideles laici, munere vel officio suo fungentes, solum et totum id agant, quod ad ipsos pertinet.[77]

---

of their work (and in the case of the ordained and instituted, their office) as decreed by the Church. In this sense, the bishop's exhortation to the candidate(s) in the ordination rite for priesthood, "Understand . . . what you do,"[1] should ring true for all who practice the liturgy, whether ordained or lay, ministering or within the faithful assembly. All are depending upon one another to do what the Church intends and expects of them in the celebration. With all giving themselves over to their parts in the liturgical action in service to the community, the entire body, the holy people (*plebis sanctae*), can expect, in turn, a graced encounter with Christ. To that end, this introductory article of Chapter III quotes 1 Peter 2:9 by citing *SC*, no. 14, the famous conciliar article equating the restoration and promotion of the liturgy with the full and active participation of all the people.

Still, the emphasis and tone of no. 91 revolves around concern for the proper ordering of liturgical ministries, which can only be realized through the hierarchical nature of the Church. Thus, the desired unity to be experienced in the eucharistic celebration is only possible if the "holy people" practice it "under the Bishop" (*scilicet plebis sanctae sub Episcopo adunatae et ordinatae*). Two points are notable about this early phrase in the article, and both are indicative of the trajectory that Vatican directives for liturgy and ministry have taken during the twenty-five years since the previous edition, *Institutio Generalis Missalis Romani* 1975 (*IGMR1975*). First, there is the concern to shore up the ordained priesthood by emphasizing its uniqueness, as found, for example, in "Some Questions Regarding Collaboration of Non-ordained Faithful in Priests' Sacred Ministry" (*Ecclesia de mysterio* [*EccMys*], 1997). This instruction, issued by eight Vatican offices, asserts that the *tria munera* comprise a unified ministry singularly founded in Christ and uniquely imparted to the ordained in the Church, and condemns "an idea of the common priesthood of the faithful which mistakes its nature and specific meaning" and "can encourage a reduction in vocations to the (ministerial) priesthood" (no. 2). Proper ordering of liturgical functions is essential to the celebration's exuding "the church's structured nature," and so "[e]very effort must be made to avoid even the appearance of confusion" (no. 7.2) between what is proper to the ordained and the laity. Citing *EccMys* and some half dozen other recent papal and Vatican missives, *Redemptionis Sacramentum* (*RedSac*, no. 45) warns against the "danger of obscuring the

1. *Rites of Ordination*, second typical edition (Washington, DC: USCCB, 2003), no. 123.

I. The Duties of Those in Holy Orders

92. Every legitimate celebration of the Eucharist is directed by the Bishop, either in person or through priests who are his helpers.[78]

Whenever the Bishop is present at a Mass where the people are gathered, it is most fitting that he himself celebrate the Eucharist and associate priests with himself as concelebrants in the sacred action. This is done not to add external solemnity to the rite but to express in a clearer light the mystery of the Church, "the sacrament of unity."[79]

I. De Officiis Ordinis Sacri

92. Omnis legitima Eucharistiæ celebratio dirigitur ab Episcopo, sive per seipsum, sive per presbyteros adiutores ipsius.[78]

Cum Episcopus Missæ interest, ubi populus est congregatus, maxime decet ipsum Eucharistiam celebrare, et presbyteros, ut concelebrantes, sibi in actione sacra consociare. Quod fit non ad sollemnitatem exteriorem ritus augendam, sed ad significandum vividiore luce mysterium Ecclesiæ, « unitatis sacramentum ».[79]

---

complementary relationship between the action of clerics and that of laypersons," which has often resulted in "a certain 'clericalization'" of lay liturgical ministries, as well as the clergy's robbing the laity of their proper parts. This phenomenon, one can conclude from both empirical observation and the logic of the text, can ironically end up rendering the faithful passive, thus contradicting the paramount objective of participation established in *SC*, no. 14.

A second notable feature about the first sentence of no. 91 is its replacement of the term "assembly" (*coetu*), as found in the opening of Chapter III of *IGMR1975* (no. 58), with "holy people" (*plebis sanctae*). This is representative of an editorial policy pervading the entire *IGMR2002* and thus, the present chapter: the regular addition of such adjectives as "sacred," "holy," and "profound" to terms that were not thus modified in the earlier edition. The intention, according to an evaluation of the 2000 draft-revision of the *IGMR* by the US Bishops' Committee on the Liturgy, is to enhance the sacred meaning of the liturgical actions, objects, and personages—an apparent correction of a perceived lack of sacredness being attributed to liturgical actions and ordained ministers in previous postconciliar documents.

The Duties of Those in Holy Orders

92. The section I title "The Duties of Those in Holy Orders" (*De officiis Ordinis sacri*) differs from *IGMR1975*'s "Offices and Ministries In the Mass" (*De officiis et ministeriis*) in regard to those in Holy Orders, seemingly to denote exclusively an official liturgical function belonging to those in Orders (see no. 97 below). In line with *Lumen Gentium* (*LG*, no. 10), all ordained priesthood is grouped together and differentiated from the "common priesthood of the faithful" as a matter of essence, and not solely of degree—a distinction that should not mask the striking and empowering nature of the affirmation granted in *LG* to all the baptized faithful by virtue of their baptism, in which all Christians have died and risen with Christ.

Even if the Bishop does not celebrate the Eucharist but has assigned someone else to do this, it is appropriate that he should preside over the Liturgy of the Word, wearing the pectoral cross, stole, and cope over an alb, and that he give the blessing at the end of Mass.[80]

Si vero Episcopus Eucharistiam non celebrat, sed alii hoc faciendum attribuit, tunc convenienter ipse, cruce pectorali, stola et pluviali super albam indutus, liturgiæ verbi præsidet, et in fine Missæ benedictionem impertit.[80]

Apart from the title, only slight differences in text distinguish this paragraph from *IGMR1975*. The role of the bishop in directing every eucharistic celebration flows seamlessly from *LG*, no. 26, "every lawful (*legitima*) celebration of the Eucharist is regulated by the bishop, to whom is confided the duty of presenting to the divine majesty the worship of the Christian religion and of ordering it in accordance with the Lord's injunctions and the church's regulation . . ." (cf. Mitchell and Baldovin, p. 11 above). In *LG* the emphasis lies on the direct accountability of the bishop to God, while in *IGMR* the use of *legitima* suggests a legal context, an idea that can be found in Ignatius of Antioch.[2]

The bishop's role as the living symbol of the unity of the local church is similarly embodied in the rite of election of the *Rite of Christian Initiation of Adults.* This rite shifts the site of the church community into which the catechumens are to be initiated from their parish to the "local" or diocesan church, with the bishop presiding as the sign of its unity.

The misconception that diocesan priests preside at the Eucharist only or principally through delegation by the bishop appears in *IGMR1969* and is corrected in *IGMR1970* to locate the priest's power to preside in his ordination to the priesthood. Nonetheless, *LG*, no. 28, elaborates on the relationship between priests and the bishop upon whom they depend for the license to exercise their sacred ministry, calling priests "prudent cooperators of the episcopal college and its support and instrument."[3]

The somewhat contrived "either [the bishop] in person or through priests who are his helpers" (*sive per seipsum, sive presbyteros adiutores ispsius*) is footnoted to a more direct formulation in *SC*, no. 42: "Since it is impossible for the bishop in his church always and everywhere to preside over the whole flock. . . ." While in the early Church a bishop would be responsible for oversight of a fairly small community of Christians, today the Church in many countries might count a large number of parishes without priests, never mind bishops, to preside regularly.

2. Ignatius of Antioch, Letter to the Smyrnaeans 8:1-2, in *Ignace d'Antioch, Polycarpe de Smyrne, Lettres. Martyre de Polycarpe*, ed. Thomas Camelot, Sources Chrétiennes 10, 4th rev. ed. (Paris: Éditions du Cerf, 1969), 138–140.

3. Emil Joseph Lengeling, *Die neue Ordnung der Eucharistiefeier* (Münster: Verlag Regensburg, 1970), 250.

93. A priest also, who possesses within the Church the power of Holy Orders to offer sacrifice in the person of Christ,[81] stands for this reason at the head of the faithful people gathered together here and now, presides over their prayer, proclaims the message of salvation to them, associates the people with himself in the offering of sacrifice through Christ in the Holy Spirit to God the Father, gives his brothers and sisters the Bread of eternal life, and partakes of it with them. When he celebrates the Eucharist, therefore, he must serve God and the people with dignity and humility, and by his bearing and by the way he says the divine words he must convey to the faithful the living presence of Christ.

93. Etiam presbyter, qui in Ecclesia sacra Ordinis potestate pollet sacrificium in persona Christi offerendi,[81] exinde populo fideli hic et nunc congregato præest, eius orationi præsidet, illi nuntium salutis proclamat, populum sibi sociat in offerendo sacrificio per Christum in Spiritu Sancto Deo Patri, fratribus suis panem vitæ æternæ dat, ipsumque cum illis participat. Cum igitur Eucharistiam celebrat, debet Deo et populo cum dignitate et humilitate servire, et in modo se gerendi et verba divina proferendi præsentiam vivam Christi fidelibus insinuare.

The specification of the vestments the bishop is to wear if he does not preside at a particular eucharistic celebration is new to the *IGMR* but can be found in the 1984 *Caeremoniale Episcoporum*, especially nos. 176 and 186.

93. The Latin formulation of this article shows no change from *IGMR1975*; however, substantial differences can be found between the 1975 and 2003 English translations (GIRM1975 and GIRM2003) that could give rise to variant interpretations by those reading only the English text. The new English text places the priest, as subject of the first sentence, in first place instead of a prepositional phrase casting the priest within the context of the community of believers. "Orders" becomes "Holy Orders," "presides over the assembly" becomes "stands at the head of the faithful people gathered here and now." In fact, the entire sentence listing the liturgical duties of the priest casts these actions as done by the priest to or on behalf of the people, with the sole exception, receiving Communion, at the end, *ipsumque cum illis participat*, translated in English by the antiquated "partakes of it with them."

The text stipulates that the priest "must convey to the faithful the living presence of Christ" (*debet . . . praesentiam vivam Christi fidelibus insinuare;* GIRM1975 had "should communicate to the faithful a sense of the living presence of Christ"). This might seem to reverse the implication of *SC*, no. 7, that (the living) Christ is present in, among others, the person of the minister. The emphasis in the English translation now falls on the minister, not the living Christ as reflected in the minister. This may be particularly ironic given the increased debate in the past two decades on eastward orientation in worship, coupled with the question of whether the personality of the priest-presider tends to dominate a eucharistic celebration, arguably leading to a de-emphasis on the transcendent nature of the liturgy.

94. After the priest, the deacon, in virtue of the sacred ordination he has received, holds first place among those who minister in the Eucharistic Celebration. For the sacred Order of the diaconate has been held in high honor in the Church even from the time of the Apostles.[82] At Mass the deacon has his own part in proclaiming the Gospel, in preaching God's word from time to time, in announcing the intentions of the Prayer of the Faithful, in ministering to the priest, in preparing the altar and serving

94. Post presbyterum diaconus, vi sacræ ordinationis acceptæ, primum locum obtinet inter eos qui in celebratione eucharistica ministrant. Sacer enim diaconatus Ordo iam a prisca Apostolorum ætate in Ecclesia in magno honore habitus est.[82] In Missa diaconus proprias habet partes in Evangelio nuntiando et quandoque verbo Dei prædicando, in orationis universalis intentiones enuntiando, in ministrando sacerdoti, in altare apparando et sacrificii celebrationi inserviendo, in Eucharistia fi-

---

The concept that the priest acts *in persona Christi* (with *capitis* implied) has been more extensively explained in *Ecclesia de Eucharistia* (nos. 29 and 52), which stresses that the worshiping community cannot provide a priest for itself but remains dependent upon the bishop, through the apostolic succession, to provide priests to connect their local eucharistic celebration to Christ's sacrifice on the cross. In this sense the phrase "with dignity and humility" (*cum dignitate et humilitate*) provides a counterbalance to the stress on ordained ministry as an exercise in power conferred by the bishop, not by the local community. Nonetheless, a recognition of the dialogical nature of the eucharistic liturgy (see no. 34 above) with its repeated acclamations, and provision for even more acclamations on the part of the assembly than have been written into the *ordo*, would cast a more practical and dynamic meaning to priestly ministry in the context of the formal ritual structure of the liturgy.

94. *IGMR2002* doubly emphasizes the "sacred" character of the deacon's ordination, by adding "in virtue of the sacred ordination he has received" (*vi sacrae ordinationis acceptae*) as well as "the sacred Order of the diaconate" (*Sacer enim diaconatus Ordo*) in the following sentence. The antiquity of the office of deacon is also marked with new emphasis, noting that the office "has been held in high honor in the Church even from the time of the Apostles" (*iam a prisca Apostolorum aetate in Ecclesia in magno honore habitus est*). *IGMR1970*, says simply "has been held in high honor since the early Church" (*iam ab initio Ecclesiae in magno honore habitus est*).

The description of the deacon's responsibilities has changed in several respects from 1969. The change from "leads the general intercessions" (*in oratione universali fidelibus praeeundo*) to "announcing the intentions of the Prayer of the Faithful" (*in orationis universalis intentiones enuntiando*) may reflect merely an updating of terminology apart from the shade of meaning that shifts the deacon's role from a leader of prayer to a presenter of petitions. The insertion of "in preparing the altar and serving the celebration of the Sacrifice" (*in altare apparando et sacrificii celebrationi inserviendo*) echoes the increased use of hieratic

the celebration of the Sacrifice, in distributing the Eucharist to the faithful, especially under the species of wine, and sometimes in giving directions regarding the people's gestures and posture.

delibus distribuenda, præcipue sub specie vini, et in gestibus et corporis habitibus populi aliquando innuendis.

II. The Duties of the People of God

95. In the celebration of Mass the faithful form a holy people, a people whom God has made his own, a royal priesthood, so that they may give thanks to God and offer the spotless Victim not only through the hands of the priest but also together with him, and so that they may learn to offer themselves.[83] They should, moreover, endeavor to make this clear by their deep religious sense and their charity toward

II. De Muneribus Populi Dei

95. In celebratione Missæ fideles efficiunt plebem sanctam, populum acquisitionis et sacerdotium regale, ut gratias Deo agant et immaculatam hostiam, non tantum per sacerdotis manus, sed etiam una cum ipso offerant et seipsos offerre discant.[83] Curent autem id manifestare per profundum sensum religiosum et per caritatem erga fratres, qui eandem celebrationem participant.

---

expressions as well as reiterating the sacrificial nature of the liturgical action at the altar. The deacon, however, does not sacrifice but rather serves. The introduction, in no. 179, of the controverted provision that the deacon is to kneel from the epiclesis until the elevation of the chalice would at first glance seem to restrict the mobility of the deacon (and introduce difficulties for older men in kneeling and rising without supports) in favor of modeling a posture of penitential piety.

The specific duties and actions of the deacon during the celebration are further specified in nos. 171–186. Article 182 repeats that, if Communion is given under both species, the deacon is to administer the cup.

The Duties of the People of God

95. Two striking changes appear in the section heading (*De muneribus populi Dei*), originally "Offices and Functions of the People of God" (*De officio et munere plebis Dei*) in *IGMR1970*. The designation "office" has been removed but "function" or "duty" remains for the people of God, suggesting another step in defining official liturgical ministries as belonging solely to the ordained. The shift from *plebs* to *populus* may not be significant in contemporary ecclesial Latin, although in classical Latin *populus* would have been a term inclusive of both leadership and the people at large.

Article 62 of previous *IGMR*s has now been divided into nos. 95, 96 and 97. The first sentence mixes scriptural paradigms denoting the dignity of the people of God as a holy people, a people acquired (by God), and a royal priesthood. In this perspective the high dignity of the people of God in offering sacrifice not only through but also together with the priest, testifies to a type of "office"

brothers and sisters who participate with them in the same celebration.

Thus, they are to shun any appearance of individualism or division, keeping before their eyes that they have only one Father in heaven and accordingly are all brothers and sisters to each other.

Vitent proinde omnes species vel singulariæ vitæ vel divisionis, præ oculis habentes se unicum Patrem habere in cælis, omnesque propterea esse inter se fratres.

96. Indeed, they form one body, whether by hearing the word of God, or by joining in the prayers and the singing, or above all by the common offering of Sacrifice and by a common partaking at the Lord's table. This unity is beautifully apparent from the gestures and postures observed in common by the faithful.

96. Unum autem corpus efficiant sive verbum Dei audiendo, sive in orationibus et in cantu partem habendo, sive præsertim in communi oblatione sacrificii et in communi participatione mensæ Domini. Hæc unitas pulchre apparet ex gestibus et corporis habitibus a fidelibus communiter servatis.

---

ineffaceably rooted in baptism and inalienably belonging to the baptized people of God, even without the word *officio* in the heading. In fact, both aspects of the offering put the assembly in a double relation to their presider before God, a paradox held in tension in the dialogical nature of the liturgy itself (cf. no. 34 above). The note that they are to offer themselves as well further marks their baptismal dignity as those who have died and risen with Christ (see *LG*, no. 11).

The second paragraph of article 95 presents an ethical counsel concerning the desired attitude of the assembly in the building up of Christian community among them. The reference to "individualism" (*singularae vitae*) suggests a critique of the dominant individualism considered in Western cultures as a norm and even a virtue. The paragraph recalls Paul's advice to the Corinthians (see 1 Cor 11). Yet taken together these two paragraphs do not represent liturgical law, strictly speaking, and they present a theological foundation of law only in the first sentence. Prescribed attitudes cannot be legislated, since penalties can be applied only to acts. A positive, mutually supportive, joyful Christian community can develop only from high morale, a sense of support and trust, and hope for the future.

96. This article too shows no textual change from *IGMR1975,* although it has been separated from the larger no. 62 in *IGMR1975.* It echoes no. 42 above. The concept of the faithful in one worshiping community forming "one body" was subject to much misunderstanding when it was first advanced by liturgical theologians linked to the early-twentieth-century liturgical movement, until the term Mystical Body of Christ gained official approbation in the 1943 encyclical *Mystici Corporis*. This passage testifies to the dynamic nature of active participation by the laity embodied in the eucharistic liturgy since Vatican II.

The phrase "this unity is beautifully apparent" (*haec unitas pulchre apparet*) represents a desired state of affairs and not liturgical legislation properly speak-

97. The faithful, moreover, should not refuse to serve the People of God gladly whenever they are asked to perform some particular ministry or function in the celebration.

97. Ne renuant autem fideles populo Dei cum gaudio servire, quoties rogantur, ut aliquod peculiare ministerium vel munus in celebratione præstent.

---

ing, as above. Yet today advocating uniformity of gesture and posture in a worshiping community would necessitate an awareness of differences in ability and a sensitivity toward those who are physically challenged within that community. Differences in theological interpretation of various postures in the liturgy, as well as local custom and the liturgical legislation of different countries, must also be factored into an understanding of posture. For example, while *IGMR2002* praises the practice of the assembly changing their stance during the Eucharistic Prayer from standing to kneeling following the *Sanctus* (no. 43 above), reflecting the longtime policy of the US Catholic bishops, a case could also be made for the appropriateness of standing to signify the dignity of the baptized faithful as a "holy priesthood" who offer sacrifice along with their presider.

97. This sentence, constituting a proper article at the conclusion of Part II of Chapter III of *IGMR2002*, is drawn from the closing statement of the first article in Part II in *IGMR1975*. The two Latin texts are nearly identical (although the official English translations are not), with one crucial exception. To the phrase "some particular ministry" (*aliquod peculiare ministerium*), *IGMR2002* adds "or function" (*vel munus*).[4] This addition is consistent with the effort throughout the new *IGMR* and other legislation in recent years, such as *Codex Iuris Canonici* (*CIC1983*, c. 907) constantly to articulate the difference between liturgical ministries practiced according to ordination (bishops, priests, and deacons) or institution (acolytes and lectors) from functions (*munus/munera*) carried out by laypeople happy (*cum gaudio*) to assist and collaborate with the pastors who call them to such service. Only those ministries done by the ordained are modified by the adjective "sacred." Other liturgical ministries, whether done by instituted or locally deputed laity, are proper to the theological principles of the Roman liturgy and its parts—e.g., a deacon or layperson, not the priest celebrant, is to announce the prayer of the faithful in the Liturgy of

4. According to Mohrmann, the concept *munus* in ancient Church documents referred to the service of worship or offering done by officials, while also at times appearing in more poetic, nontechnical language in reference to the offerings made to God. Citing ancient Church authors ("Digests"), Casel tied both of these meanings together, arguing that while the use of the term coincided with the ancient notion of liturgy, the offering of worship (the gifts) precisely by the people of the Church designated an act not only of the hierarchy but also the laity. See Christine Mohrmann, *Etudes sur le latin des chrétiens*, Vol. III: *Latin chrétien et liturgique*, Storia e letterature, Raccolta di studi e testi, no. 103 (Roma: Edizioni di stoira e letteratura, 1965), 235, n. 16; and Odo Casel, "Leitourgia-munus," *Oriens Christianus* 3, serie 7 (1932): 289–302.

the Word (see no. 71 above) and, thus, to the rich variety characteristic of the liturgical action and participation by all the members of the Church (see *CIC1983*, c. 837). *EccMys* describes all such lay collaboration with the ordained a matter "not merely of assistance but of mutual enrichment of the common Christian vocation" (no. 4). Such ministries are carried out according to *CIC1983* and, in this specific area, liturgical legislation.

Particular Ministries

The Ministry of the Instituted Acolyte and Lector

The subtitle preceding the next two articles indicates the first of two subdivisions in this third section of the chapter is dedicated to the various liturgical ministries practiced by the laity. These first two are offices conferred by institution, while the subsequent division entails ministries practiced by laymen and laywomen by deputation of the local bishop or pastor. This section in *IGMR1975* includes no such bifurcation and subtitles.

In establishing the offices of instituted acolyte and lector in his 1972 *motu proprio, Ministeria quaedam* (*MQ*), Pope Paul VI (d. 1978) eliminated the minor orders of porter, reader, exorcist, and acolyte, as well as one of the major orders, the subdiaconate. Strongly influenced by a fifth century Gallican treatise,[5] medieval Roman officials had canonized the minor orders in the Roman Pontifical, clericalizing all liturgical ministries that had developed over the centuries and placing them in the realm of the *sacerdotium*. The Council of Trent (1545–63) considered reforming the minor orders, recognizing the special value of acolyte and lector for dignified liturgical celebration, but the attempt failed, leaving the minor orders as seminary steps toward the ordained priesthood.[6] Paul VI's reform released from the clerical orbit liturgical ministries lacking intrinsic connection to ordination, situating them, rather, in the laity's share in the priesthood of Christ through baptism. The pastoral-liturgical importance of the ministries of acolyte and lector warranted their status as offices, Paul decreed, subsuming the former functions of subdeacon into the two, as well. Their function as lay ministries required a new form of conferral, "institution," as opposed to ordination. *MQ* both commits these two instituted ministries to "lay Christians" and requires them of seminarians, with only males being eligible in either case, following "the venerable tradition of the Church" (no. 7). The reason for conferring these ministries on seminarians is to provide them better preparation "for the future service of the word and of the altar" that they will perform as clerics. Why that should be so is better addressed when considering the nature and function of each of the two instituted ministries in turn.

5. *Statuta Ecclesiae Antiqua* in *Concilia Galliae A. 314–506*, ed. Charles Munier, Corpus Christianorum Series Latina 148 (Turnhout, 1963), 164–185.

6. See David N. Power, *Gifts That Differ: Lay Ministries Established and Unestablished* (New York: Pueblo, 1985), 3–8 and 86–88.

III. Particular Ministries

The Ministry of the Instituted Acolyte and Lector

98. The acolyte is instituted to serve at the altar and to assist the priest and deacon. In particular, it is his responsibility to prepare the altar and the sacred vessels and, if it is necessary, as an extraordinary minister, to distribute the Eucharist to the faithful.[84]

In the ministry of the altar, the acolyte has his own functions (cf. below, nos. 187–193), which he must perform personally.

III. De Ministeriis Peculiaribus

De ministerio acolythi et lectoris institutorum

98. Acolythus instituitur ad servitium altaris et in adiutorium sacerdotis et diaconi. Ipsius præcipue est altare atque vasa sacra parare et, si necesse est, Eucharistiam, cuius est minister extraordinarius, fidelibus distribuere.[84]

In ministerio altaris, acolythus partes proprias habet *(cf. nn. 187–193)* quas ipse exercere debet.

---

98. This article gives a general description of the service the instituted acolyte renders to the eucharistic celebration and its ordained celebrants while noting that a detailed description of these functions is to be found in Chapter IV, nos. 187–193.

That the acolyte's ministry is especially oriented to the "service of the altar," a service in "sincere love for the Mystical Body of Christ, the People of God" (*MQ*, no. 6), is attested in the prayer said by the bishop during the liturgy of institution, which addresses God as the one who has "entrusted the bread of life" to the Church and asks God that through their service, the acolytes might "grow always in faith and love, and so build up your Church."[7] The acolyte, therefore, is not a mere ritual functionary but, rather, a minister in service to the eucharistic sacrifice that nourishes the People of God for entire lives that are "spiritual sacrifices acceptable to God through Jesus Christ" (1 Pet 2:5).[8] It is not only the acolyte's duty to carry the Missal and other processional objects, as well as to prepare the altar, but he can be expected, as needed, to instruct others (laymen and laywomen) deputed for similar service (see *MQ*, no. 6). Such work, along with ministering the Eucharist to the weak and sick, would seem to contribute to the greater understanding of the liturgy that Paul VI expected the instituted office of acolyte to provide for seminarians. In addition, his *motu proprio* instructs that the acolyte should grow in eucharistic piety and study the spiritual meaning of the Blessed Sacrament so as to become exemplary in his reverent service to the liturgy and total self-gift to God.

7. *De Institutione Lectorum et Acolythorum* (1972), ch. II, no. 6, trans. ICEL in *Rites I*. 744–45.

8. See J.-M.-R. Tillard, *Flesh of the Church, Flesh of Christ: At the Source of the Ecclesiology of Communion*, trans. Madeleine Beaumont (Collegeville, MN: The Liturgical Press, 2001), 97–99.

99. The lector is instituted to proclaim the readings from Sacred Scripture, with the exception of the Gospel. He may also announce the intentions for the Prayer of the Faithful and, in the absence of a psalmist, proclaim the Psalm between the readings.

In the Eucharistic Celebration, the lector has his own proper office (cf. below, nos. 194–198), which he must exercise personally.

99. Lector instituitur ad proferendas lectiones sacræ Scripturæ, Evangelio excepto. Potest etiam intentiones orationis universalis proponere et, deficiente psalmista, psalmum inter lectiones proferre.

In celebratione eucharistica lector proprium munus habet *(cf. nn. 194–198)*, quod ipse per se exercere debet.

The other service the instituted acolyte provides is distributing the Eucharist in the capacity of an extraordinary minister of Holy Communion. That this lay liturgical function had become a cause of concern for the hierarchy over the past two decades is indicated by both the addition of a dependent clause in no. 98 that is not found in the otherwise identically worded article in *IGMR1975* (no. 65) and a difference between GIRM1975 and GIRM2003 translations of the adjective *extraordinarius*. *IGMR2002* emphasizes the supplementary quality of the acolyte's ministry of Holy Communion by adding the clause, "if it is necessary" (*si necesse est*). True, *MQ* (citing *CIC1917*, c. 845) explains the instituted acolyte's service of distributing Holy Communion, as well as publicly exposing the Blessed Sacrament for adoration, as "auxiliary" functions for "extraordinary circumstances," namely, the lack of priests or deacons, their ill health or, in the case of Communion, "great [numbers] approaching the table" (no. 6). *MQ*, however, predates *IGMR1975* by two years. The addition of "if it is necessary" to *IGMR2002* is representative of the concerns raised and reiterated in *EccMys* and *RedSac*. The former instruction repeatedly warns that the function of extraordinary ministry of Communion must "avoid generating confusion" (no. 7), namely, a generic sense of eucharistic ministry that reduces the "sacred ministry" of the ordained to a merely "functional concept" (no. 4), or elevates the laity by attributing this functional, "supplementary and extraordinary" (no. 8, citing *CIC1983*, c. 230, pars. 2 and 3) service with quasi-clerical status. Further consideration of *RedSac* on this point will be taken up with no. 100 below. The preceding should be adequate to appreciate why the GIRM1975 translation of *et Eucharistiam, cuius est minister extraordinarius, fidelibus distribuere* as "and, as *special minister* of the eucharist, to give Communion to the faithful" (no. 65), is now rendered, "and . . . as an *extraordinary minister*, to distribute the Eucharist to the faithful" (GIRM2003, no. 98).

99. This article provides a general description of the office of instituted lector as its "own proper office . . . exercise[d] personally" (*lector proprium munus habet . . . quod ipse exercere debet*), while nos. 194 to 198 below will address the lector's duties in detail.

IGMR2002's consistent priority to highlight the hierarchical distinctions of those participating in or providing ministerial service to the liturgy is especially evident in this article on the lector when compared with its equivalent in *IGMR1975* (no. 66). That constant (clericalizing) concern would seem to be the reason for eliminating *IGMR1975*'s further specification on what is proper and personal about the lector's proclamation of the readings from Sacred Scripture. Moreover, it would seem to be the cause for an unfortunate splitting of the description of this ministry, such that its value in the larger context of the Liturgy of the Word and its importance for the life of faith is (oddly) deferred to a later article, i.e., that addressing deputed readers (no. 101, below). Thus, the article on the lector in *IGMR2002* is significantly shorter than that in the prior edition and limited to consideration of the instituted office. Even at that, it fails to elaborate on this liturgical ministry. While the current text reads "the lector has his own proper office . . . which he must exercise personally" (*lector proprium munus habet . . . quod ipse per se exercere debet*), *IGMR1975* adds to the exact same statement, "and should exercise this even though ministers of higher rank may be present" (*quamvis adsint ministri gradus superioris*). Ironically, if one turns to the treatment of the ministries to the Liturgy of the Word in the introduction to the current Lectionary for Mass (*OLM1981-Pr*), the article on lectors (no. 51) begins by quoting that (now-eliminated) statement from *IGMR1975*.

Nonetheless, the main point about what is proper to the lector as specified in this article, just as it is in *MQ* (no. 5), concerns the scope of scriptural proclamation that he is to read, namely, anything but the gospel (on the proclamation of the gospel as proper to the ordained clergy, see nos. 59 and 94 above). When available, instituted lectors should proclaim the first and second biblical readings "on Sundays and festive days" (*OLM1981-Pr,* no. 51). The psalm between those two readings, however, is normally the ministry of the cantor/psalmist, for psalms and canticles, by their very nature, call for sung proclamation (see no. 102 below, also *Liturgical Music Today* [LMT], no. 35). Lack of a cantor or psalmist, however, results in the lector proclaiming the psalm. The order of responsibility for announcing the intercessions of the prayer of the faithful is "the deacon . . . or a cantor, a lector, or one of the lay faithful" (see no. 71 above; also, *OLM1981-Pr,* nos. 30 and 53). Thus, this function may fall to an instituted lector in a given liturgy.

The office of lector entails a ministry to the Word more comprehensive than mere ritual function. Indeed, *MQ* prohibits that reductionism by exhorting the lector "to make every effort and employ suitable means to acquire that increasingly warm and living love and knowledge of Scripture that will make him a more perfect disciple of the Lord" (no. 5, with citation of *SC,* no. 24). Here again, as with the office of instituted acolyte, the *motu proprio* sounds the tones of formation for the ordained priesthood, assigning the lector to "prepar[e] other faithful who by a temporary appointment are to read the Scriptures in liturgical celebrations," while the model homily for the Institution of Readers tells them: "You will proclaim that word [of God] in the liturgical assembly, instruct children and adults in the faith, and prepare them to receive the sacraments worthily" (*De Institutione Lectorum et Acolythorum*, ch. I, no. 4). Emphatically

Other Ministries

100. In the absence of an instituted acolyte, lay ministers may be deputed to serve at the altar and assist the priest and the deacon; they may carry the cross, the candles, the thurible, the bread, the wine, and the water, and they may also be deputed to distribute Holy Communion as extraordinary ministers.[85]

De ceteris muneribus

100. Deficiente acolytho instituto, ad servitium altaris et in adiutorium sacerdotis et diaconi deputari possunt ministri laici qui crucem, cereos, thuribulum, panem, vinum, aquam deferunt, vel etiam ad sacram Communionem distribuendam deputantur ut ministri extraordinarii.[85]

---

forbidden, however, is the practice of seminarians, installed lectors, or any layperson, preaching the homily within Mass (see *RedSac*, nos. 65–66 [with 146], and *EccMys*, no. 3.1).

As noted above in the introductory comments on the offices of acolyte and lector, only men are eligible for them. While Paul VI clearly envisioned other laymen than seminarians holding these offices, pastoral sensitivity to women's exclusion from them seems to have been a crucial factor preventing this from happening. The historical fact in the US has been that, with few exceptions, only seminarians have been instituted as acolytes and lectors. Thus, one could argue that even though Paul VI explicitly designated these to be lay ministries, they still practically function as milestones along the way to priestly ordination. This is reinforced when one reads in *OLM1981-Pr* that "an instituted reader must wear the distinctive vestment of their office when they go up to the ambo to read the word of God," whereas those who carry out this ministry without institution "may go to the ambo in ordinary attire" (no. 54). The treatment of "Other Ministries" (nos. 100–107), comprising the remainder of Section III of this present chapter, then, concerns what practically characterizes nearly all lay liturgical ministries and functions in US parishes, oratories, and school and hospital chapels today.

Other Ministries

100. Following the "Guidelines for Altar Servers," approved by the US bishops in 1994 and slightly revised by the Bishop's Committee on the Liturgy according to *IGMR2000*, the local bishop may permit the liturgical functions of the instituted acolyte, with the exception of distributing Holy Communion, to be performed by altar servers. According to those guidelines, "the role of server is integral to the normal celebration of the Mass" (no. 5), and so at least one should always assist the priest, two or more on Sundays and feasts. Servers should, accordingly, be well formed in the parts of the Mass, the articles used, necessary duties, and proper decorum. It is the local ordinary's decision to establish diocesan-wide policy allowing not only men and boys but also women and girls to be altar servers. The guidelines, therefore, call for the term "server" to replace "altar boy." When both males and females do function as altar servers

101. In the absence of an instituted lector, other laypersons may be commissioned to proclaim the readings from Sacred Scripture. They should be truly suited

101. Deficiente lectore instituto, alii laici deputentur ad proferendas lections sacræ Scripturæ, qui revera apti sint huic muneri adimplendo et sedulo præparati, ut fideles

---

in a diocese, there is to be no division of the various duties (e.g., carrying the cross, candles, bread, wine, etc.) by gender. In the case of boys and girls, altar servers should possess adequate maturity and have received Holy Communion. Indeed, the guidelines stipulate that altar servers of whatever age should "normally receive the Eucharist whenever they participate in the liturgy" (no. 3). Still, for all the guidelines' careful allowance for servers of both sexes and all (reasonable) ages, the Vatican's subsequent *RedSac* devotes an entire article extolling "the noble custom by which boys or youths . . . provide service at the altar," warning that it should not "be forgotten that a great number of sacred ministers over the course of the centuries have come from among boys such as these" (no. 47). The article goes on to encourage local and international associations for young male altar servers, "including also the participation and assistance of their parents."

The US bishops have distinguished the lay ministering of Communion from the other functions of the locally deputed server. As already noted in reference to the instituted acolyte (see no. 98 above), distribution of Holy Communion by a layperson is an extraordinary service always to be necessitated by an insufficient number of able-bodied ordained (sacred) ministers. Inaugurated by the 1973 Vatican instruction *Immensae caritatis*, the extraordinary ministry of Holy Communion has been subject to repeated reiterations of the conditions under which it is allowed or, conversely, forbidden (see *RedSac,* nos. 155 and 157), as well as increased specification of the titles not to be given it: "This function is to be understood strictly according to the name by which it is known, that is to say, that of extraordinary minister of Holy Communion, and not 'special minister of Holy Communion' nor 'extraordinary minister of the Eucharist' nor 'special minister of the Eucharist,' by which names the meaning of this function is unnecessarily and improperly broadened" (*RedSac,* no. 156). As noted regarding no. 98 above, *EccMys* focuses on the danger of confusing this lay function with the power of sacred ministerial office. The Instruction prohibits three specific practices: 1) extraordinary ministers giving Communion to themselves or receiving it "apart from the other faithful," 2) receiving their blessing for this ministry during the Chrism Mass on Holy Thursday, and 3) a "habitual use of extraordinary ministers of holy communion at Mass, thus arbitrarily extending the concept of a great number of the faithful [approaching the altar]" (no. 8).

101. As noted for no. 98 above, *IGMR2002* separates its treatment of the deputed reader from that of the instituted lector. Number 101 is a mildly reworded presentation of the third paragraph of *IGMR1975*, no. 66. In addition

to perform this function and should receive careful preparation, so that the faithful by listening to the readings from the sacred texts may develop in their hearts a warm and living love for Sacred Scripture.[86]

ex auditione lectionum divinarum suavem et vivum sacræ Scripturæ affectum[86] in corde concipiant.

102. The psalmist's role is to sing the Psalm or other biblical canticle that comes between the readings. To fulfill this function correctly, it is necessary that the psalmist have the ability for singing and a facility in correct pronunciation and diction.

102. Psalmistæ est psalmum vel aliud canticum biblicum, quod inter lections invenitur, proferre. Ad suum munus recte implendum necesse est, ut psalmista et arte psallendi et facultate recte pronuntiandi et dicendi polleat.

---

to the qualities expected of all liturgical ministers (see no. 107 below), suitability for proclaiming the scriptural readings entails adequate intellectual capacity, reverence for the Word of God, and the ability to articulate and project one's voice. Being able-bodied, that is, ambulatory, however, is not a criterion. Indeed, the USCCB's *Built of Living Stones* (BLS, ch. 2, no. 61) stipulates that the ambo be accessible to all, including the physically disabled. The qualities distinguishing the layperson called to this ministry emerge in the detailed outline of preparation laid out in *OLM1981-Pr,* no. 55: spiritual formation, developing "the ability to understand the readings in context and to perceive by the light of faith the central point of the revealed message"; liturgical formation, educating the reader in the structure of the Liturgy of the Word and its relation to the Liturgy of the Eucharist; and technical preparation, enhancing the reader's ability both to project one's voice and to use sound equipment effectively. *OLM1981-Pr,* no. 52, asserts the importance of the recruitment and preparation of readers, arguing that the "liturgical assembly requires readers"—a statement pointing to the entire theology of the biblical word as an essential source of the Church's liturgy (its readings but also prayers and structural elements), as well as an irreducible resource for the mission of all the faithful in the world (see *SC,* nos. 24, 52, 53; and *OLM1981-Pr,* nos. 1–7). All the baptized are called to this biblically-formed life-as-spiritual-sacrifice, and the expectation that different readers, if available, do the various readings in a given liturgy (see *OLM1981-Pr,* no. 52) reinforces the practice of this lay liturgical ministry as a symbolic call to all the assembled faithful to practice lives proclaiming the Gospel and promoting the justice and mercy of the kingdom of God.

102. The psalmist serves a highly important ministerial function. The responsorial psalm proclaimed to the assembly, as a text of Sacred Scripture, "is an integral part of the Liturgy of the Word and holds great liturgical and pastoral importance, because it fosters meditation on the word of God" (*pars integralis liturgiae verbi et magnum momentum liturgicum et pastorale prae se fert, cum verbi Dei meditationem foveat,* no. 61). Indeed, the psalm's comprehensibility relies on its being sung: "The singing of the psalm, or even the response alone, is a great help toward understanding and meditating on the psalm's spiritual meaning"

103. Among the faithful, the *schola cantorum* or choir exercises its own liturgical function, ensuring that the parts proper to it, in keeping with the different types of chants, are properly carried out and fostering the active participation of the faithful through the singing.[87] What is said about the choir also applies, in accordance with the relevant norms, to other musicians, especially the organist.

103. Inter fideles suum munus liturgicum exercet schola cantorum vel chorus, cuius est de partibus sibi propriis, iuxta diversa genera cantuum, debite exsequendis, curare, et actuosam fidelium participationem in cantu fovere.[87] Quæ de schola cantorum dicuntur, valent, servatis servandis, pro aliis etiam musicis, præsertim vero pro organista.

(*OLM1981-Pr,* no. 21). Given all this, the psalmist clearly needs more than native singing ability and well-developed diction. Just as lectors and readers need to be formed spiritually and liturgically in the Word of God, so should the psalmist. Furthermore, since psalmists, "as a rule" (*de more,* no. 61), lead the assembled faithful in their singing of the response between the verses of the psalm, they also should be formed in the necessary skills of liturgical leadership and ministerial presence (see LMT, nos. 64 and 65). From this, it is clear that the proclamation of the responsorial psalm, as a ministry to God's word, takes place at the ambo (see *OLM1981-Pr,* no. 22).

103. As noted at the end of no. 96, *IGMR2002* relocates the service of choirs, cantors, and other musicians from the second section of the chapter, concerning the people of God as a whole at worship, to this third one, enumerating the specific ministries of the laity. Perhaps *IGMR1975* situates the two articles on the choir and cantor (nos. 63–64) in the earlier section to emphasize that these ministries of music are done not as separate performances or entertainment (see also no. 104 below), but rather, as part of the *leitourgia* of the worshiping community, *inter fideles* (translated as "within the assembly" in GIRM1975; GIRM2003 renders it "among the faithful"). The choir's work is to provide the chants integral to the celebration of the liturgy on Sundays and feasts, as well as to enable the entire assembled people to sing what is proper to such celebration, e.g., the entrance and Communion songs, the Gospel acclamation, etc. (see *Musicam Sacram* [*MusSac*], no. 19). Thus do the choir, as well as other musicians (especially the organist), minister to both the Church's liturgy, helping to unify the worship of the mystical body of Christ, and the People of God, humbly building up the full, conscious, active participation of the faithful (see *SC,* nos. 14, 112–114; *Music in Catholic Worship* [MCW], no. 23). Given the choir, cantor, and other musicians' liturgical ministry of animating the faithful as a body of worship, "the space chosen for the musicians should clearly express that they are part of the assembly of worshipers." Indeed, in order for ministers and assembly to realize the musical nature of the liturgy, the acoustical features and sight-lines of "the building must support the music and song of the entire worshiping assembly" (BLS, ch. 2).

104. It is fitting that there be a cantor or a choir director to lead and sustain the people's singing. When in fact there is no choir, it is up to the cantor to lead the different chants, with the people taking part.[88]

105. The following also exercise a liturgical function:

a. The sacristan, who carefully arranges the liturgical books, the vestments, and other things necessary in the celebration of Mass.

104. Decet adesse cantorem vel magistrum chori ad cantum populi dirigendum et sustentandum. Immo, cum deficit schola, cantori competit diversos cantus moderari, populo pro sua parte participante.[88]

105. Munus liturgicum exercent etiam:

a) Sacrista, qui libros liturgicos, paramenta et alia, quæ in celebratione Missæ sunt necessaria, diligenter disponit.

---

104. What this article mandates for the cantor or choir director builds upon the rationale for the choir and other musicians just explicated, namely, fostering the people's musical participation in the liturgy and avoiding any degeneration of their ministry into individualistic performances extrinsically added onto the action of the people. *RedSac* puts all of this in perspective: "It is the right of the community of Christ's faithful that especially in the Sunday celebration there should be true and suitable sacred music" (no. 57). At several points in the Mass such music is to be done by the entire assembly. The cantor or choir director leads the assembled faithful in singing music aptly chosen for the liturgy of the day and suited to the musical aptitude of the specific community (see *MusSac,* nos. 20–21), offering their gifts as liturgical service: "While there is no place in the liturgy for display of virtuosity for its own sake, artistry is valued, and an individual singer can effectively lead the assembly, attractively proclaim the Word of God in the psalm sung between the readings, and take his or her part in other responsorial singing" (MCW, no. 35). The cantor, for obvious reasons therefore, needs to be positioned visibly for the entire assembly, providing this ministry from a podium to the side of the sanctuary, and using the ambo only for proclaiming the responsorial psalm (see BLS, ch. 2, no. 89).

105. The four liturgical functions of sacristan, commentator, collection-takers, and greeters are carried out in local communities by members who are generous in service to the less liturgically elevated tasks. The Church's liturgy is an action of Christ, head and members (*SC,* no. 7), which is to say that, while divinely initiated, it is also a human endeavor that depends on practical measures to assure its smooth and rewarding enactment. Local pastors depend on the men and women serving these four functions for their reliability and honesty in handling church property and financial contributions but, more importantly, for their care toward all who come to the liturgy, whether local members, fellow Christians, or other guests. In truly tangible ways these lay ministers are the face of the Church, symbolizing in their selfless functions various fundamental dimensions of liturgy as a work by and for the people of God. The Order for the Blessing of Altar Servers, Sacristans, Musicians, and Ushers in-

b. The commentator, who provides the faithful, when appropriate, with brief explanations and commentaries with the purpose of introducing them to the celebration and preparing them to understand it better. The commentator's remarks must be meticulously prepared and clear though brief. In performing this function the commentator stands in an appropriate place facing the faithful, but not at the ambo.

c. Those who take up the collection in the church.

d. Those who, in some places, meet the faithful at the church entrance, lead them to appropriate places, and direct processions.

106. It is appropriate, at least in cathedrals and in larger churches, to have some

b) Commentator, qui explicationes et admonitiones pro opportunitate breviter proponit fidelibus, ut in celebrationem introducantur et ad eius intellegentiam melius disponantur. Oportet monitiones commentatoris sint adamussim præparatæ et sobrietate perspicuæ. In suo munere adimplendo, commentator stat loco apto coram fidelibus, non vero in ambone.

c) Qui collectas in ecclesia faciunt.

d) Ii, qui aliquibus in regionibus, fideles ad portas ecclesiæ recipiunt eosque in locis ipsis convenientibus disponunt, et eorum processiones ordinant.

106. Expedit ut, saltem in ecclesiis cathedralibus et maioribus, habeatur aliquis

---

cludes this petition among its general intercessions: "For all the liturgical ministers of our parish, that they may deepen their commitment to serve God and their neighbor" (*Book of Blessings,* no. 1853). For their part, then, these ministers need to pray and reflect upon the nature and purpose of their service, seeking to avoid or correct (should they emerge) any tendencies toward officiousness or inordinate control that could detract from the liturgy's mission.

It is important to offer a particular word about the commentator. This ministry was quite common in the early years of the post–Vatican II reform and renewal of the liturgy but now is quite rare in the US. The great progress made over the past several decades in redacting good hymnals (that include orders of worship) and missalettes would seem to have put these printed liturgical aids in place of commentators. Should local community leadership discern a need for a commentator for a particular liturgy or even every Sunday, perhaps the "Guidelines for the Publication of Participation Aids,"[9] with its articulation of principles for printed commentary, might provide pastoral-liturgical criteria for the exercise of this ministry to the worshiping assembly. In any event, any tendency toward didacticism should be avoided (see *SC,* no. 34).

106. As with those ministries enumerated in no. 105, the recommendation of having a master of ceremonies for liturgies in cathedrals and large churches is likewise a matter of human practicality in ritual execution. The need for this

9. Originally in the *BCL Newsletter* (July, 1998), available at http://www.usccb.org/liturgy/innews/798.shtml (accessed December 2006).

competent minister, that is to say a master of ceremonies, to oversee the proper planning of sacred actions and their being carried out by the sacred ministers and the lay faithful with decorum, order, and devotion.

competens minister seu cæremoniarum magister, qui curet de actionibus sacris congrue disponendis et cum decore, ordine et pietate per ministros sacros et fideles laicos exercendis.

107. The liturgical duties that are not proper to the priest or the deacon and are listed in nos. 100–106 may also be entrusted by a liturgical blessing or a temporary deputation to suitable lay persons chosen by the pastor or rector of the church.[89] All should observe the norms established by the Bishop for his diocese regarding the office of those who serve the priest at the altar.

107. Liturgica munera, quæ non sunt propria sacerdotis vel diaconi, et de quibus superius *(nn. 100–106)* dicitur, etiam laicis idoneis a parocho vel rectore ecclesiæ selectis,[89] committi possunt liturgica benedictione vel temporanea deputatione. Quoad munus inserviendi sacerdoti ad altare, serventur normæ ab Episcopo datæ pro sua diœcesi.

"competent minister" (*competens minister*) arises not only from the added complexities or infrequency of certain rites performed in cathedrals but also the simultaneous management and support of a significant number of ministers in churches with large worshiping assemblies. A good master of ceremonies makes it possible for all the other ministers, whether ordained or lay, to serve their functions without worried distraction. While the person called to this ministry needs to be a good planner, able to think on one's feet, and knowledgeable of the rites, she or he also should find time regularly to study, pray, and reflect on the Church's worship. This enables the master of ceremonies to serve in a manner that fosters rather than detracts from the fundamentally prayerful nature of the overall liturgical action.

107. The subjects of this closing article to section III are "suitable lay persons" (*laicis idoneis*). Comment on the criteria for and formation of suitable instituted acolytes and lectors, as well as deputed readers, has already been made above (see nos. 98, 99 and 101). Liturgical blessings prepared by ICEL and approved for use in the US signal some of the qualities characterizing suitability for the other non-instituted ministries. The general intercessions ask that " the light of Christ may shine in [the] hearts" of altar servers, that by their work sacristans might encourage the faithful "to prepare [their] hearts for worship," that parish musicians produce "beauty . . . in song and praise" that affects the people at worship, and that the pastoral presence of ushers "make all who enter this church always feel welcome in God's house" (*Book of Blessings,* no. 1853). The prayer of blessing (*Book of Blessings,* no. 1854) describes these ministers as having responded to the parish's needs and committed themselves to God's service. *RedSac* provides a more precise description: "The lay Christian faithful called to give assistance at liturgical celebrations should be well instructed and must be those whose Christian life, morals and fidelity to the church's Magisterium

IV. The Distribution of Duties and The Preparation of the Celebration

108. One and the same priest celebrant must always exercise the presidential office in all of its parts, except for those parts which are proper to a Mass at which the Bishop is present (cf. no. 92).

IV. De Distributione Munerum et de Præparatione Celebrationis

108. Unus idemque sacerdos munus præsidentiale semper in omnibus eius partibus exercere debet, iis exceptis quæ propria sunt Missæ cui Episcopus interest (*cf.* supra *n.* 92).

---

recommend them. . . . No one should be selected whose designation could cause consternation for the faithful" (no. 46, with citation of *Immensae caritatis*). The local pastor oversees the various ministries and normally is the one who blesses those who serve them (see *Book of Blessings,* no. 1851), while in the case of widespread appointment of extraordinary ministers of Holy Communion, the diocesan bishop "should issue special norms by which he determines the manner in which this function is to be carried out in accordance with the law, bearing in mind the tradition of the Church" (*RedSac,* no. 160). For all such ministries, the deputation is temporary, that is, in no way signifying or participating in an office (see *CIC1983*, c. 230, par. 2).

A significant difference between this summary article and *IGMR1975* concerns the service of women in liturgical ministries (see Power and Vincie, 54–55 above). Whereas the earlier edition gives universal allowance for laymen to perform all functions "below those reserved to deacons" (*infra ea quae propria sunt diaconi*), it restricts women's possibilities to those ministries performed "outside the sanctuary" (*extra presbyterium*) with even that allowance subject to the local pastor's discretion (*IGMR1975*, no. 70). As for non-instituted readers, the former *IGMR* leaves it to conferences of bishops to decide on permitting qualified women for this service, as well as the question of whether such women readers should be allowed to proclaim the Word of God from the sanctuary or, rather, merely from some location "in the liturgical assembly" (*in coetu liturgico, IGMR1975*, no. 70). No such article exists in *IGMR2002*. The current legislation has made women eligible for all deputed ministries (although the question of altar servers is left to each diocesan bishop, per no. 100 above).

The Distribution of Duties and the Preparation of the Celebration

108. A new addition to *IGMR2002*, this article makes sense when seen as a piece with nos. 109, 110, and 111. All of these are grouped under a new section heading, "*De distributione munerum et de praeparatione celebrationis,*" again using the collective term "tasks" without speaking of "ministries." Number 108 uses "*sacerdos,*" a term referring to bishop or priest but not to a deacon. The actual designation of duties is further broken down by specifying that no. 92, with its emphasis on the prerogative of the bishop to preside at the Eucharist together with priest concelebrants, or else to preside at the Liturgy of the Word, takes precedence over this provision.

109. If there are several persons present who are able to exercise the same ministry, nothing forbids their distributing among themselves and performing different parts of the same ministry or duty. For example, one deacon may be assigned to take the sung parts, another to serve at the altar; if there are several readings, it is well to distribute them among a number of lectors. The same applies for the other ministries. But it is not at all appropriate that several persons divide a single element of the celebration among themselves, e.g., that the same reading be proclaimed by two lectors, one after the other, except as far as the Passion of the Lord is concerned.

109. Si plures adsunt qui idem ministerium exercere possunt, nihil vetat, quominus diversas partes eiusdem ministerii vel officii inter se distribuant et peragant. Ex. gr., alius diaconus adhiberi potest pro partibus in cantu proferendis, et alius pro ministerio altaris; si plures lectiones habentur, inter plures lectores eas distribuere iuvat, et sic de ceteris. Minime vero congruit ut plures unicum elementum celebrationis inter se dividant: ex. gr. eadem lectio a duobus, unus post alium, lecta, nisi agatur de Passione Domini.

The language used, "one and the same priest celebrant must always" (*Unus idemque sacerdos munus praesidentiale semper . . . debet*), strengthens the force of liturgical law on this point. The effect is to centralize the leadership of a particular celebration on one presider and to exclude any division of labor among two or more concelebrating priests, a principle consistent with the overarching emphasis on the singularity and prominence of the role of the presider in *IGMR20002*.

109. This article, taken over from the earlier *IGMR1975* with no change until the last sentence, sets up a contrast with no.108. Deacons or lectors may choose to divide the parts pertinent to their liturgical ministry (and the text retains the original 1969 term *ministerium*). Certainly at the Easter Vigil, given the number of readings and the more demanding diaconal duties, to do so would make perfect sense from the standpoint both of the structure of the liturgy and of simple human endurance. On the distribution of the parts of the Eucharistic Prayer in concelebrations, see nos. 219ff below.

The newly inserted final sentence, formulated in direct but not extreme language ("not at all appropriate," *minime congruit*), takes a position against distributing a single element of the liturgy among several deacons or lay ministers. While at first glance the English text may lend itself to some misunderstanding ("e.g., that the same reading be proclaimed by two lectors, one after the other") whether two successive lectors or two successive proclamations of the same reading were meant (apart from the example given), the Latin text says clearly *ex. gr., eadem lectio a duobus, unus post alium, lecta*. This may point directly to the practice of dividing a particularly long reading among two or more lectors to proclaim in turn. It does not seem to exclude one reading proclaimed twice in two different languages if necessary.

110. If only one minister is present at a Mass with a congregation, that minister may exercise several different duties.

111. Among all who are involved with regard to the rites, pastoral aspects, and music there should be harmony and diligence in the effective preparation of each liturgical celebration in accord with the Missal and other liturgical books. This should take place under the direction of the rector of the church and after the consultation with the faithful about things that directly pertain to them. The priest who presides at the celebration, however, always retains the right of arranging those things that are his own responsibility.[90]

110. Si in Missa cum populo unus tantum minister adest, ipse diversa munera exerceat.

111. Effectiva cuiusque celebrationis liturgicæ præparatio concordi et diligenti animo iuxta Missale et alios libros liturgicos fiat inter omnes quorum interest sive quoad ritus, sive quoad rem pastoralem et musicam, rectore ecclesiæ moderante et auditis quoque fidelibus pro iis quæ ad ipsos directe pertinent. Sacerdoti vero, qui celebrationi præest, ius semper manet disponendi de his quæ ipsi competunt.[90]

---

110. This brief article, unchanged from *IGMR1969* and nonspecific in its formulation, provides a counterbalance to no. 109 by recognizing that if only one liturgical minister (again using *minister*) can be present, that person might fulfill multiple appropriate roles. While perhaps a necessary concession particularly for daily Mass in a parish, a Sunday Eucharist should ideally manifest a broader involvement of the local worshiping community in ministerial roles (see no. 112 below) to represent more fully the diversity among the people of God.

111. The third chapter's concluding article in *IGMR2002* differs significantly in length and tone from the similar one (no. 73) in *IGMR1975*. The revised Latin (typical) text is a full third longer than its predecessor, with the content of the expanded material shifting the overall tone of the article from one of mutual collaboration of liturgical ministers with their pastor to the rector's need for diligence (*diligente*) in assuring that *Missale Romanum* and other liturgical books are properly followed. The difference between the translations of the material common to GIRM1975 and GIRM2003 for this article further accents the priority of clerical supervision. *IGMR2002* adds an entirely new sentence at the end, asserting that "the priest who presides at the celebration, however, always retains the right of arranging those things that are his own responsibility" (*Sacerdoti vero, qui celebrationi praest, ius sempter manet disponendi de his quae ipsi competent*). The footnote at the end of the article cites *SC*, no. 22, which delimits the scope of authority for regulating the liturgy (resting basically with the Apostolic See, diocesan ordinaries, and conferences of bishops) and prohibits any person, even a priest, from adding, removing, or altering anything in the liturgy. No such footnote was appended to the *IGMR1975* version of this article. Still, the new edition retains the call for the variety of ministers, ordained and lay, to understand how the liturgy functions as a whole, not as isolated parts and performances, and so to work for a harmonious execution in practice. Among the ritual, pastoral, and musical dimensions mentioned, the latter—through both sound and silence—plays no small part in unifying the liturgical action overall, as well as within each movement (entrance, Word, Eucharist, conclusion). Accordingly, then, the section "Pastoral Planning for Celebration" in MCW (nos. 10–14) could prove a helpful supplement to this article of *IGMR2002*.

Finally, given the pastoral, ritual, and leadership responsibilities of the rector (or pastor) for the liturgy in his community, *SC*'s call for liturgical formation to pervade all seminary courses (no. 16) can provide a warning against any legalistic ritualism: "Pastors must therefore realize that when the liturgy is celebrated something more is required than the mere observance of the laws governing valid and lawful celebration; it is their duty to ensure that the faithful take part fully aware of what they are doing, actively engaged in the rite, and enriched by its effects" (*SC*, no. 11).

GIRM—Notes (English)

75. Cf. Second Vatican Ecumenical Council, Constitution on the Sacred Liturgy, *Sacrosanctum Concilium*, no. 26.

76. Cf. ibid., no. 14.

77. Cf. ibid., no. 28.

78. Cf. Second Vatican Ecumenical Council, Dogmatic Constitution on the Church, *Lumen gentium*, nos. 26, 28; Constitution on the Sacred Liturgy, *Sacrosanctum Concilium*, no. 42.

79. Cf. Second Vatican Ecumenical Council, Constitution on the Sacred Liturgy, *Sacrosanctum Concilium*, no. 26.

80. Cf. *Caeremoniale Episcoporum, editio typica*, 1984, nos. 175–186.

81. Cf. Second Vatican Ecumenical Council, Dogmatic Constitution on the Church, *Lumen gentium*, no. 28; Decree on the Ministry and Life of Priests, *Presbyterorum ordinis*, no. 2.

82. Cf. Paul VI, Apostolic Letter *Sacrum diaconatus ordinem*, 18 June 1967: AAS 59 (1967), pp. 697–704; The Roman Pontifical, *Rites of Ordination of a Bishop, of Priests, and of Deacons, editio typica altera*, 1989, no. 173.

83. Cf. Second Vatican Ecumenical Council, Constitution on the Sacred Liturgy, *Sacrosanctum Concilium*, no. 48; Sacred Congregation of Rites, Instruction *Eucharisticum mysterium*, On the worship of the Eucharist, 25 May 1967, no. 12: AAS 59 (1967), pp. 548–549.

IGMR—Notes (Latin)

75. Cf. Conc. Œcum. Vat. II, Const. de sacra Liturgia, *Sacrosanctum Concilium*, n. 26.

76. Cf. *ibidem*, n. 14.

77. Cf. *ibidem*, n. 28.

78. Cf. Conc. Œcum. Vat. II, Const. dogm. de Ecclesia, *Lumen gentium*, nn. 26, 28; Const. de sacra Liturgia, *Sacrosanctum Concilium*, n. 42.

79. Cf. Conc. Œcum. Vat. II, Const. de sacra Liturgia, *Sacrosanctum Concilium*, n. 26.

80. Cf. *Cæremoniale Episcoporum*, nn. 175–186.

81. Cf. Conc. Œcum. Vat. II. Const. dogm. de Ecclesia, *Lumen gentium*, n. 28; Decretum de Presbyterorum ministerio et vita, *Presbyterorum ordinis*, n. 2.

82. Cf. Paulus VI, Litt. Ap. *Sacrum diaconatus Ordinem*, diei 18 iunii 1967: A.A.S. 59 (1967) pp. 697–704; Pontificale Romanum, *De Ordinatione Episcopi, presbyterorum et diaconorum*, edition typica altera, 1989, n. 173.

83. Conc. Œcum. Vat. II, Const. de sacra Liturgia, *Sacrosanctum Concilium*, n. 48; S. Congr. Rituum, Instr. *Eucharisticum mysterium*, diei 25 maii 1967, n. 12: A.A.S. 59 (1967) pp. 548–549.

84. Cf. *Codex Iuris Canonici*, can. 910 § 2; cf. also Interdicasterial Instruction on certain questions regarding the collaboration of the non-ordained faithful in the sacred ministry of priests, *Ecclesiae de mysterio*, 15 August 1997, art. 8: AAS 89 (1997), p. 871.

85. Cf. Sacred Congregation for the Discipline of the Sacraments, Instruction *Immensae caritatis*, 29 January 1973, no. 1: AAS 65 (1973), pp. 265–266; *Codex Iuris Canonici*, can. 230 § 3.

86. Cf. Second Vatican Ecumenical Council, Constitution on the Sacred Liturgy, *Sacrosanctum Concilium*, no. 24.

87. Cf. Sacred Congregation of Rites, Instruction *Musicam sacram*, On music in the Liturgy, 5 March 1967, no. 19: AAS 59 (1967), p. 306.

88. Cf. ibid., no. 21: AAS 59 (1967), pp. 306–307.

89. Cf. Pontifical Commission for interpreting legal texts, response to *dubium* regarding can. 230 § 2: AAS 86 (1994), p. 541.

90. Cf. Second Vatican Ecumenical Council, Constitution on the Sacred Liturgy, *Sacrosanctum Concilium*, no. 22.

84. Cf. *Codex Iuris Canonici*, can. 910 § 2; Instructio interdicasterialis de quibusdam quæstionibus circa fidelium laicorum cooperationem sacerdotum ministerium spectantem, *Ecclesiæ de mysterio*, diei 15 augusti 1997, art. 8: A.A.S. 89 (1997) p. 871.

85. Cf. S. Congr. de Disciplina Sacramentorum, Instr. *Immensæ caritatis*, diei 29 ianuarii 1973, n. 1: A.A.S. 65 (1973) pp. 265–266; *Codex Iuris Canonici*, can. 230 § 3.

86. Conc. Œcum. Vat. II, Const. de sacra Liturgia, *Sacrosanctum Concilium*, n. 24.

87. Cf. S. Congr. Rituum, Instr. *Musicam sacram*, diei 5 martii 1967, n. 19: A.A.S. 59 (1967) p. 306.

88. Cf. *ibidem*, n. 21: A.A.S. 59 (1967) pp. 306–307.

89. Cf. Pont. Cons. de Legum textibus interpretandis, responsio ad propositum dubium circa can. 230 § 2: A.A.S. 86 (1994) p. 541.

90. Cf. Conc. Œcum. Vat. II, Const. de sacra Liturgia, *Sacrosanctum Concilium*, n. 22.

CHAPTER IV.I

The Different Forms of Celebrating Mass

(DE DIVERSIS FORMIS MISSAM CELEBRANDI)

Martin Connell and Sharon McMillan

While remaining the same through all editions of the *IGMR*, the unassuming title of this section underscores the significant recovery by the Second Vatican Council (1962–65) of the understanding of the eucharistic celebration as inherently adaptable to a variety of circumstances. *Missale Romanum* of 1570 (*MR1570*) contained not a single reference to the presence of an assembly in its one set of rubrics for Mass, and its one form of the Mass was celebrated no matter what the circumstances. The simple words of this title demonstrate the fundamental decision of the Second Vatican Council to revise the texts and rites of the liturgy in order to restore it to consonance with the richness of the tradition. That there are "different forms of the Mass" is one such tradition.

The different forms described here are: I. a setting with one priest with the full complement of lay ministers together with an assembly of the faithful; II. a setting with that same complement of ministers and assembly but with a number of priests concelebrating; and III. a setting with one priest and only one minister and in the absence of any assembly. In addition, no. 112 addresses the form of the Mass celebrated by the bishop at the cathedral and no. 114 addresses the conventual or community Mass of religious orders or canons regular.

IGMR2002 has not altered the basic structure found in *IGMR1975*. While adding to and rearranging the text of individual articles, the editors chose to maintain the overall sequence and chapter design of *IGMR1975*, although important theological and ecclesial themes articulated in the previous three chapters might have suggested a different arrangement. Two such examples are worth noting. The first is that the initial form of "Mass with the people" is the form of Mass without a deacon, intimating that such was the preferred form. Despite the themes in *IGMR2002* regarding the dignity and importance of the deacon's role, the presentation of instructions for Mass with a deacon takes second place.

A second result of the editors' choosing to follow the overall design of *IGMR1975* is the absence in this text of any provision for a ferial or weekday

Chapter IV
THE DIFFERENT FORMS OF CELEBRATING MASS

112. In the local Church, first place should certainly be given, because of its significance, to the Mass at which the Bishop presides, surrounded by his presbyterate, deacons, and lay ministers,[91] and in which the holy people of God participate fully and actively, for it is there that the preeminent expression of the Church is found.

At a Mass celebrated by the Bishop or at which he presides without celebrating the Eucharist, the norms found in the *Caeremoniale Episcoporum* should be observed.[92]

Caput IV
DE DIVERSIS FORMIS MISSAM CELEBRANDI

112. In Ecclesia locali primus sane locus tribuatur, propter eius significationem, Missæ cui præest Episcopus a suo presbyterio, diaconis et ministris laicis circumdatus[91] et in qua plebs sancta Dei plene et actuose participat, ibi enim habetur præcipua manifestatio Ecclesiæ.

In Missa quam Episcopus celebrat, vel cui ipse præest quin Eucharistiam celebret, serventur normæ quæ in Cæremoniali Episcoporum inveniuntur.[92]

---

form for celebrating the Eucharist, which occurs most frequently in contemporary parish life. Although *IGMR2002* does not identify the form of Mass described in the articles that follow as exclusively a form of celebration for Sundays, many paragraphs highlight the preferred presence of a large number of ministers, e.g., a thurifer, cross-bearer, candle-bearers, instituted acolytes, different lectors for each reading before the gospel, cantor, choir, accompanying musicians, etc. This is not a ferial model of celebration. However, such a model could assist parishes in implementing the carefully nuanced rubrics in the text that follows as well as properly employing principles of progressive solemnity.[1] Perhaps the next edition of *IGMR* will provide this valuable direction.

112. This article rightly asserts that the preeminent model of eucharistic celebration is that over which the local bishop presides, surrounded by representatives of the other orders and ministries in the Church. Another vital aspect of this model is the full and active participation of the "holy people of God" (*plebs sancta Dei*). These three elements—the presidency of the bishop, the gathering of priests, deacons and lay ministers, and the full and active participation of the faithful—give rise to what *IGMR2002* calls "the preeminent expression of the Church" (*praecipua manifestatio Ecclesiae*).

The wording here has been expanded from earlier editions of *IGMR* to signal the importance of the presence of the order of deacons together with the bishop as well as the order of presbyters. Another addition to the paragraph is the use of the adjective "lay" (*laici*) to describe the other liturgical ministers (whether instituted or not) surrounding the bishop. This insertion is consistent with *IGMR*'s tendency to emphasize the unique character of ordained ministry (see no. 91 above).

1. See Anscar Chupungco, "Toward a Ferial Order of Mass," *Ecclesia Orans* 10 (1993): 11–32.

113. Great importance should also be attached to a Mass celebrated with any community, but especially with the parish community, inasmuch as it represents the universal Church gathered at a given time and place. This is particularly true in the communal Sunday celebration.[93]

114. Among those Masses celebrated by some communities, moreover, the conventual Mass, which is a part of the daily Office, or the community Mass, has a particular place. Although such Masses do not have

113. Magni etiam habeatur Missa quæ cum aliqua communitate, præsertim vero parœciali, celebratur, utpote quæ Ecclesiam universalem repræsentet tempore et loco statutis, præcipue vero in communi celebratione dominicali.[93]

114. Inter Missas autem ab aliquibus communitatibus celebratas peculiarem locum obtinet Missa conventualis, quæ pars est Officii cotidiani, aut Missa, quæ « communitatis » dicitur. Et quamvis hæ Missæ nullam specialem formam celebra-

---

The footnote to *Sacrosanctum Concilium* (*SC*, no. 41) draws attention to this singular model of the Eucharist celebrated at the cathedral (though *IGMR* makes no reference to the cathedral here), which *SC* notes should also be a model of active participation. *SC*, no. 41, also highlights the bishop's role as high priest of the local Church, presiding over the assembly surrounded by the full array of ministries. At this Eucharist, there is one bishop, one altar, one prayer in which all participate fully and actively within their own order. In this article *IGMR2002* thus articulates the core model from which every other form of eucharistic celebration is derived.

The second paragraph of this article, not in *IGMR1975*, notes simply that the norms for the celebration of the Eucharist with the bishop are to be found in the *Caeremoniale Episcoporum* (*CaerEp*, nos. 119–186).

113. Repeating previous editions of *IGMR*, this article makes it clear that the document will restrict itself to a description of eucharistic celebrations at which a priest presides, particularly the parish Sunday celebration. When the Instruction does refer to rubrics reserved to the bishop, a note in the commentary below will indicate this.

The footnotes underscore the essential relationship of every parish Mass to the ministry of the bishop (*SC*, no. 42), the sanctifying office of the presbyter under the bishop's authority (*Lumen Gentium* [*LG*], no. 28), the centrality of the eucharistic assembly for the community of the faithful entrusted to the priest (*Presbyterorum Ordinis* [*PO*], no. 5), and the role of the pastor as taking the place of the bishop at the shared celebration of Sunday Mass (*Eucharisticum mysterium*, no. 26).[2]

114. Most of this article is unchanged from previous *IGMR*s, although the final two sentences are new. Conventual Masses celebrated by religious communities or by canons are to be marked by singing and the full participation of all members according to the liturgical function proper to each (see nos.

2. *IGMR2002* reorders the sequence of these documents in the footnote in order to group together the conciliar documents and then follow those with the instruction *Eucharisticum mysterium*, issued by the Sacred Congregation of Rites in 1967.

a special form of celebration, it is nevertheless most proper that they be celebrated with singing, especially with the full participation of all members of the community, whether of religious or of canons. In these Masses, therefore, individuals should exercise the office proper to the Order or ministry they have received. It is appropriate, therefore, that all the priests who are not bound to celebrate individually for the pastoral benefit of the faithful concelebrate at the conventual or community Mass insofar as it is possible. In addition, all priests belonging to the community who are obliged, as a matter of duty, to celebrate individually for the pastoral benefit of the faithful may also on the same day concelebrate at the conventual or community Mass.[94] For it is preferable that priests who are present at a Eucharistic Celebration, unless excused for a good reason, should as a rule exercise the office proper to their Order and hence take part as concelebrants, wearing the sacred vestments. Otherwise, they wear their proper choir dress or a surplice over a cassock.

tionis præ se ferant, maxime tamen decet eas cum cantu fieri, præcipue cum plena participatione omnium sodalium communitatis sive religiosorum sive canonicorum. In iis proinde munus suum exerceant singuli iuxta Ordinem vel ministerium receptum. Expedit ideo ut omnes sacerdotes qui pro utilitate pastorali fidelium singulariter celebrare non tenentur, in iis, quantum fieri potest, concelebrent. Omnes insuper ad eam communitatem pertinentes sacerdotes qui officio in bonum pastorale fidelium singulariter celebrandi tenentur, Missam quoque conventualem aut « communitatis » eadem die concelebrare possunt.[94] Præstat enim presbyteros, qui celebrationi eucharisticæ intersunt, nisi iusta causa excusentur, munus proprii Ordinis de more exercere et proinde uti concelebrantes participare, sacris vestibus indutos. Secus habitum choralem proprium aut superpelliceum super vestem talarem gestant.

I. Mass with a Congregation

115. By "Mass with a congregation" is meant a Mass celebrated with the participation of the faithful. It is moreover

I. De Missa cum Populo

115. Missa cum populo ea intellegitur quæ cum fidelium participatione celebratur. Convenit autem ut, quantum fieri po-

---

199–251 below). Ordained members of religious orders are encouraged to concelebrate at the community Mass even if they have previously celebrated the Eucharist for an assembly of the faithful (cf. no. 199 below). These additions remind ordained religious of the importance of celebrating the Eucharist according to their proper order whenever they are present, and of being appropriately vested.

Mass with a Congregation

115. Articles 115 through 198 describe the first form of the celebration of the Eucharist: Mass with a congregation. Mass without a deacon is described first, followed by the rubrics for Mass with a deacon. *IGMR2002* refers to this form as *Missa cum populo*. By translating *populus* here as "congregation" rather than as "assembly," GIRM2003 bypassed an opportunity to allow the reader to

appropriate, whenever possible, and especially on Sundays and holy days of obligation, that the celebration of this Mass take place with singing and with a suitable number of ministers.[95] It may, however, also be celebrated without singing and with only one minister.

test, præsertim vero diebus dominicis et festis de præcepto, cum cantu et congruo numero ministrorum celebratio peragatur;[95] attamen etiam sine cantu et cum uno ministro perfici potest.

116. If a deacon is present at any celebration of Mass, he should exercise his office. Furthermore, it is desirable that, as a rule, an acolyte, a lector, and a cantor should be there to assist the priest celebrant. In fact, the rite to be described below foresees a greater number of ministers.

116. In qualibet Missæ celebratione si adest diaconus, hic suo munere fungatur. Expedit autem ut sacerdoti celebranti de more adsint acolythus, lector et cantor. Ritus vero qui infra describitur facultatem prævidet amplioris etiam numeri ministrorum.

---

recognize this term more clearly in continuity with the use of the titles from ancient tradition: *qahal* (Hebrew), *ekklesia* (Greek), and *ecclesia* (Latin), i.e., the people of God called together in holy assembly.

The first sentence of this article, found in previous *IGMR*s, overturns centuries of a very different understanding: Mass with the people is no longer Mass celebrated by others in the presence of the people. Rather, the assembly is one of the subjects of the eucharistic celebration with Christ (*SC*, no. 7; see Power and Vincie, 52 above). The participation of the baptized is to be enhanced with music designed for their participation, and with the number of lay ministers that is appropriate, especially on Sundays and holy days.

After highlighting the preeminence of the pontifical Mass at the cathedral and the full and active participation of the faithful as normative, and after citing two footnotes that commend the celebration of the Eucharist with music as being the first choice, the text notes that canonically it is possible to celebrate the Mass in a form that takes none of those principles into account. Since Mass celebrated without an assembly is considered later in the Instruction (nos. 252–272), one wonders whether this sentence might well have been omitted in order that the entire article would consistently reflect the theological and ecclesial importance of the participation of the faithful.

116. *IGMR2002* here again stresses the importance of the order of deacon. In previous *IGMR*s, the sentence referring to the deacon's presence is a separate and final sentence. Now it has been brought forward to be the opening sentence of the article, placing mention of the deacon before any lay minister. Just as presbyters present for the celebration of the Eucharist participate as presbyters, so too deacons fulfill their liturgical ministry whenever they are present.

Repeating previous *IGMR*s, this article goes on to signal the normative character of a variety of liturgical roles within the eucharistic assembly; the participation of at least an (instituted) acolyte, lector, and cantor is presumed by the nature of the liturgy itself. These would constitute a minimum. To celebrate the

The Articles to Be Prepared

117. The altar is to be covered with at least one white cloth. In addition, on or next to the altar are to be placed candlesticks with lighted candles: at least two in any celebration, or even four or six, especially for a Sunday Mass or a holy day of obligation. If the diocesan Bishop celebrates, then seven candles should be used. Also on or close to the altar, there is to be a cross with a figure of Christ crucified. The candles and the cross adorned with a figure of Christ crucified may also be carried in the Entrance Procession. On the altar itself may be placed the *Book of the Gospels,* distinct from the book of other readings, unless it is carried in the Entrance Procession.

Præparanda

117. Altare una saltem tobalea albi coloris cooperiatur. Super ipsum vero aut iuxta ipsum duo saltem in omni celebratione, vel etiam quattuor aut sex, præsertim si agitur de Missa dominicali vel festiva de præcepto, vel, si Episcopus dioecesanus celebrat, septem candelabra cum cereis accensis ponantur. Item super altare vel circa ipsum habeatur crux, cum effigie Christi crucifixi. Candelabra autem et crux effigie Christi crucifixi ornata in processione ad introitum afferri possunt. Super ipsum altare poni potest, nisi in processione ad introitum deferatur, Evangeliarium a libro aliarum lectionum distinctum.

Eucharist as the document envisions, additional ministers are called for. Excised from this paragraph is the previous reference to this form of the Mass as being the "basic form" (*forma typica, IGMR1975*, IV.I.A).

The Articles to Be Prepared

The topic of church art and environment has been among those most contended in post-conciliar reforms. In the years since Vatican II, US bishops have significantly shifted emphasis from the promulgation of *Environment and Art in Catholic Worship* (EACW) to the more recent *Built of Living Stones: Art, Architecture, and Worship* (BLS). One can characterize the change as a shift from a teaching spare in details—thereby encouraging local inculturation in church design and environment—to considerably more detailed teaching with more tightly prescribed and uniform instructions regarding the environment for worship.

From this perspective, changes in *IGMR2002* regarding the articles to be prepared for Mass are rather slight. Some changes parallel the shift toward the closer prescription perceptible as BLS displaced EACW, but in general the shifts are relatively benign.

117. Regarding the altar cloth (*tobalea*), while *IGMR1975* makes mention of it without qualification, *IGMR2002* adds a phrase describing it as "white-colored" (*albi coloris;* also, see no. 304 below). This new directive links the symbolism of the altar to Christ, as the color white is richly symbolic in the tradition, evoking, for example, Christ's transfiguration (Matt 17:2), in which the glorified Christ is transformed into dazzling white. There is also strong resonance between the color white and the newly baptized. While evoking rich symbolism from dominant strands of the tradition, such emphasis on a singular color such as white could be perceived by some as culturally questionable. The US bishops seem to recognize this, as their approved adaptation allows for additional cloths to be of other colors (GIRM2003, no. 304).

Lit candles are also richly symbolic, both of Christ who declared himself "the light of the world" (John 8:12 and 9:5), as well as of his followers called to be "the light of the world" (Matt 5:14), and presented a lighted candle at baptism. *IGMR2002* prescribes that candles be "on or next to the altar" (*super ipsum vero aut iuxta ipsum*). Later the Instruction will offer more rationale for this placement (see no. 307 below). The number of candles is increased according to the heightened festivity of the celebration: at least two in any celebration, four or six for a Sunday Mass or holy day, and seven candles for celebrations at which the bishop presides. The seven candles might have emerged as a reflection of the theology of the book of Revelation, particularly 4:5. The change in the number of candles does not signal a more efficacious celebration but the uniqueness of festival days over ordinary ferial Masses, and the sign of the Church's unity in the presence of the bishop.

A significant clarification in *IGMR2002* is the addition of the phrase "with a figure of Christ crucified" (*cum effigie Christi crucifixi)* to the description of the cross (see no. 308 below; cf. Seasoltz, 33 above). *CaerEp* presumes that the cross has a figure of Christ when that text specifies that the figure is to be facing front and that "the recommended practice" is that the processional cross serve as the altar cross (no. 128). A similar change had occurred in documents from the US bishops: EACW had been characteristically spare, describing the cross as "a basic symbol in any Christian liturgical celebration" (no. 88), whereas BLS instructs that "The cross with the image of Christ crucified is a reminder of Christ's paschal mystery. It draws us into the mystery of suffering and makes tangible our belief that our suffering when united with the passion and death of Christ leads to redemption" (no. 91). Explanations of this shift are multiple. It could be that *IGMR2002* is providing more detail, as is its pattern. It also could be that the preference for a figure of the crucified is more respectful of the doctrine concerning the Eucharist as a sacrifice (see Power and Vincie, especially 56–57 above). This interpretation would seem to be born out by the *Book of Blessings* which comments, "Of all sacred images, the 'figure of the precious, life-giving cross of Christ' is pre-eminent, because it is the symbol of the entire paschal mystery" (no. 1233). It is also possible that this move reveals a preference for a more literal reading over the inherent ambiguity of a more symbolic approach.

The Instruction adds that the candles and cross are to be carried in the procession (see no. 120b below). A fuller display of the variety of the church's ministries in the liturgy is clearly preferred (no. 91 above), especially in processions and stational liturgies that manifest both the Church's movement to the coming reign of God and a continual vigilance for Christ's second coming.

IGMR2002 acknowledges the importance of the Book of the Gospels (*Evangeliarium,* though previous editions spoke of the *liber Evangeliorum,* see *IGMR1975,* no. 79), distinctive from "the book of other readings" (*a libro aliarum*

118. The following are also to be prepared:

a. Next to the priest's chair: the Missal and, as needed, a hymnal;
b. At the ambo: the Lectionary;
c. On the credence table: the chalice, a corporal, a purificator, and, if appropriate, the pall; the paten and, if needed, ciboria; bread for the Communion of the priest who presides, the deacon, the ministers, and the people; cruets containing the wine and the water, unless all of these are presented by the faithful in procession at the Offertory; the vessel of water to be blessed, if the *asperges* occurs; the Communion-plate for the Communion of the faithful; and whatever is needed for the washing of hands.

It is a praiseworthy practice to cover the chalice with a veil, which may be either the color of the day or white.

118. Item parentur:

a) iuxta sedem sacerdotis: missale et, pro opportunitate, libellus cantuum;
b) in ambone: lectionarium;
c) in abaco: calix, corporale, purificatorium et, pro opportunitate, palla; patena et pyxides, si necessariæ sunt; panis pro Communione sacerdotis qui præest, diaconi, ministrorum et populi; urceoli cum vino et aqua, nisi hæc omnia a fidelibus in processione ad offertorium præsententur; vas aquæ benedicendæ, si fit aspersio; patina pro Communione fidelium; et ea quæ necessaria sunt ad manus lavandas.

Calix laudabiliter cooperiatur velo, quod potest esse aut coloris diei aut coloris albi.

---

lectionum distinctum). The ancient veneration for this book[3] attests to its strong Christological symbolism, and its privileged role in the proclamation of the gospel (see no. 349 below), which is a climactic moment of the Liturgy of the Word as underscored by the change in the assembly's posture, the gospel procession (see no. 37 above), the tracing of a cross and the triple signing of ministers and people before the gospel proclamation, the optional use of incense, and the very kissing of the Book of the Gospels (see no. 134 below). Because of its rich and ancient symbolism, the Book of the Gospels is the only liturgical article allowed on the altar before the preparation of the gifts, symbolically uniting the table of the Word and the table of the Eucharist. As noted in previous *IGMR*s, it may either be placed on the altar before the entrance procession, or if carried in the entrance procession, it may be placed on the altar at the end of the procession (see no. 122 below).

118. This article provides further details regarding the things to be prepared for the celebration of the Eucharist that are to be placed in the sanctuary. First, repeating *IGMR1975*, the Instruction notes that the missal is to be placed next to the priest's chair; English editions of this book published in North America are more properly categorized as sacramentaries, as they are missing key ele-

3. In *Ordo Romanus Primus* (*OR I*) no. 30, the Book of the Gospels has its own procession into the church even before the introit. See Michel Andrieu, *Les Ordines romani du haut moyen âge*, 5 vols., Spicilegium Sacrum Lovaniense 11, 23, 24, 28, 29 (Louvain, 1960), I:76.

ments for the celebration such as the readings. The text also notes that next to the priest's chair one would place a hymnal "as needed" (*pro opportunitate*). This is a strong indicator that the presider is to join his voice with the rest of the community in song (cf. no. 40 above). Placing the hymnal at the chair would be especially appropriate if the entrance procession is accompanied by an instrumental piece, or is done in silence. Since the entrance procession ordinarily includes a song (see no. 48 above), which the priest is expected to sing,[4] and since the priest-presider is usually not required to carry any other liturgical article in procession,[5] the priest should ordinarily carry the hymnal with him in the opening procession, so as to be in solidarity with the community in the opening song and contribute to the sense of unity that this song is to foster (see no. 47 above).

Like previous *IGMR*s, this article notes that the lectionary is to be at the ambo before Mass begins. Contrary to common practice in the US since the early 1970s, no *IGMR* has specifically authorized the carrying of the lectionary in the entrance procession. The practice of carrying the lectionary in the procession developed because the Book of the Gospels was not commonly available until the 1990s in English-speaking North America. Furthermore, a heightened awareness of the presence of Christ in the Scriptures (*SC*, no. 7), as well as a concern for richer symbolic action in the liturgy (cf. MCW, nos. 4–7), contributed to this virtually ubiquitous practice. The ancient tradition (see n. 3, above) and authorized practice is to carry the Book of the Gospels in the entrance procession. What *IGMR2002* and its predecessors do not address, however, are the economic and cultural questions surrounding multiple books of readings for a single celebration of the Eucharist. If a community cannot afford two books of readings, and the lectionary is the economic choice as it contains all readings including the gospels, does it *de facto* become the Book of the Gospels for such a community and have a place in the entrance procession? *IGMR* does not resolve such a question.

Finally, this article delineates those elements to be placed on the credence table before the beginning of Eucharist. Most of this repeats what is found in *IGMR1975*, no. 80c. While chalice, corporal, and purificator are presumed, the pall is to be available "if appropriate" (*pro opportunitate*), indicating its optional usage which should be dictated by some pastoral necessity (e.g., the presence of flying insects); otherwise, it is appropriate to leave the chalice uncovered. A paten is essential according to *IGMR2002*, while ciboria are present only "if needed" (*si necessariae*). Criteria for determining such need are imbedded in the next directive that bread needs to be provided for various individuals or groups: the priest-presider, the deacon (not mentioned in *IGMR1975*, no. 80c but distin-

4. The US bishops describe the opening song as one which "everyone is able to join in singing to some degree" (*Introduction to the Order of Mass* [ITTOM], no. 67).

5. One exception is if he performs the sprinkling rite during the opening procession, as the US bishops allow in ITTOM, no. 74.

119. In the sacristy, the sacred vestments (cf. nos. 337–341) for the priest, the deacon, and other ministers are to be prepared according to the various forms of celebration:

a. For the priest: the alb, the stole, and the chasuble;

b. For the deacon: the alb, the stole, and the dalmatic; the dalmatic may be omitted, however, either out of necessity or on account of a lesser degree of solemnity;

c. For the other ministers: albs or other lawfully approved attire.[96]

119. In sacristia, pro diversis formis celebrationis, parentur sacræ vestes *(cf. nn. 337–341)* sacerdotis, diaconi et aliorum ministrorum:

a) pro sacerdote: alba, stola et casula seu planeta;

b) pro diacono: alba, stola et dalmatica, quæ tamen, ob necessitatem vel minorem gradum sollemnitatis, omitti potest;

c) pro aliis ministris: albæ vel aliæ vestes legitime approbatæ.[96]

---

guished, underscoring the dignity of this office), other ministers, and the people. If all of the bread cannot fit on the paten, then ciboria become necessary. Ideally, all the bread would fit on a single large paten, signifying the "one bread" of the Eucharist (1 Cor 10:16-17), and a practice with deep roots in the liturgies of Rome.[6] Cruets with water and wine are prepared, unless brought up in the procession by the faithful, which *IGMR2002* previously noted as "praiseworthy" (*laudabiliter*, no. 73 above) and thus preferable. New to the objects on the list is the "vessel of water to be blessed, if the *asperges* occurs"[7] (*vas aquae benedicendae, si fit aspersio*), further demonstrating how *IGMR2002* gives more attention to the sprinkling rite (cf. no. 51 above). A "Communion-plate for the Communion of the faithful" (*patina pro Communione fidelium*), ordinarily held by a server under the communicant's chin during the reception of the consecrated host, is also to be prepared; there is no further mention of its use during *IGMR*'s detailing of the Communion rite. As for the chalice veil, *IGMR2002* seems less prescriptive than *IGMR1975,* which notes that "The chalice should be covered with a veil, which may always be white" (*Calix cooperiatur velo, quod potest esse semper coloris albi,* 80c). *IGMR2002* instead notes that it is a "praiseworthy practice to cover the chalice with a veil" (*Calix laudabiliter cooperiatur velo*); other "praiseworthy" practices like the procession of gifts are preferred, but not prescribed (cf. no. 73 above). The color of the chalice veil does not have to be white, and it may be the "color of the day" (*coloris diei*).

119. Repeating most of what was found in *IGMR1975* (which excludes materials pertaining to the subdeacon in *IGMR1971*, no. 81), this article delineates

6. See, for example, the sixth-century description of patens weighing 30 lbs apiece in *The Book of Pontiffs (Liber Pontificalis)*, ed. and trans. Raymond Davis, rev. ed., Translated Texts for Historians 6 (Liverpool: Liverpool University Press, 2000), 34.9.

7. In no. 51, above, GIRM2003 translates *asperges* as "sprinkling" which seems more appropriate.

All who wear an alb should use a cincture and an amice unless, due to the form of the alb, they are not needed.

When there is an Entrance Procession, the following are also to be prepared: the *Book of the Gospels;* on Sundays and festive days, the thurible and the boat with incense, if incense is used; the cross to be carried in procession; and candlesticks with lighted candles.

Omnes qui albam induunt, cingulum adhibeant et amictu utantur, nisi ob ipsius albæ formam non exigantur.

Cum introitus processione perficitur, parentur etiam Evangeliarium; in diebus dominicis et festivis thuribulum et navicula cum thure, si incensum seu thus adhibetur; crux in processione deferenda, candelabra cum cereis accensis.

---

the vestments for the priest, deacon, and other ministers. In outlining the necessary vesture for the celebration of Mass, the universal use of the alb (*alba*) for all ministers symbolizes the church's foundational sacrament of baptism as the gateway to salvation and the door to the other sacraments, including orders and Eucharist.[8]

IGMR2002 makes some minor adjustments here. Regarding the place where these are to be prepared, this Instruction changes *secretario (IGMR1975*, no. 81) to *sacristia,* both of which GIRMs have translated as "sacristy." *IGMR2002* also adds *casula* as an alternative to *planeta*, which together GIRM2003 translates in the singular as "the chasuble." The vestments for the deacon and the other ministers are the same as in previous *IGMR*s, though instead of referring to them as *ceteris ministris* (*IGMR1975*, no. 81c), they are called *aliis ministris,* which the respective GIRMs both translated as "other ministers."

Like previous *IGMR*s, the current Instruction directs that those who wear an alb "should use a cincture and an amice" (*cingulum adhibeant et amictu utantur*), although the reason for not using one changes from "unless other provision is made" (*nisi aliter provideatur, IGMR1975*, no. 81) to "unless the form of the alb makes this unnecessary" (*ob ipsius albae formam non exigantur*). This is a somewhat functional rather than prescriptive approach to vesture.

Drawing upon material noted in other articles (nos. 49, 117 and 276–77), *IGMR2002* adds a new sentence regarding the entrance procession and specifies all of those elements to be prepared when such a procession occurs. Here is another example of this Instruction offering concise summaries of materials scattered through previous *IGMR*s.

8. See Joanne Pierce, "Vestments and Objects," in *The Oxford History of Christian Worship*, ed. Geoffrey Wainwright and Karen Westerfield Tucker (New York: Oxford University Press, 2006), 841–57.

A. Mass Without a Deacon

The Introductory Rites

120. Once the people have gathered, the priest and ministers, clad in the sacred vestments, go in procession to the altar in this order:

a. The thurifer carrying a thurible with burning incense, if incense is used;
b. The ministers who carry lighted candles, and between them an acolyte or other minister with the cross;
c. The acolytes and the other ministers;
d. A lector, who may carry the *Book of the Gospels* (though not the Lectionary), which should be slightly elevated;
e. The priest who is to celebrate the Mass.

A) De Missa sine diacono

Ritus initiales

120. Populo congregato, sacerdos et ministri, sacris vestibus induti, ad altare procedunt hoc ordine:

a) thuriferarius cum thuribulo fumigante, si thus adhibetur;
b) ministri qui deferunt cereos accensos, et inter eos acolythus vel alius minister cum cruce;
c) acolythi et alii ministri;
d) lector, qui potest Evangeliarium, non autem lectionarium, parum elevatum deferre;
e) sacerdos Missam celebraturus.

Mass Without a Deacon[9]

The Introductory Rites

120. The first act of the eucharistic liturgy is the gathering of the people, the baptized faithful who "form a holy people, a people whom God has made his own, a royal priesthood" (*efficiunt plebem sanctam, populum acquisitionis et sacerdotium regale,* no. 95). Gathering with them, particularly in the Sunday assembly, will also be catechumens, baptized candidates preparing for reception into full communion, and more regularly guests and even strangers. The prerequisite act of gathering, however, is the assembling of the members of the Body of Christ as the liturgical assembly.

No directives are given regarding the place from which the procession begins, leaving the configuration of the sacred space, the liturgical season, or perhaps the degree of solemnity to suggest the most appropriate locations. The direction and goal of the procession is the altar, that central symbol of Christ in the midst of the assembly (cf. nos. 49 above and 298 below), while the procession itself "expresses visibly the unity and fullness of the assembly" (ITTOM, no. 67).

In outlining the order of the procession, *IGMR2002* offers some details and nuances not found in previous *IGMR*s. The "server" (*minister, IGMR1975,* no. 82a) with a thurible is now more accurately identified as "the thurifer" (*thuriferarius*); the use of incense continues to be an option (no. 276 below). *IGMR2002* newly prescribes that the candles are "lighted" (*accensos*). More significant is that

9. On the choice in *IGMR2002* to first describe "A Mass without a Deacon," see no. 222 below.

If incense is used, before the procession begins, the priest puts some in the thurible and blesses it with the Sign of the Cross without saying anything.

121. During the procession to the altar, the Entrance chant takes place (cf. above, nos. 47–48).

122. On reaching the altar, the priest and ministers make a profound bow.

The cross adorned with a figure of Christ crucified and perhaps carried in procession may be placed next to the altar to serve as the altar cross, in which case it ought to be the only cross used; otherwise it is put away in a dignified place. In addition, the candlesticks are placed on the altar or near it. It is a praiseworthy practice that the *Book of the Gospels* be placed upon the altar.

Si incensum adhibetur, sacerdos antequam procedatur, incensum in thuribulo imponit et signo crucis benedicit, nihil dicens.

121. Dum fit processio ad altare, cantus ad introitum peragitur *(cf. nn. 47–48).*

122. Cum ad altare pervenerint, sacerdos et ministri faciunt profundam inclinationem.

Crux effigie Christi crucifixi ornata et in processione forte delata, iuxta altare erigi potest ut fiat crux altaris, quæ una tantum esse debet, secus in loco digno reponatur. Candelabra vero super altare vel iuxta illud collocantur; Evangeliarium laudabiliter super altare deponitur.

---

the distinction is made between the role of the instituted acolyte (cf. *CaerEp*, nos. 27–29) and other ministers. The acolyte performs "the more important duties" (no. 187 below), here for example carrying the cross rather than the candles. Additional instituted acolytes and other ministers needed in the celebration follow.

All *IGMR*s prescribe that the lector may carry the Book of the Gospels. Despite that this was common pastoral practice, *IGMR*s never offer the option of lectors carrying the lectionary (see no. 118 above); *IGMR2002* specifically prohibits that practice. Also new here is the directive that the Book of the Gospels is to be "slightly elevated" (*parum elevatum*) when carried in procession. Like its predecessors, *IGMR2002* further stipulates that at the end of the procession is not simply the priest, but the one "who is to celebrate the Mass" (*sacerdos Missam celebraturus*), indicating the theological importance of the individual fulfilling this function over the ecclesial rank of any other priests or prelates who may join the opening procession.

IGMR2002 repeats the instruction that the priest blesses the incense without saying anything (*IGMR1975*, no. 236) but adds that this blessing is done "with the Sign of the Cross" (*signo crucis*). GIRM2003's capitalizations in the Sign of the Cross are not in *IGMR2002* and could be an attempt to give greater attention or respect to this gesture.

121. On the Entrance Chant, see nos. 47–48, above.

122. *IGMR2002* indicates that the normative act of the priest, the deacon, and the ministers upon entering the sanctuary is a profound bow to the altar. Removed from this article are *IGMR1975*'s directions of how to proceed if there is a tabernacle in the sanctuary (no. 84). This has been moved to no. 274 in *IGMR2002*. The general principle is that the priest, the deacon, and the other

123. The priest goes up to the altar and venerates it with a kiss. Then, as the occasion suggests, he incenses the cross and the altar, walking around the latter.

124. After doing these things, the priest goes to the chair. Once the Entrance chant is concluded, the priest and faithful, all

123. Sacerdos ad altare ascendit ipsumque veneratur osculo. Deinde, pro opportunitate, crucem et altare incensat, illud circumeundo.

124. His peractis, sacerdos sedem petit. Cantu ad introitum expleto, omnibus stantibus, sacerdos et fideles signant se signo

---

ministers genuflect before the Blessed Sacrament present in the tabernacle in the sanctuary upon approaching or departing from the altar, but not during the rest of the Mass (no. 274). *IGMR2002* again adds the prescription that the processional cross is adorned with a figure of Christ crucified (see no. 117 above). The Instruction observes that there is to be only one cross in the sanctuary, signifying an awareness of the principle that multiplication of symbols diminishes their power (cf. EACW, no. 86). While previous *IGMR*s note that processional candles are placed either on the altar or on a side table, *IGMR2002* adds that they might be placed near the altar. Number 307 below will point out that should the candles be on the altar, they are not to interfere with the faithful's view of the eucharistic action. The US bishops comment that the more appropriate place for the candles is near or around the altar (ITTOM, no. 52).

To the description found in previous *IGMR*s that the Book of the Gospels is to be placed on the altar, *IGMR*2002 adds that this is "praiseworthy" (*laudabiliter*). In noting the praiseworthy nature of the practice and still keeping it an option, *IGMR2002* is pastorally sensitive regarding the availability or cost of such a book (see no. 118 above). Traditional Roman practice is to place the Book of the Gospels flat on the altar (see no. 295 below; also BLS, no. 59), although *IGMR2002* does not prescribe any particular way for placing it on the altar.

123. Every edition of *IGMR* except *IGMR2000* notes that the priest "goes up to" (*ascendit*) the altar, reflecting the assumption that the sanctuary is elevated (cf. 295 no. below; also BLS, no. 59). *IGMR2000* has altered the text to read "the priest approaches the altar" (*sacerdos ad altare accedit*), perhaps reflecting awareness of pluriform configurations of sacred space. While that change in language is not incorporated here, the phrase appears in no. 195 in reference to the lector.

The altar, previously reverenced with a profound bow, is also "venerated" with a kiss. New in *IGMR2002* is the directive to incense the cross, and to do so before the altar (see nos. 49 and 277). Since *Inter Oecumenici* (*IntOec*), the altar has been described as "freestanding, to permit walking around it" (*IntOec* no. 91). *IGMR2002*'s note that the priest incenses the altar while walking around it corresponds with this postconciliar tradition (cf. 299 no. below).

124. The priest reaches the presidential chair and presides over the introductory rites from there; standing at the altar or ambo or other place is not permitted as an option. *IGMR2002* adds the detail that the priest and faithful "make the Sign of the Cross" (*signant se signo crucis*); here, as in other places, GIRM2003

standing, make the Sign of the Cross. The priest says, *In nomine Patris et Filii et Spiritus Sancti (In the name of the Father, and of the Son, and of the Holy Spirit)*. The people answer, *Amen*.

Then, facing the people and extending his hands, the priest greets the people, using one of the formulas indicated. The priest himself or some other minister may also very briefly introduce the faithful to the Mass of the day.

crucis. Sacerdos dicit: In nómine Patris, et Fílii, et Spíritus Sancti. Populus respondet: Amen.

Deinde, versus ad populum et manus extendens, sacerdos eum salutat, una adhibita e formulis propositis. Potest etiam ipse sacerdos vel alius minister, brevissimis verbis introducere fideles in Missam illius diei.

125. The Act of Penitence follows. Afterwards, the *Kyrie* is sung or said, in keeping with the rubrics (cf. no. 52).

125. Sequitur actus pænitentialis. Postea cantatur vel dicitur Kýrie, iuxta rubricas *(cf. n. 52)*.

---

inexplicably capitalizes the nouns. For the greeting that follows the priest faces the people (on the placement of the chair, see no. 310 below). Thus, when the chair is attached to a side wall, turning to face the people is required. The priest's hands are extended for the greeting. *CaerEp* clarifies that they are "slightly raised and outstretched. This practice appears already in the tradition of the Old Testament, and was taken over by Christians in memory of the Lord's passion" (no. 104).

The *Missale Romanum* makes several forms of the greeting available from which the priest will choose. The theological significance of the mystery of Christ's Body gathered together was previously noted (no. 50 above), and ITTOM observes that this greeting of the gathered Body is to be warm and reverent, never casual or personalized (no. 69).

A brief introduction to the Mass of the day may occur at this point. According to a 1973 instruction from Sacred Congregation for Divine Worship, it is meant to be a way "of leading the faithful to a more thorough grasp of the meaning of the sacred rites or certain of their parts and to an inner participation in them" (*Eucharistiae Participationem,* no. 14, in DOL, no. 1988). Number 50 further notes the order of preference for the one who may offer this introduction: the priest, the deacon, or a lay minister. *IGMR2002* here omits the word "appropriate" (*idoneus, IGMR1975,* no. 86) before "minister," perhaps intending to expand the number of liturgical ministers who might offer the introduction upon occasion: a lector or a musician, even others. The US bishops interpret this statement as allowing for "some other member of the congregation" (ITTOM, no. 70) to offer this introduction, which might include a catechist or catechumenate team member, among others.

125. Although the US adaptations for the Sacramentary place the Rite of Blessing and Sprinkling Holy Water at this point, and although no. 51 mentions it as an option for Sundays, *IGMR2002* does not offer any directions for the rite here or anywhere in its text (see no. 51 above).

126. For celebrations where it is prescribed, the *Gloria* is either sung or said (cf. no. 53).

127. The priest then invites the people to pray, saying, with hands joined, *Oremus (Let us pray)*. All pray silently with the priest for a brief time. Then the priest, with hands extended, says the collect, at the end of which the people make the acclamation, *Amen*.

126. In celebrationibus statutis, cantatur vel dicitur Glória *(cf. n. 53)*.

127. Deinde sacerdos populum ad orandum invitat, manibus iunctis, dicens: Orémus. Et omnes una cum sacerdote ad breve tempus silentes orant. Tunc sacerdos, manibus extensis, dicit collectam, qua expleta, populus acclamat: Amen.

The *actus paenitentialis* (literally "penitential act") is the same Latin designation as in other *IGMR*s, but GIRM2003 offers a new translation ("Act of Penitence") and introduces capitalizations not found in the original. The *Kyrie* chant that follows Form A and Form B is helpfully identified as distinct from the Act of Penitence, and there is a preference that the *Kyrie* be sung (*IGMR1975*, no. 87 states simply that the *Kyrie* and *Gloria* "are said" [*dicuntur*]). Number 52 above includes additional information regarding the *Kyrie* litany.

126. The *Gloria* is considered separately from the *Kyrie*. This article includes the preference for singing the hymn and makes reference to the fuller rubrics found in no. 53 above.

127. The prayer at the conclusion of the introductory rites was identified as the "opening prayer" in all the preceding English translations of the GIRM until GIRM2003. "Prayer" was the preferred translation for *oratio* (found in both *IGMR1969* and *IGMR1971*, no. 88) as well as the translation for *collecta* when this term replaced *oratio* in *IGMR1975*, no. 88. GIRM2003 adds precision to the translation: "collect" is the new name for this first of the presidential prayers.

The Liturgy of the Word

The lectionary introduced after Vatican II brought four major changes to the Liturgy of the Word: first, the readings could be proclaimed in the vernacular language of the local church; second, a change from two readings at Sunday Mass to three readings; third, a change from a one-year cycle to a three-year Sunday cycle; and fourth, as a result of the second and third, a dramatic increase in the number of biblical texts proclaimed and heard by the people of God. In a way the last three changes are predicated on the first, for the increase in the proportion of the Bible proclaimed would have had little impact on the church had most of the people in the assembly not known the language in which the readings were proclaimed. The three editions of the *Missale Romanum* after Vatican II reflect the settling of the ritual tradition necessary to receive this newly enriched element of the church's liturgical life.

IGMR2002 earlier addressed the rite of the Liturgy of the Word when it describes the structure of the eucharistic rite and the particular elements of the

The Liturgy of the Word

128. After the collect, all sit. The priest may, very briefly, introduce the faithful to the Liturgy of the Word. Then the lector goes to the ambo and, from the Lectionary already placed there before Mass, proclaims the first reading, to which all listen. At the end, the lector says the acclamation *Verbum Domini (The word of the Lord)*, and all respond, *Deo gratias (Thanks be to God)*.

Then, as appropriate, a few moments of silence may be observed so that all may meditate on what they have heard.

129. Then the psalmist or even a lector proclaims the verses of the Psalm and the people sing or say the response as usual.

Liturgia verbi

128. Collecta conclusa, omnes sedent. Sacerdos potest, brevissimis verbis, fideles in liturgiam verbi introducere. Lector vero ad ambonem pergit, et ex lectionario ibi iam ante Missam posito proclamat primam lectionem, quam omnes auscultant. In fine lector profert acclamationem Verbum Dómini, omnibus respondentibus Deo grátias.

Tunc breve spatium silentii, pro opportunitate, servari potest, ut omnes, ea quæ audierunt meditentur.

129. Deinde psalmista, vel ipse lector, profert versus psalmi, populo de more responsum proferente.

Mass (see nos. 29 and 55–64 above). Although not included in this part, the Instruction addresses the order of the readings in nos. 357–362, with a fuller theology of the ordering of the readings in the revised *Ordo Lectionum Missae* (*OLM1981-Pr*, nos. 58–110).

128. *IGMR2002* gives much more information about the execution of the Liturgy of the Word than previous *IGMR*s. New is the option that the priest may briefly introduce the Liturgy of the Word (cf. no. 31 above). Such an introduction of the Word is not usually required. Perhaps when the readings to be proclaimed are complex or unfamiliar, from books not often used in proclamation, such an introduction may deepen the assembly's preparation for or appreciation of the meaning of the readings. Wisely *IGMR* notes that when given, such an introduction should be very brief.

A second addition is the specification that the lector proclaims the first reading "from the Lectionary already placed there before Mass" (*ex lectionario ibi iam ante Missam posito*). This is a corollary to no. 120d, which notes that the lectionary is not to be carried in procession by the lector (as has been common practice in many places in the US), and thus needs to be placed on the ambo before Mass begins. A third addition here is the allowance that a few moments of silence may be observed after the first reading. While not obligatory ("as appropriate," *servari potest*), this addition acknowledges that such silence has become customary in some communities in their celebration of the Liturgy of the Word. It also seems to be an implicit acknowledgement that silence between the readings contributes to a community's capacity for encountering God's presence in the Word.

129. There was no change to this paragraph between *IGMR1969* and *IGMR1975*, in which the minister of the psalm could have been the "the psalmist or cantor of the psalm, or even the reader" (*psalmista vero, seu cantor, vel ipse lector*, no. 90). In *IGMR2002* the cantor has been omitted while the psalmist and

130. If there is to be a second reading before the Gospel, the lector proclaims it from the ambo. All listen and at the end respond to the acclamation, as noted above (no. 128). Then, as appropriate, a few moments of silence may be observed.

131. Afterwards, all rise, and the *Alleluia* or other chant is sung as required by the liturgical season (cf. nos. 62–64).

132. During the singing of the *Alleluia* or other chant, if incense is used, the priest puts some into the thurible and blesses it. Then, with hands joined, he bows profoundly before the altar and quietly says, *Munda cor meum (Almighty God, cleanse my heart).*

130. Si habenda sit secunda lectio ante Evangelium, lector eam ex ambone proclamat, omnibus auscultantibus, atque in fine acclamationi respondentibus, ut dicitur supra *(n. 128)*. Deinde, pro opportunitate, breve spatium silentii servari potest.

131. Postea omnes surgunt et canitur Allelúia vel alius cantus, prout tempus liturgicum postulat *(cf. nn. 62–64)*.

132. Dum canitur Allelúia vel alius cantus, sacerdos incensum, si adhibetur, imponit et benedicit. Deinde, manibus iunctis, et profunde inclinatus ante altare, dicit secreto: Munda cor meum.

---

lector are retained. Also dropped was the phrase "when the reading is finished" (*lectione finita*), which might have been needed after Vatican II because the responsorial psalm sung by a lay minister had not been part of the tradition for centuries; now, after more than three decades of experience of the psalm between the first and second reading, the phrase is no longer necessary. This paragraph finds its foundation in an earlier section of *IGMR2002*, which signals the importance of singing in the liturgy and the inculturation of the musical idiom of the local church (nos. 39–41 above). The action of the minister was changed from "says" (*dicit*, *IGMR1975*, no. 89) to "offers" (*profert*). This slight change suggests that local custom will dictate whether the psalm will be spoken, chanted, or sung. The insertion of the phrase "as usual" (*de more*) at the end of this paragraph seems to underscore this point.

130. New here is a sentence allowing for a period of silence after the reading, similar to no. 128 above. As then, the opportunity is offered to those celebrating for a brief moment of reflection on the reading. This silence also allows for an appropriate interval before the gospel acclamation, thus contributing to its ritual effectiveness.

131. *IGMR2002* adds the phrase "Afterwards, all rise" (*Postea omnes surgunt*). This is one of the many places where the Instruction provides directives for a practice that had been common in the worship tradition for a long time. Pastorally this addition suggests that the community should already be standing for the beginning of the gospel acclamation, rather than the acclamation serving to announce a change in the community's posture.

132. Virtually unchanged from *IGMR1975*, this is the second of three articles addressing the actions during the Alleluia or other gospel acclamation. It provides the specifics for the optional use of incense before the gospel which the priest blesses (cf. no. 277 below) and puts into the thurible. The *apologia* (see

133. If the *Book of the Gospels* is on the altar, the priest then takes it and goes to the ambo, carrying the *Book of the Gospels* slightly elevated and preceded by the lay ministers, who may carry the thurible and the candles. Those present turn towards the ambo as a sign of special reverence to the Gospel of Christ.

134. At the ambo, the priest opens the book and, with hands joined, says, *Dominus vobiscum (The Lord be with you)*, and the

133. Tunc Evangeliarium, si est in altari, accipit et, præcedentibus ministris laicis, qui thuribulum et cereos deferre possunt, ad ambonem accedit, Evangeliarium parum elevatum deferens. Adstantes ad ambonem se convertunt, singularem reverentiam erga Evangelium Christi manifestantes.

134. In ambone sacerdos aperit librum et, manibus iunctis, dicit: Dóminus vobíscum, populo respondente: Et cum spíritu

---

no. 33 above) is said only by the priest, and not by the deacon if he is to proclaim the gospel (see no. 175 below). *IGMR2002* newly specifies that the priest bows "profoundly" (*profunde*) before the altar, i.e., this is a bow of the body and not just the head. *IGMR2002* presumes that all of this activity is happening while the *Alleluia* is being chanted, which could diminish its power as a processional chant, accompanying the movement of the Book of the Gospels.

133. This third article covering the actions during the Alleluia (or other chant) provides one of the more specific references in *IGMR2002* to the gospel procession, and implicitly recognizes the accompanying chant here as a processional chant (cf. no. 37 above). A number of additions have been introduced that are not present in *IGMR1975*, no. 94. True to its tendency to draw sharper distinctions between the clergy and the laity (see 91, above), *IGMR2002* newly notes that those who precede the priest are "lay ministers" (*ministris laicis*). This Instruction also specifies that the Book of the Gospels is to be carried "slightly elevated" (*parum elevatum*), as was noted in the entrance procession (no. 120d above). A completely new sentence then instructs that all are to turn towards the ambo "as a sign of special reverence to the Gospel of Christ" (*singularem reverentiam erga Evangelium Christi manifestantes*). Here *IGMR2002* offers a particular example for the general principle articulated in no. 311 below, that the community requires a worship space that both allows them to move easily during the eucharistic liturgy (e.g., turning toward the ambo), and to see (and hear) the various rituals in the Mass without difficulty.

134. As elsewhere, this paragraph adds details of the assembly's ritual practices that had never been mentioned in an *IGMR*. Here *IGMR2002* prescribes that the priest says "The Lord be with you" with "joined hands" (*manibus iunctis*), which seems to contradict other directions in *IGMR2002* indicating that when the priest offers a greeting it is done while "extending hands" (*manus extendens*, nos. 124, 146, 148 and 167). *IGMR2002* also explicates that the people respond "And also with you" (*Et cum spiritu tuo*). Similarly, while *IGMR1975* indicates that the priest would make the triple signing on forehead, mouth, and breast before the gospel (no. 95), *IGMR2002* adds that "everyone else does [this] as well" (*quod faciunt et ceteri omnes*).

people respond, *Et cum spiritu tuo (And also with you)*. Then he says, *Lectio sancti Evangelii (A reading from the holy Gospel)*, making the sign of the cross with his thumb on the book and on his forehead, mouth, and breast, which everyone else does as well. The people say the acclamation *Gloria tibi, Domine (Glory to you, Lord)*. The priest incenses the book, if incense is used (cf. nos. 276–277). Then he proclaims the Gospel and at the end says the acclamation *Verbum Domini (The Gospel of the Lord)*, to which all respond, *Laus tibi, Christe (Praise to you, Lord Jesus Christ)*. The priest kisses the book, saying quietly, *Per evangelica dicta (May the words of the Gospel)*.

tuo, et deinde Léctio sancti Evangélii, pollice signans librum et seipsum in fronte, ore et pectore, quod faciunt et ceteri omnes. Populus acclamat, dicens: Glória tibi, Dómine. Sacerdos librum, si incensum adhibetur, thurificat *(cf. nn. 276–277)*. Deinde proclamat Evangelium, et in fine profert acclamationem: Verbum Dómini, omnibus respondentibus: Laus tibi, Christe. Sacerdos librum osculatur, secreto dicens: Per evangélica dicta.

135. If no lector is present, the priest himself proclaims all the readings and the Psalm, standing at the ambo. If incense is used, remaining at the ambo he puts some into the thurible, blesses it, and, bowing profoundly, says, *Munda cor meum (Almighty God, cleanse my heart)*.

135. Si non adest lector, sacerdos ipse omnes lectiones et psalmum profert, stans in ambone. Ibidem, si adhibetur, incensum imponit et benedicit, et, profunde inclinatus, dicit: Munda cor meum.

136. The priest, standing at the chair or at the ambo itself or, when appropriate, in another suitable place, gives the homily. When the homily is completed, a period of silence may be observed.

136. Sacerdos, stans ad sedem vel in ipso ambone vel, pro opportunitate, in alio loco idoneo, profert homiliam; qua finita, spatium silentii servari potest.

While the assembly's response "Praise to you, Lord Jesus Christ" (*Laus tibi, Christe)* is also included for the first time in *IGMR2002*, missing at the end of this paragraph is the phrase included in previous *IGMR*s that after the proclamation of the gospel, "the people make the acclamation customary to the region" (*fit acclamatio populi, iuxta consuetudinem regionem, IGMR1975*, no. 95). This appears to be at least an oversight if not an unwelcome removal of previous *IGMR*s' awareness that different cultures could honor this privileged Christological event in particular ways.

135. While it is possible for the priest to proclaim all of the readings and the psalm, the absence of a reader is clearly an exception, especially given the way *IGMR2002* underscores the value of a full range of ministers within the Eucharist (cf. nos. 112 and 120 above). Here, as previously (see no. 132 above), this Instruction notes that the bow is to be done "profoundly" (*profunde*).

136. *IGMR2002* introduces two changes into this paragraph. First concerns the appropriate location for the homily. While previous *IGMR*s had noted the possibility of preaching from the chair or ambo, *IGMR2002* acknowledges that,

137. The Creed is sung or recited by the priest together with the people (cf. no. 68) with everyone standing. At the words *et incarnatus est (by the power of the Holy Spirit . . . and became man)* all make a profound bow; but on the solemnities of the Annunciation and of the Nativity of the Lord, all genuflect.

138. After the recitation of the Creed, the priest, standing at the chair with hands joined, by means of a brief introduction invites the faithful to participate in the Prayer of the Faithful. Then the cantor, the

137. Symbolum cantatur vel recitatur a sacerdote una cum populo *(cf. n. 68)*, omnibus stantibus. Ad verba Et incarnátus est, etc. omnes profunde se inclinant; in sollemnitatibus vero Annuntiationis et Nativitatis Domini genua flectunt.

138. Dicto symbolo, sacerdos stans ad sedem, manibus iunctis, brevi monitione fideles invitat ad orationem universalem. Deinde cantor vel lector vel alius, ex ambone aut ex alio loco convenienti, intentio-

---

when appropriate, the homilist can preach from another place. Implicit here is the pastoral realization that the ambo or chair may not be the most audible, visible, or dynamic place for enacting this critical liturgical event (cf. no. 311 below). In some contexts, standing in front of the altar is preferable. This addition thus prods homilists to consider not only what they say, but from where their proclamation is most effective.

The second change concerns the option for some silence after the homily. Consonant with the proposed possibilities of silence after the first and second readings (see nos. 128 and 130 above), and the richer treatment of silence in chapter 3 (no. 45 above), such silence can help dispose worshippers to hear the Holy Spirit at work in the preaching (*Institutio Generalis de Liturgia Horarum* [*IGLH*] no. 202). The pastoral challenge is to welcome such silence without allowing it to impede the dynamic of the liturgical action (*SC*, no. 7) as the Liturgy of the Word prepares to move to its conclusion.

137. As for the Creed, *IGMR1975*, no. 98, indicates that it "is said" (*dicitur*). In order to underscore the musical possibilities for this element, *IGMR2002* clarifies that it may be "sung or recited" (*cantatur vel recitatur*). This article also gives considerable attention to the shared posture of ministry and assembly during the Creed. New is the specification that the Creed is done "with everyone standing" (*omnibus stantibus*). Previous *IGMR*s note that priest and assembly bow at "He became man" (*et incarnatus est*); this Instruction specifies that the bow is "profound" (*profunde*). As in previous *IGMR*s, priest and people together genuflect at this moment on the Feasts of the Annunciation and Christmas, illustrating how changes in the church year affect the celebration of the Eucharist.

138. What is a single sentence in *IGMR1975*, no. 99, has been expanded to three here. *IGMR2002* no longer allows the option for the priest to stand at the ambo for this prayer; instead he must be at the chair. *IGMR2002* adds details concerning the priest's gestures, e.g., hands are folded for the introduction, and

lector, or another person announces the intentions from the ambo or from some other suitable place while facing the people, who take their part by responding in supplication. After the intentions, the priest, with hands extended, concludes the petitions with a prayer.

nes versus populum proponit, populo pro sua parte suppliciter respondente. Postremo sacerdos, minibus extensis, precationem oratione concludit.

The Liturgy of the Eucharist

139. When the Prayer of the Faithful is completed, all sit, and the Offertory chant begins (cf. no. 74).

An acolyte or other lay minister arranges the corporal, the purificator, the chalice, the pall, and the Missal upon the altar.

140. It is appropriate for the faithful's participation to be expressed by an offering, whether of the bread and wine for the celebration of the Eucharist or of other gifts for the relief of the needs of the Church and of the poor.

Liturgia eucharistica

139. Oratione universali absoluta, omnes sedent et incipit cantus ad offertorium *(cf. n. 74)*.

Acolythus vel alius minister laicus corporale, purificatorium, calicem, pallam et missale super altare collocat.

140. Expedit ut participatio fidelium manifestetur per oblationem sive panis et vini ad Eucharistiæ celebrationem, sive aliorum donorum, quibus necessitatibus ecclesiæ et pauperum subveniatur.

---

hands extended during the closing oration. Also, there is more specification regarding who should announce the intentions. The cantor is listed first here, underscoring the lyrical, even musical nature of this litany, even though *IGMR* does not mention music in relationship to this prayer. *IGMR2000* mentions the deacon first, an odd insertion in a section entitled "Mass without a deacon," which was subsequently removed (cf. no. 177 below).

The Liturgy of the Eucharist

139. Similar to previous editions, *IGMR2002* adds a few details. It specifies that "all sit" (*omnes sedent*) as the Liturgy of the Eucharist begins, indicating that the priest and assembly here assume a common posture. On the difficulty with the language for the "Offertory chant" (*cantus ad offertorium*) see no. 37 above. Whereas previous editions indicate that ministers or "servers" (*ministri*) prepare the altar (*IGMR1975*, no. 100), this edition specifies that "an acolyte or other lay minister" (*acolythus vel alius minister laicus*) prepares the altar, giving more prominence to the role of the instituted acolyte (cf. no. 120 above). It also mentions the pall (*pallam*) as one of the items brought to the altar (cf. no. 118 above).

140. The first paragraph in this article is identical with that found in *IGMR1975*, no. 101. The presumption of the paragraph is that the priest-presider and assembly continue to sit during the taking of the collection, rather than the priest standing at the altar saying the prayers of blessing while the collection is being taken.

The offerings of the faithful are received by the priest, assisted by the acolyte or other minister. The bread and wine for the Eucharist are carried to the celebrant, who places them upon the altar, while other gifts are put in another appropriate place (cf. no. 73).

141. At the altar the priest accepts the paten with the bread. With both hands he holds it slightly raised above the altar and says quietly, *Benedictus es, Domine (Blessed are you, Lord)*. Then he places the paten with the bread on the corporal.

142. After this, as the minister presents the cruets, the priest stands at the side of the altar and pours wine and a little water

Oblationes fidelium a sacerdote accipiuntur, adiuvantibus acolytho vel alio ministro. Panis et vinum pro Eucharistia ad celebrantem deferuntur, qui ea super altare deponit, alia autem dona alio apto loco collocantur *(cf. n. 73)*.

141. Sacerdos, ad altare, accipit patenam cum pane, eamque ambabus minibus aliquantulum elevatam super altare tenet, dicens secreto Benedíctus es, Dómine. Deinde patenam cum pane super corporale deponit.

142. Postea, sacerdos stans ad latus altaris, infundit vinum et parum aquæ in calicem, dicens secreto: Per huius aquæ,

---

The second paragraph adds the clarification that only the priest places the bread and wine on the altar. The wording of the text does not prohibit assisting ministers from helping to carry the elements into the sanctuary, but seems only to prohibit them from placing the bread and wine on the altar, an action restricted to the ordained (see no. 73 above).

141. In previous *IGMR*s the priest received "the paten with the bread from a minister" (*a ministro patenam cum pane, IGMR1975*, no. 102). *IGMR2002* drops the phrase "from a minister" (*a ministro*), something of a holdover from *MR1570*, which indicated that the deacon held out the paten and the priest accepted the paten with the host from him (*diaconus porrigit celebranti patenam cum hostia; secus sacerdos ipse accipit patenam cum hostia . . ."*). The English translation of *accipit* as "accepts" rather than "takes" could give the impression that some minister is yet offering the paten to the presider, which *IGMR2002* clearly does not intend. Concerning further information on the paten, see no. 331 below.

Previous *IGMR*s and *MR*s indicate that the text with the cup at the preparation of the gifts is to be said *secreto* (GIRM1975 translates "softly" while the 1974 Sacramentary has "quietly," cf. no. 33 above). *IGMR2002* adds this directive for the first time in reference to praying the text over the bread. This new consistency is typical of this Instruction and further seems to support the preference for music during the preparation of the gifts (see nos. above 74 and 142 below). During this modest action, the paten with the bread is held "slightly raised above the altar" (*aliquantulum elevatam super altare*), a directive found in previous *IGMR*s and *MR*s, and clearly distinguished from the chest-high gesture that accompanies the offering of the bread in *MR1570*.

142. A minister (not an acolyte) presents the cruets to the priest, suggesting that this is not "one of the more important duties" (no. 187 below) during the celebration of the Mass. While all *IGMR*s make reference to "cruets" (*urceoli*),

into the chalice, saying quietly, *Per huius aquae (By the mystery of this water)*. He returns to the middle of the altar, takes the chalice with both hands, raises it a little, and says quietly, *Benedictus es, Domine (Blessed are you, Lord)*. Then he places the chalice on the corporal and covers it with a pall, as appropriate.

If, however, there is no Offertory chant and the organ is not played, in the presentation of the bread and wine the priest may say the formulas of blessing aloud, to which the people make the acclamation, *Benedictus Deus in saecula (Blessed be God for ever)*.

143. After placing the chalice upon the altar, the priest bows profoundly and says quietly, *In spiritu humilitatis (Lord God, we ask you to receive us)*.

ministro urceolos porrigente. Reversus ad medium altaris, acceptum calicem ambabus manibus parum elevatum tenet, dicens secreto Benedíctus es, Dómine, et deinde calicem super corporale deponit, et palla pro opportunitate cooperit.

Si vero cantus ad offertorium non peragitur vel non pulsatur organum, sacerdoti licet, in præsentatione panis et vini, elata voce proferre formulas benedictionis, quibus populus acclamat: Benedíctus Deus in sǽcula.

143. Calice super altare deposito, sacerdos, profunde inclinatus, dicit secreto: In spíritu humilitátis.

---

a cruet for wine would seem to be the exception, given the preference for a procession with the gifts (no. 73 above; also ITTOM, no. 105) that would include a vessel with the wine. Furthermore, since it is "most desirable" that the faithful receive Communion under both forms when permitted (no. 85 above), a cruet of wine would ordinarily be insufficient for this. While *Redemptionis Sacramentum* (*RedSac*) instructs that the pouring of consecrated wine is to be avoided (no. 106), and notes the appropriateness of multiple chalices on the table (no. 105), presumably at the preparation of the gifts, there exists no directive to pour water into each chalice on the altar at this time. The priest's prayers during this action are said "quietly" (*secreto*).

New here is the inclusion of the *incipit* for the prayer during the pouring of the water (see *Veronense*, no. 1239), the blessing prayer, and the people's acclamation.

The second paragraph of this article, which repeats the rubric found in *MR2002*, is a helpful addition, underscoring the preference for music here and its precedence over the audible speaking of these texts. Even if there is no music, the texts may be prayed inaudibly, and there is no requirement for liceity that the people's acclamation be said by anyone. Since these texts form a single unit, they need to be performed identically; reciting one quietly and the second aloud should never happen (ITTOM, no. 106). The option for complete silence here accentuates the preparatory, even secondary nature of this liturgical unit. The 1969 *Appendix to the General Instruction for the Dioceses of the United States* (no. 50) wisely noted that muting this preparatory rite was a good thing before demanding the full attention of the community during the Eucharistic Prayer (cf. no. 74 above).

144. If incense is used, the priest then puts some in the thurible, blesses it without saying anything, and incenses the offerings, the cross, and the altar. A minister, while standing at the side of the altar, incenses the priest and then the people.

145. After the prayer *In spiritu humilitatis (Lord God, we ask you to receive us)* or after the incensation, the priest washes his hands standing at the side of the altar and, as the minister pours the water, says quietly, *Lava me, Domine (Lord, wash away my iniquity)*.

146. Upon returning to the middle of the altar, the priest, facing the people and extending and then joining his hands, invites the people to pray, saying, *Orate, fratres (Pray, brethren)*. The people rise and make their response: *Suscipiat Dominus (May the Lord accept)*. Then the priest, with hands extended, says the prayer over the offerings. At the end the people make the acclamation, *Amen*.

147. Then the priest begins the Eucharistic Prayer. In accordance with the rubrics (cf. no. 365), he selects a Eucharistic Prayer

144. Deinde, si incensum adhibetur, sacerdos illud in thuribulo imponit, benedicit nihil dicens atque oblata, crucem et altare incensat. Minister stans ad latus altaris sacerdotem incensat, deinde populum.

145. Post orationem In spíritu humilitátis vel post incensationem, sacerdos, stans ad latus altaris, manus lavat, secreto dicens: Lava me, Dómine, ministro aquam fundente.

146. Ad medium altaris deinde reversus, sacerdos, stans versus populum, extendens et iungens manus, populum ad orandum invitat, dicens: Oráte, fratres. Populus surgit et responsionem dat: Suscípiat Dóminus. Deinde sacerdos, manibus extensis, dicit orationem super oblata. In fine populus acclamat: Amen.

147. Tunc sacerdos incipit Precem eucharisticam. Iuxta rubricas *(cf. n. 365)* seligit unam ex iis quæ in Missali Romano inve-

---

143. New in this article is the precision that, after the chalice is placed upon the altar, the priest bows "profoundly" (*profunde*) while quietly speaking the text from Daniel 3:39-40, an *apologia* made obligatory in *MR1570*.

144. As previously, *IGMR2002* here newly adds that the cross (cf. nos. 49 and 123 above) as well as the offerings and altar are to be incensed. *IGMR2002* also specifies that the minister (*minister*, not *acolythus*) who incenses the priest does so "while standing at the side of the altar" (*stans ad latus altaris*). It is presumed that when the same minister goes on to incense the people, it is necessary to move from this position to a more central place for incensing the assembly.

145. As it has done in other places (e.g., no. 142), *IGMR2002* newly adds the *incipit* for the text said quietly by the priest as he washes his hands. A minister (not an acolyte) pours the water.

146. New in this article is *IGMR2002*'s directive that the people are standing as they make their response to the priest's invitation to pray (reiterating the directives of no. 43). Pastorally this could suggest that the people are standing even before the priest offers the invitation, so that his text is a true invitation to pray, rather than a cue to stand. Also new is the inclusion of the *incipit*s for the priest and people for this invitation and response.

from those found in the *Roman Missal* or approved by the Apostolic See. The Eucharistic Prayer demands, by its very nature, that the priest say it in virtue of his ordination. The people, for their part, should associate themselves with the priest in faith and in silence, as well as through their parts as prescribed in the course of the Eucharistic Prayer: namely the responses in the Preface dialogue, the *Sanctus*, the acclamation after the consecration, the acclamatory *Amen* after the final doxology, as well as other acclamations approved by the Conference of Bishops and recognized by the Holy See.

It is very appropriate that the priest sing those parts of the Eucharistic Prayer for which musical notation is provided.

niuntur, vel ab Apostolica Sede probatæ sunt. Prex eucharistica natura sua exigit ut solus sacerdos, vi ordinationis, eam proferat. Populus vero sacerdoti in fide et cum silentio se societ, necnon interventibus in eucharisticæ Precis cursu statutis, qui sunt responsiones in dialogo Præfationis, Sanctus, acclamatio post consecrationem et acclamatio Amen post doxologiam finalem, necnon aliæ acclamationes a Conferentia Episcoporum probatæ et a Sancta Sede recognitæ.

Valde convenit ut sacerdos partes Precis eucharisticæ, quæ notis ditantur, cantu proferat.

148. As he begins the Eucharistic Prayer, the priest extends his hands and sings or

148. Precem eucharisticam incipiens, sacerdos, manus extendens, cantat vel dicit:

---

147. This is the first of five articles in this section on the Eucharistic Prayer. Aside from the opening sentence, this article is a new addition in *IGMR2002*. It first notes that a Eucharistic Prayer needs to be selected, an action presuming forethought done in view of the spiritual needs of the people (cf. no. 352 below). *IGMR2002* reiterates that only approved prayers are allowed (cf. *RedSac*, no. 10), but the Instruction later will reference only four Eucharistic Prayers (no. 365 below).

The directives that distinguish the specific eucharistic acclamations and responses of the people from the rest of the prayer, to be said only by the priest, underscore *IGMR2002*'s strong tendency to emphasize the distinction between the ministerial priesthood and the priesthood of the faithful and to avoid any confusion about what is proper to the ordained and to the laity within the eucharistic liturgy (cf. no. 91, above). The people's participation in the Eucharistic Prayer is not meant to be diminished by this distinction, for as both *SC* (no. 48) and *IGMR2002* itself note, the people are joined to Christ in offering the sacrifice during this great thanksgiving (no. 78) and can rightly be considered a subject of the eucharistic action (cf. Power and Vincie, 52; also no. 27 above).

Additional eucharistic acclamations may be used, provided they are approved. This could be an implicit reference to the Eucharistic Prayers for children and for Masses for Various Needs and Occasions with their multiple eucharistic acclamations, which are not explicitly mentioned in *IGMR2002*, as they have only been approved *ad experimentum*. The final note is an encouragement to the priest to sing the Eucharistic Prayer.

says, *Dominus vobiscum (The Lord be with you)*. The people respond, *Et cum spiritu tuo (And also with you)*. As he continues, *Sursum corda (Lift up your hearts)*, he raises his hands. The people respond, *Habemus ad Dominum (We lift them up to the Lord)*. Then the priest, with hands outstretched, adds, *Gratias agamus Domino Deo nostro (Let us give thanks to the Lord, our God)*, and the people respond, *Dignum et iustum est (It is right to give him thanks and praise)*. Next, the priest, with hands extended, continues the Preface. At its conclusion, he joins his hands and, together with everyone present, sings or says aloud the *Sanctus* (cf. no. 79b).

Dóminus vobíscum, populo respondente: Et cum spíritu tuo. Cum prosequitur: Sursum corda, manus elevat. Populus respondet: Habémus ad Dóminum. Deinde sacerdos, manibus extensis, subdit: Grátias agámus Dómino Deo nostro, et populus respondet: Dignum et iustum est. Postea sacerdos prosequitur, manibus extensis, Præfationem; eaque conclusa, iunctis manibus, una cum omnibus adstantibus, cantat vel clara voce dicit: Sanctus *(cf. n. 79 b)*.

149. The priest continues the Eucharistic Prayer in accordance with the rubrics that are set forth in each of the Prayers.

If the celebrant is a Bishop, in the Prayers, after the words *Papa nostro N. (N., our Pope)*, he adds, *et me, indigno famulo tuo (and me,*

149. Sacerdos prosequitur Precem eucharisticam iuxta rubricas, quæ in singulis Precibus exponuntur.

Si celebrans est Episcopus, in Precibus, post verba: Papa nostro N. subiungit: et me indígno fámulo tuo, vel post verba: Papæ

---

148. *IGMR2002* newly notes that the first preference is for the priest to sing the preface dialogue. Since the priest next "continues the Preface" (*prosequitur . . . Praefationem*) it is presumed that the priest would sing the preface if he sang the preface dialogue. *IGMR2002* also adds all of the people's responses to the dialogue (only *Dignum et iustum est* is in *IGMR1975*, no. 108). This article no longer refers to the *Sanctus-Benedictus* (as in *IGMR1975*, no. 108) but only to the *Sanctus*, and more simply notes that it is prayed by the priest "together with everyone present" (*cum omnibus adstantibus*) rather than "with ministers and people" *(cum ministris et populo, IGMR1975*, no. 108).

149. The parallel article in *IGMR1969* (no. 109) provides one sentence at this point instructing that the priest continues the Eucharistic Prayer. That same article is expanded in *IGMR1975* to include directives concerning how a bishop-presider is to name himself (in and outside his own diocese) and how a priest-presider is to pray for his local bishop, auxiliary bishops or their equivalents. *IGMR2002* provides even more information concerning how a visiting bishop is to refer to the bishop of the diocese and which specific names the priest uses for a list of those equivalent to the bishop (singular and plural). Bishop- and priest-presiders are also reminded to include in the Eucharistic Prayer only the names of the local bishop, the coadjutor, and the auxiliary bishops; naming other bishops who may be present as an honorific gesture would be inappropriate, since the eucharistic celebrations of a local church are profoundly rooted in the priesthood of the diocesan bishop as the focus of their unity (see no. 92 above).

your unworthy servant). If, however, the Bishop is celebrating outside his own diocese, after the words *Papa nostro N. (N., our Pope),* he adds, *et me indigno famulo tuo, et fratre meo N., Episcopo huius Ecclesiae N. (me, your unworthy servant, and my brother N., the Bishop of this Church of N.).*

The diocesan Bishop or anyone equivalent to him in law must be mentioned by means of this formula: *una cum famulo tuo Papa nostro N. et Episcopo (or Vicario, Prelato, Praefecto, Abbate) (together with your servant N., our Pope, and N., our Bishop [or Vicar, Prelate, Prefect, Abbot]).*

It is permitted to mention Coadjutor and Auxiliary Bishops in the Eucharistic Prayer, but not other Bishops who happen to be present. When several are to be named, this is done with the collective formula *et Episcopo nostro N. eiusque Episcopis adiutoribus (N., our Bishop and his assistant Bishops).*

In each of the Eucharistic Prayers, these formulas are to be modified according to the requirements of grammar.

150. A little before the consecration, when appropriate, a server rings a bell as a signal to the faithful. According to local custom, the server also rings the bell as the priest shows the host and then the chalice.

nostri N., subiungit: mei indígni fámuli tui. Si autem Episcopus extra diœcesim suam celebrat, post verba: Papa nostro N. subiungit: et me indígno fámulo tuo, et fratre meo N., Epíscopo huius Ecclésiæ N., vel post verba: Papæ nostri N., subiungit: mei indígni fámuli tui, et fratris mei N., Epíscopi huius Ecclésiæ N.

Episcopus diœcesanus, aut qui eidem in iure æquiparatus est, nominari debet hac formula: una cum fámulo tuo Papa nostro N. et Epíscopo (vel: Vicário, Præláto, Præfécto, Abbáte) nostro N.

Episcopos Coadiutorem et Auxiliares, non autem alios Episcopos forte præsentes, nominari licet in Prece eucharistica. Quando plures nominandi sunt, dicitur sub formula generali: et Epíscopo nostro N. eiúsque Epíscopis adiutóribus.

In unaquaque Prece eucharistica, prædictæ formulæ aptandæ sunt, normis grammaticorum attentis.

150. Paulo ante consecrationem, minister, pro opportunitate, campanulæ signo fideles monet. Item pulsat campanulam ad unamquamque ostensionem, iuxta cuiusque loci consuetudinem.

Furthermore, the intercession during the Eucharistic Prayer in which the local church is mentioned also includes a reference to all bishops.

150. *IGMR2002* has taken material about ringing bells, found in previous *IGMR*s, and set it apart into a distinctive paragraph with additional information about incensation. Regarding bell ringing before the consecration, *IGMR2002* adds the phrase "when appropriate" (*pro opportunitate*), possibly suggesting that several decades of catechesis, vernacular liturgy and the rearrangement of altars facing the people may have made the use of such a signal unnecessary. No cue is given for when this ringing of the bells may take place, but only the ambiguous "a little before the consecration" (*Paulo ante consecrationem*). The parallel to the Tridentine practice of ringing a bell at the *Hanc igitur* (never in the official rubrics, but often found in manuals for serving Mass) would be the ringing of the bell at the consecratory epiclesis. The problem with such an interpretation, however, is that the consecratory epiclesis is integral to the act of consecration (cf. no. 78c above), and so does not really signal "a little before the consecration."

If incense is used, a server incenses the host and the chalice when each is shown to the people after the consecration.

Si incensum adhibetur, cum hostia et calix populo post consecrationem ostenduntur, minister ea incensat.

151. After the consecration when the priest has said, *Mysterium fidei (Let us proclaim the mystery of faith)*, the people sing or say an acclamation using one of the prescribed formulas.

At the end of the Eucharistic Prayer, the priest takes the paten with the host and the chalice and elevates them both while alone singing or saying the doxology, *Per ipsum (Through him)*. At the end the people make the acclamation, *Amen*. Then the priest places the paten and the chalice on the corporal.

151. Post consecrationem, dicto a sacerdote: Mystérium fídei, populus acclamationem profert, adhibita una ex formulis præscriptis.

In fine Precis eucharisticæ, sacerdos, accipiens patenam cum hostia et calicem et utrumque elevans, doxologiam: Per ipsum, solus profert. Populus in fine acclamat: Amen. Postea sacerdos patenam et calicem super corporale deponit.

152. After the Eucharistic Prayer is concluded, the priest, with hands joined, says the introduction to the Lord's Prayer. With hands extended, he then says this prayer together with the people.

152. Expleta Prece eucharistica, sacerdos, manibus iunctis, dicit monitionem ante Orationem dominicam, quam deinde una cum populo profert, manibus extensis.

Also new are instructions for the optional incensations during the showings of the host and of the chalice (see no. 277 below).

151. This new article details rubrics found in *MR2002* regarding the second eucharistic acclamation and the doxology. Regarding the invitation to the second eucharistic acclamation, GIRM2003 could give the impression that while the people "sing or say an acclamation" (*acclamationem profert*), the invitation is "said" (*dicto*) by the priest. If the people are to sing the acclamation, the priest should sing the invitation.

IGMR2002 reiterates that during the doxology the priest "elevates . . . both" elements (*utramque elevans*), distinguishing this moment from the showing (*ad unamquamque ostensionem)* following the "consecration" (no. 150; also, cf. no. 84 above). Since *IGMR2002* recognizes that a paten can be large enough to hold the bread for other ministers and the faithful as well as the priest (no. 331), the directive to "take the paten with the host" (*accipiens patenam cum hostia)* cannot be taken too literally. The pastoral context, shape of the vessels and care for the consecrated species (cf. *RedSac*, no. 92) will dictate whether a single host or the full paten is to be elevated.

IGMR2002 directs that the priest alone prays the doxology; even when there are concelebrants, their participation is optional (no. 236). The faithful do not join the priest in this text. It is only after the people's *Amen* that the priest returns the paten and chalice to the corporal, implying that during any extended singing of the acclamation, the priest sustains the elevation until the end.

153. After the Lord's Prayer is concluded, the priest alone, with hands extended, says the embolism *Libera nos (Deliver us)*. At the end, the people make the acclamation, *Quia tuum est regnum (For the kingdom)*.

153. Oratione dominica conclusa, sacerdos, manibus extensis, solus dicit embolismum Líbera nos, quo completo, populus acclamat: Quia tuum est regnum.

154. Then the priest, with hands extended, says aloud the prayer, *Domine Iesu Christe, qui dixisti (Lord Jesus Christ, you said)*. After this prayer is concluded, extending and then joining his hands, he gives the greeting of peace while facing the people and saying, *Pax Domini sit s[e]mper vobiscum (The peace of the Lord be with you always)*. The

154. Deinde sacerdos, manibus extensis, clara voce dicit orationem Dómine Iesu Christe, qui dixísti; eaque conclusa, extendens et iungens manus, pacem annuntiat, versus ad populum, dicens: Pax Dómini sit semper vobíscum. Populus respondet: Et cum spíritu tuo. Postea, pro opportunitate, sacerdos subiungit: Offérte vobis pacem.

---

152. This article provides directions for the introduction to and performance of the Lord's Prayer. The opening sentence is slightly changed from *IGMR1975*, which places the introduction to the Lord's Prayer "After the doxology at the end of the Eucharistic prayer" (*Expleta doxologia, quae in fine Precis eucharisticae*, no. 110) to "After the Eucharistic Prayer is concluded" (*Expleta Prece eucharistica*). The change seems more respectful of the unitary nature of the Eucharistic Prayer, which although composed of various elements, is still a single presidential prayer (cf. nos. 30 and 79 above).

For the performance of the Lord's Prayer, *IGMR*s make reference to the priest praying "with hands extended" *(manibus extensis)*, but offer no instruction regarding the people's gesture during the Our Father. Previous instructions, which noted the need to pay attention both to traditional practice as well as to what serves the common spiritual good of the faithful (no. 42 above), recommend that the faithful pray the Our Father with open hands as well.

153. In discussing the embolism and the doxology after the Lord's Prayer, *IGMR2002* introduces one slight variation, changing the verb from *Oratione dominica finita* (which GIRM1975 rendered "After the Lord's Prayer is finished") to *Oratione dominica conclusa* ("After the Lord's Prayer is concluded"). While the change in itself has little significance, it does draw attention to the presumption of *IGMR2002* and its predecessors that this prayer is not yet "finished." Quite different from *MR1570*, which inserted an "Amen" before the embolism, *MR2002* and its post-conciliar predecessors suspend the "Amen" until after the embolism and the doxology, suggesting that it is only after these that this liturgical unit is "finished." The recovery of the doxology after the Lord's Prayer is ecumenically important, though the placement of the doxology after the embolism continues to distinguish the way Roman Catholics pray this prayer from most other Christians.

154. As is its pattern, *IGMR2002* adds the detail that the prayer "Lord Jesus Christ" (*Domine Iesu Christe)* is said with "hands extended" (*manibus extensis*).

people answer, *Et cum spiritu tuo (And also with you)*. Afterwards, when appropriate, the priest adds, *Offerte vobis pacem (Let us offer each other the sign of peace)*.

The priest may give the sign of peace to the ministers but always remains within the sanctuary, so as not to disturb the celebration. In the dioceses of the United States of America, for a good reason, on special occasions (for example, in the case of a funeral, a wedding, or when civic leaders are present) the priest may offer the sign of peace to a few of the faithful near the sanctuary. At the same time, in accord with the decisions of the Conference of Bishops, all offer one another a sign that expresses peace, communion, and charity. While the sign of peace is being given, one may say, *Pax Domini sit semper tecum (The peace of the Lord be with you always)*, to which the response is *Amen*.

Sacerdos pacem potest dare ministris, semper tamen intra presbyterium remanens, ne celebratio turbetur. Item faciat si e rationabili causa aliquibus paucis fidelibus pacem dare velit. Omnes vero, iuxta ea quæ a Conferentia Episcoporum statuta sunt, pacem, communionem et caritatem sibi invicem significant. Dum pax datur, dici potest: Pax Dómini sit semper tecum, cui respondetur: Amen.

It also adds four new sentences regarding to whom the ordained priest can offer the sign of peace. The priest is to remain in the sanctuary "so as not to disturb the celebration" (*ne celebratio turbetur*), whether sharing the sign of peace with ministers or "a few of the faithful" (*aliquibus paucis fidelibus*). The value of this circumscription is its underscoring that the sign of peace does not begin at the altar and move outward to the faithful, but is an act that naturally emerges from the gathered assembly. Yet such circumscription could contribute to an image of the presider as isolated from the assembly. GIRM2003 includes an approved adaptation for dioceses of the US allowing the priest to "offer the sign of peace to a few of the faithful near the sanctuary," which would seem to require the priest to leave the sanctuary. This is allowed "for a good reason" and "on special occasions" (for example, in the case of a funeral, a wedding, or when civic leaders are present).

Previous *IGMR*s teach that the significance of the sign of peace is its expression of peace and charity (*IGMR1975*, no. 112). The current Instruction adds communion to this official interpretation of the ritual, consonant with the communion ecclesiology in ascendancy during the shaping of this Instruction (cf. no. 82 above). This addition suggests that it is ordinarily important for the priest-presider to share the peace with some members of the faithful, in order to symbolize the communion of the ministerial priesthood with the common priesthood of the baptized, rather than ritually segregate these. Furthermore, in view of the approved adaptation for dioceses in the US, it is possible to suggest that the pastoral care of the community is always a good reason for the

155. The priest then takes the host and breaks it over the paten. He places a small piece in the chalice, saying quietly, *Haec commixtio (May the mingling)*. Meanwhile the *Agnus Dei* is sung or said by the choir and congregation (cf. no. 83).

155. Postea sacerdos accipit hostiam, eamque super patenam frangit, et particulam immittit in calicem, dicens secreto: Hæc commíxtio. Interim a choro et a populo cantatur vel dicitur Agnus Dei *(cf. n. 83)*.

156. Then the priest, with hands joined, quietly says the preparatory prayer of Communion: *Domine Iesu Christe, Fili Dei vivi (Lord Jesus Christ, Son of the living God)* or *Perceptio Corporis et Sanguinis (Lord Jesus Christ, with faith in your love and mercy)*.

156. Tunc sacerdos secreto et manibus iunctis dicit orationem ad Communionem Dómine Iesu Christe, Fili Dei vivi vel Percéptio Córporis et Sánguinis.

157. When the prayer is concluded, the priest genuflects, takes the host consecrated in the same Mass, and, holding it slightly raised above the paten or above the chalice, while facing the people, says, *Ecce Agnus Dei (This is the Lamb of God)*. With the people he adds, *Domine, non sum dignus (Lord, I am not worthy)*.

157. Oratione conclusa, sacerdos genuflectit, accipit hostiam in eadem Missa consecratam, eamque aliquantulum elevatam super patenam vel super calicem tenens, versus ad populum, dicit: Ecce Agnus Dei, et una cum populo subdit: Dómine, non sum dignus.

---

clergy to share peace with the faithful, and that the Sunday eucharistic gathering by definition is always a special occasion for such sharing.

155. This article is a verbatim repetition of previous *IGMR*s. Given that a commonly enacted second part of the fraction rite, i.e., the pouring of wine from flagons into Communion cups for the faithful, has been transferred to the preparation of the gifts, it is important that the breaking of "larger breads" (ITTOM, no. 131), and the transfer of consecrated hosts from the large paten to other vessels for the Communion of the faithful, be carried out with the due reverence befitting a ritual gesture which "gave the eucharistic actions its name in apostolic times" (no. 83 above). Eliminating any breaking of the bread at the institution narrative (*RedSac,* no. 55) helps give appropriate emphasis to this rite. On the performance of the *Agnus Dei,* see no. 83 above.

156. Providing directions for this priestly *apologia* (cf. no. 33 above) recited in preparation for Communion, *IGMR2002* adds a small detail that the prayer "Lord Jesus Christ" (*Domine Iesu Christe*) is said "with hands joined" (*manibus iunctis*), underscoring that this is a private prayer, and thus performed without the traditional *orans* gesture that marks the public prayers of the Eucharist.

157. Two slight additions appear in this article. First, *IGMR2002* notes that the priest takes the host "consecrated in the same Mass" (*in eadem Missa consecratam*), thus reemphasizing a point made earlier (no. 85 above). Second, whereas previous *IGMR*s note that the consecrated host is held slightly raised above the paten, *IGMR2002* adds "or above the chalice" (*vel super calicem*), which has more ritual integrity, especially if the assembly will be receiving

158. After this, standing and turned toward the altar, the priest says quietly, *Corpus Christi custodiat me in vitam aeternam (May the Body of Christ bring me to everlasting life)* and reverently receives the Body of Christ. Then he takes the chalice, saying quietly, *Sanguis Christi custodiat me in vitam aeternam (May the Blood of Christ bring me to everlasting life)*, and reverently receives the Blood of Christ.

158. Postea, stans ad altare conversus, sacerdos secreto dicit: Corpus Christi custódiat me in vitam ætérnam, et reverenter sumit Corpus Christi. Deinde accipit calicem, secreto dicens: Sanguis Christi custódiat me in vitam ætérnam, et reverenter sumit Sanguinem Christi.

159. The Communion chant begins while the priest is receiving the Sacrament (cf. no. 86).

159. Dum sacerdos sumit Sacramentum, inchoatur cantus ad Communionem *(cf. n. 86)*.

160. The priest then takes the paten or ciborium and goes to the communicants, who, as a rule, approach in a procession.

The faithful are not permitted to take the consecrated bread or the sacred chalice by

160. Sacerdos deinde accipit patenam vel pyxidem, et accedit ad communicandos, qui de more processionaliter appropinquant.

Non licet ipsis fidelibus panem consecratum neque calicem sacrum per semetipsos

---

Communion under both forms, which the Instruction highly values (cf. nos. 72, 84 and 85 above).

As in previous *IGMR*s, this article notes that the priest *accipit hostiam*, and in the following article he *accipit calicem*. While GIRM2003 translates these as "takes the host" and "takes the chalice," there is a real sense that these gifts are "accepted" or "received" on the part of the priest, and not simply taken. *IGMR2002* insists that the faithful "receive" the consecrated elements and never "take" them (no. 160, below). This literal distinction between the way the priest and the faithful communicate does not eliminate the spiritual reality that the eucharistic elements are always a gift from God to be received and not taken.

158. There is virtually no change in this article, other than the minor explication that, as when receiving the host, the priest "says quietly" (*secreto dicens*) the text *Sanguis Christi* before drinking from the chalice. The directive here that the priest communicates first is now bolstered by *IGMR2002*'s further instruction that ministers of Communion do not approach the table before the priest has received Communion (no. 162 below), thus assuring that the priest must communicate before them. Furthermore, *RedSac* insists that the priest-presider (or a concelebrant) is never to delay his Communion until the people's Communion is concluded (no. 97 above). Such instructions are consonant with *IGMR2002*'s overall tendency to emphasize the distinction between the ministerial priesthood and the priesthood of the faithful (cf. no. 91 above).

159. See no. 86 above, for commentary pertinent to this article, unaltered from previous editions.

160. Most of this article is new. First is the added detail that communicants, "as a rule, approach in procession" (*de more processionaliter approprinquant*), an

themselves and, still less, to hand them from one to another. The norm for reception of Holy Communion in the dioceses of the United States is standing. Communicants should not be denied Holy Communion because they kneel. Rather, such instances should be addressed pastorally, by providing the faithful with proper catechesis on the reasons for this norm.

When receiving Holy Communion, the communicant bows his or her head before the Sacrament as a gesture of reverence and receives the Body of the Lord from the minister. The consecrated host may be received either on the tongue or in the hand, at the discretion of each communicant. When Holy Communion is received under both kinds, the sign of reverence is also made before receiving the Precious Blood.

accipere eo minus de manu in manum inter se transmittere. Fideles communicant genuflexi vel stantes, prout Conferentia Episcoporum statuerit. Cum autem stantes communicant, commendatur ut debitam reverentiam, ab iisdem normis statuendam, ante susceptionem Sacramenti faciant.

---

implicit acknowledgement that most of the faithful not only receive Communion standing, but do so in a processional line. This movement recalls the processional nature of classic Roman liturgy[10] and the symbolic inference that the whole of the Christian life is a pilgrimage (ITTOM, no. 135).

The new second paragraph provides further instructions on the reception of Communion. The prescription that the faithful are not to take the eucharistic elements by themselves or hand them on to others is an affirmation of a foundational sacramental principle that the sacraments are signs of God's grace and pure gifts which are accepted or received, not taken. This directive also contributes to the previously noted pattern in *IGMR2002* of emphasizing distinctions between the ministerial priesthood and the priesthood of the faithful (cf. no. 91 above), since the priest-presider does take the eucharistic elements for his self-communication, actions accentuated by the translation in GIRM2003 (see nos. 157–58 above).

While *IGMR2002* notes that the faithful may receive either kneeling or standing, GIRM2003 includes the approved adaptation for the US that the norm is standing. This pastorally sensitive addition also notes that kneeling communicants should not be denied Communion (cf. *RedSac*, no. 91), and that proper catechesis is the appropriate response if this norm is not followed.

IGMR2002 also adds that if the faithful receive Communion standing, a gesture of reverence is recommended (*commendatur ut debitam reverentiam*).

10. See, for example, Thomas Mathews, "An Early Roman Chancel Arrangement and Its Liturgical Functions," *Rivista di Archeologia Cristiana* 38 (1962): 73–95.

161. If Communion is given only under the species of bread, the priest raises the host slightly and shows it to each, saying, *Corpus Christi (The Body of Christ)*. The communicant replies, *Amen,* and receives the Sacrament either on the tongue or, where this is allowed and if the communicant so chooses, in the hand. As soon as the communicant receives the host, he or she consumes it entirely.

If, however, Communion is given under both kinds, the rite prescribed in nos. 284–287 is followed.

161. Si Communio sub specie tantum panis fit, sacerdos hostiam parum elevatam unicuique ostendit dicens: Corpus Christi. Communicandus respondet: Amen, et Sacramentum recipit, ore vel, ubi concessum sit, manu, pro libitu suo. Communicandus statim ac sacram hostiam recipit, eam ex integro consumit.

Si vero Communio fit sub utraque specie, servetur ritus suo loco descriptus *(cf. nn. 284–287)*.

What constitutes a gesture of reverence differs across cultures. GIRM2003 here again includes the approved adaptation for the US, and directs that before receiving the consecrated bread and wine, communicants bow their heads "before the Sacrament." Having this common gesture of reverence on the part of all communicants is commendable. Missing here is the language of "recommendation" found in *IGMR2002*; the gesture does not appear to be optional in GIRM2003. Finally, *IGMR2002* explicates that it is at the discretion of each communicant whether to receive on the tongue or in the hand.

161. Here *IGMR2002* combines materials found in two different paragraphs in *IGMR1975* (nos. 117–18) and adds new material. New is the explication, noted in no. 160 as well, that the communicant may receive either on the tongue or in the hand. GIRM2003's translation "either on the tongue or, where this is allowed and if the communicant so chooses, in the hand" (*ore vel, ubi concessum sit, manu, pro libitu suo*) shows more of a prejudice for receiving on the tongue than the Latin text, which has no *et* ("*and* if the communicant so chooses") and in which the phrase *pro libitu suo* can refer both to *ore* or *manu. RedSac* clearly shows a preference for receiving Communion on the tongue (no. 92).

Gone is *IGMR1975*'s reference to the Communion plate held under the chin of the communicant (*tenens patinam sub ore,* no. 117), although *RedSac,* no. 92, notes that it should be retained. Also new here is the instruction that once the host has been received, the communicant is to immediately and entirely consume it (*statim ac sacram hostiam recipit, eam ex integro consumit*). While *IGMR2002* gives no theological or pastoral reason for this addition, a parallel passage in *RedSac* speaks of the "risk of profanation" (*profanationis periculum,* no. 92).

Given *IGMR2002*'s emphasis on the importance of Communion under both forms (cf. nos. 72, 84 and 85 above and 284–87 below), it is somewhat disconcerting that this article focuses almost exclusively on Communion under the

162. The priest may be assisted in the distribution of Communion by other priests who happen to be present. If such priests are not present and there is a very large number of communicants, the priest may call upon extraordinary ministers to assist him, e.g., duly instituted acolytes or even other faithful who have been deputed for this purpose.[97] In case of necessity, the priest may depute suitable faithful for this single occasion.[98]

These ministers should not approach the altar before the priest has received Communion, and they are always to receive from the hands of the priest celebrant the vessel containing either species of the Most Holy Eucharist for distribution to the faithful.

162. In distribuenda Communione sacerdotem adiuvare possunt alii presbyteri forte præsentes. Si isti præsto non sunt et communicantium numerus valde magnus, sacerdos in adiutorium sibi vocare potest ministros extraordinarios, idest acolythum rite institutum aut etiam alios fideles, qui ad hoc rite deputati sint.[97] In casu necessitatis, sacerdos potest fideles idoneos, ad actum deputare.[98]

Hi ministri ad altare ne accedant antequam sacerdos Communionem sumpserit, semperque vas ubi continentur Ss.mæ Eucharistiæ species, fidelibus distribuendæ, e manu sacerdotis celebrantis accipiant.

163. When the distribution of Communion is finished, the priest himself immediately and completely consumes at the altar any consecrated wine that happens to remain; as for any consecrated hosts that are

163. Distributione Communionis expleta, sacerdos vinum consecratum forte remanens ipse ad altare statim ex integro consumit; hostias vero consecrates quæ supersunt, aut ad altare sumit aut

---

species of bread alone. Only at the end of the article is there reference to nos. 284–87 below, which offer directions for Communion under both species.

162. This article, largely concerned with who is to distribute Communion, is completely new. These pastoral directives also have a strong theological subtext and, as noted previously (e.g., no. 160 above), clearly demarcate boundaries between the ministerial priesthood and the priesthood of the faithful (cf. no. 91 above). Consistent with other Roman instructions, *IGMR2002* notes the "extraordinary" (*extraordinarios*) nature of the assistance by the non-ordained in the distribution of Communion and indicates that such is permissible only in well-defined circumstances (cf. nos. 100 above and 284 below; also *RedSac*, nos. 154–60). Yet *IGMR2002* also gives the priest new latitude in deputing "suitable faithful" (*fideles idoneos*) to help in cases of necessity (cf. no. 107 above), although the Instruction does not indicate what constitutes this suitability. Consistent with previous directives (e.g., no. 160 above), *IGMR2002* ensures that the priest communicates first, even before extraordinary ministers approach the altar, and that extraordinary ministers never take the consecrated species from the altar, but receive them from the hands of the priest.

163. The first paragraph of this number is new, directing that the priest must "immediately and completely" (*statim ex integro*) consume all remaining consecrated wine at the altar. Fulfilling this directive could be pastorally challenging if a large amount of consecrated wine remains. The *Norms for the Celebration*

left, he either consumes them at the altar or carries them to the place designated for the reservation of the Eucharist.

Upon returning to the altar, the priest collects any fragments that may remain. Then, standing at the altar or at the credence table, he purifies the paten or ciborium over the chalice, then purifies the chalice, saying quietly, *Quod ore sumpsimus (Lord, may I receive)*, and dries the chalice with a purificator. If the vessels are purified at the altar, they are carried to the credence table by a minister. Nevertheless, it is also permitted, especially if there are several vessels to be purified, to leave them suitably covered on a corporal, either at the altar or at the credence table, and to purify them immediately after Mass following the dismissal of the people.

164. Afterwards, the priest may return to the chair. A sacred silence may now be

defert ad locum Eucharistiæ asservandæ destinatum.

Sacerdos, ad altare reversus, colligit fragmenta, si quæ sint; deinde, stans ad altare vel ad abacum, purificat patenam vel pyxidem super calicem, postea purificat calicem, dicens secreto: Quod ore súmpsimus, et calicem purificatorio exterget. Si vasa purificata sunt ad altare, a ministro deferuntur ad abacum. Licet tamen vasa purificanda, præsertim si sint plura, opportune cooperta, in altari vel in abaco super corporale relinquere eaque statim post Missam, populo dimisso, purificare.

164. Postea sacerdos ad sedem redire potest. Sacrum silentium, per aliquod tem-

---

and Reception of Holy Communion under Both Kinds in the Dioceses of the United States of America allow for eucharistic ministers to help the priest in such situations (no. 52). The consecrated bread is to be consumed by the priest as well, with the option that it can be carried "to the place designated for the reservation" (*ad locum . . . asservandae destinatum*).

IGMR2002 eliminates the reference to cleaning the vessels at the "side of the altar" (*stans ad latus altaris, IGMR1975*, no. 120). Concerns about hygiene suggest that the second option of purifying vessels after Mass is more appropriate, allowing for a thorough cleaning of the vessels, and the avoidance of drying them with a purificator that may have been used previously. Such would also respect the view of the US bishops that such purification should be done "briefly and inconspicuously" (ITTOM, no. 138). Similarly, a Canadian commentary on *Inaestimabile Donum* (1980), originating with the National Liturgy Office, notes that, rather than purifying the vessels after Communion, this time is better spent in prayer and reflection, purifying the vessels "after the people have gone."[11]

164. After Communion all *IGMR*s note that the priest "may return to the chair" (*sacerdos ad sedem redire potest*), although this seems more a requirement than an option since, after an appropriate silence, he will soon be required to offer the prayer after Communion from the chair (cf. no. 165 below). As for the silence after Communion, the US bishops offer a thoughtful reflection, noting

11. *National Bulletin on Liturgy* 13 (1980): 225; also, 15 (1982): 77.

observed for some period of time, or a Psalm or another canticle of praise or a hymn may be sung (cf. no. 88).

165. Then, standing at the chair or at the altar and facing the people the priest, with hands joined says, *Oremus (Let us pray)*; then, with hands extended, he recites the prayer after Communion. A brief period of silence may precede the prayer, unless this has been already observed immediately after Communion. At the end of the prayer the people say the acclamation, *Amen*.

The Concluding Rites

166. When the prayer after Communion is concluded, brief announcements to the people may be made, if they are needed.

167. Then the priest, extending his hands, greets the people, saying, *Dominus vobiscum (The Lord be with you)*. They

poris spatium, servari, vel psalmus aut aliud laudis canticum aut hymnus proferri potest *(cf. n. 88)*.

165. Deinde, stans ad sedem vel ad altare, sacerdos, versus ad populum, dicit, manibus iunctis: Orémus et, extensis manibus, orationem post Communionem recitat, cui præmitti potest breve spatium silentii, nisi iam præcesserit statim post Communionem. In fine orationis populus acclamat: Amen.

Ritus conclusionis

166. Expleta oratione post Communionem, fiant, si habendæ sunt, breves annuntiationes ad populum.

167. Deinde sacerdos, extendens manus, salutat populum, dicens: Dóminus vobíscum, cui respondetur a populo: Et cum

---

that true stillness is achieved only if all ministers and congregation take part. They further note that it should not be interrupted by second collections, announcements, or the recitation of devotional materials (ITTOM, no. 139). *IGMR2002* adds hymnody to the list of options for singing, which may replace the period of silence.

165. As in other places, *IGMR2002* adds details about gestures, here specifying that the priest has his "hands joined" (*manibus iunctis)* when he says, "Let us pray" (*Oremus*). As in previous editions, this Instruction notes that silence occurs either before or after the invitation to prayer, indicating that it is one of the four constitutive elements (cf. no. 54 above) of this presidential prayer.

The Concluding Rites

166. Announcements are optional and, if made, are to be brief since the assembly is standing with the ritual presumption that the liturgy is coming to a close. Any appropriate member of the assembly may make the announcements and the priest may wish to offer the announcements himself (see no. 184 below). The suitable place for making such announcements would not be the ambo but some other location. As "pastoral announcements . . . [they should] help the people make the transition from worship into renewed Christian witness in society" (ITTOM, no. 143). The time before the dismissal is also a fitting moment for any concluding comments by the priest (see no. 31 above).

167. This expanded text in *IGMR2002* provides new details for the final blessing, prescribing that the priest joins his hands after the greeting, and during

answer, *Et cum spiritu tuo (And also with you)*. The priest, joining his hands again and then immediately placing his left hand on his breast, raises his right hand and adds, *Benedicat vos omnipotens Deus (May Almighty God bless you)* and, as he makes the Sign of the Cross over the people, continues, *Pater, et Filius, et Spiritus Sanctus (the Father, and the Son, and the Holy Spirit)*. All answer, *Amen*.

On certain days and occasions this blessing, in accordance with the rubrics, is expanded and expressed by a prayer over the People or another more solemn formula.

A Bishop blesses the people with the appropriate formula, making the Sign of the Cross three times over the people.[99]

spíritu tuo. Et sacerdos, manus denuo coniungens, et statim, manum sinistram super pectus ponens et manum dexteram elevans, subdit: Benedícat vos omnípotens Deus et, signum crucis super populum faciens, prosequitur: Pater, et Fílius, et Spíritus Sanctus. Omnes respondent: Amen.

Quibusdam diebus et occasionibus, hæc benedictio, iuxta rubricas, oratione super populum vel alia formula sollemniore ditatur et exprimitur.

Episcopus populo benedicit congruenti formula, ter signum crucis super populum faciens.[99]

168. Immediately after the blessing, with hands joined, the priest adds, *Ite, missa est (The Mass is ended, go in peace)*, and all answer, *Deo gratias (Thanks be to God)*.

168. Statim post benedictionem sacerdos, manibus iunctis, subiungit: Ite, missa est; et omnes respondent: Deo grátias.

---

the actual blessing places his "left hand on his breast" (*manum sinistram super pectus*) and "raises his right hand" (*manum dexteram elevans*). Although *IGMR2002* provides directives about the people's action during parallel rituals (e.g., no. 124 above), a reference to them signing themselves is missing here.

The second paragraph of this article is a thoughtful clarification of *IGMR1975*, that a prayer over the people or a solemn blessing does not "precede" (*praemittitur, IGMR1975*, no. 124) the blessing but is an optional expansion of it. These blessings and prayers are fitting options that contribute to realizing the principle of progressive solemnity (*IGLH*, no. 273). GIRM2003 curiously capitalizes part of "prayer over the People" (also no. 90b, but not no. 185), not in *IGMR2002*. A final paragraph inserts limited information for episcopal blessings from *CaerEp*, nos. 1118–1121.

168. This article is identical to that of previous *IGMR*s. With hands joined, the priest dismisses the assembly. The directives here would suggest that there is only one formulary for this dismissal, when various sacramentaries and other ritual texts provide several options for the dismissal. The 1975 Sacramentary's option C ("Go in peace to love and serve the Lord") is particularly effective in making explicit the presumption of no. 90c that the dismissal of the faithful is so that "each may go out to do good works" (*ut unusquisque ad opera sua bona revertatur*).

169. Then, as a rule, the priest venerates the altar with a kiss and, after making a profound bow with the lay ministers, departs with them.

170. If, however, another liturgical action follows the Mass, the concluding rites, that is, the greeting, the blessing, and the dismissal, are omitted.

169. Tunc sacerdos altare de more osculo veneratur, et facta illi cum ministris laicis profunda inclinatione, cum eis recedit.

170. Si vero Missam sequitur aliqua actio liturgica, ritus conclusionis, idest salutatio, benedictio et dimissio, omittuntur.

B. Mass with a Deacon

171. When he is present at the Eucharistic Celebration, a deacon should exercise his ministry, wearing sacred vestments. For the deacon

B) De Missa cum Diacono

171. Quando celebrationi eucharisticæ interest, diaconus, sacris vestibus indutus, suo ministerio fungatur. Ipse enim.

---

169. While *IGMR1975,* no. 125 notes that the priest "made the appropriate reverence with the ministers" (*facta . . . debita reverentia cum ministris*), *IGMR2002* prescribes that this is a "profound bow with the lay ministers" (*cum ministris laicis profunda inclinatione*). Furthermore, *IGMR2002* explicates that the priest-presider not only "departs" (*recedit, IGMR1975,* no. 124), but does so with the ministers (*cum eis recedit),* presumably departing in the same order as their entrance. Consistent with other *IGMR*s, there is no reference to any music, as closing hymns or instrumental recessional music are optional and silence is an acceptable option (see no. 90 above; also ITTOM, no. 147).

170. As in other *IGMR*s, this article notes that concluding rites are omitted should another liturgical action follow, e.g., the final commendation at a funeral. Parallel to this is the omission of elements of the introductory rites when other liturgical actions precede the opening collect, e.g., the first two forms of the commemoration of the Lord's entrance into Jerusalem on Palm Sunday of the Lord's Passion (cf. no. 46 above).

Mass with a Deacon

Three overall tendencies are apparent in this description of a eucharistic celebration with a deacon. First, as is generally true of *IGMR2002*, there is more detail and description of the deacon's ministry. Second, some of that detail helps to clearly distinguish the deacon (as with the priest-presider) from other ministers and the laity. Finally, some of that detail will also more distinctively cast the deacon in an unmistakably auxiliary role to the priest. In this regard, *IGMR2002* does what it can to alleviate any confusion of roles in the celebration of the Eucharist.

171. While a comparable article is present in previous *IGMR*s (e.g., *IGMR1975,* no. 127), it is expanded here, better reflecting the understanding of diaconal ministry embedded in *De Ordinatione Diaconorum* (1990). When a deacon is

a. Assists the priest and remains at his side;
b. Ministers at the altar, with the chalice as well as the book;
c. Proclaims the Gospel and, at the direction of the priest celebrant, may preach the homily (cf. above, no. 66);
d. Guides the faithful by appropriate introductions and explanations, and announces the intentions of the Prayer of the Faithful;
e. Assists the priest celebrant in distributing Communion, and purifies and arranges the sacred vessels;
f. As needed, fulfills the duties of other ministers himself if none of them is present.

a) sacerdoti assistit et ad eius latus procedit;
b) ad altare, sive ad calicem sive ad librum ministrat;
c) Evangelium proclamat et potest, de mandato sacerdotis celebrantis, homiliam habere *(cf. n. 66)*;
d) populum fidelem per opportunas monitiones dirigit et intentiones orationis universalis enuntiat;
e) sacerdotem celebrantem adiuvat in distribuenda Communione, et vasa sacra purificat et componit;
f) officia aliorum ministrorum, pro necessitate, ipse adimplet si nullus eorum adsit.

The Introductory Rites

172. Carrying the *Book of the Gospels* slightly elevated, the deacon precedes the priest as he approaches the altar or else walks at the priest's side.

Ritus initiales

172. Evangeliarium parum elevatum deferens, diaconus sacerdotem accedentem ad altare præcedit, secus ad eius latus incedit.

---

present, he exercises his ministry as would any other ordained minister, and fittingly wears the sacred vestments of his office. *Diakonia* characterizes the deacon's liturgical ministry, as he is the proper minister to accompany the priest throughout the celebration of the Eucharist, to proclaim the gospel and the general intercessions, to be minister of the cup and of the book, to serve as minister of Communion and to purify and arrange the vessels. In the absence of the lay ministers, he may also fulfill their roles.

The Introductory Rites

172. Since proclamation of the gospel is properly a diaconal ministry, it belongs to the deacon to carry the Book of the Gospels in the procession. This text is altered only slightly from *IGMR1975*. The reference to sacred vestments has been moved to the previous article, and *IGMR2002* notes as in other places (cf. nos. 120d and 130) that the Book of the Gospels is "slightly elevated" (*parum elevatum*) when the deacon carries it. If there is another deacon (or several), one deacon walks by the side of the priest; such would also be the case if there were no Book of the Gospels to carry in procession. When the deacon does carry the Book of the Gospels, he walks behind the lector (who would not be carrying the lectionary, cf. no. 118 above) and precedes any concelebrants and the priest-presider.

173. When he reaches the altar, if he is carrying the *Book of the Gospels*, he omits the sign of reverence and goes up to the altar. It is particularly appropriate that he should place the *Book of the Gospels* on the altar, after which, together with the priest, he venerates the altar with a kiss.

If, however, he is not carrying the *Book of the Gospels*, he makes a profound bow to the altar with the priest in the customary way and with him venerates the altar with a kiss.

Lastly, if incense is used, he assists the priest in putting some into the thurible and in incensing the cross and the altar.

174. After the incensation of the altar, he goes to the chair together with the priest, takes his place there at the side of the priest and assists him as necessary.

The Liturgy of the Word

175. If incense is used, the deacon assists the priest when he puts incense in the

173. Cum ad altare pervenerit, si Evangeliarium defert, omissa reverentia, ad altare ascendit. Deinde Evangeliario laudabiliter super altare deposito, simul cum sacerdote altare osculo veneratur.

Si vero Evangeliarium non defert, profundam facit altari inclinationem more solito cum sacerdote, et cum ipso altare osculo veneratur.

Demum si adhibetur incensum, sacerdoti assistit ad incensum imponendum et ad crucem et altare thurificandum.

174. Altari incensato, sedem una cum sacerdote petit, ibique ad latus sacerdotis consistit eique pro necessitate ministrat.

Liturgia verbi

175. Dum Allelúia vel alter cantus profertur, si adhibetur incensum, ad impositionem

---

173. Much expanded from *IGMR1975* (no. 127), this article includes useful precisions regarding the deacon's actions during the introductory rites. If he is carrying the Book of the Gospels, he does not make the "sign of reverence" (*reverentia*) before the altar but continues moving without a pause to the altar table and places the Book of the Gospels on it. He waits there for the priest and then together they kiss the altar. Placing the Book of the Gospels on the altar is called "particularly appropriate" (*laudabiliter*), signaling the importance of the Book of the Gospels itself and its placement on the altar (cf. no. 122 above). Should the deacon not carry the Book of the Gospels, *IGMR2002* newly notes (as also in no. 135 above, etc.) that he makes a "profound bow" (*profundam . . . inclinationem*) to the altar with the priest, and together they approach and venerate the altar. Fulfilling his role of assisting the priest and remaining at his side (no. 171 above), the deacon is available to offer any needed help as the priest places incense in the thurible, and then he accompanies the priest as he incenses the cross and then the altar.

174. On the seat for the deacon at the side of the priest, cf. no. 310 below.

Liturgy of the Word

175. This article, parallel to no. 134 above, adds many details missing from previous *IGMR*s. The deacon is now instructed to make a "profound bow"

thurible during the singing of the *Alleluia* or other chant. Then he makes a profound bow before the priest and asks for the blessing, saying in a low voice, *Iube, domine [sic], benedicere (Father, give me your blessing)*. The priest blesses him, saying, *Dominus sit in corde tuo (The Lord be in your heart)*. The deacon signs himself with the Sign of the Cross and responds, *Amen*. Having bowed to the altar, he then takes up the *Book of the Gospels* which was placed upon it. He proceeds to the ambo, carrying the book slightly elevated. He is preceded by a thurifer, carrying a thurible with smoking incense, and by servers with lighted candles. There the deacon, with hands joined, greets the people, saying, *Dominus vobiscum (The Lord be with you)*. Then, at the

thuris sacerdoti ministrat, deinde, ante sacerdotem profunde inclinatus, benedictionem petit, submissa voce dicens: Iube, domne, benedícere. Sacerdos eum benedicit, dicens: Dóminus sit in corde tuo. Diaconus signat se signo crucis et respondet: Amen. Deinde Evangeliarium, quod super altare collocatum est, facta altari inclinatione, sumit et ad ambonem pergit librum parum elevatum deferens, præcedentibus thuriferario cum thuribulo fumigante atque ministris cum cereis accensis. Ibi populum salutat dicens, manibus iunctis: Dóminus vobíscum, dein ad verba Léctio sancti Evangélii, pollice signat librum et postea seipsum in fronte, ore et pectore, librum incensat et proclamat Evangelium. Quo finito, acclamat: Verbum Dómini, omnibus respondentibus:

(*profunde inclinatus*) before the priest and signs himself during the priest's blessing. The deacon bows to the altar (*facta altari inclinatione*) before taking the Book of the Gospels. Where *IGMR1975* (no. 131) merely indicates that he greets the people, incenses the book and proclaims the gospel, *IGMR2002* adds many details here. All of these details were in the postconciliar *MR*s, but missing from *IGMR*s until now. The expansion from ten words in *IGMR1975* to almost forty words of detail in *IGMR2002* (indicating how his hands are to be closed during the greeting of the people, noting how the book is to be signed with the thumb, etc.) underscores one of the penchants of this Instruction to offer more precision in describing the celebration of the Eucharist. New also is the inclusion of directives concerning how the ritual is slightly altered if a bishop is presiding (cf. *CaerEp*, no. 141).

A final new paragraph concerns the disposition of the Book of the Gospels after the gospel proclamation. With no previous parallel when describing the proclamation of the gospel if no deacon is present (no. 134 above), this addition not only continues the Instruction's emphasis on the dignity of the Book of the Gospels (cf. no. 117 above), but suggests a useful liturgical principle: that the book—as any significant liturgical symbol—cannot be ignored once its primary purpose has been fulfilled, but must be treated with respect throughout the whole celebration.

Eliminated is the note found in *IGMR1975* that if there is no homily or profession of faith, the deacon may remain at the ambo for the prayer of the faithful (no. 132), possibly underscoring the normative role of the homily (see no. 65 above) in what is clearly a description of a non-ferial Eucharist (see no. 262 below).

words *Lectio sancti Evangelii (A reading from the holy Gospel)*, he signs the book with his thumb and, afterwards, himself on his forehead, mouth, and breast. He incenses the book and proclaims the Gospel reading. When the reading is concluded, he says the acclamation *Verbum Domini (The Gospel of the Lord)*, and all respond, *Laus tibi, Christe (Praise to you, Lord Jesus Christ)*. He then venerates the book with a kiss, saying privately, *Per evangelica dicta (May the words of the Gospel)*, and returns to the priest's side.

When the deacon is assisting the Bishop, he carries the book to him to be kissed, or else kisses it himself, saying quietly, *Per evangelica dicta dicta [sic] (May the words of the Gospel)*. In more solemn celebrations, as the occasion suggests, a Bishop may impart a blessing to the people with the *Book of the Gospels*.

Lastly, the deacon may carry the *Book of the Gospels* to the credence table or to another appropriate and dignified place.

Laus tibi, Christe. Deinde librum osculo veneratur, secreto dicens: Per evangélica dicta, et ad sacerdotem redit.

Quando diaconus Episcopo ministrat, librum ei defert osculandum vel ipse osculatur, secreto dicens: Per evangélica dicta. In celebrationibus sollemnioribus Episcopus, pro opportunitate, benedictionem cum Evangeliario populo impertit.

Evangeliarium demum ad abacum vel aliud locum aptum et dignum deferri potest.

176. If, in addition, there is no other suitable lector present, the deacon should proclaim the other readings as well.

176. Si alius quoque idoneus lector absit, diaconus etiam alias lectiones proferat.

177. After the introduction by the priest it is the deacon himself who normally announces the intentions of the Prayer of the Faithful, from the ambo.

177. Intentiones orationis fidelium, post introductionem sacerdotis, ipse diaconus de more ex ambone profert.

---

176. This new article prescribes that the deacon proclaims the other reading or readings if there is no "suitable lector" (*idoneus lector*) present.[12]

177. As previously noted (no. 171d above), the deacon is the first option for announcing the intentions of the prayer of the faithful. While he "normally" (*de more*) carries out this function, it is not required. Unlike *IGMR2002*, no. 138, which allows other ministers to announce these intentions from the ambo or other "suitable place," here the deacon is not given that same option (as is allowed in *IGMR1975*, no. 132). This again draws a distinction between lay and ordained ministers.

12. On the characteristics of a suitable lector, see above no. 59, n. 45.

The Liturgy of the Eucharist

178. After the Prayer of the Faithful, while the priest remains at the chair, the deacon prepares the altar, assisted by the acolyte, but it is the deacon's place to take care of the sacred vessels himself. He also assists the priest in receiving the people's gifts. Next, he hands the priest the paten with the bread to be consecrated, pours wine and a little water into the chalice, saying quietly, *Per huius aquae (By the mystery of this water)*, and after this presents the chalice to the priest. He may also carry out the preparation of the chalice at the credence table. If incense is used, the deacon assists the priest during the incensation of the gifts, the cross, and the altar; afterwards, the deacon himself or the acolyte incenses the priest and the people.

Liturgia eucharistica

178. Oratione universali absoluta, sacerdote ad sedem remanente, diaconus altare præparat, acolytho adiuvante; ipsius tamen est sacrorum vasorum curam gerere. Assistit etiam sacerdoti ad dona populi recipienda. Tradit deinde sacerdoti patenam cum pane consecrando; infundit vinum et parum aquæ in calicem, dicens secreto: Per huius aquæ, et postea calicem sacerdoti præsentat. Hanc præparationem calicis, ad abacum peragere potest. Si incensum adhibetur, in thurificandis oblatis, cruce et altari sacerdoti ministrat, et postea ipse, vel acolythus, sacerdotem et populum incensat.

Liturgy of the Eucharist

178. This article describes the deacon's actions as he fulfills his role "as minister of the altar" (*Rites of Ordination,* no. 199). Minor variations in the *IGMR2002* version of this article underscore several recurring patterns noted above. Regarding the confusion as to whether the liturgical unit is a preparation rite or an offertory (see no. 28 above), *IGMR2002* here emphasizes the former by changing the reference from "At the offertory" (*Ad offertorium, IGMR1975,* no. 133) to "After the Prayer of the Faithful" (*Oratione universali absoluta*). Next, *IGMR2002* repeats the language for the elements found in previous *IGMRs* which, when presented by the people, are here called "gifts" (*dona;* also, nos. 44, 73, 74, 75 and 79), although when set on the table and incensed are *oblata* (also nos. 73 and 75), which GIRM2003 yet translates as "gifts" (cf. no. 73 above). Given the different theological resonance in these terms, it would be helpful if future editions would offer clarifications on these terms. Here it appears that the terminology changes because gifts are now placed on the altar, although *IGMR2002* still refers to them as "gifts" (*dona)* during the Eucharistic Prayer (no. 79c above).

There is a clear preference in *IGMR2002* for the instituted acolyte to assist the deacon in these preparatory rites, underscored by the removal of the reference to "other ministers" (*aliis ministris*) found in *IGMR1975* (no. 133). *IGMR1975* first gave to the deacon the prayer "By the mystery" (*Per huius aquae)* previously spoken by the priest during the mixing of water with wine. This practice is retained, and it is notable that it is the ritual action and not the presidential role that dictates who recites the prayer.

179. During the Eucharistic Prayer, the deacon stands near the priest but slightly behind him, so that when needed he may assist the priest with the chalice or the Missal.

From the epiclesis until the priest shows the chalice, the deacon normally remains kneeling. If several deacons are present, one of them may place incense in the thurible for the consecration and incense the host and the chalice as they are shown to the people.

179. Durante Prece eucharistica, diaconus stat prope sacerdotem, aliquanto tamen post ipsum, ut, quando opus sit, ad calicem vel ad missale ministret.

Inde ab epiclesi usque ad ostensionem calicis diaconus de more genuflexus manet. Si adsunt plures diaconi, unus ex eis ad consecrationem immittere potest incensum in thuribulum atque ad ostensionem hostiæ et calicis incensare.

180. At the final doxology of the Eucharistic Prayer, the deacon stands next to the priest, holding the chalice elevated while the priest elevates the paten with the host, until the people have responded with the acclamation, *Amen*.

180. Ad doxologiam finalem Precis eucharisticæ, stans ad latus sacerdotis, calicem elevatum tenet, dum sacerdos patenam cum hostia elevat, usquedum populus Amen acclamaverit.

The language describing the preparation of the chalice has been shortened and simplified, and repeats the option of these actions taking place at the credence table (see no. 73 above).

179. This article treats the role of the deacon during the Eucharistic Prayer where he stands at the side of the priest slightly back from the altar, always ready to assist the priest, particularly with the chalice and with the Sacramentary. New to *IGMR2002* is the instruction that the deacon "normally remains kneeling" (*de more genuflexus manet*) from the epiclesis until the showing of the chalice, a directive previously found in *CaerEp*, no. 155. Such an insertion highlights the tendency in *IGMR2002* not only to make clear distinctions between the ordained and lay ministers (cf. no. 91 above), but also to distinguish clearly between the deacon who serves the priest (cf. no. 94, above), and the priest who "offer[s] the sacrifice in the person of Christ" (*sacrificium in persona Christi offerendi*, no. 93 above).

The usual criteria for not kneeling during the Eucharistic Prayer (see no. 43 above) apply. If a deacon were unable to kneel and then to rise without assistance, he would not kneel; if among several deacons, one were unable to do so, then no deacon would kneel. Also new here is the instruction that, if several deacons are present, one may take over the responsibilities for the incensation.

180. Found in previous *IGMR*s, this article concerns the deacon's role during the doxology as he stands at the priest's side, elevating the chalice until the people's "Amen" is concluded. This action recalls a traditional image of the deacon as the cupbearer, who was eventually restricted to dispensing the chalice

181. After the priest has said the prayer at the Rite of Peace and the greeting *Pax Domini sit semper vobiscum (The peace of the Lord be with you always)* and the people have responded, *Et cum spiritu tuo (And also with you)*, the deacon, if it is appropriate, invites all to exchange the sign of peace. He faces the people and, with hands joined, says, *Offerte vobis pacem (Let us offer each other the sign of peace)*. Then he himself receives the sign of peace from the priest and may offer it to those other ministers who are closer to him.

181. Postquam sacerdos dixit orationem ad pacem et: Pax Dómini sit semper vobíscum, et populus respondit: Et cum spíritu tuo, diaconus, pro opportunitate, invitationem facit ad pacem, dicens, manibus iunctis et versus ad populum: Offérte vobis pacem. Ipse vero pacem a sacerdote recipit, aliisque ministris sibi propioribus potest offerre.

182. After the priest's Communion, the deacon receives Communion under both

182. Communione a sacerdote facta, diaconus Communionem sub utraque spe-

---

alone (and not the consecrated bread).[13] While the Tridentine Rite required that the deacon stand at the right of the priest for the doxology,[14] the current Instruction does not stipulate.

181. This article offers no substantial changes from previous editions but provides new details regarding the sign of peace, i.e., the deacon invites members of the assembly to offer one another the sign of peace facing the people and with hands joined (*manibus iunctis*). While the instruction that the deacon receives the sign of peace from the priest is not new, *IGMR2002*'s tendency to draw clearer distinctions between the deacon and the priest (cf. no. 179 above) casts new light on this rubric that does not indicate that this is a mutual exchange of peace—an explicit presumption of the ritual invitation "Let us offer each other the sign of peace" (*Offerte vobis pacem*)—but one which the priest initiates and the deacon receives. Also, the new instructions for the priest during the sign of peace (no. 154 above) offer an appropriate hermeneutic for understanding why the deacon apparently stays in the sanctuary for this ritual gesture extended only "to those other ministers who are closer to him" *(aliisque ministris sibi propioribus)*. The pastoral exceptions for the priest would also seem to apply to the deacon.

In its description of concelebrated Mass, *IGMR2002* notes that deacons may also join in helping the priest with the fraction rite (no. 240 below). While no explicit mention is made of this here, it would be appropriate for the deacon to provide this same assistance outside of concelebrated Masses.

182. Offering directives for the deacon's Communion, this and previous *IGMR*s indicate that the deacon waits until the priest's Communion is finished,

13. See Thomas Aquinas, *ST* III, 1. 82, art. 3, obj. 1.

14. See, for example, Adrian Fortescue, *The Ceremonies of the Roman Rite Described*, 5th ed. rev. by J. B. O'Connell (London: Burns, Oates and Washbourne, 1936), 125.

kinds from the priest himself and then assists the priest in distributing Communion to the people. If Communion is given under both kinds, the deacon himself administers the chalice to the communicants; and, when the distribution is completed, he immediately and reverently consumes at the altar all of the Blood of Christ that remains, assisted if necessary by other deacons and priests.

cie ab ipso sacerdote accipit, et sacerdotem deinde adiuvat in Communione populo distribuenda. Quod si Communio sub utraque specie fit, ipse calicem sumentibus ministrat et, distributione peracta, statim totum Christi Sanguinem qui remansit ad altare reverenter consumit, adiuvantibus, si casus fert, aliis diaconis et presbyteris.

183. When the distribution of Communion is completed, the deacon returns to the altar with the priest and collects the fragments, if any remain, and then carries the chalice and other sacred vessels to the credence table, where he purifies them and arranges them in the usual way while the priest returns to the chair. It is also permissible to leave the vessels that need to be purified, suitably covered, at the credence table on a corporal, and to purify them immediately after Mass following the dismissal of the people.

183. Distributione Communionis expleta, diaconus cum sacerdote ad altare revertitur, colligit fragmenta, si quæ sint, deinde portat calicem et alia vasa sacra ad abacum, ibique ea purificat et de more componit, dum sacerdos ad sedem redit. Licet tamen vasa purificanda, opportune cooperta, in abaco super corporale relinquere eaque statim post Missam, populo dimisso, purificare.

---

and receives Communion from the priest rather than taking it himself. These directives contribute to a clear distinction between the priest-presider and the deacon (cf. no. 179 above). At the same time, *IGMR*s prescribe that the deacon, like the priest, must receive Communion "under both kinds" (*sub utraque specie)*, even when Communion under both forms is not available for the rest of the assembly, underscoring the distinction between the ordained and the laity at Eucharist (cf. no. 91 above).

In the distribution of Communion under both forms the deacon fulfills his traditional role (cf. no. 180 above) by administering the cup to the people. Similar to no. 163 above, *IGMR2002* here includes the new directive that, after the distribution of the chalice, the deacon "immediately and reverently consumes . . . all of the Blood of Christ that remains" (*statim totum Christi Sanguinem qui remansit ad altare reverenter consumit*). This could be pastorally challenging, even when assisted by other deacons and priests. *Norms for the Distribution and Reception of Holy Communion Under Both Kinds in the Diocese of the United States of America* permits extraordinary ministers of Holy Communion to aid in the consumption of whatever Precious Blood remains (no. 52).

183. These unchanged directives regarding the deacon's role in the removal and cleansing of vessels parallel those of priests in Masses without a deacon and are consistent with the vision of diaconal ministry outlined above (no. 171). As previously noted, hygienic concerns seem to recommend the second option of purifying the vessels after Mass (cf. no. 163 above).

The Concluding Rites

184. Once the prayer after Communion has been said, the deacon makes brief announcements to the people, if indeed any need to be made, unless the priest prefers to do this himself.

185. If a prayer over the people or a solemn formula for the blessing is used, the deacon says, *Inclinate vos ad benedictionem (Bow your heads and pray for God's blessing).* After the priest's blessing, the deacon, with hands joined and facing the people, dismisses them, saying, *Ite, missa est (The Mass is ended, go in peace).*

186. Then, together with the priest, the deacon venerates the altar with a kiss, makes a profound bow, and departs in a manner similar to the procession beforehand.

Ritus conclusionis

184. Dicta oratione post Communionem, diaconus facit breves annuntiationes populo, quæ forte faciendæ sunt, nisi ipse sacerdos malit eas facere.

185. Si adhibetur oratio super populum vel formula benedictionis sollemnis diaconus dicit: Inclináte vos ad benedictiónem. Data benedictione a sacerdote, diaconus populum dimittit dicens, manibus iunctis, ad populum versus: Ite, missa est.

186. Deinde, una cum sacerdote, altare osculo veneratur, et, facta profunda inclinatione, simili modo quo processerat, recedit.

The Concluding Rites

184. As in previous *IGMR*s, this first of three paragraphs on the concluding rites reaffirms the deacon's role as someone who communicates directly to the assembly in preaching, offering petitions, making invitations, or here making announcements. At the same time, the deacon is again cast in an auxiliary position to the priest (cf. no. 179, above), who can perform this ministry if he prefers.

185. As in no. 167, *IGMR2002* here provides more nuanced information on the possible use of a prayer over the people or a solemn form of the blessing, both missing from the parallel passages in previous *IGMR*s (e.g., *IGMR1975*, no. 140). This Instruction notes that the deacon invites the community to bow their heads and pray. Also, this article provides new details about the deacon offering the dismissal "with hands joined and facing the people" (*manibus iunctis, ad populum versus*). While the Instruction provides only one text for the dismissal ("The Mass is ended, go in peace," *Ite, missa est*), approved sacramentaries offer multiple possibilities here (cf. no. 168 above).

186. As in no. 169 and frequently at other times (cf. nos. 122, 123, 132, 135, 137, 143, 169, 173 and 175), *IGMR2002* here specifies that a "profound bow" *(profunda inclinatione)* follows the kissing of the altar, rather than the more ambiguous "due reverence"*(debita reverentia)* of *IGMR1975* (no. 141).

The Duties of the Acolyte

Although there are numerous changes in this subdivision of *IGMR2002*, this section is one of those for which the greatest change came between 1969 and

C. The Duties of the Acolyte

187. The duties that the acolyte may carry out are of various kinds and several may coincide. Hence, it is desirable that these duties be suitably distributed among several acolytes. If, however, only one acolyte is present, he should perform the more important duties while the rest are to be distributed among several ministers.

The Introductory Rites

188. In the procession to the altar, the acolyte may carry the cross, walking between two ministers with lighted candles. Upon reaching the altar, the acolyte places the cross upright near the altar so that it may serve as the altar cross; otherwise, he puts it in a worthy place. Then he takes his place in the sanctuary.

189. Through the entire celebration, the acolyte is to approach the priest or the

C) De muneribus acolythi

187. Munera quæ acolythus exercere potest varii sunt generis; plura autem ex iis simul occurrere possunt. Expedit proinde ut opportune inter plures distribuantur; si vero unus tantum acolythus præsens adest, ea quæ potioris sunt momenti ipse exsequatur, cetera vero inter plures ministros distribuantur.

Ritus initiales

188. In accessu ad altare crucem, medius inter duos ministros cum cereis accensis, deferre potest. Cum autem ad altare pervenerit, crucem apud altare erigit, ut fiat crux altaris, secus eam in loco digno reponit. Deinde locum suum in presbyterio occupat.

189. Per totam celebrationem, acolythi est ad sacerdotem vel diaconum, quoties

---

1975 rather than from 1975 to 2002.[15] *IGMR1969* presents the duties of the subdeacon in nos. 142–152. In *IGMR1975* that entire section is omitted, and in its stead are new ritual instructions for the deacon (nos. 127–141), the acolyte (nos. 142–147), and the lector (nos. 148–152). *IGMR2002* follows that design.

187. This unchanged paragraph supports the consistent effort of *IGMR2002* to note differences between liturgical actions done by instituted ministers from functions carried out by laypeople (cf. no. 97, above). Specific examples of how the acolyte is relegated the "more important duties" (*quae potioris sunt momenti*) have been noted above (e.g., nos. 120, 139 and 178).

Introductory Rites

188. The proper role of the acolyte in the procession is that of cross-bearer, whose appropriate location is between the candle-bearers (see no. 120b above). On the placement of the cross in the sanctuary, which *IGMR2002* stipulates in a different way from its predecessors, see nos. 122 above and 308 below.

The Liturgy of the Eucharist

189. The role of the acolyte is to assist ordained ministers in the execution of their roles. One of the frequent tasks in this work is holding the liturgical

15. See above, Chapter III, section III: also no. 98 above.

deacon, whenever necessary, in order to present the book to them and to assist them in any other way required. Thus it is appropriate, insofar as possible, that the acolyte occupy a place from which he can conveniently carry out his ministry either at the chair or at the altar.

opus sit, accedere, ut ipsis librum præbeat et in aliis quæ necessaria sunt eos adiuvet. Convenit proinde ut, quantum fieri possit, locum occupet e quo ministerium suum commode possit implere, sive ad sedem sive ad altare.

The Liturgy of the Eucharist

190. If no deacon is present, after the Prayer of the Faithful is concluded and while the priest remains at the chair, the acolyte places the corporal, the purificator, the chalice, the pall, and the Missal on the altar. Then, if necessary, the acolyte assists the priest in receiving the gifts of the people and, if appropriate, brings the bread and wine to the altar and hands them to the priest. If incense is used, the acolyte presents the thurible to the priest and assists him while he incenses the gifts, the cross, and the altar. Then the acolyte incenses the priest and the people.

191. A duly instituted acolyte, as an extraordinary minister, may, if necessary, assist the priest in giving Communion to the people.[100] If Communion is given under both kinds, when no deacon is present, the acolyte administers the chalice to the communicants or holds the chalice if Communion is given by intinction.

Liturgia eucharistica

190. Absente diacono, expleta oratione universali, dum sacerdos ad sedem manet, acolythus super altare ponit corporale, purificatorium, calicem, pallam et missale. Deinde, si opus est, sacerdotem adiuvat in accipiendis donis populi et, pro opportunitate, panem et vinum ad altare defert et sacerdoti tradit. Si incensum adhibetur, sacerdoti thuribulum exhibet eique assistit in thurificandis oblatis, cruce et altari. Deinde sacerdotem et populum incensat.

191. Acolythus rite institutus, qua minister extraordinarius, sacerdotem, si necesse est, adiuvare potest in Communione populo distribuenda.[100] Quod si Communio sub utraque specie fit, absente diacono, ipse calicem sumentibus ministrat, vel calicem sustinet si Communio per intinctionem præbetur.

---

book for the priest or deacon when they pray from it. To this end, the acolyte should be conveniently located for this service.

190. A significant part of the ministry of acolyte occurs at the altar, and he is to bring the objects to the altar for the Eucharist while the priest stays in the presider's chair; as before, *IGMR2002* mentions the pall as one of these objects (cf. no. 118 above). If there is a procession of the gifts for the Eucharist and there are more items than can be carried by the priest alone, the acolyte serves the priest in meeting those bearing the gifts. He also assists during the incensation at the preparation of the gifts, and *IGMR2002* adds that it is the acolyte who "incenses the priest and the people" (*sacerdotem et populum incensat*).

191. While lay ministers may also be deputed to serve as extraordinary ministers of Communion (cf. nos. 100 above and 284 below), the instituted acolyte takes precedence in this role. This article seems to ally the acolyte closely with the

192. Likewise, when the distribution of Communion is completed, a duly instituted acolyte helps the priest or deacon to purify and arrange the sacred vessels. When no deacon is present, a duly instituted acolyte carries the sacred vessels to the credence table and there purifies, wipes, and arranges them in the usual way.

193. After the celebration of Mass, the acolyte and other ministers return in procession to the sacristy, together with the deacon and the priest in the same way and order in which they entered.

192. Itemque acolythus rite institutus, distributione Communionis expleta, sacerdotem vel diaconum in vasis sacris purificandis et componendis adiuvat. Absente vero diacono, acolythus rite institutus vasa sacra ad abacum defert ibique more solito ea purificat, abstergit et componit.

193. Celebratione Missæ expleta, acolythus aliique ministri, una cum diacono et sacerdote ad sacristiam revertuntur processionaliter eodem modo et ordine quo venerunt.

D. The Duties of the Lector

Introductory Rites

194. In coming to the altar, when no deacon is present, the lector, wearing approved

D) De muneribus lectoris

Ritus initiales

194. In accessu ad altare, absente diacono, lector, veste probata induttus,

---

cup, underscoring the substitution role of the acolyte for the deacon ("when no deacon is present," *absente diacono*; also no. 190 above) who has a traditional ministry with the cup (see no. 180 above). This is the first reference to intinction in *IGMR2002* (cf. nos. 285b and 287 below), which was not mentioned in the parallel passage describing the deacon's role in ministering the cup (no. 182 above).

192. In liturgical practice after Vatican II, non-instituted acolytes and extraordinary ministers of Communion often helped the ordained to purify the sacred vessels after the Communion rite. *IGMR2002* circumscribes this so that non-instituted acolytes cannot purify the vessels. In 2002 the US bishops received an indult which allowed extraordinary ministers to purify the vessels "when this is a necessity,"[16] but permission to extend the indult was denied in October, 2006.[17] On the preference for purifying the vessels after Mass, cf. no. 163 above.

193. As is common in *IGMR2002*, this new paragraph makes explicit practices that were presumed but were never noted in previous *IGMR*s. Here instructions are provided for how the acolyte with the other ministers process to the sacristy after the celebration of Mass, paralleling the information in no. 188 above.

The Duties of the Lector

In the five paragraphs on the liturgical role of the lector, there were no major changes from *IGMR1975* to *IGMR2002* (cf. Chapter III, section III, and no. 99

16. *BCL Newsletter* (March–April, 2002).

17. Letter of Francis Cardinal Arinze, Prefect of the Congregation for Divine Worship and the Discipline of the Sacraments (Prot. no. 468/05/L), of 12 October 2006 at http://www.usccb.org/liturgy/cleansingofvessels.pdf (accessed December, 2006).

attire, may carry the *Book of the Gospels,* which is to be slightly elevated. In that case, the lector walks in front of the priest but otherwise along with the other ministers.

Evangeliarium parum elevatum deferre potest: tunc ante sacerdotem incedit; secus cum aliis ministris.

195. Upon reaching the altar, the lector makes a profound bow with the others. If he is carrying the *Book of the Gospels,* he approaches the altar and places the *Book of the Gospels* upon it. Then the lector takes his own place in the sanctuary with the other ministers.

195. Cum ad altare pervenerit, cum aliis facit profundam inclinationem. Si Evangeliarium defert, ad altare accedit et Evangeliarium supra illud deponit. Deinde in presbyterio una cum aliis ministris locum suum occupat.

The Liturgy of the Word

196. The lector reads from the ambo the readings that precede the Gospel. If there

Liturgia verbi

196. Lectiones, quæ Evangelium præcedunt, ex ambone legit. Deficiente vero

---

above). As noted above (see Chapter IV, section I.C), the major changes occurred between 1969 and 1975.

Introductory Rites

194. Drawing on no. 126 above, *IGMR2002* here newly speaks about vesture for the lector, noting that the lector is "wearing approved attire" (*veste probata indutus*). The addition of a vestment for proclaiming the Word ennobles the ministry. Like the acolyte (cf. no. 191 above), the lector sometimes substitutes for the deacon, as in carrying the Book of the Gospels. As previously mentioned (no. 120d above), *IGMR2002* adds that the Book of the Gospels should be "slightly elevated" (*parum elevatum*) when carried by the lector in procession. Since the Book of the Gospels holds a privileged place in the Mass, it is placed toward the end of the procession preceding the priest, whether a deacon or a lector carries it.

195. As is its pattern, *IGMR2002* here indicates that the proper reverence upon reaching the altar is a "profound bow" (*profundam inclinationem*). On the change in the verb here from "goes up" (*ascendit* in *IGMR1975*, no. 149) to "approaches" (*accedit*) the altar, see no. 123 above. On the relationship of the Book of the Gospels to the altar, see no. 117 above.

The Liturgy of the Word

The description of the role of the lector in the actual rite of the Liturgy of the Word here is virtually identical to that found in *IGMR1975*.

196. Because of his or her commission to proclaim the Word, it is appropriate that in the absence of a psalmist, the lector proclaims the responsorial psalm, which is also the Word of God (cf. no. 57 above).

is no psalmist, the lector may also proclaim the responsorial Psalm after the first reading.

psalmista, potest et psalmum responsorium post primam lectionem proferre.

197. When no deacon is present, the lector, after the introduction by the priest, may announce from the ambo the intentions of the Prayer of the Faithful.

197. Absente diacono, post introductionem a sacerdote dictam, intentiones orationis universalis ex ambone proferre potest.

198. If there is no singing at the Entrance or at Communion and the antiphons in the Missal are not recited by the faithful, the lector may read them at the appropriate time (cf. nos. 48, 87).

198. Si ad introitum vel ad Communionem non habetur cantus, et antiphonæ in Missali propositæ a fidelibus non recitantur, tempore conveniente eas proferre potest *(cf. nn. 48, 87).*

---

197. While the intentions of the prayer of the faithful are more aptly proclaimed by the deacon (cf. no. 177 above), in the absence of a deacon the lector may fulfill this function, but this is not required, and others may also do so (see no. 138 above).

198. As noted previously (nos. 48 and 87 above), it is preferred that there is singing at the entrance and Communion processions. In the absence of singing, or the adaptation of the antiphon by the priest in his introductory remarks, these antiphons are recited, preferably by the faithful. The recitation of these antiphons by a lector is a last and ritually least satisfactory option.

GIRM—Notes (English)

91. Cf. Second Vatican Ecumenical Council, Constitution on the Sacred Liturgy, *Sacrosanctum Concilium,* no. 41.

92. Cf. *Caeremoniale Episcoporum, editio typica,* 1984, nos. 119–186.

93. Cf. Second Vatican Ecumenical Council, Constitution on the Sacred Liturgy, *Sacrosanctum Concilium,* no. 42; Dogmatic Constitution on the Church, *Lumen gentium,* no. 28; Decree on the Ministry and Life of Priests, *Presbyterorum ordinis,* no. 5; Sacred Congregation of Rites, Instruction *Eucharisticum mysterium,* On the worship of the Eucharist, 25 May 1967, no. 26: AAS 59 (1967), p. 555.

94. Cf. Sacred Congregation of Rites, Instruction *Eucharisticum mysterium,* On the worship of the Eucharist, 25 May 1967, no. 47: AAS 59 (1967), p. 565.

95. Cf. ibid., no. 26: AAS 59 (1967), p. 555; Sacred Congregation of Rites, Instruction *Musicam sacram,* On music in the Liturgy, 5 March 1967, nos. 16, 27: AAS 59 (1967), pp. 305, 308.

IGMR—Notes (Latin)

91. Cf. CONC. ŒCUM. VAT. II, Const. de sacra Liturgia, *Sacrosanctum Concilium,* n. 41.

92. Cf. *Cæremoniale Episcoporum,* nn. 119–186.

93. Cf. CONC. ŒCUM. VAT. II, Const. de sacra Liturgia, *Sacrosanctum Concilium,* n. 42; Const. dogm. de Ecclesia, *Lumen gentium,* n. 28; Decr. de Presbyterorum ministerio et vita, *Presbyterorum ordinis,* n. 5; S. CONGR. RITUUM, Instr. *Eucharisticum mysterium,* diei 25 maii 1967, n. 26: A.A.S. 59 (1967) p. 555.

94. Cf. S. CONGR. RITUUM, Instr. *Eucharisticum mysterium,* diei 25 maii 1967, n. 47: A.A.S. 59 (1967) p. 565.

95. Cf. *ibidem,* n. 26: A.A.S. 59 (1967) p. 555; Instr. *Musicam sacram,* diei 5 martii 1967, nn. 16, 27: A.A.S. 59 (1967) pp. 305, 308.

96. Cf. Interdicasterial Instruction on certain questions regarding the collaboration of the non-ordained faithful in the sacred ministry of priests, *Ecclesiae de mysterio*, 15 August 1997, art. 6: AAS 89 (1997), p. 869.

97. Cf. Sacred Congregation for the Sacraments and Divine Worship, Instruction *Inaestimabile donum*, 3 April 1980, no. 10: AAS 72 (1980), p. 336; Interdicasterial Instruction on certain questions regarding the collaboration of the non-ordained faithful in the sacred ministry of priests, *Ecclesiae de mysterio*, 15 August 1997, art. 8: AAS 89 (1997), p. 871.

98. Cf. below, Appendix, Order of Commissioning a Minister to Distribute Holy Communion on a Single Occasion, p. 1253.

99. Cf. *Caeremoniale Episcoporum, editio typica*, 1984, nos. 1118–1121.

100. Cf. Paul VI, Apostolic Letter *Ministeria quaedam*, 15 August 1972: AAS 64 (1972), p. 532.

96. Cf. Instructio interdicasterialis de quibusdam quæstionibus circa fidelium laicorum cooperationem sacerdotum ministerium spectantem, *Ecclesiæ de mysterio*, diei 15 augusti 1997, art. 6: A.A.S. 89 (1997) p. 869.

97. Cf. S. Congr. pro Sacramentis et Cultu Divino, Instr. *Inæstimabile donum*, diei 3 aprilis 1980, n. 10: A.A.S. 72 (1980) p. 336; Instructio interdicasterialis de quibusdam quæstionibus circa fidelium laicorum cooperationem sacerdotum ministerium spectantem, *Ecclesiæ de mysterio*, diei 15 augusti 1997, art. 8: A.A.S. 89 (1997) p. 871.

98. Cf. *infra*, Appendix, Ritus ad deputandum ministrum sacræ Communionis ad actum distribuendæ, p. 1161.

99. Cf. *Cæremoniale Episcoporum*, nn. 1118–1121.

100. Cf. Paulus VI, Litt. Apost. *Ministeria quædam*, diei 15 augusti 1972: A.A.S. 64 (1972) p. 532.

CHAPTER IV.II

Concelebrated Mass

(*DE MISSA CONCELEBRATA*)

Gilbert Ostdiek and Andrew Ciferni

Introduction

In 1963 *Sacrosanctum Concilium* (*SC*) extended permission for concelebration. It notes, "Concelebration, which is an appropriate way of manifesting the unity of the priesthood, has remained in use to this day both in the east and in the west" (no. 57).

The history of that practice is complex.[1] In the early Church the primary concern was for the unity of the eucharistic assembly. Within that unity, there were some early indications of a differentiation of roles.[2] By the third century, the role of presbyters in the assembly clearly differed from that of the laity. For example, the presbyters laid hands on the offerings at the consecration of a bishop and on priests at their ordination.[3] History records a number of instances in which visiting bishops were invited to say all or part of the words of institution. Robert Taft has theorized that this exercise of "eucharistic hospitality" for visiting bishops was the origin of what we now know as concelebration.[4] The intent of this hospitality was to express the unity of sister churches. This fourth-century practice eventually spread to suffragan bishops and then to priests. By the seventh and eighth centuries, there are documents attesting to the practice

1. For a standard treatment of the history, see Archdale A. King, *Concelebration in the Christian Church* (London: Mowbray, 1966); Jean Carroll McGowan, *Concelebration: Sign of the Unity of the Church* (New York: Herder and Herder, 1964). For a summary of that history, see Pierre Jounel, *The Rite of Concelebration and of Communion under Both Species: History—Texts in English and Commentaries* (New York: Desclée, 1967), 13–24. For corrections from recent scholarship, see Robert Taft, "Ex Oriente Lux? Some Reflections on Eucharistic Concelebration," *Worship* 54 (1980): 308–325.

2. E.g., in the letters of Ignatius of Antioch, Barnabas, and Clement of Rome. For citations, see Taft, "Ex Oriente," 314–316.

3. *ApTrad* 4, 7 in Bernard Botte, *La Tradition Apostolique d'après les anciennes versions. Introduction, traduction et notes,* Source Chrétiennes 11-bis (Paris: Les Éditions du Cerf, 1989), 46 and 56.

4. Taft, "Ex Oriente," 318.

of concelebration as we have come to know it, that is, "verbal co-consecration." That practice was enshrined in the medieval rites of presbyteral ordination, in which the newly ordained priests were to recite all the prayers in consort with the ordaining bishop. Little further thought was given to theology and practice of concelebration in the Latin Church until the modern liturgical movement.

In the 1920s and 1930s, concelebration again became a topic of lively discussion.[5] Concern for the communal dimension of the Eucharist stood in strong contrast both to the passive participation of the faithful and the practice of "private" Masses by priests. That practice had a number of roots. One was the multiplication of Masses and of priests ordained without pastoral care of a community, dating back into the early Middle Ages. Another was the spiritual ideal, strengthened under the pontificate of Pius IX (d. 1878), that every priest should say Mass daily, even if there was no congregation (cf. no. 19 above). Since canon law at that time restricted the use of concelebration to presbyteral ordinations and episcopal consecrations, other ways were sought to alleviate the isolation priests experienced in multiple individual celebrations. One solution was simultaneous Masses, "synchronized" so that one server/congregation could respond and be present for all of them.[6] Another was a communal Mass (the *messe communautaire*) in which priests attended the celebration vested in alb and stole, as was then the traditional Holy Thursday practice.

The discussions of that era raised many questions around both ritual practice and theology. Paradoxically, the experience of the *messe communautaire* highlighted the unity among priests themselves at the expense of the unity of the gathered community: ". . . in the middle of a period in which the liturgy was going to be de-clericalized, there arose a tendency toward clericalization of concelebration."[7] Theological discussion centered on such issues as nonverbal or "ceremonial" concelebration as opposed to verbal or "sacramental" concelebration; whether valid concelebration requires all priests to recite the entire Eucharistic Prayer, or at least the words of consecration; the unity of the sacrifice and the question of stipends; and perhaps most importantly, the relationship between the communal character of the liturgy, the hierarchical nature of the Church, and the unity of the priesthood—a question that was to resurface. Several papal and curial interventions in the decades just before Vatican II (1962–65) set limits to some aspects of the discussion.

5. See Hendrik Manders, "Concelebration," in *The Church and the Liturgy*, ed. Johannes Wagner, Concilium 2 (Glen Rock, NJ: The Paulist Press, 1963), 136–144; Gilbert Ostdiek, "Concelebration Revisited," in *Shaping English Liturgy: Studies in Honor of Archbishop Denis Hurley*, ed. Peter C. Finn and James M. Schellman (Washington, DC: The Pastoral Press, 1990), 140–144.

6. In a chapter entitled "Convention Concelebration," Gerald Ellard describes such a future celebration of synchronized masses on a grand scale. Accompanying drawings depict a convention space with 105 altars for 128 celebrants and seating to accommodate 17,000 worshipers. In his *The Mass of the Future* (Milwaukee, WI: Bruce, 1948), 309–321.

7. Manders, "Concelebration," 143.

"On the eve of the Council, a number of theological boundaries seemed effectively established: the value of private celebration, the requirement of verbal consecration for true concelebration, a minimalist theory of consecration as constituting the essence of the eucharistic sacrifice, the theological definition of the priesthood in terms of its unique power to act in the name of Christ, and a strong emphasis on the unity of the priesthood as the symbolic meaning of concelebration."[8]

The Vatican II Reform

The proposal to extend concelebration found great support before and during the Council.[9] From a theological perspective, conciliar discussion clearly favored a more inclusive view integrating the unity of the church, of the priesthood, and of the liturgical assembly. However, the final version of *SC*, no. 57, narrowed that focus to the unity of the priesthood.

The "new rite of concelebration" mandated by Vatican II was drawn up in a very short time, as religious communities and priests in situations of individual celebration of the Mass anxiously waited to put the rite into practice. After an intense period of experimental use of a provisional rite, *Ritus Concelebrationis (RitCon)* was finalized. The *editio typica* promulgated by the Consilium of the Sacred Congregation of Rites[10] began with *praenotanda* (nos. 1–17), a form of theological-liturgical introduction that was to become standard for all the reformed rites. The *RitCon* then described in detail how concelebration was to take place in a variety of situations.[11] Although it was called a "new rite," it clearly followed the medieval model of presbyteral ordination, in keeping with the narrower focus on the unity of the priesthood (*SC*, no. 57), which was placed verbatim at the head of the *praenotanda* of the rite (*RitCon*, no. 1).

The text of the rite of concelebration entered into a second phase with the publication of the *Missale Romanum (MR)* and accompanying Instructions. *Institutio Generalis Missalis Romani* 1970 and 1975 (*IGMR1970* and *IGMR1975*) incorporated a revised version of the *RitCon*. In place of the separate descriptions of the various forms of concelebration, the *IGMR*s provided a unified, shortened

8. Ostdiek, "Concelebration Revisited," 144.

9. For a full discussion, see Annibale Bugnini, *The Reform of the Liturgy 1948–1975*, trans. Matthew J. O'Connell (Collegeville, MN: The Liturgical Press, 1990), 123–134.

10. Sacred Congregation of Rites (Consilium), "Decree *Ecclesiae semper*, promulgating the *editio typica* of the rites of concelebration and of Communion under both kinds, 7 March 1965," in DOL, nos. 1788–1792.

11. Namely: a pontifical Mass (*RitCon*, nos. 18–60); a solemn Mass (*RitCon*, nos. 61–78); a sung Mass (*RitCon*, nos. 79–108); a Mass in which presbyteral ordination is conferred (*RitCon*, nos. 109–121); a Mass in which episcopal consecration is conferred (*RitCon*, nos. 122–132); a Mass in which an abbot is blessed (*RitCon*, nos. 133–139); and a Mass concelebrated by infirm priests (*RitCon*, nos. 140–155). An English translation of the complete text, together with commentary, can be found in Jounel, *The Rite of Concelebration and of Communion under Both Species*.

II. Concelebrated Mass

199. Concelebration, which appropriately expresses the unity of the priesthood, of the Sacrifice, and also of the whole People of God, is prescribed by the rite itself for the Ordination of a Bishop and of priests, at the blessing of an abbot, and at the Chrism Mass.

Unless the good of the Christian faithful requires or suggests otherwise, concelebration is also recommended at:

a. The Evening Mass of the Lord's Supper;
b. The Mass during Councils, meetings of Bishops, and synods;
c. The conventual Mass and the principal Mass in churches and oratories;
d. Masses at any kind of meeting of priests, either secular or religious.[101]

II. De Missa Concelebrata

199. Concelebratio qua unitas sacerdotii et sacrificii necnon totius populi Dei opportune manifestatur ipso ritu præcipitur: in ordinatione Episcopi et presbyterorum, in benedictione abbatis et in Missa chrismatis.

Commendatur autem, nisi utilitas christifidelium aliud requirat aut suadeat:

a) ad Missam vespertinam in Cena Domini;
b) ad Missam in Conciliis, Conventibus Episcoporum et Synodis;
c) ad Missam conventualem et ad Missam principalem in ecclesiis et oratoriis;
d) ad Missas in conventibus cuiusvis generis sacerdotum tum sæcularium tum religiosorum.[101]

---

version of the ritual provisions of the rite. More importantly, the fuller threefold meaning of concelebration was recovered from the conciliar discussion and inserted into the first paragraph. This broader statement of the symbolic meaning of concelebration, however, is counteracted in many ways by the shape of the rite itself. There are small editorial variations between *IGMR1970* and *IGMR1975*; one noteworthy change is the elimination of the role of subdeacon in 1972 (cf. Morrill and Roll, 208 above) and taken into account in *IGMR1975*. Another change, the shift in language from *elevatio* to *ostensio* (*IGMR1975*, nos. 174, 180, 184, and 188), will be taken up in the following commentary. For our purposes, *IGMR1970* and *IGMR1975* are so close to each other that they can be taken together as a single stage in the development of the rite.

IGMR2000 and *IGMR2002* represent the third stage. Comparison of the second and third stages of the rite shows that the rite prescribed in *IGMR2002* has few substantial revisions compared to what was found in *IGMR1970* and *IGMR1975*. The ways in which the most recent *IGMR* has amended those earlier versions of the rite will be noted in the commentary. Note will also be made of the pastoral and theological questions that concelebration continues to raise.[12]

199. This article reproduces in substance the provisions for concelebration set down in *SC*, no. 57, and *RitCon*, no. 1, with some slight rearrangement and

12. See John F. Baldovin, "Concelebration: A Problem of Symbolic Roles in the Church," *Worship* 59 (1985): 32–47; Eligius Dekkers, "Concelebration–Limitations of Current Practice," *Doctrine and Life* 22 (1972): 190–202; Ostdiek, "Concelebration Revisited," 159–170; Taft, "Ex Oriente," 319–324.

An individual priest is, however, permitted to celebrate the Eucharist individually, though not at the same time as a concelebration is taking place in the same church or oratory. On Holy Thursday, however, and for Mass of the Easter Vigil, it is not permitted to celebrate individually.

200. Visiting priests should be gladly welcomed to eucharistic concelebration, as long as their priestly standing is ascertained.

Singulo tamen sacerdoti liceat Eucharistiam individuali modo celebrare, non vero eo tempore, quo in eadem ecclesia aut oratorio concelebratio habetur. Attamen feria V in Cena Domini et in Missa Vigiliæ paschalis modo individuali sacrum litare non permittitur.

200. Presbyteri peregrini libenter ad concelebrationem eucharisticam accipiantur, dummodo eorum condicio sacerdotalis cognoscatur.

---

adjustment.[13] The first paragraph lists occasions on which concelebration is prescribed. The second paragraph lists the recommended occasions, which are subject to the restriction of what is required for the good of the faithful. What that "good of the Christian faithful" *(utilitas christifidelium)* might be is left unspecified. It could be the need for community celebration of the Eucharist at other times or places; it might also include cases such as religious communities where the number of concelebrants may obscure the presence and participation of non-ordained members. The permission of the ordinary, formerly required for the occasions listed in no. 199c-d, has been dropped. Concelebration on those occasions is now accepted as a matter of course. Number 199d raises questions regarding the image of church that is being portrayed and modeled when concelebrants are the only ones present at a Eucharist celebrated during gatherings of priests. The last three lines of no. 199, not found in *IGMR1975* (no. 153), have been added from *SC,* no. 57. They allow individual celebrations of Mass, except for Holy Thursday and the Easter Vigil.

The theological rationale for concelebration has undergone significant fluctuations.[14] In preconciliar and conciliar discussions it often took the three-fold form used here: "the unity of the priesthood, of the Sacrifice, and also of the whole People of God" *(unitas sacerdotii et sacrificii necnon totius populi Dei).* Somewhat surprisingly in light of the vigorous conciliar debate over this matter, *SC,* no. 57, and *RitCon,* no. 1, had reduced that rationale to the unity of the priesthood only. Although the three-fold rationale had been restored in *IGMR1975* (no. 153) and here in *IGMR2002,* some have suggested that it is the unity of the priesthood that stands out most clearly in concelebration, to the detriment of the unity of the gathered church.[15]

200. This is a new statement, which reintroduces the element of eucharistic hospitality for visiting clergy so important in the early centuries. This ought

13. The blessing of an abbot has been moved from the listing in the first paragraph. In *SC,* no. 57, *RitCon,* no. 1, and *IGMR1975,* no. 153, it had been included in the listing.

14. On these fluctuations, see Ostdiek, "Concelebration Revisited," 144–159 *passim.*

15. E.g., see Baldovin, "Concelebration," 32–47.

201. Where there is a large number of priests, concelebration may take place even several times on the same day, wherever necessity or pastoral benefit suggest it. Nevertheless, it must be held at different times or in distinct sacred places.[102]

202. It is for the Bishop, in accordance with the norm of law, to regulate the discipline for concelebration in all churches and oratories of his diocese.

201. Ubi magnus habetur numerus sacerdotum, concelebratio pluries etiam in eodem die fieri potest, ubi necessitas vel pastoralis utilitas id suadeat; fieri tamen debet temporibus subsequentibus vel in locis sacris diversis.[102]

202. Episcopi est, ad normam iuris, concelebrationis disciplinam in omnibus ecclesiis et oratoriis suæ diœcesis moderari.

---

not be interpreted to mean that every visiting priest automatically has the right to concelebrate. GIRM2003's translation that visiting priests "should be gladly welcomed" to concelebrate might be taken too readily to imply such a right. The Latin subjunctive *libenter accipiantur* allows other translations, e.g., "they may be welcomed," or "let them be welcomed."[16]

201. Like *IGMR1975* (no. 154), this article allows concelebration, with restrictions, on occasions when there are a large number of priests. However, permission of "the authorized superior" *(superior competens)* is no longer required. The subsequent omission of the theological rationale originally found in *RitCon*, no. 2 (the manifestation of the unity of the priesthood), has reduced this provision to a purely practical matter to be decided locally.

202. This article slightly rewords *IGMR1975*, no. 155. *RitCon*, no. 3, had assigned a threefold regulatory oversight to ordinaries and major superiors of

16. This reading is supported by the limitations set down in the 2003 USCCB *Guidelines for Concelebration of the Eucharist* (GCE). GCE, no. 11 (based on *RitCon*, no. 2) reads: "Each Ordinary or the Major Superior of clerical non-exempt religious and of societies of clerics living in common may limit the number of concelebrants if, in consideration of the size of the church and the altar and whether the faithful's view of the rite is impaired, he decides 'that the dignity of the rite requires this.'" This guideline is in conflict with GCE, no. 7 regarding visiting priests. Number 7 repeats GIRM2003, no. 200 *verbatim* and adds: ". . . and a superior may not prohibit a priest from concelebrating." The added phrase is excerpted from a statement of the Congregation for Divine Worship and Discipline of the Sacraments, *"Responsa officialia," Notitiae* 35:396–397, nos. 7–8 (1999) 307–309. However, the phrase has been taken out of context and applied inaccurately. It is clear from the Congregation's introduction and the *responsa* themselves that the three cases being addressed all concern priests belonging to an institute whose members enjoy the indult of celebrating Mass according to the pre–Vatican II rite, i.e., using *MR1962*. The question at issue is whether such priests can celebrate (first two *dubia*) or concelebrate (third *dubium*) using the current Roman rite *(Missale romanum vigens)*. The specific intent of the third *responsum*, from which the added phrase has been taken, is that a major superior or local ordinary cannot, by reason of the indult alone, prohibit priests who normally celebrate the Tridentine liturgy from joining in a concelebration using the current post–Vatican II rite *(Missale romanum vigens)*. In addition, the response explicitly refers to both superiors and local ordinaries, not just superiors. Thus, the Congregation's *responsum* by no means grants priests, whether visiting or local, an absolute right to concelebrate if a local ordinary or superior, in keeping with GCE, no. 11, has decided to limit the number of concelebrants on specific occasions for appropriate pastoral reasons.

203. To be held in high regard is that concelebration in which the priests of each diocese concelebrate with their own Bishop at a stational Mass, especially on the more solemn days of the liturgical year, at the Ordination Mass of a new Bishop of the diocese or of his Coadjutor or Auxiliary, at the Chrism Mass, at the Evening Mass of the Lord's Supper, at celebrations of the Founder Saint of a local Church or the Patron of the diocese, on anniversaries of the Bishop, and, lastly, on the occasion of a Synod or a pastoral visitation.

For this same reason, concelebration is recommended whenever priests gather together with their own Bishop either on the occasion of a retreat or at any other meeting. In these instances the sign of the unity of the priesthood and also of the Church inherent in every concelebration is made more clearly manifest.[103]

203. In singulari honore illa concelebratio habenda est, qua presbyteri alicuius diœcesis cum proprio Episcopo concelebrant, in Missa stationali præsertim in diebus sollemnioribus anni liturgici, in Missa ordinationis novi Episcopi diœcesis aut eius Coadiutoris vel Auxiliaris, in Missa chrismatis, in Missa vespertina in Cena Domini, in celebrationibus Sancti Fundatoris Ecclesiæ localis vel Patroni diœcesis, in anniversariis Episcopi, occasione denique Synodi vel visitationis pastoralis.

Eadem ratione concelebratio commendatur quoties presbyteri cum proprio Episcopo conveniunt, sive occasione exercitiorum spiritualium, sive alicuius conventus. In his casibus illud signum unitatis sacerdotii, necnon Ecclesiæ, omni concelebrationi proprium, magis perspicuo modo manifestatur.[103]

---

clerical nonexempt religious and of societies of clerics living in common but without vows, namely, "to judge whether concelebration is opportune and to grant permission for it in their churches and oratories, as well as to fix the number of those who may concelebrate." Number 155 of *IGMR1970* and *IGMR1975* retains the oversight of all major superiors in their own churches and oratories, but omit the phrase allowing them and the bishop to restrict the number of concelebrants. The role of all major superiors is omitted completely in *IGMR2000* and thereafter. Number 202 thus makes the local ordinary the sole authority in general law for regulating concelebration in all churches and oratories of his diocese; it does not preclude the possibility that particular law or local guidelines might make provision for a regulatory role for major superiors.[17]

203. This is an expanded version of *IGMR1975,* no. 157. The thread common to all these occasions, except for "the celebrations of the Founder Saint of a local Church or the Patron of the diocese" *(in celebrationibus Sancti Fundatoris Ecclesiae localis vel Patroni dioecesis)* is the bond between the concelebrants and their

17. Thus, the regulatory role of major superiors, including limiting the number of concelebrants, has resurfaced as a guideline in the GCE, no. 11 (cited above, n. 16). Religious profession would be an occasion on which a major superior or an abbot might consider limiting the number of concelebrants. That ceremony is meant to focus on the unity of the community, including both ordained and non-ordained members, rather than on the unity of the ordained.

204. For a particular reason, having to do either with the significance of the rite or of the festivity, the faculty is given to celebrate or concelebrate more than once on the same day in the following cases:

a. A priest who has celebrated or concelebrated the Chrism Mass on Holy Thursday may also celebrate or concelebrate the Evening Mass of the Lord's Supper;

b. A priest who has celebrated or concelebrated the Mass of the Easter Vigil may celebrate or concelebrate Mass during the day on Easter Sunday;

c. On the Nativity of the Lord (Christmas Day), all priests may celebrate or

204. Ob peculiarem causam, sive significationis ritus sive festivitatis, facultas fit pluries celebrandi vel concelebrandi eodem die, sequentibus in casibus:

a) si quis, feria V Hebdomadæ sanctæ, Missam chrismatis celebravit aut concelebravit, etiam Missam vespertinam in Cena Domini celebrare aut concelebrare potest;

b) si quis Missam Vigiliæ paschalis celebravit aut concelebravit, potest Missam in die Paschæ celebrare aut concelebrare;

c) in Nativitate Domini omnes sacerdotes tres Missas celebrare vel concelebrare possunt, dummodo hæ suo tempore celebrentur;

---

bishop. These occasions are said to manifest more clearly "the sign of the unity of the priesthood and also of the Church inherent in every concelebration" *(signum unitatis sacerdotii, necnon Ecclesiae, omni concelebrationi)*. Again, the unity of the priests around their bishop takes center stage ritually. The expression of the unity of the Church will need to be carefully fostered in how the Eucharist is celebrated on those occasions.

204. This article repeats the provisions of *IGMR1975*, no. 158, with one addition. Allowance has now been made in no. 204d for priests to concelebrate or celebrate three times on All Souls' Day. As with the three Masses at Christmas, which are to be celebrated at their proper times of day, the three celebrations on All Souls' Day are to take place at different times. The recent custom of celebrating those three Masses continuously is thus to be discontinued. There is also an added reference to the application of the second and third Masses.[18]

18. *RitCon*, no. 10, had approved the acceptance of stipends by concelebrants, in accordance with the law. Current canon law states: "A priest who concelebrates a second Mass on the same day may not take an offering for it under any title" (c. 951, par 2). For a brief commentary on the issue of stipends for concelebration, see John Huels. "Concelebration," in his *Disputed Questions in the Liturgy Today* (Chicago: Liturgy Training Publications, 1988), 42. For a fuller theological discussion on the fruits of the Mass and stipends, see Edward Kilmartin, "The One Fruit or the Many Fruits of the Mass," *Proceedings of the Catholic Theological Society of America* 21 (1966): 37–69; Gilbert Ostdiek, "The Threefold Fruits of the Mass: Notes and Reflections on Scotus' Quodlibetal Questions, q. 20," in *Essays Honoring Allan B. Wolter*, ed. William A. Frank and Girard J. Etzkorn (St. Bonaventure, NY: The Franciscan Institute, 1985), 203–219; Karl Rahner and Angelus Häussling, *The Celebration of the Eucharist*, trans. W. J. O'Hara (New York: Herder and Herder, 1968), 61–127.

concelebrate three Masses, provided the Masses are celebrated at their proper times of day;

d. On the Commemoration of All the Faithful Departed (All Souls' Day), all priests may celebrate or concelebrate three Masses, provided that the celebrations take place at different times, and that the norms established regarding the application of second and third Masses are observed;[104]

e. A priest who concelebrates with the Bishop or his delegate at a Synod or pastoral visitation, or concelebrates on the occasion of a meeting of priests, may celebrate Mass again for the benefit of the faithful. This holds also, with due regard for the prescriptions of law, for groups of religious.

d) die Commemorationis omnium fidelium defunctorum omnes sacerdotes tres Missas celebrare vel concelebrare possunt, dummodo celebrationes diversis temporibus fiant et servatis iis quæ circa applicationem secundæ et tertiæ Missæ statuta sunt;[104]

e) si quis in Synodo et in visitatione pastorali cum Episcopo vel eius delegato aut occasione cuiusdam conventus sacerdotum concelebrat, Missam ad utilitatem fidelium iterum celebrare potest. Idem valet, servatis servandis, pro cœtibus religiosorum.

205. A concelebrated Mass, whatever its form, is arranged in accordance with the norms commonly in force (cf. above, nos. 112–198), except for those matters that are to be observed, even with appropriate adaptation to circumstances, as set forth below.

205. Missa concelebrata ordinatur, pro qualibet forma, iuxta normas communiter servandas *(cf. nn. 112–198),* iis tamen servatis aut mutatis quæ infra exponentur.

206. No one is ever to enter into a concelebration or to be admitted as a concelebrant once the Mass has already begun.

206. Nemo umquam ad concelebrandum accedat neque admittatur incepta iam Missa.

207. In the sanctuary there should be prepared[:]

207. In presbyterio parentur:

---

205. This article repeats the directive of *IGMR1975,* no. 159. The referenced norms are those revised above (no. 112–198).

206. Here the requirement of *RitCon,* no. 8, and *IGMR1975,* no. 156, are repeated. This seems to be a requirement of discipline and good order, rather than a theological requirement.

207. This article is a new addition, mentioning only two items from the long list originally given in *RitCon,* no. 17. At first glance, this number simply deals with practical arrangements. However, the worship space itself is part of the larger complex of communicative liturgical symbols (cf. no. 288 below), and the symbolism of the seating arrangement merits further reflection. Seating for the concelebrants becomes an especially acute problem when the number of concelebrants is large. The interior design of the worship space will determine what is possible in a given situation. *RitCon,* no. 17, had specified the seating

a. Seats and texts for the concelebrating priests;

b. On the credence table: a chalice of sufficient size or else several chalices.

208. If a deacon is not present, his proper duties are to be carried out by some of the concelebrants.

In the absence also of other ministers, their proper parts may be entrusted to other suitable members of the faithful; otherwise, they are carried out by some of the concelebrants.

a) sedes et libelli pro sacerdotibus concelebrantibus;

b) in abaco: calix sufficientis magnitudinis, aut plures calices.

208. Si diaconus non adsit, munera ipsi propria ab aliquibus concelebrantibus perficiuntur.

Si neque alii ministri adsint, partes ipsis propriæ aliis fidelibus idoneis committi possunt; secus ab aliquibus concelebrantibus absolvuntur.

---

arrangement somewhat when it directed that the chairs or benches for the concelebrants are to be "close to the chair of the principal celebrant, or in some suitable place in the sanctuary." One celebrated arrangement is that of the typical *presbyterium* found in ancient basilicas. More recent church design, especially of the sanctuary area, may require other arrangements. In deciding those arrangements, three related aspects need to be kept in balance. One is the relationship of the concelebrants' seating to that of the other liturgical ministers and members of the assembly (see nos. 310–11 below), represented in seating patterns that neither intermingle concelebrants with the assembly nor form a visual barrier between the assembly and the liturgical action (see no. 294 below). Another aspect is the unity of the priesthood, represented by seating concelebrants close to the principal celebrant. The third aspect is the unique role of the principal celebrant, whether bishop or priest, as the one who presides over the celebration, represented by a certain distinctiveness in design and/or place from the seating of the concelebrants. The same will be true for the other forms of liturgical expression to be addressed later: posture, gesture, word, and song. Visual and ritual clarity about the unique leadership role of the presider in relation to the concelebrants is subtle and may be difficult to maintain in the present practice of concelebration. Concelebration is neither synchronized celebration nor co-presiding.[19]

208. The parallel material from *IGMR1975,* no. 160, is substantially unchanged here. The provision that concelebrants may perform the functions of the deacon[20] and other liturgical ministers in their absence only highlights what seems ecclesiologically anomalous. *SC,* nos. 27–28, envision the presence of an assembly and a distribution of ministerial roles in every liturgical celebration (cf. no. 112 above). A concelebration in the absence of an assembly would seem

19. On the physical arrangements for concelebration, cf. GCE, nos. 14–15.

20. *RitCon,* no. 15 had required that a priest filling the ministry of a deacon was to abstain from concelebrating at the same Mass, which preserved clarity in the exercise of distinct ministerial roles.

209. In the vesting room or other suitable place, the concelebrants put on the sacred vestments they customarily wear when celebrating Mass individually. Should, however, a good reason arise, (e.g., a large number of concelebrants or a lack of vestments), concelebrants other than the principal celebrant may omit the chasuble and simply wear the stole over the alb.

209. Concelebrantes in secretario, vel alio loco apto, sacras vestes induunt, quas sumere solent cum Missam singuli celebrant. Accedente tamen iusta causa, v. gr. frequentiore concelebrantium numero et deficientia paramentorum, concelebrantes, excepto semper celebrante principali, omittere possunt casulam seu planetam, adhibita stola super albam.

The Introductory Rites

210. When everything has been properly arranged, the procession moves as usual through the church to the altar, the concelebrating priests walking ahead of the principal celebrant.

Ritus initiales

210. Omnibus rite dispositis, fit de more processio per ecclesiam ad altare. Sacerdotes concelebrantes incedunt ante celebrantem principalem.

---

to reduce the Eucharist to a corporate version of a "private" celebration. A concelebration without a distribution of ministerial roles would seem to revert to a past ritual practice in which only the priests were seen to be necessary for a celebration of the Eucharist. Both cases would proclaim that the presence and participation of non-ordained faithful are neither required nor essential, raising the earlier question regarding what image of church is being modeled (see no. 199 above).

209. Basically reiterating *IGMR1975*, no. 161, this article highlights one of the areas in which careless pastoral practice may detract significantly from the proper dignity and beauty[21] of the concelebration. Mismatched or slovenly worn vesture communicates a lack of appropriate reverence and respect for the sacred mysteries being celebrated. It can also emphasize an individualism and detract from the presidential role of the principal celebrant.[22] One solution adopted in some places is the designation of a "diocesan/community chasuble" which all priests are to bring to concelebrations.

The Introductory Rites

210. Unchanged from the previous edition, it is noteworthy that nothing is said here about gathering the faithful as one and preparing them for celebration of Word and table, which *IGMR2002* sets down as the primary purpose of the entrance rites (no. 46 above). A lengthy procession of concelebrants can call attention to the concelebrants rather than to the entire assembly, or to some other

21. Vestments are also part of the complex of liturgical symbols and their beauty is not insignificant, see no. 335 below.

22. This point is made in GCE, no. 20.

211. On reaching the altar, the concelebrants and the principal celebrant, after making a profound bow, venerate the altar with a kiss, then go to their designated seats. The principal celebrant, if appropriate, also incenses the cross and the altar and then goes to the chair.

211. Cum ad altare pervenerint, concelebrantes et celebrans principalis, facta profunda inclinatione, altare osculo venerantur, deinde sedem sibi assignatam petunt. Celebrans vero principalis crucem et altare, pro opportunitate, incensat, ac deinde sedem petit.

The Liturgy of the Word

212. During the Liturgy of the Word, the concelebrants remain at their places, sitting or standing whenever the principal celebrant does.

When the *Alleluia* is begun, all rise, except for a Bishop, who puts incense into the thurible without saying anything and blesses the deacon or, if there is no deacon, the concelebrant who is to proclaim the Gospel. In a concelebration where a priest presides, however, the concelebrant who in the absence of a deacon proclaims the Gospel neither requests nor receives the blessing of the principal celebrant.

Liturgia verbi

212. Durante liturgia verbi concelebrantes locum suum occupant et sedent et surgunt eadem ratione ac celebrans principalis.

Incepto Allelúia, omnes surgunt, excepto Episcopo, qui imponit incensum nihil dicens et benedicit diaconum vel, eo absente, concelebrantem qui Evangelium est proclamaturus. In concelebratione tamen cui presbyter præest, concelebrans qui, absente diacono, Evangelium proclamat, benedictionem celebrantis principalis nec petit nec accipit.

---

appropriate focus in the worship, e.g., the bride and groom in a wedding or the body in a funeral.

211. There is one slight change here from *IGMR1975,* no. 163, namely, the prescribed reverence to be made before kissing the altar is now specified as a "profound bow" (*profunda inclinatione,* cf. no. 186 above). When the number of concelebrants is large, the reverencing of the altar requires good coordination with the entrance song, lest the assembly be kept waiting in silence. The placement of the "designated seats" *(sedem . . . assignatam)* can also be problematic when the number of concelebrants is large (cf. nos. 207 above and 215, below).

The Liturgy of the Word

212. The first paragraph of this article is taken verbatim from *IGMR1975,* no. 164. The second paragraph is an addition.[23] There is an internal inconsistency between the first and second paragraphs. The first requires concelebrants to conform to the postures of the principal celebrant; the second requires them to stand for the Alleluia even though the bishop is to remain seated for putting incense in the thurible and blessing the deacon. Rising when the Alleluia is

23. *RitCon,* nos. 26, 69, 86, and 101 had made similar provisions.

213. The homily is usually given by the principal celebrant or by one of the concelebrants.

213. Homiliam habet de more celebrans principalis, vel unus e concelebrantibus.

The Liturgy of the Eucharist

Liturgia eucharistica

214. The Preparation of the Gifts (cf. nos. 139–146) is carried out by the principal celebrant, while the other concelebrants remain at their places.

214. Præparatio donorum *(cf. nn. 139–146)* perficitur a celebrante principali, aliis concelebrantibus suis locis manentibus.

215. After the prayer over the offerings has been said by the principal celebrant,

215. Post dictam a celebrante principali orationem super oblata, concelebrantes ad

---

begun, however, fosters the unity of the concelebrants with the rest of the assembly. The nuances in asking/receiving a blessing prior to proclaiming the gospel clearly highlight the hierarchical nature of three grades of sacred orders and the equality of status among presbyters.

213. The provisions of *IGMR1975,* no. 165, are unchanged here. Earlier, no. 66 allowed that the principal celebrant may entrust the homily to a deacon as well, "occasionally, according to the circumstances" *(quandoque, pro opportunitate)*. Presumably the same would hold true for concelebrations, although this provision is not repeated here. Number 66 also provides that, in certain circumstances "the homily may even be given by a Bishop or a priest who is present at the celebration but cannot concelebrate" *(homilia haberi potest etiam ab Episcopo vel presbytero qui celebrationi interest quin concelebrare possit)*.[24]

The Liturgy of the Eucharist

214. This article repeats materials found in *IGMR1975,* no. 166. In the earliest form of the reformed rite, the concelebrants were to approach the altar with the principal celebrant and stand there during the preparation of the gifts (*RitCon,* nos. 28, 72, and 104). Having the concelebrants remain at their places during the preparation of the gifts lends greater clarity and simplicity to the presentation of the gifts. Presumably the principal celebrant is assisted by the deacon, if one is present. Number 208 had stated earlier that concelebrants are to carry out the functions of the deacon if none is present. Thus it would be consistent for a concelebrant to perform this diaconal function, as concelebrants are explicitly invited to do at other moments in a celebration when there is no deacon (cf. nos. 212, 239, 240, and 246a-b).

215. This first paragraph has been taken from *IGMR1975,* no. 167. The concelebrants are to approach the altar after the prayer over the gifts has been said, although in practice this sometimes does not happen until during or after the

24. This wording, unlike *Eucharisticum mysterium,* no. 43, envisions the presence and participation of non-concelebrating priests.

the concelebrants approach the altar and stand around it, but in such a way that they do not obstruct the execution of the rites and that the sacred action may be seen clearly by the faithful. They should not be in the deacon's way whenever he needs to go to the altar to perform his ministry.

The deacon exercises his ministry at the altar whenever he needs to assist with the chalice and the Missal. However, insofar as possible, he stands back slightly, behind the concelebrating priests standing around the principal celebrant.

altare accedunt et circa illud consistunt, ita tamen ut impedimento non sint in ritibus peragendis, et actio sacra a fidelibus bene conspiciatur, neque impedimento sint diacono quando ad altare, ratione sui ministerii, accedere debet.

Diaconus suo ministerio prope altare fungatur, quando opus est calici et missali ministrando. Attamen, quantum fieri potest stat aliquantulum retro, post sacerdotes concelebrantes, qui circa celebrantem principalem consistunt.

Sanctus, which interrupts the flow and integrity of the Eucharistic Prayer and implies that the preface is not really part of the prayer.[25] The prescription that the concelebrants stand around the altar is one of the spatial aspects of concelebration most difficult to arrange appropriately. Two requirements are "that they do not obstruct the execution of the rites and that the sacred action may be seen clearly by the faithful" *(impedimento non sint in ritibus peragendis, et actio sacra a fidelibus bene conspiciatur)*. It can be difficult to distinguish the principal celebrant from a phalanx of concelebrants arrayed around or higher than him on the steps of the old high altar. His presiding role might be visually enhanced if he were to stand alone at the altar without concelebrants immediately next to him but rather at a slight distance from the altar.[26] More significantly, it can happen that the view of the faithful becomes completely impeded, e.g., at presbyteral ordinations with many concelebrants. If concelebrants occupy pews in the center of the nave, they become a visual barrier to the faithful who are kneeling behind them, who can see nothing of the sacred action at the altar.[27] If concelebrants leave the pews and stand behind the principal celebrant, there can be a sizeable void between the altar and the assembly, creating a sense of separation from the sacred action. If the arrangement of the church allows it, concelebrants

25. GCE, no. 25 notes: "The principal celebrant begins the Eucharistic Prayer only after the concelebrants have taken their places." Also, see no. 43 above.

26. That the concelebrants are to "approach the altar and stand around it" *(ad altare accedunt et circum illud consistunt)* does not necessarily imply that any of them can immediately touch it. See also *RitCon,* no. 4.

27. This problem does not occur in countries where, in keeping with the general provisions of *IGMR*s, the faithful remain standing for the Eucharistic Prayer. In the dioceses of the United States they are to kneel after the *Sanctus* through the doxology. Note, however, that exceptions are allowed in US dioceses, "on occasion" and for a "good reason" (see no. 43 above). Enabling people to participate as fully as possible in the Eucharistic Prayer would surely qualify as a "good reason."

The Manner of Speaking the Eucharistic Prayer

216. The Preface is sung or said by the principal priest celebrant alone; but the *Sanctus* is sung or recited by all the concelebrants, together with the congregation and the choir.

217. After the *Sanctus,* the priest concelebrants continue the Eucharistic Prayer in the way described below. Unless otherwise indicated, only the principal celebrant makes the gestures.

218. The parts spoken by all the concelebrants together and especially the words of consecration, which all are bound to say, are to be said in such a way that the concelebrants speak them in a very low voice and that the principal celebrant's voice be

De modo proferendi Precem eucharisticam

216. Præfatio cantatur vel dicitur a solo sacerdote celebrante principali; Sanctus vero ab omnibus concelebrantibus una cum populo et schola cantatur vel recitatur.

217. Sanctus expleto, sacerdotes concelebrantes Precem eucharisticam modo infra descripto prosequuntur. Solus celebrans principalis gestus facit, nisi aliter notetur.

218. Partes quæ ab omnibus concelebrantibus simul proferuntur, et præsertim consecrationis verba, quæ exprimere omnes tenentur, in recitatione ita dicendæ sunt, ut eas concelebrantes submissa voce proferant et vox celebrantis principalis

---

could stand to the sides, or it might be appropriate, other than at ordinations, to limit the number of concelebrants.[28]

The second paragraph of this article is new. It reflects a similar concern found in *RitCon,* no. 16, that deacons and other ministers not stand among the concelebrants. Effective performance of the ritual is surely at issue here; obscuring the distinct identity of the priesthood might also be at stake.

The Manner of Speaking the Eucharistic Prayer

216. This material is identical to *IGMR1975,* no. 168. Whenever concelebrants are to sing or recite prayers along with the congregation, great care needs to be taken they do not overpower the voice of the assembly. It is at points such as this that the unity of the priesthood and the unity of the eucharistic assembly can come into symbolic tension.

217. The solo performance of some of the words and gestures of the Eucharistic Prayer highlights the role of the principal celebrant as the one who presides over the whole celebration. Surrounded by concelebrants, he would do well to support that role by appropriately amplifying the sense of "presence" he communicates to the assembly through these words and gestures.

218. While unchanged from *IGMR1975,* GIRM2003 has translated *submissa voce* as "in a very low voice," whereas GIRM1975 translated the phrase "in a softer voice." This new translation should help to alleviate the problem of concelebrants overriding the voice of the principal celebrant due to the sheer volume of the concelebrants' voices, especially when numerous, and if there is

28. In keeping with GCE, no. 11, based on *RitCon,* no. 4.

clearly heard. In this way the words can be better understood by the people.

It is a praiseworthy practice for the parts that are to be said by all the concelebrants together and for which musical notation is provided in the Missal to be sung.

clare audiatur. Hac ratione verba a populo facilius percipiuntur.

Partes ab omnibus concelebrantibus simul dicendæ, quæ notis in missali ornantur, laudabiliter cantu proferuntur.

Eucharistic Prayer I, or The Roman Canon

219. In Eucharistic Prayer I, or the Roman Canon, the prayer *Te igitur (We come to you, Father)* is said by the principal celebrant alone, with hands extended.

220. It is appropriate that the commemoration of the living (*the Memento*) and the *Communicantes (In union with the whole Church)* be assigned to one or other of the concelebrating priests, who then speaks these prayers aloud, with hands extended.

221. The *Hanc igitur (Father, accept this offering)* is likewise said by the principal celebrant alone, with hands extended.

Prex eucharistica I, seu Canon romanus

219. In Prece eucharistica I, seu Canone romano Te ígitur a solo celebrante principali, extensis manibus, dicitur.

220. Meménto vivorum et Communicántes uni alterive e sacerdotibus concelebrantibus committi convenit, qui solus has preces, manibus extensis, et elata voce profert.

221. Hanc ígitur a solo celebrante principali iterum dicitur, manibus extensis.

---

timid vocal leadership on the part of the principal celebrant. The purpose of this vocal discipline is so that "the words can be better understood by the people" *(verba a populo facilius percipiuntur). SC*'s pastoral goal of full, conscious, and active participation of all the faithful (no. 14) needs to be safeguarded with special care in concelebrations, which place such strong emphasis on the unity of the ministerial priesthood.

The second paragraph of no. 218 has been added here. It simply collects into one place the multiple directives in *IGMR1975* (nos. 178, 182, 186, and 190) about concelebrants singing those parts of the Eucharistic Prayer that are to be proclaimed in common. Although "praiseworthy" *(laudabiliter)*, this practice requires suitable musical settings and rehearsal of concelebrants.

Eucharistic Prayer I, or The Roman Canon

219–225. These are substantially the same as *IGMR1975*, nos. 171–177.[29] There are a few alternative translations between GIRM1975 and GIRM2003[30] and the Latin incipits of the prayers have been kept in the English translation. Several issues concerning ritual practice need to be addressed. First, the ritual

29. Nos. 221–222 replicate the simpler set of directives originally given in *RitCon*, no. 39.

30. E.g., "with hands extended" instead of "with hands outstretched" for *manibus extensis*.

222. From the *Quam oblationem (Bless and approve our offering)* up to and including the *Supplices (Almighty God, we pray that your angel)*, the principal celebrant alone makes the gestures, while all the concelebrants speak everything together, in this manner:

222. A Quam oblatiónem usque ad Súpplices, celebrans principalis gestus facit, omnes vero concelebrantes omnia simul proferunt, hoc modo:

---

gestures of the concelebrants presume that their hands are free for them to perform these gestures,[31] which presumes that the prayers to be proclaimed in common are known by heart. Second, the provision in nos. 220 and 223 that individual concelebrants may be invited to proclaim parts of the Eucharistic Prayer[32] sometimes results in an awkward break in the proclamation, e.g., because of pausing to assign the commemoration and intercessions in the midst of the prayer, passing the book around, or having concelebrants move to the book on the altar.[33] Third, differences in voice and tone, or the lack of microphones for concelebrants, can make the prayer sound uneven. Parceling out the prayer so that as many concelebrants as possible have something to say is

31. The various stages of the rite of concelebration have consistently required the extension of both hands for the epiclesis before the words of institution, but leave the extension of the hand (right hand only) optional for the words of institution. Regarding the gesture during the epiclesis, GCE no. 29 notes: "The full impact of this gesture can be achieved if the concelebrants adopt the same gesture as the principal celebrant," i.e., an imposition of hands with palms down. There has been discussion of how the second, optional gesture is to be made, with palms down in an epicletic gesture, or turned sideways in a demonstrative gesture. Good ritual practice would require that the decisions about whether and how to make the gesture during the words of institution be made beforehand. For a scholarly exchange over the relative merits of the epicletic vs. the demonstrative gesture, see Cyprien Vagaggini, "L'extension de la main au moment de la consécration: geste indicatif ou épiclétique?" *Paroisse et liturgie* 51 (1969): 46–53; Aimé-Georges Martimort, "Le Geste des Concélébrants, lors des Paroles de la Consécration: Indicatif ou Épiclétic?" *Notitiae* 18, 193–194, nos. 8–9 (1982): 408–412; Cipriano Vagaggini, "Ancora sulla estensione della mano dei concelebranti al momento della consecrazione: gesto indicativo o epicletico?" *Ephemerides Liturgicae* 97, no. 2 (1983): 224–241. Nothing official has been determined about the nature of the gesture. An affirmative response was given to the question of whether the right hand extended at the words of consecration could be turned to the side and interpreted as demonstrative. But a prefatory note says that the solutions proposed to the *dubia* are only "orienting" and have no official value *("Solutio quae proponitur nullam induit vestem officialem. Solummodo habet valorem orientativum.")*. See: *Dubia* n. 39c, *Notitiae* 1 (1965): 143.

32. *IGMR2002* says that the commemorations and intercessions "are appropriately assigned" *(committi convenit)* to one or the other concelebrant (nos. 220 and 223). *IGMR1975* and *IGMR1970* say that "they may be assigned" (*committi possunt*, no. 175). *IGMR2002* thus expresses a preference for but does not mandate the entrusting of these parts to concelebrants.

33. To avoid this problem, GCE, no. 34 recommends that cards or booklets containing the Eucharistic Prayer should be provided for those who will say the intercessions. This, however, makes extending their hands difficult.

a. The *Quam oblationem (Bless and approve our offering)* with hands extended toward the offerings;
b. The *Qui pridie (The day before he suffered)* and the *Simili modo (When supper was ended)* with hands joined;
c. While speaking the words of the Lord, each extends his right hand toward the bread and toward the chalice, if this seems appropriate; as the host and the chalice are shown, however, they look toward them and afterwards bow profoundly;
d. The *Unde et memores (Father, we celebrate the memory)* and the *Supra quae (Look with favor)* with hands extended;
e. From the *Supplices (Almighty God, we pray that your angel)* up to and including the words *ex hac altaris participatione (as we receive from this altar)*, they bow with hands joined; then they stand upright and cross themselves at the words *omni benedictione et gratia repleamur (let us be filled with every grace and blessing)*.

a) Quam oblatiónem, manibus ad oblata extensis;
b) Qui prídie et Símili modo, manibus iunctis;
c) verba Domini, manu dextera, si opportunum videtur, ad panem et ad calicem extensa; ad ostensionem autem hostiam et calicem aspicientes ac postea profunde se inclinantes;
d) Unde et mémores et Supra quæ, manibus extensis;
e) Súpplices, inclinati et manibus iunctis usque ad verba ex hac altáris participatióne, ac deinde erecti et se signantes ad verba omni benedictióne cæléstí et grátia repleámur.

223. The commemoration of the dead (*Memento*) and the *Nobis quoque peccatoribus (Though we are sinners)* are appropriately assigned to one or other of the concelebrants, who speaks them aloud alone, with hands extended.

223. Meménto defunctorum et Nobis quoque peccatóribus uni alterive e concelebrantibus committi convenit, qui solus ea, manibus extensis et elata voce, profert.

---

even more disruptive of the flow of the prayer and distracting for the faithful.[34] Care must be taken so that concelebrants do not appear as co-presiders. It is important to maintain coherence and integrity in the proclamation of the Eucharistic Prayer, the "center and summit of the entire celebration" *(centrum et culmen totius celebrationis)*, to which the faithful are to "listen . . . with reverence and in silence" (*omnes reverentia et silentio . . . auscultent*, no. 78).

34. In no other rite are extended euchological texts divided up among various proclaimers. Exercising the option for the principal celebrant to say the *memento* and intercessions might be helpful in preserving both the integrity of the prayer and the symbolism of his presidential role.

224. At the words *Nobis quoque peccatoribus (Though we are sinners)* all the concelebrants strike their breast.

225. The *Per quem haec omnia (Through him you give us all these gifts)* is said by the principal celebrant alone.

Eucharistic Prayer II

226. In Eucharistic Prayer II the *Vere sanctus (Lord, you are holy indeed)* is spoken by the principal celebrant alone, with hands extended.

227. From the *Haec ergo dona (Let your Spirit come upon)* to the *Et supplices (May all of us who share)* inclusive, all the concelebrants speak all the following together:

a. The *Haec ergo dona (Let your Spirit come upon)* with hands extended toward the offerings;
b. The *Qui cum passioni (Before he was given up to death)* and the *Simili modo (When supper was ended)* with hands joined;
c. While speaking the words of the Lord, each extends his right hand toward the bread and toward the chalice, if this seems appropriate; as the host

224. Ad verba Nobis quoque peccatóribus omnes concelebrantes pectus sibi percutiunt.

225. Per quem hæc ómnia a solo celebrante principali dicitur.

Prex eucharistica II

226. In Prece eucharistica II Vere Sanctus a solo celebrante principali, extensis manibus, profertur.

227. Ab Hæc ergo dona usque ad Et súpplices omnes concelebrantes omnia simul proferunt, hoc modo:

a) Hæc ergo dona, manibus ad oblata extensis;
b) Qui cum passióni et Símili modo, manibus iunctis;
c) verba Domini, manu dextera, si opportunum videtur, ad panem et ad calicem extensa; ad ostensionem autem hostiam et calicem aspicientes ac postea profunde se inclinantes;

In these and the parallel paragraphs for the other Eucharistic Prayers, one of the principles underlying the Vatican II rite of concelebration becomes abundantly clear. The official position taken by Pius XII (d. 1958) and reaffirmed by the Council is that verbal co-consecration is required for valid celebration by the concelebrants. This follows the medieval practice adopted for presbyteral ordination and episcopal consecration, as opposed to the nonverbal practices found in the early church. From another angle, the rite departs from the medieval practice in that the concelebrants are not required to say all the words of the Eucharistic Prayer along with the principal celebrant. To that extent it relies on the more minimalist medieval theological approach to what is essential for the confection of a sacrament.

Eucharistic Prayer II

226–228. These articles are substantially the same as *IGMR1975*, nos. 179–181. See the parallel comments for nos. 219–225 above.

and the chalice are shown, however, they look toward them and afterwards bow profoundly;

d. The *Memores igitur (In memory of his death)* and the *Et supplices (May all of us who share)* with hands extended.

d) Mémores ígitur atque Et súpplices, manibus extensis.

228. The intercessions for the living, *Recordare, Domine (Lord, remember your Church),* and for the dead, *Memento etiam fratrum nostrorum (Remember our brothers and sisters),* are appropriately assigned to one or other of the concelebrants, who speaks them aloud alone, with hands extended.

228. Intercessiones pro vivis: Recordáre, Dómine, et pro defunctis: Meménto étiam fratrum nostrórum, uni alterive e concelebrantibus committi convenit, qui solus eas, manibus extensis et elata voce, profert.

Eucharistic Prayer III

229. In Eucharistic Prayer III, the *Vere sanctus (Father, you are holy indeed)* is spoken by the principal celebrant alone, with hands extended.

230. From the *Supplices ergo te, Domine (And so, Father, we bring you these gifts)* to the *Respice, quaesumus (Look with favor)* inclusive, all the concelebrants speak all the following together:

a. The *Supplices ergo te, Domine (And so, Father, we bring you these gifts)* with hands extended toward the offerings;

b. The *Ipse enim in qua nocte tradebatur (On the night he was betrayed)* and the *Simili modo (When supper was ended)* with hands joined;

c. While speaking the words of the Lord, each extends his right hand toward the bread and toward the chalice, if this seems appropriate; as the host and the chalice are shown, however, they look at them and, afterwards, bow profoundly;

Prex eucharistica III

229. In Prece eucharistica III Vere Sanctus a solo celebrante principali, extensis manibus, profertur.

230. A Súpplices ergo te, Dómine, usque ad Réspice, quǽsumus, omnes concelebrantes omnia simul proferunt hoc modo:

a) Súpplices ergo te, Dómine, manibus ad oblata extensis;

b) Ipse enim in qua nocte tradebátur et Símili modo, manibus iunctis;

c) verba Domini, manu dextera, si opportunum videtur, ad panem et ad calicem extensa; ad ostensionem autem hostiam et calicem aspicientes ac postea profunde se inclinantes;

d) Mémores ígitur et Réspice, quǽsumus, manibus extensis.

Eucharistic Prayer III

229–231. These articles are substantially the same as *IGMR1975*, nos. 183–185. See the parallel comments for nos. 219–225, above. *IGMR2002* adds the commemoration of the dead *(Fratres nostros)* to the list of those portions of the

d. The *Memores igitur (Father, calling to mind)* and the *Respice, quaesumus (Look with favor)* with hands outstretched.

231. The intercessions *Ipse nos (May he make us an everlasting gift), Haec hostia nostrae reconciliationis (Lord, may this sacrifice),* and *Fratres nostros (Welcome into your kingdom)* are appropriately assigned to one or other of the concelebrants, who speaks them aloud alone, with hands extended.

231. Intercessiones: Ipse nos, Hæc hóstia nostræ reconciliatiónis, et Fratres nostros uni alterive e concelebrantibus committi convenit, qui solus eas, minibus extensis et elata voce, profert.

Eucharistic Prayer IV

232. In Eucharistic Prayer IV, the *Confitemur tibi, Pater sancte (Father, we acknowledge)* up to and including the words *omnem sanctificationem compleret (bring us the fullness of grace)* is spoken by the principal celebrant alone, with hands extended.

233. From the *Quaesumus, igitur, Domine (Father, may this Holy Spirit)* to the *Respice, Domine (Lord, look upon the sacrifice)* inclusive, all the concelebrants speak all the following together:

a. The *Quaesumus igitur, Domine (Father, may this Holy Spirit)* with hands extended toward the offerings;

b. The *Ipse enim, cum hora venisset (He always loved those)* and the *Simili modo (When supper was ended)* with hands joined;

c. While speaking the words of the Lord, each extends his right hand toward the bread and toward the chalice, if this seems appropriate; as the host and the chalice are shown, however, they look toward them and afterwards bow profoundly;

Prex eucharistica IV

232. In Prece eucharistica IV Confitémur tibi, Pater sancte, usque ad omnem sanctificatiónem compléret, a solo celebrante principali, extensis manibus, profertur.

233. A Quǽsumus ígitur, Dómine, usque ad Réspice, Dómine, omnes concelebrantes omnia simul proferunt, hoc modo:

a) Quǽsumus ígitur, Dómine, manibus ad oblata extensis;

b) Ipse enim, cum hora venísset et Símili modo, manibus iunctis;

c) verba Domini, manu dextera, si opportunum videtur, ad panem et ad calicem extensa; ad ostensionem autem hostiam et calicem aspicientes ac postea profunde se inclinantes;

d) Unde et nos et Réspice, Dómine, manibus extensis.

---

prayer that can be said by a single concelebrant (no. 231). This brings it into line with the distribution of parts in the other Eucharistic Prayers.

Eucharistic Prayer IV

232–234. These articles are substantially the same as *IGMR1975,* nos. 187–189. See the parallel comments for nos. 219–225 above.

d. The *Unde et nos (Father, we now celebrate)* and the *Respice, Domine (Lord, look upon this sacrifice)* with hands outstretched.

234. The intercessions *Nunc ergo, Domine, omnium recordare (Lord, remember those)* and *Nobis omnibus (Father, in your mercy)* are appropriately assigned to one or other of the concelebrants, who speaks them aloud alone, with hands extended.

234. Intercessiones: Nunc ergo, Dómine, ómnium recordáre, et Nobis omnibus uni alterive e concelebrantibus committi convenit, qui solus eas, minibus extensis et elata voce, profert.

235. As to other Eucharistic Prayers approved by the Apostolic See, the norms established for each one are to be observed.

235. Quoad alias Preces eucharisticas ab Apostolica Sede approbatas, serventur normæ pro singulis statutæ.

236. The concluding doxology of the Eucharistic Prayer is spoken solely by the principal priest celebrant and, if this is desired, together with the other concelebrants, but not by the faithful.

236. Doxologia finalis Precis eucharisticæ solummodo a sacerdote celebrante principali et, si placuerit, una cum aliis concelebrantibus profertur, non autem a fidelibus.

---

235. Because new Eucharistic Prayers have appeared since the rite of concelebration first appeared in *MR1970*, this paragraph has been added. One discrepancy here concerns the curial document introducing the Eucharistic Prayers for Masses with Children, which stated: "The rubrics for the individual Eucharistic Prayers appearing in the Latin text are all to be incorporated into the vernacular text. Special rubrics for concelebration as are found in the four Eucharistic Prayers already in use are lacking in these prayers. In view of the psychology of children it seems better to refrain from concelebration when Mass is celebrated with them."[35] Nonetheless, published versions of the Eucharistic Prayers for Masses with Children contain rubrics indicating which parts of the prayer are said by the principal celebrant alone, which are said by all the concelebrants, and which may be said by one concelebrant. Although concelebration at Masses with children may be less likely to occur in places like the US as the number of priests declines, this discrepancy is still worth noting and pondering as part of the larger question of what the "psychology of children" might have to say about the composition and performance of Eucharistic Prayers.

236. The one addition to this article from *IGMR1975*, no. 191, is the final phrase instructing that the faithful are not to join in speaking the doxology (cf. nos. 79h and 151 above). The first option given here is that the principal celebrant alone speaks the doxology; the other concelebrants are to join in "if this

35. Sacred Congregation for Divine Worship, *Eucharistic Prayers for Masses with Children and for Masses of Reconciliation, Introduction*, no. 22, in DOL, no. 2020.

The Communion Rite

237. Then the principal celebrant, with hands joined, says the introduction to the Lord's Prayer. Then, with hands extended, he says the prayer itself together with the other concelebrants, who also pray with hands extended and with the people.

238. *Libera nos (Deliver us)* is said by the principal celebrant alone, with hands extended. All the concelebrants, together with the people, sing or say the final acclamation *Quia tuum est regnum (For the kingdom).*

239. After the deacon or, when no deacon is present, one of the concelebrants has said the invitation *Offerte vobis pacem (Let us offer each other the sign of peace)*, all exchange the sign of peace with one another. The concelebrants who are nearer the principal celebrant receive the sign of peace from him before the deacon does.

Ritus Communionis

237. Deinde celebrans principalis, iunctis manibus, dicit monitionem ante Orationem dominicam ac deinde, manibus extensis, una cum ceteris concelebrantibus, qui et manus extendunt, et cum populo ipsam Orationem dominicam.

238. Líbera nos dicitur a solo celebrante principali, manibus extensis. Omnes concelebrantes, una cum populo, acclamationem finalem proferunt: Quia tuum est regnum.

239. Post monitionem diaconi vel, eo absente, unius e concelebrantibus: Offérte vobis pacem, omnes sibi invicem pacem tradunt. Qui propiores sunt celebranti principali pacem ab ipso recipiunt ante diaconum.

---

is desired" *(si placuerit)*, a phrase added in *MR2002*. Honoring the first preference emphasizes the presidential role of the principal celebrant[36] and enhances the doxology, especially when it is sung.

The Communion Rite

237. *IGMR1975*, no. 192 is ammended here, with the addition that the other concelebrants also extend their hands during the Lord's Prayer. As the Lord's Prayer is the prayer of the whole assembly, a problem could arise if the faithful are not invited to share this gesture as well (cf. no. 42 above), or the concelebrants' voices overpower the voices of the assembled faithful.

238. Identical to previous Instructions, *IGMR* here notes that concelebrants are not to extend their hands during the embolism, and their voices should not overpower the assembly in saying or singing the final acclamation.

239. This article repeats *IGMR1975*, no. 194, with a slight change of wording. If the number of concelebrants is large, caution should be taken so that their exchange of peace does not unduly lengthen the peace, interrupting the flow of the Communion rite.[37]

36. The principal celebrant alone would thus both initiate the Eucharistic Prayer and bring it to a close.

37. Cf. *IGMR2002*, no. 82; GIRM2003, no. 154; and GCE, no. 40.

240. While the *Agnus Dei* is sung or said, the deacons or some of the concelebrants may help the principal celebrant break the hosts for Communion, both of the concelebrants and of the people.

241. After the commingling, the principal celebrant alone, with hands joined, privately says the prayer *Domine Iesu Christe, Fili Dei vivi (Lord Jesus Christ, Son of the living God)* or *Perceptio Corporis et Sanguinis (Lord Jesus Christ, with faith in your love and mercy).*

242. When this prayer before Communion is finished, the principal celebrant genuflects and steps back a little. Then one after another the concelebrants come to the middle of the altar, genuflect, and reverently take the Body of Christ from the altar. Then holding it in their right hand, with the left hand placed below, they return to their places. The concelebrants may, however, remain in their places and take the Body of Christ from the paten presented to them by the principal celebrant or by

240. Dum Agnus Dei profertur, diaconi vel aliqui e concelebrantibus celebrantem principalem adiuvare possunt ad hostias frangendas, sive pro concelebrantium sive pro populi Communione.

241. Immixtione peracta, solus celebrans principalis, manibus iunctis, dicit secreto orationem Dómine Iesu Christe, Fili Dei vivi vel Percéptio Córporis et Sánguinis.

242. Oratione ante Communionem expleta, celebrans principalis genuflectit et paulum recedit. Concelebrantes vero unus post alium ad medium altaris accedunt, genuflectunt et Corpus Christi reverenter ex altari accipiunt, atque manu dextera illud tenentes, eique manum sinistram supponentes, ad loca sua recedunt. Possunt tamen concelebrantes suis locis remanere et Corpus Christi e patena sumere, quam celebrans principalis aut unus vel plures e concelebrantibus tenent, ante ipsos

---

240. The current Instruction newly notes that deacons may also join in the fraction rite, something without a parallel in "Mass with a Deacon" (cf. no. 181 above).

241. While there are no changes here in the Latin text, GIRM2003 changes the translation of *secreto* from "inaudibly" to "privately," although the former translation could be pastorally more helpful (cf. no. 33 above).

242. The alternate manner of distributing the Body of Christ to concelebrants seems less time-consuming and ritually obtrusive than having them come to the altar one by one, especially if the number of concelebrants is large. More thought is needed regarding how the hosts are broken and shared in a way that effectively symbolizes the unity of both concelebrants and assembly.[38]

38. GCE, no. 42, notes, "It is not necessary that each concelebrant receive one-half of a large host. But at least some of the Eucharistic bread should be broken for the concelebrants and the people." This is a question of symbolically expressing the unity not only of the priesthood, but also of the entire assembly at the eucharistic table. See *IGMR2002,* nos. 242 and 321. The guideline in GCE, no. 43, that concelebrants must receive hosts consecrated at that Mass but that this is only recommended for the faithful, is a remnant of two-tiered thinking about participation in the celebration.

one or more of the concelebrants, or by passing the paten one to another.

transeundo, vel etiam tradendo patenam sequenti et ita usque ad ultimum.

243. Then the principal celebrant takes a host consecrated in the same Mass, holds it slightly raised above the paten or the chalice, and, facing the people, says the *Ecce Agnus Dei (This is the Lamb of God).* With the concelebrants and the people he continues, saying the *Domine, non sum dignus (Lord, I am not worthy).*

243. Deinde celebrans principalis accipit hostiam in eadem Missa consecratam, eamque aliquantulum elevatam super patenam vel super calicem tenens, versus ad populum dicit: Ecce Agnus Dei, et prosequitur cum concelebrantibus et populo, dicens: Dómine, non sum dignus.

244. Then the principal celebrant, facing the altar, says quietly, *Corpus Christi custodiat me ad vitam aeternam (May the body of Christ bring me to everlasting life),* and reverently receives the Body of Christ. The concelebrants do likewise, communicating themselves. After them the deacon receives the Body and Blood of the Lord from the principal celebrant.

244. Deinde celebrans principalis, ad altare versus, secreto dicit: Corpus Christi custódiat me in vitam æternam, et Corpus Christi reverenter sumit. Similiter faciunt concelebrantes seipsos communicantes. Post eos diaconus a celebrante principali Corpus et Sanguinem Domini accipit.

245. The Blood of the Lord may be received either by drinking from the chalice directly, or by intinction, or by means of a tube or a spoon.

245. Sanguis Domini sumi potest vel ex ipso calice directe bibendo, vel per intinctionem, vel cum calamo, vel cum cochleari.

---

243. Only the principal celebrant shows the consecrated host to the people. This presumes that the concelebrants continue to hold the host in their hands (no. 242 above) during the invitation to Communion; they do not elevate their hosts.[39] This maintains the clarity of the presidential role.

244. Reflective of its penchant for adding details that were part of common practice but missing from previous Instructions (cf. no. 174 above), *IGMR2002* here notes that the deacon also receives the "Blood of the Lord" *(Sanguinem Domini).* The wording is open to misinterpretation, as it indicates that the deacon receives the Body and Blood of the Lord after the concelebrants,[40] who will have received only the host at this point. That same lack of clarity occurs in no. 247 below. *IGMR1975* states more clearly that the "deacon receives Communion last" (*Ultimus accedit diaconus,* no. 204), which is also the intention of this article.

245. No new material is included in this article, and the further directions for reception by tube or spoon, found in *IGMR1975,* nos. 202–203 have been eliminated. While both of these options, as well as intinction, are allowed (although they have been eliminated as options for the Communion of the faithful,

39. Thus GCE, no. 46.

40. *IGMR1975,* no. 199 had spoken only of the deacon receiving the Body of Christ at this point.

246. If Communion is received by drinking directly from the chalice, one or other of two procedures may be followed:

a. The principal celebrant, standing at the middle of the altar, takes the chalice and says quietly, *Sanguis Christi custodiat me in vitam aeternam (May the Blood of Christ bring me to everlasting life)*. He consumes a little of the Blood of Christ and hands the chalice to the deacon or a concelebrant. He then distributes Communion to the faithful (cf. nos. 160–162).

   The concelebrants approach the altar one after another or, if two chalices are used, two by two. They genuflect, partake of the Blood of Christ, wipe the rim of the chalice, and return to their seats.

b. The principal celebrant normally consumes the Blood of the Lord standing at the middle of the altar.

   The concelebrants may, however, partake of the Blood of the Lord while remaining in their places and drinking from the chalice presented to them by the deacon or by one of the concelebrants, or else passed from one to the other. The chalice is always wiped either by the one who drinks from it or by the one who presents it. After communicating, each returns to his seat.

246. Si Communio fit bibendo directe ex calice, unus ex his modis potest adhiberi:

a) Celebrans principalis, stans in medio altaris, accipit calicem et secreto dicit: Sanguis Christi custódiat me in vitam ætérnam, et paulum Sanguinis sumit et calicem diacono vel concelebranti tradit. Communionem fidelibus deinde distribuit *(cf. nn. 160–162)*.

   Concelebrantes unus post alium, vel bini si duo calices adhibentur, ad altare accedunt, genuflectunt, Sanguinem sumunt, labrum calicis abstergunt et ad suam sedem redeunt.

b) Celebrans principalis Sanguinem Domini sumit de more stans in medio altaris.

   Concelebrantes vero Sanguinem Domini sumere possunt locis suis manendo et ex calice, ipsis a diacono vel ab uno concelebrante oblato, bibendo; aut etiam tradendo sibi deinceps calicem. Calix semper abstergitur vel ab eo qui bibit vel ab illo qui calicem præsentat. Singuli, cum communicaverint, ad suam sedem redeunt.

---

see Schaefer and Pierce, 337 below) they are clearly exceptions; the fullness of the sacramental sign is in eating the host and drinking from the chalice (see no. 281 below).

246. In describing Communion from the chalice, this article includes a few minor changes from *IGMR1975*. In the first option, when concelebrants individually approach the altar, *IGMR2002* adds the directive that each is to genuflect before partaking. Furthermore, the wiping of the chalice by a deacon or concelebrant (*IGMR1975*, no. 201) has been omitted from the text. The purpose of handing the chalice to a deacon is left unstated here. Presumably, since the deacon is to receive Communion only after the concelebrants have finished (no. 244 above), the intent here is that the deacon will serve the chalice to the

247. The deacon reverently drinks at the altar all of the Blood of Christ that remains, assisted, if necessary, by some of the concelebrants. He then carries the chalice over to the credence table and there he or a duly instituted acolyte purifies, wipes, and arranges it in the usual way (cf. no. 183).

247. Diaconus totum Christi Sanguinem qui remansit ad altare reverenter sumit, adiuvantibus, si casus fert, aliquibus concelebrantibus, dein calicem ad abacum transfert, ibique ipse vel acolythus rite institutus more solito eum purificat, abstergit et componit *(cf. n. 183)*.

248. The Communion of the concelebrants may also be arranged so that each concelebrant communicates the Body of the Lord at the altar and, immediately afterwards, the Blood of the Lord.

248. Communio concelebrantium ita etiam potest ordinari, ut singuli ad altare Corpori et, statim postea, Sanguini Domini communicent.

---

concelebrants, an action that could seem superfluous when the concelebrants come to the altar to receive from the chalice,[41] but also seems to respect the traditional role of the deacon as cupbearer (see no. 180 above). When the concelebrants approach the altar two by two, the role of the deacon in wiping the chalice is dropped, and that action is now left to the concelebrants themselves (no. 246a). These changes simplify the procedure a little. The second option, in which concelebrants receive from the chalice while remaining in their places, seems more effective in not prolonging the rite unduly.

Notable is the directive that the principal celebrant distributes Communion to the faithful immediately after he has received, without waiting for the concelebrants to finish receiving. Waiting would introduce a long delay between the invitation to Communion and the actual distribution to the other members of the assembly, interrupting the flow of the Communion rite for them.[42]

247. This article (like no. 244 above) is less clear than *IGMR1975,* no. 204. The latter clearly states that the deacon receives last. Since concelebration will normally involve a greater number of vessels to be purified, it would be appropriate to cover them suitably and purify them later.[43]

248. *IGMR2002* provides yet another alternative for the concelebrants' Communion, in which they approach the altar to receive both the Body and Blood of the Lord. Since nothing is said about the concelebrants genuflecting before communicating from the chalice (as in no. 246), one can presume that the genuflection at the middle of the altar before receiving the host suffices. The "rite chosen . . . for Communion from the chalice" *(ritu pro Communione calicis*

41. At an earlier time in the church, Communion was administered to all, including the presider. See Taft, "Receiving Communion–A Forgotten Symbol," *Worship* 57 (1983): 412–18.

42. GCE, no. 51, states: "If there are many concelebrating priests, the Communion of the liturgical assembly should not be delayed. There is no need for all the concelebrants to finish receiving Holy Communion before distribution to the assembly can commence."

43. See above, nos. 163 and 183; also GCE, no. 52, allows this option.

In this case the principal celebrant receives Communion under both kinds in the usual way (cf. no. 158), observing, however, the rite chosen in each particular instance for Communion from the chalice; and the other concelebrants should follow suit.

After the principal celebrant's Communion, the chalice is placed on another corporal at the side of the altar. The concelebrants approach the middle of the altar one after another, genuflect, and receive the Body of the Lord; then they go to the side of the altar and consume the Blood of the Lord, following the rite chosen for Communion from the chalice, as has just been said.

The Communion of the deacon and the purification of the chalice take place as already described.

249. If the concelebrants' Communion is by intinction, the principal celebrant receives the Body and Blood of the Lord in the usual way, but making sure that enough of the precious Blood remains in the chalice for the Communion of the concelebrants. Then the deacon, or one of the concelebrants, arranges the chalice as appropriate in the center of the altar or at the side on another corporal together with the paten containing particles of the host.

The concelebrants approach the altar one after another, genuflect, and take a particle, dip it partly into the chalice, and, holding

Hoc in casu, celebrans principalis sub utraque specie Communionem more solito sumit *(cf. n. 158),* servato tamen ritu pro Communione calicis singulis in casibus electo, quem ceteri concelebrantes sequantur.

Communione autem celebrantis principalis peracta, calix ad latus altaris super aliud corporale deponitur. Concelebrantes unus post alium ad medium altaris accedunt, genuflectunt et Corpori Domini communicant; transeunt deinde ad latus altaris, et Sanguinem Domini sumunt, iuxta ritum pro Communione calicis electum, ut supra dictum est.

Eodem modo ac supra fiunt et Communio diaconi et purificatio calicis.

249. Si Communio concelebrantium fit per intinctionem, celebrans principalis more solito Corpus et Sanguinem Domini sumit, attendens tamen ut in calice satis Sanguinis remaneat ad Communionem concelebrantium. Diaconus deinde, vel unus e concelebrantibus, calicem aut in medio altaris, aut ad latus eius super aliud corporale, una cum patena continente particulas hostiæ, opportune disponit.

Concelebrantes, unus post alium, ad altare accedunt, genuflectunt, particulam accipiunt, eam partim in calicem intingunt et, purificatorium ori submittentes, intinc-

---

. . . *electo)* by the concelebrants presumably refers to the options named in no. 245: by drinking, intinction, tube, or spoon. In order not to separate symbolically the concelebrants from the assembly, it would be appropriate to have all in the assembly communicate from the chalice and to adopt the same manner of communicating for all. This raises questions about the use of the tube or spoon, which are not listed as options for Communion under both forms for the faithful (see no. 285 below).

249. In describing how concelebrants would receive Communion by intinction, this article repeats the provisions of *IGMR1975,* no. 206 with one small change: as they receive the intincted particle, the concelebrants hold a purificator rather than a paten under their chins.

a purificator under their chin, consume the intincted particle. They then return to their places as at the beginning of Mass.

The deacon also receives Communion by intinction and to the concelebrant's words *Corpus et Sanguis Christi (The Body and Blood of Christ)* makes the response, *Amen*. The deacon, however, consumes at the altar all that remains of the Precious Blood, assisted, if necessary, by some of the concelebrants. He carries the chalice to the credence table and there he or a duly instituted acolyte purifies, wipes and arranges it in the usual way.

tam particulam sumunt, ac deinde ad loca sua recedunt ut initio Missæ.

Per intinctionem Communionem accipit etiam diaconus, qui Amen respondet concelebranti sibi dicenti: Corpus et Sanguis Christi. Diaconus autem ad altare totum Sanguinem qui remansit sumit, adiuvantibus, si casus fert, aliquibus concelebrantibus, calicem ad abacum transfert, ibique ipse vel acolythus rite institutus more solito eum purificat, abstergit et componit.

The Concluding Rites

250. Everything else is done by the principal celebrant in the usual way until the end of Mass (cf. nos. 166–168), while the other concelebrants remain at their seats.

251. Before leaving the altar, the concelebrants make a profound bow to the altar. For his part the principal celebrant, along with the deacon, venerates the altar with a kiss in the usual way.

Ritus conclusionis

250. Cetera usque ad finem Missæ fiunt more solito *(cf. nn. 166–168)* a celebrante principali, concelebrantibus suis sedibus remanentibus.

251. Concelebrantes, antequam ab altari discedant, altari profundam inclinationem faciunt. Celebrans vero principalis cum diacono altare de more osculo veneratur.

The Concluding Rites

250–251. These two articles repeat the parallel material in *IGMR1975,* nos. 207–208, with one addition: the deacon reverences the altar with the principal celebrant. Nothing is said about the dismissal. According to no. 185 above, the deacon is to dismiss the people. The earlier provision for one of the concelebrants to perform the functions of the deacon if no deacon is present (nos. 208, 212, 239, 240, and 246a-b) suggests that one of the concelebrants might also carry out the function of dismissing the people.

Concluding Reflections

The rite of concelebration promulgated in 1965 was incorporated into *IGMR1970* in a simplified form. *IGMR2002* leaves the 1970 version virtually unchanged and does not address concerns raised by four decades of pastoral practice. Three such concerns woven through the preceding commentary deserve to be highlighted in conclusion.

1. **Clarity of sign** is a principle underlying the Vatican II renewal of the liturgy (see *SC*, nos. 34, 50, and 59). All *IGMR*s have used the sign of unity as the leading descriptor for "concelebration, which appropriately expresses the unity

of the priesthood, of the Sacrifice, and also of the whole People of God" (*Concelebratio qua unitas sacerdotii et sacrificii necnon totius populi Dei opportune manifestatur,* no. 199). The above commentary has named two areas of concern about how unity is symbolized in actual practice. One is that the unity of the priesthood can obscure the presidential role visually, ritually, and audibly. The other is that the unity of the priesthood can obscure and diminish the fundamental unity of the whole People of God. This can be especially problematic when there is a large number of concelebrants. In each of these two areas of concern, attention must be paid in pastoral practice to questions of vesture, seating, gesture, and the proclamation of the Eucharistic Prayer if concelebration is to communicate an integral unity clearly and effectively.

2. **Fully effective liturgy** requires engagement of the faithful that is not only outward, but also inward (*SC,* no. 11). The example of priests is key (*SC,* no. 19). The commentary has noted ways in which the performance of the concelebrants can distract the faithful from prayer or hinder their full participation. Chief among such instances are seating arrangements that block the view of the assembly or put them at a distance during the proclamation of the Eucharistic Prayer, an uncoordinated and fragmented proclamation of the Eucharistic Prayer, a protracted exchange of peace among the concelebrants, a long delay between the invitation to Communion and the distribution to the other members of the assembly, leaving them to wait while the concelebrants receive, and a disparity in the manner of sharing the cup by concelebrants and the rest of the faithful. In these and other ways of performing the rites, the concelebrants can either enhance or detract from the unity of the assembly and the prayerful dignity and beauty of the celebration.

3. **"A simple and attractive beauty** in everything that is said or done in the liturgy is the most effective invitation" to encountering the mystery of God.[44] *IGMR2002* instructs that "The gestures and posture of the priest, the deacon, and the ministers, as well as those of the people, ought to contribute to making the entire celebration resplendent with beauty and noble simplicity, so that the true and full meaning of the different parts of the celebration is evident and that the participation of all is fostered" (*Gestus et corporis habitus tum sacerdotis, diaconi, et ministrorum, tum populi eo contendere debent ut tota celebratio decore nobilique simplicitate fulgeat, diversarum eius partium vera plenaque significatio percipiatur et omnium participatio foveatur,* no. 42). The commentary has drawn attention to things which either foster or militate against that sense of beauty, e.g., vestments that match, the harmonious design of the seating for the presider and concelebrants, a dignified pace and tone of voice worthy of the Eucharistic Prayer being proclaimed, and unison singing by concelebrants which enhances the beauty of the Eucharistic Prayer. It is the beauty of all the symbols from

44. See EACW, no. 12. See also John Paul II, *Letter to Artists* (Chicago: Liturgy Training Publications, 1999), nos. 6 and 16.

which the celebration is woven,[45] including the worship space itself,[46] that bears an unspoken invitation to the faithful to enter into God's presence and embrace. Concelebration is certainly worthy of pastoral attention to that kind of beauty if it is to be effective in gathering the faithful into oneness in Christ at "the table both of God's word and of Christ's Body" (*mensa tam verbi Dei quam Corporis Christi*, no. 28).

45. See *Catholicae Ecclesiae Catechismus*, no. 1145.
46. *Built of Living Stones*, nos. 44 and 142ff.

GIRM—Notes (English)

101. Cf. Second Vatican Ecumenical Council, Constitution on the Sacred Liturgy, *Sacrosanctum Concilium*, no. 57; *Codex Iuris Canonici*, can. 902.

102. Cf. Sacred Congregation of Rites, Instruction *Eucharisticum mysterium*, On the worship of the Eucharist, 25 May 1967, no. 47: AAS 59 (1967), p. 566.

103. Cf. ibid., p. 565.

104. Cf. Benedict XV, Apostolic Constitution *Incruentum altaris sacrificium*, 10 August 1915: AAS 7 (1915), pp. 401–404.

IGMR—Notes (Latin)

101. Cf. Conc. Œcum. Vat. II, Const. de sacra Liturgia, *Sacrosanctum Concilium*, n. 57; *Codex Iuris Canonici*, can. 902.

102. Cf. S. Congr. Rituum, Instr. *Eucharisticum mysterium*, diei 25 maii 1967, n. 47: A.A.S. 59 (1967) p. 566.

103. Cf. *ibidem*, p. 565.

104. Cf. Benedictus XV, Const. Ap. *Incruentum altaris sacrificium*, diei 10 augusti 1915: A.A.S. 7 (1915) pp. 401–404.

CHAPTER IV.III

Mass at Which Only One Minister Participates

(*DE MISSA, CUIUS UNUS TANTUM MINISTER PARTICIPAT*)

Mary Schaefer and Joanne M. Pierce

Overview

The title of this subsection in previously published *Institutio Generalis Missalis Romani* (*IGMR*) was "Mass without a Congregation" (*De Missa Sine Populo*); in *IGMR2002*, however, this is changed to the more positive description "Mass at which Only One Minister Participates" (*De Missa, cuius Unus tantum Minister Participat*). The change in title implies a significant theological trajectory in referring to "private" Mass.[1]

1. The descriptive definition of a "private" Mass given by Josef A. Jungmann remains useful: "a mass celebrated for its own sake, with no thought of anyone participating, a mass where only the prescribed server is in attendance or even where no one is present, as was the case with the *missa solitaria*." See his *The Mass of the Roman Rite*, trans. Francis Brunner, 2 vols. (Westminster: Christian Classics, 1986), I:215. Discussion of Masses at which, however large the congregation, only the priest communicates indicates that these were considered private at the Council of Trent (1545–62). See *Concilium Tridentinum. Diarorum, actorum, epistularum, tractatuum nova collectio*, ed. Görres-Gesellschaft, Vol. XIII, *Tractatuum pars altera, volumen prius*, ed. H. Jedin (Freiburg im Br.: Herder, 1967), 712, ll. 1–2. Paul VI's 1965 definition, a Mass celebrated "with no one present except the server," shows current usage; *Mysterium fidei*, no. 32, in DOL, no. 1176. Mass in which a single priest takes over all functions of other ministers also may be called "private."

The origins of the private Mass, of which nascent Western monasticism is an important locus, are still debated. Scholars have offered several theories. Otto Nussbaum and Cyrille Vogel explored the growing sacerdotalization of the liturgy in keeping with the increase in the numbers of monk-priests and the offering of Mass to satisfy devotion and concern for salvation of priest or donor. Votive Masses were connected with the stipend system of clerical support in private chapels (priests given "absolute ordination," i.e. without official responsibility for a community, celebrated such Masses). The stipend was also adopted to support parish priests. Angelus Häussling proposed that ordinary, intimate celebrations such as those for small groups in house or shrine or at a grave later on developed, in monasteries and ca-

Carolingian and later decrees forbade Mass said by the priest alone.[2] Mass said with the assistance of only one server and no congregation was recognized as an anomaly throughout the Middle Ages, since the Latin greeting *Dominus vobiscum* in the second person plural is addressed to multiple participants and the reference to those standing around the altar, the *omnes circumstantes* commemorated in the Roman Canon, presumes them.[3] The normative "read" Mass thus included presider, at least two ministers, and congregation. Ministers represented the congregation participating in the Mass. When the congregation no longer responded to the priest[4] or when the congregation was altogether absent, the presence of the two ministers maintained the plural character of the assembly.

From the first discussions of the new *Ordo Missae* in 1967, the basic distinction between forms of celebration "was not the presence or the absence of singing but the participation of the faithful."[5] The *Ordo Missae* of Paul VI (d. 1978) published in 1969 includes the apostolic constitution *Missale Romanum*, *IGMR1969*, the prefaces, and the four Eucharistic Prayers. Pope Paul VI addressed the issue of the *Ordo Missae* with only one server when he asked that the plural form *Dominus vobiscum*, rather than the singular form *Dominus tecum*, be kept as the opening greeting; and that the *Orate, fratres* (earlier considered for omission even in the *Missa normativa*) be said in order to safeguard the communal nature of Mass without a congregation.[6]

Two specific issues arise concerning the general title of this section of Chapter IV. First, it is significant that *IGMR2002* opts for the conciliar (*Sacrosanctum*

---

thedrals, into imitation by simultaneous celebration of the liturgy of the city-church of Rome. See "Excursus: The 'Private' Mass," in Cyrille Vogel, *Medieval Liturgy*, rev. and trans. William Storey and Niels Rasmussen (Washington, DC: The Pastoral Press, 1986), 156–58.

2. "*Ne presbyter missam solus cantet*"; "*Sacerdos missam solus nequaquam celebret*" in J.M. Hanssens, "*Fungiturne minister missae privatae diaconi et subdiaconi vicibus*," *Ephemerides liturgicae* 48 (1934): 410–12.

3. In his influential *Micrologus* (ca. 1089) Bernold of Constance cites what he thought were the decrees of popes Anacletus (first century) and Soter (d. ca. 175) which established that the priest should be joined by at least two others, viz. server and member of the assembly (*PL* 151:979c). The medievals recognized the anomaly presented by a priest with one server and the plural greetings *Dominus vobiscum*, the *Orate, fratres*, and the blessings. Among the list of abuses against the sacrifice of the Mass drawn up at the Council of Trent on 8 August 1562 was the saying of Mass with fewer than two *auditores*. "*Item missa privata non dicatur, nisi duae utrimque candelae accendantur et ad minimum duo adsint auditores*" (Council of Trent. *Concilium Tridentinum*, Vol. VIII, *Actorum pars quinta*, ed. S. Ehses [Freiburg im Br.: Herder, 1964], 918, ll. 29–30), also Hanssens, "Fungiturne minister?" 412.

4. Bernold's *Micrologus* affirmed that the lay members of the congregation should join in the responses (*PL* 151:979C-D).

5. Annibale Bugnini, *The Reform of the Liturgy 1948–1975* (Collegeville, MN: The Liturgical Press, 1990), 116.

6. *Ordo Missae* (Vatican: Polyglot Press, 1969), 174, as reported by Bugnini, *Reform of the Liturgy*, 383–84. Bugnini's footnote referred to the "truthfulness" which would be manifested by *Dominus tecum*.

III. Mass at which Only One Minister Participates

252. At a Mass celebrated by a priest with only one minister to assist him and to make the responses, the rite of Mass with

III. De Missa, cuius Unus tantum Minister Participat

252. In Missa quæ celebratur a sacerdote cui unus tantum minister assistit et respondet, servatur ritus Missæ cum populo *(cf.*

Concilium [*SC*], no. 14) language of "participation" in the title[7] rather than the more traditional language of the ministers "assisting" at Mass. This raises the question, however, whether this shift in language is accompanied by a concomitant shift in the theological model at work in this chapter of *IGMR2002*. This question is raised in light of the wording of no. 252's opening sentence, "At a Mass celebrated by a priest with only one minister to assist him . . ." *(In Missa quae celebratur a sacerdote cui unus tantum minister assistit*). This language and image originated under the influence of a scholastic theological model in which Mass was understood primarily as the work of the celebrating priest. This theology, dominant from the late twelfth century until Vatican Council II (1962–65), undergirded practices surrounding the "private" Mass. Studies of the early and medieval Church show that focus on the celebrating priest to the exclusion of the whole assembly represents a reversal of the patristic and monastic understandings of the Eucharist as an integral action of the whole gathered Church. The twentieth-century liturgical movement and its accompanying scholarship were influential in recovering this broader theological understanding of the liturgy as the work of Christ, head and members, in which the assembly, presided over by priest or bishop, together offers the sacrifice and is an active subject of the liturgical action (see Power and Vincie, 52 above).

In predicating the theological notion of "participation" of the assisting minister, the English title of this section is evidently inspired by *SC*'s call for the people's "full, conscious, and active participation" (nos. 14 and 50). This theological concept implies that the minister represents an assembly which is absent and so functions in its stead. A preliminary translation of the title into English by the International Commission on English in the Liturgy in June of 2001 read "assists." Retaining the notion of "assisting at" (the wording found in no. 252) rather than "participating in" may suggest that "participates" in the title of this section is an afterthought.

252. This article is a conflation of two statements that began the section in *IGMR1975*, nos. 209 and 210. These virtually unchanged texts provided a more explicit transition to the new *Ordo Missae* for priests who were used to the practice of saying a "private" Mass every day, explaining how the minister was

7. Language of the "participation" of the people in the liturgy was in evidence in papal writings of the twentieth century, e.g., the introduction of the 1903 *motu proprio Tra le Sollecitudini* from Pius X (d. 1914), the 1928 apostolic constitution *Divini cultus* (no. 9) of Pius XI (d. 1939) and the 1947 encyclical *Mediator Dei* (e.g., no. 5) of Pius XII (d. 1958).

a congregation is followed (cf. nos. 120–169) the minister saying the people's parts as appropriate.

nn. 120–169), ministro, pro opportunitate, partes populi proferente.

"to assist him and to make the responses" (*tantum minister assistit et respondet*). All versions of *IGMR* clearly state that the "rite of Mass with a congregation" (*ritus Missae cum populo*) is to be used, and assume that a priest (or bishop) will usually celebrate Mass with at least one minister.

The word "assist" is already found in the formulation of 1917 *Codex Iuris Canonici (CIC1917)*, c. 813, par. 1: "A priest should not celebrate Mass without a minister who assists him and responds." The Latin *adsisto, adsistere, adstiti/astiti* (and its variant *assist-*) mean literally "to place oneself near" or "to stand by." GIRM2003's translation as "assist," which connotes help, prescinds from the issue of posture. Given the regulation in *IGMR2002* requiring kneeling by people (no. 43) and even by the deacon (no. 179) during portions of the Eucharistic Prayer, "assist" serves as a neutral term which permits different postures for priest and people, a clerical-lay differentiation not common in the pre-Scholastic and Byzantine traditions.

In summary, there appears to be some tension within *IGMR2002*. The minister is defined both as one who "participates" and one who "assists." Emphasis on the latter diminishes the notion of the active participation of the minister acting on behalf of an absent assembly[8] to the more secondary role of "assisting" the priest-presider. However, the minister is to say the people's parts "as appropriate" (*pro opportunitate*). This suggests that the responses manifesting "participation" have priority over actions which materially "assist" the priest. *CIC1917*, c. 2, par. 1 instructed that "The minister serving at Mass should not be a woman unless, in the absence of a man, for a just cause, it is so arranged that the woman respond from afar and by no means approach the altar."[9] In this instance a woman is viewed as server because she is making the responses. Thus, even *CIC1917* seems to affirm that the responses constitute the essential collaboration of the "minister serving."

8. For Thomas Aquinas the server "represents the whole Catholic people, and in that capacity answers the priest in the plural." *Summa Theologiae*, III, q. 83, art. 5, ad 12; quoted in James Coriden, Thomas Green and Donald Heintschel, eds., *The Code of Canon Law: A Text and Commentary* (New York: Paulist Press, 1985), 648; and John P. Beal, James A. Coriden, Thomas J. Green, eds., *New Commentary on the Code of Canon Law* (New York: Paulist Press, 2000), 1102.

9. On the present discipline which allows female altar servers see John M. Huels, "Female Altar Servers: The Legal Issues," in idem, *Disputed Questions in the Liturgy Today* (Chicago: Liturgy Training Publications, 1988), 27–38; *Pontificium Consilium de Legum Textibus Interpretandis, "Responsio ad propositum dubium," AAS* 86 (1994): 541–42.

253. If, however, the minister is a deacon, he performs his proper duties (cf. nos. 171–186) and likewise carries out the other parts, that is, those of the people.

254. Mass should not be celebrated without a minister or at least one of the faithful, except for a just and reasonable cause. In this case, the greetings, the introductory or explanatory remarks, and the blessing at the end of Mass are omitted.

253. Si tamen minister est diaconus, ipse munera sibi propria peragit *(cf. nn. 171–186)*, necnon alias partes populi adimplet.

254. Celebratio sine ministro vel aliquo saltem fideli ne fiat nisi iusta et rationabili de causa. Hoc in casu salutationes, monitiones et benedictio in fine Missæ omittuntur.

---

253. Only *IGMR2002* states that the minister may be a deacon. It is clear throughout this section that the term minister is to be understood more broadly than the office of deacon. If the deacon is the only minister, he has a dual role: he is to assume the "parts" (*partes*) that would be assigned to any assisting minister representing the larger congregation; in addition, "he performs his proper duties" (*ipse munera sibi propria peragit*, cf. nos. 171–186 above). This is another example in which more than thirty years of liturgical and pastoral experience, including the restoration of the permanent diaconate, has led to further clarity in *IGMR2002*.

If the minister is a deacon, he carries out the functions proper to the deacon, server, and people. To enshrine this principle in a regulation affirms the important liturgical role of the deacon and implies that Mass with a congregation and all of its diverse ministries remains normative. In some liturgical periods in our history the "higher" order (viz., *sacerdos*) claimed the responsibilities of "lower" orders.[10] At a Mass with only a deacon participating, it is a liturgical "abuse"[11] if the priest assumes any part of the deacon's role. The converse is also true: the lower order may not claim the responsibilities of the higher order. Thus *CIC1983*, c. 907, prohibits deacons and laypersons from saying the prayers and performing the actions "proper to the celebrating priest."

254. The wording of this text in *IGMR2002* differs slightly from its predecessors (e.g. *IGMR1975*, no. 211). Whereas previous editions had only spoken of Mass "without a minister" (*sine ministro*), *IGMR2002* here speaks of Mass *sine ministro vel aliquo saltem fideli*, which the US bishops render as "without a minister or at least one of the faithful." Canadian bishops offer "without a

10. Bernold of Constance's *Micrologus* recommends that, in the absence of vested ministers, the priest take over the lesser ministries (*PL* 151:982A-B). Vestiges of this practice are detectable in Masses with a congregation when, for instance, the Sacramentary is placed on a stand rather than held by a server or the vessels are placed within reach of the priest so that a server's assistance is unnecessary.

11. In the technical language of canon law an "abuse" is an action contrary to the law.

minister or at least some of the faithful."[12] Both make clear that the celebration of Mass without a congregation is to be understood very much as an "exceptional" practice. Earlier *IGMR*s put the case a bit more strongly, and noted that Mass without a minister should not be celebrated "except in serious necessity" (*nisi ex gravi necessitate*). *IGMR2002* indicates it should not be celebrated "except for a just and reasonable cause" (*nisi iusta et rationabili de causa*).

The relaxation of the prohibition against Mass without a server, something for which Pius XII in 1949 would not grant an indult unless a member of the assembly was present,[13] may have originated with Paul VI's 1965 encyclical *Mysterium fidei*.[14] Early in the Vatican II reform suggestions were made for a Mass without a congregation, for example, that there should be only one reading, or "longer or more numerous formulas that may augment the devotion of the celebrant."[15] But the idea was discarded. There is no *Ordo Missae* for the celebration of Mass without a congregation.

CIC1983, c. 906, allows a priest "for a just and reasonable cause"[16] (*iusta et rationabili de causa*) to celebrate Mass when only one member of the faithful or one server is available and the priest is otherwise unable to participate in communal celebrations.[17] *CIC1983* has been adjusted to the wording *justa de causa* of *Mysterium fidei*, no. 32. Here the canon gives priority to a member of the assembly, allowing a priest to say Mass when one member of the faithful (not designated as minister or server) is present. On the other hand, in this article

12. The plural in the Canadian text presents what has always been considered the desirable minimum rather than the minimal number necessary for a eucharistic celebration according to current legislation.

13. Instruction *Quam plurimum*, October 1, 1949; AAS 41 (1949): 508; four exceptions are listed. See *Canon Law Digest*, ed. T. Lincoln Bouscaren, Vol. III: 1942–53 (Milwaukee: Bruce, 1954), 334–36; Coriden, Green, Heintschel, eds., *The Code of Canon Law: A Text and Commentary*, 648; Beal, Coriden, Green, eds., *New Commentary on the Code of Canon Law*, 1102.

14. In *Mysterium fidei*, no. 33 (in DOL, no. 1177), Paul VI expressed the desire that priests exercise their consecratory and sacrificial power to obtain the fruits of the Mass for themselves and for the faithful, living and dead.

15. As well, such celebrations would require a "smaller space without all the liturgical centers" (Bugnini, *The Reform of the Liturgy 1948–1975*, 340, reporting on comments and discussions of April 1964–October 1965; 356 on 1967; and 389.

16. Coriden et al., eds., *The Code of Canon Law: A Commentary*, 647–48; Beal et al., eds., *New Commentary*, 1102–1103. Translations in the British tradition read "good and reasonable cause," *Code of Canon Law*, New revised English translation (London: HarperCollins, 1997), 209.

17. These reasons include illness, infirmity, and travel but not "mere convenience" or "preference." See Coriden et al., eds., *The Code of Canon Law: A Commentary*, 648; Beal et al., eds., *New Commentary*, 1103. The "serious" causes envisioned by the Consilium members as the Order of Mass was developed in the mid-1960s included the life-situations of priests interned in concentration camps or working in remote locales. Giving a generous interpretation to c. 906, the unofficial manual written by Peter J. Elliott includes two numbers (538, 539) on "celebrating alone." The tenor of the comments suggests that this practice continues to enjoy some popularity. Elliott admits that the omissions (greetings, final blessing) which are recommended "in practice do not work for the rest of the rite" (*Ceremonies of the Modern Roman Rite* [San Francisco: Ignatius Press, 1995], 198–99 and n. 5).

255. Before Mass, the necessary vessels are prepared either at the credence table or on the righthand side of the altar.

255. Ante Missam vasa necessaria parantur vel ad abacum, vel super altare ad latus dexterum.

The Introductory Rites

256. The priest approaches the altar and, after making a profound bow along with the minister, venerates the altar with a kiss and goes to the chair. If he wishes, the priest may remain at the altar; in this case, the Missal is likewise prepared there. Then the minister or the priest says the Entrance Antiphon.

Ritus initiales

256. Sacerdos ad altare accedit et, facta cum ministro profunda inclinatione, osculo veneratur altare et sedem petit. Si libet, sacerdos potest ad altare manere; hoc in casu, ibi etiam missale paratur. Tunc minister vel sacerdos dicit antiphonam ad introitum.

IGMR2002 seems to present a hierarchy of participants in descending order, preferring a "minister" (deacon or server) to "at least one of the faithful." This seems to contradict the central role of the assembly in *SC*'s vision of the liturgy. The differences between the present liturgical regulation giving preference to a server and canon law requiring the presence of a member of the faithful may explain why the GIRM2003 title for section III equivocates.

All *IGMR*s note that "greetings" (*salutationes*) and "the blessing at the end of Mass" (*benedictio in fine Missae*) are dropped for a solitary celebration, viz., one lacking server and member of the faithful. *IGMR2002* adds that "the introductory or explanatory remarks" (*monitiones*) are also to be dropped.

255. This article is a reworking of *IGMR1975* (no. 212). The "necessary vessels" (*vasa necessaria*, not "chalice," *calix*) are prepared before Mass, either on a "credence table" (*abacus*, used in both documents) or on the "righthand side" (*ad latus dexteram*) of the altar (*IGMR1975* simply states "on the altar itself," *super altare*). *IGMR1975* also directs that the Missal be "placed on the left side of the altar" (*ad latus sinistrum altaris collocatur*). *IGMR2002* drops this directive here, but in no. 256 will note that, if the presider does not move to the chair for the Introductory Rites but remains at the altar, "the Missal is likewise prepared there" (*ibi etiam missale paratur*).

Here one can detect vestiges of post-Tridentine practices. Given the regulation in no. 306 below, that the altar-table is to hold only what is required for the sacrificial action, and given that Section III of Chapter IV presumes the assistance of a server, there seems little reason for provisions for placing cruets, bowl, and towel on the altar.

The Introductory Rites

256. *IGMR1975* (no. 213) states that the priest venerates the altar. Then he faces the server, makes the sign of the cross, and greets the server. The location of both priest and minister according to *IGMR1975* is at "the foot of the altar"

257. Then the priest, standing, makes with the minister the sign of the Cross as the priest says, *In nomine Patris (In the name of the Father)*. Facing the minister, he greets the minister choosing one of the formulas of greeting.

258. Then the Act of Penitence takes place, and, if required by the rubrics, the *Kyrie* and *Gloria* are said.

257. Deinde sacerdos cum ministro, stans, signat se signo crucis et dicit: In nómine Patris; conversus ad ministrum eum salutat, unam e formulis propositis eligendo.

258. Deinde peragitur actus pænitentialis, et, iuxta rubricas, dicitur Ký́rie et Glória.

(*ad pedes altaris*) through the penitential rite. The *IGMR1975* directive applied best to a pre-Vatican II sanctuary or traditional side-chapel in which the altar was raised on a platform of several steps and attached to the wall; possibly chair and lectern were lacking. These directives are amplified and rearranged in *IGMR2002*, implying a different configuration of the presbiterium with the altar centrally located and accessible from all sides, a presider's chair and, as we will see in no. 260, an ambo or lectern. The priest and the minister are first to make "a profound bow" (*profunda inclinatione*), then the priest alone venerates the altar "with a kiss" (*osculo*). *IGMR2002* indicates that the priest "goes to the chair" (*sedem petit*), but "if he wishes" (*si libet*), he may stay at the altar.

IGMR1975 (no. 215) notes that the priest read the entrance antiphon. In *IGMR2002* the minister or priest (in that order) recites the entrance antiphon. This preference acknowledges that recitation of the antiphon does not properly belong to the priest (see no. 48 above). The practice of the priest saying the antiphon alone, even at community Masses, is reminiscent of private Mass practice.

257. In this article *IGMR2002* relocates a section of *IGMR1975* (no. 213). The wording is almost identical with that of the earlier Instruction; however, the reference to standing at the foot of the altar (see no. 256 above) is omitted. Both priest and minister sign themselves with the cross. Then the priest, facing the minister, gives the greeting.

During the development of the introductory rites much thought was given to the opening rites, including reducing their number. Although Pope Paul VI judged the use of the greeting in a private Mass "extreme,"[18] the directive that the priest "greets the minister" (*eum salutat*) has been included in all *IGMR*s.

258. This section is a reworking of *IGMR1975*, no. 215. The reference to the recitation of the entrance antiphon was addressed above in no. 256. Next follows the "Act of Penitence" (*actus paenitentialis*, translated in GIRM1975, no. 213 as "the penitential rite"), then the *Kyrie* and *Gloria* "if required by the rubrics" (*iuxta rubricas*). Including the *Gloria* as a standard rather than exceptional element implies that in some places Mass without a congregation is normal even on Sundays and important feast days. Both *Kyrie* and *Gloria* are ordinarily sung (see nos. 52 and 53 above).

18. Bugnini, *Reform of the Liturgy*, 381.

259. Then, with hands joined, the priest says, *Oremus (Let us pray)*. After a suitable pause, with hands extended he says the collect. At the end the minister makes the acclamation, *Amen*.

259. Deinde, manibus iunctis, dicit Orémus et, interposita mora convenienti, manibus extensis, profert collectam. In fine minister acclamat: Amen.

The Liturgy of the Word

260. The readings should whenever possible be proclaimed from the ambo or a lectern.

261. After the collect, the minister reads the first reading and Psalm, the second reading, when it is to be said, and the verse for the *Alleluia* or other chant.

Liturgia verbi

260. Lectiones, quantum fieri potest, ex ambone vel ex pluteo proferuntur.

261. Dicta collecta, minister legit primam lectionem et psalmum, et, quando dicenda est, secundam lectionem atque versum ad Allelúia vel alterum cantum.

---

259. The Latin text of this section is identical to that of *IGMR1975*, no. 216. In the English texts the only change is that the earlier term "the opening prayer" is now translated as "the collect." The Latin term is the same in both (*collectam*, see no. 127 above). The priest offers the greeting and then says the collect "after a suitable pause" (*interposita mora convenienti*), providing another brief nod to the role of silence in the rite (see no. 45 above). It is the minister who responds with *Amen*.

IGMR2002 has previously noted the great importance of singing, especially those parts to be sung by the priest with the people responding (see no. 40 above). That principle applies even here. Singing a collect at Mass with one minister should never be ruled out altogether.

The Liturgy of the Word

260. This is a new directive, for *IGMR1975* does not specify a preference for reading "from the ambo or a lectern" (*ex ambone vel ex pluteo*). The inclusion of this preference underscores the importance of the ambo (see no. 309 below) and also gives the impression that the altar at which this Mass is being celebrated is a main altar table in a fully-appointed sanctuary. The presider may find himself, whether seated or standing, in the awkward position of viewing the back of the minister as the latter proclaims the Scriptures to an empty assembly hall.

261. Here, *IGMR2002* presents a slight reworking of *IGMR1975*, no. 217. The minister is to read the (non-gospel) readings, the responsorial psalm, and the verse of the gospel acclamation. This directive presumes that the minister will be literate and of sufficient age to read. Directions for singing the Alleluia or Lenten acclamation are not given. As previously noted, the Alleluia or verse before the gospel may be omitted if not sung in Masses when there is only one reading before the gospel (see no. 63c above).

262. Then the priest bows profoundly and says the *Munda cor meum (Almighty God, cleanse my heart)* and, afterwards, reads the Gospel. At the conclusion he says, *Verbum Domini (The Gospel of the Lord)*, to which the minister responds, *Laus tibi, Christe (Praise to you, Lord Jesus Christ)*. The priest then venerates the book with a kiss, saying quietly the *Per evangelica dicta (May the words of the Gospel)*.

262. Deinde sacerdos, profunde inclinatus, dicit: Munda cor meum, et postea legit Evangelium. In fine dicit: Verbum Dómini, cui minister respondet: Laus tibi, Christe. Sacerdos deinde librum osculo veneratur, secreto dicens: Per evangélica dicta.

263. Afterwards, if required by the rubrics, the priest says the Creed together with the minister.

263. Sacerdos postea symbolum, iuxta rubricas, una cum ministro recitat.

264. The Prayer of the Faithful follows, which may be said even in this form of Mass. The priest introduces and concludes it, with the minister announcing the intentions.

264. Sequitur oratio universalis, quæ etiam in hac Missa dici potest. Sacerdos introducit et concludit orationem, minister vero intentiones profert.

IGMR1975's option that the priest himself could read these lessons has been eliminated. This provision that the priest not proclaim the scriptural passages prior to the gospel is an important one, underscoring the extraordinary nature of the earlier provision that, at Masses with an assembly but where no lector is present, "the priest himself proclaims all the readings and the Psalm" (*sacerdos ipse omnes lectiones et psalmum profert*, no. 135). This statement reminds pastors and communities to nurture liturgical ministries such as that of the lector among the people. It further affirms *IGMR2002*'s earlier instruction that, whether ordained or lay, in fulfilling liturgical offices or duties, people "should carry out solely but completely that which pertains to them" (*solum et totum id agant, quod ad ipsos pertinet*, no. 91).

262. This article reworks *IGMR1975*, no. 218. The earlier reference to the priest remaining "in the same place" (*manens in eodem loco*) is dropped. As in multiple other places in this Instruction (e.g., no. 49), his bow is now described as "profound" (*profunde inclinatus*). While all editions stipulate that he recite the *Munda cor meum*, as is its tendency the current Instruction includes more details regarding the concluding verses at the end of the gospel and clarifies the sequence. *IGMR2002* adds that the priest first says *Verbum Domini* and specifies that the minister responds with *Laus tibi*. Only then does the priest kiss the gospel book and quietly recite the *Per evangelica dicta*.

263. The Latin text of this section regarding the recitation of the Creed is identical to that of *IGMR1975* (no. 219). GIRM2003 differs slightly but not significantly from GIRM1975, e.g., besides a change in the word order, it translates *symbolum* as "Creed" rather than "profession of faith."

264. The first sentence of this article is the same as in *IGMR1975*, no. 220, indicating that the "Prayer of the Faithful" (*oratio universalis*, translated in

The Liturgy of the Eucharist

265. In the Liturgy of the Eucharist, everything is done as in a Mass with a congregation, with the following exceptions.

266. After the acclamation at the end of the embolism that follows the Lord's Prayer, the priest says the prayer *Domine Iesu Christe, qui dixisti (Lord Jesus Christ, you said).* He then adds, *Pax Domini sit semper vobiscum (The peace of the Lord be with you always),* and the minister answers, *Et cum spiritu tuo (And also with you).* The priest gives the sign of peace to the minister, if appropriate.

Liturgia eucharistica

265. In Liturgia eucharistica omnia fiunt sicut in Missa cum populo, præter ea quæ sequuntur.

266. Expleta acclamatione in fine embolismi qui sequitur Orationem dominicam, sacerdos dicit orationem Dómine Iesu Christe, qui dixísti; ac deinde subiungit: Pax Dómini sit semper vobíscum, cui minister respondet: Et cum spíritu tuo. Pro opportunitate sacerdos dat pacem ministro.

GIRM1975 as "general intercessions") "may be said" (*dici potest*) but is not required at this kind of eucharistic celebration. More significantly, however, the roles of the priest and minister have been changed. In *IGMR1975* the priest "gives the intentions and the server makes the response" *(sacerdote intentiones proferente, ministro respondente*). In *IGMR2002,* however, the roles are both clarified and reversed: the priest "introduces and concludes" (*Sacerdos introducit et concludit*) the prayer of the faithful, while it is the minister who "announc[es] the intentions" (*intentiones profert*). This might again indicate a different focus after several decades of liturgical celebration: in 1970 it was reasonable to stress the acclamation following each intention (a new element for both priest and people), but by 2002 the stress had shifted instead to an awareness that the announcement of the intentions is not proper to the role of the priest but belongs first to the deacon, then to cantor, lector, or some other member of the assembly (nos. 138 and 171c above).

The Liturgy of the Eucharist

265. In turning to the Liturgy of the Eucharist, *IGMR2002* adds a new introductory statement, emphasizing that this liturgical unit is structurally identical to a Mass with a congregation. However, there are some exceptions to be noted and explained more fully in the following paragraphs. Note that the priest does not act as his own server even if the single minister has already served as lector.

266. At this point, *IGMR2002* begins the list of exceptions (signaled in no. 265 above) with the Lord's Prayer. Omitted entirely are three earlier sections dealing with the preparation of the gifts and the Eucharistic Prayer (*IGMR1975,* nos. 221–223), which were redundancies easily eliminated in view of no. 265. *IGMR1975*, nos. 224 and 225 dealing with the Lord's Prayer are conflated here. The Latin is virtually identical between the two; so is the English, with the exception of the direction concerning the sign of peace. In the GIRM1975 text, the

267. Then, while he says the *Agnus Dei (Lamb of God)* with the minister, the priest breaks the host over the paten. After the *Agnus Dei,* he performs the commingling, saying quietly the *Haec commixtio (May this mingling).*

267. Deinde, dum dicit Agnus Dei cum ministro, sacerdos frangit hostiam super patenam. Expleto Agnus Dei, facit immixtionem, dicens secreto: Hæc commíxtio.

268. After the commingling, the priest quietly says the prayer *Domine Iesu Christe, Fili Dei vivi (Lord Jesus Christ, Son of the living God)* or *Perceptio (Lord Jesus Christ, with faith in your love and mercy).* Then he genuflects, takes the host, and, if the minister is to receive Communion, turns to the min-

268. Post immixtionem, sacerdos dicit secreto orationem Dómine Iesu Christe, Fili Dei vivi vel Percéptio; deinde genuflectit, hostiam accipit et, si minister Communionem recipit, versus ad eum et hostiam aliquantulum elevatam super patenam vel super calicem tenens, dicit: Ecce Agnus Dei

---

priest "may give" (no. 225) the sign of peace to the minister, but in GIRM2003 the priest does so "if appropriate"; the Latin for both is *pro opportunitate.* The change in translation could suggest that the sign of peace is not to be regarded as optional but should be exchanged unless other circumstances dictate. It is not clear what circumstances would make exchanging the sign of peace seem inappropriate here (see no. 82 above).

267. The Latin text of this section concerning the *Agnus Dei,* fraction and the commingling is identical with that of *IGMR1975,* no. 226. The English texts differ slightly: in GIRM1975 the priest "places a particle in the chalice," but in the US and Canadian versions of GIRM2003 he "performs the commingling."

268. This lengthy section deals with the *Agnus Dei* and reception of Communion during a Mass with one minister. The first sentences are almost identical with those found in *IGMR1975* (no. 227). One minor change is made to the gesture accompanying the invitation "This is the Lamb of God" (*Ecce Agnus Dei*). In the earlier *IGMR,* if the minister is going to receive Communion the priest turns to him and holds the host "a little above the paten" (*aliquantulum elevatam super patenam, IGMR1975,* no. 227), then recites the *Ecce Agnus Dei*; in *IGMR2002* the priest may hold the host above either the paten "or the chalice" (*vel super calicem*), as in no. 84 above. Both priest and minister are to make the response "Lord, I am not worthy" (*Domine, non sum dignus*). *IGMR1975* specifies that this response is made "once" (*semel*), a word that is dropped in *IGMR2002.*

If "the minister does not receive communion" (*minister Communionem non recipit; IGMR1975* instead uses the phrase *Corpus Christi non participat*), the priest is directed to perform the same actions as in *IGMR1975*: genuflect, take the host, and "quietly" (*secreto*) recite "Lord, I am not worthy." In keeping with its tendency to note more details, *IGMR2002* includes here the recitation of the Communion formula "May the Body of Christ bring" *(Corpus Christi custodiat)* not found in *IGMR1975.* GIRM1975 translates *Corpus Christi sumit* as "eats the body

ister and, holding the host a little above the paten or the chalice, says the *Ecce Agnus Dei (This is the Lamb of God)*, adding with the minister the *Domine, non sum dignus (Lord, I am not worthy)*. Facing the altar, the priest then partakes of the Body of Christ. If, however, the minister does not receive Communion, the priest, after genuflecting, takes the host and, facing the altar, says quietly the *Domine, non sum dignus (Lord, I am not worthy)* and the *Corpus Christi custodiat (May the Body of Christ bring)* and then receives the Body of Christ. Then he takes the chalice and says quietly, *Sanguis Christi custodiat (May the Blood of Christ bring)*, and then consumes the Blood of Christ.

et cum ipso subdit: Dómine, non sum dignus. Deinde, ad altare conversus, Corpus Christi sumit. Si vero minister Communionem non recipit, facta genuflexione, sacerdos hostiam accipit et, ad altare conversus, dicit secreto: Dómine, non sum dignus, et Corpus Christi custódiat ac dein Christi Corpus sumit. Deinde accipit calicem et secreto dicit: Sanguis Christi custódiat et Sanguinem sumit.

269. Before Communion is given to the minister, the Communion Antiphon is said by the minister or by the priest himself.

269. Antequam Communio detur ministro, dicitur a ministro vel ab ipso sacerdote antiphona ad Communionem.

---

of Christ," while the US and Canadian versions of GIRM2003 read "partakes of the Body of Christ."

The directions for the cup are also slightly different. *IGMR1975* simply states that "The blood of Christ is received as directed in the Order of Mass with a congregation" *(Sumptio Sanguinis Christi fit ut in Ordine Missae cum populo describitur)*. *IGMR2002* drops this line; it substitutes a directive that the priest takes the cup and "says quietly" (*secreto dicit*) the Communion formula for the cup (*Sanguis Christi custodiat*).

Curiously the rubrics for the minister's Communion are omitted. Perhaps they should have been included to indicate that Communion of both priest and minister is the normative practice. Sharing the host is the logical outcome of the fraction rite and, in light of no. 321 below, it is presumed that the minister receives a portion of the priest's host which has been broken. Also, given the many affirmations in *IGMR2002* about Communion under both kinds (e.g., nos. 72 and 85 above), it is presumed that the minister also receives from the chalice. The missing rubrics should be supplied in the next edition of *IGMR* to safeguard the principles of full, conscious and active participation (*SC*, no. 14); in the absence of such specific directives, contrary practices may prevail.

269. One change here, parallel to that found in no. 256 above, is that *IGMR2002* indicates that the Communion antiphon "is said by the minister or by the priest himself" *(dicitur a ministro vel ab ipso sacerdote)*, whereas *IGMR1975* indicates that it is only to be said by the priest (no. 228). Furthermore, by mentioning the minister first, *IGMR2002* again suggests that the priority is for this action to be fulfilled by the minister, not the priest (cf. no. 264 above). This reso-

270. The priest purifies the chalice at the credence table or at the altar. If the chalice is purified at the altar, it may be carried to the credence table by the minister or may again be placed on the altar at the side.

270. Sacerdos calicem purificat ad abacum vel ad altare. Si calix ad altare purificatur, potest ad abacum a ministro deferri, aut super altare ad latus reponi.

271. After the purification of the chalice, the priest should observe some moments of silence, after which he says the prayer after Communion.

271. Purificatione calicis expleta, oportet ut sacerdos aliquam pausam silentii servet; postea vero dicit orationem post Communionem.

The Concluding Rites

272. The concluding rites are carried out as at a Mass with a congregation, but the dismissal formula is omitted. The priest venerates the altar in the usual way with a kiss and, after making a profound bow with the minister, departs.

Ritus conclusionis

272. Ritus conclusionis perficiuntur sicut in Missa cum populo, Ite, missa est omisso. Sacerdos altare de more osculo veneratur et, facta profunda inclinatione cum ministro, recedit.

---

nates with the pattern through this section of limiting the presider to actions that are truly proper to him (cf. no. 261 above). Because of the order of priority clearly stated here, access to the text of the Communion antiphon by the minister should be assured.

270. Following the directives outlined in no. 163 above, the chalice is to be purified either at the credence table or at the altar. *IGMR1975* instructs that this was to take place "at the side of the altar" (*ad latus altaris*, no. 229). The preferred place for the purification of the chalice is now the credence table.

271. This article further stresses the importance of silence in the ritual action, noting that "the priest should observe some moments of silence" *(oportet ut sacerdos aliquam pausam silentii servet*). This is a stronger statement than that found in *IGMR1975*, which notes that "the priest may observe a period of silence" (*sacerdos aliquam pausam silentii servare potest*, no. 230).

Rather than immediately purifying the chalice, it might be more seemly for the priest and minister to observe some moments of silence immediately following Communion and prior to the prayer after Communion. The chalice can be purified after Mass is concluded.

The Concluding Rites

272. The text of *IGMR2002* makes slight changes in word order in the first sentence, but no substantial change from what is found in *IGMR1975*, no. 231. GIRM2003 mandates the omission of the dismissal phrase (*Ite, missa est*, etc.*)*. Unlike *IGMR1975* (no. 231), *IGMR2002* adds a final sentence on kissing the altar and bowing profoundly with the minister before leaving.

Conclusion

This section of Chapter IV in *IGMR2002* expresses both a sense of clarity and an underlying tension. Clearly the Order of Mass with a Congregation (treated in the previous two sections of Chapter IV) is normative for celebrating Eucharist. The directions for celebrating Masses in which only one minister participates are based on the normative structure. On the other hand, this Instruction continues to exhibit an undercurrent influenced by medieval and early modern understandings of the role of the priest and of his "private" Mass. Such understandings are revealed, for example, in Masses with a congregation in which properly ministerial activities (reading all the lessons, chanting the gospel acclamation when it might be done by another, dispensing with book-bearer and server, and presenting all the biddings of the intercessory prayer) may be reappropriated by the priest-presider. In addition, there has been a tendency in some places since Vatican Council II towards a minimizing of the rite, i.e., a celebration of Mass shorn of any solemnity, devoid of singing, without a variety of ministers, no homily, and omitting the prayer of the faithful and the sign of peace. Ironically, such celebrations can still be experienced as "virtually private," i.e., celebrations that seem to ignore the congregation and the potential ministers who could emerge from the assembly. It is therefore important in reviewing this section to recognize the exceptional character of the rite of Mass with one minister. It should not become in any way an unacknowledged "norm" for weekday or other simpler celebrations of Mass.

CHAPTER IV.IV

Some General Norms for All Forms of Mass

(*QUAEDAM NORMAE GENERALIORES PRO OMNIBUS FORMIS MISSAE*)

Mary Schaefer and Joanne M. Pierce

IV. Some General Norms for All Forms of Mass

Veneration of the Altar and the Book of the Gospels

273. According to traditional practice, the altar and the *Book of the Gospels* are venerated by means of a kiss. Where, however, a sign of this kind is not in harmony with the traditions or the culture of some region, it is for the Conference of Bishops to establish some other sign in its place, with the consent of the Apostolic See.

IV. Quædam Normæ Generaliores pro omnibus Formis Missæ

De veneratione altaris et Evangeliarii

273. Iuxta morem traditum, veneratio altaris et Evangeliarii osculo perficitur. Attamen, ubi huiusmodi signum non congruit cum traditionibus aut ingenio alicuius regionis, ibi est Conferentiæ Episcoporum aliud signum statuere loco illius adhibendum, consentiente Sede Apostolica.

Overview

This last section of Chapter IV of the new *Institutio Generalis Missalis Romani* (*IGMR2002*) parallels the same section in *IGMR1975* (nos. 232–253), and covers the same general subtopics: veneration of the altar and Book of the Gospels; genuflections and bows; purifications (covering both the usual purification of the vessels and purifications to be done in the case of other "accidents"); and the distribution of Communion under both kinds.

Veneration of the Altar and the Book of the Gospels

273. *IGMR2002* generally repeats *IGMR1975* (no. 232) in this article, with one major change concerning the process for substituting signs of veneration. The 1975 text permitted the local conference of bishops to "substitute some other sign" (*aliud signum statuere*) in areas where kissing the altar and Book of the Gospels was not "in harmony with the traditions or the culture of some region" (*non congruit cum traditionibus aut ingenio alicuius regionis*). This substitution was to be done "after informing the Apostolic See" (*hac de re certiore facta Sede Apostolica*). In *IGMR2002*, such a substitution must be done "with the

Genuflections and Bows

274. A genuflection, made by bending the right knee to the ground, signifies adoration, and therefore it is reserved for the Most Blessed Sacrament, as well as for the Holy Cross from the solemn adoration during the liturgical celebration on Good Friday until the beginning of the Easter Vigil.

During Mass, three genuflections are made by the priest celebrant: namely, after the showing of the host, after the showing of the chalice, and before Communion.

De genuflexione et inclinatione

274. Genuflexio, quæ fit dextero genuflectendo usque ad terram, adorationem significat; ideoque reservatur Ss.mo Sacramento, et sanctæ Cruci inde a sollemni adoratione in Actione liturgica feriæ VI in Passione Domini usque ad initium Vigiliæ paschalis.

In Missa tres genuflexiones fiunt a sacerdote celebrante, hoc est: post ostensionem hostiæ, post ostensionem calicis et ante Communionem. Peculiaritates in

---

consent of the Apostolic See" (*consentiente Sede Apostolica*). This change is reflective of the new attention *IGMR2002* gives, particularly in the new Chapter IX below, to the role of conferences of bishops and the Holy See in enacting liturgical adaptations (e.g., see no. 388 below).

All *IGMR*s direct that the altar, a symbol of Christ (see nos. 49 above and 298 below) is to be kissed only before the greeting which commences the liturgy and at its end, following the dismissal. The kissing of the altar at the beginning of the Mass seems to have been a custom borrowed from both civic and domestic ancient culture.[1] In early Roman papal liturgy, there is evidence that the pope would have greeted others at the altar with a kiss, then kissed both the gospel book and the altar at the beginning of Mass.[2] Later, the altar alone—symbolizing Christ the cornerstone—was kissed. In the Tridentine *Missale Romanum* (*MR1570*) the altar was kissed whenever the priest-presider turned away from it to greet the people with *Dominus vobiscum*. All *IGMR*s also direct that the Book of the Gospels, which also symbolizes Christ (see no. 117 above), is to be kissed at the conclusion of its proclamation as the deacon, priest, or bishop says, "May the words of the Gospel wipe away our sins" (see nos. 134 and 175 above). This reduction in gestures of veneration toward the Book of the Gospels, and especially to the altar, marks a turn to the noble simplicity predicated on classic Roman liturgy and mandated by *Sacrosanctum Concilium* (*SC*, no. 34).

Genuflections and Bows

274. *IGMR2002* includes a new opening sentence to material taken from *IGMR1975*, no. 233. This lengthy sentence defines a genuflection "made by bending the right knee to the ground" (*dextero genu flectendo usque ad terram*), notes that it "signifies adoration" (*adorationem significant*), and is "reserved"

1. Josef Jungmann, *The Mass of the Roman Rite*, trans. Francis Brunner, 2 vols. (Westminster: Christian Classics, 1986), I:314.

2. Jungmann, *The Mass of the Roman Rite*, I:311.

Certain specific features to be observed in a concelebrated Mass are noted in their proper place (cf. nos. 210–251).

If, however, the tabernacle with the Most Blessed Sacrament is present in the sanctuary, the priest, the deacon, and the other ministers genuflect when they approach the altar and when they depart from it, but not during the celebration of Mass itself.

Otherwise all who pass before the Most Blessed Sacrament genuflect, unless they are moving in procession.

Ministers carrying the processional cross or candles bow their heads instead of genuflecting.

Missa concelebrata servandæ suis locis notantur *(cf. nn. 210–251).*

Si vero tabernaculum cum SS.mo Sacramento sit in presbyterio, sacerdos, diaconus et alii ministri genuflectunt, cum ad altare perveniunt et ab eo recedunt, non autem durante ipsa Missæ celebratione.

Secus genuflectunt omnes qui ante Ss.mum Sacramentum transeunt, nisi processionaliter incedant.

Ministri qui crucem processionalem vel cereos deferunt, loco genuflexionis inclinationem capitis faciunt.

(*reservatur*) for the Blessed Sacrament and the adoration of the Cross from the liturgy of Good Friday until the Easter Vigil.

While Jungmann suggests that the custom arises in the fourteenth century of the priest's genuflecting "before and after every touching of the Blessed Sacrament" between the consecration and Communion of the Mass,[3] the first printed *Missale Romanum* (*MR1474*) contained no indication of either genuflections or elevations (see Mitchell and Baldovin, 19 above). Since the thirteenth century a bow by the priest was considered sufficient reverence at the time of the consecration. The influential 1502 *Ordo Missae* of John Burckard, on the other hand, contained genuflections before and after each consecration, a practice incorporated in *MR1570*.[4]

The second paragraph of this *IGMR2002* article largely repeats *IGMR1975* (no. 233), with two clarifications. The first is the specification that the three genuflections at Mass are to be made by the "priest celebrant" (*sacerdote celebrante*). The second is a new sentence admitting "certain specific features" (*peculiaritates*) that arise in the case of concelebration with a cross-reference to the pertinent earlier articles (nos. 210–251).

The next paragraph repeats previous directives on when the tabernacle with the Blessed Sacrament is to be reverenced with a genuflection during Mass (if one "is present in the sanctuary," *sit in presbyterio*), but includes more detail on when genuflections are made, and by whom. *IGMR2002* specifically states that the priest, deacon, and "other ministers" (*alii ministri*) genuflect to the tabernacle in the sanctuary, but only when they approach and depart from the altar. Priest,

3. Jungmann, *The Mass of the Roman Rite*, I:123.

4. Leonard and Mitchell, *The Postures of the Assembly*, 72; also, Mitchell and Baldovin, 21 above.

275. A bow signifies reverence and honor shown to the persons themselves or to the signs that represent them. There are two kinds of bows: a bow of the head and a bow of the body.

a. A bow of the head is made when the three Divine Persons are named together and at the names of Jesus, of the Blessed Virgin Mary, and of the Saint in whose honor Mass is being celebrated.

b. A bow of the body, that is to say a profound bow, is made to the altar; dur-

275. Inclinatione significatur reverentia et honor quæ personis ipsis vel eorum signis tribuitur. Duæ species inclinationum habentur, scilicet capitis et corporis:

a) Inclinatio capitis fit cum tres Divinæ Personæ simul nominantur, et ad nomen Iesu, beatæ Mariæ Virginis et Sancti in cuius honorem celebratur Missa.

b) Inclinatio corporis seu inclinatio profunda, fit: ad altare; ad orations Munda cor meum et In spíritu humilitátis; in symbolo ad verba Et incarnátes est; in

---

deacon, and other ministers do not genuflect before the tabernacle "during the celebration of Mass itself" (*non autem durante ipsa Missae celebratione*).

The article ends with two new directives. First, others are to genuflect if they pass before the tabernacle unless they are "moving in procession" (*nisi processionaliter incedant*); the contrast between these persons and those mentioned in the previous paragraph is heightened by the use of the adverb *secus* ("otherwise") at the beginning of the sentence. A second clarification concerns the ministers in a procession who carry the processional cross and lighted candles who do not genuflect, but instead "bow their heads" (*inclinationem capitis faciunt*), as would have been the case in the rubrics for the Tridentine rite as well.[5] *Caeremoniale Episcoporum* offers the helpful clarification that those who are carrying articles used in worship neither make a genuflection "nor a deep bow" (no. 70). Genuflections may be impossible or very difficult for persons not fully able-bodied, with poor balance, or suffering from other physical issues. As priests grow older, they may find difficulty in following these directives. The insight of no. 43 above, regarding kneeling, provides a useful hermeneutic. When ministers are prevented by good reason from genuflecting, the profound bow seems the appropriate option.

275. Like previous editions, *IGMR2002* distinguishes between a bow of the head and a bow of the body. New here is the added clarification about the significance of the bow, which symbolizes "reverence and honor" (*reverentia et honor*) both "to persons themselves or to the signs that represent them" (*personis ipsis vel eorum signis tribuitur*). An example of this is the custom of the mutual

5. Neither the subdeacon, carrying the Book of the Gospels, nor acolytes carrying candles, were to genuflect with the priest and others during a "missa solemnis"; see *Missale Romanum. Rubricae Generales Missalis,* XVII, no. 4 (New York: Benziger, 1942); also Adrian Fortescue and J. O'Connell, *The Ceremonies of the Roman Rite Described* (Westminster, MD: Newman Press, 1953), 21–23, 77–78, 149–150.

ing the prayers *Munda cor meum (Almighty God, cleanse my heart)* and *In spiritu humilitatis (Lord God, we ask you to receive)*; in the Creed at the words *Et incarnatus est (by the power of the Holy Spirit . . . and became man)*; in the Roman Canon at the words *Supplices te rogamus (Almighty God, we pray that your angel)*. The same kind of bow is made by the deacon when he asks for a blessing before the proclamation of the Gospel. In addition, the priest bows slightly as he speaks the words of the Lord at the consecration.

Canone romano ad verba Súpplices te rogámus. Eadem inclinatio fit a diacono, cum petit benedictionem ante proclamationem Evangelii. Sacerdos insuper parum se inclinat cum, in consecratione, verba Domini profert.

---

bow made by the thurifer as well as the ministers or assembly being incensed (see no. 277 below). Aside from this clarification, the remainder of the article repeats directives found in *IGMR1975* (no. 234); the notation that the altar is reverenced with a bow "if there is no tabernacle with the blessed sacrament" (*si tabernaculum cum SS. Sacramento non adsit*) is dropped in *IGMR2002*, as that situation was already dealt with in no. 274 above. As for the English translations, while the Latin in *IGMR1975* and *IGMR2002* are identical in noting that a bow is made *ad nomen . . . B. Maria Virginis*, GIRM1975 translates "at the name of . . . Mary," while GIRM2003 is more exact with "Blessed Virgin Mary."

While there is a general directive for a head bow "when the Three Divine Persons are named together" (*cum tres Divinae Personae simul nominantur*), the practice is more appropriate during the first section of the minor doxology (*Gloria Patri*) rather than during the sign of the cross at the commencement of Mass, for which *IGMR2002* never stipulates a bow. There is widespread tradition for bowing at the name of Jesus, though the prescription to bow at the name of the Blessed Virgin or the saint commemorated in the Mass is less well known. It could be helpful if future *IGMR*s distinguished between a bow at the divine name and that for a saint,[6] so there is no confusion between worship paid to God (*latria*) and the honor due to a holy person (*hyperdulia* for the Blessed Virgin, *dulia* for other saints).

While only providing two categories of bows (i.e., of the head and of the body), *IGMR2002* and its predecessors seem to distinguish between a "profound bow" (*inclinatio profunda*) employed, for example, during the Creed, and the

6. Fortescue and O'Connell make such a distinction in their discussion of Tridentine ceremonial for priests and other altar ministers: "the head is bowed less deeply at the name 'Mary' of the Blessed Virgin, at the mention of the name of the saint of the day, at that of the Pope and of the Bishop," *The Ceremonies of the Roman Rite Described*, 22.

Incensation

276. Thurification or incensation is an expression of reverence and of prayer, as is signified in Sacred Scripture (cf. Ps 141 [140]:2, Rev 8:3).

Incense may be used if desired in any form of Mass:

a. During the Entrance procession;
b. At the beginning of Mass, to incense the cross and the altar;
c. At the Gospel procession and the proclamation of the Gospel itself;
d. After the bread and the chalice have been placed upon the altar, to incense the offerings, the cross, and the altar, as well as the priest and the people;
e. At the showing of the host and the chalice after the consecration.

De incensatione

276. Thurificatio seu incensatio reverentiam exprimit et orationem, ut in Sacra Scriptura significatur *(cf. Ps* 140, 2; *Apoc* 8, 3*)*.

Incensum ad libitum adhiberi potest in qualibet forma Missæ:

a) durante processione ingressus;
b) initio Missæ, ad crucem et altare thurificandum;
c) ad processionem et ad proclamationem Evangelii;
d) pane et calice super altare depositis, ad thurificanda oblata, crucem et altare, necnon sacerdotem et populum;
e) ad ostensionem hostiæ et calicis post consecrationem.

---

gesture at the institution narrative for which *IGMR2002* indicates "the priest bows slightly" (*Sacerdos . . . parum se inclinat*). The latter is a more restrained gesture that respects the narrative quality of this segment of the Eucharistic Prayer. In the earliest Roman *ordines*, the surrounding clergy, as well as all members of the congregation, were to bow from the beginning of the *Sanctus* to the end of the Roman Canon, although the bishop stood upright.[7] By the ninth century in some places, kneeling was already replacing bowing as the expected posture especially for the assembly during the Eucharistic Prayer, as well as at several other points during the Mass.[8]

Incense

276. In this article on the use of incense, *IGMR2002* again adds a new opening sentence offering a theological statement on the significance of incense, which is both "an expression of reverence and of prayer" (*reverentiam exprimit et orationem*). To underscore this point, the Instruction cites Psalm 140:2 and Revelation 8:3, something that would have also been useful in reference to the kiss, the genuflection, and the bow (nos. 273–275 above). The remainder of the article repeats directives found in *IGMR1975*, with three minor adjustments. Consistent with an earlier addition (no. 123 above), no. 276b here adds that the

7. *Ordo Romanus I (OR I)*, nos. 88–89. While it is clear that ministers who had specific tasks during the Canon (such as the subdeacon in no. 89) stood upright when necessary, everyone else continued to bow. See Leonard and Mitchell, *The Postures of the Assembly*, 65.

8. Leonard and Mitchell, *The Postures of the Assembly*, 66–67; also Jungmann, *The Mass of the Roman Rite*, I:240, 370ff.

277. The priest, having put incense into the thurible, blesses it with the sign of the Cross, without saying anything.

Before and after an incensation, a profound bow is made to the person or object that is incensed, except for the incensation of the altar and the offerings for the Sacrifice of the Mass.

The following are incensed with three swings of the thurible: the Most Blessed Sacrament, a relic of the Holy Cross and images of the Lord exposed for public veneration, the offerings for the sacrifice of the Mass, the altar cross, the *Book of the Gospels*, the Paschal Candle, the priest, and the people.

The following are incensed with two swings of the thurible: relics and images of the Saints exposed for public veneration, which should be done, however, only at

277. Sacerdos, cum incensum ponit in thuribulum, illud benedicit signo crucis, nihil dicens.

Ante et post thurificationem fit profunda inclinatio personæ vel rei quæ incensatur, altari et oblatis pro Missæ sacrificio exceptis.

Tribus ductibus thuribuli incensantur: Ss.mum Sacramentum, reliquia sanctæ Crucis et imagines Domini publicæ venerationi expositæ, oblata pro Missæ sacrificio, crux altaris, Evangeliarium, cereus paschalis, sacerdos et populus.

Duobus ductibus incensantur reliquiæ et imagines Sanctorum publicæ venerationi expositæ, et quidem unice initio tantum celebrationis, post incensationem altaris.

Altare incensatur singulis ictibus hoc modo:

---

cross is to be censed along with the altar at the beginning of Mass, and actually lists it before the altar. In no. 276d *IGMR2002* then clarifies that at the preparation of gifts the proper time to incense the gifts is "after the bread and chalice have been placed upon the altar" (*pane et calicem super altare depositis*). Further, no. 276d (like no. 276b) adds the cross to the list of persons and objects to be censed at that time.

IGMR2002 notes that incense may be used "in any form of Mass" (*in qualibet forma Missae*), suggesting that one does not need to reserve its use only for more festive times of the year. The US bishops offer a further helpful insight when they note that, when incense is used, it does not need to be used at every possible point in the Mass, and may simply "enhance a particular moment within a celebration" (*Introduction to the Order of Mass* [ITTOM], no. 58).

When using incense one needs to exhibit caution, as incense can have deleterious effects on some worshipers, e.g., triggering asthmatic or allergic reactions. Special caution must be exercised in churches with poor ventilation or low ceilings. It is helpful, where possible, to publicize its use, search for hypoallergenic types of incense, and experiment with alternate scent-producing forms that might be more culturally appropriate for different groups of worshippers, e.g. cedar shavings or sweet grass for Native Americans or First Nations People.

277. *IGMR2002* here provides a fuller description for incensing than was found in *IGMR1975* (no. 236). The first directive repeats previous *IGMR*s: incense is added to the thurible and is blessed by the priest silently, using only

the beginning of the celebration, after the incensation of the altar.

The altar is incensed with single swings of the thurible in this way:

a. If the altar is freestanding with respect to the wall, the priest incenses walking around it;
b. If the altar is not freestanding, the priest incenses it while walking first to the righthand side, then to the left.

The cross, if situated on or near the altar, is incensed by the priest before he incenses the altar; otherwise, he incenses it when he passes in front of it.

The priest incenses the offerings with three swings of the thurible or by making the sign of the cross over the offerings with the thurible before going on to incense the cross and the altar.

a) si altare est a pariete seiunctum, sacerdos illud circumeundo incensat;
b) si vero altare non est a pariete seiunctum, sacerdos transeundo incensat primo partem dexteram, deinde partem sinistram.

Crux, si est super altare vel apud ipsum, thurificatur ante altaris incensationem, secus cum sacerdos transit ante ipsam.

Oblata incensat sacerdos tribus ductibus thuribuli, ante incensationem cruces et altaris, vel signum crucis super oblata thuribulo producens.

---

the sign of the cross. Several new clarifications and stipulations then follow. First, there is to be a "profound bow" (*profunda inclinatio*) before incensing persons and things (except for the altar and the offerings). Second, *IGMR2002* newly stipulates that three swings of the thurible are used for several groups of objects and persons (including the Blessed Sacrament, the gifts on the altar, the Book of the Gospels, the priest and people); two swings are to be used for relics and images of the saints used for "public veneration" (*publicae venerationi*); and single swings are employed to incense the altar.

The manner of incensing the altar presented next is essentially the same as is found in previous *IGMR*s. The movement of the priest around the altar is described both for a free-standing altar (which the priest incenses as he walks around it), and a non-freestanding altar (which he incenses walking back and forth in front of it, starting from the center and moving first to the right and then to the left side).

The directives on incensing the altar cross are also virtually unchanged: it is incensed before the altar if it is placed "on or near the altar" (*super altare vel apud ipsum*), otherwise, it is incensed as the priest "passes in front of it" (*transit ante ipsam*). While according to *IGMR1975* this latter option occurred if the cross is "behind the altar" (*post altare*), *IGMR2002* leaves the position of the cross unspecified, and simply states that this second option occurs if the cross is in any position other than on or near the altar. This article concludes with a new directive concerning the method of incensing the gifts on the altar. These are to be incensed before either the cross or the altar with a triple swing of the

The Purification

278. Whenever a fragment of the host adheres to his fingers, especially after the fraction or the Communion of the faithful, the priest is to wipe his fingers over the paten or, if necessary, wash them. Likewise, he should also gather any fragments that may have fallen outside the paten.

279. The sacred vessels are purified by the priest, the deacon, or an instituted acolyte after Communion or after Mass, insofar as possible at the credence table. The purification of the chalice is done with water alone or with wine and water, which is then drunk by whoever does the purification. The paten is usually wiped clean with the purificator.

Care must be taken that whatever may remain of the Blood of Christ after the

De purificatione

278. Quoties aliquod fragmentum hostiæ digitis adhæserit, præcipue post fractionem vel fidelium Communionem, sacerdos digitos super patenam abstergat vel pro necessitate abluat. Similiter fragmenta, si quæ extra patenam sint, colligat.

279. Vasa sacra purificantur a sacerdote vel a diacono vel ab acolytho instituto post Communionem vel post Missam, quantum fieri potest ad abacum. Purificatio calicis fit cum aqua vel cum aqua et vino, quæ ab ipso qui purificat, sumitur. Patena de more purificatorio detergeatur.

Attendendum est ut quod de Sanguine Christi post Communionis distributionem forte remanet statim ex integro sumatur ad altare.

---

thurible (as noted earlier in this article). *IGMR2002* then notes that they may also be incensed "by making the sign of the cross over the offerings with the thurible" (*signum crucis super oblata thuribulo producens*).

Purifications

278. This is the first of three articles concerned with the purification of the priest's hands or vessels during the celebration of the Eucharist. Identical to *IGMR1975* (no. 237), the main concern here is about fragments of the host adhering to the fingers of the priest. In such cases the priest is to "wipe his fingers over the paten" (*digitos super patenam abstergat*, GIRM1975 has "cleanses his fingers"). The use of *digitos* confirms that the priest can use fully both hands when touching the hosts, rather than just *index* and *pollex* (index finger and thumb), as noted in the rubrics for the Canon of the Mass in *MR1570.* Another option is for the priest to wash his fingers, presumably employing the same vessels used for the washing of the hands at the preparation of the gifts. There is no indication here or in *MR2002* that this is to be done over the chalice as required in the Tridentine Rite. Finally, this article enjoins the priest to gather any eucharistic fragments "that may have fallen outside the paten" (*si quae extra patenam sint*).

279. The first section of this article, on the time and place for the purification of vessels, is virtually identical to the text of *IGMR1975* (no. 238). The indication that this cleansing "insofar as possible" should take place at the credence table (*quantum fiere potest ad abacum*) underscores that this is the preferred location for cleansing the vessels rather than the center of the altar. Previously, *IGMR2002*

distribution of Communion is consumed immediately and completely at the altar.

280. If a host or any particle should fall, it is to be picked up reverently. If any of the Precious Blood is spilled, the area where the spill occurred should be washed with water, and this water should then be poured into the sacrarium in the sacristy.

280. Si hostia vel aliqua particula dilabatur, reverenter accipiatur; si quid vero Sanguinis fundatur, locus ubi ceciderit aqua lavetur, et hæc aqua postea in sacrarium in sacristia collocatum mittatur.

---

offered the third option of leaving the vessels so that they can be purified after Mass (see no. 163 above).

IGMR2002 makes two changes in the text from *IGMR1975.* The first concerns which ministers may purify the vessels. Both *IGMR*s list the priest and the deacon. For a third possibility *IGMR1975* refers to the acolyte (*ab acolytho*) while, consistent with its more hieratic understanding of ministries (see no. 187 above), *IGMR2002* specifies an "instituted acolyte" (*ab acolytho instituto,* also no. 284b below). While an indult extended to the United States allowed extraordinary ministers to participate in purification of vessels, it expired and a request to extend it was denied in 2006 (see no. 192 above).

A small change is found in the description of the method of purifying the chalice. *IGMR1975* specifies that this may be done "with wine and water, or with water only" (*cum vino et aqua vel cum aqua tantum*). *IGMR2002* reverses this order and the first preference is for "water alone or with wine and water" (*cum aqua vel cum aqua et vino*). Here, again, *IGMR2002* distinguishes itself from Tridentine practice, in which the chalice was purified using a little wine, then the priest celebrant would purify his thumb and index fingers with water and wine over the chalice, and drink the liquid before wiping out the chalice with the purificator.[9]

A new final sentence in *IGMR2002* urges particular caution in dealing with any of the consecrated wine that may remain after Communion. Here, the directive states that any such remnant must be "consumed immediately and completely at the altar" (*statim ex integro sumatur ad altare*) by a priest, deacon, or instituted acolyte (see no. 284b below).[10] This directive about immediate and complete consumption of the elements parallels the newly inserted text concerning the Communion of the faithful in no. 161 above.

280. As with other articles in this section, this article dealing with the accidental dropping of a host or spilling of the precious blood is substantially the same as that found in *IGMR1975* (no. 239). A minor addition is that, while *IGMR1975* notes that water used to wash the area where precious blood may

9. *MR1570, Ritus servandus* X, 5.

10. "Pouring the Precious Blood into the ground or into the sacrarium is strictly prohibited," ITTOM, no. 138, with its references to the 1983 *Codex Iuris Canonici (CIC1983),* c. 1367, and the US Bishops' *Norms for the Distribution and Reception of Holy Communion Under Both Kinds in the Dioceses of the United States of America* (2001), no. 55.

have been spilled is to be poured into the sacrarium, *IGMR2002* specifies that the sacrarium is "in the sacristy" (*in sacristia*).

IGMR2002 does not cover all possible circumstances with regard to possible accidents during distribution of Communion. Confusion may still arise concerning, for example, where a host dropped from someone's mouth is to be disposed of; pastorally it could be inappropriate to offer this to the communicant, or to have the minister consume it. There may also be confusion, if precious blood spills, how much cleansing of the area should be done during the Communion rite, and how much is best deferred until after Mass.[11] Without the detail of *MR1570*'s *De defectibus*, future editions of *IGMR* could offer further direction on these matters

Communion under Both Kinds

Early church practice that Communion be received by all the baptized at every eucharistic liturgy was widely and relatively quickly recovered after Vatican Council II.[12] The reception of Communion under both kinds, in abeyance for some eight hundred years for all but the presiding bishop or priest, developed in a much more gradual fashion and still is not the practice in various parts of Roman Catholicism. Eight centuries of nonavailability of the cup to laity and non-ordained religious have created for some laypeople a kind of inertia regarding Communion under both species. Some modern Catholics have their own reasons for abstaining from the cup: unwillingness on the part of both pastors and parishioners to change old habits; in some cases a distaste for wine and objection to its cost; the fear of infection from sharing a common cup; or the fact that grape wine is not an indigenous drink in many countries around the world. Commitment to full restoration of the cup in the Latin rite would be aided by reflection upon and instruction about the Communion practices of other Christians, especially Eastern Rite Catholics and the Orthodox.

SC, no. 55, proposes offering Communion under both kinds on certain occasions, and in 1965 the rite of Communion under both kinds in favor of specified categories of individuals was made available to the universal Church.[13] The Congregation for Divine Worship's instruction *Sacramentali Communione*

11. Peter J. Elliott, *Ceremonies of the Modern Roman Rite: The Eucharist and the Liturgy of the Hours*, rev. ed. (San Francisco: Ignatius Press, 2005) includes a short, incomplete appendix entitled "Accidents," 314–16.

12. The restoration of Communion under both kinds and the interaction of the various Vatican congregations with the Consilium charged with developing it are sketched by Annibale Bugnini, *The Reform of the Liturgy 1948–1975* (Collegeville, MN: Liturgical Press, 1990), 626–34. See also R. Kevin Seasoltz, "Sacraments: Eucharist (Communion and Worship)," in *New Liturgy, New Laws* (Collegeville: Liturgical Press, 1980), 99–111.

13. Congregation of Rites, *Rite of Communion under Both Kinds* (March 7, 1965), in DOL, nos. 2105–2107. The bishop of the place is to choose one of three rites using tube, spoon, or intinction. Curiously, drinking from the chalice is not mentioned.

(29 June 1970) broadened the practice.[14] Authority was given to episcopal conferences to regulate Communion under both kinds for their country; it was the responsibility of the local ordinary to grant permission and to supervise its use, determining "instances that are of special significance in the spiritual life of any community or group of the faithful."[15] To ensure reverence, the document forbade offering consecrated wine in celebrations involving large crowds. Drinking from the chalice was preferred, but intinction was also recommended as "easier" and "safer." Although *Fidei custos* (30 April 1969) had already made provision for additional ministers of Communion, *Sacramentali Communione* stated, "When they are available other priests or deacons or even acolytes should be chosen to present the chalice."[16]

By 1970 reception under both kinds had been inaugurated for the universal church as a special privilege for individuals, e.g., for the newly baptized on the day of their initiation, the bride and bridegroom at their wedding Mass, and virgins on the day of their consecration. *IGMR1970* underscores the exceptional nature of this act when it notes that Communion under both kinds may be given "to those ordained, in the Mass of their ordination" (*ordinates in Missa suae Ordinationis*).[17] While Vatican initiatives may have been cautious, bishops' conferences seemed to have a better sense of what was both liturgically apt and culturally possible. In 1970 the US bishops, exercising the authority given to them in *Sacramentali communione*, extended the privilege of Communion under both kinds to laity at weekday Masses that were not holy days.[18] In 1978 the US bishops further extended this privilege to Sundays and holy days, but they did not receive the *recognitio* from Rome until 1984.[19]

14. *AAS* 62 (1970): 664–666, in *DOL*, no. 2115. If "other priests or deacons or even acolytes" are not available to present the chalice, the priest himself should present first the bread, then the cup, or give Communion by intinction.

15. The bishops of the United States (16–20 November 1970) determined that the ordinary could allow Communion under both kinds at the Mass of the Lord's Supper on Holy Thursday and at the Easter Vigil as well as at Masses of special religious or civic significance (*BCL Newsletter* 6 [Nov. 1970]: 251).

16. The "acolytes" referred to were not "instituted" since that lay ministry would be inaugurated by *Ministeria quaedam* (15 August 1972). It is unclear whether the clerical minor order of acolyte was the intended reference.

17. The emended Canadian list in GIRM1975 specifies that these ordained persons were "deacons at the Mass of their ordination." See *New Introductions to the Sacramentary and Lectionary* (Ottawa: Publications Service, 1983), no. 242 and n. 71.

18. *BCL Newsletter* 6 (November 1970): 251. The chronology of developing practice can be readily followed in the *BCL Newsletter* for these years.

19. *BCL Newsletter* 15 (January 1979): 651–54, vol. 20 (November 1984): 934, and vol. 21 (January 1985): 942; John Huels, *The Interpretation of the Law on Communion under Both Kinds*, CUA Canon Law Studies, no. 505 (Washington DC: Catholic University of America, 1982), 304; idem, "Communion Under Both Kinds," in *New Dictionary of Sacramental Worship* (Collegeville, MN: The Liturgical Press, 1990), 240–41; idem, "The Cup of Blessing," in *One Table, Many Laws: Essays on Catholic Eucharistic Practice* (Collegeville, MN: The Liturgical Press, 1986), 37.

Communion under Both Kinds

281. Holy Communion has a fuller form as a sign when it is distributed under both kinds. For in this form the sign of the Eucharistic banquet is more clearly evident and clear expression is given to the divine will by which the new and eternal Covenant is ratified in the Blood of the Lord, as also the relationship between the Eucharistic banquet and the eschatological banquet in the Father's Kingdom.[105]

De Communione sub utraque specie

281. Formam ratione signi pleniorem habet sacra Communio cum fit sub utraque specie. In ea enim forma signum eucharistici convivii perfectius elucet, et clarius exprimitur voluntas divina qua novum et æternum Testamentum in Sanguine Domini ratum habetur, necnon ratio inter convivium eucharisticum et convivium eschatologicum in regno Patris.[105]

IGMR2002's section "Communion under Both Kinds" (nos. 281–287) has been reduced in length and detail from *IGMR1970* and *IGMR1975* (nos. 240–252). These earlier instructions described in detail four possible forms for receiving the Blood of Christ: drinking directly from the chalice or reception by intinction, tube, or spoon.[20] *IGMR2002* reduces these to two: drinking from the cup, the form which corresponds more closely to Christ's command, and intinction; the option of a tube or spoon has been dropped altogether, although it is mentioned with regard to the Communion of concelebrants (no. 245 above). Directions concerning these forms (nos. 285–287) are brief, since reception of both species is now customary in many places.

281. Here, *IGMR2002* repeats the theological rationale for preferring Communion under both kinds found in *IGMR1970* and *IGMR1975* (no. 240). The text is taken almost verbatim from *Eucharisticum mysterium* (no. 32). There are three key theological themes or images that are linked together here: the "Eucharistic banquet" (*eucharistici convivii*), the "new and eternal covenant . . . ratified in the Blood of the Lord" (*novum et aeternum Testamentum in Sanguine Domini ratum habetur*), and the eschatological banquet (*convivium eschatologicum*).

While in other sections of *IGMR2002* there seems to be more emphasis on sacrifice than banquet (see Power and Vincie, 56ff. above; also no. 72 above) the first emphasis here is on the image of eucharistic banquet, and particularly how Communion in its "fuller form" (*formam . . . pleniorem*) makes the sign of the eucharistic banquet "more clearly evident" (*perfectius elucet*). The cup of wine was traditionally linked to the Greco-Roman banquet which clearly

20. The final two forms had been added to its second schema by the commission charged with implementing the rite of Communion under both kinds (30 May 1964). See Bugnini, *Reform of the Liturgy*, 628. The tube *(pugillaris)* or reed *(calamus, fistula)* was in use for the pope's Communion at solemn Mass until modern times, and for the people's according to *OR I*, no. 111. Communicating with a tube or straw was not much attempted in the reform of Paul VI. In various Eastern Rites today (e.g., the Byzantine liturgy) the bread is immersed in the wine and then given in the mouth by means of a spoon.

influenced Jewish festival meals as well as early Christian banquets.[21] It is this Greco-Roman, Jewish, and early Christian tradition which is more fully evoked when the cup is shared along with the eucharistized bread.

While it will return to banquet imagery, following the sequence of *Eucharisticum mysterium,* the article then turns to sacrificial imagery. It asserts that Communion under both forms clearly expresses the divinely willed ratification of the new Covenant in Christ's blood. Drinking of the cup in the New Testament is clearly an image of Christ's acceptance of God's will unto death (see Mark 14:36), and in four New Testament institution narratives Christ's own blood is identified as the medium by which the new covenant is established (Matt 26:28, Mark 14:24, Luke 22:20, 1 Cor 11:25). Furthermore, the invitation to his disciples to drink of the cup, repeated at every eucharistic liturgy, is an invitation to sacrificial living and dying for them and us as well.[22] Without the cup, the faithful are deprived of this potent symbol of Christ's sacrifice and the new covenant into which they were baptized.

Finally, the article notes the strong bond between the eucharistic liturgy of the Church and the eschatological banquet "in the Father's Kingdom" (*in regno Patris*). The linkage between Eucharist and eschatology is one of the more underdeveloped aspects of contemporary sacramental theology,[23] and *IGMR2002* makes few eschatological references (exceptions are nos. 79b above and 318 below). Thus it is welcome that *IGMR2002* would rely on *Eucharisticum mysterium* in its final theological assertion about the eschatological importance of Communion under both forms. While the Instruction does not elaborate on how Communion under both forms gives clear expression to the linkage between the Eucharist of this world and the next, John Paul II (d. 2005) did speak of how Eucharist not only "makes present what occurred in the past . . . [but] also impels us towards the future, when Christ will come again at the end of history" (*Mane nobiscum Domine,* no. 15). From this perspective Eucharist is both a source of hope and also a call to mission (cf. no. 89 above). *IGMR2002* implicitly suggests, therefore, that Communion under both forms is both a potent symbol of Christian hope in the coming reign of God and an important symbol for expressing and sustaining the *missio Dei* among the baptized who are inspired by the eschatological Spirit (see Power and Vincie, 56 above) to help realize God's reign.

21. See Dennis E. Smith, *From Symposium to Eucharist: The Banquet in the Early Christian World* (Minneapolis: Fortress Press, 2003), especially 29–30 and 145–50.

22. See Xavier Léon-Dufour, *Sharing the Eucharistic Bread,* trans. Matthew O'Connell (New York: Paulist Press, 1987), 64.

23. A groundbreaking exception continues to be Geoffrey Wainwright, *Eucharist and Eschatology* (London: Epworth Press, 1971).

282. Sacred pastors should take care to ensure that the faithful who participate in the rite or are present at it are as fully aware as possible of the Catholic teaching on the form of Holy Communion as set forth by the Ecumenical Council of Trent. Above all, they should instruct the Christian faithful that the Catholic faith teaches that Christ, whole and entire, and the true Sacrament, is received even under only one species, and consequently that as far as the effects are concerned, those who receive under only one species are not deprived of any of the grace that is necessary for salvation.[106]

282. Curent sacri pastores fidelibus, qui ritum participant, vel ei intersunt, aptiore quo fieri potest modo doctrinam catholicam de forma sacræ Communionis in mentem revocare iuxta Concilium Œcumenicum Tridentinum. In primis christifideles moneant fidem catholicam docere etiam sub altera tantum specie totum atque integrum Christum verumque Sacramentum sumi, ac propterea, quod ad fructum attinet, nulla gratia necessaria ad salutem eos defraudari qui unam speciem solam recipiant.[106]

---

282. The next two paragraphs of this and previous *IGMR*s (e.g., *IGMR1975*, no. 241) are taken from the 1965 Rite of Communion under Both Kinds issued by the Congregation of Rites.[24] In the first paragraph, *IGMR2002* emphasizes the preparation necessary for the faithful to participate in Communion under both species. As an "Instruction," it is appropriate and consistent that *IGMR*s are insistent on preparation both for the laity and the clergy before celebrating the Eucharist (cf. nos. 1, 11, and 12 above). The current text is identical to that of *IGMR1975*.

The final sentence of the first paragraph sets out the doctrine of concomitance, which holds for the coexistence of the body and blood of Christ in each of the eucharistic elements. According to this theological stance—which arose in the twelfth century, was defended by Thomas Aquinas (d. 1274) and confirmed by the Council of Trent (1545–63)—Christ is present, whole and entire, under each species alone.[25] While the doctrine explains how the whole Christ is present in those extraordinary circumstances when only one species is received (e.g., in the special case of the sick), it also provides theological support for withdrawing the cup from the laity, which had begun in western Christianity by the ninth century and became more widespread in the thirteenth century with this doctrinal support.[26] This paragraph maintains the doctrinal accuracy of Trent's teaching in view of various challenges to the practice of Communion

24. See DOL, no. 2106, for the relevant sections.

25. Thomas Aquinas, *Summa Theologica*, q. 76, art. 2, repond; Council of Trent, Session 21, ch. 3, in Tanner, ed., *Decrees of the Ecumenical Councils*, 2:727. On the doctrine of concomitance see J. J. Megivern, *Concomitance and Communion: A Study in Eucharistic Doctrine and Practice*, Studia Friburgensia, NS 33 (Fribourg: University Press, 1963).

26. Nathan Mitchell, *Cult and Controversy: The Worship of the Eucharist Outside Mass* (New York: Pueblo Publishing, 1982), 92 and 159.

They are to teach, furthermore, that the Church, in her stewardship of the Sacraments, has the power to set forth or alter whatever provisions, apart from the substance of the Sacraments, that she judges to be most conducive to the veneration of the Sacraments and the well-being of the recipients, in view of changing conditions, times, and places.[107] At the same time, the faithful should be encouraged to seek to participate more eagerly in this sacred rite, by which the sign of the Eucharistic banquet is made more fully evident.

Doceant insuper Ecclesiam potestatem habere in Sacramentorum dispensatione, salva eorum substantia, statuendi vel mutandi quæ ipsorum venerationi vel suscipientium utilitati pro rerum, temporum et locorum varietate magis expedire iudicaverit.[107] Simul tamen fideles moneantur ut sacrum ritum, quo signum eucharistici convivii plenius elucet, impensius participare velint.

---

under one form. One result of this caution is that the Tridentine teaching, repeated here, is expressed negatively, i.e., "those who receive only one form are not cheated of any grace necessary for salvation."[27] This teaching makes it difficult to suggest that there is any spiritual advantage to receiving Communion under both rather than one species.

The second paragraph of no. 282 begins with what could appear to be a somewhat apologetic statement, defending the Church's right "to set forth or alter whatever provisions . . . that she judges to be most conducive to the veneration of the Sacraments and the well-being of the recipients" (*statuendi vel mutandi quae ipsorum venerationi vel suscipientium utilitati . . . magis expedire iudicaverit*). On the other hand, given that this is a citation from the groundbreaking 1965 "Rite of Communion under Both Kinds," the statement can be rightly interpreted as an affirmation that—following the imperative of Vatican II for the full, conscious, and active participation of the people (*SC*, no. 14)—Communion under both forms is the practice judged to be most conducive to the veneration of the Sacrament and the well-being of the recipients. This interpretation seems validated by the closing sentence that encourages the faithful "to seek participation more eagerly in this sacred rite, by which the sign of the eucharistic banquet is made more fully evident" (*ut sacrum ritum, quo signum eucharistici convivii plenius elucet, impensius participare velint*). Number 281 above explicates that it is Communion under both forms which is the fuller sign, and it is this practice rather than Communion under one form which redounds to the greater spiritual good of the faithful.

27. Council of Trent, Session 21, ch. 3, in Tanner, ed., *Decrees of the Ecumenical Councils*, 2:727. This cautious approach is reflected in *CIC1983,* which seems to give a priority to receiving Communion by bread alone: "Holy communion is to be given under the form of bread alone, or under both species according to the norm of the liturgical laws, or even under the form of wine alone in a case of necessity" (c. 925).

283. In addition to those cases given in the ritual books, Communion under both kinds is permitted for[:]

a. Priests who are not able to celebrate or concelebrate Mass;
b. The deacon and others who perform some duty at the Mass;
c. Members of communities at the conventual Mass or "community" Mass, along with seminarians, and all who are engaged in a retreat or are taking part in a spiritual or pastoral gathering.

283. Communio sub utraque specie permittitur, præter casus in libris ritualibus expositos:

a) sacerdotibus qui sacrum celebrare vel concelebrare non possunt;
b) diacono et ceteris qui aliquod officium in Missa implent;
c) sodalibus communitatum in Missa conventuali vel in illa quæ « communitatis » dicitur, alumnis seminariorum, omnibus qui exercitiis spiritualibus vacant vel conventum spiritualem aut pastoralem participant.

---

283. In this article *IGMR2002* offers a much revised version of *IGMR1975* (no. 242), which in itself is a revision of *IGMR1970*.[28] These revisions are understandable in view of the liturgical developments that have taken place over the past thirty years. Because a number of "ritual books" (*libris ritualibus*) now indicate as standard practice the giving of Communion under both kinds to persons celebrating important moments in their faith-lives, *IGMR2002* first provides a general directive referring the reader to the texts of these books themselves. Next, it lists three cases beyond those given in the ritual books.

The first in no. 283a concerns "priests who are not able to celebrate or concelebrate Mass" (*celebrare vel concelebrare non possunt*); the previous stipulation that this occurs at "large celebrations" (*magnis celebrationibus, IGMR1975*, no. 242.9) has been dropped. In addition, no. 283b simplifies and extends a permission that was spelled out in a more limited fashion in earlier editions: that Communion under both kinds is permitted for "the deacon and others who perform some duty at Mass" (*diacono et ceteris qui aliquod officium in Missa implent*). In comparison, *IGMR1970*, no. 242.8a states that at concelebrations the cup may be given to all who exercise "a genuine liturgical function" (*vero ministerio liturgico*) "including the laity" (*etiam laicis*),[29] and also to all seminarians.

Number 283c combines and edits two earlier elements of *IGMR1975* (nos. 242.8b and 242.10), offering permission for Communion under both forms to members of religious communities at their community Mass, as well as seminarians, and those on retreat or participating in any other "spiritual or pastoral gathering" (*conventum spiritualem aut pastoralem participant*).

28. *IGMR1970*, no. 242.3 gives permission to "those ordained, in the Mass of their ordination" *(ordinates in Missa suae Ordinationis)* as well as in no. 242.7 "to the deacon, the subdeacon, and the servers exercising their office in a sung Mass *(diacono, subdiacono et ministries, officium suum implentibus in Missa cum cantu)*" to receive Communion from the cup as well as the host.

29. *IGMR1975* drops the specific reference to the laity.

The diocesan Bishop may establish norms for Communion under both kinds for his own diocese, which are also to be observed in churches of religious and at celebrations with small groups. The diocesan Bishop is also given the faculty to permit Communion under both kinds whenever it may seem appropriate to the priest to whom, as its own shepherd, a community has been entrusted, provided that the faithful have been well instructed and there is no danger of profanation of the Sacrament or of the rite's becoming difficult because of the large number of participants or some other reason.

In all that pertains to Communion under both kinds, the *Norms for the Distribution and Reception of Holy Communion under Both Kinds in the Dioceses of the United States of America* are to be followed (see nos. 27–54).

Episcopus diœcesanus normas circa Communionem sub utraque specie pro sua diœcesi definire potest, etiam in ecclesiis religiosorum et in parvis cœtibus servandas. Eidem Episcopo facultas datur Communionem sub utraque specie permittendi, quoties id sacerdoti cui, uti pastori proprio, communitas commissa est, opportunum videatur, dummodo fideles bene instructi sint et absit omne periculum profanationis Sacramenti, vel ritus difficilior evadat ob multitudinem participantium aliamve causam.

Quod autem ad modum distribuendi fidelibus sacram Communionem sub utraque specie, et ad facultatis extensionem Conferentiæ Episcoporum normas edere possunt, actis a Sede Apostolica recognitis.

The final paragraph of no. 283 goes well beyond *IGMR1975* (no. 242) in enlarging the prerogative of the diocesan bishop to permit Communion under both kinds, at the discretion of pastors, in well-prepared parish communities. In so doing, *IGMR2002* has largely eliminated the need for pastors to seek the explicit permission of the bishop to give Communion under both forms, "thus presenting Communion under both kinds as the expected way that Communion is given during every Mass."[30] This further regularizes a situation which was already underway in the United States, when the ordinary was given the right to determine when laity might be permitted to receive Communion in both kinds on weekdays (1970) and on Sundays (1978).

The paragraph continues by providing a general directive that it is within the prerogative of conferences of bishops to adapt the norms for receiving Communion under both forms, which will then require the *recognitio* of the Holy See (see no. 390 below). GIRM2003 refers readers to the 2001 document "Norms for the Distribution and Reception of Holy Communion Under Both Kinds in the Dioceses of the United States of America"[31] (singling out nos. 27–54) for consultation "in all that pertains to Communion under both kinds."

30. Dennis Smolarski, *The General Instruction of the Roman Missal, 1969–2002: A Commentary* (Collegeville, MN: The Liturgical Press, 2003), 60.

31. "Norms for the Distribution and Reception of Holy Communion Under Both Kinds in the Dioceses of the United States of America" (2001); the text is available at http://www.usccb.org/liturgy/current/norms.shtml (accessed December, 2006).

284. When Communion is distributed under both kinds,

a. The chalice is usually administered by a deacon or, when no deacon is present, by a priest, or even by a duly instituted acolyte or another extraordinary minister of Holy Communion, or by a member of the faithful who, in case of necessity, has been entrusted with this duty for a single occasion;

b. Whatever may remain of the Blood of Christ is consumed at the altar by the priest or the deacon or the duly instituted acolyte who ministered the chalice. The same then purifies, wipes, and arranges the sacred vessels in the usual way.

Any of the faithful who wish to receive Holy Communion under the species of bread alone should be granted their wish.

284. Cum Communio sub utraque specie distribuitur:

a) ad calicem de more ministrat diaconus vel, eo absente, presbyter; vel etiam acolythus rite institutus aut alius minister extraordinarius sacræ Communionis; aut fidelis, cui, in casu necessitatis, hoc officium ad actum concreditur;

b) quod de Sanguine Christi forte remanet sumitur ad altare a sacerdote, vel diacono, vel ab acolytho rite instituto, qui calici ministravit et vasa sacra more solito purificat, abstergit et componit.

Fidelibus, qui forte sub specie tantum panis communicare volunt, sacra Communio hac forma præbeatur.

---

284. This new article presents a fresh summary of the parameters for the distribution of Communion under both species, including: who may minister the chalice, how any extra consecrated wine is to be consumed, and a stress on the freedom of communicants to receive Communion under the form of bread alone.

The chalice is "usually" (*de more*) ministered by the deacon; if there is no deacon, then a priest, instituted acolyte, or another "extraordinary minister" (*minister extraordinarius*) of Communion assumes this role. In their absence, even a member of the assembly may be asked to serve in this capacity for a single occasion "in case of necessity" (*in casu necessitatis*).

This provision goes far beyond what was permitted by *IGMR1970* (no. 244). In that Instruction only a priest, with or without the assistance of a deacon, was permitted to minister Communion. If a deacon is assisting, he may give the chalice. *IGMR1970*, no. 245 describes the rite when the priest is without the assistance of a deacon; in such situations, the Instruction envisioned two processions of the faithful, one for the eucharistized bread followed by a second to receive from the chalice.

IGMR1975 (no. 244) demonstrates significant differences from its predecessor. Most important is the addition of the acolyte to the list of deacon or other assisting priest who may help with Communion under both forms. Consequently, *IGMR1975* speaks more generically of the priest giving the chalice "to the minister" (*ministro*, no. 244c) to assist in giving Communion under both forms. Such changes occurred in light of Paul VI's restoration of the permanent diaconate in 1972,[32] and more importantly, his establishment of the instituted acolyte at the same time (see no. 98 above). One of the duties of the acolyte was to serve as a special minister of Communion; this duty was recognized as an "extraordinary" one, both in *Ministeria quaedam* (*MQ*, no. 6) and later in *CIC1983* (c. 910, par. 2).

Even though *MQ* reserved instituted ministries to men, a Vatican spokesperson at the time noted that "nothing therefore prevents women's continuing to be deputed for public readings during liturgical celebrations. . . . Similarly, according to the norms now in effect, bishops may always request the Holy See for the authorization of women as special ministers of holy communion."[33]

Already in 1970, the instruction from the Congregation for Divine Worship, *Liturgicae instaurationes* ("On the orderly carrying out of the Constitution on the Liturgy"), declared that, apart from priests, deacons, and instituted acolytes, "The Holy See has the power to permit the appointment of other known and worthy persons as ministers, if they have received a mandate" (no. 6d).[34] The issue of who might receive such a mandate had been clarified in the 1969 instruction *Fidei custos* from the Congregation for the Discipline of the Sacraments treating of special ministers of Communion. According to that document bishops, other authorities, and their delegates might seek permission from the Holy See to allow "fit persons to administer communion to themselves and to the faithful" because of a shortage of ministers, when it was difficult for the regular minister, or whenever the numbers for Communion would unduly lengthen the celebration (no. 1). The order of preference for choosing such a person was: subdeacon, cleric in minor orders, one who had received tonsure, male religious, woman religious, male catechist (unless a male catechist is preferable to a woman religious), a layman, and finally a laywoman (no. 3).[35] In 1971 the US

32. See his motu proprio *Ad pascendum* (15 August 1972), in *AAS* 64 (1972): 534–40, in DOL, nos. 2576–2591.

33. *L'Osservatore Romano* (6 October 1972); *Notitiae* 9 (1973): 16; see DOL, no. 2932, R1. Papal rescripts authorizing women religious to give Communion under the form of bread alone when an ordinary minister of the Eucharist was absent for a time were granted for specific situations in Brazil (1965) and Canada (1966). Under similar conditions male laity or superiors of cloistered women's convents were authorized for West Germany (1968). Kingston, Jamaica (1968) and Duluth, Minnesota (1969) received rescripts which allowed laity to function as Communion ministers. These special cases paved the way for the special ministers of Communion required once Communion under both forms was undertaken. See DOL, nos. 2035, 2039–42 and 2070–71.

34. *AAS* 62 (1970): 692–704, in DOL, no. 524d.

35. DOL, nos. 2044 and 2046. An original Latin text was never published. A 1969 version was sent to the presidents of bishops' conferences. See Bugnini, *Reform of the Liturgy*, 636–40. In Canada an issue of the *National Bulletin on Liturgy* was dedicated to the topic (4:31 [1970]).

bishops' conference received permission to appoint qualified lay persons as Communion ministers, apparently without regard to their state of life.[36]

The 1973 instruction *Immensae caritatis* of the Congregation for the Discipline of the Sacraments (on facilitating Communion) added that the "fit persons" for this ministry were to be chosen by local ordinaries by name "in a given instance or for a set period or even permanently" (no. 1).[37] Individual priests might appoint such a person for a specific occasion. These ministers were to be chosen according to the preferred order of reader, major seminarian, male religious, woman religious, catechist, one of the faithful (a man or a woman). A rite was later published by which the *mandatum* (commission) was to be given.[38] *Minister extraordinarius* was translated by ICEL as "special minister."[39] In a 1976 letter to the US bishops, Paul VI referred to these as "extraordinary ministers duly deputed"[40]; the language of "extraordinary minister" (*extraordinarius minister*) is repeated in *CIC1983*, c. 910.

IGMR2002, no. 284 also deals with the issue of consecrated wine left over after the distribution of Communion, and on respecting the preference of those who might choose to receive under the form of bread alone. On the first point, the text limits this act to the priest, deacon, or "the duly instituted acolyte who ministered the chalice" (*vel acolytho rite instituto qui calici ministravit*).[41] This is specifically to be done *ad altare*. The purification of the chalice itself, however, is to be done as earlier described.[42] The US bishops sought an indult to permit

36. Congregation for the Discipline of the Sacraments, *Rescript* to the Conference of Bishops, authorizing laypersons to give Communion (9 March 1971), see DOL, nos. 2071–2072. Cf. the 14 February 1971 statement by the US Bishops' Committee on the Liturgy in *BCL Newsletter* 7 (April–May 1971): 282.

37. AAS 65 (1973): 264–71, in DOL, no. 2075.

38. *Notitiae* 9 (1973): 165–67, in DOL, nos. 2949–2952. For the rite in Canada see "Auxiliary Ministers," *National Bulletin on Liturgy* 11, no. 66 (1978): 301–308; and Canadian Conference of Catholic Bishops, *Celebrations of Installation and Recognition* (Ottawa: Publications Service, 2005), 96–105.

39. *Immensae caritatis* (January 29, 1973), in DOL 265, no. 2074; and in the rite of commissioning issued by the Congregation for Divine Worship in *Notitiae* 83 (1973): 165–67. See also *BCL Newsletter* 14 (April–May 1978): 622; John P. Beal, James A. Coriden, Thomas J. Green, eds., *New Commentary on the Code of Canon Law* (New York: Paulist, 2000), 1105–1106. But now see Congregation for Divine Worship and the Sacraments, *Redemptionis Sacramentum (RedSac)*, no. 156, which mandates the term "extraordinary minister of holy communion."

40. *AAS* 68 (1976): 406–15, in DOL, no. 562.

41. Smolarski notes that *IGMR2002* (nos. 163, 182, and 247) mentions only priests and deacons as those who may consume any remaining consecrated wine after Communion, *The General Instruction of the Roman Missal*, 66.

42. The wording of this sentence might be taken to refer to the altar as an appropriate place for cleansing the vessels and it is allowed for Mass without a deacon (no. 163). A deacon carries the vessels to the credence table, cleansing them at that time or after Mass (nos. 183 and 247). *RedSac* (no. 119) seems to prefer that the priest (and deacon also) purifies the vessels at the altar immediately following the distribution of Communion. Their cleansing is also permissible after Mass. An instituted acolyte purifies them at the credence table.

285. For Communion under both kinds the following should be prepared:

a. If Communion from the chalice is carried out by communicants' drinking

285. Ad Communionem sub utraque specie distribuendam, parentur:

a) si Communio calicis fit bibendo directe ex calice, vel calix sufficientis magni-

---

lay eucharistic ministers to consume whatever remained in their chalices. The Congregation for Divine Worship and Discipline of the Sacraments in 2002 responded that neither an indult nor permission of the diocesan bishop was needed since anyone, minister or communicant, may help consume whatever remains of the excess species in case of need.[43]

Given the catechetical points listed in no. 282 above, the next directive clarifying that communicants may still choose to receive Communion under the form of bread only, even when Communion is being distributed under both forms, seems a logical insertion.[44] In future editions of *IGMR* the reverse concern of any of the faithful who wish to receive Holy Communion under the species of wine alone should also be addressed. Paralysis, tracheotomy, or other medical conditions including those common to the dying may render ingestion of the host impossible.[45] More common is celiac disease which excludes reception of the sacramental bread (cf. no. 320 below). Sufferers from celiac disease cannot sip from a chalice in which even a fragment of the host has been placed. Thus it is important that, where people who suffer from this disease are present, a cup free from contamination by any wheat by-products be reserved for them. The dilemma facing priests who suffer from celiac disease is spelled out in a 2003 letter from the Congregation for the Doctrine of the Faith.[46] Such a priest may be able to participate only as a concelebrant of Mass. The laity's dilemma is that in most parishes they will be unable to receive Communion at all, despite *CIC1983*, c. 843, giving every Catholic in good standing the right to receive Holy Communion (cf. *RedSac*, no. 91).

285. This article edits and condenses the directives found in *IGMR1975* (no. 243) on preparations for the distribution of Communion under both species. Consistent with no. 280 above, references to the distribution of Communion

43. *BCL Newsletter* 38 (2002): 64.

44. For analysis of the biochemistry of baking Communion breads as well as liturgical issues see J. Frank Henderson, "Eucharistic Bread: Actual Food," *National Bulletin on Liturgy*, 12, no. 69 (1979): 129–43.

45. See the negative judgments in respect to canon 852 on Communion through a stomach tube in T. Lincoln Bouscaret and James I. O'Connor, *Canon Law Digest* 6 (1963–1967): 562–65.

46. The letter of Cardinal Ratzinger of 24 July 2003 (Prot. 89/78–174 98) is reprinted in *BCL Newsletter* (2003) at http://www.nccbuscc.org/liturgy/innews/1103.shtml (accessed December 2006); other pertinent references to this issue include *BCL Newsletter* 31 (1995): 1449–50; 31 (November 1995): 1467–68; and 36 (April–May 2000): 1688–90; also, Canadian Conference of Catholic Bishops, National Liturgy Office, "Celiac Disease and Communion," available at www.cccb.ca/site/content/view/2124/1172/lang,eng/.

directly from the chalice, a chalice of a sufficiently large size or several chalices are prepared. Care should, however, be taken in planning lest beyond what is needed of the Blood of Christ remains to be consumed at the end of the celebration.

b. If Communion is carried out by intinction, the hosts should be neither too thin nor too small, but rather a little thicker than usual, so that after being dipped partly into the Blood of Christ they can still easily be distributed to each communicant.

tudinis, vel plures calices, cauto semper tamen ut prævideatur ne copia Sanguinis Christi plus æquo remaneat in fine celebrationis sumenda;

b) si per intinctionem fit, hostiæ ne sint nimis tenues neque nimis parvæ, sed paulum spissiores solito, ut, Sanguine partim intinctæ, possint commode distribui.

286. If Communion of the Blood of Christ is carried out by communicants' drinking from the chalice, each communicant, after receiving the Body of Christ,

286. Si Communio Sanguinis fit bibendo e calice, communicandus postquam Corpus Christi accepit, transit ad calicis ministrum et stat coram eo. Minister dicit:

---

by tube or spoon have been dropped from no. 285b. The instructions for Communion by intinction, dealing with thickness of the host ("a little thicker than usual," *paulum spissiores solito*) have been retained almost word for word. It is notable that the Instruction speaks of intincted hosts as "distributed" (*distribui*), clarifying that the communicant does not have the option of dipping the host in the chalice (cf. no. 287 below). Consonant with no. 85 above, the faithful are to receive Communion rather than take it.[47]

Most notable in this article, however, are the new directives (no. 285a) concerning the preparation for Communion from the cup. Beginning this article with a discussion of "drinking directly from the chalice" *(bibendo directe ex calice)* underscores the primacy of this symbol. The chalice should either be large enough[48] to use by itself (*sufficientis magnitudinis*), or several cups should be used. A caution is added here on the need for an accurate judgment of the amount of wine needed, so that there is not a large amount left to be consumed at the end of Mass.

286. In this article, *IGMR2002* has condensed what was a much longer article in *IGMR1975* (no. 244). The practice over three decades of distributing Communion directly from the chalice renders many of the previous step-by-step instructions unnecessary. The directives on the priest's Communion and on his

47. See Robert F. Taft, "Receiving Communion: a Forgotten Symbol?" *Beyond East and West: Problems in Liturgical Understanding* (Washington DC: Pastoral Press, 1984), 101–109.

48. In discussing the procession with the gifts, the US bishops state that the vessels containing the bread and wine should be such "that can be easily seen," ITTOM, no. 105.

moves and stands facing the minister of the chalice. The minister says, *Sanguis Christi (The Blood of Christ)*, the communicant responds, *Amen*, and the minister hands over the chalice, which the communicant raises to his or her mouth. Each communicant drinks a little from the chalice, hands it back to the minister, and then withdraws; the minister wipes the rim of the chalice with the purificator.

Sanguis Christi; communicandus respondet: Amen, et minister porrigit ei calicem, quem communicandus ipse manibus suis ori admovet. Communicandus paulum e calice bibit, eum ministro restituit et recedit; minister autem labrum calicis purificatorio abstergit.

(and the minister's) positioning themselves before distributing Communion to the congregation (*IGMR1975*, no. 244a-b) have been dropped. In addition, the 1975 subsection detailing the rite of distribution of the consecrated host (no. 244c) is also dropped, including the earlier notations that the communicants approach one by one (*singuli*), and that they "make the proper reverence" (*debitam reverentiam faciunt*) before receiving.

The focus of this article in *IGMR2002* is the Communion of the faithful from the chalice. Similar to *IGMR1975* (no. 244d), communicants are simply to move to and stand in front of the "minister of the chalice" (*calicis ministrum; ad diaconum* in *IGMR1970*). The minister speaks the distribution formula, communicants respond "Amen," take the proffered chalice into their own hands and lift it to drink. The communicant drinks "a little from the chalice" (*paulum e calice*), hands the cup back to the minister and "withdraws" (*recedit*). The minister then wipes the "rim" (*labrum*) of the chalice with the purificator. Other details from *IGMR1975* have been dropped: the reference to the communicants taking the cup themselves "if convenient" (*pro opportunitate*), the stipulation that the communicant hold the purificator "in the left hand" (*tenens manu sinistra*), under the mouth, and the admonition that the communicant "take care not to spill [the Blood]" (*attendens ne quid Sanguinis defluat*).

An entire article from *IGMR1975* (no. 245), detailing how Communion is to be distributed under both species if only a priest is present, has been dropped. A parallel section, on how intinction is to be done by an unassisted priest, has also been deleted (*IGMR1975*, no. 247).

While detailing some of the rubrics of Communion under both forms, this and the surrounding articles of *IGMR2002* say nothing about the manner of this exchange. To express the ritual significance of encounter and communion with God and neighbor, the minister's expression and demeanor are to be inviting, unhurried, and engage the communicant; and the communicant is to respond in a fully human way, appropriate to one's context and culture.

The ritual descriptions in nos. 285 and 286 make no reference to bowing the head or other sign of reverence immediately prior to the reception of Commun-

287. If Communion from the chalice is carried out by intinction, each communicant, holding a communion-plate under the chin, approaches the priest who holds a vessel with the sacred particles, a minister standing at his side and holding the chalice. The priest takes a host, dips it partly into the chalice and, showing it, says, *Corpus et Sanguis Christi (The Body and Blood of Christ).* The communicant responds, *Amen*, receives the Sacrament in the mouth from the priest, and then withdraws.

287. Si Communio calicis fit per intinctionem, communicandus, patinam sub ore tenens, accedit ad sacerdotem, qui vas cum sacris particulis tenet et ad cuius latus sistit minister qui calicem sustinet. Sacerdos hostiam accipit, partem eius in calicem intingit et eam ostendendo dicit: Corpus et Sanguis Christi; communicandus respondet: Amen, a sacerdote Sacramentum ore recipit, ac postea recedit.

---

ion. Earlier, GIRM2003 states that communicants bow their heads before receiving either or both species (see no. 160 above).[49]

287. This last article in this section of *IGMR2002* is concerned with Communion by intinction. Placing a consideration of intinction in this place implicitly recognizes the stronger symbol of drinking directly from the cup, as well as the increased rarity of this form of Communion under both forms which is not always recommended.[50] Viruses like AIDS and SARS have lessened eagerness for sharing the common cup, despite the fact that medical research has yet to produce any evidence that a disease such as AIDS can be transmitted by drinking from a common cup. Intinction has, by consequence, become a substitute for the fuller sign of drinking directly from the chalice. Dissemination of medical research would go far to address this issue.[51] Also helpful for promoting Communion from the common cup is effective training of Communion ministers and sacristans in rules of good hygiene, and sensitive catechesis for the faithful concerning when it might be appropriate for them to refrain from drinking from a common cup (e.g., when suffering from the common cold or flu).

In *IGMR1975* intinction is given its own subheading and is addressed in two separate articles (nos. 246 and 247). *IGMR2002* discusses intinction by condensing the first of these earlier articles (no. 246) and dropping the subheading. The

49. The Canadian adaptation states, "[w]hen receiving Holy Communion standing, the faithful should make a simple bow of the head before the minister. . . . The simple bow of the head is not repeated before receiving the Precious Blood" (no. 160).

50. The proposed Canadian version of GIRM makes this addition to no. 287: "In the dioceses of Canada, the preferred manner for giving Communion under both kinds is the direct administration of the chalice. Intinction is not recommended." Intinction has proved to be a more difficult form to minister, and there has been some comment about its inappropriateness for lay ministers. Intinction has never been recommended in Canada (English sector).

51. Canadian Conference of Catholic Bishops, Episcopal Commission for Liturgy—English Sector, "Communion from the Cup." See www.cccb.ca/site/content/view/2125/1226/lang,eng/ (accessed 31 January 2007).

other article (no. 247), concerned with intinction without a deacon, assisting priest or acolyte present, has been dropped. Thus, *IGMR2002* (given the provisions of no. 284 above) envisions that there will always be an assisting minister if Communion is distributed by intinction.

The directives for intinction are much the same as in *IGMR1975*. The communicant holds "a communion-plate under the chin" (*patinam sub ore tenens*), and approaches the priest,[52] who holds a container of hosts, while a minister next to him holds a chalice. The priest takes a host and dips it partially into the chalice, holds it up, and recites the distribution formula. The communicant responds "Amen" and receives the host in the mouth.

Other articles that followed in *IGMR1975*, concerning Communion under both species using a tube (nos. 248–250) and spoon (nos. 251–252), have been omitted. As noted in no. 280 above, these are no longer specified options in the Roman Rite. The norms issued by the US bishops in 2001 state that "distribution of the Precious Blood by a spoon or through a straw is not customary in the Latin dioceses of the United States of America."[53]

52. All references to communicants approaching one by one and making a gesture of reverence, found in *IGMR1975*, no. 246b have been dropped.

53. "Norms for the Distribution and Reception of Holy Communion Under Both Kinds in the Dioceses of the United States of America," no. 48.

GIRM—Notes (English)

105. Cf. Sacred Congregation of Rites, Instruction *Eucharisticum mysterium*, On the worship of the Eucharist, 25 May 1967, no. 32: AAS 59 (1967), p. 558.

106. Cf. Council of Trent, session 21, *Doctrina de communione sub utraque specie et parvulorum*, 16 July 1562, chaps. 1–3: Denz-Schön, 1725–1729.

107. Cf. ibid., chap. 2: Denz-Schön, 1728.

IGMR—Notes (Latin)

105. Cf. S. Congr. Rituum, Instr. *Eucharisticum mysterium*, diei 25 maii 1967, n. 32: A.A.S. 59 (1967) p. 558.

106. Cf. Conc. Œcum. Trid., Sessio XXI, diei 16 iulii 1562, Decr. de communione eucharistica, capp. 1–3: Denz.-Schönm. 1725–1729.

107. Cf. *ibidem*, cap. 2: Denz.-Schönm. 1728.

CHAPTER V

The Arrangement and Furnishings of Churches for the Celebration of the Eucharist

(*DE ECCLESIARUM DISPOSITIONE ET ORNATU AD EUCHARISTIAM CELEBRANDAM*)

Mark E. Wedig and Richard S. Vosko

It is said that the spaces we shape will, in turn, shape us.[1] The power of a place in the formation of the behavior and attitudes of humans in that place is so significant it cannot be overlooked. Fundamentally, this is the reason why the *Institutio Generalis Missalis Romani* (*IGMR*) includes instructions for preparing a proper setting for the enactment of the eucharistic rites. Chapter V in *IGMR2002* presumes not only a faithful adherence to the strength of the Church's traditions but also a steadfast desire to implement the guidelines in an appropriate manner.

This commentary will consider some of the theoretical and practical underpinnings of each article in Chapter V so that the decisive application of the principles in the actual environment for worship will, in some way, abide by the spirit of the Instruction and contribute to a sense of unity throughout the Church. This foundation is important because local adaptations respectful of diverse cultural milieus will inevitably result in remarkably different artistic and architectural solutions. For example, the ecclesiological perspective of *IGMR2002* seems to emphasize a hierarchical arrangement of space (see no. 295 below) with distinct areas in each place of worship for clergy and laity. Yet there are already a number of new and renovated church settings in the Americas that align liturgical settings in architecturally creative ways without denying or impeding the expression of the Church's hierarchical nature.

1. This quote is attributed to Winston Churchill, who apparently made the remark during the reconstruction of the House of Commons in Great Britain after World War II.

Because the local bishop is the chief liturgist (cf. Seasoltz, 33–35 and no. 92 above) he is responsible not only for the celebration of all sacramental rituals in his jurisdiction but also the construction of churches and the requisites for the celebration of the rites. This responsibility must be exercised with pastoral sensitivity. The stewardship of individual bishops in these matters will also result in diverse expressions not only in liturgical practice but also in the interior design of the church buildings. Thus, in some dioceses, the tabernacle may be found in its own distinct chapel; in others, it may be found very near the central altar used for the celebration of the Eucharist.

The stylistic manner in which every church is designed and organized will also depend on a number of non-liturgical issues. In some regions of the Americas, cultural influences foster popular devotional practices and the presence of multiple images of saints dominate the worship environment. In other places the church might appear barren and devoid of artistic embellishment. Other factors that can have an impact on the design of a church include media arts, energy efficiency, the economy, environmental stewardship, the merging of parishes, and the lack of appropriate models.[2]

A number of areas that comprise the worship environment are excluded from this chapter, presumably because it focuses on the celebration of the Eucharist and not other sacraments. Nevertheless, a comprehensive plan for a church building cannot overlook the significance of pathways, portals, public gathering areas and baptisteries or factors like acoustics, light, and ornamentation. Although these elements are often discussed in national and local pastoral instructions, it would have been helpful if they had been considered here.[3] Similarly, references to the *CaerEp* would have been helpful in topics that also pertain to the arrangement and furnishings of cathedrals.

Finally, there is the question of the implementation of Chapter V in places of worship built or renovated prior to the date of the promulgation of *IGMR2002*. Canons 7, 8 and 9 in the 1983 *Codex Iuris Canonici* (*CIC1983*) imply that if plans were approved or if places of worship were built or renovated before the effective date of 25 July 2000, the norms in *IGMR2002* are not retroactive.[4] However, the local ordinary who has the authority in such matters may insist that a particular facet of *IGMR2002* be implemented according to his particular guidelines.

2. *Ceremoniale Episcopale* (*CaerEp*) notes that the "cathedral church should be a model for the other churches in the dioceses" (no. 46). Yet, it is apparent that not all cathedrals have been entirely refashioned to conform to directives in liturgical documents. For example, many cathedrals do not have a chapel for the tabernacle (*CaerEp*, no. 49), a baptistery (*CaerEp*, no. 52), or a gathering place for people (*CaerEp*, no. 54).

3. See *Our Place of Worship*, Canadian Conference of Catholic Bishops (Ottawa, Ontario, 1999), and *Built of Living Stones* (BLS).

4. John M. Huels, "Effective Date of Revised General Instruction of the Roman Missal," in F. Stephen Pedone and James I. Donlon, eds., *Roman Replies and CLSA Advisory Opinions 2004* (Washington, DC: Canon Law Society of America, 2004), 77–80.

Chapter V
THE ARRANGEMENT AND FURNISHINGS OF CHURCHES FOR THE CELEBRATION OF THE EUCHARIST

I. General Principles

288. For the celebration of the Eucharist, the people of God normally are gathered together in a church or, if there is no church or if it is too small, then in another respectable place that is nonetheless worthy of so great a mystery. Churches, therefore, and other places should be suitable for carrying out the sacred action and for ensuring the active participation of the faithful. Sacred buildings and requisites for divine worship should, moreover, be truly worthy

Caput V
DE ECCLESIARUM DISPOSITIONE ET ORNATU AD EUCHARISTIAM CELEBRANDAM

I. Principia Generalia

288. Ad Eucharistiam celebrandam, populus Dei plerumque in ecclesiam congregatur vel, ea deficiente aut insufficiente, in alium locum honestum qui tamen sit tanto mysterio dignus. Ecclesiæ igitur, aliave loca, ad sacram actionem exsequendam et ad fidelium actuosam participationem obtinendam apta sint. Ædes sacræ insuper et res ad cultum divinum pertinentes vere sint dignæ, pulchræ, atque rerum supernarum signa et symbola.[108]

The overall interpretative framework of this commentary on Chapter V of *IGMR2002* is best understood as ecclesiological. This interpretation presumes that "The Arrangement and Furnishings of Churches for the Celebration of the Eucharist" mediates particular visions of the Church. The commentary will follow the schema of Chapter V: a) general principles for arrangement and furnishing of churches, b) the arrangement of the sanctuary, and c) the arrangement of the rest of the church building.

General Principles

288. Chapter V begins by envisioning the Church, specifically a local Church, gathered and actively participating in a beautiful environment that symbolizes heavenly and transcendent realities. Although this introductory article recognizes the importance of the community and its active participation (*Sacrosanctum Concilium* [*SC*], no. 14) in transcendent realities, emphasis is placed on the church building as symbol of the divine. *IGMR2002* underlines that the church edifice needs to feature an otherworldly character over any other distinctiveness.

What the Instruction does not emphasize, however, is that there are two poles of ecclesiological self-realization that must be considered by each community of faith.[5] Besides considering the Church as God's divine gift, one also needs to reflect on the Church as a human endeavor. *IGMR2002* begins here with an emphasis on "heavenly realities;" perhaps an ascending ecclesiology, beginning with the human and earthly metaphors, is a more realistic and proper place to start this reflection.

5. Joseph Komonchak, "The Church: God's Gift and Our Task," *Origins* 16 (1987): 735–741.

and beautiful and be signs and symbols of heavenly realities.[108]

289. Consequently, the Church constantly seeks the noble assistance of the arts and admits the artistic expressions of all peoples and regions.[109] In fact, just as she is intent on preserving the works of art and the artistic treasures handed down from past centuries[110] and, insofar as necessary, on adapting them to new needs, so also she strives to promote new works of art that are in harmony with the character of each successive age.[111]

On account of this, in commissioning artists and choosing works of art to be admitted into a church, what should be required is that true excellence in art which nourishes faith and devotion and accords authentically with both the meaning and the purpose for which it is intended.[112]

289. Proinde, Ecclesia nobile subsidium artium continenter quærit, et omnium gentium atque regionum artis significationes admittit.[109] Immo, sicut studet artis opera atque thesauros a sæculis anteactis tradita servare[110] et, quatenus opus est, novis necessitatibus aptare, nova cuiusque ætatis indoli consona promovere contendit.[111]

Quapropter in instituendis artificibus necnon in seligendis operibus in ecclesiam admittendis, vera artis præstantia exquiratur, quæ fidem et pietatem alat et cum veritate significationis et finis cui destinatur congruat.[112]

Assurance of the participation of the assembly can be achieved in the arrangement and design of a church without compromising either the physical beauty of a building or the sacramental nature of the gathering. Worshiping in a "worthy and beautiful" environment is always balanced by a concern with factors like sightlines, acoustics, distance, comfort, and safety (see no. 293 below). The challenge is to create places of worship and to utilize liturgical symbols in ways that will stimulate all the senses and stir the imagination. Ultimately, it is the assembly that is called to transcendence.[6]

289. This article stresses that the Church always has sought the gracious support of the arts and collaboration with artists and artisans in preserving its heritage. The Church's involvement in the arts has been inclusive of a diversity of cultural expressions, playing a major role in preserving aesthetic treasures over the ages. Local churches give diverse and unique expression to artistic and architectural treasures, standing behind artists and artisans whose work represents a great religious aesthetic tradition and also shapes pathways for new aesthetic expression.

IGMR2002 here shows a strong preference for the commissioning of works of art instead of purchasing mass-produced objects in order to promote excellence in the aesthetics of the liturgical environment. Excellence in liturgical art is characterized by the use of authentic materials, the application of appropriate scale

6. For a helpful reflection on the search for transcendence, see Richard R. Gaillardetz, "North American Culture and the Liturgical Life of the Church: The Separation of the Quests for Transcendence and Community," *Worship* 68 (1994): 403–16.

290. All churches should be dedicated or, at least, blessed. Cathedrals and parish churches, however, are to be dedicated with a solemn rite.

290. Ecclesiæ omnes dedicentur vel saltem benedicantur. Cathedrales tamen et parœciales ecclesiæ sollemni ritu dedicentur.

---

and proportion, the installation in specific settings, a resonance with an indigenous (local community) narrative and some expression of faith on the part of the artist. *IGMR2002* makes claims for excellence, rightly noting the long-standing ecclesial tradition of art patronage, although there have been controversies over this claim in contemporary settings. Often there is a divide between aesthetic culture and the Church in the modern and postmodern worlds.[7]

Personal taste can govern artistic expression in church buildings. While one can point to the history of art and architecture to find examples that have outlasted trends, it is also important to look to more contemporary designers or artists for fresh interpretations of biblical texts or theological doctrines. Likewise ritual furnishings should be designed and fabricated with the same attention afforded fine works of art in terms of scale, proportion, materiality, and color. Here ritual appropriateness is more significant than stylistic patterns. It is important to distinguish among works of art that are required for public worship, those that are seasonal, and those that may be important for popular devotions.[8]

290. This article is a radical simplification of *IGMR1975*, no. 255. "The Rite of Dedication of a Church and an Altar" guides the local parish or oratory in shaping the normative public ritual for offering a new space, especially the altar, to a local assembly and a local Church.[9] The revised rite (1977) focuses on the centrality of the altar, signifying Christ (cf. no. 49 above), in the dedication of a new ecclesial environment. The ritual treats the whole space as if it were a candidate for ecclesial initiation; the space is thus sprinkled and chrismated, not to become itself a member of the Body of Christ, but so that the local assembly might gather there around the altar (the central Christological axis) and find unity as the Body of Christ in this space for the Eucharist.[10]

In this sense the building is a resonator of the Body of Christ, the Church, and is "awakened" during these dedicatory rites. This metaphorical expression becomes especially apparent: 1) when the building materials themselves are natural and environmentally sustainable; 2) when the shape of the room reveals

7. R. Kevin Seasoltz, *A Sense of the Sacred: Theological Foundations of Christian Architecture and Art* (New York: Continuum, 2005), 221–251.

8. Richard S. Vosko, "A House for the Church: Structures for Public Worship in a New Millennium," *Worship* 74, no. 3 (May 2000): 194–212.

9. For a practical commentary on the *Rite of Dedication*, see Thomas Simons, *Holy People, Holy Place* (Chicago: Liturgy Training Publications, 1991).

10. See Ignazio M. Calabuig, *The Dedication of a Church and an Altar: A Theological Commentary* (Washington, DC: U.S. Catholic Conference, 1980), 12.

291. For the proper construction, restoration, and remodeling of sacred buildings, all who are involved in the work are to consult the diocesan commission on the sacred Liturgy and sacred Art. The diocesan Bishop, moreover, should use the counsel and help of this commission whenever it comes to laying down norms on this matter, approving plans for new buildings, and making decisions on the more important issues.[113]

292. Church decor should contribute toward the church's noble simplicity rather

291. Ad sacras ædes recte exstruendas, reficiendas atque disponendas, omnes quorum interest Commissionem diœcesanam de sacra Liturgia et de Arte sacra consulant. Episcopus autem diœcesanus eiusdem Commissionis consilio et adiutorio utatur, quando agitur de normis in hac re tradendis, aut de novarum ædium adumbrationibus approbandis aut de quibusdam quæstionibus nonnullius momenti diiudicandis.[113]

292. Ornatus ecclesiæ ad nobilem ipsius simplicitatem conferat, potius quam ad

---

both illumination and shadow; and 3) when the symbolic elements used in the rite (water, oil, candle light, incense, bread, and wine) are likewise organic and abundant.

291. This article clearly sets up the proper method for shaping the construction, restoration, and remodeling of sacred buildings. The diocese depends on the stewardship of the bishop and the collaboration of knowledgeable advisors. The ordinary, in consultation with a diocesan commission (*SC*, nos. 44–46 refers to three commissions: liturgy, art, music), guides and oversees the processes for new and remodeled buildings, recognizing the particular liturgical and aesthetic character of the Church and the vision articulated by the bishop and that commission for that diocese. The work of the bishop with the diocesan commission in shaping the edifices and art of the diocese embodies the missionary character of the Church, making an indelible mark on that place for years to come.

The construction, renovation, and maintenance of church buildings can represent the largest budget item in any given diocese. A complete environment for worship will also include appropriate ritual furnishings and works of art. These are compelling reasons for having competent resources on art and architecture, to assist liturgical commissions or offices in advising the local bishop about the environment for worship.

Because of shifting demographics, many dioceses have had to close or merge parishes. The fate of unused church buildings and their contents is a sensitive issue. On the other hand, in some regions the growing Catholic population and dwindling presbyterate are creating a need for much larger church buildings. The design of these can challenge the standard aesthetic formularies as well as the liturgical practice of the community. Responsible real estate stewardship implies that every diocese should create a master plan to guide the future development of all properties.

292. Here *IGMR2002* offers a considerable re-ordering of material from *IGMR1975* in order to bring greater logic and coherence to addressing the

than ostentation. In the choice of materials for church appointments there should be a concern for genuineness of materials and an intent to foster the instruction of the faithful and the dignity of the entire sacred place.

293. A proper arrangement of a church and its surroundings that appropriately meets contemporary needs requires attention not only to the elements related more directly to the celebration of the sacred actions but also to those things conducive to the appropriate comfort of the faithful that are normally forthcoming in places where people regularly gather.

pompam. In elementis autem seligendis quæ ad ornatum pertinent, rerum veritas curetur, atque eo contendatur, ut ad fidelium institutionem conferat et ad dignitatem totius loci sacri.

293. Apta ecclesiæ eiusque adiunctorum dispositio, quæ necessitatibus nostræ ætatis opportune respondeat, requirit ut non ea solummodo curentur quæ ad sacras actiones celebrandas directius pertineant, sed ut ea quoque prævideantur, quæ ad fidelium convenientem commoditatem tendunt, quæque in locis ubi populus congregatur habitualiter prævideri solent.

---

general plan of church in relationship to its method of construction (see no. 291 above). This article recognizes that much of the effort (and impact) made by the local diocese in shaping a proper vision of Church depends on emphasizing the dignity of its sacred spaces. It advises that a sacred dignity be achieved through simplicity and modesty of forms and not ostentation or pretension.[11] Simplicity does not mean adhering to a particular style, and does not necessarily imply austerity or minimalism. The strengths of the local Church environment are dependent, on the one hand, on the educational processes that reveal how contemporary aesthetics relates to Church and culture. On the other hand, the document recognizes that the materials chosen for church appointments are formative in constituting dignity of place and the formation of community. The space itself is mystagogical.

293. This article affirms that the fundamental human needs of contemporary cultures affect our consideration of the expectations of a public building. One example of how contemporary culture has raised our awareness of human needs can be seen in the emerging culture of disability and how it has influenced the construction and renovation of churches around concerns for accessibility.[12] Here *IGMR2002* correlates the accessibility of the building and people's comfort. Civil codes about the safety and security of buildings alter the arrangement of public spaces as well as require clearly marked entrances and exits. Many of these considerations challenge our traditional understanding of who and what constitutes the Church.

In this sense dignity is not merely a matter of aesthetics. The respect for all members of the assembly must resonate throughout the environment.

11. Mark E. Wedig, "Edifice and Image: Reform of the Roman Catholic Worship Environment," *New Theology Review* 15, no. 3 (August 2002): 5–15.

12. United States Conference of Catholic Bishops, *Guidelines for the Celebration of the Sacraments with Persons with Disabilities* (Washington, DC: USCCB, 1995); Edward Foley, ed., *Developmental Disabilities and Sacramental Access* (Collegeville, MN: The Liturgical Press, 1994).

294. The People of God, gathered for Mass, has a coherent and hierarchical structure, which finds its expression in the variety of ministries and the variety of actions according to the different parts of the celebration. The general ordering of the sacred building must be such that in some way it conveys the image of the gathered assembly and allows the appropriate ordering of all the participants, as well as facilitating each in the proper carrying out of his function.

The faithful and the choir should have a place that facilitates their active participation.[114]

The priest celebrant, the deacon, and the other ministers have places in the sanctuary. Seats for concelebrants should also be prepared there. If, however, their number is great, seats should be arranged in another part of the church, but near the altar.

All these elements, even though they must express the hierarchical structure and the diversity of ministries, should nevertheless bring about a close and coherent unity that is clearly expressive of the unity of the entire holy people. Indeed, the character and beauty of the place and all its furnishings should foster devotion and show forth the holiness of the mysteries celebrated there.

294. Populus Dei, qui ad Missam congregatur, cohærentem et hierarchicam habet ordinationem, quæ diversis ministeriis diversaque actione pro singulis celebrationis partibus exprimitur. Generalis itaque dispositio ædis sacræ ea sit oportet quæ cœtus congregati imaginem quodammodo præ se ferat, atque congruam omnium ordinationem permittat necnon rectam muneris exsecutionem uniuscuiusque foveat.

Fideles atque schola cantorum locum obtinebunt, qui ipsorum actuosam participationem faciliorem reddat.[114]

Sacerdos celebrans, diaconus et alii ministri locum capient in presbyterio. Ibidem parentur sedes concelebrantium; si vero eorum numerus magnus sit, sedes in alia ecclesiæ parte, sed prope altare, disponantur.

Hæc omnia, quamvis hierarchicam dispositionem et munerum diversitatem exprimere debeant, intimam tamen et cohærentem unitatem efficiant, qua unitas totius plebis sanctæ clare eluceat. Natura vero et pulchritudo loci universæque supellectilis pietatem foveant et sanctitatem mysteriorum quæ celebrantur ostendant.

Sustainable design and energy conservation are important ingredients in the composition of all buildings. Many architectural firms are now LEED[13] accredited to help their clients develop green buildings. The application of these principles will also likely affect the design and the cost of churches and cathedrals. Nevertheless, older churches, like newer ones, need to comply with civic standards. More and more church members consider this issue a critical ethical one.[14]

294. The conclusion of the General Principles section describes the makeup of the *ecclesia* and the way the church building should effectively mirror the

13. Leadership in Energy and Environmental Design (LEED) was developed by the nonprofit, nongovernmental United States Green Building Council in 1993.

14. Larry L. Rasmussen, *Earth Community, Earth Ethics* (Maryknoll, NY: Orbis Books, 1996).

II. Arrangement of the Sanctuary for the Sacred Synaxis (Eucharistic Assembly)

295. The sanctuary is the place where the altar stands, where the word of God is proclaimed, and where the priest, the deacon, and the other ministers exercise their offices. It should suitably be marked off from the body of the church either by its being somewhat elevated or by a particular structure and ornamentation. It should, however, be large enough to allow the Eucharist to be celebrated properly and easily seen.[115]

II. De Presbyterii Ordinatione ad Sacram Synaxim

295. Presbyterium locus est ubi altare exstat, verbum Dei proclamatur, et sacerdos, diaconus et alii ministri munus suum exercent. Ab aula ecclesiæ opportune distinguatur aut per aliquam elevationem, aut per peculiarem structuram et ornatum. Talis autem amplitudinis sit, ut Eucharistiæ celebratio commode peragi et conspici possit.[115]

---

structure and ordering of the People of God, both as a communion (cf. no. 82 above) and also for ministerial service (cf. nos. 69, 73, 89, and 90 above). Much in this article is new material, different from *IGMR1975*, stressing the strong ecclesiological reality of the church building. The overall normative organization of the local Church must be reflected in the careful design of its environment for worship. *IGMR2002* asserts that there are a variety of ministries and each has its place in the assembly (cf. no. 112 above). Each of these ministries plays a vital role in the overall unity of the assembly. Nevertheless, the traditional ordering of the Church and its ministry is hierarchical (cf. no. 91 above) and therefore a gradation of functions and roles flow out from the place where priest-presider, deacon, and concelebrants minister; this is marked off by their place in the sanctuary. Finally, stress is placed on the active participation of the faithful (*SC*, no. 14) and on the role that the choir plays in that participation (cf. no. 113 above). In addition, this conclusion to the first section underscores the need for quality in all furnishings, in order to foster devotion and reinforce the sacredness of the environment itself.

Arrangement of the Sanctuary for the Sacred Synaxis (Eucharistic Assembly)

295. This article presents new material, not found in *IGMR1975*. It notes that the sanctuary (*presbyterium*) "should suitably be marked off" (*opportune distinguatur*) or distinguished from the body of the church building. The sanctuary is the locus for the ambo and altar, specifying the area where Word is proclaimed and the Eucharist is celebrated. In turn, the sanctuary is the place where the ministers of the Word and the Eucharist carry out their functions. Either through an elevated platform or through other architectural structure or device, the faithful should know that the sanctuary is the location for sacred actions that remain unique to that area of the church environment.

Demarcating the sanctuary or *presbyterium* is clearly for the sake of the participation of the people and the accommodation of the rite. It is also there to

The Altar and Its Appointments

296. The altar on which the Sacrifice of the Cross is made present under sacramental signs is also the table of the Lord to which the People of God is called together to participate in the Mass, as well as the center of the thanksgiving that is accomplished through the Eucharist.

De altari eiusque ornatu

296. Altare, in quo sacrificium crucis sub signis sacramentalibus præsens efficitur, est etiam mensa Domini, ad quam participandam in Missa populus Dei convocatur; atque centrum gratiarum actionis, quæ per Eucharistiam perficitur.

---

enhance the visible participation of the faithful in the liturgical actions. This article emphasizes that there needs to be a clear separation between the people and the *presbyterium*, therefore correcting the practice of shaping liturgical environments where that demarcation has been purposely blurred in order to stress a different ecclesiology. *IGMR2002* here clearly critiques church designs that reflect what could be considered more collaborative ecclesiologies.[15]

There are already churches and cathedrals in the United States and Canada where a distinct sanctuary setting is no longer apparent. The age-old monastic choral plan has provided a model for many parishes. More centralized seating plans have assembled the clergy and laity together around the ritual furnishings. This reorganization of the entire worship area can contribute to a different liturgical experience, one that embodies the entire assembly without diminishing the hierarchical nature of the Church.[16]

In the spirit of this article, in a new or renovated church or cathedral the placement of the font, altar, ambo, and chair should maximize the participation of the entire assembly. The designs for the architectural settings for all ritually required furnishings are determined by the distinct liturgical actions that occur in each place. For example, the font setting is suitable for a water bath; the place of the ambo is designed for proclamation; the area for the altar accommodates sacrifice and banquet; the location of the chair or *cathedra* is designed for presiding and teaching. Lighting, acoustics, posture, and body movement accompanied by the use of symbols that are "perceptible to all the senses" (*SC*, no. 7) will serve the liturgical engagement of the entire assembly.

The Altar and Its Appointments

296. This article offers three complementary metaphors of the altar: altar, table, and center of thanksgiving. The first metaphor underscores "the altar" as the place of sacrifice and the second as the "table of the Lord," the locus of

15. On collaborative ecclesiologies, see Nathan Mitchell, "Liturgy and Ecclesiology," in *Handbook for Liturgical Studies*, Vol. 2: *Fundamental Liturgy*, ed. Anscar J. Chupungco (Collegeville, MN: The Liturgical Press, 1998), 113–127.

16. Richard S. Vosko, *God's House Is Our House: Re-imagining the Environment for Worship* (Collegeville, MN: Liturgical Press, 2006), 60–67.

297. The celebration of the Eucharist in a sacred place is to be carried out on an altar; but outside a sacred place, it may be carried out on a suitable table, always with the use of a cloth, a corporal, a cross, and candles.

298. It is appropriate to have a fixed altar in every church, since it more clearly and permanently signifies Christ Jesus, the living stone (1 Pt 2:4; cf. Eph 2:20). In other places set aside for sacred celebrations, the altar may be movable.

An altar is called "fixed" if it is attached to the floor so as not to be removeable; otherwise it is called "moveable."

297. Celebratio Eucharistiæ, in loco sacro, peragenda est super altare; extra locum sacrum vero, etiam super mensam convenientem, peragi potest, retentis semper tobalea et corporali, cruce et candelabris.

298. Expedit in omni ecclesia altare fixum inesse, quod Christum Iesum, Lapidem vivum (*1 Petr* 2, 4; cf. *Eph* 2, 20), clarius et permanenter significat; ceteris vero locis, sacris celebrationibus dicatis, altare potest esse mobile.

Altare fixum dicitur, si ita exstruatur ut cum pavimento cohæreat ideoque amoveri nequeat; mobile vero si transferri possit.

---

the eschatological banquet. A purposeful tension among these three gives a sense of the altar as a metaphor for the Church in adoration and thanksgiving before the Lord's own self-sacrifice on the Cross and the Church supping upon the food hosted by the Lord's bountiful love.[17] Two meanings (altar and table) are communicated as God's gift to the people in Christ, emphasizing the central Christological significance of all activity associated with the altar. What is clarified and underlined here in *IGMR2002* is the third meaning of the altar, where the local assembly in union with the whole Church offers thanksgiving.

297. In this article *IGMR2002* rearranges slightly materials from the parallel article in *IGMR1975* (no. 260), moving the entire discussion of fixed or movable altars to no. 298 below. The place of the eucharistic celebration, though proper to the sacred axis of the church setting, may also take place outside of the sacred building. The Church finds its home not only in designated locations; since the love of Christ abounds on the earth, the eucharistic action of the Church makes its way to places other than its official sanctuaries. The Eucharist may be celebrated on a suitable table in shrines, homes, and on pilgrimage where the Lord is found. Nevertheless, the eucharistic action is always conducted with certain decorum, expressed by the use of a cloth, corporal, cross, and candles.

298. These next articles (nos. 298–301) delineate precise norms concerning the character, the placing, and the material construction of an altar. First, *IGMR2002* emphasizes that proper to official church buildings is a fixed and unmovable altar, attached to the floor. This article places stronger emphasis on the fixity of the altar than *IGMR1975* (no. 261), giving less leeway for having a movable altar as an alternative in the sanctuary.

17. David Power, "Words that Crack: The Uses of 'Sacrifice' in Eucharistic Discourse," *Worship* 53, no. 5 (1979): 386–404.

299. The altar should be built apart from the wall, in such a way that it is possible to walk around it easily and that Mass can be celebrated at it facing the people, which is desirable wherever possible. The altar should, moreover, be so placed as to be truly the center toward which the attention of the whole congregation of the faithful naturally turns.[116] The altar is usually fixed and is dedicated.

300. An altar whether fixed or movable is dedicated according to the rite prescribed in the Roman Pontifical; but it is permissible for a movable altar simply to be blessed.

301. In keeping with the Church's traditional practice and the altar's symbolism, the table of a fixed altar is to be of stone and indeed of natural stone. In the dioceses of the United States of America, however, wood which is worthy, solid, and well-crafted may be used, provided that the altar is structurally immobile. The supports or base for upholding the table, however, may be made of any sort of material, provided it is worthy and solid.

A movable altar may be constructed of any noble and solid materials suited to liturgical use, according to the traditions and usages of the different regions.

299. Altare exstruatur a pariete seiunctum, ut facile circumiri et in eo celebratio versus populum peragi possit, quod expedit ubicumque possibile sit. Altare eum autem occupet locum, ut revera centrum sit ad quod totius congregationis fidelium attentio sponte convertatur.[116] De more sit fixum et dedicatum.

300. Altare tum fixum tum mobile iuxta ritum in Pontificali Romano descriptum dedicetur; altare tamen mobile potest tantum benedici.

301. Iuxta traditum Ecclesiæ morem et significationem, mensa altaris fixi sit lapidea, et quidem ex lapide naturali. Attamen etiam alia materia digna, solida et affabre effecta, de iudicio Conferentiæ Episcoporum, adhiberi potest. Stipites vero aut basis ad mensam sustentandam ex qualibet materia, dummodo sit digna et solida, confici possunt.

Altare mobile ex quibuslibet materiis nobilibus et solidis atque usui liturgico, iuxta diversarum regionum traditiones et mores, convenientibus, exstrui potest.

---

299. A second norm delineated in this article is that the altar is to be built apart from the wall, facing the people, so that the altar anchors both the assembly's worship and its adoration, and that the presider and ministers can "walk around it easily" (*facile circumiri*), and so that Mass "can be celebrated at it facing the people, which is desirable whenever possible" (*in eo celebratio versus populum peragi possit, quod expedit ubicumque possibile sit*). The spatial location of the altar embodies and supports the central Christological metaphors of sacrifice, table of the Lord, and center of thanksgiving.

300. Fixed and immoveable altars are ritually "dedicated" (*dedicetur*), whereas moveable altars may be dedicated or are "simply to be blessed" (*potest tantum benedici*, see *The Rite of Dedication of a Church and an Altar*, ch. 5, no.1).

301. The third norm delineated in these numbers regards the materials for constructing an altar. The traditional material for the construction of the altar top is "natural stone" (*lapide naturali*), yet *IGMR2002* allows other solid materials to be used at the discretion of the conference of bishops. Thus GIRM2003

302. The practice of placing relics of Saints, even those not Martyrs, under the altar to be dedicated is fittingly retained. Care should be taken, however, to ensure the authenticity of such relics.

302. Usus deponendi sub altari dedicando reliquias Sanctorum, etsi non Martyrum, opportune servetur. Caveatur tamen ut de huiusmodi reliquiarum veritate certo constet.

---

notes that wood is permitted in the United States, as long as the wooden structure is immovable and the materials are genuine and strong. The support base of the altar top can be made of any "worthy and solid" (*digna et solida*) materials indigenous to traditions of the region.

Articles 298–301, with their precise norms, provide the support for further theological reflection on the meaning and significance of the altar for the worship and adoration of the local assembly. For example, because of its position in the church building, and the dignity and significance of its material construction, the altar provides a way for the local Church to identify itself gathered around that altar in the act of offering as the Body of Christ itself (cf. *SC*, no. 48). Both the church building and the altar together symbolize the post-resurrection Church gathered in the Lord's presence.[18] Furthermore, as a locus of the risen Christ in the gathered assembly, the altar challenges the local Church to discover ways of translating that equivalence into a culturally relevant language, both for the altar itself and the larger arrangement of the sanctuary.[19]

302. This article recognizes the ancient Christian practice of linking the tombs of the martyrs and saints with the eucharistic altars of the local churches. *IGMR2002* underscores that in contemporary church buildings there should be a fitting place for the reservation of relics in the construction and design of the altar. *IGMR2002* prescribes that relics should be placed only "under the altar" (*sub altari*), whereas *IGMR1975* (no. 266) also allows the practice of placing relics in the altar as well as under it. In addition *IGMR2002* accentuates that communities of faith need to ensure that its relics are authentic. Maybe even more important than the authenticity of the relics for the community is the catechesis that has been carried out about the devotion to the martyrs and saints of the Church in order to recover its significance as it relates to relics.[20]

Two methods for reserving relics beneath an altar have recently emerged. Relics that are not venerated during the year may be stored in a container recessed into the floor beneath an altar table designed with columns or alongside one that has a solid base. The place of the container is then sealed and engraved with a cross or the name(s) of the saint(s) whose relics are reserved. The other

18. Calabuig, *The Dedication of a Church and an Altar*, 12–26.

19. Anscar J. Chupungco, *Liturgical Inculturation: Sacramentals, Religiosity, and Catechesis* (Collegeville, MN: The Liturgical Press, 1992), 76–78.

20. Mark E. Wedig, "Recovering the *Concilium Sanctorum*: A Contemporary Ecclesiology Inclusive of the Communion of the Saints," *Liturgical Ministry* 12 (2003): 1–8.

303. In building new churches, it is preferable to erect a single altar which in the gathering of the faithful will signify the one Christ and the one Eucharist of the Church.

In already existing churches, however, when the old altar is positioned so that it makes the people's participation difficult but cannot be moved without damage to its artistic value, another fixed altar, of artistic merit and duly dedicated, should be erected and sacred rites celebrated on it alone. In order not to distract the attention of the faithful from the new altar, the old altar should not be decorated in any special way.

303. In novis ecclesiis exstruendis præstat unum altare erigi, quod in fidelium cœtu unum Christum unamque Ecclesiæ Eucharistiam significet.

In ecclesiis vero iam exstructis, quando altare vetus ita situm est, ut difficilem reddat participationem populi nec transferri possit sine detrimento valoris artis, aliud altare fixum, arte confectum et rite dedicandum, exstruatur; et tantum super illud sacræ celebrationes peragantur. Ne fidelium attentio a novo altari distrahatur, altare antiquum ne sit peculiari modo ornatum.

---

option is to place the relics in a solid decorated container set directly beneath an altar table designed with columns. Here the reliquary is visible to all and could be accessible when desired.

303. This article is a new and distinct entry that underscores the value of a single altar, which signifies the one Christ and one Eucharist of the Church. It also provides guidelines for accommodating those circumstances in which an "old altar" (*altare vetus*) continues to exist. No reference is made here to side altars and the ecclesiological problem they embody (cf. Schaefer and Pierce).

Liturgical theology after Vatican II (1962–65) has underlined the importance of one altar for the worship and piety of the people. The multiplication of altars obscures the recognition of the one Christ and the one Eucharist in the life of the Church. This article suggests displacing the value of these structures as *the* altar by instructing that they "should not be decorated in any special way" (*ne sit peculiari modo ornatum*). *IGMR2002* seems to be referring to an old "high" altar, rather than numerous "side" altars. By refraining from decorating or adorning these as well, their historical value and reference remains, while their visible impact on the setting is reduced and the liturgical focus shifts appropriately to the one single main altar in use.

The sensitive illumination of a retablo or reredos on the central axis of the church could be used to emphasize its artistic importance at different times. For example, it could be highlighted before and after but not during the eucharistic liturgy. This would be especially appropriate when an older altar, directly behind the newer one used for the Eucharist, is the place for the reservation of the sacrament (see no. 315 below).

304. Out of reverence for the celebration of the memorial of the Lord and for the banquet in which the Body and Blood of the Lord are offered on an altar where this memorial is celebrated, there should be at least one white cloth, its shape, size, and decoration in keeping with the altar's design. When, in the dioceses of the United States of America, other cloths are used in addition to the altar cloth, then those cloths may be of other colors possessing Christian honorific or festive significance according to long-standing local usage, provided that the uppermost cloth covering the *mensa* (i.e., the altar cloth itself) is always white in color.

304. Ob reverentiam erga celebrationem memorialis Domini et erga convivium in quo Corpus et Sanguis Domini præbentur, super altare ubi celebratur saltem una tobalea albi coloris ponatur, quæ ad formam, mensuram et ornatum quod attinet cum ipsius altaris structura conveniat.

305. Moderation should be observed in the decoration of the altar.

During Advent the floral decoration of the altar should be marked by a moderation suited to the character of this season, without expressing prematurely the full joy of the Nativity of the Lord. During Lent it is forbidden for the altar to be decorated with flowers. *Laetare* Sunday (Fourth Sunday of Lent), solemnities, and feasts are exceptions.

Floral decorations should always be done with moderation and placed around the altar rather than on its *mensa*.

305. In altaris ornatu moderatio servetur.

Tempore Adventus altare floribus ornetur ea moderatione, quæ indoli huius temporis conveniat, quin tamen plenam lætitiam Nativitatis Domini præveniat. Tempore Quadragesimæ altare floribus ornari prohibetur. Excipiuntur tamen dominica Lætáre (IV in Quadragesima), sollemnitates et festa.

Florum ornatus semper sit temperatus, et potius quam supra mensam altaris, circa illud disponatur.

---

304. This article, concerned with altar coverings, parallels *IGMR1975,* no. 268. New in *IGMR2002* is the prescription that there be "at least one white cloth" (*saltem una tobalea albi coloris*). GIRM2003 includes the US indult allowing that, when other cloths are used in dioceses of the US, they may be of other colors, although the uppermost cloth must remain white. Similar to the next article (no. 305), this article shows concern for the quantity and quality of decoration for the altar, and proposes a norm of simplicity and moderation. The careful consideration of material construction of the altar (cf. no. 301 above), identifies the fundamental way to enhance it. Because of its intrinsic attractiveness and quality, the altar need not be improved or augmented for the sake of beauty. Therefore, the simplicity of a single white cloth—or the moderate use of other cloths in the US—embodies the straightforwardness of this aesthetic norm.

305. Mirroring the aesthetic concerns of no. 304, this new article addresses the "moderation" (*moderatio*) of altar decoration, particularly "floral decoration" (*floribus ornetur*). As with the altar cloth, restraint in floral or other decoration,

306. Only what is required for the celebration of the Mass may be placed on the *mensa* of the altar: namely, from the beginning of the celebration until the proclamation of the Gospel, the *Book of the Gospels;* then from the Presentation of the Gifts until the purification of the vessels, the chalice with the paten, a ciborium, if necessary, and, finally, the corporal, the purificator, the pall, and the Missal.

In addition, microphones that may be needed to amplify the priest's voice should be arranged discreetly.

306. Super enim mensam altaris ea tantummodo quæ ad Missæ celebrationem requiruntur deponi possunt, scilicet: Evangeliarium ab initio celebrationis usque ad Evangelii proclamationem; a præsentatione vero donorum usque ad purificationem vasorum calix cum patena, pyxis, si necesse est, tandem corporale, purificatorium, palla et missale.

Disponantur insuper modo discreto quæ forte ad amplificationem vocis sacerdotis necessaria sunt.

---

and even no decorations at all (e.g., during Lent), underscores this aesthetic norm of moderation and simplicity. In *IGMR2002* it is the feast that sets the decoration, and this article emphasizes fundamental theological principles rooted in the nature of the liturgical year that should determine the altar's décor. Prohibitions against floral decoration for Lent, for example, symbolize the solemn austerity of the season. Not only should the local Church community think of natural flowers as the sanctuary's decoration but also trees, living plants, and fruits of the earth, exemplifying the bountiful harvest of the Lord.

306. This article, drawing together previously noted materials (e.g., nos. 73 and 190) stresses that only what is required for Mass may be placed on the altar, i.e., the Book of the Gospels, chalice with paten, ciborium, corporal, purificator, pall, and missal. In addition, the Instruction recognizes that there may be a need to use microphones "arranged discreetly" (*Disponantur insuper modo discreto*). *IGMR2002* never specifies that microphones need to be on the altar, and seems to discourage their visibility on the altar. All other objects and enhancements take away from the sacred action and diminish the symbolism of the altar itself.

The size of the altar table should be generous enough that the symbolic presence of the altar table, the cup, and the plate are evident to the assembly. It should be scaled "for the action of a community and the functioning of a single priest—not concelebrants."[21] Also, the placement of multiple vessels upon the altar table to assure the proper distribution of the Eucharist to all members of the assembly (see *Redemptionis Sacramentum,* no. 105) should not result in the design of altar tables that are out of scale in a given architectural context.

21. See "Guidelines for Concelebrating the Eucharist," *Study Text 5: Eucharistic Concelebration* (Washington, DC: USCCB Publications Office, 1978), VI, 7.

307. The candles, which are required at every liturgical service out of reverence and on account of the festiveness of the celebration (cf. no. 117), are to be appropriately placed either on or around the altar in a way suited to the design of the altar and the sanctuary so that the whole may be well balanced and not interfere with the faithful's clear view of what takes place at the altar or what is placed on it.

308. There is also to be a cross, with the figure of Christ crucified upon it, either on the altar or near it, where it is clearly visible to the assembled congregation. It is appropriate that such a cross, which calls to mind for the faithful the saving Passion of the Lord, remain near the altar even outside of liturgical celebrations.

307. Candelabra, quæ pro singulis actionibus liturgicis, venerationis et festivæ celebrationis causa, requiruntur *(cf. n. 117)*, aut super altare, aut circa ipsum, attenta structura tum altaris tum presbyterii, opportune collocentur, ita ut totum concinne componatur, neque fideles impediantur ab iis facile conspiciendis, quæ super altare aguntur vel deponuntur.

308. Item super altare vel prope ipsum crux, cum effigie Christi crucifixi, habeatur, quæ a populo congregato bene conspiciatur. Expedit ut huiusmodi crux, ad salutiferam Domini passionem in mentem fidelium revocandam, etiam extra celebrationes liturgicas prope altare permaneat.

---

307. This article underscores the requirement of candles at every liturgical celebration for reason of reverence and festiveness. Light is a strong Christological image that particularly illustrates the paschal significance of the Church's ritual (see no. 117 above). Nevertheless, the candles should not detract from the liturgical act and need to blend in with the basic contours of the altar itself as well as the design of the sanctuary. Whether placed on the altar or set next to it, the candles should be aligned to the fundamental design of the space. Concerns about their arrangement arise from the standpoint of the people's ocular participation.

Consideration could be given to the greater use of taller candlesticks that can be carried in processions and placed in the different liturgical settings (e.g., near the font, the altar table, and ambo) at appropriate times. By their height these sizable lights also help demarcate those areas in the church set aside for various liturgical actions.

308. This last article in this section on "The Altar and Its Appointments" links the altar with the saving mystery of the cross, thus the need to display "a cross with the figure of the crucified Christ upon it" (*cum effigie Christi crucifixi*) always on or near the altar, even outside of liturgical celebrations. The singularity of the altar corresponds to the one cross. The crucifix correlates the altar with the one sacrifice of Jesus Christ and addresses the need for the faithful to continually see the correspondence between the cross and the altar as Body of the Lord.

As noted previously (see no. 117; also Seasoltz, 33), there is a major change between *IGMR1975* and *IGMR2002* concerning the requirement that the cross contain the figure of the crucified Christ. *IGMR1975* only mentions *crux*, which

The Ambo

309. The dignity of the word of God requires that the church have a place that is

De ambone

309. Dignitas verbi Dei requirit ut in ecclesia locus congruus exsistat e quo an-

---

GIRM1975 consistently translates as "cross" (e.g., no. 270), widely interpreted as permitting the option of either a cross without a corpus or a crucifix. The emphasis on the "figure of the crucified," however, could be understood as a preference for a more literal approach to the eucharistic liturgy and its theology rather than a preference for the inherent ambiguity of a more symbolic approach.

Mindful that the paschal event celebrates the passion, death, and resurrection of Christ, it has become customary in many places to venerate a cross without a corpus during Lent, on Good Friday, and during the Easter season. In order to foster devotion to the cross, consideration should be given to securing it to the floor rather than displaying it on a wall or suspending it overhead, which would render it inaccessible.

Although a processional cross with a body of the crucified Jesus would suffice as the cross of the altar, a larger crucifix is also a possibility. In this case appropriate proportions and scale should be considered in the design of the crucifix near an altar to assure that it does not dominate the space. If there is a crucifix fixed near the altar table or ambo, the processional cross or crucifix should be placed elsewhere when not being carried in procession (see no. 122 above).

The Ambo

SC, no. 7, stresses the multiple modes of Christ's presence in the priest, the eucharistic elements, the sacraments, the Word, and the assembly. The theological revolution in this teaching directly relates to the reconfiguration of liturgical space especially as it pertains to the Liturgy of the Word. One of the most comprehensive innovations in the reform of the liturgy following Vatican II was the uncompromised role that the Word played in every rite, especially enriching the Eucharist for the people in the Liturgy of the Word. The Lectionary for Mass orchestrates and arranges the texts of Scripture as ritual encounter and the proclamation of the Word as a central liturgical event. As a consequence, Roman Catholics have a renewed relationship with the Scriptures of the Old and New Testaments and a hunger for intelligible interpretations of the Word in the homily.[22]

309. In light of these reforms, *IGMR2002* requires that the sanctuary must provide a "suitable place" (*locus congruus*) where the Liturgy of the Word is to

22. See nos. 28, 55, and 65, above; also, Mark E. Wedig, "A Practical Liturgical Theology of the Word," *Liturgical Ministry* 13 (2004): 192–199.

suitable for the proclamation of the word and toward which the attention of the whole congregation of the faithful naturally turns during the Liturgy of the Word.[117]

It is appropriate that this place be ordinarily a stationary ambo and not simply a movable lectern. The ambo must be located in keeping with the design of each church in such a way that the ordained ministers and lectors may be clearly seen and heard by the faithful.

From the ambo only the readings, the responsorial Psalm, and the Easter Proclamation (*Exsultet*) are to be proclaimed; it may be used also for giving the homily and for announcing the intentions of the Prayer of the Faithful. The dignity of the ambo requires that only a minister of the word should go up to it.

It is appropriate that a new ambo be blessed according to the rite described in the Roman Ritual[118] before it is put into liturgical use.

nuntietur et ad quem, inter liturgiam verbi, attentio fidelium sponte convertatur.[117]

Convenit ut generatim locus huiusmodi sit ambo stabilis et non simplex pluteus mobilis. Ambo, pro cuiusque ecclesiæ structura, ita dispositus esse debet, ut ministri ordinati et lectores a fidelibus bene conspici et audiri possint.

Ex ambone unice proferuntur lectiones, psalmus responsorius atque præconium paschale; item proferri possunt homilia et intentiones orationis universalis. Ambonis dignitas exigit ut ad eum solus minister verbi ascendat.

Convenit ut novus ambo benedicatur, antequam usui liturgico destinetur, iuxta ritum in Rituali Romano descriptum.[118]

---

be proclaimed. A stationary ambo is preferred to a moveable lectern, and its placement must ensure that the ministers of the Word be seen and heard. Alternative locations for the ambo are possible in places of worship that have choral or centralized seating plans, where the entire assembly (including the clergy) is arranged around the altar and ambo. According to the *Book of Blessings*, the ambo is to be blessed before it is used by the local Church (nos. 1173–91).

The ambo is more than a pulpit or lectern and for that reason it is better appreciated as a second table, anchored to the sanctuary in a similar way that the altar is anchored there. It should be understood as a table for the Word, and the locus for proclamation and preaching. Here a unique modality of Christ's presence is encountered in the Word. Therefore the dignity of the ambo should reflect the unique ministry of the Word that takes place in it. The reading of the Scriptures, the chanting of the responsorial psalm, the singing of the Easter proclamation "are to be proclaimed" (*proferuntur*) from the ambo, and it "may be used" (*proferri possunt*) for the homily and the intentions of the prayer of the faithful. To this end, *IGMR2002* only notes that it is a place from which "ordained ministers and lectors may be clearly seen and heard by the faithful" (*ministri ordinati et lectores a fidelibus bene conspici et audiri possint*), whereas *IGMR1975* simply speaks more generally of "ministers" (*ministri*, no. 272). And while *IGMR1975* cautions that "It is better for the commentator, cantor, or choir

The Chair for the Priest Celebrant and Other Seats

310. The chair of the priest celebrant must signify his office of presiding over the gathering and of directing the prayer. Thus the best place for the chair is in a position facing the people at the head of the sanctuary, unless the design of the building or other circumstances impede this: for example, if the great distance would interfere

De sede pro sacerdote celebrante aliisque sedibus

310. Sedes sacerdotis celebrantis debet munus eius præsidendi cœtui atque orationem dirigendi significare. Proinde locus eius magis congruus est versus ad populum in vertice presbyterii, nisi ædis structura vel alia adiuncta id impediant, ex. gr. si propter nimiam distantiam communicatio inter sacerdotem et cœtum congrega-

---

director not to use the lectern" (*Minus vero congruit ad ambonem ascendere commentatorem, cantorem aut moderatorem chori*), *IGMR2002* is more prescriptive, noting that "only a minister of the word should go up to it" (*ad eum solus minister verbi ascendat*).

The ambo does not also function as a repository for the Sacred Scriptures. The practice of displaying the Book of Gospels or a Bible on a ledge in front of the ambo is without historical or theological precedent.[23] A more satisfying means of reserving the Word of God would be to incorporate in the church an ambry or repository for all Scripture books not unlike an Ark in a synagogue.

In principle, like all ritual furnishings and appointments, the design and placement of the ambo is in the service of the liturgy. Its scale and proportions should permit more than one person to use it especially when singing psalms and the *Exultet*. The design of adjustable ambos to accommodate persons of various statures and physical abilities is becoming popular and appropriate. The approach to and space around the ambo should be gracious enough to accommodate processions with lights and incense.

The culture of disability offers certain critiques of the sanctuary (cf. no. 293 on "comfort"), specifically an ambo that inhibits the accessibility of wheelchairs. People with disabilities can help us to rethink some fundamental ecclesial relationships and how they are embodied in our churches.[24] Along these lines communities also must consider changes in the sacred space when the Word is signed for the deaf by an additional minister of the Word.

The Chair for the Priest Celebrant and Other Seats

310. Besides the altar and ambo, the chair of the priest celebrant is integral to the design of the sanctuary. As Christ is present in the Word, the eucharistic

23. BLS notes that "it has become customary to provide a place for the permanent display of the Scriptures in the sanctuary area," no. 62.

24. Jennie Weiss Block, *Copious Hosting: A Theology of Access for People with Disabilities* (New York: Continuum, 2002), 83–128.

with communication between the priest and the gathered assembly, or if the tabernacle is in the center behind the altar. Any appearance of a throne, however, is to be avoided.[119] It is appropriate that, before being put into liturgical use, the chair be blessed according to the rite described in the Roman Ritual.[120]

Likewise, seats should be arranged in the sanctuary for concelebrating priests as well as for priests who are present for the celebration in choir dress but who are not concelebrating.

The seat for the deacon should be placed near that of the celebrant. Seats for the other ministers are to be arranged so that they are clearly distinguishable from those for the clergy and so that the ministers are easily able to fulfill the function entrusted to them.[121]

tum difficilis evadat, aut si tabernaculum locum habeat in media parte retro altare. Omnis autem species throni vitetur.[119] Convenit ut sedes benedicatur, antequam usui liturgico destinetur, iuxta ritum in Rituali Romano descriptum.[120]

Item in presbyterio sedes disponantur pro sacerdotibus concelebrantibus necnon pro presbyteris, qui veste chorali induti, celebrationi intersunt, quin concelebrent.

Sedes diaconi prope sedem celebrantis ponatur. Pro aliis ministris sedes ita collocentur, ut clare distinguantur a sedibus cleri et ipsi munus sibi concreditum facile implere possint.[121]

---

species, the sacraments and the assembly, Christ is also present in the person of the minister (*SC*, no. 7). The priest's chair signifies his office of presiding over the people and directing prayer. It is best positioned at the center or head of the sanctuary facing the people. If there is a great distance between the chair and the assembly, or if the tabernacle is positioned at the head of the church, another suitable place needs to considered. Like the ambo, the chair is to be blessed before it is employed in the liturgy (*Book of Blessings*, nos. 1150–73).

The style and size of the chair and its positioning is significant because it mediates the way the local community conceptualizes itself in relationship to the priest-presider. *IGMR2002* underlines that any appearance of a "throne" (*throni*) should be avoided. The placement of the chair has profound ecclesiological significance. How the chair is situated in relationship to the assembly and eucharistic action signifies how the Church understands and represents itself. *IGMR2002* emphasizes that the chair should be "facing the people at the head of the sanctuary" (*versus ad populum in vertice presbyterii*), contributing to a stronger relationship between presider and people.

Alternative locations for the presider's chair and the *cathedra* are possible in places of worship that have choral or centralized seating plans, where the entire assembly, including the clergy, is arranged around the altar and ambo. The chairs for the presiding priest and the deacon would be placed in the first row of seats. In order to assure good visibility and communication between the presider and the assembly the chair would be elevated accordingly for sightline purposes.

III. The Arrangement of the Church

The Places for the Faithful

311. Places should be arranged with appropriate care for the faithful so that they are able to participate in the sacred celebrations visually and spiritually, in the proper manner. It is expedient for benches or seats usually to be provided for their use. The custom of reserving seats for private persons, however, is reprehensible.[122] Moreover, benches or chairs should be arranged, especially in newly built churches, in such a way that the people can easily take up the postures required for the different parts of the celebration and can easily come forward to receive Holy Communion.

III. De Ecclesiæ Ordinatione

De locis fidelium

311. Loca fidelium congrua cura disponantur, ut ipsi oculis et animo sacras celebrationes debite participare possint. Expedit ut de more scamna seu sedilia ad eorum usum ponantur. Consuetudo tamen personis quibusdam privates sedes reservandi reprobanda est.[122] Scamna autem seu sedilia, præsertim in ecclesiis noviter exstructis, ita disponantur, ut fideles corporis habitus a diversis celebrationis partibus requisitos facile sumere possint et expedite ad sacram Communionem recipiendam accedere valeant.

The Arrangement of the Church

The Places for the Faithful

Following *SC*, no. 7, *IGMR2002* stresses the multiple modes of Christ's presence in the eucharistic liturgy. Even though the ordering of these modes differs in several of the contemporary Church documents, all of them include the presence of Christ in assembly, minister, Word, and sacramental species.[25] All of Chapter V can be understood as concerned with ways to express the theology of Christ's presence in concrete ecclesial form. The interior arrangement of a church building embodies a theology of the space and is a prominent ecclesiological symbol.[26] Contemporary eucharistic theology has placed great emphasis on developing a mature and comprehensive understanding of the role of the assembly in relationship to ideas and practices concerning the Body of Christ.[27]

311. *IGMR2002* sketches out the significance of the physical arrangement of the places for the faithful in order to accentuate the importance of a local Church embodying the faithful as a eucharistic people. Therefore, the Instruction teaches that there need to be places for the assembly to participate "visually and spiritually" (*oculis et animo*) as that people. Care needs to be given so that

25. Judith Marie Kubicki, "Recognizing the Presence of Christ in the Liturgical Assembly," *Theological Studies* 65, no. 4 (2004): 817–837.

26. Ibid., 831–837.

27. See Power and Vincie, p. 51ff. above; also Mark Francis, "The Liturgical Assembly," in *Handbook for Liturgical Studies*, Vol. 2: *Fundamental Liturgy*, edited by Anscar J. Chupungco (Collegeville, MN: The Liturgical Press, 1998), 129–160.

Care should be taken that the faithful be able not only to see the priest, the deacon, and the lectors but also, with the aid of modern technical means, to hear them without difficulty.

Caveatur ut fideles sive sacerdotem sive diaconum et lectores non tantum videre, sed etiam, hodiernis instrumentis technicis adhibitis, commode audire valeant.

---

the assembly may see and hear the priest, deacon, and lector. Benches or chairs are recommended, and their design should not interfere with the space requirements that allow the postures and movements of the assembly during Mass. Reserved seats are seen as "reprehensible" (*reprobanda est*). The liturgy makes distinction between persons based on their liturgical function, but no special honors are to be given in the liturgy to private persons or classes of persons (cf. *SC*, no. 32).

IGMR2002 does not show a preference for either fixed or movable seating plans. Movable chairs or benches make it possible to use a church building for more than one purpose when a different seating plan is desired. Fixed pews are more practical in churches with sloped floors. The installation of a combination of fixed and movable seats is becoming more prominent.

Whether or not the seating plan is fixed, it should permit persons who are physically challenged to choose their places without embarrassment. This would mean that, throughout and within the assembly seating area, spaces should be made available for people with physical disabilities and a companion. Local codes can be helpful in determining just how many spaces should be provided.

There are seating issues that do not surface in *IGMR2002* related to the full, conscious, active participation of the faithful, one of the prominent principles in the document (e.g., Power and Vincie, 52). One of these concerns the question of whether participation is merely a matter of seeing and hearing. Full, conscious, and active participation involves more, including processing and movement. As a result, it is imperative that the space is arranged to allow for the different postures and movements of the people.

The layout of the place of worship has an effect on the assembly's participation. One key environmental factor is distance. Beyond a certain point (some studies suggest sixty feet or about eighteen meters)[28] it becomes more difficult to see and hear what is going on. Thus it is helpful, especially in newer and larger church buildings, to design seating plans that link people more comfortably and closely to the liturgical actions, to one another and to all liturgical ministers. In older churches every imaginative effort should be made to reduce the distance factor, for example, by moving the focal points (altar, ambo, chair) closer to the assembly.

28. Vosko, ibid., 56–59.

The Place for the Choir and the Musical Instruments

312. The choir should be positioned with respect to the design of each church so as to make clearly evident its character as a part of the gathered community of the faithful fulfilling a specific function. The location should also assist the choir to exercise its function more easily and conveniently allow each choir member full, sacramental participation in the Mass.[123]

313. The organ and other lawfully approved musical instruments are to be

De loco scholæ cantorum et instrumentorum musicorum

312. Schola cantorum, attenta cuiusque ecclesiæ dispositione, ita collocetur, ut clare appareat eius natura, eam nempe fidelium communitatis congregatæ partem esse, et peculiare munus agere; eiusdem muneris executio facilior evadat; singulis scholæ sodalibus plena in Missa participatio sacramentalis commode permittatur.[123]

313. Organum aliaque instrumenta musica legitime probata apto loco collocentur,

---

The Place for the Choir and the Musical Instruments

312. The choir, organist, instrumentalists, and other ministers of music need to be understood to be part of the gathered community. The choir's location should assist in allowing its members to participate fully in the liturgical celebration. Their placement should link the role of the choir to the rest of the assembly, rather than it appearing as a performance group separated from the faithful. The role of the choir and other musicians is analogous to that of liturgical music itself, i.e., to support and enhance the singing of the whole community and add beauty and solemnity to the liturgy (see nos. 40, 48, 52, 53, and 68 above; also *SC*, nos. 112–13 and 118; Liturgical Music Today, nos. 33–36).

313. *IGMR2002* indicates the organ and other "lawfully approved musical instruments" (*aliaque instrumenta musica legitime probata*, cf. *SC*, no. 120) are to be situated so as to sustain the singing of choir and assembly. Also, they must be heard by all with ease when played alone. In Advent the organ and other instruments are to be used with "moderation" (*moderatione*); in Lent they are used "only to support the singing" (*ad cantum sustentandum*), with some exceptions (e.g., *Laetare* Sunday). Thus, like the decoration of the altar (see no. 305 above), it is the liturgical year that provides important guidelines for the employment of music in the Eucharist. *IGMR2002* calls for the blessing of the organ before it is used for the liturgy (*Book of Blessing*, nos. 1328–1340).

The continual use of choir lofts or galleries, especially when an historic or functioning pipe organ is located there, may make the linkage between the choir and the assembly difficult. Additionally, the culture of disability reminds us of the problems of lofts and galleries that are not barrier-free. Persons with disabilities should be able to participate in music ministries wherever they are located in the church.

*IGMR*s do not treat tonal space. The acoustical character of the church is vital for supporting the participation of the community. The resonance of the church building should be considered when deciding the best location for choirs

placed in an appropriate place so that they can sustain the singing of both the choir and the congregation and be heard with ease by all if they are played alone. It is appropriate that, before being put into liturgical use, the organ be blessed according to the rite described in the Roman Ritual.[124]

In Advent the organ and other musical instruments should be used with a moderation that is consistent with the season's character and does not anticipate the full joy of the Nativity of the Lord.

In Lent the playing of the organ and musical instruments is allowed only to support the singing. Exceptions are *Laetare* Sunday (Fourth Sunday of Lent), solemnities, and feasts.

ut tum scholæ tum populo cantanti subsidio esse possint, atque, si sola pulsentur, commode ab omnibus audiri queant. Convenit ut organum benedicatur, antequam usui liturgico destinetur, iuxta ritum in Rituali Romano descriptum.[124]

Tempore Adventus organum aliaque musica instrumenta adhibeantur ea moderatione, quæ indoli huius temporis conveniat, quin tamen plenam lætitiam Nativitatis Domini præveniat.

Tempore in Quadragesima sonus organi aliorumque instrumentorum permittitur tantum ad cantum sustentandum. Excipiuntur tamen dominica Lætáre (IV in Quadragesima), sollemnitates et festa.

The Place for the Reservation of the Most Holy Eucharist

314. In accordance with the structure of each church and legitimate local customs, the Most Blessed Sacrament should be reserved in a tabernacle in a part of the church that is truly noble, prominent, readily visible, beautifully decorated, and suitable for prayer.[125]

De loco asservationis sanctissimæ eucharistiæ

314. Pro cuiusque ecclesiæ structura et iuxta legitimas locorum consuetudines, Ss.mum Sacramentum asservetur in tabernaculo in parte ecclesiæ pernobili, insigni, conspicua, decore ornata, et ad orationem apta.[125]

---

and musicians, as well as the placement of a major instrument, e.g., a pipe organ. The acoustical requirements for singing and playing instruments must be determined before building or renovating churches. The shape and materials of the building determine how well sound travels naturally in the space.

The Place for the Reservation of the Most Holy Eucharist

314. Many of the norms articulated in nos. 314–317 reiterate existing liturgical laws pertaining to the reserved Eucharist. The Blessed Sacrament needs to be reserved in a tabernacle in a part of the church building that is "noble, prominent, readily visible, beautifully decorated and suitable for prayer" (*pernobili, insigni, conspicua, decore ornata, et ad orationem apta*). The Instruction recognizes that this needs to be done according to the design of the building and legitimate local customs. The tabernacle should be a locked fixture and made of solid and inviolable materials instead of transparent ones. It is appropriately blessed before being used in the liturgy (*Book of Blessings,* nos. 1192–1202).

The one tabernacle should be immovable, be made of solid and inviolable material that is not transparent, and be locked in such a way that the danger of profanation is prevented to the greatest extent possible.[126] Moreover, it is appropriate that, before it is put into liturgical use, it be blessed according to the rite described in the Roman Ritual.[127]

Tabernaculum de more unicum sit, inamovibile, materia solida atque inviolabili non transparenti confectum, et ita clausum ut quam maxime periculum profanationis vitetur.[126] Convenit insuper ut benedicatur, antequam usui liturgico destinetur, iuxta ritum in Rituali Romano descriptum.[127]

315. It is more in keeping with the meaning of the sign that the tabernacle in which the Most Holy Eucharist is reserved not be on an altar on which Mass is celebrated.[128]

Consequently, it is preferable that the tabernacle be located, according to the judgment of the diocesan Bishop,

a. Either in the sanctuary, apart from the altar of celebration, in a form and place more appropriate, not excluding on an old altar no longer used for celebration (cf. no. 303);
b. Or even in some chapel suitable for the faithful's private adoration and prayer[129] and organically connected to the church and readily visible to the Christian faithful.

315. Ratione signi magis congruit ut in altari in quo Missa celebratur non sit tabernaculum in quo Ss.ma Eucharistia asservatur.[128]

Præstat proinde tabernaculum collocari, de iudicio Episcopi diœcesani:

a) aut in presbyterio, extra altare celebrationis, forma et loco magis convenientibus, non excluso vetere altari quod ad celebrationem amplius non adhibetur *(cf. n. 303)*.
b) aut etiam in aliquo sacello ad privatam fidelium adorationem et precationem idoneo,[129] quod sit cum ecclesia organice coniunctum et christifidelibus conspicuum.

316. In accordance with traditional custom, near the tabernacle a special lamp,

316. Secundum traditam consuetudinem, iuxta tabernaculum peculiaris perenniter

---

315. *IGMR2002* indicates that the Blessed Sacrament should not be reserved on an altar where Mass is celebrated. It is preferable that the location of the tabernacle be determined by the judgment of the diocesan bishop, in one of two ways: a) either in the sanctuary, but "apart from the altar of celebration" (*extra altare celebrationis*), which could include an old altar no longer employed for the eucharistic liturgy, or b) in a chapel for private adoration and prayer, "organically connected to the church building and readily visible" (*cum ecclesia organice coniunctum et . . . conspicuum*).

One important issue that arises in view of these two options is whether a single space can be suited for both reservation and liturgical action. Option "a" points to this dilemma, but *IGMR2002* neither addresses nor resolves the question (see *Environment and Art in Catholic Worship*, no. 78).

316. This article states that the tabernacle requires a special lamp nearby that is "fueled by oil or wax" (*oleo vel cera nutrienda*), thus indicating the inappropriateness of an electronic candle for this use.

fueled by oil or wax, should be kept alight to indicate and honor the presence of Christ.[130]

317. In no way should all the other things prescribed by law concerning the reservation of the Most Holy Eucharist be forgotten.[131]

luceat lampas, oleo vel cera nutrienda, qua indicetur et honoretur Christi præsentia.[130]

317. Minime obliviscantur etiam cetera omnia quæ de asservatione Ss.mæ Eucharistiæ ad normam iuris præscribuntur.[131]

Sacred Images

318. In the earthly Liturgy, the Church participates, by a foretaste, in that heavenly Liturgy which is celebrated in the holy city of Jerusalem toward which she journeys as a pilgrim, and where Christ is sitting at the right hand of God; and by venerating the memory of the Saints, she hopes one day to have some part and fellowship with them.[132]

De imaginibus sacris

318. Ecclesia in terrena Liturgia cælestem illam prægustando participat, quæ in sancta civitate Ierusalem, ad quam peregrina tendit, celebratur, ubi Christus est in dextera Dei sedens, et memoriam Sanctorum venerando partem aliquam et societatem cum iis sperat se habituram.[132]

---

317. This brief article simply states that all other laws pertaining to the reservation of the Blessed Sacrament must not be "forgotten" (*obliviscantur*). It is also important to remember the official doctrine and theology regarding the reserved Sacrament, e.g., "the principal reason for reserving the sacrament is . . . sacramental communion . . . especially the sick and the aged."[29]

Sacred Images

318. The first paragraph of this article, which articulates the basic principle concerning sacred images housed in the parish church or oratory, is new to the *IGMR*. The overarching principle is that all images in a church building participate in the grander eschatological narrative of Christianity and need to be harmonized to indicate as such.[30] The article makes the claim that Church art is narrative art and from that perspective contributes to the unfolding of God's Word to God's people in nonverbal form. Images in the edifice for worship can reveal that the Eucharist we celebrate on earth is a foretaste of a heavenly one. Therefore our liturgical life, like the *Sanctus* we sing as part of the preface, places us on the threshold between this life and God's eternal communion.

29. Decree of the Sacred Congregation for Divine Worship (21 June 1973) promulgating *Forms of Worship of the Eucharist: Exposition, Benediction, Processions, Congresses* (Washington, DC: USCC Publications Office, 1976), 1.

30. This can be compared to the approach to sacred images in the Introduction to the *Directory on Popular Piety and the Liturgy* (Vatican, 2001), that roots sacred images in the faith of people from age to age (no. 18).

Thus, images of the Lord, the Blessed Virgin Mary, and the Saints, in accordance with the Church's most ancient tradition, should be displayed for veneration by the faithful in sacred buildings[133] and should be arranged so as to usher the faithful toward the mysteries of faith celebrated there. For this reason, care should be taken that their number not be increased indiscriminately, and that they be arranged in proper order so as not to distract the faithful's attention from the celebration itself.[134] There should usually be only one image of any given Saint. Generally speaking, in the ornamentation and arrangement of a church as far as images are concerned, provision should be made for the devotion of the entire community as well as for the beauty and dignity of the images.

Itaque Domini, beatæ Mariæ Virginis et Sanctorum imagines, iuxta antiquissimam Ecclesiæ traditionem, in ædibus sacris fidelium venerationi exhibeantur[133] et ibi ita disponantur ut fideles manuducant ad mysteria fidei quæ ibi celebrantur. Ideoque caveatur ne eorum numerus indiscrete augeatur, hinc ut earum dispositio debito ordine fiat, ne fidelium attentionem ab ipsa celebratione avocent.[134] Unius autem eiusdemque Sancti plus quam una imago de more ne habeatur. Generatim in ornamento et dispositione ecclesiæ ad imagines quod attinet, pietati totius communitatis prospiciatur atque pulchritudini et dignitati imaginum.

This article also makes a claim for a "proper order" in displaying Christian imagery beginning with the Lord, extending to Mary, and followed by the saints. *IGMR2002* directs that the multiplication of images in churches should be avoided, and that this art, meant for devotion, should not "distract" (*avocent*) the faithful from the eucharistic celebration. It also notes that, in the design and ornamentation of a church, provision should be made both for "the devotion" (*pietati*) of the faithful, as well as for the "beauty and dignity of the images" (*pulchritudini et dignitati imaginum*).

This last section of the Instruction on images generates numerous questions. For example, communities that have a strong and well-developed history and practice of popular religion may offer some critique of the norms that restrict the multiplication of images. Many of these communities, especially Hispanic or Latino, have a radically different history and Christian anthropology that arose from the visible pieties of those devotions.[31]

The provision of appropriate devotional places in the church should not be an afterthought. The development of a master plan for art is valuable whether or not the church is new or old. This will help avoid clutter and confusion when it comes to furnishing the worship environment with devotional as well as ritual works of art. In every case, all works of art should be perceived as the expressions of the culture and faith of the entire community and not just of particular groups or individuals.

31. Roberto S. Goizueta, "Fiesta: Life in the Subjunctive," in Orlando O. Espín and Miguel H. Diaz, eds., *From the Heart of Our People: Latino/a Explorations in Catholic Systematic Theology* (Maryknoll, NY: Orbis, 1999), 84–99.

Conclusion

This chapter is a valuable tool for church building and renovation projects. Its purpose needs to be understood in light of *SC*'s concern for the active participation of the worshiping community (no. 14), and an awareness that church buildings are ecclesiological statements. In shaping spaces for worship, therefore, it is necessary to provide places that, in the words of *IGMR2002*'s Preamble, are "a witness to unbroken traditions" (*Traditio non intermissa declaratur*, no. 6) while they are also an "accommodation to new conditions" (*Ad novas rerum condiciones accommodatio*, no. 10).

Overall, the chapter seems stronger regarding the witness to tradition, and not as developed in accommodating to new conditions. For example, the basic definition of the sanctuary does not seem to allow for alternative understandings prompted by emerging centralized or choral church plans, which often blur boundaries between the ministry (especially the ordained) and the faithful. Similarly, practices of popular piety imbedded in rich cultural traditions were not given much attention, for example, regarding the cross of the altar, which is not only a liturgical artifact but also an important object of personal piety for many cultural groups, affecting its location and size.

The next edition of this chapter will need to address more directly some of the complex and challenging issues of culture. For example, it could offer some direction regarding the architectural style of church buildings in different regions and how a place of worship and its ornamentation serves not only as a metaphor for the heavenly liturgy, and the universal Church, but also as a metaphor for the living, local community of believers who worship there.

GIRM—Notes (English)

108. Cf. Second Vatican Ecumenical Council, Constitution on the Sacred Liturgy, *Sacrosanctum Concilium*, nos. 122–124; Decree on the Ministry and Life of Priests, *Presbyterorum ordinis*, no. 5; Sacred Congregation of Rites, Instruction *Inter Oecumenici*, On the orderly carrying out of the Constitution on the Sacred Liturgy, 26 September 1964, no. 90: AAS 56 (1964), p. 897; Sacred Congregation of Rites, Instruction *Eucharisticum mysterium*, On the worship of the Eucharist, 25 May 1967, no. 24: AAS 59 (1967), p. 554; *Codex Iuris Canonici*, can. 932 § 1.

109. Cf. Second Vatican Ecumenical Council, Constitution on the Sacred Liturgy, *Sacrosanctum Concilium*, no. 123.

110. Cf. Sacred Congregation of Rites, Instruction *Eucharisticum mysterium*, On the worship of the Eucharist, 25 May 1967, no. 24: AAS 59 (1967), p. 554.

111. Cf. Second Vatican Ecumenical Council, Constitution on the Sacred Liturgy, *Sacrosanctum Concilium*, nos. 123, 129; Sacred Congregation of Rites, Instruction *Inter Oecumenici*, On the orderly carrying out of the Constitution on the Sacred Liturgy, 26 September 1964, no. 13c: AAS 56 (1964), p. 880.

112. Cf. Second Vatican Ecumenical Council, Constitution on the Sacred Liturgy, *Sacrosanctum Concilium*, no. 123.

113. Cf. ibid., no. 126; Sacred Congregation of Rites, Instruction *Inter Oecumenici*, On the orderly carrying out of the Constitution on the Sacred Liturgy, 26 September 1964, no. 91: AAS 56 (1964), p. 898.

114. Cf. Sacred Congregation of Rites, Instruction *Inter Oecumenici*, On the orderly carrying out of the Constitution on the Sacred Liturgy, 26 September 1964, nos. 97–98: AAS 56 (1964), p. 899.

115. Cf. ibid., no. 91: AAS 56 (1964), p. 898.

116. Cf. ibid.

117. Cf. Sacred Congregation of Rites, Instruction *Inter Oecumenici*, On the orderly carrying out of the Constitution on the Sacred Liturgy, 26 September 1964, no. 92: AAS 56 (1964), p. 899.

118. Cf. The Roman Ritual, *Book of Blessings, editio typica*, 1984, Order for a Blessing

IGMR—Notes (Latin)

108. Cf. Conc. Œcum. Vat. II, Const. de sacra Liturgia, *Sacrosanctum Concilium*, nn. 122–124; Decr. de Presbyterorum ministerio et vita, *Presbyterorum ordinis*, n. 5; S. Congr. Rituum, Instr. *Inter Œcumenici*, diei 26 septembris 1964, n. 90: A.A.S. 56 (1964) p. 897; Instr. *Eucharisticum mysterium*, diei 25 maii 1967, n. 24: A.A S. 59 (1967) p. 554; *Codex Iuris Canonici*, can. 932 § 1.

109. Cf. Conc. Œcum. Vat. II, Const. de sacra Liturgia, *Sacrosanctum Concilium*, n. 123.

110. Cf. S. Congr. Rituum, Instr. *Eucharisticum mysterium*, diei 25 maii 1967, n. 24: A.A S. 59 (1967) p. 554.

111. Cf. Conc. Œcum. Vat. II, Const. de sacra Liturgia, *Sacrosanctum Concilium*, nn. 123, 129; S. Congr. Rituum, Instr. *Inter Œcumenici*, diei 26 septembris 1964, n. 13 c: A.A.S. 56 (1964) p. 880.

112. Cf. Conc. Œcum. Vat. II, Const. de sacra Liturgia, *Sacrosanctum Concilium*, n. 123.

113. Cf. *ibidem*, n. 126; S. Congr. Rituum, Instr. *Inter Œcumenici*, diei 26 septembris 1964, n. 91: A.A.S. 56 (1964) p. 898.

114. Cf. S. Congr. Rituum, Instr. *Inter Œcumenici*, diei 26 septembris 1964, nn. 97–98: A.A.S. 56 (1964) p. 899.

115. Cf. *ibidem*, n. 91: A.A.S. 56 (1964) p. 898.

116. Cf. *ibidem*.

117. Cf. S. Congr. Rituum, Instr. *Inter Œcumenici*, diei 26 septembris 1964, n. 96: A.A.S. 56 (1964) p. 899.

118. Cf. Rituale Romanum, *De Benedictionibus*, editio typica 1984, Ordo benedictio-

on the Occasion of the Installation of a New Ambo, nos. 900–918.

119. Cf. Sacred Congregation of Rites, Instruction *Inter Oecumenici*, On the orderly carrying out of the Constitution on the Sacred Liturgy, 26 September 1964, no 92: AAS 56 (1964), p. 898.

120. Cf. The Roman Ritual, *Book of Blessings, editio typica*, 1984, Order for a Blessing on the Occasion of the Installation of a New Cathedra or Presidential Chair, nos. 880–899.

121. Cf. Sacred Congregation of Rites, Instruction *Inter Oecumenici*, On the orderly carrying out of the Constitution on the Sacred Liturgy, 26 September 1964, no. 92: AAS 56 (1964), p. 898.

122. Cf. Second Vatican Ecumenical Council, Constitution on the Sacred Liturgy, *Sacrosanctum Concilium*, no. 32.

123. Cf. Sacred Congregation of Rites, Instruction *Musicam sacram*, On music in the Liturgy, 5 March 1967, no. 23: AAS 59 (1967), p. 307.

124. Cf. The Roman Ritual, *Book of Blessings, editio typica*, 1984, Order for the Blessing of an Organ, nos. 1052–1067.

125. Cf. Sacred Congregation of Rites, Instruction *Eucharisticum mysterium*, On the worship of the Eucharist, 25 May 1967, no. 54: AAS 59 (1967), p. 568; cf. also Sacred Congregation of Rites, Instruction *Inter Oecumenici*, On the orderly carrying out of the Constitution on the Sacred Liturgy, 26 September 1964, no. 95: AAS 56 (1964), p. 898.

126. Cf. Sacred Congregation of Rites, Instruction *Eucharisticum mysterium*, On the worship of the Eucharist, 25 May 1967. no. 52: AAS 59 (1967), p. 568; Sacred Congregation of Rites, Instruction *Inter Oecumenici*, On the orderly carrying out of the Constitution on the Sacred Liturgy, 26 September 1964, no. 95: AAS 56 (1964), p. 898; Sacred Congregation for the Sacraments, Instruction *Nullo umquam tempore*, 28 May 1938, no. 4: AAS 30 (1938), pp. 199–200; The Roman Ritual, *Holy Communion and Worship of the Eucharist outside Mass, editio typica*, 1973, nos. 10–11; *Codex Iuris Canonici*, can. 938 § 3.

127. Cf. The Roman Ritual, *Book of Blessings, editio typica*, 1984, Order for a Blessing

nis occasione data auspicandi novum ambonem, nn. 900–918.

119. Cf. S. Congr. Rituum, Instr. *Inter Œcumenici,* diei 26 septembris 1964, n. 92: A.A.S. 56 (1964) p. 898.

120. Cf. Rituale Romanum, *De Benedictionibus,* editio typica 1984, Ordo benedictionis occasione data auspicandi novam cathedram seu sedem præsidentiæ, nn. 880–899.

121. Cf. S. Congr. Rituum, Instr. *Inter Œcumenici,* diei 26 septembris 1964, n. 92: A.A.S. 56 (1964) p. 898.

122. Cf. Conc. Œcum. Vat. II, Const. de sacra Liturgia *Sacrosanctum Concilium,* n. 32.

123. Cf. S. Congr. Rituum, Instr. *Musicam sacram,* diei 5 martii 1967, n. 23: A.A.S. 59 (1967) p. 307.

124. Cf. Rituale Romanum, *De Benedictionibus,* editio typica 1984, Ordo benedictionis organi, nn. 1052–1067.

125. Cf. S. Congr. Rituum, Instr. *Eucharisticum mysterium,* diei 25 maii 1967, n. 54: A.A S. 59 (1967) p. 568; Instr. *Inter Œcumenici,* diei 26 septembris 1964, n. 95: A.A.S. 56 (1964) p. 898.

126. Cf. S. Congr. Rituum, Instr. *Eucharisticum mysterium,* diei 25 maii 1967, n. 52: A.A.S. 59 (1967) p. 568; Instr. *Inter Œcumenici,* diei 26 septembris 1964, n. 95: A.A.S. 56 (1964) p. 898; S. Congr. de Sacramentis, Instr. *Nullo umquam tempore,* diei 28 maii 1938, n. 4: A.A.S. 30 (1938) pp. 199–200; Rituale Romanum, *De sacra Communione et de cultu mysterii eucharistici extra Missam,* editio typica 1973, nn. 10–11; *Codex Iuris Canonici,* can. 938 § 3.

127. Cf. Rituale Romanum, *De Benedictionibus,* editio typica 1984, Ordo benedictionis

on the Occasion of the Installation of a New Tabernacle, nos. 919–929.

128. Cf. Sacred Congregation of Rites, Instruction *Eucharisticum mysterium,* On the worship of the Eucharist, 25 May 1967, no. 55: AAS 59 (1967), p. 569.

129. Cf. ibid., no. 53: AAS 59 (1967), p. 568; The Roman Ritual, *Holy Communion and Worship of the Eucharist outside Mass, editio typica,* 1973, no. 9; *Codex Iuris Canonici* can. 938 § 2; John Paul II, Apostolic Letter *Dominicae Cenae,* 24 February 1980, no. 3: AAS 72 (1980), pp. 117–119.

130. Cf. *Codex Iuris Canonici,* can. 940; Sacred Congregation of Rites, Instruction *Eucharisticum mysterium,* On the worship of the Eucharist, 25 May 1967, no. 57: AAS 59 (1967), p. 569; The Roman Ritual, *Holy Communion and Worship of the Eucharist outside Mass, editio typica,* 1973, no. 11.

131. Cf. particularly in Sacred Congregation for the Sacraments, Instruction *Nullo umquam tempore,* 28 May 1938: AAS 30 (1938), pp. 198–207; *Codex Iuris Canonici,* cann. 934–944.

132. Cf. Second Vatican Ecumenical Council, Constitution on the Sacred Liturgy, *Sacrosanctum Concilium,* no. 8.

133. Cf. The Roman Pontifical: *Order of the Dedication of a Church and an Altar, editio typica,* 1984, Chapter 4, no. 10; The Roman Ritual, *Book of Blessings, editio typica,* 1984, Order for the Blessing of Images for Public Veneration by the Faithful, nos. 984–1031.

134. Cf. Second Vatican Ecumenical Council, Constitution on the Sacred Liturgy, *Sacrosanctum Concilium,* no. 125.

occasione data auspicandi novum tabernaculum eucharisticum, nn. 919–929.

128. Cf. S. Congr. Rituum, Instr. *Eucharisticum mysterium,* diei 25 maii 1967, n. 55: A.A.S. 59 (1967) p. 569.

129. *Ibidem,* n. 53: A.A.S. 59 (1967) p. 568; Rituale Romanum, *De sacra Communione et de cultu mysterii eucharistici extra Missam,* editio typica 1973, n. 9; *Codex Iuris Canonici,* can. 938 § 2; Ioannes Paulus II, Epist. *Dominicæ Cenæ,* diei 24 februarii 1980, n. 3: A.A.S. 72 (1980) pp. 117–119.

130. Cf. *Codex Iuris Canonici,* can. 940; S. Congr. Rituum, Instr. *Eucharisticum mysterium,* diei 25 maii 1967, 57: A.A.S. 59 (1967) p. 569; cf. Rituale Romanum, *De sacra Communione et de cultu mysterii eucharistici extra Missam,* editio typica 1973, n. 11.

131. Cf. præsertim S. Congr. de Sacramentis, Instr. *Nullo umquam tempore,* diei 28 maii 1938: A.A.S. 30 (1938) pp. 198–207; *Codex Iuris Canonici,* cann. 934–944.

132. Cf. Conc. Œcum. Vat. II, Const. de sacra Liturgia, *Sacrosanctum Concilium,* n. 8.

133. Cf. Pontificale Romanum, *Ordo Dedicationis ecclesiæ et altaris,* editio typica 1977, cap. IV, n. 10; Rituale Romanum, *De Benedictionibus,* editio typica 1984, Ordo ad benedicendas imagines quæ fidelium venerationi publicæ exhibentur, nn. 984–1031.

134. Cf. Conc. Œcum. Vat. II, Const. de sacra Liturgia, *Sacrosanctum Concilium,* n. 125.

CHAPTER VI

Requisites for the Celebration of Mass

(DE IIS QUAE AD MISSAE CELEBRATIONEM REQUIRUNTUR)

Richard E. McCarron and Anne C. McGuire

Introduction

Chapter VI (nos. 319–351) of *Institutio Generalis Missalis Romani* (*IGMR2002*) continues with prescriptions for the material things needed for the celebration of the Mass. While the major architectural symbols like the altar and ambo and their furnishings are treated in Chapter V, this chapter takes up the central symbols of bread and wine; the sacred vessels used for them; the sacred vesture for celebrating the Mass; and, in a more summary way, liturgical books, the altar cross, the processional cross, and other objects for the celebration. Arranged in five major subsections (on the Bread and Wine for Celebrating the Eucharist; Sacred Furnishings in General; Sacred Vessels; Sacred Vestments; and Other Things Intended for Church Use), this section should be read in conjunction with the commentary of *Redemptionis Sacramentum* (*RedSac*) as well as with any local guidelines for liturgical objects, like the US Bishops' *Built of Living Stones* (BLS).[1]

While addressed under the functional heading "those things that are required for the celebration of Mass," the elements discussed in this chapter form an essential part of the nonverbal dimension of the liturgical celebration. As *Sacrosanctum Concilium* (*SC*) explains, these nonverbal signs and symbols are a central part of the liturgical celebration: "human sanctification is given expression in symbols perceptible to the senses" (no. 7, also no. 33). Imbued with the deeply Catholic sacramental principle, *SC* affirms that "there is scarcely any proper use of material things that cannot be directed toward human sanctification and the praise of God" (no. 61). This affirmation also reveals how attention cannot be given only to isolated things in themselves, but always to those things in relation to God and to the human persons who use them. The objects, vessels, and vestments used in liturgy are in service of the action of the liturgy, not articles that are ends in themselves. While they do serve a functional purpose—

1. Especially BLS, nos. 91–92, 146–149, and 164–165.

one needs a container for the bread—they are also media for the faith and theology of the celebration, as they mark the festivity of the celebration and call our attention to our central relationship with God through Christ in the Holy Spirit. As such, the quality of these items demands careful consideration.

A recurring expression in this section—"noble simplicity" (*nobilis simplicitas*) —echoes the expression used in *SC* that speaks of the renewal of the liturgical rites in terms of a "noble simplicity" (no. 34). This expression has been used to describe the so-called "genius of the Roman Rite," although that term is not without scholarly contention.[2] At issue here is a liturgical aesthetic regarding what is "noble simplicity," as well as who makes that decision. *SC* speaks to the quality of the furnishings and objects used at liturgy when it calls for "worthy, becoming, beautiful signs and symbols" (no. 122) and cautions against the extremes of mediocrity and sumptuous display (no. 124). While *SC* entrusts this judgment to local ordinaries in consultation with experts and commissions (see no. 126), it provides no criteria for judgment; neither does *IGMR2002* (cf. no. 390). This will remain a critical pastoral issue. A cue can be taken from *SC*'s approach that urges a wide consultation for a communal standard, rather than the personal taste or piety of an individual bishop or presbyter.

Such aesthetic judgments become even more acute with regard to the way that what is beautiful, worthy, and noble is inextricably tied to local culture (e.g., no. 325 below). *SC* speaks of the critical embrace of the cultural "genius and talents of various races and peoples" (no. 37, also no. 123). This necessarily entails a plurality of standards of excellence that are to be guided by the customs of the various regions of the world in which the Church is incarnated (cf. *Ad Gentes*, no. 22). While *IGMR2002* regularly appeals to local standards and the spirit of the contemporary ages, there is a certain predilection in this chapter to affirm notions of excellence and beauty in terms that some African, Asian, and South American local churches might regard as more typical of an affluent European and European-American aesthetic (cf. no. 397 below).

When treating the material provisions necessary for the celebration of the liturgy, there is further an ethical consideration to be taken into account. While affirming the need for noble and beautiful things for the liturgy, *IGMR2002*, like its predecessors, does not address the issue of cost of materials in local context (cf. no. 118 above), how they are obtained, or appropriate compensation for artists and purveyors. Centuries ago Bartolomé de las Casas (d. 1566) questioned what he was doing when celebrating Mass with bread stolen from the poor.[3] Today the same concern remains, as do others: the migrant workers who

2. See, for example, Burkhard Neunheuser, "Roman Genius Revisited," in *Liturgy for the New Millennium: A Commentary on the Revised Sacramentary*, ed. Mark R. Francis and Keith Pecklers (Collegeville, MN: The Liturgical Press, 2000), 35–48.

3. See the account of Enrique Dussell, "The Bread of the Eucharistic Celebration and the Sign of Justice in the Community," in *Can We Always Celebrate the Eucharist?* ed. Mary Collins and David Power, Concilium 152 (New York: Seabury, 1982), 56–65.

Chapter VI
THE REQUISITES FOR THE CELEBRATION OF MASS

I. The Bread and Wine for Celebrating the Eucharist

319. Following the example of Christ, the Church has always used bread and wine with water to celebrate the Lord's Supper.

Caput VI
DE IIS QUÆ AD MISSÆ CELEBRATIONEM REQUIRUNTUR

I. De Pane et Vino ad Eucharistiam Celebrandam

319. Exemplum Christi secuta, Ecclesia panem et vinum cum aqua ad celebrandum dominicum convivium semper adhibuit.

---

harvest the grapes for wine; the slave labor mining the gold to line chalices; the sweatshop labor making the fabrics of the vestments; the commitment and talent of the liturgical artists trying to support their families. *IGMR2002* does not provide clear criteria for reasonable expenditures for local communities who, in love of and fidelity to the Church's liturgical law, might make great sacrifice to purchase material goods for the appropriate celebration of the liturgy. No edition of *IGMR* has given any consideration to a poor and debt-ridden community or a mission where obtaining even the simplest of these "requirements for the celebration of Mass" might entail great hardship and expense.

Each of these aspects—the liturgical, the aesthetic, and the ethical—needs to be taken into consideration when implementing the directives in Chapter VI. Holding out a standard of excellence, these documents urge Christians to bring their best to the liturgy. Within this larger frame, comment is now given for the individual paragraphs.

The Bread and Wine for Celebrating the Eucharist

319. This section remains unchanged from *IGMR1975*. It calls attention to the central symbols of bread and wine for the celebration of the Mass. As the prayers at the preparation of the altar and gifts name them, bread and wine are both fruits of creation *(fructum terrae . . . fructum vitis)* and the work of human hands *(operis manuum hominum, Missale Romanum* 2002 [*MR2002*], nos. 23 and 25). As such, bread and wine themselves are multivalent. As fruits of the earth, bread and wine help us recall God's gracious gift to us and the sacramentality of all creation. For many cultures, bread is the daily nourishment and wine is the mark of festivity. As Saint Augustine (d. 430) preached, the process of making a Christian through the rites of initiation can be likened to the process of making bread: the crushing of the grain evokes fasting and exorcism; the admixture of water bringing many grains into one is like the water of baptism; and the baking is represented by the oil of chrism and the Holy Spirit.[4] The bread, thus, is symbol of all the baptized who gather. In the Hebrew Bible, wine

4. *Sermo* 227, in *Sermons pour la Pâque*, ed. Suzanne Poque, Sources Chrétiennes 116 (Paris: Éditions du Cerf, 1966), 234–243.

320. The bread for celebrating the Eucharist must be made only from wheat, must be recently baked, and, according to the ancient tradition of the Latin Church, must be unleavened.

320. Panis ad Eucharistiam celebrandam debet esse mere triticeus, recenter confectus et, secundum antiquam Ecclesiæ latinæ traditionem, azymus.

---

is often called the "blood of grapes" *(dam anavim)* and its use recalls images of liberation, covenant, and sacrifice. The crushing of wheat and grapes and the preparation of bread and wine to sustain us recall the mystery of death and life. As fruits of the earth, bread and wine call us to attend with care to creation; as work of human hands they point us to just relationships for the laborers who harvest and manufacture them.

The amount of water that is to be added to the wine in the chalice is "small" (*modica aqua* in *Codex Iuris Canonici* 1983 [*CIC1983*] c. 924, par. 1). This practice reflects the Church's inheritance of local table customs in Jesus' day that were, by the third century, invested with further ecclesial or Christological meaning, as reflected in the current prayer at the preparation, "through the mystery of this water and wine" *(per huius aquae et vini mysterium)*, whose roots trace back to a collect for the Nativity in the *Sacramentarium Veronense* (no. 1239).[5]

320. A change of wording brings this paragraph in harmony with the language of *CIC1983*, and deletes the explanation that the use of wheat bread is according to the tradition of the whole Church *(iuxta traditionem totius Ecclesiae,* cf. *IGMR1970* and *IGMR1975*, no. 282). Following *CIC1983*, c. 924, par. 2, the bread is to be "only wheat" *(mere triticeus)* and recently made *(recenter confectus)*. In accord with *CIC1983*, c. 926, *IGMR2002* explains further that the bread should be unleavened "according to the ancient tradition of the Latin Church" *(secundum antiquam Ecclesiae latinae traditionem)*. Up to the late eighth century, the bread for the celebration of the Eucharist was what was provided by the faithful and did not differ in substance from their ordinary bread.[6] Thus, the bread's composition varied according to local custom, "unleavened or leavened, with or without salt, even with oil, as was noted occasionally in times past for Eastern countries. It is not ruled out that it was prepared just for the Eucharist."[7] Preferences for the use of unleavened bread of pure wheat flour for the Eucharist are

5. For the textual history, see P. Tirot, "Histoire des prières d'offertoire dans la liturgie romaine du VIIe au XVIe siècle," *Ephemerides Liturgicae* 98 (1984): 179–181. The full current text reads: "Per huius aquae et vini mysterium eius efficiamur divinitatis consortes, qui humanitatis nostrae fieri est particeps" (*MR2002*, no. 24). The current ICEL translation specifies that the reference is to Christ: "By the mystery of this water and wine may we come to share in the divinity of Christ who humbled himself to share in our humanity."

6. George Galavaris, *Bread and the Liturgy: The Symbolism of Early Christian and Byzantine Bread Stamps* (Madison, WI and London: University of Wisconsin Press, 1970), 13.

7. Vincenzo Raffa, *Liturgia eucaristica. Mistagogia della Messa: dalla storia e dalla teologia alla pastorale practica*, new ed., Bibliotheca Ephemerides Liturgicae, Subsidia 100 (Rome: CLV-Edizioni Liturgiche, 2003), 390. Galavaris notes the evidence of special attention given to the

found from the late eighth century.[8] "Recently made" refers to the necessity of avoiding stale, moldy, or otherwise spoiled bread. That the bread be only wheat continues to exclude the use of other grains and the admixture of other ingredients like oil, salt, sugar, honey, or milk in its preparation. Such admixture is named a grave abuse by *RedSac*, no. 48. The 1980 instruction *Inaestimabile Donum* further clarifies that the preparation of the bread requires "attentive care" so that "nothing diminishes the dignity that is due to the eucharistic bread, its fraction may be done with dignity, does not give rise to excessive fragments and does not offend the sensibilities of the faithful when they eat it" (no. 8).[9] No canonical objection has been raised to the use of whole wheat flour or unbleached, all-purpose flour for white flour.

The restriction of the "matter" to purely wheat flour raises pastoral issues for those who suffer with celiac disease (cf. no. 284 above).[10] Such persons may be given permission by the Ordinary or his delegate to receive hosts that are deemed "low-gluten," that is, those that contain a "sufficient amount of gluten to obtain the confection of bread."[11] Bread or a host that is completely without gluten is considered invalid matter for the Eucharist.[12] The argument proceeds from the criterion of *common estimation:* bread with no gluten is not considered to be bread according to the common estimation of its contents, although

quality of the bread that was for the Church or given to the sick—*panis siligineus* of carefully sifted flour—and the marking of the bread (Galavaris, 14).

8. Raffa argues that the frequently-cited letter of Alcuin in 798 deals primarily with the exclusion of adding salt to the bread, which was the custom in Spanish regions but not for Alcuin (see *Epistola XC Ad Fratres Lugdunenses* [*PL* 100:289A-B]. According to Raffa, the first clear testimony to unleavened bread comes from Rabanus Maurus (d. 856), *De clericorum institutione,* book 1, chap. 31 (*PL* 107:318C-D–319); his expressed preference for unleavened bread would have had considerable weight because of Rabanus's authority. Raffa posits that the spread of the exclusive use of unleavened bread comes when the monasteries, particularly Cluniac monasteries, began preparing their own bread for the monk's increasing number of Masses and the bread of the faithful was no longer used for the Eucharist. Further, "unleavened bread" then came to mean not only that yeast was not added, but became synonymous with small, thin, round, pure white hosts whose preparation was given minute detail. By the time of Rupert of Deutz (d. 1129), the practice of this unleavened bread in the West had come to be seen as normative to the extent that Rupert declared that the Roman Church had always used unleavened bread (*Liber De Divinis Officiis*, book 2, part 22 *[De Azymo et fermento]*; CCL, Continuatio Mediaevalis 7:52-56, here at 52). See the presentation in Raffa, 390–394. See further Mary Collins, "Critical Questions for Liturgical Theology," in her *Worship: Renewal to Practice* (Washington, DC: Pastoral Press, 1987), 115–132, for a theological study of the layers of meaning in the change of the bread sign.

9. English Translation from *Origins* 10, no. 3 (5 June 1980): 43. The Latin reads: "Eius confectio attenti animi postulat curam ita ut compositio nihil detrimenti afferat dignitati, quae eucharistico pani debetur, eius fractio digne fieri possit, neque nimia fragmenta oriri, neque in manducatione sensum religiosum fidelium offendi contingat." *AAS* 72, no. 3 (30 April 1980): 336.

10. Also known as coeliac or coeliac-sprue disease.

11. CDF letter 2003, Prot. 89/78–17498, no. A-2.

12. CDF letter, no. A-1.

321. The meaning of the sign demands that the material for the Eucharistic celebration truly have the appearance of food. It is therefore expedient that the Eucharistic bread, even though unleavened and baked in the traditional shape, be made in such a way that the priest at Mass with a congregation is able in practice to break it into parts for distribution to at least some of the faithful. Small hosts are, however, in no way ruled out when the number of those receiving Holy Communion or other pastoral needs require it. The action of the fraction or breaking of bread, which gave

321. Ratio signi postulat ut materia celebrationis eucharisticæ revera ut cibus appareat. Expedit ergo ut panis eucharisticus, quamvis azymus et forma tradita confectus, tali modo efficiatur, ut sacerdos in Missa cum populo celebrata revera hostiam frangere possit in diversas partes, easque saltem aliquibus fidelibus distribuere. Parvæ tamen hostiæ minime excluduntur, quando numerus sacram Communionem sumentium aliæque rationes pastorales id exigunt. Gestus autem fractionis panis, quo simpliciter Eucharistia designabatur tempore apostolico, apertius manifestabit vim

---

common estimation may vary across cultural lines. While stating that the presence of gluten is necessary for validity, the Congregation for the Doctrine of the Faith (CDF) does not specify the exact quantity that must be present. This is of concern for many persons with celiac disease who suffer deleterious internal effects from even minuscule amounts of gluten, even in the absence of overt symptoms.[13]

321. Taking into account the importance of the value of the bread as a "sign" *(ratio signi)*, *IGMR2002* explains that the bread should actually look like food and be able to be broken into pieces for the Communion of "at least some of the faithful" (*saltem aliquibus fidelibus*). This gives visible expression to the unity of the participants in Christ, sharing the one bread as the final sentence of the paragraph explains. The earlier *Inaestimabile Donum* explains that the criterion "appear as actual food" (here referring to *IGMR1975*, no. 283) is linked to the consistency of the bread, not its shape, which should remain traditional (no. 8). *IGMR2002* continues the specification that the "traditional shape" should be maintained *(forma tradita confectus)*. It does not describe what the "traditional shape" is. In early centuries when people brought bread from home, it could have had a variety of sizes and shapes. There is evidence of round, cruciform, rectangular, and square bread stamps.[14] The mosaics of Ravenna depict both small round loaves and a more elaborate ring shape, which is also described by Gregory the Great (d. 604), who speaks of the *coronae oblationum*.[15] References

13. For a more detailed discussion, see Aidan McGrath, "Coeliacs, Alcoholics, the Eucharist and the Priesthood," *Irish Theological Quarterly* 67 (2002): 125–144.

14. See Galavaris, 46–62.

15. See Raffa, 394–395; see Gregory the Great, *Dialogue* 4, ch. 57 in *Grégoire le Grand, Dialogues, Livre 4, Texte critique*, ed. A. de Vogüé, trad. P. Antin, Sources Chrétiennes 265 (Paris: Éditions du Cerf, 1980), 186.

its name to the Eucharist in apostolic times, will bring out more clearly the force and importance of the sign of unity of all in the one bread, and of the sign of charity by the fact that the one bread is distributed among the brothers and sisters.

et momentum signi unitatis omnium in uno pane, et caritatis ex eo quod unus panis inter fratres distribuitur.

322. The wine for the Eucharistic celebration must be from the fruit of the grapevine (cf. Lk 22:18), natural, and unadulterated, that is, without admixture of extraneous substances.

322. Vinum pro celebratione eucharistica debet esse ex genimine vitis (cf. *Lc* 22, 18), naturale et merum, idest extraneis substantiis non admixtum.

---

to the eucharistic bread having the size and shape of coins *(in modum denarii)* appear in the twelfth century.[16]

Today some parishes have retrieved the practice of people carefully baking loaves of unleavened bread each week for Sunday Mass. *RedSac* cautions that people who prepare the bread for the Eucharist should be "not only distinguished by their integrity, but also their skill" (no. 48). While extolling the sign value of the fraction and sharing in one bread, *IGMR2002* explains that the use of "small hosts" *(parvae hostiae)* is not in the least excluded when the number of communicants or "other pastoral reasons" (*aliaeque rationes pastorales*) require. *RedSac* gives further specification that "indeed small hosts requiring no further fraction ought customarily to be used for the most part" (no. 49). This observation seems in line with the caution at *IGMR2002* that the fraction rite "should not be unnecessarily prolonged" (*ne tamen innecessarie protrahatur*, no. 83). Both of those statements, however, seem to be in tension with the more expansive description of the fraction as a sign of unity and charity that concludes this article (cf. no. 83 above).

322. The wine for Mass is to be pure and natural, made only from grapes.[17] Wine that has turned to vinegar, is souring or cloudy, or in any other way spoiled, is excluded. The wine must not have any artificial additives (that is, additives other than those made from grapes). Thus, care should be taken with regular commercial wines in this regard (cf. *RedSac*, no. 50). In fact, while not a canonical requirement, so-called "altar wine" is usually lightly fortified to help it last longer. In the past, most canonical experts specified an alcohol content at a minimum five percent and maximum twenty percent, the point being that fermentation must have begun and any added alcohol is not in so great a

16. See Honorius of Autun (d. ca. 1151), *Gemma animae*, book 1, ch. 35 (*PL* 172:555); and further Sicard of Cremona (d. 1215), *Mitrale (sive de officiis ecclesiasticis summa)*, book 3, ch. 6 (*PL* 213:118–119), and the discussion by Raffa, 395.

17. Cf. *CIC1983*, c. 924, par. 3.

323. Diligent care should be taken to ensure that the bread and wine intended for the Eucharist are kept in a perfect state of conservation: that is, that the wine does not turn to vinegar nor the bread spoil or become too hard to be broken easily.

324. If the priest notices after the consecration or as he receives Communion that

323. Sedula cura caveatur ut panis et vinum ad Eucharistiam destinata perfecto statu conserventur; id est, caveatur ne vinum acescat, neve panis corrumpatur vel nimis durus fiat, ita ut difficulter frangi possit.

324. Si post consecrationem aut cum Communionem sumit, sacerdos animad-

---

quantity as to alter its nature (e.g., some ports).[18] There is no restriction on whether red wine or white wine is used, dry or sweet, but some have noted the visual impact of red wine with regard to blood symbolism.[19]

The presence of alcohol is a major concern for priests, deacons, and lay faithful with alcoholism or alcohol intolerance. Priests who are unable to consume even a minimal amount of wine may, with the permission of the local Ordinary or his delegate, use *mustum*.[20] *Mustum* is pure "grape juice that is either fresh or preserved by methods that suspend its fermentation without altering its nature (for example, freezing)."[21] With *mustum*, fermentation has started, but is arrested so the alcohol content is minimal. Commercial pasteurized grape juice is invalid matter because the heat of pasteurization removes any residual alcohol.[22] Dealcoholized wine—wine with all of its alcohol content extracted by human means—is considered wine whose nature has been altered *(corruptus)* and is, therefore, not admissible.[23]

323. This section emphasizes the care that should be taken with the bread and wine for the celebration of the Eucharist, lest they spoil. Proper care should be taken to keep the wine in a cool and dark place, and the hosts well wrapped; one task of a sacristan might be that they are both checked for integrity before use.

324. This paragraph remains unchanged from *IGMR1975*. It might seem odd to switch topics here to a discussion of required ritual actions if the priest-celebrant discovers that only water was in the chalice during the recitation of

18. The figure of five percent is what is considered common estimation of true wine. Determination of the validity of lower percentages depends on how it was produced. For further detail on these matters, see Patrick J. McSherry, *Wine as Sacramental Matter and the Use of Mustum* (Washington, DC: National Clergy Council on Alcoholism, 1986), 42–44, and McGrath, 133–134.

19. See Pierre-Marie Gy, "Le vin rouge, est-il préférable pour l'Eucharistie?" in *Liturgia et Unitas: In honorem Bruno Bürki*, ed. Martin Klöckener and Arnaud Join-Lambert (Freiburg Schweiz: Universitätsverlag; Genève: Labor and Fides, 2001), 178–184.

20. CDF letter 2003, Prot. 89/78–17498, no. C-1.

21. CDF letter 2003, Prot. 89/78–17498, no. A-3.

22. This is the determination of the U.S. Bishops' Committee on the Liturgy, *Newsletter* 39 (November 2003): 45 and 49. McSherry argued differently in 1986; see 80–88.

23. See McSherry, 43.

not wine but only water was poured into the chalice, he pours the water into some container, then pours wine with water into the chalice and consecrates it. He says only the part of the institution narrative related to the consecration of the chalice, without being obliged to consecrate the bread again.

vertat vinum non fuisse infusum, sed aquam, deposita aqua in aliquo vase, vinum cum aqua infundat in calicem, illud consecret, partem narrationis dicens quæ ad consecrationem calicis pertinet, quin tamen teneatur iterum panem consecrare.

II. Sacred Furnishings in General

325. As in the case of the building of churches, so also regarding all sacred furnishings the Church admits the artistic style of each region and accepts those adaptations that are in keeping with the culture and traditions of each people, provided

II. De Sacra Supellectile in Genere

325. Sicut pro ecclesiis ædificandis, ita et pro sacra supellectile universa, Ecclesia genus artis cuiusque regionis admittit, et eas aptationes recipit, quæ cum singularum gentium ingenio et traditionibus congruant, dummodo omnia usui ad quem

---

the institution narrative; however, these details formed part of the *De Defectibus Missae* of *MR1570* regarding wine.[24]

Sacred Furnishings in General

325. Parallel to its discussion of the church building in Chapter V, *IGMR2002* here offers some criteria for church furnishings. It explains that the Church welcomes the contributions of local art and adaptations that may be introduced that reflect the talents of the people and their traditions. It also qualifies that the purpose of the various furnishing should always be borne in mind. Further, *IGMR2002* presents the concept of "noble simplicity" *(nobilis simplicitas)*, which is presented as "the best companion of genuine art" (*cum arte vera optime copulatur*). The adjective *nobilis* is used twelve times in *IGMR2002* and combined with *simplicitas* three other times (see nos. 42, 292, and 351). The term is found in *SC*, no. 34, which explains that the rites should "radiate a noble simplicity" and be "short, clear, and free from useless repetition." Like its predecessors, *IGMR2002* admits the embrace of local art traditions, but it appears to impose a particular aesthetic associated with the Roman Rite, that of "noble simplicity." In some cultures, a complex composition is aesthetically pleasing in art, while simplicity is not (see no. 318 above). It might be helpful to review *SC*, nos. 122–123, with regard to making particular judgments at the local level, especially where different aesthetics might clash with the claim that simplicity makes for the best art. *SC* explains that what is used in worship should praise God and "extend his glory" by turning "people's spirit devoutly to God." The objects are not tied to any particular time period or cultural temperament. Further,

24. Title 4.

that all fit the purpose for which the sacred furnishings are intended.[135]

In this matter as well, a noble simplicity should be ensured such as is the best companion of genuine art.

326. In the choice of materials for sacred furnishings, besides those which are traditional, others are acceptable if by contemporary standards they are considered to be noble, are durable, and are well suited for sacred use. In the dioceses of the United States of America these materials may include wood, stone, or metal which are solid and appropriate to the purpose for which they are employed.

ipsa sacra supellex destinatur apte respondeant.[135]

Etiam in hac parte sedulo curetur nobilis illa simplicitas, quæ cum arte vera optime copulatur.

326. In seligendis materiis pro sacra supellectile, præter eas quæ usu traditæ sunt, eæ quoque admitti possunt quæ, iuxta mentem nostræ ætatis, nobiles æstimantur, durabiles sunt et usui sacro bene accommodantur. Qua de re iudex erit Conferentia Episcoporum pro singulis regionibus *(cf. n. 390).*

III. Sacred Vessels

327. Among the requisites for the celebration of Mass, the sacred vessels are held in special honor, especially the chalice and

III. De Sacris Vasis

327. Inter ea quæ ad Missam celebrandam requiruntur, speciali honore habentur vasa sacra, et inter hæc calix et patena, in

---

these should be things "set apart for use" and be "worthy, becoming, and beautiful signs and symbols of things supernatural." *SC* makes clear that liturgical furnishings and art are not ends in themselves, for "sumptuous display" (no. 124). Further, not only is what is "repugnant to faith and morals" to be kept well away from churches, but also things that are mediocre or merely for pretense (no. 124). In *SC*, decisions are not based on the piety or taste of the individual bishop, but rather are made in consultation with others (no. 126). While *SC* entrusts this process to the local ordinary, similar criteria could be used to help local leadership.

326. Here *IGMR* explains that in addition to what is considered traditional, for example, marble altars or gold chalices, local churches may also employ what is now considered durable and noble. The judge of these matters is the local conference of bishops. The current terminology of *conferentia episcoporum* differs from *IGMR1975 (conferentia episcopalis)* and a cross-reference to no. 390 has been added since *IGMR2000*. It is now the custom of the *recognitio* process to include in the approved translation what the local conference of bishops has decided rather than, for example, include them in an appendix. Thus GIRM2003 here provides specific options for materials that may be used for fabricating sacred furnishings in the dioceses of the US.

Sacred Vessels

327. This paragraph calls special attention to the vessels used to hold the bread and wine for Mass: the chalice and the paten.

paten, in which the bread and wine are offered and consecrated, and from which they are consumed.

quibus vinum et panis offeruntur, consecrantur et sumuntur.

328. Sacred vessels are to be made from precious metal. If they are made from metal that rusts or from a metal less precious than gold, then ordinarily they should be gilded on the inside.

328. Vasa sacra ex metallo nobili conficiantur. Si ex metallo conflata sint quod robiginem producat vel auro minus nobilis sit, interius plerumque inaurentur.

329. In the dioceses of the United States of America, sacred vessels may also be made from other solid materials that, according to the common estimation in each region, are precious, for example, ebony or other hard woods, provided that such materials are suited to sacred use and do not easily break or deteriorate. This applies to all vessels which hold the hosts, such as the paten, the ciborium, the pyx, the monstrance, and other things of this kind.

329. De iudicio Conferentiæ Episcoporum, actis ab Apostolica Sede recognitis, vasa sacra confici possunt etiam aliis ex materiis solidis et, secundum communem æstimationem cuiusque regionis, nobilibus, ex. gr. ebeno aut aliis lignis durioribus, dummodo usui sacro aptæ sint. Hoc in casu, præferantur semper materiæ quæ facile non frangantur neque corrumpantur. Quod valet pro omnibus vasis quæ ad hostias recipiendas destinata sunt, uti patena, pyxis, theca, ostensorium et alia huiusmodi.

---

328. *IGMR2002* changes the treatment of what materials can be used for sacred vessels from earlier editions. *IGMR1975*, no. 290, begins by stating that vessels are made from materials that are solid and that are regarded by the common estimation of the local region as noble or precious *(e materiis solidis et . . . nobilibus)*. Then *IGMR1975*, no. 294, explains that vessels made from metal that might rust are generally gilded; if made from metals that are immune to rust or more noble than gold, gilding is not necessary.

IGMR2002 now specifies first that the vessels are to be made "from precious metal" (although "noble metal" might have been a more accurate translation of *ex metallo nobili*). If the metal might rust or is less noble than gold, the interior (i.e., the part that comes in contact with the bread or wine) "generally should be gilded" *(plerumque inaurentur)*. The reference to metal more noble than gold or immune to rust is dropped. There is no mention here of the need for common estimation of what *"ex metallo nobili"* entails.

329. This article incorporates topics previously treated in *IGMR1975*, nos. 290 and 292. The conference of bishops, with the *recognitio* of the Apostolic See, can allow the sacred vessels to be made from other materials that are solid (*solidis*) and noble according to the "common estimation" of the local region. *IGMR1975*, no. 292, speaks of materials that are held in high esteem in the region *(magis aestimatis)*. *Solidus* can carry a range of meaning from solid or dense to lasting or real. What would be excluded would be something porous (see no. 330 below), like bone, or material that was easily breakable, like porcelain.

330. As regards chalices and other vessels that are intended to serve as receptacles for the Blood of the Lord, they are to have bowls of nonabsorbent material. The base, on the other hand, may be made of other solid and worthy materials.

330. Quoad calices aliaque vasa, quæ ad recipiendum Sanguinem Domini destinata sunt, cuppam habeant ex tali materia confectam, quæ liquida non absorbeat. Pes vero ex aliis materiis solidis et dignis confici potest.

IGMR2002 offers the example of ebony[25] as a suitable material. It specifies that whatever material is used should not be easily broken or corrupted and be suitable for a sacred purpose (this would rule out plastic, for example). It adds here that this judgment also applies to other vessels like the paten or the pyx, which were treated in *IGMR1975*, no. 292. As also occurred above (see no. 326), GIRM2003 replaces the reference to the conference of bishops with the phrase, "In the Dioceses of the United States of America," and continues with the article with no further changes.

A review of the history of vessels for liturgical use demonstrates that a wide range of materials have been used, including glass. Eventually legislation limited vessels to gold or silver with gilded interior.[26] The use of these two metals for at least the cup of the chalice became the law, with the exception of alloy or tin *(stannum)* in case of need.[27]

In the common estimation of many parishes, following the directives of the *IGMR1970* and *IGMR1975*, specially crafted chalices of solid glass, heavy crystal, and hand-crafted pottery served as sacred vessels. More recently, *RedSac*, no. 117, excludes the use of "vessels made from glass, earthenware, clay, or other materials that break easily." But that text should be read in light of this *IGMR* article. In many cases, the weight and proportion of vessels from solid glass, crystal or pottery make them not easily breakable and their crafting by artists makes them noble, meeting the criteria of *IGMR2002* (see also no. 332 below).

330. Explaining further the conditions set forth in no. 328 above, this paragraph specifies that the vessels that hold the Blood of the Lord have a cup that is nonabsorbent. The "base" *(pes)* of the vessel can be crafted from other solid and worthy materials. This seems to give some freedom to artistic designers if the use of precious metals is a financial burden for the community or is not lo-

25. Corrected to *ebeno* compared to *IGMR1975*, no. 292, and *IGMR2000*, no. 329, which have *ebure*.

26. For example, see Decretals of Gratian, part. 3, dist. 1, c. 45 (*PL* 187:1719C).

27. See *MR1570*, *Ritus servandus*, tit. 1, n. 1, and *De defectibus*, tit. 10, no. 1. In all of this discussion, one is reminded of St. John Chrysostom's admonition, "Do you wish to honor the Body of the Savior? Do not despise it when it is naked. Do not honor it in church with silk vestments while outside it is naked and numb with cold. He who said, 'This is my body,' and made it so by his word, is the same who said, 'You saw me hungry and you gave me no food. As you did it not to the least of these, you did it not to me.' Honor him then by sharing your property with the poor. For what God needs is not golden chalices but golden souls." *On the Gospel of St. Matthew*, 50:3 (*PG* 58:508).

331. For the consecration of hosts, a large paten may appropriately be used; on it is placed the bread for the priest and the deacon as well as for the other ministers and for the faithful.

332. As to the form of the sacred vessels, the artist may fashion them in a manner that is more in keeping with the customs of each region, provided each vessel is suited to the intended liturgical use and is clearly distinguishable from those intended for everyday use.

333. For the blessing of sacred vessels, the rites prescribed in the liturgical books are to be followed.[136]

331. Ad hostias consecrandas patena amplior convenienter adhiberi potest, in qua ponatur panis tum pro sacerdote et diacono tum pro aliis ministris et fidelibus.

332. Ad formam vasorum sacrorum quod attinet, artificis est ea opportuniore modo conficere, qui moribus respondeat singularum regionum dummodo ad usum liturgicum, ad quem destinantur, singula vasa sint apta, et clare distinguantur ab iis quæ usui cotidiano destinantur.

333. Quoad vasorum sacrorum benedictionem, serventur ritus in libris liturgicis præscripti.[136]

---

cally so esteemed. There is no specification that a knob *(nodus)* be part of the stem.

331. This article is in harmony with the theological concept of "one bread" when circumstances dictate the use of hosts. While *IGMR1975* speaks of "one rather large paten" *(unica patena amplior*, no. 293*)*, *IGMR2002* now deletes *"unica,"* although it would seem that in many situations one large paten is perhaps all that is needed. The mention of the deacon as a communicant is an addition not in *IGMR1975* and another example of the more detailed attention that *IGMR2002* gives to the deacon (cf. no. 94 above).

Consideration of the need for providing for Communion under both species is not addressed here. For Communion under both species (both for the faithful and for concelebrants), *IGMR2002* speaks in other places of the use of one chalice of "sufficient size" *(sufficientis magnitudinis*, no. 207b*)* or the use of "several chalices" *(plures calices*, no. 285a). *RedSac* notes that when many chalices are used, it is laudable "by reason of the sign" *(ratione signi)* to use a principal chalice *(calix principalis)* that is larger than the other chalices (see *RedSac*, no. 105).

332. There is a new phrase added in this article of *IGMR2002* clarifying that each sacred vessel "is clearly distinguishable from those intended for daily use" (*clare distinguantur ab iis quae usui cotidiano destinantur*). This helps to qualify the judgment required in no. 329 above and give some parameters to the principle of common estimation. The recognition of the artist's judgment is significant here, and should be understood in harmony with the overarching concern of *SC*, no. 127.

333. The blessing for vessels can be found in various places, as the new footnote indicates, the most accessible of which is in the appendix of the *MR* itself. The current article drops the phrase "or consecration" (*vel consecrationem*, *IGMR1975*, no. 296) to align it with the current prescribed rites that bless, not consecrate, vessels destined for liturgical use.

334. The practice is to be kept of building a sacrarium in the sacristy, into which are poured the water from the purification of sacred vessels and linens (cf. no. 280).

334. Mos servetur exstruendi in sacristia sacrarium, in quod aqua ablutionis sacrorum vasorum et linteaminum fundatur *(cf. n. 280).*

IV. Sacred Vestments

335. In the Church, which is the the Body of Christ, not all members have the same office. This variety of offices in the celebration of the Eucharist is shown outwardly by the diversity of sacred vestments, which should therefore be a sign of the office proper to each minister. At the same time, however, the sacred vestments should also contribute to the beauty of the sacred action itself. It is appropriate that the vestments

IV. De Sacris Vestibus

335. In Ecclesia, quæ est Corpus Christi, non omnia membra eodem munere funguntur. Hæc diversitas munerum in Eucharistiæ celebratione exterius manifestatur diversitate sacrarum vestium, quæ proinde signum exstare debent muneris cuique ministro proprii. Eædem tamen sacræ vestes ad decorem quoque ipsius actionis sacræ conferant oportet. Vestes quibus sacerdotes et diaconi, necnon ministri laici

---

334. This is a new article. Historically, the *sacrarium* was a place set aside for storing sacred things. The term came to be applied to the sink in the sacristy down which the ablution waters and first rinse water for sacred linens were poured.[28] Rather than allow this water to enter the local gray water or even sewage systems, the *sacrarium* diverts it directly to the earth. In previous eras, leftover blessed ashes or water from washing blessed oil vessels or used baptismal water were also poured down the *sacrarium.*

Sacred Vestments

335. Very little is changed from *IGMR1975* regarding sacred vestments. In this particular paragraph, however, there are some shifts in language. Whereas *IGMR1975* speaks of a "diversity of ministries in worship" (*diversitas ministeriorum cultu sacro,* no. 297), *IGMR2002* speaks of a "variety of offices in the celebration of the Eucharist" (*diversitas munerum in Eucharistiae celebratione,* cf. no. 97 above). According to *IGMR2002,* vestments mark outwardly the "office" (*muneris*) of particular ministers, while in *IGMR1975,* the translation speaks of vestments symbolizing the "function" (*muneris*) of particular ministers. This change clarifies the nature of the vestments mentioned in the following paragraphs: alb, stole, dalmatic, chasuble, and cope. Each of these sacred vestments defines the office of the minister wearing it, as well as the liturgical rite for which it is worn. Adapted from imperial Roman apparel, specific vesture of a liturgical nature emerges early in Christianity, although there was no uniformity

28. See also *RedSac,* no. 120.

to be worn by priests and deacons, as well as those garments to be worn by lay ministers, be blessed according to the rite described in the Roman Ritual[137] before they are put into liturgical use.

induuntur opportune benedicuntur antequam usui liturgico destinentur, iuxta ritum in Rituali Romano descriptum.[137]

336. The sacred garment common to ordained and instituted ministers of any rank is the alb, to be tied at the waist with a cincture unless it is made so as to fit even without such. Before the alb is put on, should this not completely cover the ordinary clothing at the neck, an amice should be put on. The alb may not be replaced by a surplice, not even over a cassock, on occasions when a chasuble or dalmatic is to be worn or when, according to the norms, only a stole is worn without a chasuble or dalmatic.

336. Vestis sacra omnibus ministris ordinatis et institutis cuiusvis gradus communis est alba, circa lumbos cingulo astringenda, nisi tali modo confecta sit, ut corpori adhæreat etiam sine cingulo. Antequam vero alba assumatur, si hæc habitum communem circa collum non cooperit, amictus adhibeatur. Alba cum superpelliceo commutari nequit, ne quidem super vestem talarem, quando casula vel dalmatica vel, iuxta normas, sola stola sine casula vel dalmatica induenda est.

---

across the Mediterranean world even by the beginning of the fifth century.[29] By the sixth century, each of these five vestments appears in paintings and mosaics, most notably at San Vitale, in Ravenna, Italy. The distinguishing office or ministry marked by one's vesture contributes to the dignity of the liturgical action and the beauty of the liturgy celebrated by that ministry.

This paragraph includes a reference to lay ministries as well as to those ordained to a specific office, particularly deacons and priests. The entire section focuses on the vestments defined by the liturgy for the offices of diaconate and priesthood, but indicates also that dignified vesture is both appropriate and expected for those lay persons who serve in the variety of liturgical ministries. *IGMR2002* adds a reference to the *Book of Blessings,* which includes a blessing for vestments worn for the celebration of the Mass (no. 1352). Similar to the requirements for the vessels for the bread and wine, the vestments for the ministers of the liturgy should "contribute to the beauty of the sacred action itself" (*ad decorem quoque ipsius actionis sacrae conferant oportet*). Noble simplicity, rooted in *SC,* no. 34, and extended to all sacred furnishings in *SC,* nos. 122–130, is to be characteristic of the vestments used and marks their worthiness to serve the dignity of worship.

336. A common garment for liturgical ministry is the alb, which identifies any instituted or ordained minister. *IGMR2002* also clarifies liturgical situations

29. Augustine of Hippo, for example, does not seem to have owned a *casula,* or chasuble, and it is not known what vesture he wore during the celebration of the Eucharist; see F. van der Meer, *Augustine the Bishop,* trans. Brian Battershaw and G. R. Lamb (London and New York: Sheed and Ward, 1961), 235–236.

337. The vestment proper to the priest celebrant at Mass and other sacred actions directly connected with Mass is, unless otherwise indicated, the chasuble, worn over the alb and stole.

337. Sacerdotis celebrantis vestis propria, in Missa aliisque sacris actionibus quæ cum Missa directo conectuntur, est casula seu planeta, nisi aliud caveatur, super albam et stolam induenda.

338. The vestment proper to the deacon is the dalmatic, worn over the alb and stole. The dalmatic may, however, be omitted out of necessity or on account of a lesser degree of solemnity.

338. Diaconi vestis propria est dalmatica, super albam et stolam induenda; dalmatica tamen ob necessitatem vel minorem gradum sollemnitatis omitti potest.

339. In the dioceses of the United States of America, acolytes, altar servers, lectors, and other lay ministers may wear the alb or other suitable vesture or other appropriate and dignified clothing.

339. Acolythi, lectores, aliique ministri laici albam vel aliam vestem in singulis regionibus a Conferentia Episcoporum legitime probatam induere possunt *(cf. n. 390)*.

---

when a cassock and surplice cannot be substituted for an alb. Occasions for the liturgical use of a surplice is never defined by *IGMR2002*; in addition, it seems to imply that its use by priests and deacons is more restricted than by others, for example, acolytes, altar servers, or masters of ceremonies (cf. no. 339 below).

337. According to *IGMR*s, the "chasuble" (*casula seu planeta*) is the vestment which marks both the office of the priest (or bishop) and his ministry (cf. no. 119 above). It also signifies the dignity and holiness of the entire liturgical action over which he is presiding. This Instruction, like its predecessors, indicates that the chasuble is worn over both the alb and the stole (cf. Seasoltz, 33 above).

338. As the chasuble visually defines the liturgical role of the priest, the dalmatic visually defines the liturgical role of the deacon. Also rooted in the liturgical practices of the early Church, the dalmatic along with the stole identifies the deacon and his liturgical ministry. While the dalmatic is not necessary (cf. no. 119 above), it is preferred unless the eucharistic liturgy has a "lesser degree of solemnity" (*minorem gradum sollemnitatis*) or because of some other "necessity" (*necessitatem*). *IGMR2002* newly explicates this permission not to wear a dalmatic.

339. The alb or "white garment," is the mark of all of the baptized, and visually expresses the dignity of all who wear it (*Ordo initiationis christianae adultorum*, no. 33). Although no. 336 depicts the alb as a garment common to ordained and instituted ministers, no. 339 notes that the alb may be worn by "acolytes, altar servers, lectors and other lay ministers" (*acolythi, lectores, aliique ministri laici*), if approved by the local conference of bishops. *IGMR2002* indicates that the US bishops have granted this permission. The alb, however, is not required by the ministers enumerated here, who may also wear other vesture or clothing, which *IGMR2002* notes is to be "appropriate and dignified." Such ensures that

340. The stole is worn by the priest around his neck and hanging down in front. It is worn by the deacon over his left shoulder and drawn diagonally across the chest to the right side, where it is fastened.

341. The cope is worn by the priest in processions and other sacred actions, in keeping with the rubrics proper to each rite.

342. Regarding the design of sacred vestments, Conferences of Bishops may determine and propose to the Apostolic See adaptations that correspond to the needs and the usages of their regions.[138]

343. In addition to the traditional materials, natural fabrics proper to each region may be used for making sacred vestments; artificial fabrics that are in keeping with the dignity of the sacred action and the

340. Stola defertur a sacerdote circa collum et ante pectus pendens; a diacono vero ab umero sinistro per transversum super pectus ducitur ad partem dexteram corporis, ibique retinetur.

341. Pluviale, seu cappa pluvialis, assumitur a sacerdote in processionibus aliisque actionibus sacris, iuxta rubricas proprias singulorum rituum.

342. Ad formam sacrarum vestium quod attinet, Conferentiæ Episcoporum possunt definire et proponere Apostolicæ Sedi aptationes, quæ necessitatibus et moribus singularum regionum respondeant.[138]

343. Ad sacras vestes conficiendas, præter traditas materias, fibræ naturales cuiusque loci propriæ adhiberi possunt, necnon aliquæ fibræ artificiales, quæ respondeant dignitati actionis sacræ et

---

whatever vesture is chosen will contribute to the beauty of the liturgical action (cf. no. 335 below).

340. The stole, worn by deacons and priests, is rooted in the garb worn by imperial Roman officials and, along with other vesture, gradually came to signify specific offices within the Church. Stoles are today prescribed for deacons, priests, and bishops. The placement of the stole differs between deacons and priests/bishops, although in all cases the stole is always worn immediately over the alb (see Seasoltz, 33 above).

341. The cope is most commonly used outside of the eucharistic liturgy, although it is an option, for example, at the beginning of the Liturgy for Passion Sunday. As noted in no. 92 above, a bishop who is not presiding over the Eucharist, but is in attendance, should preside over the Liturgy of the Word wearing, along with the other appropriate vesture for his office, a cope. Although not specified in this Instruction, the cope is worn over the alb and stole. Thus the *Institutio Generalis de Liturgia Horarum* states that a priest may wear a cope, while a deacon may wear a dalmatic (no. 255).

342. The conference of bishops determines any adaptations or requirements in the design and fabrication of the vestments. This is in keeping with *SC*, no. 128. Here again, aesthetic and ethical principles respectful of the local context must be weighed along with the liturgical principles (see the Introduction, 384–385 above).

343. This article discusses fabrics employed for producing vestments. While *IGMR*s first attend to "traditional materials" (*traditas materias*)—e.g., wool, silk,

person wearing them may also be used. The Conference of Bishops will be the judge in this matter.[139]

personæ. De qua re iudicabit Episcoporum Conferentia.[139]

344. It is fitting that the beauty and nobility of each vestment derive not from abundance of overly lavish ornamentation, but rather from the material that is used and from the design. Ornamentation on vestments should, moreover, consist of figures, that is, of images or symbols, that evoke sacred use, avoiding thereby anything unbecoming.

344. Decet pulchritudinem et nobilitatem cuiusque vestis non ex abundantia ornamentorum quæ superadduntur exquiri, sed e materia quæ adhibeatur et a forma. Ornamenta autem figuras seu imagines vel symbola præbeant, quæ usum sacrum indicent, remotis iis quæ usum sacrum dedeceant.

345. The purpose of a variety in the color of the sacred vestments is to give effective expression even outwardly to the specific character of the mysteries of faith being celebrated and to a sense of Christian life's passage through the course of the liturgical year.

345. Diversitas colorum in sacris vestibus eo contendit, ut hinc proprietas mysteriorum fidei celebrandorum, hinc sensus progredientis vitæ christianæ, decursu anni liturgici, efficacius etiam exterius exprimatur.

---

and linen—both natural and artificial fabrics are permitted. The two principles provided by *IGMR2002* and its predecessors in judging these materials are their capacity for conforming to "the dignity of the sacred action and the person wearing them" (*dignitati actionis sacrae et personae*). While the artisans who craft vestments will recognize the suitability of some fabrics over others, any decisions concerning appropriate fabric are left to the conference of bishops.

344. This article notes a concern about the inappropriateness of overly lavish ornamentation (*abundantia ornamentorum*) on vestments, parallel to a previously-voiced concern about the ornamentation of church buildings (no. 318 above). In view of the two principles articulated in no. 344, such ornamentation should not detract from the dignity of the liturgical action nor from the person wearing the vesture. As *SC* states, all sacred art, including that of sacred vestments, "should strive after noble beauty rather than mere sumptuous display" (no. 124). Thus *IGMR2002* notes a concern about anything unbecoming, a judgment that requires liturgical, aesthetic, and ethical perspectives (see the Introduction, 384–385 above).

345. This is the first of three articles on colors of liturgical vestments. Such colors have two primary purposes: they give expression to the "specific character of the mysteries of faith" (*proprietas mysteriorum fidei*) as well as "to a sense of Christian life's passage" (*sensus progredientis vitae christianae*), both of which are celebrated through the liturgical year. One should also bear in mind that the interpretation of colors varies greatly from culture to culture.

346. As to the color of sacred vestments, the traditional usage is to be retained: namely,

a. White is used in the Offices and Masses during the Easter and Christmas seasons; also on celebrations of the Lord other than of his Passion, of the Blessed Virgin Mary, of the Holy Angels, and of Saints who were not Martyrs; on the Solemnities of All Saints (November 1) and of the Nativity of St. John the Baptist (June 24); and on the Feasts of St. John the Evangelist (December 27), of the Chair of St. Peter (February 22), and of the Conversion of St. Paul (January 25).

b. Red is used on Palm Sunday of the Lord's Passion and on Good Friday, on Pentecost Sunday, on celebrations of the Lord's Passion, on the feasts of the Apostles and Evangelists, and on celebrations of Martyr Saints.

346. Ad colorem sacrarum vestium quod attinet, servetur usus traditus, nempe:

a) Color albus adhibetur in Officiis et Missis temporis paschalis et Nativitatis Domini; insuper in celebrationibus Domini, quæ non sint de eius Passione, beatæ Mariæ Virginis, SS. Angelorum, Sanctorum non Martyrum, in sollemnitatibus Omnium Sanctorum (1 nov.) et S. Ioannis Baptistæ (24 iunii), in festis S. Ioannis Evangelistæ (27 dec.), Cathedræ S. Petri (22 febr.) et Conversionis S. Pauli (25 ian.).

b) Color ruber adhibetur in dominica Passionis et feria VI Hebdomadæ sanctæ, in dominica Pentecostes, in celebrationibus Passionis Domini, in festis nataliciis Apostolorum et Evangelistarum et in celebrationibus Sanctorum Martyrum.

c) Color viridis adhibetur in Officiis et Missis temporis « per annum ».

---

346. An obligatory liturgical color scheme first appeared in *MR1570*, although in the twelfth century Innocent III (d. 1216) explained the four colors used throughout the liturgical year for vestments (white, red, black, and green, nuanced with scarlet, violet, and saffron).[30] *IGMR1971* (no. 308) basically follows the principles outlined in *MR1570*, which has been repeated with little variation in succeeding editions. The changing colors reflect the changing feasts and seasons of the liturgical year in both the sanctoral and temporal cycles. The liturgical color is always applied to both the offices and the Masses for the feasts and seasons dictated. The assignment of colors listed here does not include an explanation of the colors themselves.[31]

GIRM2003 notes some differences for the dioceses of the US. At offices and Masses for the dead (no. 346e), white vestments are approved along with the black and violet colors noted in *IGMR2002* (no. 346d-e). "On more solemn days" (*Diebus sollemnioribus*, no. 346g) is entirely new to *IGMR2002*, and *IGMR2002* adds that "gold- or silver-colored vestments" may be used on these more solemn days.

30. Innocent III, *De Sacro Altaris Mysterio*, no. 10 (*PL* 217:799–802).

31. Standard interpretations of these colors can be found in a variety of liturgical sources, including Janet Mayo, *A History of Ecclesiastical Dress* (New York: Homes & Meier Publishers, Inc., 1984) and Herbert Norris, *Church Vestments: Their Origin & Development* (Mineola, NY: Dover Publications, Inc., [1940] 2002).

c. Green is used in the Offices and Masses of Ordinary Time.
d. Violet or purple is used in Advent and Lent. It may also be worn in Offices and Masses for the Dead (cf. below).
e. Besides violet, white or black vestments may be worn at funeral services and at other Offices and Masses for the Dead in the dioceses of the United States of America.
f. Rose may be used, where it is the practice, on *Gaudete* Sunday (Third Sunday of Advent) and on *Laetare* Sunday (Fourth Sunday of Lent).
g. On more solemn days, sacred vestments may be used that are festive, that is, more precious, even if not of the color of the day.
h. Gold- or silver-colored vestments may be worn on more solemn occasions in the dioceses of the United States of America.

d) Color violaceus adhibetur tempore Adventus et Quadragesimæ. Assumi potest etiam in Officiis et Missis defunctorum.
e) Color niger adhiberi potest, ubi mos est, in Missis defunctorum.
f) Color rosaceus adhiberi potest, ubi mos est, in dominicis Gaudéte (III Adventus) et Lætáre (IV in Quadragesima).
g) Diebus sollemnioribus adhiberi possunt sacræ vestes festivæ seu nobiliores, etsi non sunt coloris diei.

Conferentiæ tamen Episcoporum possunt definire, ad colores liturgicos quod attinet, et proponere Apostolicæ Sedi aptationes, quæ necessitatibus et ingenio populorum respondeant.

347. Ritual Masses are celebrated in their proper color, in white, or in a festive color; Masses for Various Needs, on the other hand, are celebrated in the color proper to the day or the season or in violet if they are of a penitential character, for example, in the *Roman Missal,* no. 31 (in Time of War or Conflict), no. 33 (in Time of Famine), or no. 38 (for the Forgiveness of Sins); Votive Masses are celebrated in the color suited to the Mass itself or even in the color proper to the day or the season.

347. Missæ rituales dicuntur cum colore proprio vel albo vel festivo; Missæ autem pro variis necessitatibus cum colore proprio diei vel temporis aut cum colore violaceo, si indolem pænitentialem manifestant, v. gr. nn. 31, 33, 38; Missæ votivæ cum colore convenienti Missæ quæ celebratur aut etiam cum colore proprio diei vel temporis.

---

347. Most ritual Masses and Masses for Various Needs have no assigned color. Rather, the color of the season or the day applies, with the exception of those rites that call for a "festive" color, wedding Masses (white), certain votive Masses, and those Masses with a "penitential character" (*indolem paenitentialem*), when violet would be the most appropriate color (cf. no. 373 below). This Instruction is in keeping with the nature of the cycle of feasts and seasons, as well as the overall understanding that the assigned vestment color coincides with a cycle of the mysteries of faith and the passage of Christian life (no. 345).

V. Other Things Intended for Church Use

348. Besides sacred vessels and sacred vestments for which some special material is prescribed, other furnishings that either are intended for strictly liturgical use[140] or are in any other way admitted into a church should be worthy and suited to their particular purpose.

349. In a special way, care must be taken that the liturgical books, particularly the *Book of the Gospels* and the Lectionary, which are intended for the proclamation of the word of God and hence enjoy special veneration, really serve in a liturgical action as signs and symbols of heavenly realities and hence are truly worthy, dignified, and beautiful.

V. De Aliis Rebus ad usum Ecclesiæ Destinatis

348. Præter vasa sacra aut vestes sacras, pro quibus aliqua peculiaris materia statuitur, alia supellex, quæ aut ipsi usui liturgico destinatur[140] aut quolibet alio modo in ecclesiam admittitur, digna sit atque respondens fini cui unaquæque res destinatur.

349. Peculiari modo curandum est ut libri liturgici, Evangeliarium et lectionarium præsertim, quæ ad verbi Dei proclamationem destinantur et proinde peculiari veneratione gaudent, sint revera in actione liturgica rerum supernarum signa et symbola, et proinde vere digni, decori et pulchri.

Other Things Intended for Church Use

This short section is a reminder that any item associated with either the liturgy directly or for use in a church should be worthy and suited to their purpose. Like the church building itself (cf. no. 292 above), these things are formative of the community and their active participation, shaping their faith and their response. The criterion of "worthiness" described for sacred vessels and vestments (e.g., no. 325 above) must be applied to all items intended for use within the body of the church, for liturgical or devotional use. They should be well-made artistically and aesthetically, and should function appropriately.

348. The introductory article is a reminder that, even though something may not be specifically mentioned in *IGMR*, the same principles of worthiness, noble simplicity, and dignity due the liturgy apply. The reference to the *Book of Blessings*, part III, indicates some specific items for consideration: pyx, monstrance, hymnals and service books (nos. 1341–1359), bells (nos. 1305–1324) and crosses (nos. 1233–1256). The list is not exhaustive, but a reminder that all things liturgical should be crafted well, given appropriate places of honor, and used with dignity.

349. All liturgical books are to be given places of honor, and those from which the Word of God are proclaimed are to enjoy special reverence. This article pays particular attention to the Book of the Gospels and the Lectionary, not addressed in *IGMR1975*. In an age when mass reproduction of text is so prevalent, the faithful need to experience the proclamation of the Word of God from books of such quality that they communicate how God's Word is deserving

350. Furthermore, great attention is to be paid whatever is directly associated with the altar and the Eucharistic celebration, e.g., the altar cross and the cross carried in procession.

351. Every effort should be made to ensure that even as regards objects of lesser importance the canons of art be appropriately taken into account and that noble simplicity come together with elegance.

350. Insuper omni cura attendendum est ad ea quæ directe cum altari et celebratione eucharistica conectuntur, uti sunt, ex. gr., crux altaris et crux quæ in processione defertur.

351. Sedulo contendatur ut etiam in rebus minoris momenti artis postulata opportune serventur, et nobilis semper simplicitas cum munditie societur.

---

of honor and reverence both within the liturgical action and outside it (see nos. 60 and 122 above).

350. Like the sacred vessels (nos. 327–34 above), all that is directly associated with the altar deserves worthy artistic attention. While the altar cloth and candles were considered earlier (nos. 117, 297, 304, and 307), this article mentions the cross carried in procession and the altar cross (cf. nos. 117 and 308 above).

351. The dignity and beauty of the liturgy require that the design of all objects, even those "of lesser importance" (*minoris momenti*) comply with what GIRM2003 translates as "canons of art" (*artis postulata*), but may better be rendered as "claims" or "demands," which better admits the enormous cultural and aesthetic diversity that marks even the fine arts today. The article ends with proposing that, in shaping materials for worship, there should be a wedding of noble simplicity (*nobilis simplicitas*) with elegance (*munditie*). While interpreted differently across times and cultures, this is a laudable standard.

GIRM—Notes (English)

135. Cf. ibid, no. 128.

136. Cf. The Roman Pontifical: *Order of the Dedication of a Church and an Altar, editio typica*, 1984, Chapter 7, Order of the Blessing of a Chalice and a Paten; The Roman Ritual, *Book of Blessings, editio typica*, 1984, Order for the Blessing of Articles for Liturgical Use, nos. 1068–1084.

137. Cf. The Roman Ritual, *Book of Blessings, editio typica*, 1984, Order for the Blessing of Articles for Liturgical Use, no. 1070.

138. Cf. Second Vatican Ecumenical Council, Constitution on the Sacred Liturgy, *Sacrosanctum Concilium*, no. 128.

139. Cf. ibid., no. 128.

140. For blessing objects that are designed for liturgical use in churches, cf. The Roman Ritual, *Book of Blessings, editio typica*, 1984, part III.

IGMR—Notes (Latin)

135. Cf. Conc. Œcum. Vat. II, Const. de sacra Liturgia, *Sacrosanctum Concilium*, n. 128.

136. Cf. Pontificale Romanum, *Ordo Dedicationis ecclesiæ et altaris*, editio typica 1977 Ordo benedictionis calicis et patenæ; Rituale Romanum, *De Benedictionibus*, editio typica 1984, Ordo benedictionis rerum quæ in liturgicis celebrationibus usurpantur, nn. 1068–1084.

137. Cf. Rituale Romanum, *De Benedictionibus*, editio typica 1984, Ordo benedictionis rerum quæ in liturgicis celebrationibus usurpantur, n. 1070.

138. Cf. Conc. Œcum. Vat. II, Const. de sacra Liturgia, *Sacrosanctum Concilium*, n. 128.

139. Cf. *ibidem*.

140. Quoad benedictionem rerum quæ in domibus ecclesiæ ad usum liturgicum destinantur, cf. Rituale Romanum, *De Benedictionibus*, editio typica 1984, pars III.

CHAPTER VII

The Choice of the Mass and Its Parts

(*DE MISSA EIUSQUE PARTIBUS ELIGENDIS*[1])

Joyce Ann Zimmerman

Introduction

Of the nine chapters of the new *Institutio Generalis Missalis Romani* (*IGMR2002*), Chapter VII is the only one which includes "choice" (*eligendis*) in its title. A short chapter, nonetheless it is as significant in its title as it is in its content. "Choice" suggests alternatives and options, painting a rich picture of legitimate variances in the celebration of Mass from assembly to assembly. The word "choice" refutes any claim that *IGMR2002* demands rigid conformity or invariable celebrations; indeed, *IGMR2002* not only suggests but actively promotes an intelligent approach to the preparation of liturgy which weighs an array of performance possibilities. Other chapters in *IGMR2002* spell out the essentials of the Mass which cannot be ignored in either its preparation or performance. This chapter presupposes respect for and adherence to those essentials, while at the same time it takes seriously the pastoral good of the whole assembly when laying down norms for the Mass and its parts to be chosen.

Chapter VII is comprised of sixteen paragraphs (nos. 352–367). Its organization is simple enough: there is an introductory paragraph followed by two main divisions: I. The Choice of Mass (with no subdivisions), and II. The Choice of Mass Texts, which is further subdivided into The Readings, The Orations, The Eucharistic Prayer, and The Chants. *IGMR2002* basically follows the order of *IGMR1975*, with one notable exception. *IGMR1975* (and its predecessors) collapses discussion of the orations and the Eucharistic Prayer under one subtitle, "Prayers" (*De orationibus*), beginning with a consideration of the Eucharistic Prayer (*IGMR1975*, nos. 321–322) followed by comments on the orations (no. 323). *IGMR2002* places the paragraph on orations first (no. 363), which is then followed by the two paragraphs on the Eucharistic Prayer in its own subsection

1. A more literal translation would be "On the Mass and Its Parts to Be Chosen." Using the gerundive verb form rather than a noun underscores an ongoing, engaging process when preparing for Mass.

Chapter VII
THE CHOICE OF THE MASS AND ITS PARTS

352. The pastoral effectiveness of a celebration will be greatly increased if the texts of the readings, the prayers, and the liturgical songs correspond as closely as possible to the needs, spiritual preparation, and culture of those taking part. This is achieved by appropriate use of the wide options described below.

The priest, therefore, in planning the celebration of Mass, should have in mind the common spiritual good of the people of God, rather than his own inclinations. He should, moreover, remember that the selection of different parts is to be made in agreement with those who have some role in the celebration, including the faithful, in regard to the parts that more directly pertain to each.

Caput VII
DE MISSA EIUSQUE PARTIBUS ELIGENDIS

352. Efficacitas pastoralis celebrationis profecto augebitur, si textus lectionum, orationum et cantuum necessitatibus et præparationi animi et ingenio participantium apte, quantum fieri potest, respondebunt. Quod obtinetur congrue adhibita multiplici facultate electionis, quæ infra describitur.

Sacerdos proinde, in ordinanda Missa, ad commune bonum spirituale populi Dei, potius quam ad suam propensionem attendet. Memor sit insuper huiusmodi electionem partium concordi ratione esse faciendam cum iis qui partem aliquam in celebratione exercent, fidelibus minime exclusis, in iis quæ ad ipsos magis directo spectant.

(nos. 364–365). This change serves to highlight the importance and centrality of the Eucharistic Prayer in its own right (cf. no. 78 above).

No fewer than six paragraphs evidence great respect for the pastoral and spiritual growth, particular needs, and culture of all those celebrating the Mass (cf. nos. 352, 358, 359, 360, 361, and 363). Indeed, this is the fundamental purpose for making choices concerning the celebration of Mass. Clearly, the priest-presider's "inclinations" are secondary to the larger pastoral good (see no. 352 below). In a subtle way this respect highlights the essential role of the assembly at the Mass (see Power and Vincie, 51–52 above).

The rubrical notes in both the Roman Missal and Lectionary are essential for understanding and implementing the content of this chapter. The Introduction to the Lectionary (*OLM1981-Pr*) spells out in more detail much of the material contained in Chapter VII. The *General Norms for the Liturgical Year and the Calendar* (GNLYC), nos. 59–61, gives in greater detail what is concisely summarized in this chapter. Another helpful document is the *Directory on Popular Piety and the Liturgy* (DPPL), which develops a sound theology of liturgical prayer and shows how popular piety is related to it but is always secondary. This document also includes numerous references to the saints and their importance for modeling Christian living.

352. This introductory paragraph for Chapter VII makes two important points which set the tone for the whole chapter. First, the preparation for every single Mass includes making choices about "the texts of the readings, the prayers, and the liturgical songs" (*textus lectionum, orationum et cantuum*), but

Since, indeed, a variety of options is provided for the different parts of the Mass, it is necessary for the deacon, the lectors, the psalmist, the cantor, the commentator, and the choir to be completely sure before the celebration about those texts for which each is responsible is to be used and that nothing be improvised. Harmonious planning and carrying out of the rites will be of great assistance in disposing the faithful to participate in the Eucharist.

Cum vero multiplex afferatur facultas seligendi diversas Missæ partes, necesse est ut ante celebrationem diaconus, lectores, psalmista, cantor, commentator, schola, unusquisque pro sua parte, probe sciant quinam textus ad se spectans adhibeatur, nihilque ex tempore quodammodo eveniat. Harmonica enim ordinatio et exsecutio rituum multum confert ad componendos fidelium animos ad Eucharistiam participandam.

those choices are always made for the spiritual good of the whole.[2] "Songs" has been qualified in GIRM2003 as "liturgical songs," which emphasizes further that all elements of the liturgy serve the liturgy, not personal piety. Further, these choices are "to be made in agreement with those who have some role in the celebration" (*electionem partium concordi ratione esse faciendam cum iis qui partem aliquam in celebratione exercent*). This unmasks a subtle tension which ensues throughout the chapter: generally, it is assumed that the priest-presider makes these choices (e.g., especially no. 353; also nos. 355 and 360 below), but this is not always the case in actual pastoral practice; sometimes the liturgy or music director makes these choices. In every case it is essential that all ministers (especially priest-presider, deacon, lectors, music ministers) be engaged in the determination of these choices.

Second, this opening paragraph makes clear that every Mass includes different ministers with particular functions proper to each (cf. no. 112 above). Further, the paragraph puts forward that there are not only different ministers and functions, but twice intimates that the assembly themselves are indispensable ministers at every Mass when it specifies "including the faithful" (*fidelibus minime exclusis*) and notes that "Harmonious planning . . . will be of great assistance in disposing the faithful to participate in the Eucharist" (*Harmonica enim ordinatio . . . multum confert ad componendos fidelium animos ad Eucharistiam participandam*).

2. The US document *Introduction to the Order of Mass* (no. 63) reiterates the importance of the principle of progressive solemnity (cf. *Institutio Generalis de Liturgia Horarum*, no. 273). This document also endorses options so that "every celebration, in whatever circumstances, will fully consider the needs, capabilities, and situation of the community that assembles for it" (no. 60). In this context the question of liturgical inculturation is particularly important.

I. The Choice of Mass

353. On solemnities the priest is bound to follow the calendar of the church where he is celebrating.

354. On Sundays, on the weekdays of the Advent, Christmas, Lenten, and Easter Seasons, on feasts, and on obligatory memorials:

a. If Mass is celebrated with a congregation, the priest should follow the calendar of the church where he is celebrating;

I. De Missa Eligenda

353. In sollemnitatibus sacerdos sequi tenetur calendarium ecclesiæ in qua celebrat.

354. In dominicis, in feriis Adventus, Nativitatis, Quadragesimæ et Paschæ, in festis et memoriis obligatoriis:

a) si Missa celebratur cum populo, sacerdos sequatur calendarium ecclesiæ in qua celebrat;

The Choice of Mass

353. The first major division of the chapter speaks to the choice of Masses for the seasons of the liturgical year as well as the various ranks of feast days on the liturgical calendar. Because it begins the division and stands in a paragraph by itself, this article underscores the importance of celebrating solemnities (cf. GNLYC, no. 11), even when they belong to a particular liturgical calendar and regardless of whether celebrating with a congregation or with only one minister present.

Various calendars govern the celebration of the liturgy, including the General Roman Calendar (1969) and those which supplement it: national calendar (determined by bishops' conferences), diocesan calendar (which, for example, includes the diocesan patrons, dedication of the cathedral, etc.), parish calendar (including the titular and the dedication of the church), and, for some, a calendar specific to religious orders and congregations (founder[s], patrons, etc.). Coordination of all these calendars must be considered (usually this work is already carried out in *ordo*s published at the national, diocesan, or order/congregation levels).[3] When a priest is in his home parish and/or diocese, he would naturally follow the *ordo* specific to his diocese. When elsewhere (e.g., on study leave, sabbatical, etc.) he is bound to follow the *ordo* of the church where he is celebrating for solemnities, which may differ from his home church. A religious priest assigned to a parish is required on solemnities to follow the local church *ordo* rather than that of his order/congregation.

354. It is unusual for liturgical seasons (Advent, Christmas, Lent, and Easter) to be grouped with Sundays and with degrees of feast day celebrations (feasts and obligatory memorials). *IGMR2002* combines days in this section according to the norms governing choice of texts.[4]

3. Also, *IGMR2002*, no. 394; GNLYC nos. 48–55; *Calendaria particularia* (Rome: Sacred Congregation for Divine Worship, 24 June 1970), passim.

4. See GNLYC, nos. 3–44: in the section titled "Liturgical Days," I. The Liturgical Year in General; II. Sunday; III. Solemnities, Feasts, and Memorials; IV. Weekdays; and in the section

b. If Mass is celebrated with the participation of one minister only, the priest may choose either the calendar of the church or his own proper calendar.

355. On optional memorials:

a. On the weekdays of Advent from December 17 to December 24, on days within the Octave of Christmas, and on the weekdays of Lent, except Ash Wednesday and during Holy Week, the Mass for the current liturgical day is to be used; but the collect may be taken from a memorial which happens to be listed in the General Calendar for that day, except on Ash Wednesday and during Holy Week. On weekdays of the Easter Season, memorials of Saints may rightly be celebrated fully.

b. On the weekdays of Advent before December 17, the weekdays of the Christmas Season from January 2, and

b) si Missa celebratur, cuius unus tantum minister participat, sacerdos eligere potest aut calendarium ecclesiæ aut calendarium proprium.

355. In memoriis ad libitum:

a) In feriis Adventus a die 17 ad 24 decembris, diebus infra octavam Nativitatis et in feriis Quadragesimæ, exceptis feriis IV Cinerum et Hebdomadæ sanctæ, dicitur Missa de die liturgico occurrente; de memoria autem in calendario generali eo die forte inscripta sumi potest collecta, dummodo non occurrat feria IV Cinerum aut feria Hebdomadæ sanctæ. In feriis temporis paschalis memoriæ Sanctorum rite ex integro peragi possunt.

b) In feriis Adventus ante diem 17 decembris, in feriis temporis Nativitatis a die 2 ianuarii et in feriis temporis paschalis, eligi potest aut Missa de feria, aut Missa de Sancto, vel de uno

---

Number 354a repeats for this category of celebration with a congregation what no. 353 above said about solemnities (with no distinction between celebrating with a congregation or with only one minister present). When a congregation is present, following the *ordo* which governs their church assures continuity of celebration for the local community.

Number 354b allows the option for a priest to follow either the calendar of the church or his own proper calendar in choosing a Mass when he is celebrating with only one minister present. This number also echoes an important difference between *IGMR1975* and *IGMR2002*. Where the former notes "if Mass is celebrated without a congregation" (*si Missa celebratur sine populo*, no. 315b), the current Instruction reads "If Mass is celebrated with the participation of one minister only" (*si Missa celebratur, cuius unus tantum minister participat*). The change in text seems to imply that celebrating Mass "without a congregation" is not envisioned, for the priest celebrates with at least one minister present (see nos. 308–10 above).

355. It is telling that the longest paragraph in Chapter VII deals with optional memorials; there is more latitude for choice on these days than for other days.

Number 355a states that, as a norm, on weekdays during specific liturgical seasons with proper Masses, these are to be used; the collect from an optional

titled "The Yearly Cycle," I. Easter Triduum; II. Easter Season; III. Lent; IV. Christmas Season; V. Advent; VI. Ordinary Time.

the weekdays of the Easter Season, it is possible to choose either the weekday Mass, or the Mass of the Saint, or the Mass of one of the Saints whose memorial is observed, or the Mass of any Saint listed in the Martyrology for that day.

c. On the weekdays in Ordinary Time, it is possible to choose either a weekday Mass, or the Mass of an optional memorial which happens to occur on that day, or the Mass of any Saint listed in the Martyrology for that day, or a Mass for Various Needs, or a Votive Mass.

If he celebrates with a congregation, the priest will take care not to omit the readings assigned for each day in the Lectionary for weekdays too frequently and without sufficient reason, since the Church desires that a richer portion at the table of God's word be provided for the faithful.[141]

For the same reason he should use Masses for the Dead in moderation, since every Mass is offered for both the living and the dead, and there is a commemoration of the dead in the Eucharistic Prayer.

Where, however, the optional memorials of the Blessed Virgin Mary or of the Saints are dear to the faithful, the priest should satisfy their legitimate devotion.

When, on the other hand, the option is given of choosing between a memorial

e Sanctis quorum fiat memoria, aut Missa de aliquo Sancto eo die in Martyrologio inscripto.

c) In feriis per annum, eligi potest aut Missa de feria, aut Missa de memoria ad libitum forte occurrente, aut Missa de aliquo Sancto eo die in Martyrologio inscripto, aut Missa pro variis necessitatibus vel votiva.

Si celebrat cum populo, sacerdos curabit ne frequentius et sine sufficienti causa lectiones omittat singulis diebus in lectionario pro feriis assignatas: Ecclesia enim cupit ut ditior mensa verbi Dei paretur fidelibus.[141]

Ob eandem causam moderate sumet Missas defunctorum: quælibet enim Missa tam pro vivis quam pro defunctis offertur, et in Prece eucharistica memoria defunctorum habetur.

Ubi autem fidelibus cordi sunt memoriæ ad libitum beatæ Mariæ Virginis vel Sanctorum, satisfiat legitimæ eorum pietati.

Cum vero facultas datur eligendi inter memoriam calendario generali inscriptam et memoriam calendario diœcesano aut religioso insertam, præoptetur, ceteris paribus et iuxta traditionem, memoria particularis.

---

memorial in the General Roman Calendar may be used on such days, "except Ash Wednesday and during Holy Week" (*exceptis feriis IV Cinerum et Hebdomadae sanctae*). *IGMR2002* adds an important final sentence which is not found in earlier editions, namely, that during the Easter season memorials may be observed. This norm reminds us that during the Easter season we celebrate the risen life of Christ and also that of the saints who already share in his glory. So, celebrating saints during this time—even optional memorials—is truly a celebration of resurrection.

Number 355b allows a wide option for the choice of Mass at times other than the liturgical season weekdays with their own proper Masses. This norm simply makes clear that on these days the same choices may be observed as on weekdays of Ordinary Time, except the latter weekdays also permit a Mass for Various Needs or a Votive Mass to be chosen (no. 355c).

found in the General Calendar and one found in a diocesan or religious calendar, preference should be given, all things being equal and in keeping with tradition, to the memorial inscribed in the particular calendar.

II. The Choice of Mass Texts

356. In the choice of texts for the several parts of the Mass, whether of the Season or of the Saints, the following norms should be observed.

II. De Missæ Partibus Eligendis

356. In seligendis textibus diversarum partium Missæ tum de Tempore tum de Sanctis, serventur normæ quæ sequuntur.

The next part of no. 355 is abbreviated from *IGMR1975*; omitted is the caution about the priest being mindful of the good of the people and not making choices based on his personal preference. This article also preserves the continuity of the Lectionary's semi-continuous selections and warns that these ought not be replaced very often and "without sufficient reason" (*sine sufficienti causa*). Both continuity and more Scripture are provided to the assembly when this norm is observed (cf. *SC,* no. 51).

In order to promote a wider use of Scripture (cf. *SC,* no. 51), *IGMR2002* admonishes against too frequent use of Masses for the Dead (quite common in a pre–Vatican II church). It also adds a second reason for this moderation, i.e., every Eucharistic Prayer includes a commemoration of the dead. DPPL does endorse liturgical celebrations in memory of the deceased, while at the same time it cautions that this is not simply a matter of relating to the dead who are relatives and friends, but these are always celebrations of the whole church (no. 255).

The corrected English translation in the next sentence offers another reason for choosing optional memorials of either Mary or the saints: to "satisfy their *legitimate* devotion" (*satisfiat legitimae eorum pietati*); "legitimate" was omitted in GIRM1970 but included in GIRM1975 and GIRM2003. The qualifier suggests that, as the priest's preferences are not to take priority, neither should individual's preferences. DPPL endorses a Saturday memorial of the Blessed Virgin Mary (no. 188) and speaks of the importance of veneration of the saints (no. 209).

The final sentence of no. 355 gives priority of choice for diocesan or religious calendars over the General Roman Calendar with regard to memorials. Earlier, no. 354 mentioned a priest's "own proper calendar" (*calendarium proprium*); here it is specified as a "religious" (*religioso*) calendar.

The Choice of Mass Texts

356. This second major division of the chapter begins with a simple statement that the norms which follow for the choice of texts (including readings, orations, Eucharistic Prayer, and the chants) are to be observed.

The Readings

357. For Sundays and solemnities, three readings are assigned: that is, from a Prophet, an Apostle, and a Gospel. By these the Christian people are brought to know the continuity of the work of salvation according to God's wonderful plan. These readings should be followed strictly. During the Easter Season, according to the tradition of the Church, instead of the reading from the Old Testament, the reading is taken from the Acts of the Apostles.

For feasts, on the other hand, two readings are assigned. If, however, according to the norms a feast is raised to the rank of a solemnity, a third reading is added, taken from the Common.

For memorials of Saints, unless strictly proper readings are given, the readings assigned for the weekday are customarily used. In certain cases, readings are provided that highlight some particular aspect of the spiritual life or activity of the Saint. The use of such readings is not to be insisted upon, unless a pastoral reason suggests it.

De lectionibus

357. Dominicis et sollemnitatibus assignantur tres lectiones, scilicet Prophetæ, Apostoli et Evangelii, quibus populus christianus ad continuitatem operas salutis, secundum mirabile propositum divinum, educatur. Hæ lectiones stricte adhibeantur. Tempore paschali, iuxta Ecclesiæ traditionem, loco Veteris Testamenti, lectio ex Actibus Apostolorum sumitur.

Festis vero duæ lectiones assignantur. Si tamen festum iuxta normas ad gradum sollemnitatis elevatur, additur tertia lectio, quæ e Communi desumitur.

In memoriis Sanctorum, nisi habeantur propriæ, leguntur de more lectiones feriæ assignatæ. In quibusdam casibus proponuntur lectiones appropriatæ, quæ scilicet peculiarem aspectum vitæ spiritualis aut actuositatis Sancti in luce ponunt. Usus harum lectionum non est urgendus, nisi ratio pastoralis revera id suadeat.

The Readings

357. For the first part of this article, GIRM2003 provides a more literal translation of the Latin by referring to the Old Testament as a reading from "a Prophet" (*Prophetae*), a departure from both GIRM1970 and GIRM1975 (no. 318). On the other hand, the Latin is misleading because readings other than from the prophetic writings are selected for some Sundays and solemnities. The Instruction here reiterates one of the principles at work in the post–Vatican II Lectionary regarding the use of an Old Testament reading, which reminds the assembly that Christianity is in continuity with the work of salvation begun by God from Adam and Eve's fall and continuing throughout the history of Israel.

This article provides no latitude concerning a choice about these three readings. The Instruction notes that during the Easter season the first reading is taken from the Acts of the Apostles, not from the Old Testament; this is likewise true for the Solemnity of the Apostles Ss. Peter and Paul, as well as for the Solemnity of All Saints when the first reading is from the book of Revelation. *IGMR2002* omits any reference to using only two readings on Sundays and solemnities, which its predecessors permitted for "pastoral reasons and by decree of the

358. In the Lectionary for weekdays, readings are provided for each day of every week throughout the entire year; as a result, these readings are for the most

358. In lectionario pro feriis, lectiones proponuntur pro singulis diebus cuiusque hebdomadæ per universum cursum anni: proinde hæ lectiones plerumque sumentur,

---

conference of bishops" (*propter rationes ordinis pastoralis et ex decreto Conferentiae Episcopalis, IGMR1975,* no. 318), which was repeated in *OLM1981-Pr,* no. 79. Also, the *Directory for Masses with Children* allows the number of readings to be decreased to two or one on weekdays or Sundays (no. 42), and *OLM1981-Pr* permitted changing the readings for children as well (nos. 66–68, 78, and 84).

The remarks on feasts and memorials are new to *IGMR2002*. Normally only two readings are assigned to celebrations with the rank of feast. On occasion a first reading from the Old Testament is given as an option (e.g., Visitation; Birth of Mary; Michael, Gabriel, and Raphael); for all other feasts, the first reading is from the writings of the Apostles. This is to be expected, since the feasts help us enter into the mystery of Christ and redemption. Some dominical feasts (including the Exaltation of the Holy Cross) are assigned three readings because they may replace a Sunday in Ordinary Time where they will need three readings. When these feasts occur on a weekday, however, only two readings are used and then a choice may be made between the first two readings given in the Lectionary (cf. *OLM1981-Pr,* no. 84.3). One non-dominical feast that is assigned three readings and also takes precedence over a Sunday in Ordinary Time is the Dedication of the Lateran Basilica. Finally, if a feast or memorial has only two readings assigned but in a local church takes the rank of solemnity (e.g., the titular feast), then the third reading is taken from the Common (cf. *OLM1981-Pr,* no. 70).

The last part of this paragraph addresses readings proclaimed on memorials (cf. *OLM1981-Pr,* nos. 70 and 83). Ordinarily the readings assigned for the weekday are preferred in order to respect the continuity of readings given in the Lectionary. If proper readings are provided (e.g., the proper gospel for the Beheading of John the Baptist), they must be used because they explain a biblical event concerning the saint (cf. *OLM1981-Pr,* no. 83). *OLM1981-Pr* makes a further distinction between readings provided which are directly related to the memorial being celebrated and "accommodated readings" (no. 83) which pertain to "the spiritual life or activity of the Saint"; these may be used but are "not to be insisted upon," which even more clearly respects the continuity and breadth of readings given in the Lectionary.

358. Next *IGMR2002* turns to the weekday readings and begins with an explanatory statement of two parts. First, the Lectionary provides readings for each day of the year (cf. *OLM1981-Pr,* no. 82) and they are normally followed. Once again, this preserves the continuity of the Lectionary for good pastoral effectiveness. Second, when a festival occurs, its proper readings are used (see no. 357 above).

part to be used on the days to which they are assigned, unless there occurs a solemnity, feast, or memorial that has its own proper New Testament readings, that is to say, readings in which mention is made of the Saint being celebrated.

If, however, the continuous reading during the week is interrupted by the occurrence of some solemnity or feast, or some particular celebration, then the priest, taking into consideration the entire week's scheme of readings, is allowed either to combine parts omitted with other readings or to decide which readings are to be preferred over others.

In Masses with special groups, the priest is allowed to choose texts more suited to the particular celebration, provided they are taken from the texts of an approved lectionary.

359. In addition, the Lectionary has a special selection of texts from Sacred Scripture for Ritual Masses into which certain

diebus quibus sunt assignatæ, nisi occurrat sollemnitas vel festum, vel memoria lectiones proprias Novi Testamenti habens, in quibus scilicet mentio fiat de Sancto celebrato.

Si tamen aliquando lectio continua in hebdomada intermittitur ob aliquam sollemnitatem, aliquod festum vel aliquam peculiarem celebrationem, sacerdoti licebit, præ oculis habita ordinatione lectionum totius hebdomadæ, aut partes omittendas una cum aliis componere aut statuere quinam textus aliis præferendi sint.

In Missis pro peculiaribus cœtibus, sacerdoti licebit textus peculiari celebrationi aptiores eligere, dummodo ex approbati lectionarii textibus seligantur.

359. Peculiaris insuper selectio textuum sacræ Scripturæ datur in lectionario pro Missis ritualibus, in quas aliqua Sacra-

---

Even when the weekday semi-continuous readings must be interrupted by the readings proper to a feast day, there remains such great respect for the overall plan of the Lectionary that missed readings may be combined with other readings or used to replace the reading on another day. Decisions about this would depend largely upon the literary genre of texts. This is especially crucial, for example, when a lengthy narrative of a biblical event is given over several weekdays and a critical part of the story might be omitted, rendering the story as a whole less comprehensible.

Finally, this paragraph allows great latitude in choosing readings when Mass is taking place to mark a special occasion (e.g., an anniversary or jubilee). In this case, the only restriction given in *IGMR2002* is that the readings be from an approved Lectionary. Sometimes the Votive Masses provide some guidance for finding suitable readings for such occasions.

359. This article addresses the choice of readings for Masses in which another sacrament or sacramental is inserted (e.g., baptism, confirmation, etc.) or celebrated for certain needs (e.g., for peace and justice). In special sections in the Lectionary, these readings are grouped by Old Testament readings, New Testament readings, responsorial psalms, gospel acclamations, and gospels (cf. *OLM1981-Pr*, nos. 72 and 85–88). Other than to advise pastoral sensitivity and the use of options so that the readings pertain to the occasion, no other guide-

Sacraments or Sacramentals are incorporated, or for Masses that are celebrated for certain needs.

Selections of readings of this kind have been established in this way, so that through a more apt hearing of the word of God the faithful may be led to a fuller understanding of the mystery in which they are participating and may be brought to a more ardent love of the word of God.

As a result, texts spoken in the celebration are to be chosen keeping in mind both a suitable pastoral reason and the options allowed in this matter.

360. At times, a longer and shorter form of the same text is given. In choosing between these two forms, a pastoral criterion must be kept in mind. At such times, attention should be paid to the capacity of the faithful to listen with understanding to a reading of greater or lesser length, and to their capacity to hear a more complete text, which is then explained in the homily.[142]

menta vel Sacramentalia inseruntur, aut pro Missis, quæ pro quibusdam necessitatibus celebrantur.

Huiusmodi lectionaria ideo statuta sunt, ut per aptiorem verbi Dei auditionem fideles ad mysterium quod participant plenius percipiendum ducantur, et ad incensiorem amorem verbi Dei instituantur.

Textus proinde, qui in celebratione proferuntur, determinandi sunt præ oculis habitis tum congrua ratione pastorali tum eligendi facultate in hac re facta.

360. Datur quandoque forma longior et forma brevior eiusdem textus. In eligendo inter has duas formas criterium pastorale præ oculis habeatur. Tunc attendatur oportet ad facultatem fidelium auscultandi cum fructu lectionem magis vel minus longam; ad eorum facultatem audiendi textum magis completum, per homiliam explicandum.[142]

---

lines are given. The text implies that the readings are taken from those which are given in the Lectionary, so there is not the same latitude with ritual Masses as is given for Masses on special occasions (see no. 358 above).

It would make pastoral sense to follow the norms given for Sundays, solemnities, and feasts in the choice of readings for ritual Masses. If a ritual Mass is celebrated on a Sunday or on more solemn occasions (for example, when the bishop is present for Confirmation), three readings would be chosen. In other circumstances (e.g., celebrating the Sacrament of the Sick within Mass on a weekday), only one reading before the gospel need be chosen.

360. This article is new to *IGMR2002*, but reiterates almost verbatim what is found in *OLM1981-Pr* (no. 80; cf. also no. 75). It ought not be automatically assumed that a longer reading is preferred because the faithful would hear more Scripture or a shorter reading is preferred because they will pay greater attention. Nor should it be assumed that longer gospels (e.g., the Parable of the Good Samaritan) are so well known as to be ineffective when proclaimed.

In addition to the "pastoral criterion" (*criterium pastorale*) given, namely, the "capacity of the faithful" (*facultatem fidelium*), another consideration for the choice of a longer or shorter alternative reading would pertain to the catechetical value of some of the longer readings as well as their theological and/or hermeneutical import. Sometimes, especially with longer or shorter forms of

361. When a choice is allowed between alternative texts, whether they are fixed or optional, attention must be paid to what is in the best interests of those taking part, whether it is a matter of using the easier text or one more appropriate in a given group, or of repeating or setting aside a text that is assigned as proper to some particular celebration while being optional for another,[143] as pastoral advantage may suggest.

Such a situation may arise when the same text would have to be read again within a few days, as, for example, on a Sunday and on a following weekday, or when it is feared that a certain text might create some difficulties for a particular group of the Christian faithful. Care should, however, be taken that, when choosing scriptural passages, parts of Sacred Scripture are not permanently excluded.

362. The adaptations to the *Ordo Lectionum Missae* as contained in the Lectionary for Mass for use in the dioceses of the United States of America should be carefully observed.

361. Quando autem facultas tribuitur seligendi inter unum vel alterum textum iam definitum, vel ad libitum propositum, attendendum erit ad utilitatem participantium, prout nempe agitur de adhibendo textu, qui facilior est vel magis conveniens cœtui congregato, vel de textu iterando vel reponendo, qui alicui celebrationi tamquam proprius assignatur, alteri vero tamquam ad libitum adhibendus, quoties utilitas pastoralis id suadeat.[143]

Quod evenire potest aut quando idem textus diebus proximioribus iterum legi debeat ex. gr. die dominica et in feria subsequenti aut quando timeatur ne textus aliquis quasdam gignat difficultates in aliquo christifidelium cœtu. Caveatur tamen ne, in seligendis textibus Scripturæ Sacræ, partes eius permanenter excludantur.

362. Præter facultates eligendi quosdam textus aptiores, de quibus supra, facultas fit Conferentiis Episcoporum, in peculiaribus adiunctis, aliquas aptationes indicandi ad lectiones quod attinet, ea tamen lege, ut textus seligantur e lectionario rite approbato.

---

the gospel, the longer form includes a parable or explanation which radically affects the meaning of the text. At times shorter readings omit more offensive or difficult material, taken up in the next paragraph which is also new to *IGMR2002* but follows closely *OLM1981-Pr,* no. 81.

361. This paragraph also restates what is in *OLM1981-Pr* (no. 81) and repeats the often cited principle that pastoral good determines choices. "Fixed" (*definitum*) alternative texts would include, for example, the choice between a longer or shorter reading. An "optional" (*ad libitum*) alternative text, for example, would refer to a legitimate choice of texts from the selections given for a ritual or votive Mass. Other examples of situations when an alternative text would be chosen are given: texts more appropriate for a particular group of people, or potential for the repetition of texts. This article also directs that no texts ought to be excluded permanently, but ought to be proclaimed on at least some occasions.

362. This article in GIRM2003 provides a pastoral adaptation approved for use in dioceses of the US, which *IGMR2002* allows. An example of such a pastoral adaptation for the US is the introduction to the gospel which uses "Saint"

The Orations

363. In any Mass the orations proper to that Mass are used, unless otherwise noted.

On memorials of Saints, the collect proper to the day is used or, if none is available, one from an appropriate Common. The prayer over the offerings, however, and the prayer after Communion, unless they are proper, may be taken either from the Common or from the weekdays of the current Season.

On the weekdays in Ordinary Time, however, besides the orations from the previous Sunday, orations from another Sunday in Ordinary Time may be used, or one of the prayers for various needs provided in the Missal. It is always permissible, however, to use the collect alone from these Masses.

In this way a richer collection of texts is available, by which the prayer life of the faithful is more abundantly nourished.

During the more important seasons of the year, however, the proper seasonal orations appointed for each weekday in the Missal already make provision for this.

De orationibus

363. In qualibet Missa, nisi aliter notetur, dicuntur orationes ipsi Missæ propriæ.

In memoriis Sanctorum, dicitur collecta propria vel, si deest, de Communi congruenti; orationes vero super oblata et post Communionem, nisi sint propriæ, sumi possunt aut e Communi aut e feriis temporis currentis.

In feriis autem « per annum », præter orationes dominicæ præcedentis, sumi possunt vel orationes alius dominicæ « per annum », vel una ex orationibus pro variis necessitatibus, quæ in Missali recensentur. Semper tamen licebit ex iisdem Missis etiam solam collectam adhibere.

Hoc modo ditior copia præbetur textuum, quibus precatio fidelium abundantius nutritur.

In potioribus tamen anni temporibus, hæc accommodatio iam fit per orationes iisdem temporibus proprias, in Missali, pro singulis feriis, exstantes.

---

rather than a more literal translation of *beati*. Also, where a Mass specific to the US (for example, for Thanksgiving Day) is given, the choice for readings may be taken only from those given for that Mass. The Lectionary for the US may be published with sense lines as an aid to proclamation; it is understood that this pastoral aid would be taken seriously.

The Orations

363. Chapter VII now turns to the orations which, as noted above (405), are transposed in *IGMR2002* to a place in this chapter before the norms on the Eucharistic Prayer and have their own subheading. In this paragraph the "orations" refer to the collect ("opening prayer" in previous GIRMs, see no. 127 above), the prayer over the offerings, and the prayer after Communion. The same principles at work for the choice of readings apply to the choice of orations.

The first principle is that the orations proper to any Mass are to be used. In the case of the collect, the 1975 US Sacramentary includes an alternative opening prayer for most Sundays and solemnities; one is free to choose either the

The Eucharistic Prayer

364. The purpose of the many prefaces that enrich the *Roman Missal* is to bring out more fully the motives for thanksgiving within the Eucharistic Prayer and to set out more clearly the different facets of the mystery of salvation.

De Prece eucharistica

364. Plurimæ præfationes, quibus Missale Romanum ditatur, eo spectant ut argumenta gratiarum actionis in Prece eucharistica plenius eniteant, et variæ rationes mysterii salutis pleniore luce proponantur.

---

opening prayer or its alternative. Good pastoral practice might suggest, for example, that the prayer which best relates to the Liturgy of the Word would be used.

On memorials, if proper orations are given they are to be used, otherwise orations may be chosen from the suitable Common. Additionally, if no proper orations are given, the prayer over the offerings and the prayer after Communion may also be taken from the ferial Mass. Since this last option is not given for collects, this opening prayer will always speak at least generically to the memorial being celebrated; this highlights the importance of the opening prayer for setting a tone for the entire Mass.

On ferial days (weekdays when no feastday is observed during Ordinary Time), orations may be taken from the previous Sunday's Mass or from another Sunday in Ordinary Time; in other words, no proper orations are provided for the weekdays in Ordinary Time. This paragraph also allows these ferial orations to be taken from the prayer for various needs (Masses and Prayers for Various Needs and Occasions, cf. no. 373 below). Although it is permitted to use only the collect, in pastoral practice generally an entire set of orations is used since, not being proper, there is no real pastoral value in taking the orations from different Masses. There is a desire that a variety of orations be used so that "the prayer life of the faithful is more abundantly nourished" (*precatio fidelium abundantius nutritur*). The last sentence in this paragraph simply indicates that a rich variety of prayers is already provided for the faithful during the seasons when proper orations are assigned.

No mention of votive Masses is made in this paragraph, but it would seem appropriate also to select orations from these Masses when no proper ones are assigned.

The Eucharistic Prayer

364. Eighty-four prefaces are given in the Sacramentary in addition to the proper ones for Eucharistic Prayers II and IV, the two Eucharistic Prayers for Children, the three Eucharistic Prayers for Masses of Reconciliation and Eucharistic Prayers for Various Needs and Occasions I–IV. Especially on the Sundays in Ordinary Time and weekdays, care ought to be taken that all the prefaces given as options are used over a period of time. Often on festivals with proper

365. The choice among the Eucharistic Prayers found in the Order of Mass is suitably guided by the following norms:

a. Eucharistic Prayer I, that is, the Roman Canon, which may always be used, is especially suited to be sung or said on days when there is a proper text for the *Communicantes (In union with the whole Church)* or in Masses endowed with a proper form of the *Hanc igitur (Father, accept this offering)* and also in the celebrations of the Apostles and of the Saints mentioned in the Prayer itself; it is likewise especially appropriate for Sundays, unless for pastoral considerations Eucharistic Prayer III is preferred.

b. Eucharistic Prayer II, on account of its particular features, is more appropriately used on weekdays or in special circumstances. Although it has been

365. Electio inter Preces eucharisticas, quæ in Ordine Missæ inveniuntur, his normis opportune regitur:

a) Prex eucharistica prima, seu Canon romanus, qui semper adhiberi potest, opportunius profertur diebus quibus assignantur Communicántes propria, aut in Missis quæ Hanc ígitur propriis ditantur, necnon in celebrationibus Apostolorum et Sanctorum, quorum mentio fit in ipsa Prece; itemque diebus dominicis, nisi, ob rationes pastorales, præferatur Prex eucharistica tertia.

b) Prex eucharistica secunda, ob peculiares ipsius notas, opportunius sumitur diebus infra hebdomadam, vel in peculiaribus rerum adiunctis. Quamvis præfatione propria instructa sit, adhiberi potest etiam cum aliis præfationibus; cum iis præsertim quæ mysterium

---

prefaces, the preface provides somewhat of a commentary on the readings as well as theological insight into the meaning of the feast. The prefaces offer rich homiletic content.

Since *IGMR2002* includes a separate paragraph on orations, beginning this subsection on the Eucharistic Prayer with the paragraph on prefaces more clearly presents the preface as the first part of the Eucharistic Prayer and integral to it (cf. nos. 43 and 79 above).

365. This important paragraph suggests norms for choosing among the four Eucharistic Prayers (cf. no. 147 above).[5] Nothing, however, is said about the Eucharistic Prayers for children, reconciliation, or for various occasions. A first point to be made is that this paragraph subtly emphasizes that there truly is a *choice* of the Eucharistic Prayer for each Mass and this choice ought to be given some thought before Mass begins.

Number 365a considers Eucharistic Prayer I (EP I) and recommends that it "may always be used" (*qui semper adhiberi potest*); "always" is a new addition to *IGMR2002* not contained in its predecessors which implies a preference for this venerable Roman canon. The Instruction goes on to note when this prayer "is especially suited to be sung or said" (*opportunius profertur; IGMR1975* has *opportunius dicitur*, no. 322a); GIRM2003's translation encourages prefaces to

5. Also useful are the "Norms on the Use of Eucharistic Prayers I–IV" (Rome: Sacred Congregation for Rites, 23 May 1968).

provided with its own Preface, it may also be used with other Prefaces, especially those that summarize the mystery of salvation, such as the common Prefaces. When Mass is celebrated for a particular dead person, the special formula may be inserted in the place indicated, namely, before the *Memento etiam (Remember our brothers and sisters)*.

c. Eucharistic Prayer III may be said with any Preface. Its use is preferred on Sundays and feast days. If, however, this Eucharistic Prayer is used in Masses for the Dead, the special formula for the dead may be used, to be included at the proper place, namely, after the *Omnes filios tuos ubique dispersos, tibi, clemens Pater, miseratus coniunge (In mercy and love unite all your children)*.

d. Eucharistic Prayer IV has an invariable Preface and gives a fuller summary of salvation history. It may be used when a Mass has no Preface of its own and on Sundays in Ordinary Time. Because of its structure, no special formula for the dead may be inserted into this prayer.

salutis compendiose repræsentant, v. gr. cum præfationibus communibus. Quando Missa pro aliquo defuncto celebratur, adhiberi potest peculiaris formula, suo loco, nempe ante Meménto étiam proposita.

c) Prex eucharistica tertia cum qualibet præfatione dici potest. Eius usus præferatur diebus dominicis et festis. Si autem hæc Prex in Missis defunctorum adhibeatur, usurpari potest peculiaris formula pro defuncto, suo loco inserenda, nempe post verba: Omnes fílios tuos ubíque dispérsos, tibi, clemens Pater, miserátus coniúnge.

d) Prex eucharistica quarta præfationem immutabilem habet et summarium plenius historiæ salutis præbet. Adhiberi potest quando Missa præfatione propria caret, et in dominicis « per annum ». In hanc Precem, ratione structuræ, inseri nequit peculiaris formula pro defuncto.

---

be sung, especially on more solemn occasions. When a proper *Communicantes* and *Hanc igitur* are provided (e.g., on Christmas) or when a saint named in EP I is celebrated, this is a most suitable choice. The last sentence states that EP I is "especially appropriate for Sundays" (*itemque diebus dominicis*) but then seems to permit only Eucharistic Prayer III to be substituted for it (cf. no. 365d below), whereas its predecessors allowed a broader choice.[6] Since Sunday is the usual day for Catholics to celebrate Mass, no. 365a strongly endorses EP I. EP I is unique in especially two ways. First, the diptychs before and after the institution narrative may be used in total or most may be omitted (omission indicated by the typography of the Sacramentary). Second, EP I is really a conflation of short prayers, each ending with a Christological mediation ("Through Christ

6. Whereas *IGMR2002* indicates that EP I is appropriate "unless for pastoral considerations Eucharistic Prayer III is preferred" *(nisi, ob rationes pastorales, praeferatur Prex eucharistica tertia)*, *IGMR1975* notes its appropriateness unless for pastoral considerations "another eucharistic prayer is preferred *(praeferatur alia Prex eucharistica—tertia vs. alia,* no. 322a*)*.

The Chants

366. It is not permitted to substitute other chants for those found in the Order of Mass, such as at the *Agnus Dei*.

De cantibus

366. Cantibus in Ordine Missæ positis, v. gr. ad Agnus Dei, non licet substituere alios cantus.

---

our Lord. Amen."); the typography indicates that these responses may also be omitted and when they are it helps to unify the prayer.[7]

Number 365b states that EP II is especially suitable for weekdays since it has its own preface; other prefaces may also be substituted. Also, a special intercession for the dead may be added in the appropriate place. Because EP II is recommended for weekdays, its own proper memento for the dead seems to be reminiscent of the pre–Vatican II practice of many weekday Masses being *Requiem* Masses. This is the shortest of the Eucharistic Prayers and tends to be overused in actual pastoral practice, especially on Sundays, often to the almost total exclusion of the other Eucharistic Prayers. Greater care in the choice of a Eucharistic Prayer would address this pastoral difficulty.

Number 365c notes that EP III has no proper preface and so any preface may be used with it. The norm indicates that this Eucharistic Prayer would be "preferred" (*praeferatur*) on Sundays, feastdays, and for Masses for the Dead—it, too, has a special memento which, in a lengthy insertion, slightly rewords the entire conclusion for EP III. Similar to EP I (although this is a new, post–Vatican II composition), EP III includes motifs of sacrifice and offering, although the former is not so apparent in EP III as in EP I.

Finally, no. 365d addresses the use of EP IV. With an invariable preface, EP IV cannot be used on any day with a proper preface. An addition in *IGMR2002* makes two points: first, EP IV may be used on Sundays in Ordinary Time (which seems to contradict no. 365a above); second, no special memento for the dead may be inserted into it. Eucharistic Prayer IV is the one Roman prayer we have which is structured most closely like an Eastern *anaphora* and gives the richest account of salvation history. Of these four prayers, EP IV is the longest. Perhaps because of its length, or because in translation it has the most exclusive language of any Eucharistic Prayer, it is rarely prayed in parishes; this is a pastoral concern which needs to be redressed.

366. This article governing chants pertains to those chant texts which are fixed in the Mass, traditionally considered the "ordinary." The example given is for the *Agnus Dei*, but presumably the norm governs also the *Kyrie*, *Gloria*, *Credo*, and *Sanctus*. Since other chants cannot be substituted, it is also presumed that paraphrases of these chants cannot be used. The Instruction does, however, allow for troping of the *Kyrie* (no. 52 above), although it does not comment on this practice for the *Agnus Dei* (no. 83 above).

7. On some of the theological questions about this prayer, see Power and Vincie, especially 64.

367. The norms laid down in their proper places are to be observed for the choice of the chants between the readings, as well as of the chants at the entrance, at the offertory, and at Communion (cf. nos. 40–41, 47–48, 61–64, 74, 86–88).

367. In eligendis cantibus inter lectiones occurrentibus, necnon cantibus ad introitum, ad offertorium et ad Communionem, normæ serventur, quæ suis locis statuuntur *(cf. nn. 40–41, 47–48, 61–64, 74, 86–88).*

---

367. This article concerns chants that traditionally have been considered "proper," including the chants between the readings (the responsorial psalm, the sequence when used, and the gospel acclamation), as well as chants at the entrance, "offertory" (cf. no. 37 above on this problematic designation), and Communion. This paragraph simply references the norms governing all these chants in Chapter II of *IGMR2002*, rather than repeating all that information here.

GIRM–Notes (English)

141. Cf. Second Vatican Ecumenical Council, Constitution on the Sacred Liturgy, *Sacrosanctum Concilium*, no. 51.

142. *The Roman Missal, Lectionary for Mass, editio typica altera*, 1981, Introduction, no. 80.

143. Ibid., no. 81.

IGMR–Notes (Latin)

141. Cf. Conc. Œcum. Vat. II, Const. de sacra Liturgia, *Sacrosanctum Concilium*, n. 51.

142. Missale Romanum, *Ordo lectionum Missæ*, editio typica altera 1981, Prænotanda, n. 80.

143. *Ibidem*, n. 81.

CHAPTER VIII

Masses and Prayers for Various Circumstances and Masses for the Dead

(*DE MISSIS ET ORATIONIBUS AD DIVERSA ET DE MISSIS DEFUNCTORUM*)

Joanne M. Pierce and Richard Rutherford

Chapter VIII follows naturally in theme from the preceding chapter, on "Choice of Mass Texts." Here the document moves to a more specific discussion of choices available for the celebration of the Eucharist, that is, to those groups of Mass formularies to accompany other ritual acts, and those "optional" Mass formularies composed "not to observe a feast or season of the liturgical year but to celebrate a chosen devotional theme or to petition for a particular intention (*votum*)."[1] *Institutio Generalis Missalis Romani* 2002 (*IGMR2002*) expands this chapter, from the fifteen sections found in the *IGMR1975* (nos. 326–341), to seventeen (nos. 368–385). The chapter retains its original two subsections: "Masses and Prayers for Various Circumstances" (*De Missis et Orationibus ad Diversa*) and "Masses for the Dead" (*De Missis Defunctorum*).[2]

Masses and Prayers for Various Circumstances

The composition and use of Mass formularies for specific intentions or in veneration of Mary and other saints is an ancient practice. These Masses would have been celebrated for smaller groups gathered to venerate a particular saint or to pray for a particular intention[3]; the earliest direct liturgical evidence for

1. Christopher Walsh, "Votive Mass," in Paul Bradshaw, ed., *The New Westminster Dictionary of Liturgy and Worship* (Louisville/London: Westminster John Knox Press, 2002), 472.

2. The *Directory on Popular Piety and the Liturgy* (DPPL) offers helpful insights into these categories of Masses. See, for example, nos. 84 (on ecclesiological context), 90 (on private revelation), 183–188 (on Mary), 208–212 and 223–227 (on the saints), 213–215 (on the angels), and 248–260 (on "suffrage" for the dead).

3. "The smaller groups who gathered at the shrines on ordinary days celebrated the Eucharist not only to honor the saints and martyrs, but took the opportunity to intensify the intercessory aspect of the celebration: to give thanks for recovery from sickness, to ask for safe

some of these Masses dates from the fifth to sixth century.[4] The practice of offering Mass for a specific request, or in time of some urgent need, is essentially rooted in the Christian concept of the nature of prayer itself. As *Catholicae Ecclesiae Catechismus* (*CEC*) states, it is the Holy Spirit "who teaches the Church . . . and also form[s] her in the life of Prayer" (no. 2623). There are five "*forms of prayer* revealed in the apostolic and canonical Scriptures [that] remain normative for Christian prayer" (*CEC*, no. 2625): blessing and adoration; prayer of petition; prayer of intercession; prayer of thanksgiving; prayer of praise (*CEC*, nos. 2626–2642). And it is the "Eucharist [that] contains and expresses all forms of prayer" (*CEC*, no. 2643).

Many of these Mass formularies are intended to be used in times of need (e.g., "In Time of Famine or For those Who Suffer From Famine," *Tempore Famis, vel Pro Fame*[5]), for certain persons or groups of people (e.g., "For Those Who Serve in Public Office," *Pro Rempublicam Moderantibus*[6]) or to request certain virtues or blessings from God (e.g., "For Unity of Christians," *Pro Unitate Christianorum*[7]). The practice of prayer of petition or intercession is not an empty gesture. Christian prayer is "efficacious" because it is rooted in "the economy of salvation," which reveals that "faith rests in God's action in history" (*CEC*, no. 2738). It is essentially Trinitarian, "founded on the prayer of the Spirit in us and on the faithful love of the Father who has given us his only Son" (*CEC*, no. 2739). Ultimately, it is in Jesus Christ that our prayer is made fruitful:

> The prayer of Jesus makes Christian prayer an efficacious petition . . . [he] prays for us—in our place and on our behalf. All our petitions were gathered up, once for all, in his cry on the Cross and, in his Resurrection, heard by the Father. That is why he never ceases to intercede for us with the Father. If our prayer is resolutely united with that of Jesus . . . we obtain all that we ask in his name, even more than any particular thing: the Holy Spirit himself, who contains all gifts (*CEC*, nos. 2740–2741).

IGMR2002 uses *IGMR1975* as the base text for this chapter. Changes include the transposition or augmentation of certain words or phrases, the addition of

childbirth, to pray for the departed, etc." Cyrille Vogel, *Medieval Liturgy: An Introduction to the Sources*, trans. and rev. William Storey and Niels Rasmussen (Washington, DC: The Pastoral Press, 1986), 157.

4. Some of the Masses contained in the *Sacramentarium Veronense* (see Mitchell and Baldovin above, 5–6) arranged according to month; Vogel, 38–46. Note, too, a reference made by Augustine (d. 430) in *The City of God* (written 413–26 C.E.) to a bedside Eucharist celebrated for the healing of a sick man (Book 22, Chapter 8); see *Medieval Sourcebook* (http://www.fordham.edu/halsall/source/augustine-cityofgod-22-9-10.html).

5. *MR2002*, under the subheading *Pro Circumstantiis Publicis*, no. 33 (1136–37).

6. Ibid., no. 22 (1123–24).

7. *MR2002*, no. 17, A, B, C (111–15). Here, the introductory rubric specifies in more detail than in previous *MR*s the seasons and other occasions when this Mass formulary may not be used.

Chapter VIII
MASSES AND PRAYERS FOR VARIOUS CIRCUMSTANCES AND MASSES FOR THE DEAD

I. Masses and Prayers for Various Circumstances

368. Since the liturgy of the Sacraments and Sacramentals causes, for the faithful who are properly disposed, almost every event in life to be sanctified by divine grace that flows from the paschal mystery,[144] and because the Eucharist is the Sacrament of Sacraments, the Missal provides formularies for Masses and orations that may be used in the various circumstances of Christian life, for the needs of the whole world or for the needs of the Church, whether universal or local.

369. In view of the rather broad range of choice among the readings and orations,

Caput VIII
DE MISSIS ET ORATIONIBUS AD DIVERSA ET DE MISSIS DEFUNCTORUM

I. De Missis et Orationibus ad Diversa

368. Quoniam liturgia Sacramentorum et Sacramentalium id efficit ut fidelibus bene dispositis omnis fere eventus vitæ sanctificetur gratia divina manante ex mysterio paschali,[144] et quoniam Eucharistia est sacramentum sacramentorum, Missale suppeditat exempla Missarum et orationum, quæ in diversis occasionibus vitæ christianæ adhiberi possunt pro necessitatibus totius mundi aut Ecclesiæ universæ vel localis.

369. Perspecta ampliore facultate eligendi lectiones et orationes, expedit ut

---

new phrases to already extant sentences, and the addition or interpolation of new material altogether.

A first change in the English translation is evident in the title of the chapter heading, and that of the first subsection. The title in GIRM1975 is "Masses and Prayers for Various Needs and Occasions," while in GIRM2003 it is "Masses and Prayers for Various Circumstances," although the Latin text (*De missis et orationibus ad diversa*) is the same for both.

368. This first paragraph is identical in the Latin to *IGMR1975* (no. 326), although GIRM2003 combines shorter sentences to form one single long sentence, and the last phrase modifying "Church" is transposed from the GIRM1975 reading of "both local and universal" to the more literal "whether universal or local" (*aut Ecclesiae universae vel localis*). This reflects a general pattern throughout the Instruction in which the universal Church is given priority over any local Church.

This and previous *IGMR*s stress the paschal mystery as source of the divine grace of all of the worship of the Church. The phrase "divine grace that flows from the paschal mystery" (*gratia divina manante ex mysterio paschali*) is clarified by a reference to *Sacrosanctum Concilium* which highlights the central role of Christ in worship, as well as the inherent goodness and real capacity of all creation to be used rightly for "people's sanctification and the praise of God" (no. 61).

369. The English translation of this paragraph has also changed: the range of readings is now described as "rather broad" (*ampliore*; GIRM1975, no. 327 had "broad") and the recommended frequency of use of these Masses is now

it is best if Masses for various circumstances be used in moderation, that is, when the occasion truly requires.

Missæ ad diversa moderate, idest quando opportunitas id exigit, adhibeantur.

370. In all the Masses for various circumstances, unless otherwise expressly indicated, it is permissible to use the weekday readings and also the chants between them, if they are suited to the celebration.

370. In omnibus Missis ad diversa, nisi aliter expresse caveatur, licet adhibere lectiones feriales, necnon cantus inter ipsas occurrentes, si cum celebratione conveniant.

371. Among Masses of this kind are included Ritual Masses, Masses for Various Needs, Masses for Various Circumstances, and Votive Masses.

371. In huiusmodi Missis adnumerantur Missæ rituales, pro variis necessitatibus, ad diversa et votivæ.

---

directed to be "in moderation" (*moderate*) rather than "sparingly" (GIRM1975, no. 327), when the occasion "truly requires" (*id exigit*). Since the Latin text has not changed, this change in the English text might be taken by some as suggesting more frequent use of these Masses.

370. While this paragraph in *IGMR2002* is identical to *IGMR1975*, GIRM2003 notes that the weekday readings and chants may be used at the celebration of these Masses unless "expressly" (*expresse,* not "otherwise" as in GIRM1975, no. 328) indicated. Their use also depends on "if they are suited to the celebration" (*si cum celebratione convenient*), although the Instruction gives no criteria for making that judgment. The Introduction to the Lectionary (*OLM1981-Pr*) offers some guidance here when it suggests texts "that can be of assistance in adapting such celebrations to the situation, circumstances, and concerns of the particular groups taking part" (no. 86).

371. The listing of types of these Masses ("Ritual Masses, Masses for Various Needs, Masses for Various Circumstances, and Votive Masses," *Missae rituales, pro variis necessitatibus, ad diversa et votivae*) has been simplified from that found in *IGMR1975* (no. 329). Such attempts at simplification have occurred regularly in the Latin West. For example, the number of some of these types of Masses was much smaller in the Tridentine Missal (*MR1570*) than the multiple texts known in an earlier period.[8] In the face of later encroachments, popes of the twentieth century similarly tried to reassert the priority of Sundays and Lent over a new proliferation of votive masses and feasts of the saints.[9]

8. ". . . the liturgical cycle was relieved of a multitude of saints' feasts with which the Middle Ages had overburdened it, causing the Sundays to disappear . . . in like manner, the celebration of votive Masses was regulated in such a way as to prevent their multiplication." Robert Cabié, *The Church at Prayer*, Vol. II: *The Eucharist* (Collegeville, MN: The Liturgical Press, 1986), 175. See also Walsh, 472.

9. "[At the beginning of the twentieth century] An ordinary saint's feast . . . could obliterate the celebration of Sunday and usually did . . . There were a considerable number of votive Masses that could be celebrated on Sunday and the ferial days of Lent were usually overlaid

372. Ritual Masses are connected to the celebration of certain Sacraments or Sacramentals. They are prohibited on Sundays of Advent, Lent, and Easter, on solemnities, on the days within the Octave of Easter, on the Commemoration of All the Faithful Departed (All Souls' Day), on Ash Wednesday, and during Holy Week, taking due account of the norms given in the ritual books or in the Masses themselves.

373. Masses for Various Needs or Masses for Various Circumstances are used in cer-

372. Missæ rituales cum celebratione quorundam Sacramentorum vel Sacramentalium conectuntur. Prohibentur in dominicis Adventus, Quadragesimæ et Paschæ, in sollemnitatibus, in diebus infra octavam Paschæ, in Commemoratione omnium fidelium defunctorum et in feriis IV Cinerum et Hebdomadæ sanctæ, servatis insuper normis quæ in libris ritualibus vel in ipsis Missis exponuntur.

373. Missæ pro variis necessitatibus vel ad diversa assumuntur quibusdam in

---

Some of the longer descriptions and definitions of these types of Masses found in the parallel paragraph of *IGMR1975* have been moved to the individual paragraphs dealing with each type specifically, as will be discussed below.

372. "Ritual Masses" (*Missae rituales*) are defined more fully at the beginning of this paragraph, as those "connected to the celebration of certain Sacraments or Sacramentals" (*cum celebratione quorundam Sacramentorum vel Sacramentalium conectuntur*). Eucharistic celebrations for sacraments include: key moments during the Initiation of Adult Christians like the Election or Enrollment of Names; Baptism or Confirmation outside of the Easter Vigil; Holy Orders; and Marriage. Other ritual Masses include those during which viaticum is distributed, or vows are professed.[10]

MR2002 expands several of these earlier categories, and adds new ones.[11] For example, the scrutinies have been expanded to list specifically the first, second, and third scrutinies; Holy Orders now includes several options (e.g., one bishop, many bishops, one priest, many priests, priests and deacons together); and Religious Profession is subdivided into first vows, perpetual vows, and renewal of vows. New Masses include: the anointing of the sick, the blessing of abbots and abbesses, the institution of lectors and acolytes, and the dedication of churches and altars.

The paragraph continues with a list of seasons and feasts for which such Masses may not be celebrated; these are identical to those found in *IGMR1975* (no. 330), with the exception that GIRM2003 adds the proper title to All Souls' Day ("Commemoration of All the Faithful Departed").

373. The "Masses for Various Needs or Masses for Various Circumstances" (*Missae pro variis necessitatibus vel ad diversa*) are more fully defined in this

---

with votive Masses of the 'Holy Winding Sheet' and such like." J. D. Crichton, *Christian Celebration: The Mass* (London: Geoffrey Chapman, 1971), 107. See also Cabié, 183.

10. Some of these have proper prefaces assigned as well: for example, Christian Marriage (*MR2002*, no. 1024); and Religious Profession (*MR2002*, no. 1052).

11. *MR2002*, nos. 971–1067.

tain situations either as matters arise or at fixed times.

Days or periods of prayer for the fruits of the earth, prayer for human rights and equality, prayer for world justice and peace, and penitential observances outside Lent are to be observed in the dioceses of the United States of America at times to be designated by the diocesan Bishop.

In all the dioceses of the United States of America, January 22 (or January 23, when January 22 falls on a Sunday) shall be observed as a particular day of penance for violations to the dignity of the human person committed through acts of abortion, and of prayer for the full restoration of the legal guarantee of the right to life. The Mass "For Peace and Justice" (no. 22 of the "Masses for Various Needs") should be celebrated with violet vestments as an appropriate liturgical observance for this day.

rerum adiunctis, sive interdum sive statis temporibus occurrentibus. Ex his ab auctoritate competenti seligi possunt Missæ pro supplicationibus, quæ decursu anni a Conferentia Episcoporum statuentur.

---

paragraph, which greatly expands the rather simple directions for their use found in previous *IGMR*s.[12] In *MR1975*, these Mass formularies—which often included a complete set of orations and other times only the opening prayer[13]—are divided into four groups: "For the Church" (*Pro Sancta Ecclesia*), "For Civil Needs" (*Pro Rebus Publicis*), "For Various Public Needs" (*In Variis Circumstantiis Publicis*), and "For Particular Needs" (*Pro Quibusdam Necessitatibus Particularibus*).[14] In *MR2002*, these Masses are grouped into three sections: "For the Holy Church" (*Pro Sancta Ecclesia*), "For Public Needs" (*Pro Circumstantiis Publicis*), and "For Various Circumstances" (*Ad Diversa*).[15] The first group of Masses "For the Holy Church" has been expanded from sixteen to twenty, with the addition of three Masses for the celebration of a wedding anniversary (one year, twenty-

12. "Ritual Masses are prohibited on the Sundays of Advent, Lent, and the Easter season, on solemnities, on days within the octave of Easter, on All Souls, on Ash Wednesday, and during Holy Week. In addition, the norms in the ritual books or in the Masses themselves also apply" (*Prohibentur in dominicis Adventus, Quadragesimae et Paschae, in sollemnitatibus, in diebus infra octavam Paschae, in Commemoratione omnium fidelium defunctorum et in feriis IV Cinerum et Hebdomadae sanctae, servatis insuper normis quae in libris ritualibus vel in ipsis Missis exponuntur. IGMR1975*, no. 330).

13. Examples of the latter exist in the current Missal, e.g., texts "For Christian Unity" (*Pro Unitate Christianorum, MR2002*, nos. 1111–1115).

14. The headings in the earlier *MR1970* are identical, with one slight difference in wording in the third group: *In Diversis Circumstantiis Publicis*.

15. *MR2002*, nos. 1075–1153.

five years, and fifty years), and the transfer of two Masses ("For the Family" and "For Promoting Harmony") from the now-defunct fourth group.[16] The second new group, "For Public Needs," contains sixteen Mass formularies, combining all of the texts from the former second group ("For Civil Needs") and several from the former third group ("For Various Public Needs"). The new third group is composed of six Masses from this former third group, five from the former fourth group ("For Particular Needs"), and one new formulary "For Continence" (*Ad postulandam continentiam*).

The rubrics introducing this section in *MR2002* have also been expanded.[17] The first rubric is the same as that of *MR1975*, concerning the use of these Masses with or without a congregation. The second rubric notes days on which it is forbidden to use these Mass formularies (solemnities; Sundays of Advent, Lent, and Easter Sunday; days in the octave of Easter; All Souls' Day; Ash Wednesday; and Holy Week). The formularies in the first three parts of this section may be used either in Masses with a congregation or Masses without a congregation. The third rubric repeats, with slightly different wording, the third found in *MR1975* regarding their use in Ordinary Time, but adds a specific list of days when they cannot be used (i.e., solemnities, Sundays of Advent, Lent, and Easter, days in the octave of Easter, All Souls' Day, Ash Wednesday, and Holy Week). The new fourth rubric refers the reader to Appendix I, *Ad Ordinem Missae*,[18] for further information on the use of the Eucharistic Prayers for these Masses. The fifth and the sixth rubrics repeat the fourth and fifth directives in *MR1975* describing the change of grammatical forms (feminine for women from masculine for men, and single forms for plural forms, when necessary), and liturgical colors to be used (the color of the day or season, or the color violet for a Mass with a penitential theme).

These rubrics are in keeping with *General Norms for the Liturgical Year and the Calendar* (GNLYC, no. 1), which present a "hierarchy" of precedence in the liturgical week and the liturgical year that must be respected in its theological and pastoral integrity when the celebration of these Masses is considered. At the same time, GNLYC seems to implicitly admit the use of Masses for various needs or circumstances when it notes that "During the different seasons of the liturgical year, the Church, in accord with traditional discipline, carries out the formation of the faithful by means of devotional practices, both interior and exterior, instruction, and works of penance and mercy." [19]

16. As is the case with the marriage anniversary Masses, other Masses have been expanded by the addition of an anniversary Mass: one for the anniversary of a priest's ordination, and another for the twenty-fifth or fiftieth anniversary of religious profession.

17. *MR2002*, no. 1074.

18. *Quoad precem eucharisticam, quae cum formularies missarum pro variis necessitatibus adhiberi potest*, cf. *Appendix I ad Ordinem Missae*, 674.

19. No. 1, in DOL, no. 3767; cf. also nos. 46–47, in DOL, nos. 3811–3813.

374. In cases of serious need or pastoral advantage, at the direction of the diocesan Bishop or with his permission, an appropriate Mass may be celebrated on any day except solemnities, the Sundays of Advent, Lent, and Easter, days within the Octave of Easter, the Commemoration of All the Faithful Departed (All Souls' Day), Ash Wednesday, and Holy Week.

375. Votive Masses of the mysteries of the Lord or in honor of the Blessed Virgin

374. Occurrente aliqua graviore necessitate vel utilitate pastorali, Missa ipsi conveniens celebrari potest, de mandato vel licentia Episcopi diœcesani, omnibus diebus, exceptis sollemnitatibus, dominicis Adventus, Quadragesimæ et Paschæ, diebus infra octavam Paschæ, Commemoratione omnium fidelium defunctorum et feriis IV Cinerum et Hebdomadæ sanctæ.

375. Missæ votivæ de mysteriis Domini aut in honorem beatæ Mariæ Virginis vel

---

Some of the expansions in the third paragraph of this article in GIRM2003 were previously listed in the "Appendix to the General Instruction for the Dioceses of the United States of America" (1973, no. 331). Many of these stipulations have been moved into the text of GIRM2003 itself.

Similar to *IGMR1975* (no. 329b), *IGMR2002* indicates that these Masses "are used in certain situations either as matters arise or at fixed times" (*assumuntur quibusdam in rerum adiunctis, sive interdum sive statis temporibus occurrentibus*). GIRM2003 then lists certain "situations" for dioceses in the United States: 1) prayer for "the fruits of the earth"; 2) "for human rights and equality"; 3) "for world justice and peace"; and 4) "penitential observances outside Lent." The specific "times" for these are left to the decision of the diocesan bishop. One key "fixed time" for dioceses in the United States is January 22 (or 23, if that date is a Sunday) for an anti-abortion and right-to-life Mass, in "penance for violations to the dignity of the human person committed through acts of abortion, and . . . for the full restoration of the legal guarantee of the right to life." The Mass formulary "For Peace and Justice" is strongly suggested for this day, as is the use of violet vestments, since this is understood to be a "day of penance."[20]

374. While the choice of these Mass texts ordinarily is the prerogative of the priest-presider in dialogue with the local community (see Zimmerman, 406 and no. 352 above; also no. 376 below), this article extends permission to the diocesan bishop for deciding if and when one of these Masses may be celebrated in or throughout the diocese "in cases of serious need or pastoral advantage" (*occurrente aliqua graviore necessitate vel utilitate pastorali*). Such may occur even on Sundays, with the exception of the certain seasons and feast days that were also noted in no. 372 above.

375. This article considers the topic of "Votive Masses" (*Missae votivae*) of the Lord, of the Virgin Mary, of the Angels, "or of any given Saint or of all the Saints" (*vel cuiusdam Sancti vel omnium Sanctorum*). The USCCB defines a votive

20. The Mass texts are to be found in *MR2002*, no. 30 (1131): *Pro Pace et Iustitia Servanda*.

Mary or of the Angels or of any given Saint or of all the Saints may be said for the sake of the faithful's devotion on weekdays in Ordinary Time, even if an optional memorial occurs. It is not, however, allowed to celebrate as Votive Masses, those that refer to mysteries related to events in the life of the Lord or of the Blessed Virgin Mary, with the exception of the Mass of the Immaculate Conception, since their celebration is an integral part of the unfolding of the liturgical year.

Angelorum vel cuiusdam Sancti vel omnium Sanctorum, pro fidelium pietate dici possunt in feriis per annum, etiamsi occurrit memoria ad libitum. Celebrari tamen nequeunt, tamquam votivæ, Missæ quæ referuntur ad mysteria vitæ Domini vel beatæ Mariæ Virginis, excepta Missa eiusdem Immaculatæ Conceptionis, quia eorum celebratio cohæret cum anni liturgici cursu.

Mass as one that "celebrates a mystery of the Lord or a saint to which the faithful may have a special devotion . . . . [e.g.,] Masses in honor of the Trinity, the Triumph of the Cross, the Eucharist, the Sacred Heart, the Precious Blood, the Holy Name, the Holy Spirit, [and] the Apostles."[21]

As in *IGMR1975*, no. 329c, these Masses are provided "for the sake of the faithful's devotion" (*pro fidelium pietate dicti*). However, *IGMR2002* newly specifies their general restriction to "weekdays in Ordinary Time, even if an optional memorial occurs" (*in feriis per annum, etiamsi occurrit memoria ad libitum*). To set these comments in historical context, by the late eighth century various days of the week had been assigned certain Mass formularies, or sets of prayers, to express certain themes or "intentions." On Tuesdays, for example, the presider could choose between a votive mass *ad postulanda Angelica suffragia* (to request Angelic favor/support), or *pro tentationibus cogitationum* (for assistance with "temptations of/in thoughts").[22] For Saturday, however, both Mass formularies were composed for the commemoration of the BVM.[23]

Mass formularies in commemoration of the saints also have an ancient history. From the sixth through the sixteenth centuries, the number of saints commemorated in what became the official Roman calendar grew to 220; after the Council of Trent (1545–63), that number was reduced to 130. However, by the middle of the twentieth century, the number had again increased, this time to some 270; the reform of the calendar in 1969 mandated by the Second Vatican Council (1962–65) trimmed this number by roughly 100. In addition, 95 of these memorials or commemorations were listed as "optional," opening up the possibility of

21. US Conference of Catholic Bishops, "Frequently Asked Questions." http://www.nccbuscc.org/nab/faq.htm, (accessed 26 December 2006).

22. A Mass formulary for assistance "against temptations of the flesh" (*contra tentationes carnis*) was one of the two assigned to Thursday. See Ignazio M. Calabuig, "The Liturgical Cult of Mary in the East and West," in Anscar Chupungco, ed., *Handbook for Liturgical Studies*, Vol. 5: *Liturgical Time and Space* (Collegeville, MN: The Liturgical Press, 2000), 277.

23. Ibid., 277–279.

376. On obligatory memorials, on the weekdays of Advent up to and including December 16, of the Christmas Season from January 2, and of the Easter Season after the Octave of Easter, Masses for Various Needs, Masses for Various Circumstances, and Votive Masses are as such forbidden. If, however, required by some real need or pastoral advantage, according to the judgment of the rector of the church or the priest celebrant himself, a Mass corresponding to such a need or advantage may be used in a celebration with a congregation.

376. In diebus quibus occurrit memoria obligatoria aut feria Adventus usque ad diem 16 decembris inclusive, temporis Nativitatis a die 2 ianuarii, et temporis paschalis post octavam Paschatis, Missæ pro variis necessitatibus, ad diversa et votivæ per se prohibentur. Si autem aliqua vera necessitas vel utilitas pastoralis id postulet, in celebratione cum populo adhiberi potest Missa huic necessitati vel utilitati respondens, de iudicio rectoris ecclesiæ vel ipsius sacerdotis celebrantis.

---

more localized commemorations ("particular calendars"), appropriate to the time and the location.[24] *MR2002* lists 19 Votive Masses; all 15 of the Masses contained in *MR1970*, plus four more (*De Dei misericordia, De D.N. Iesu Christo summo et aeterno sacerdote, De S. Ioanne Baptista*, and a Mass formulary to commemorate both Saints Peter and Paul together, *De Ss. Petro et Paulo, apostolis*).[25] In addition, the single Mass of the Blessed Virgin Mary (BVM) has been expanded by the addition of three more Masses, in honor of the Blessed Virgin Mary as Mother of the Church and as Queen of the Angels, and of the holy name of Mary.

This article continues with a further clarification, forbidding the celebration of votive Masses "that refer to the mysteries related to events in the life of the Lord or the Blessed Virgin Mary, with the exception of the Mass of the Immaculate Conception, since their celebration is an integral part of the unfolding of the liturgical year" (*quae referuntur ad mysteria vitae Domini vel Beatae Mariae Virginis, excepta Missa eiusdem Immaculatae Conceptionis, quia eorum celebratio cohaeret cum anni liturgici cursu*). This clarification seems to be concerned with halting potential abuses of votive Masses whose celebration could violate the theological progression and structure of the liturgical year.

376. Similar to *IGMR1975* (no. 333), this article lists categories of weekdays on which Masses for various needs and circumstances as well as votive Masses "are as such forbidden" (*pro se prohibentur*). First, they may not be used on any weekday that is assigned an obligatory memorial. Next, they are prohibited on weekdays during "Advent up to and including December 16; the Christmas season from January 2; and the Easter season after the octave of Easter" (*Adventus usque ad diem 16 decembris inclusive, temporis Nativitatis a die 2 ianuarii, et*

24. Summarized from Philippe Rouillard, "The Cult of the Saints in the East and the West," in Aimé-Georges Martimort, ed., *The Church at Prayer,* Vol. IV: *Liturgical Time and Prayer,* trans. Matthew O'Connell (Collegeville, MN: The Liturgical Press, 1986), 306–309. See also GNCLY, nos. 49–55, in DOL, nos. 3815–3821.

25. *MR2002*, nos. 1157–1187.

377. On weekdays in Ordinary Time when there is an optional memorial or the Office is of the weekday, it is permissible to use any Mass or oration for various circumstances, though not from the Ritual Masses.

377. In feriis per annum in quibus occurrunt memoriæ ad libitum vel fit Officium de feria, licet celebrare quamlibet Missam vel adhibere quamlibet orationem ad diversa, exceptis tamen Missis ritualibus.

---

temporis paschalis post octavam Paschatis).[26] The reasons are the same as those underlying the repetition of prohibited times and days in earlier articles of the chapter (e.g., no. 372 above).

The text notes, however, that this is not an absolute prohibition. As in no. 374 above, such Masses may be celebrated even during these times "if . . . required by some real need or pastoral advantage" (*Si . . . aliqua vera necessitas vel utilitas pastoralis*). The final decision rests with "the rector of the church or the priest celebrant himself" (*de iudicio rectoris ecclesiae vel ipsius sacerdotis celebrantis*). Since this permission pertains to eucharistic celebrations "with a congregation" (*in celebratione cum populo*), however, the choice of these or other Mass texts are not to be dictated by the personal instincts of the priest-presider. Rather, it is essential to attend to the larger pastoral good and the needs of the worshiping community in making such decisions (see Zimmerman, 406 and no. 352 above).

It could appear that the exceptions granted in this article for celebrating these Masses seem to mute if not cancel out the prohibitions regarding when these texts are not to be used. On the other hand, the prohibition serves to underscore the need to respect the cycle of established feasts and seasons, while the exceptions emphasize the need for pastoral care and attention to the authentic needs of the faithful in making liturgical choices. Both of these values need to be kept in balance, while recalling the medieval axiom that sacraments are for people, and not the other way around (see Seasoltz, 44 above).

Very little has been added to this paragraph, which is substantially that found in previous *IGMR*s. The minor changes that do occur are clarifications, e.g., a remark on the status of the date December 16 ("including," *inclusive*); the addition of Masses *ad diversa* in the list of prohibited Mass formularies; and the use of the singular, "a Mass corresponding to such a need or advantage" (*Missa huic necessitate vel utilitati respondens*) instead of the plural "the Masses" (*Missae, IGMR1975*, no. 333).

377. Similar to *IGMR1975* (no. 344), this article offers the presider the option to use "any Mass or oration for various circumstances" (*quamlibet Missam vel adhibere quamlibet orationem ad diversa*), exclusive of those for Ritual Masses, on most weekdays in Ordinary Time, that is, on weekdays with only an "optional memorial" (*memoriae ad libitum*) or with no other commemoration assigned.

26. Cf. rubrics in *MR2002*, no. 1156.

378. It is especially recommended to celebrate the commemoration of the Blessed Virgin Mary on Saturday, because it is to the Mother of the Redeemer in the Liturgy of the Church that in the first place and before all the Saints veneration is given.[145]

378. Peculiari modo, memoria sanctæ Mariæ in sabbato commendatur, quia Redemptoris Matri in Liturgia Ecclesiæ imprimis et præ omnibus Sanctis veneratio tribuitur.[145]

---

378. The final paragraph in this section is new, and highlights a fresh reappropriation of the role of the Blessed Virgin Mary in the liturgy. Masses in "commemoration" of the BVM are "especially recommended . . . on Saturday" (*peculiari modo . . . in sabbato commendatur*) because of her unique role in salvation history and special status within the communion of saints. The tradition of marking Saturday as a day dedicated to the commemoration of the BVM is an ancient one (cf. no. 375 above), dating back to the era of Frankish augmentation of the Roman papal sacramentary (the *Hadrianum*) in the late eighth century.[27]

The footnote added here in *IGMR2002* refers first to *Lumen Gentium* (*LG*) which spoke of "both the role of the Blessed Virgin in the mystery of the Incarnate Word and in the mystical body, and the duties of the redeemed towards the Mother of God, who is mother of Christ and mother of humanity, and especially of those who believe" (no. 54; also cf. *OLM1981-Pr,* no. 18). Clearly, the liturgical veneration of the BVM is to be considered as one among the "duties" mentioned in *LG*. A second footnoted source is *Marialis cultus*. This 1974 apostolic exhortation by Paul VI (d. 1978) first speaks about the place of Mary in the General Roman Calendar and individual calendars of local Churches. One example of such a "local" feast is the memorial of Our Lady of Guadalupe (December 12), patroness of the Americas as well as of several dioceses in the United States. *Marialis cultus* also endorses "frequent commemorations of the Blessed Virgin . . . through the use of the Saturday Masses of our Lady." The text goes on to note that "This is an ancient and simple commemoration and one that is made very adaptable and varied by the flexibility of the modern Calendar and the number of formulas provided by the Missal."[28]

In *MR2002*, texts for these Marian Masses are found under the Common of the Blessed Virgin Mary (*Commune Beatae Mariae Virginis*)[29] rather than in the section on votive Masses. They are divided into four sections: "Ordinary Time" (*Tempore "per annum"*); Advent (*Tempore Adventus*); Christmas (*Tempore Nativitatis*); and Easter (*Tempore Paschali*).[30] By contrast, in *MR1975*, there are three

27. See Calabuig, 277–279.

28. *Marialis cultus*, no. 9, in DOL, no. 3907.

29. *MR2002*, nos. 897–908.

30. *MR2002*: Ordinary Time, nos. 897–905; Advent, nos. 905–906; Christmas Season, nos. 906–907; Easter Season, no. 908.

general Masses listed first, and then one each for Advent, the Christmas season, and the Easter season, as well as a final formulary entitled: "Other Prayers for Masses of the Blessed Virgin Mary" (*Aliae Orationes in Missis de B. Maria Virgine*).[31] The number of Marian Votive Masses found in *MR1975* was greatly expanded by the publication of a *Collectio Missarum de Beata Maria Virgine* (1987). An English version for interim use was offered in 1990, and finalized in 1992 with the publication of this separate set of two books containing additional votive Masses in honor of the BVM for use in the United States: the *Collection of Masses of the Blessed Virgin Mary*.[32] Here, the Mass formularies are grouped according to liturgical season: three for Advent, six for the Christmas Season, five for Lent, four for the Easter Season, and three separate sections of Masses for use during Ordinary Time (a total of twenty-eight). In all, forty-six Mass formularies in honor of the BVM can be found in this collection. It is not clear whether a similar collection will be offered as a supplement to *MR2002*.

Conclusion

This section of *IGMR2002* on "Masses and Prayers for Various Circumstances" seems generally concerned both with addressing pressing pastoral concerns as well as clarifying practices and procedures in light of the past thirty years of liturgical experience. In cases where the legal prescription and urgent pastoral need (or even "pastoral advantage") appear to be in tension, it is normally the pastoral need that takes precedence (cf. nos. 374 and 376). When read in the light of the contents of both *IGMR2002* and *MR2002*, the role of these Masses has been notably refocused to reflect the dynamics of local pastoral practice and need. This can be clearly seen in the elaboration of occasions for Ritual Masses, the increase in the number of "special occasions" marked by the celebration of the Eucharist (e.g., anniversaries of various kinds), and the renewed emphasis on liturgical devotion to Mary and the saints as manifested by individual groups or parish communities.

Masses for the Dead

Seven paragraphs make up this short section of Chapter VIII. Similarities between both *IGMR2002* and GIRM2003 and their predecessors far outnumber any differences; for all intents and purposes they are identical. Pastoral implementation of *IGMR2002* must place this section in the larger theological context of the paschal character of Christian death, the principal mark of all liturgical expression at death following Vatican II. This was the intention of the original

31. *MR1975*, nos. 670–677. The introductory rubric clearly states that these are to be used both for Saturday commemorations, as well as votive masses: "*Hae Missae adhibentur etiam pro celebranda memoria sanctae Mariae in sabbato, et in missis votivis de beata Maria Virgine.*"

32. *Collection of Masses of the Blessed Virgin Mary. Volume I: Sacramentary, Volume II: Lectionary* (Collegeville, MN: The Liturgical Press, 1992).

framers of *IGMR1970*.[33] Yet, from its inception the *IGMR*s on Masses for the dead have preserved only a partial expression of this fuller paschal context. In this regard, given its intention to correct and update the Roman Missal for today's Church, *IGMR2002* misses a unique opportunity. Although familiar to current pastoral practice, the fuller context of the magisterium is worth noting in view of future application of the *IGMR2002* and its North American editions.

CEC summarizes, "The Christian meaning of death is revealed in the light of the Paschal mystery of the death and resurrection of Christ in whom resides our only hope" (no. 1680). Nowhere is the full Catholic teaching on Masses and suffrages for the dead more clearly expressed than in the reformed funeral liturgy, recommended by the *SC*[34] and embodied in the opening paragraphs of the 1969 *Ordo exsequiarum* (*OrEx*)—still the *editio typica* for the vernacular editions, such as the *Order of Christian Funerals* (OCF) in North America. There we see, first of all, the ancient and renewed tradition: "At the funerals of its children the Church confidently celebrates Christ's Paschal Mystery. Its intention is that those who by Baptism were made one with the dead and risen Christ with him may pass from death to life" (OCF, no. 1). At the same time concern for the interim lot of the separated soul remains part of the tradition: "In soul they are to be cleansed and taken up into heaven with the saints and elect; in body they await the blessed hope of Christ's coming and the resurrection of the dead" (OCF, no. 1). Finally, in this theologically balanced context reflecting Catholic tradition, *OE* makes a clear link with the paschal mystery when noting, "The Church, therefore, offers the eucharistic sacrifice of Christ's Passover for the dead . . ." (OCF, no. 1). The remaining text—"and pours forth prayers and petitions for them. Because of the communion of all Christ's members with each other, all of this brings spiritual aid to the dead and the consolation of hope to the living" (OCF, no. 1)[35]—expresses clearly the classic understanding of the interaction among the living and the dead in the communion of saints.

Just prior to the promulgation of *IGMR2002*, the *Directory on Popular Piety and the Liturgy* (DPPL) developed even more fully this larger articulation of Church teaching on Mass and suffrages for the dead.[36] To ensure that popular piety toward death and the dead is inspired by Christian faith, DPPL sets out

33. Annibale Bugnini, *The Reform of the Liturgy 1948–1975* (Collegeville, MN: The Liturgical Press, 1990), 401.

34. "Funeral rites should express more clearly the paschal character of Christian death" (*SC*, no. 81).

35. The English text here follows the ICEL translation of *OrdEx* as emended by the Congregation for the Sacraments and Divine Worship, 12 September 1983. The parallel in *IGMR2002*, no. 379) is more literal and follows the earlier ICEL translation of the *Rite of Funerals* (1970).

36. Nos. 248–260. For a thorough and theologically well-documented review of this document see also Peter Phan, "Popular Religion, The Liturgy, and the Cult of the Dead," *East Asian Pastoral Review* 42 (2005). Accessed online at http://eapi.admu.edu.ph/eapr005/peter%20phan.htm. His critical evaluation of the theology of Mass and other suffrages offered

II. Masses for the Dead

379. The Church offers the Eucharistic Sacrifice of Christ's Passover for the dead so that, since all the members of Christ's body are in communion with each other, the petition for spiritual help on behalf of some may bring comforting hope to others.

II. De Missis Defunctorum

379. Sacrificium eucharisticum Paschatis Christi pro defunctis offert Ecclesia ut, inter se communicantibus omnibus Christi membris, quæ aliis impetrent spiritualem opem, aliis afferant spei solacium.

---

the principles to be followed. It leaves no doubt that the paschal mystery is the hub around which all the rest revolves.[37] This "paschal meaning of Christian death" is the faith of the Church and thus the cornerstone of the following commentary.

379. At first reading, the opening words of this article appear to present the rationale for celebrating Masses for the dead principally as the paschal character of Christian death. Yet, when compared to *OrdEx*, no. 1 (its apparent source text, cf. 436 above), this partial segment of the fuller text with a significant omission provides a more narrow statement about why we celebrate Mass for the dead: a communion of mutual benefit in suffrage and consolation. Omitted is any mention of the deceased's participation in the paschal mystery through his or her Baptism and sacramental life. Finally, by omitting the phrase of the *OrdEx* text, "and offers prayers and petitions for them," *IGMR2002* misses an opportunity of keeping the celebration of Mass for the dead in its early Christian context of all prayer for the dead.

While this article and its predecessors are identical in the Latin, minor but noteworthy differences mark the English translations. By changing from "Christ's paschal sacrifice" (GIRM1970, no. 335) to "*Eucharistic* Sacrifice of Christ's Passover," GIRM2003 clearly intends to follow a more literal reading of *IGMR2002*'s *Sacrificium eucharisticum Paschatis Christi*. However, to translate *omnibus Christi membris* as "all the members of Christ's *body*"—while accurate and perhaps colloquially familiar—is not consistent with the principle

---

on behalf of the dead in the *Directory* clarifies the elements conspicuously missing in *IGMR2002*.

37. "It is always necessary to ensure that popular piety is inspired by the principles of the Christian faith. Thus, they should be made aware of the paschal meaning of the death undergone by those who have received Baptism and who have been incorporated into the mystery of the death and resurrection of Christ (cf. Rom 6:3-10); the immortality of the soul (cf. Luke 23:43); the communion of Saints, through which 'union with those who are still on their pilgrim journey with the faithful who repose in Christ is not in the least broken, but strengthened by a communion of spiritual goods, as constantly taught by the Church' (footnote reference to *LG*, no. 49): 'our prayer for them is capable not only of helping them, but also of making their intercession for us effective' (footnote reference to *CEC*, no. 958); the resurrection of the body; the glorious coming of Christ, who will 'judge the living and the dead' (footnote reference to Denzinger, no. 150 and the *Symbolum Nicaeno-Constantinopolitanum* of the *Ordo Missae*); the reward given to each according to his deeds; life eternal."

380. Among the Masses for the Dead, the Funeral Mass holds first place. It may be celebrated on any day except for solemnities that are holy days of obligation, Holy Thursday, the Easter Triduum, and the Sundays of Advent, Lent, and Easter, with due regard also for all the other requirements of the norm of the law.[146]

380. Inter Missas defunctorum primum locum tenet Missa exsequialis, quæ celebrari potest omnibus diebus, exceptis sollemnitatibus de præcepto, feria V Hebdomadæ sanctæ, Triduo paschali et dominicis Adventus, Quadragesimæ et Paschæ, servatis insuper omnibus servandis ad normam iuris.[146]

---

of translating literally and does not improve upon the theologically closer "all Christ's members" of the earlier GIRMs (e.g., GIRM1970, no. 335) and OCF (no. 1). Finally, translating the conjunctive introduction to the ablative clause *inter se communicantibus omnibus Christi membris* with "since" in GIRM2003 instead of "on the basis of" (GIRM1975, no. 335) better accentuates the mutual effectiveness of the relationship between members of the communion of saints, a traditional marker of the consolation of the faith among Catholics.

380. *IGMR2002* reiterates here the primacy of place held by the actual funeral Mass among Masses for the dead. Preserving this emphasis is especially important today in North America where substituting a so-called memorial Mass without either body or cremated remains present is becoming common practice. The funeral Mass should be the centerpiece of Catholic funeral rites, the uniquely Christian ritual of leave-taking. By bringing the death of a member of the faithful into the eucharistic celebration of the paschal sacrifice, especially with the body or cremated remains present, the *lex orandi* of the Church professes most fully the *lex credendi* that in Christ risen life rather than death has the last word. Yet, even when circumstances prevent gathering for the funeral Mass in the presence of the mortal remains of the deceased—for example, when the person has been lost at sea or when interment has preceded the Mass—the Mass celebrated is still the funeral Mass and deserves its proper emphasis (see no. 384 below).

Finally, on those Sundays, holy days, and solemnities when only the Mass of the day itself is permitted, the funeral liturgy may take place with the celebration of the Liturgy of the Word and Final Commendation. Since the prohibition to celebrate a funeral Mass on these days flows from the nature of the Sunday or solemnity (e.g., a Sunday in Advent), those preparing the funeral are to preserve the liturgical nature of the day and allow its own special character to inform the funeral Liturgy of the Word. The principles in the Lectionary guiding the choice of readings for such occasions (*OLM1981-Pr*, nos. 85–88) offer direction for determining whether and where to substitute one of the orations from the options provided for funeral Masses in the Roman Missal. Any such substitution requires both liturgical sensitivity and pastoral awareness that "the spiritual welfare of the participants must be the primary consideration" (*OLM1981-Pr*, no. 88).

381. A Mass for the Dead may be celebrated on receiving the news of a death,

381. Missa defunctorum post acceptum mortis nuntium, vel in ultima sepultura

---

The primary difference between *IGMR2002* and its predecessors in this article is the addition of the phrase, "with due regard also for all the other requirements of the norm of the law" (*servatis insuper omnibus servandis ad normam iuris*). This is a significant addition for it clarifies the relationship of *IGMR2002* to existing norms without having to be exhaustive itself and ensures that it will remain current in the event of new legislation. The associated footnote (n. 146) refers to both the 1983 Code of Canon Law (*CIC1983*) and the *editio typica* of *OrdEx*. *CIC1983* codifies ecclesiastical legislation on both the celebration of funeral liturgy and laws regarding to whom funeral rites are to be granted or denied (cc. 1176–1185). *OE* embodies normative liturgical law that, in accord with *CIC1983* (c. 2), remains in force except for norms that are contrary to the revised canons. To address those cases, the Congregation for Divine Worship and the Discipline of the Sacraments (then Congregation for the Sacraments and Divine Worship) published the required emendations in 1983.[38] With regard to Masses for the dead the emendations concern only nos. 14 and 15 of *OrdEx*.

OrdEx, no. 14, reflects the substantial change to include catechumens among those for whom funeral rites are to be celebrated and together with catechumens "children whose baptism was intended by their parents but who died before being baptized" and "baptized members of another Church or non-Catholic Ecclesial Community" under specified circumstances. *MR1970*, following closely upon the *OrdEx*, included a funeral Mass for children who died before baptism; *MR2002* moved this Mass—together with its Mass for baptized children—from its place as the last of the Masses for the dead forward to a position as a proper funeral Mass (Section I, F). This move gives both of these funeral Masses for children more appropriate pride of place and makes them pastorally more accessible.

OrdEx, no. 15, on funeral rites for those who have chosen cremation, simply updates the language in accord with *CIC1983*, dropping the now-redundant reference to the May 1963 Instruction lifting the prior prohibition on cremation.[39]

38. *Emendations in the Liturgical Books following upon the new Code of Canon Law* (Washington, DC: ICEL, 1984).

39. Although that legislation is no longer required in the text of the *OE* or pertinent to *IGMR2002* as such, including reference to it here is historically appropriate. The Instruction from the Holy Office (8 May 1963) was approved by the Holy Father on 5 July 1963 and transmitted to local ordinaries *in forma reservata*. Because of widespread and sometimes misleading publicity, the Holy See decided to make the Instruction public. It appeared first in Italian (*L'Osservatore Romano*, 30 September 1964), and the official Latin text appeared in the *AAS* 56 (1964): 822–823.

for the final burial, or the first anniversary, even on days within the Octave of Christmas, on obligatory memorials, and on weekdays, except for Ash Wednesday or weekdays during Holy Week.

Other Masses for the Dead, that is, "daily" Masses, may be celebrated on weekdays in Ordinary Time on which optional memorials occur or when the Office is of the weekday, provided such Masses are actually applied for the dead.

defuncti, vel in primo anniversario die, celebrari potest etiam diebus infra octavam Nativitatis, diebus quibus occurrit memoria obligatoria aut feria quæ non sit IV Cinerum aut Hebdomadæ sanctæ.

Aliæ Missæ defunctorum, seu Missæ « cotidianæ » celebrari possunt in feriis per annum, in quibus occurrunt memoriæ ad libitum vel fit Officium de feria, dummodo pro defunctis revera applicentur.

---

381. As an *editio typica* for the universal Latin Church, *IGMR2002*, like its predecessors, includes customs and practices that are not necessarily common in all regions. While the practice of celebrating a Mass for the dead on receiving the news of a death is not widespread in North America, it is customary in other parts of the world. With the growing cultural diversity in North America, familiarity with such usages can open new pastoral opportunities for multicultural communities. Further, the reference since *IGMR1970* to "final burial" (*ultima sepultura,* no. 337) mostly applies in cultures where a second burial with appropriate rites follows a first interment, which takes place at the time of death. In North America, a Mass for the dead at the time of a "final burial" may be celebrated, for example, when a body has been exhumed and reburied in its final resting place or when cremated remains have been moved from one resting place to another one.

What is most important in this article for Roman Catholic liturgical practice in North America is an appreciation for the breadth with which *IGMR2002* authorizes the celebration of Masses for the Dead. Although not widely customary, a Mass for the dead, (e.g. the funeral Mass or Mass on the first anniversary of a death), may appropriately be celebrated—sometimes even necessarily celebrated, given the scarcity of ordained presbyters or other limiting circumstances—on a Sunday. On the other hand, it is not clear why the first anniversary of a death here receives priority over later anniversaries, especially in light of contemporary research on the nature and duration of normal bereavement beyond first or second anniversaries of death. Yet, not only does *IGMR2002* repeat this preference of its predecessors (e.g., *IGMR1970*, no. 337), but *MR2002* itself has added the specification in its introduction to the section on anniversary Masses.[40]

40. *In Anniversario: Haec Missa celebrari potest in primo anniversario die . . . . In aliis anniversaries, celebrari potest in feriis "per annum"* ("This Mass may be celebrated on the day of the first anniversary . . . On other anniversaries, it may be celebrated on weekdays throughout the year"), *MR2002*, no. 1199.

382. At the Funeral Mass there should, as a rule, be a short homily, but never a eulogy of any kind.

382. In Missis exsequialibus habeatur de more brevis homilia, secluso tamen quovis genere laudationis funebris.

The second part of this article repeats *IGMR1975* (no. 337) with very minor adjustments. Significant here since *IGMR1970* is the emphasis that daily Masses for the dead are understood to be "actually applied for the dead" (*pro defunctis revera applicentur*). While no longer an issue in North America, this paragraph clarifies that Masses for the dead are indeed to be celebrated for specific deceased persons and prohibits the daily "black" Mass, once so familiar before Vatican II. At the same time, this is one of those places in *IGMR2002* where the language of applying the (fruits of the) Mass (see no. 89 above) implies an earlier theology of efficacious intercession for the remission of temporal punishment due sin. It is worth noting the same emphasis stated in no. 355 above, albeit in language more reflective of the contemporary *magisterium*, that daily Masses for the dead are to be selected "in moderation, since every Mass is offered for both the living and the dead, and there is a commemoration of the dead in the Eucharistic Prayer" (*moderate . . . quaelibet enim Missa tam pro vivis quam pro defunctis offertur, et in Prece eucharistica memoria defunctorum habetur*).

382. This paragraph on the homily both reflects and challenges pastoral practice at funeral Masses. The simple exhortation of *OrdEx*, "A brief homily should be given after the gospel, but without any kind of funeral eulogy" (no. 41), has opened the door to much discussion and not a few controversies. Nevertheless, it can now be taken for granted that those planning funeral Masses, and often other Masses for the dead with a congregation as well, will prepare what they believe to be a "homily." Yet, commentators since *OrdEx* and *IGMR* first appeared have lamented the inadequate quality of funeral homilies and the lingering tendency to preach a eulogy instead. The best directive in this regard is still that appended to the United States 1970 edition of the *Rite of Funerals*: "The homily may properly include an expression of praise and gratitude to God for [his] gifts, particularly the gift of a Christian life, to the deceased person. The homily should relate Christian death to the paschal mystery of the Lord's victorious death and resurrection and to the hope of eternal life" (no. 41). The present rendering of this directive in OCF elaborates effectively to note how, "attentive to the grief of those present, the homilist should dwell on God's compassionate love. . ." (no. 27), and further help the participants understand that the mysteries of God's love and of Jesus' paschal mystery, present in the life and death of the deceased, are active in their own lives as well. "Through the homily members of the family and community should receive consolation and strength to face the death of one of their members with a hope nourished by the saving word of God" (no. 25).

383. The faithful, and especially the family of the deceased, should be urged to participate in the Eucharistic Sacrifice offered for the deceased person also by receiving Holy Communion.

383. Incitentur fideles, præsertim e familia defuncti, ut etiam per sacram Communionem sacrificium eucharisticum pro defuncto oblatum participent.

The more participants understand that the funeral liturgy is first of all about God and God's saving word and the homily is a "living commentary on the word" as established in *SC*, nos. 7, 33, and 52, and articulated in no. 29 above, the less satisfied they are with a eulogy in lieu of a homily.

In addressing the final commendation, OCF states, "A member or a friend of the family may speak in remembrance of the deceased before the final commendation begins" (no. 170). In contemporary North America the Roman Catholic funeral Mass for the deceased, as centerpiece of a larger set of funeral rites, is becoming more and more countercultural. Many would prefer a simple, efficient, final disposition of the deceased followed by an equally simple "Memorial" Mass. The directive that the homily not be a eulogy is all the more difficult to achieve when the cultural trend is turning the entire funeral event into a public demonstration of "celebrating the life" of the deceased.

Finally, in this paragraph *IGMR2002* omits a second sentence found in its predecessors: "The homily is also recommended at other Masses for the dead celebrated with a congregation" (*Homilia etiam in ceteris Missis defunctorum cum populo suadetur, IGMR1970*, no. 338). Given the pride of place of the homily in *IGMR2002* (cf. nos. 65–66 above), omitting this recommendation does not imply omitting the homily in those other Masses. Rather it fits well with the intention of the framers of *IGMR2002* to simplify this Instruction where possible.

383. This paragraph reminds us of the importance of full, active, and conscious participation in the funeral Mass. While *IGMR2002* encourages such participation in Roman Catholic constituencies where it appears to be lacking, in North America it is rather the success of full, active, and conscious participation that has caused a greater concern, namely intercommunion. Open sacramental sharing with Protestant Christians even in the pastorally sensitive situation of funeral liturgy remains prohibited by both *CIC1983* (c. 844) and the 1993 revised Ecumenical Directory. Nevertheless, in the early years of this century several high-profile exceptions to the usual limits governing intercommunion at funeral Mass as well as the ongoing debate about sacramental sharing at the wedding of couples of mixed religion are positive signs of a greater openness to further exceptions to official ecumenical policy.[41]

41. Two exceptions occurred at the funeral of Pope John Paul II (8 April 2005), when Taizé's founder Brother Roger Schutz received communion from then Cardinal Ratzinger, and at Schutz' own funeral (23 August 2005) when Cardinal Walter Kasper, President of the Pontifical Council for the Promotion of Christian Unity, presiding at the concelebrated Funeral Mass, distributed Holy Communion according to the strict ecumenical policy of Taizé. In this regard,

384. If the Funeral Mass is directly joined to the burial rite, once the prayer after Communion has been said and omitting the concluding rite, the rite of final commendation or farewell takes place. This rite is celebrated only if the body is present.

385. In the arranging and choosing of the variable parts of the Mass for the Dead, especially the Funeral Mass (e.g., orations, readings, Prayer of the Faithful), pastoral considerations bearing upon the deceased, the family, and those attending should rightly be taken into account.

384. Si Missa exsequialis directo conectitur cum ritu exsequiarum, dicta oratione post Communionem, et omisso ritu conclusionis, fit ritus ultimæ commendationis seu valedictionis; qui ritus nonnisi præsente cadavere celebratur.

385. In ordinandis ac seligendis iis partibus Missæ pro defunctis, præsertim Missæ exsequialis, quæ variari possunt (ex. gr. orationibus, lectionibus, oratione universali), præ oculis habeantur, ut par est, rationes pastorales, quoad defunctum, eius familiam, et astantes.

---

384. This article addresses the situation when a funeral Mass is joined to the burial rite. Since "The rite of final commendation and farewell is to be held only in the funeral celebration itself, that is, with the body present" (*OrdEx,* no. 10), this means that the once-familiar empty catafalque has been relegated to its place in history. Approved adaptations in North America permit the celebration of the final commendation service without catafalque even when the body or cremated remains are not able to be present. When the rite of final commendation does not follow immediately upon the funeral Mass (e.g., to be celebrated at the place of committal), the Mass concludes in the ordinary manner with final blessing and dismissal.

385. This paragraph on arranging and choosing of variable parts of Masses for the dead, apart from minor editorial adjustments, follows earlier *IGMRs* in preserving the pastoral thrust of *SC* and *OrdEx*. As the pastoral principles are worked out in the *Missae defunctorum* themselves, significant differences between *MR2002* and earlier postconciliar editions as well as the *OrdEx* become apparent. Bugnini wrote of the conscious decision of the framers of *OrdEx* (and by extension of *IGMR1970*) to be holistic in their choice of prayers, "namely, that our thoughts must be focused not exclusively on the 'souls' of the deceased but on the deceased as total human beings, and therefore on the body that is

---

Cardinal Kasper's intervention at the 2005 Synod of Bishops on the inappropriateness of the term "intercommunion" throws broader light on the entire question: "It should be avoided. Since this is not an 'inter' communion, that is a 'between' two communions (two Communities), rather a communion in the communion of the one body of Christ, which is the Church" (XI Ordinary General Assembly of the Synod of Bishops 2–23 October 2005). For details on "Sacramental Sharing with Other Christians," see John M. Huels, *More Disputed Questions in the Liturgy* (Chicago: Liturgy Training Publications, 1996), 113–127; for a recommendation to include the funeral Mass among exceptions when intercommunion might be permitted according to *CIC1983*, c. 844, see H. Richard Rutherford, *Death of a Christian* (Collegeville, MN: The Liturgical Press, 1990), 245–247; 291–292.

Pastors should, moreover, take into special account those who are present at a liturgical celebration or who hear the Gospel on the occasion of the funeral and who may be non-Catholics or Catholics who never or rarely participate in the Eucharist or who seem even to have lost the faith. For priests are ministers of Christ's Gospel for all.

Specialem insuper rationem habeant pastores de iis qui, per occasionem exsequiarum, liturgicis celebrationibus adsunt vel Evangelium audiunt, sive sunt acatholici sive catholici qui Eucharistiam numquam vel vix umquam participant, vel fidem etiam amisisse videntur: sunt enim sacerdotes ministri Evangelii Christi pro omnibus.

---

called to share in the resurrection of Christ."[42] After nearly four decades of developing a language of prayer that reflects a more holistic anthropology of praying for and offering Mass for the person who had died, *MR2002* has begun to reintroduce a euchology of praying for the soul of the deceased.

Of the 111 orations that *MR2002* and *MR1975* share in common, only two in *MR1975* retained the use of "soul" (*anima)* as object of supplication. Both are in the Mass "For Relatives, Friends and Benefactors" (*Pro Defunctis Fratribus, Propinquis et Benefactoribus*)." In *MR1975* the remaining 109 orations offer prayers for the person (*famulus/famula*). In *MR2002*, however, 29 of these 109 orations (26%) return to the use of "the soul of your servant " (*anima famuli tui*). There is no explanation offered for this change either in *IGMR2002* or in *MR2002*. Neither does there seem to be a liturgical nor theological rationale for the place of these orations in the Mass, for of the 29 revised prayers: 9 are Collects, 9 are Prayers over the Gifts, and 10 are Post-Communion Prayers. An initial survey of Pierre Bruylants[43] reveals a consistent pattern of the use of *anima* throughout the medieval manuscripts and earliest printed editions of the *Missale Romanum* catalogued there. That usage, however, reflected a different anthropology and a theology from a different time.

Throughout the renewal of Roman Catholic funeral rites since Vatican Council II, pastoral renewal has been its hallmark. The second part of this paragraph reminds us that liturgical pastoral care for the faithful dead and bereaved reaches out to all who participate in funeral Masses, the Liturgy of the Word at funeral liturgy outside Mass or still other rites embodied in *OrdEx*. Once again, at the conclusion of this Chapter VIII, the recent DPPL issued the previous December 2001, helps place *IGMR2002* in its larger context. Together with Masses for the dead, prayers and other suffrages, the Church touches those who are present, for example, by joining them in almsgiving, in works of mercy on behalf of others; on prayerful visits to the cemetery as an expression of the bonds between the living and the dead in the communion of saints; through

42. Bugnini, 777.

43. Pierre Bruylants, *Les Oraisons du Missel Romain: Texte et Histoire*, 2 vols. (Louvain: Centre de Documentation et d'Information Liturgiques, 1952).

assisting with funeral and cemetery plans in light of the Christian vision of death; or through providing a supportive community for the relatives of the dead.

Despite its previously noted goal of "safeguarding 'things old,' that is, the deposit of tradition" (*custodiens "vetera," id est depositum traditionis)* and fulfilling the duty "of examining and prudently bringing forth 'things new'" (*considerandi prudenterque adhibendi "nova,"* no. 15 above), *IGMR2002* is notably inconsistent in this section of Chapter VIII. The "new" is an acknowledgement of the centrality of the paschal mystery without the emphasis it receives in earlier and contemporary postconciliar documents; the "old" is the accentuation and support of a spirituality that finds hope in applying the fruits of the Sacrifice of the Mass for the purgation of the souls of the dead. The "new" is a holistic anthropology that affirms the integrity of person in death and resurrection—"the resurrection of the dead;" the "old" is the preservation of an emphasis on the separated soul suffering a temporal punishment for sins forgiven but not appeased, awaiting its completion at the General Judgment—"the resurrection of the body." Both of these theologies of death and resurrection weave their way through these paragraphs, just as they did *mutatis mutandis* in the preceding editions of *IGMR*s. Nevertheless, the residual tendency in *MR1970* and *MR1975* to "preserve" certain aspects of an earlier piety appears to take on new energy in *IGMR2002*, which also seems to reclaim an earlier worldview as well.

Conclusion

The prevailing tone of this short section of *IGMR2002* on Masses for the dead is pastoral. This is apparent from the opening paragraph identifying the Church's offering of the "Eucharistic sacrifice of Christ's Passover for the dead" (*Sacrificium eucharisticum Paschatis Christi pro defunctis*) as characteristic of Catholic spirituality in face of death (no. 379), to its closing emphasis on the pastoral responsibility of the Church to be truly evangelical in her care for the deceased, the bereaved, and all who participate in liturgy on that occasion (no. 385). When implemented in its larger pastoral and theological context, *IGMR2002*'s instruction on Masses for the dead will stand in the long and venerable tradition to which St. Augustine at the funeral of his mother St. Monica bears witness[44] and in which the renewed spirit of Vatican II invites the Church of the twenty-first century to mark the death of today's "saints."

44. ". . . the sacrifice of our redemption was offered up in her behalf, with the corpse already placed beside the grave before being lowered into it, as is the custom of that place. . . ." *The Confessions of St. Augustine*, trans. John K. Ryan (Garden City, New York: Doubleday, 1960), IX:12.

GIRM—Notes (English)

144. Cf. Second Vatican Ecumenical Council, Constitution on the Sacred Liturgy, *Sacrosanctum Concilium*, no. 61.

145. Cf. Second Vatican Ecumenical Council, Dogmatic Constitution on the Church, *Lumen gentium*, no. 54; Paul VI, Apostolic Exhortation *Marialis cultus*, 2 February 1974, no. 9: AAS 66 (1974), pp. 122–123.

146. Cf. particularly *Codex Iuris Canonici*, can. 1176–1185; The Roman Ritual, *Order of Christian Funerals, editio typica*, 1969.

IGMR—Notes (Latin)

144. Cf. CONC. ŒCUM. VAT. II, Const. de sacra Liturgia, *Sacrosanctum Concilium*, n. 61.

145. Cf. CONC. ŒCUM. VAT. II, Const. dogm. de Ecclesia, *Lumen gentium*, n. 54; PAULUS VI, Adhort. Ap., *Marialis cultus*, diei 2 februarii 1974, n. 9: A.A.S. 66 (1974) pp. 122–123.

146. Cf. præsertim *Codex Iuris Canonici*, cann. 1176–1185; RITUALE ROMANUM, *Ordo Exsequiarum*, editio typica 1969.

CHAPTER IX

Adaptations Within the Competence of Bishops and Bishops' Conferences

(DE APTATIONIBUS QUAE EPISCOPIS EORUMQUE CONFERENTIIS COMPETUNT)

Mark Francis and Gary Neville

Introduction

Chapter IX is an entirely new chapter in *Institutio Generalis Missalis Romani* (*IGMR2002*), dealing with issues of liturgical adaptation in the *Missale Romanum* (*MR*), although similar material dealing with adaptations within the competence of bishops and bishops' conferences appears in the introductions to other liturgical books of the Roman Rite. This addition points to the increasing relevance of questions regarding adapting the *Ordo Missae* since the promulgation of *IGMR1975*. This chapter needs to be considered in conjunction with nos. 23–26 above that deal with the "first level" of adaptation that is the responsibility of the priest celebrant. The possibility of these adaptations is contained within the *Ordo Missae* itself and largely has to do with "the choice of certain rites or texts . . . chants, readings, prayers, explanations, and gestures that may respond better to the needs, preparation, and culture of the participants" (*in electione quorundam rituum aut textuum . . . cantuum, lectionum, orationum, monitionum et gestuum, qui sint necessitatibus, praeparationi et ingenio participantium magis respondentes*, no. 24). Chapter IX deals with what could be considered the second and third level of adaptations that are entrusted to the diocesan bishop and the national episcopal conferences, as well as those more profound alterations in the liturgy referred to in *Sacrosanctum Concilium* (*SC*, no. 40) that, if judged pastorally necessary by both bishops' conferences and the Congregation for Worship, depart in a significant way from the Roman Rite.[1]

1. See Anthony Ward, "Features and Significance of the New Chapter of the *Institutio Generalis Missalis Romani*," *Ephemerides Liturgicae* 114 (2000): 499.

Cardinal Jorge Medina, then Prefect of the Congregation of Divine Worship and the Discipline of the Sacraments, noted in his presentation of *MR2002* that this new chapter,

> . . . contains the principles and criteria to be used when a Conference of Bishops judges it necessary to introduce adaptations in the Missal beyond those that are foreseen by the Missal itself. Such adaptations are to be considered as special and exceptional; their justification can be none other than the need for providing for the spiritual good of the local churches involved, provided that the substantial unity of the Roman rite is safeguarded.[2]

These remarks parallel the approach of the Congregation's 1994 Instruction *Varietates legitimae* (*VarLeg*). Of particular note is the way both these documents use the words "adaptation" and "inculturation." *VarLeg*, no. 4, had announced that since the term "adaptation (*aptatio*) could lead one to think of modifications of a somewhat transitory and external nature," the term "inculturation" (*inculturatio*) would better express a more profound level of cultural adaptation of the liturgy. This change in vocabulary was spurred by Pope John Paul II (d. 2005) in his encyclical *Redemptoris Missio*, no. 52, quoted in *VarLeg*: "by inculturation the church makes the Gospel incarnate in different cultures and at the same time introduces peoples, together with their cultures, into her own community" (no. 4). This double movement of inculturation was seen by the Pope to establish a dialogue between the Church and the local culture that enriches both parties. Nevertheless, like latter sections of *VarLeg* (no. 52ff.) that continue to describe proposed changes in the rite as "adaptations," *IGMR2002* also reverts to the use of the term "adaptation" when discussing liturgical changes proposed by episcopal conferences. The term "inculturation" does appear in the historical and theological discussion of the Roman Rite in nos. 397 and 398, but in a way that suggests that while inculturation had taken place in the past, the most recent *editiones typicae* are already "inculturated," and hence further inculturation would be an activity of "last resort," since such changes might threaten "the substantial unity of the Roman Rite." Discussion of inculturation as a dialogue that is capable of enriching the Universal Church (*Redemptoris Missio*, no. 52) falls out of the discussion. Similarly, nos. 391–392, on biblical and liturgical translations, while echoing some of the principles already enunciated by the Concilium's 1969 document on liturgical translation *Comme le prévoit*, announce an emphasis on a formal correspondence approach to translation, an approach sharply criticized by *Comme le prévoit*, but which reappears in the

2. *"Presentazione del nuovo messale romano" intervento del Cardinale Jorge Arturo Medina Estévez*, (Lunedì, 18 marzo 2002), available in Italian from the web site of the Holy See http://www.vatic.va/roman_curia/congregations/ccdds/documents/rc_con_ccdds_doc_20020327_card-medina-estevez_it.html (accessed October 2006).

Chapter IX

ADAPTATIONS WITHIN THE COMPETENCE OF BISHOPS AND BISHOPS' CONFERENCES

386. The renewal of the *Roman Missal,* carried out in our time in accordance with the decrees of the Second Vatican Ecumenical Council, has taken great care that all the faithful may engage in the celebration of the Eucharist with that full, conscious, and active participation that is required by the nature of the Liturgy itself and to which the faithful, in virtue of their status as such, have a right and duty.[147]

In order, however, to enable such a celebration to correspond all the more fully to the norms and the spirit of the Sacred Liturgy, certain further adaptations are set forth in this Instruction and in the Order of Mass and entrusted to the judgment either of the diocesan Bishop or of the Bishops' Conferences.

Caput IX

DE APTATIONIBUS QUÆ EPISCOPIS EORUMQUE CONFERENTIIS COMPETUNT

386. Missalis Romani instauratio, ad normam decretorum Concilii Œcumenici Vaticani II ætate nostra effecta, assidue curavit ut fideles universi, in celebratione eucharistica, plenam illam, consciam atque actuosam participationem præstare possint, quæ ab ipsius Liturgiæ natura postulatur, et ad quam ipsi fideles, vi suæ condicionis, ius habent et officium.[147]

Quo autem celebratio normis et spiritui sacræ Liturgiæ plenius respondeat, in hac Institutione et in Ordine Missæ ulteriores aliquæ aptationes proponuntur, quæ iudicio vel Episcopi diœcesani vel Conferentiarum Episcoporum committuntur.

Congregation's 2001 document on liturgical translation *Liturgiam authenticam* (*LitAuth*).

386. For the purpose of the renewal of the *Missale Romanum*, the first paragraph of this article restates significant theological and liturgical principles found in both conciliar and postconciliar documents. Reiterated is that all the faithful are to "engage in the celebration of the Eucharist with that full, conscious, and active participation that is required by the nature of the liturgy itself" (*in celebratione eucharistica, plenam illam, consciam atque actuosam participationem praestare possint, quae ab ipsius Liturgiae natura postulatur*). The faithful have this "right and duty" (*ius habent*) in "virtue of their status" (*vi suae condicionis*). Quoted almost verbatim here is *SC*, no. 14, which adds that such active participation is required because the Christian people are "a chosen race, a royal priesthood, a holy nation, a redeemed people" (1 Pet 2:9; cf. 2:4-5); hence, they enjoy this right and duty "by reason of their baptism." This is because "in the celebration of the sacraments it is . . . the whole assembly that is *leitourgos*, each according to his function, but in the 'unity of the Spirit' who acts in all"; thus, "each person, minister or layman, who has an office to perform, should carry out all and only those parts which pertain to his office by the nature of the rite and the norms of the liturgy" (*Catholicae Ecclesiae Catechismus* [*CEC*], no. 1144; cf. *CEC*, no. 1142; also *SC*, nos. 28–29).

The second paragraph of this article states that in order to respect the norms and spirit of the liturgy, further adaptations have been required by *IGMR2002*.

387. The diocesan Bishop, who is to be regarded as the high priest of his flock, and from whom the life in Christ of the faithful under his care in a certain sense derives and upon whom it depends,[148] must promote, regulate, and be vigilant over the liturgical life in his diocese. It is to him that in this Instruction is entrusted the regulating of the discipline of concelebration (cf. nos. 202, 374) and the establishing of norms regarding the function of serving the priest at the altar (cf. no. 107), the distribution of Holy Communion under both kinds (cf. no. 283), and the construction and ordering of churches (cf. no. 291). With him lies responsibility above all for fostering the spirit of the Sacred Liturgy in the priests, deacons, and faithful.

387. Episcopus diœcesanus, qui ut sacerdos magnus sui gregis habendus est, a quo vita suorum fidelium in Christo quodammodo derivatur et pendet,[148] vitam liturgicam fovere, moderari eique invigilare debet in sua diœcesi. Ipsi, in hac Institutione, committitur concelebrationis disciplinam moderari *(cf. nn. 202, 374)*, normas statuere circa munus inserviendi sacerdoti ad altare *(cf. n. 107)*, circa sacram Communionem sub utraque specie distribuendam *(cf. n. 283)*, circa domos ecclesiæ exstruendas et ordinandas *(cf. n. 291)*. Sed ad ipsum primarie spectat spiritum sacræ Liturgiæ in presbyteris, diaconis et fidelibus alere.

They are "entrusted to the judgment either of the diocesan Bishop or of the Bishops' Conferences" (*quae iudicio vel Episcopi dioecesani vel Conferentiarum Episcoporum committuntur*) and will be further explained in the articles that follow. While adding nothing new to *SC*, no. 14, this article does lay the groundwork for a significant role for liturgical supervision and implementation by bishops and their conferences in order to ensure the full and active participation of all the faithful in the celebration of the Eucharist.

387. This article highlights liturgical adaptations within the competence of the diocesan bishop. Numerous Church documents teach that by their episcopal consecration, bishops, successors of the Apostles, are constituted pastors in the Church, teachers of doctrine, priests of sacred worship and ministers of governance (*Codex Iuris Canonici* [*CIC1983*] c. 375; see also *Lumen Gentium* [*LG*], nos. 19–20; *Christus Dominus* [*ChrDom*], no. 2; *CEC*, nos. 888–896 and 1558). The bishop is charged to insist on the observance of all ecclesiastical laws and to guarantee that abuses are avoided in ecclesiastical discipline, particularly in the ministry of the word, in the celebration of the sacraments and sacramentals, and in the worship of God and the cult of the saints (*CIC1983*, c. 392; see also *LG*, no. 23; *ChrDom*, no. 16). The bishops are "guardians of the entire liturgical life in the Churches entrusted to their care" (*CIC1983*, c. 835; see also c. 838, par. 1; *SC*, no. 41; *LG*, no. 26; *ChrDom*, nos. 11 and 15). It is the responsibility of the diocesan bishop "to lay down for the Church entrusted to his care, liturgical regulations which are binding on all" (*CIC1983*, c. 838, par. 4; see also *SC*, no. 22; *LG*, no. 26; *ChrDom*, nos. 15 and 35).

In light of these teachings, this article places the responsibility for the promotion, regulation, and vigilance over the liturgical life of the diocese with the

388. The adaptations spoken of below that call for a wider degree of coordination are to be decided, in accord with the norm of law, by the Conference of Bishops.

388. Aptationes, de quibus infra, quæ ampliorem coordinationem expetunt, in Conferentia Episcoporum, ad normam iuris, sunt determinandæ.

---

diocesan bishop, "the high priest of his flock" (*SC*, no. 41). Specifically entrusted to the diocesan bishop is "the discipline of concelebration, . . . establishing norms for serving at the altar, the distribution of Holy Communion under both kinds, and the construction and ordering of churches" (*concelebrationis disciplinam . . . normas statuere circa munus inserviendi sacerdoti ad altare, circa sacram Communionem sub utraque specie distribuendam, circa domos ecclesiae exstruendas et ordinandas*). In the broad spectrum, he is responsible "for fostering the spirit of the sacred Liturgy in the priests, deacons, and faithful" (*spiritum sacrae Liturgiae in presbyteris, diaconis et fidelibus alere*). Bishops may choose to issue local norms and directives on their own, working with diocesan offices of worship and/or of art and environment. At times a national episcopal conference may address such issues and provide guidelines, but unless the universal law or mandate of the Holy See has granted the conference authority to issue decrees in these areas, the competence of the individual diocesan bishop is not altered (*CIC1983*, c. 455, par. 4). As a teacher, the bishop would well serve his diocese with appropriate and well-presented catechesis on all norms issued.

388. The third article of Chapter IX moves directly from a discussion of the matters assigned to individual diocesan bishops to that of the conferences of bishops. This article notes that the adaptations that follow (nos. 389–392 below) will "call for a wider degree of coordination" (*ampliorem coordinationem expetunt*), and should thus be decided by the conference of bishops following the norms of law.[3] While the reference to the conference is frequent in these articles, the conference actually plays a limited role in making law when compared to the governing authority of the diocesan bishop.[4]

3. Besides those areas listed in *IGMR2002*, *CIC1983* also charges the Conference with issuing complementary norms for the universal law. The USCCB website notes that there are 84 canons authorizing legislative activity by the conference. The Conference has acted in the following areas that touch upon liturgy: c. 230, par. 1, Liturgical functions; c. 276, Permanent Deacons and the Liturgy of the Hours; c. 766, Lay Preaching; c. 788, par. 3, Norms for the Catechumenate; c. 877, par. 3, Norms for recording baptisms of adopted children; c. 891, Age of Confirmation; c. 961, par. 1, 2°, General Absolution; c. 964, par. 2, Place of Celebration of the Sacrament of Reconciliation; c. 1031, Minimum Age of Ordination of Permanent Deacons; c. 1067, Norms for Pre-Marital Investigation; c. 1112, Lay Witnesses for Marriage; c. 1126, Declaration and Promises; c. 1127, par. 2, Dispensation from the Form of Marriage; c. 1246, Holy Days of Obligation; c. 1252, Observance of Fast and Abstinence.

4. See Thomas J. Green, "The Legislative Competency of the Episcopal Conference: Present Situation and Future Possibilities in Light of Eastern Synodal Experience," *The Jurist* 64, no. 2 (2004): 284–331, especially 295–300.

389. It is the competence of the Conferences of Bishops in the first place to prepare and approve an edition of this *Roman Missal* in the authorized vernacular languages, for use in the regions under their care, once their decisions have been accorded the *recognitio* of the Apostolic See.[149]

The *Roman Missal*, whether in Latin or in lawfully approved vernacular translations, is to be published in its entirety.

389. Ad Conferentias Episcoporum competit imprimis huius Missalis Romani editionem in probatis linguis vernaculis apparare atque approbare, ut, actis ab Apostolica Sede recognitis, in regionibus ad quas pertinet adhibeatur.[149] Missale Romanum sive in textu latino sive in versionibus vernaculis legitime approbatis integre edendum est.

CIC1983, c. 455, pars. 2 and 3 outline the procedures. For a decree to be enacted validly at a plenary meeting, it must be approved by a minimum vote of two-thirds of those conference members who possess a deliberative vote. The decree, however, does not become the law of the Conference until it has been reviewed (*recognitio*) by the Apostolic See (see Seasoltz, 37 above). Once reviewed, it is up to the conference to determine the manner of promulgation and the effective date.

In May of 1998, John Paul II issued, *motu proprio*, the decree, *Apostolos suos*. Section IV of *Apostolos Suos* deals specifically with the complementary norms that are the responsibility of the Episcopal Conference. The intervention of Rome through the *recognitio*,

> Serves . . . to guarantee that, in dealing with new questions posed by the accelerated social and cultural changes characteristic of present times, the doctrinal response will favor communion and not harm it, and will rather prepare an eventual intervention of the universal magisterium (*Apostolos suos*, no. 22).[5]

Apostolos suos gives a history of episcopal conferences and theologically treats the collegial union that exists among bishops (nos. 1–13; see also *LG*, nos. 9, 20, 22, and 23; *ChrDom*, no. 36).

389. This article spells out the specific competencies that belong to conferences of bishops. It is within their "competence" (*competit*) to prepare and approve a vernacular translation of the new edition of the Roman Missal, but not without the prior *recognitio* of the Apostolic See. Whether in Latin or in an approved vernacular language, the Missal is to be published in its entirety.[6] The

5. Translation posted on the Web Site of the Holy See, http://benedettoxvi.va/holy_father/john_paul_ii/motu_proprio/documents/hf_jp-ii_motu-proprio_22071998_apostolos-suos_en.html (accessed October 2006).

6. *IGMR2002*, no. 389, cites *CIC1983*, c. 838, par. 3: "It pertains to Episcopal Conferences to prepare vernacular translations of liturgical books, with appropriate adaptations as allowed by the books themselves and, with the prior review of the Holy See, to publish these translations." See also *SC*, nos. 22, 36, 39, and 40.

390. It is up to the Conferences of Bishops to decide on the adaptations indicated in this General Instruction and in the Order of Mass and, once their decisions have been accorded the *recognitio* of the Apostolic See, to introduce them into the Missal itself. These adaptations include

- The gestures and posture of the faithful (cf. no. 43);
- The gestures of veneration toward the altar and the *Book of the Gospels* (cf. no. 273);
- The texts of the chants at the entrance, at the presentation of the gifts, and at Communion (cf. nos. 48, 74, 87);
- The readings from Sacred Scripture to be used in special circumstances (cf. no. 362);
- The form of the gesture of peace (cf. no. 82);
- The manner of receiving Holy Communion (cf. nos. 160, 283);
- The materials for the altar and sacred furnishings, especially the sacred vessels, and also the materials, form, and color of the liturgical vestments (cf. nos. 301, 326, 329, 339, 342–346).

390. Conferentiarum Episcoporum est aptationes definire et, actis a Sede Apostolica recognitis, in ipsum Missale introducere, quæ in hac Institutione generali et in Ordine Missæ indicantur, uti sunt:

- fidelium gestus et corporis habitus (*cf.* supra, *n. 43*);
- gestus venerationis erga altare et Evangeliarium (*cf.* supra, *n. 273*);
- textus cantuum ad introitum, ad præsentationem donorum et ad Communionem (*cf.* supra, *nn. 48, 74, 87*);
- lectiones e Sacra Scriptura peculiaribus in adiunctis desumendæ (*cf.* supra, *n. 362*);
- forma pro pace tradenda (*cf.* supra, *n. 82*);
- modus sacræ Communionis recipiendæ (*cf.* supra, *nn. 160, 283*);
- materia altaris et sacræ supellectilis, præsertim sacrorum vasorum, necnon materia, forma et color vestium liturgicarum (*cf.* supra, *nn. 301, 326, 329, 339, 342–346*).

Congregation's *LitAuth* provided very detailed directions for how the translations are to be undertaken and the *recognitio* obtained from the Holy See (*LitAuth*, nos. 79–84). This document also announced a change in procedure that significantly departs from the principle contained in *SC* that the bishops' conferences alone are responsible for translations of the *editiones typicae*. *LitAuth*, no. 76, declares that because "the major languages are widely and frequently employed" in liturgical celebrations in the "Diocese of Rome" the "Congregation for Divine Worship and the Discipline of the Sacraments" will now be "involved more directly in the preparations of translations into these major languages." The "major languages" are nowhere named in *LitAuth*, but one may assume that the principal European languages—French, German, English, and Spanish—are being referenced here. Since to date there has never been an official, complete translation of *LitAuth* into Italian, one wonders if Italian—"widely and frequently employed" in the Diocese of Rome—is to be included in this list.

390. *IGMR2002* here cites seven specific areas of adaptation left to the conference of bishops: the gestures and posture of the faithful; the gestures of veneration toward the altar and the Book of the Gospels; the texts of the chants

Directories or pastoral instructions that the Conferences of Bishops judge useful may, with the prior *recognitio* of the Apostolic See, be included in the *Roman Missal* at an appropriate place.

391. It is up to the Conferences of Bishops to provide for the translations of the biblical texts used in the celebration of Mass, exercising special care in this. For it is out of the Sacred Scripture that the readings are read and explained in the homily and that psalms are sung, and it is drawing upon the inspiration and spirit of Sacred Scripture that prayers, orations, and liturgical songs are fashioned in such a way that from them actions and signs derive their meaning.[150]

Directoria vero aut Instructiones pastorales, quas Conferentiæ Episcoporum utiles iudicaverint, prævia Apostolicæ Sedis recognitione, in Missale Romanum, loco opportuno, induci poterunt.

391. Iisdem Conferentiis spectat versionibus textuum biblicorum qui in Missæ celebratione adhibentur, peculiari cura attendere. Ex Sacra Scriptura enim lectiones leguntur et in homilia explicantur, psalmi canuntur, atque ex eius afflatu instinctuque preces, orationes et carmina liturgica effusa sunt, ut ex ea significationem suam actiones et signa accipiunt.[150]

---

at the entrance, at the presentation of the gifts, and at Communion; the readings from Sacred Scripture to be used in special circumstances; the form of the gesture of peace; the manner of receiving Holy Communion; the materials for the altar and sacred furnishings, and the materials, form, and color of the liturgical vestments. Several adaptations made for the United States by the USCCB may be found in earlier articles of GIRM2003.[7] The areas for adaptation outlined in this article also need to be read in tandem with *VarLeg*, 38–45, which describes in even greater detail the possibility of adapting music and singing, gestures and posture, dance, art and popular religious devotions due to the cultural needs of assembly.

IGMR2002, no. 283, which states when Communion under both species is permitted in addition to the times referenced in the ritual books, is cited both here and in no. 387. While no. 390 delegates the conference of bishops to prepare this adaptation, no. 387 also leaves to the diocesan bishop the regulation of Communion under both kinds.

One cannot overstate the need for adequate sacramental catechesis in preparing both people and clergy for the adaptations listed here, especially since there is a great deal of variation in practice from parish to parish in countries such as the United States and Canada—for example, in the gestures of the faithful during the rite of peace and in the gestures of veneration that accompany the reception of Holy Communion.

391. This and the following article speak directly of the episcopal conference's responsibility to provide translations of liturgical texts. Number 391 speaks specifically of the biblical texts used in the celebration of the Mass. There is a specific reference to *SC*, no. 24:

7. See nos. 43, 48, 74, 87, 160, 283, 301, 326, 329, 339, and 362.

Language should be used that can be grasped by the faithful and that is suitable for public proclamation, while maintaining those characteristics that are proper to the different ways of speaking used in the biblical books.

Sermo adhibeatur qui captui fidelium respondeat et publicæ proclamationi aptus sit, notis tamen servatis quæ propriæ sunt diversis modis loquendi in libris biblicis adhibitis.

> Sacred scripture is of the greatest importance in the celebration of the liturgy. For from it are drawn the lessons which are read and which are explained in the homily; from it too come the psalms which are sung. It is from scripture that the petitions, prayers and hymns draw their inspiration and their force, and that actions and signs derive their meaning. Hence, in order to achieve the restoration, progress, and adaptation of the sacred liturgy it is essential to promote that warm and lively appreciation of sacred scripture to which the venerable tradition of eastern and western rites gives testimony.[8]

The first *editio typica* of the Order of Readings for Mass was published in 1969. A new edition was promulgated by the Sacred Congregation for the Sacraments and Divine Worship on 21 January 1981. The first volume of the Lectionary for Mass in the vernacular (Sundays, Solemnities, Feasts of the Lord and the Saints) was approved by the US Conference of Bishops on 20 June 1992. The *recognitio* of Rome was received on 6 October 1997. The second, third, and fourth volumes of the Lectionary were also approved by the Conference in June of 1992; approval by the Congregation of Divine Worship and the Discipline of the Sacraments was received on 6 June 2001.

Meanwhile, *LitAuth* (promulgated in March 2001) called for a consistent approach to translation, which it proposed and summarized as follows:

> The words of the Sacred Scriptures, as well as the other words spoken in liturgical celebrations, especially in the celebration of the Sacraments, are not intended primarily to be a sort of mirror of the interior dispositions of the faithful; rather, they express truths that transcend the limits of time and space. Indeed, by means of these words God speaks continually with the Spouse of his beloved Son, the Holy Spirit leads the Christian faithful into all truth and causes the word of Christ to dwell abundantly within them, and the Church perpetuates and transmits all that she herself is and all that she believes, even as she offers the prayers of all the faithful to God, through Christ and in the power of the Holy Spirit (no. 19).[9]

8. See also *SC*, nos. 37–40, for the norms concerning the adaptation of the liturgy to the culture and traditions of peoples.

9. Translation posted on the Web Site of the Holy See, http://www.vatic.va/roman_curia/congregations/ccdds/documents/rc_con_ccdds_doc_20010507_liturgiam-authenticam_en.html (accessed October 2006).

392. It will also be up to the Conferences of Bishops to prepare, by means of careful study, a translation of the other texts, so that, even though the character of each language is respected, the meaning of the original Latin text is fully and faithfully rendered. In accomplishing this task, it is expedient to take account of the different literary genres used at Mass, such as the presidential prayers, the antiphons, the acclamations, the responses, the litanies of supplication, and so on.

392. Item Conferentiarum Episcoporum erit versionem aliorum textuum assiduo studio apparare, ut, etiam servata indole cuiusque linguæ, sensus textus primigenii latini plene et fideliter reddatur. In hoc opere efficiendo, spectare expedit diversa litterarum genera quæ in Missa adhibentur, uti sunt orationes præsidentiales, antiphonæ, acclamationes, responsa, supplicationes litanicæ, etc.

LitAuth rightly desires a version of the Scriptures that has been prepared following the principles of sound exegesis and high literary quality (no. 34). *LitAuth* also desires that the faithful be able to commit to memory important scriptural texts. To do this, however, requires that the translation be characterized by a "certain uniformity and stability" (no. 36). It is in this spirit that it attributes massive authority to the *Nova Vulgata* version of the Scriptures, making it "the point of references as regards the delineation of the sacred text" (*LitAuth*, no. 37). How this problematic requirement will be carried out practically remains to be seen.[10]

Episcopal conferences are free to establish a commission of experts to prepare draft translations for the approval of the conference and eventually of Rome. If such a commission is lacking, two or three bishops with the required expertise can be assigned the responsibility.[11] Sensitivity to cultural adaptations in liturgy is most essential. However, the principles and directives, as laid down in these documents, do not guarantee smooth sailing through the drafting and approval processes, as will be noted in the next article.

392. The conference of bishops is also responsible for preparing translation of the other liturgical texts in such a way that "the character of each [target] language is respected [and] the meaning of the original Latin text is fully and faithfully rendered" (*etiam servata indole cuiusque linguae, sensus textus primigenii latini plene et fideliter reddatur*). Moreover, the "primary purpose of the translation of the texts is not . . . meditation, but rather that they be proclaimed or sung during an actual celebration" (*textuum versio non spectat imprimis ad medi-*

10. On *LitAuth*, see the 2001 statement of the Catholic Biblical Association of America addressed to the prelates of the US Conference of Catholic Bishops at http://cba.cua.edu/usccbdoc.cfm (accessed October 2006); also, Joseph Jensen, "*Liturgiam authenticam* and the New Vulgate," *America* 185 (13–20 August 2001): 11–23; and Richard J. Clifford, "The Authority of the Nova Vulgata," *The Catholic Biblical Quarterly* 63 (2001): 197–202.

11. For the norms governing preparation of translations and the establishment of commissions, see *LitAuth*, nos. 70–78.

It should be borne in mind that the primary purpose of the translation of the texts is not with a view to meditation, but rather that they be proclaimed or sung during an actual celebration.

Language should be used that is accommodated to the faithful of the region, but is noble and marked by literary quality, and there will always remain the need for some catechesis on the biblical and Christian meaning of certain words and expressions.

It is, indeed, of advantage that in regions using the same language, the same translation be used whenever possible for liturgical texts, especially for biblical texts and for the Order of Mass.[151]

Præ oculis habeatur quod textuum versio non spectat imprimis ad meditationem, sed potius ad proclamationem vel cantum in actu celebrationis.

Sermo adhibeatur fidelibus regionis accommodatus, attamen nobilis ac litteraria qualitate præditus, firma semper manente necessitate alicuius catechesis de sensu biblico et christiano nonnullorum verborum et sententiarum.

Præstat vero, in regionibus eandem linguam habentibus, pro textibus liturgicis, præsertim vero pro textibus biblicis et pro Ordine Missæ eandem versionem, quantum fieri potest, haberi.[151]

---

tationem, sed potius ad proclamationem vel cantum in actu celebrationis). The language used should be accommodated to the faithful of the region, as well as being "noble and marked by literary quality" (*nobilis ac litteraria qualitate praeditus*). This article further recognizes that there will always remain a need for catechesis on the meaning of certain words and expressions.

LitAuth gives significant direction in translating liturgical texts into the vernacular using an approach that emphasizes a literal fidelity to the Latin text that could be described as "formal correspondence."[12] In this vein, *LitAuth* directs that

> translations of liturgical texts in various localities stand in need of improvement through correction or through a new draft. The omissions or errors which affect certain existing vernacular translations—especially in the case of certain languages—have impeded the progress of the inculturation that actually should have taken place. Consequently, the Church has been prevented from laying the foundation for a fuller, healthier and more authentic renewal (no. 6).

As provided for in *LitAuth*, the International Committee on English in the Liturgy (ICEL) was established during the Second Vatican Council by eleven English-speaking conferences to translate the liturgical texts into English. ICEL worked from 1982 to 1998 producing a revised translation of the Roman Missal. The draft was critiqued for taking a "dynamic equivalence" (rather than a

12. Compare for example *LitAuth*, no. 57, with Anscar Chupungco's description of the "formal correspondence" approach to translation in "The Translation of Liturgical Texts," *A Handbook for Liturgical Studies*, Vol. I: *Introduction to the Liturgy*, edited by Anscar Chupungco (Collegeville, MN: The Liturgical Press, 1997), 390.

393. Bearing in mind the important place that singing has in a celebration as a necessary or integral part of the Liturgy,[152] all musical settings of the texts for the people's responses and acclamations in the Order of Mass and for special rites that occur in the course of the liturgical year must be submitted to the Secretariat for the

393. Attento loco eminenti, quem in celebratione cantus obtinet, utpote liturgiæ pars necessaria vel integralis,[152] Conferentiarum Episcoporum est melodias aptas approbare, præsertim pro textibus Ordinarii Missæ, pro populi responsionibus et acclamationibus, et pro peculiaribus ritibus per annum liturgicum occurrentibus.

"formal correspondence") approach to the translation process, for its use of inclusive language, and for English texts that some felt took liberties with the Latin text. In recent years ICEL's statutes and translation personnel have been changed in an effort to comply with the translation principles found in *LitAuth.*

In 2002, Pope John Paul II appointed the *Vox Clara* Committee. In a message dated 20 April 2002 to the Prefect of the Congregation for Divine Worship and the Discipline of the Sacraments (CDWDS) on the occasion of the first meeting of the new committee, the Pope stated that the purpose of *Vox Clara* is "to assist and advise the Congregation for Divine Worship and the Sacraments in fulfilling its responsibilities with regard to the English translation of liturgical texts."[13] Specifically stated was their responsibility to follow the norms of the instruction *LitAuth.* The Pope had hoped to make available as quickly as possible official translations of the third edition of the *Missale Romanum* which he had approved in 2001. *Vox Clara* is unique in that no other language group has such an oversight committee. This underscores the Holy See's understanding of the importance of the English texts, since these often serve as points of reference for other modern language translations of the *editiones typicae.*

These first seven articles of Chapter IX address the responsibilities and rights afforded the people of God, the diocesan bishop, the conference of bishops, and, ultimately, the supreme authority of the Church. The directives found in all the documents referenced above have as their goal the active participation of all the people of God in the Church's liturgy. Experience has shown that there exists among these constituencies diverse understanding, expectations, and agendas. While the ultimate authority rests in Rome, it is obvious that there is a need for dialogue among the constituencies that respects the diversity found in the Church, the role of custom and the lived experience of the local church to interpret and give life to the law.

393. Citing SC, no. 112, this article underlines the importance of singing as an integral part of the liturgy. Because both the texts and their musical expres-

13. Message of Pope John Paul II to Cardinal Jorge Medina, April 20, 2002, Zenit News Agency http://www.zenit.org/english/visualizza.phtml?sid=19669 (accessed October 2006).

Liturgy of the United States Conference of Catholic Bishops for review and approval prior to publication.

While the organ is to be accorded pride of place, other wind, stringed, or percussion instruments may be used in liturgical services in the dioceses of the United States of America, according to longstanding local usage, provided they are truly apt for sacred use or can be rendered apt.

Item iudicare quasnam formas musicales, melodias, instrumenta musica in cultum divinum admittere liceat, quatenus usui sacro vere apta sint vel aptari possint.

---

sion are so important, these must now be submitted to the National Conference of Catholic Bishops for approval before publication. The original Latin version of the article mentions that this stipulation is "especially for" *(praesertim pro)* the ordinary texts of the Mass, the acclamations and responses of the people, and the "special rites that occur in the course of the liturgical year" *(pro peculiaribus ritibus per annum liturgicum occurrentibus),* for example, the sung texts that accompany the special observances of Holy Week, Washing of the Feet, Veneration of the Cross as well as the Easter Proclamation *(Exultet)* at the Easter Vigil. Specific mention of these occasions seems to indicate that the appropriateness of other compositions, including hymnody—though included in this provision—is of less immediate concern to the CDWDS.

In a letter directed to the USCCB dated 2001, Cardinal Medina, then Prefect of the CDWDS, indicated his satisfaction that the USCCB had taken steps to implement this provision in order to "encourage a new era of responsible creativity among liturgical musicians and composers" and expressed his opinion that the USCCB should specifically extend this provision to also include melodies in order "to set in place a filter to exclude inappropriate settings for the future."[14]

The last provision of this article (about use of the organ) has been slightly amended for the dioceses of the US. The original Latin text does not speak specifically of "the organ having pride of place," since many of the churches in Africa and Asia are much more accustomed to other musical instruments in the liturgy. The point of this provision is to underline the importance of instrumental accompaniment provided that they are "truly apt for sacred use or can be rendered apt" (*usui sacro vere apta sint vel aptari possint*). This clearly raises the need for liturgical/musical judgments that must be made in the context of the musical traditions of the local community. The use of drums and other

14. Letter from Jorge Cardinal Medina to Bishop Fiorenza (25 October 2001), *Congregatio de Culto Divino et Disciplina Sacramentorum*—Prot n. 138/10/L. *Adoremus* Online Edition Vol. VII, No. 9: December 2001–January 2002. http://www.adoremus.org/1201-0102AmAdaptations.html (accessed October 2006).

394. Each diocese should have its own Calendar and Proper of Masses. For its part, the of Bishops' Conference should draw up a proper calendar for the nation or, together with other Conferences, a calendar for a wider territory, to be approved by the Apostolic See.[153]

In carrying this out, to the greatest extent possible the Lord's Day is to be preserved and safeguarded, as the primordial holy day, and hence other celebrations, unless they be truly of the greatest importance, should not have precedence over it.[154] Care should likewise be taken that the liturgical year as revised by decree of the Second Vatican Council not be obscured by secondary elements.

In the drawing up of the calendar of a nation, the Rogation and Ember Days should be indicated (cf. no. 373), as well as the forms and texts for their celebration,[155] and other special measures should also be taken into consideration.

It is appropriate that in publishing the Missal, celebrations proper to an entire nation or territory be inserted at the correct place among the celebrations of the General Calendar, while those proper to a region or diocese be placed in a special appendix.

394. Oportet ut quævis diœcesis suum Calendarium et Proprium Missarum habeat. Conferentia vero Episcoporum, pro sua parte, conficiat calendarium proprium nationis, vel, una cum aliis Conferentiis, calendarium amplioris dicionis, ab Apostolica Sede approbandum.[153]

In hoc opere perficiendo, maxime servanda et tuenda est dies dominica, ut primordialis dies festus, exinde aliæ celebrationes, nisi revera sint maximi momenti, ipsi ne præponantur.[154] Item curetur ne annus liturgicus ex decreto Concilii Vaticani II recognitus elementis secundariis obscuretur.

In calendario nationis conficiendo, dies indicentur *(cf. n. 373)* Rogationum et Quattuor anni Temporum, et formæ et textus ad illas celebrandas,[155] aliæque peculiares determinationes præ oculis habeantur.

Convenit ut, in edendo Missali, celebrationes quæ toti nationi vel dicioni sunt propriæ suo loco inter celebrationes calendarii generalis inserantur, quæ vero regioni vel diœcesi in Appendice particulari locum habeant.

---

percussion instruments in the African-American and Hispanic communities throughout the US would be examples of instruments "rendered apt" by several generations of use in Catholic worship.

394. This article mandates that each diocese have its own liturgical calendar, a stipulation that underlines the theological importance of the local church and the need to promote a sense of local Christian tradition and identity through celebrations of saints who are of especial importance to the people of a given diocese. In a like manner, national conferences of bishops should also draw up a celebration proper to the nation; if appropriate, these celebrations are to be proposed in consultation with the conferences of neighboring nations. The article's insistence on developing local calendars is tempered, however, by the value of maintaining Sunday as the "primordial holy day" (*primordialis dies festus*). This is in keeping with the principle enunciated in *SC*: "Other celebrations,

395. Finally, if the participation of the faithful and their spiritual welfare requires variations and more thoroughgoing adaptations in order that the sacred celebration respond to the culture and traditions of the different peoples, then Bishops' Conferences may propose such to the Apostolic See in accordance with article 40 of the *Constitution on the Sacred Liturgy* for introduction with the latter's consent, especially in the case of peoples to whom the Gospel has been more recently proclaimed.[156] The special norms given in the *Instruction On the Roman Liturgy and Inculturation*[157] should be carefully observed.

Regarding procedures to be followed in this matter, the following should be followed:

In the first place, a detailed preliminary proposal should be set before the Apostolic See, so that, after the necessary faculty has been granted, the detailed working out of the individual points of adaptation may proceed.

Once these proposals have been duly approved by the Apostolic See, experiments should be carried out for specified periods and at specified places. If need be, once the period of experimentation is concluded, the Bishops' Conference shall decide upon pursuing the adaptations and shall propose a mature formulation of the matter to the Apostolic See for its decision.[158]

395. Demum, si fidelium participatio et eorum spirituale bonum varietates et profundiores aptationes requirant, ut sacra celebratio ingenio et traditionibus diversarum gentium respondeat, Conferentiæ Episcoporum illas Sedi Apostolicæ, ad normam art. 40 Constitutionis de sacra Liturgia proponere poterunt, de ipsius consensu introducendas, præsertim pro gentibus quibus Evangelium recentius nuntiatum est.[156] Attente serventur peculiares normæ quæ per Instructionem « De Liturgia romana et inculturatione » traditæ sunt.[157]

Ad modum autem in hac re procedendi, hæc serventur:

Imprimis prævia propositio Sedi Apostolicæ particulatim exponatur, ut, debita facultate concessa, ad singulas aptationes elaborandas procedatur.

His propositis ab Apostolica Sede rite approbatis, experimenta pro temporibus et locis statutis peragentur. Si casus fert, experimenti tempore expleto, Conferentia Episcoporum aptationum prosecutionem determinabit et rei maturam formulationem Apostolicæ Sedis iudicio proponet.[158]

---

unless they be truly of greatest importance, shall not have precedence over the Sunday, the foundation and kernel of the entire liturgical year" (no. 106).

395. This article is largely a repetition of the provisions already published in *VarLeg,* nos. 65–68, regarding the process to be followed in initiating, carrying, and obtaining final approval for "a more thoroughgoing adaptation" (*profundiores aptationes*). In effect, this article in *IGMR2002* and its parallel references in *VarLeg* serve as a kind of gloss on *SC,* no. 40, which deals with "even more radical adaptation of the liturgy"—presumably those that go beyond the possibilities for adaptation already provided in the *editiones typicae.* Clearly, the responsibility of proposing such changes rests with the national bishops' conferences, who are to submit a detailed preliminary proposal to the CDWDS in

396. Before, however, proceeding to new adaptations, especially those more thoroughgoing, great care should be taken to promote the proper instruction of clergy and faithful in a wise and orderly fashion, so as to take advantage of the faculties already foreseen and to implement fully the pastoral norms concerning the spirit of a celebration.

397. Furthermore, the principle shall be respected according to which each particular Church must be in accord with the universal Church not only regarding the doctrine of the faith and sacramental signs, but also as to the usages universally handed down by apostolic and unbroken tradition. These are to be maintained not only so that errors may be avoided, but also so that the faith may be passed on in its integrity, since the Church's rule of prayer (*lex orandi*) corresponds to her rule of belief (*lex credendi*).[159]

The Roman Rite constitutes a notable and precious part of the liturgical treasure and patrimony of the Catholic Church. Its riches are of benefit to the universal Church, so that were they to be lost, the Church would be seriously harmed.

Throughout the ages, the Roman Rite has not only preserved the liturgical usages that arose in the city of Rome but has also in a deep, organic, and harmonious way incorporated into itself certain other usages derived from the customs and culture of different peoples and of various particular

396. Antequam tamen ad novas aptationes, profundiores præsertim, deveniatur, sedulo curandum erit ut cleri et fidelium debita institutio sapienter ordinateque promoveatur, facultates iam prævisæ ad effectum ducantur et normæ pastorales, spiritui celebrationis respondentes, plene applicentur.

397. Principium quoque servetur, iuxta quod unaquæque Ecclesia particularis concordare debet cum universali Ecclesia non solum quoad fidei doctrinam et signa sacramentalia, sed etiam quoad usus universaliter acceptos ab apostolica et continua traditione, qui servandi sunt non solum ut errores vitentur, verum etiam ad fidei integritatem tradendam, quia Ecclesiæ lex orandi eius legi credendi respondet.[159]

Ritus romanus partem notabilem et pretiosam liturgici thesauri et patrimonii Ecclesiæ catholicæ constituit, cuius divitiæ ad bonum universæ Ecclesiæ iuvant, ita ut earum amissio ei graviter noceret.

Ritus ille sæculorum decursu non solum usus liturgicos ex urbe Roma ortos servavit sed etiam profundo, organico et harmonico modo alios quosdam in se integravit, qui e consuetudinibus et ingenio diversorum populorum variarumque Ecclesiarum particularium sive Occidentis sive Orientis derivabantur, indolem quandam supraregionalem sic acquirens. Nostris vero temporibus identitas et expressio unitaria huius Ritus invenitur in editionibus typicis libro-

---

order to obtain the necessary faculty (permission) for beginning the adaptation *ad experimentum*. It is only after having evaluated a liturgical change tried experimentally on a limited basis that a national bishops' conference would present its "mature" (*maturam*) request for adaptation to the Holy See.

396. This article serves as a common-sense admonition that liturgical changes, especially those of a more radical nature, require preparation of both the clergy and the faithful. It echoes no. 387 above and parallels a similar provision found in *VarLeg*, no. 69.

Churches of both West and East, so that in this way, the Roman Rite has acquired a certain supraregional character. In our own times, on the other hand, the identity and unitary expression of this Rite is found in the typical editions of the liturgical books promulgated by authority of the Supreme Pontiff, and in those liturgical books corresponding to them approved by the Bishops' Conferences for their territories with the *recognitio* of the Apostolic See.[160]

rum liturgicorum ex auctoritate Summi Pontificis promulgatis et in libris liturgicis illis respondentibus, a Conferentiis Episcoporum pro suis dicionibus probatis atque a Sede Apostolica recognitis.[160]

---

397. Having stated the need for pastoral preparation, this final section of *IGMR2002* departs from its rather detailed discussion of the process by which adaptations are to be enacted. Instead, nos. 397–399 contain observations regarding the relationship of liturgy—especially the Roman Rite—to culture, and how the liturgy serves as a means and expression of ecclesial identity and communion. The first paragraph of no. 397 speaks of the transcultural aspect of this relationship, emphasizing that all particular churches must be in accord with the Universal Church not only regarding the "doctrine of the faith and sacramental signs, but also as to those usages universally handed down by apostolic and unbroken tradition" (*fidei doctrinam et signa sacramentalia, sed etiam quoad usus universaliter acceptos ab apostolica et continua traditione*). These aspects of the liturgy had been recognized in *SC* as "unchangeable elements divinely instituted, and . . . elements subject to change" (no. 21), and hence could not be objects of cultural adaptation. Many of these usages are identified in *VarLeg*, including,

> daily prayer, sanctification of Sunday and the rhythm of the week, the celebrations of Easter, and the unfolding of the mystery of Christ throughout the liturgical year, the practice of penance and fasting, the sacraments of Christian initiation, the celebration of the memorial of the Lord and the relationship between the Liturgy of the Word and the Eucharistic liturgy, the forgiveness of sins, the ordained ministry, marriage and the anointing of the sick (no. 26).

Then, invoking the patristic adage *lex orandi, lex credendi* (the Church's rule of prayer corresponds to its rule of belief), the first paragraph of this article emphasizes that these basic elements of the liturgy are to be maintained in order to hand down the faith in an integral manner to succeeding generations.

While the first paragraph seems to be a general statement that would apply to all the Rites of the Church, no. 397 then specifically declares that the Roman Rite is a "notable and precious part of the liturgical treasure and patrimony of the Catholic Church" and if this richness "were . . . to be lost, the Church would be seriously harmed" (*partem notabilem et pretiosam liturgici thesauri et patrimonii Ecclesiae catholicae . . . ita ut earum amissio ei graviter noceret*). The text does not describe these riches nor say whether some would be more important to preserve than others. This paragraph needs to be read in light of *SC*, no. 21, which speaks not only of unchangeable elements of the liturgy, but also declares that there are parts of the liturgical tradition that are subject to change and in fact "ought to be changed with the passage of time if they have suffered from the intrusion of anything out of harmony with the inner nature of the liturgy or have become less suitable." This second paragraph of no. 397 is not saying, therefore, that *everything* about the Roman Rite is to be retained without change.

The final paragraph of no. 397 offers a particular interpretation of the characteristics of the Roman Rite that flow from its history. Since the liturgy of Rome was able to incorporate into itself in a "deep, organic, and harmonious way" (*profundo, organico et harmonico modo*) other liturgical usages from East and West in addition to those that arose in Rome itself, it has acquired "a certain supra-regional character" (*indolem quandam supraregionalem*). This statement is complimented by a similar assertion contained in *VarLeg*:

> During the course of the centuries, the Roman Rite has known how to integrate texts, chants, gestures and rites from various sources and to adapt itself in local cultures in mission territories, even if at certain periods a desire for liturgical uniformity obscured this fact (no. 17).

Examples of such borrowing by the Roman Rite from non-Roman sources are further specified in n. 32 to *VarLeg*, no. 17, and include such items as the *Improperia* and adoration of the Cross of Good Friday, the hymns of the liturgy of the hours, sprinkling of holy water, use of incense, genuflection, hands joined, and the rogations. On closer investigation one also notes that there are various cultural styles of prayer in the Roman liturgy. To the collection of original Roman texts composed by such authors as Popes St. Leo the Great (d. 461), Gelasius (d. 496) and Vigilius (d. 555), which are characterized as simple, sober, and rather cerebral, subsequent compositions from the Franco-Germanic lands were added to the Roman sacramentaries, and these latter show a marked difference in style. The prayers from northern European sources are more effusive and emotional, and supplement the original "layer" of classical Roman prayers (one only need think of Easter Vigil's *Exultet*). There are also prayers celebrating feasts of the Lord that arose in later centuries, such as the Sacred Heart, or particular prayers for saints' days incorporated into the Roman Rite that exhibit a style in contrast to that of the sober "pure" Roman collects. Thus, many euchological styles are found in *MR1970*. [15]

15. See Antoine Dumas, "Les sources du nouveau Missel romain," *Notitiae* 7 (1971): 37–42, 74–77, 94–95, 134–136, 276–279, and 409–410.

398. The norm established by the Second Vatican Council—that in the liturgical reform there should be no innovations unless required in order to bring a genuine and certain benefit to the Church, and taking care that any new forms adopted should in some way grow organically from forms already existing[161]—must also be applied to efforts at the inculturation of the same Roman Rite.[162] Inculturation, moreover, requires a necessary length of time, lest the authentic liturgical tradition suffer contamination due to haste and a lack of caution.

Finally, the purpose of pursuing inculturation is not in any way the creation of new families of rites, but aims rather at meeting the needs of a particular culture in such a way that adaptations introduced either in the Missal or in combination with other liturgical books are not at variance with the distinctive character of the Roman Rite.[163]

398. Norma a Concilio Vaticano II statuta, ut innovationes in instauratione liturgica ne fiant nisi vera et certa utilitas Ecclesiæ id exigat, et adhibita cautela ut novæ formæ ex formis iam exstantibus organice quodammodo crescant,[161] ad ipsius quoque Ritus romani inculturationem operandam applicari debet.[162] Inculturatio insuper necessariam temporis copiam requirit ne festinatim et incaute authentica traditio liturgica contaminetur.

Inculturationis denique inquisitio minime contendit ad novas familias rituales creandas, sed culturæ datæ exigentiis consulere eo tamen modo, ut aptationes inductæ sive in Missali sive in aliis libris liturgicis compositæ indoli propriæ Ritus romani non sint noxiæ.[163]

It is in light of the complicated history of the Roman Rite (see Mitchell and Baldovin, especially 11–17 above) that the final assertion of no. 397 needs to be understood. The liturgy's "identity and unitary expression" (*identitas et expressio unitaria*) is to be found in the *editiones typicae*, as well as in their corresponding approved translations of the Roman Rite into the many vernacular languages in which the Rite is celebrated. When read alongside a parallel passage in *VarLeg* (no. 36), the final paragraph of article 397 seems to be saying that, given the diversity of styles present in the current Missal, "identity and unitary expression" is not to be found in one particular style of text and rite, but simply within the range of options and styles now found in the approved liturgical books. It is this which constitutes the "substantial unity of the Roman Rite" mentioned in *SC*, no. 38.

398. This article adds yet another note of caution to those who would propose inculturation, repeating the caveat found in *SC*, no. 23, and reiterated in *VarLeg*, no. 46, that changes in the liturgy should only be done for well-established pastoral benefit, and that they should grow organically from forms already existing. At this point no. 398 adds that inculturation requires a fair amount of time "lest the authentic liturgical tradition suffer contamination due to haste and a lack of caution" *(ne festinatim et incaute authentica traditio liturgica contaminetur).* Given the many stipulations regarding enacting cultural adaptations of the liturgy, such contamination would be very unlikely. The article ends with a statement already found in *VarLeg*, no. 36, that inculturation is not to result in

399. And so, the *Roman Missal,* even if in different languages and with some variety of customs,[164] must be preserved in the future as an instrument and an outstanding sign of the integrity and unity of the Roman Rite.[165]

399. Itaque Missale Romanum, quamvis in linguarum diversitate atque in quadam consuetudinum varietate,[164] in posterum servari debet veluti instrumentum et præclarum signum integritatis et unitatis Ritus romani.[165]

---

the creation of new families of rites, but aims to address particular needs of given cultures "in such a way that . . . [they] are not at variance with the distinctive character of the Roman Rite" *(eo tamen modo, ut . . . indoli propriae Ritus romani non sint noxiae).* As we have seen, given the wide scope of cultural styles contained in the *editiones typicae,* as well as in the approved vernacular versions of the liturgical books, there is a generous range of possibilities that could still be described as falling within the distinctive character of the Roman Rite.

399. This final article of *IGMR2002* invokes Pope Paul VI's (d. 1978) concern, voiced in the apostolic constitution that promulgated *MR1970,* that this same Missal be an instrument and sign of the integrity and unity of the Roman Rite. Even though this Rite is celebrated in an amazing number of languages, and although many particular usages can be proposed by local churches and allowed by the Holy See, no. 399 contends that Missale Romanum, by preserving the substantial unity of the Roman Rite, safeguards this unity.

GIRM—Notes (English)

147. Cf. Second Vatican Ecumenical Council, Constitution on the Sacred Liturgy, *Sacrosanctum Concilium,* no. 14.

148. Cf. ibid., no. 41.

149. Cf. *Codex Iuris Canonici,* can. 838 § 3.

150. Cf. Second Vatican Ecumenical Council, Constitution on the Sacred Liturgy, *Sacrosanctum Concilium,* no. 24.

151. Cf. ibid., no. 36 § 3.

152. Cf. ibid., no. 112.

153. Cf. *General Norms for the Liturgical Year and the Calendar,* nos. 48–51, p. 99; Sacred Congregation for Divine Worship, Instruction *Calendaria particularia,* 24 June 1970, nos. 4, 8: AAS 62 (1970), pp. 652–653.

154. Cf. Second Vatican Ecumenical Council, Constitution on the Sacred Liturgy, *Sacrosanctum Concilium,* no. 106.

155. Cf. *General Norms for the Liturgical Year and Calendar,* no. 46, p. 98; cf. also Sacred Congregation for Divine Worship, Instruction *Calendaria particularia,* 24 June 1970, no. 38: AAS 62 (1970), p. 660.

IGMR—Notes (Latin)

147. Cf. Conc. Œcum. Vat. II, Const. de sacra Liturgia, *Sacrosanctum Concilium,* n. 14.

148. Cf. *ibidem,* n. 41.

149. Cf. *Codex Iuris Canonici,* can. 838 § 3.

150. Cf. Conc. Œcum. Vat. II, Const. de sacra Liturgia, *Sacrosanctum Concilium,* n. 106.

151. Cf. *ibidem,* n. 36 § 3.

152. Cf. *ibidem,* n. 112.

153. Cf. *Normæ Universales de Anno liturgico et de Calendario,* nn. 48–51, *infra,* pp. 68–69; S. Congr. pro Cultu Divino, Instr. *Calendaria particularia,* diei 24 iunii 1970, nn. 4, 8: A.A.S. 62 (1970) pp. 652–653.

154. Cf. Conc. Œcum. Vat. II, Const. de sacra Liturgia, *Sacrosanctum Concilium,* n. 106.

155. Cf. *Normæ Universales de Anno liturgico et de Calendario,* 46, *infra,* p. 68; S. Congr. pro Cultu Divino, Instr. *Calendaria particularia,* diei 24 iunii 1970 n. 38: A.A.S. 62 (1970) p. 660.

156. Cf. Second Vatican Ecumenical Council, Constitution on the Sacred Liturgy, *Sacrosanctum Concilium*, nos. 37–40.

157. Cf. Congregation for Divine Worship and the Discipline of the Sacraments, Instruction *Varietates legitimae*, 25 January 1994, nos. 54, 62–69: AAS 87 (1995), pp. 308–309, 311–313.

158. Cf. ibid., nos. 66–68: AAS 87 (1995), p. 313.

159. Cf. ibid., nos. 26–27: AAS 87 (1995), pp. 298–299.

160. Cf. John Paul II, Apostolic Letter *Vicesimus Quintus Annus*, 4 December 1988, no. 16: AAS 81 (1989), p. 912; Congregation for Divine Worship and the Discipline of the Sacraments, Instruction *Varietates legitimae*, 25 January 1994, nos. 2, 36: AAS 87 (1995), pp. 288, 302.

161. Cf. Second Vatican Ecumenical Council, Constitution on the Sacred Liturgy, *Sacrosanctum Concilium*, no. 23.

162. Cf. Congregation for Divine Worship and the Discipline of the Sacraments, Instruction *Varietates legitimae*, 25 January 1994, no. 46: AAS 87 (1995), p. 306.

163. Cf. ibid., no. 36: AAS 87 (1995), p. 302.

164. Cf. ibid., no. 54: AAS 87 (1995), pp. 308–309.

165. Cf. Second Vatican Ecumenical Council, Constitution on the Sacred Liturgy, *Sacrosanctum Concilium*, no. 38; Paul VI, Apostolic Constitution *Missale Romanum*, p. 14.

156. Conc. Œcum. Vat. II, Const. de sacra Liturgia, *Sacrosanctum Concilium*, nn. 37–40.

157. Cf. Congr. de Cultu Divino et Disciplina Sacramentorum, Instr. *Varietates legitimæ*, diei 25 ianuarii 1994, nn. 54, 62–69: A.A.S. 87 (1995) pp. 308–309, 311–313.

158. Cf. *ibidem*, nn. 66–68: A.A.S. 87 (1995) p. 313.

159. Cf. *ibidem*, nn. 26–27: A.A.S. 87 (1995) pp. 298–299.

160. Cf. Ioannes Paulus II, Litt. Ap. *Vicesimus quintus annus*, diei 4 decembris 1988, n. 16: A.A.S. 81 (1989) p. 912; Congr. de Cultu Divino et Disciplina Sacramentorum, Instr. *Varietates legitimæ*, diei 25 ianuarii 1994, nn. 2, 36: A.A.S. 87 (1995) pp. 288, 302.

161. Cf. Conc. Œcum. Vat. II, Const. de sacra Liturgia, *Sacrosanctum Concilium*, n. 23.

162. Cf. Congr. de Cultu Divino et Disciplina Sacramentorum, Instr. *Varietates legitimæ*, diei 25 ianuarii 1994, n. 46: A.A.S. 87 (1995) p. 306.

163. Cf. *ibidem*, n. 36: A.A.S. 87 (1995) p. 302.

164. Cf. *ibidem*, n. 54: A.A.S. 87 (1995) pp. 308–309.

165. Cf. Conc. Œcum. Vat. II, Const. de sacra Liturgia, *Sacrosanctum Concilium*, n. 38; Paulus VI, Const. Ap. *Missale Romanum: supra*, p. 11.

List of Contributors

John F. Baldovin, SJ, PhD, is professor of historical and liturgical theology at Weston Jesuit School of Theology, Cambridge, MA.

Andrew D. Ciferni, OPraem, STL, PhD, is a Norbertine priest of Daylesford Abbey, Paoli, PA, where he is the subprior, rector of the abbey church, and director of associates.

Martin Connell, PhD, is associate professor of theology at Saint John's University in Collegeville, MN, and the College of Saint Benedict in Saint Joseph, MN.

Edward Foley, Capuchin, PhD, is professor of liturgy and music and founding director of the Ecumenical Doctor of Ministry Program at Catholic Theological Union.

Mark R. Francis, CSV, SLD, is superior general of the Clerics of St. Viator (Viatorians). He teaches liturgical inculturation at the Pontifical Liturgical Institute of Sant' Anselmo in Rome.

Margaret Mary Kelleher, OSU, PhD, is associate professor in the School of Theology and Religious Studies at The Catholic University of America, Washington, DC.

Richard E. McCarron, PhD, is associate professor of liturgy at Catholic Theological Union in Chicago, IL.

Anne C. McGuire, PhD, is associate professor of theology at Saint Gregory's University, Shawnee, OK.

Sharon McMillan, SNDdeN, SLD, is associate professor of liturgy at Saint Patrick's Seminary, Menlo Park, CA.

Nathan D. Mitchell, PhD, teaches liturgical studies in the Department of Theology at the University of Notre Dame, and is concurrently an associate director of the Notre Dame Center for Liturgy.

Bruce T. Morrill, SJ, PhD, is associate professor in the Department of Theology at Boston College.

Gary J. Neville, OPraem, JCD, is abbot of Saint Norbert Abbey in De Pere, WI.

Gilbert Ostdiek, OFM, STD, is professor of liturgy at Catholic Theological Union in Chicago, IL.

Keith F. Pecklers, SJ, is professor of liturgy at the Pontifical Gregorian University and professor of liturgical history at the Pontifical Liturgical Institute in Rome.

Joanne M. Pierce, PhD, is associate professor in the Department of Religious Studies at the College of the Holy Cross in Worcester, MA.

David N. Power, OMI, is professor emeritus at The Catholic University of America in Washington, DC.

Susan K. Roll, PhD, is associate professor of liturgy and sacraments at Saint Paul University in Ottawa, Canada.

H. Richard Rutherford, CSC, is professor in the Department of Theology at the University of Portland in Portland, OR.

Mary M. Schaefer, PhD, is professor (retired) at Atlantic School of Theology in Halifax, Canada.

R. Kevin Seasoltz, OSB, STL, JCD, is professor of theology at Saint John's University in Collegeville, MN.

Catherine Vincie, RSHM,PhD, is associate professor of liturgical and sacramental theology at the Aquinas Institute of Theology in Saint Louis, MO.

Richard S. Vosko, PhD, HON AIA, is a design consultant for planning places of worship and a priest of the Diocese of Albany.

Mark E. Wedig, OP, PhD, is chair and associate professor of theology in the Department of Theology and Philosophy, and associate dean for graduate studies in the School of Arts and Sciences at Barry University.

Joyce Ann Zimmerman, CPPS, STD, PhD, is the director of the Institute for Liturgical Ministry in Dayton, OH.

Index

Note: Page numbers shown in roman refer to the English edition of the General Instruction of the Roman Missal; page numbers shown in bold refer to the commentary.

Absolution 141

69, 141, 451

Acclamation 122, 123, 125, 142, 143, 147, 151, 152, 154, 170, 174, 179, 191, 239, 240, 241, 243, 247, 248, 249, 252, 253, 261, 267, 301, 318, 320, 456, 458

31, 50, 58, 120, 122, 123, 124, 127, 132, 142, 143, 145, 151, 154, 155, 172, 173, 174, 175, 179, 204, 215, 241, 243, 247, 249, 252, 301, 318, 320, 324, 414, 422, 459

Acolyte 209, 212, 228, 235, 245, 246, 259, 268, 273, 274, 275, 305, 307, 333, 343, 398

9, 21, 26, 53, 207, 208, 209, 210, 211, 212, 213, 218, 225, 228, 236, 245, 246, 248, 268, 272, 273, 274, 275, 276, 328, 334, 336, 343, 344, 345, 350, 398, 427

Action 78, 83, 88, 100, 101, 103, 117, 120, 122, 128, 132, 133, 134, 164, 176, 183, 193, 199, 201, 218, 263, 292, 353, 357, 358, 388, 396, 398, 399, 403, 454

vii, viii, 8, 15, 25, 28, 30, 40, 49, 50, 51, 52, 54, 56, 58, 59, 60, 63, 64, 66, 67, 68, 69, 70, 71, 72, 73, 82, 83, 90, 93, 95, 99, 100, 101, 104, 105, 106, 113, 114, 115, 118, 119, 122, 124, 132, 137, 140, 148, 149, 151, 162, 163, 164, 166, 172, 175, 177, 178, 180, 184, 185, 186, 188, 189, 190, 193, 199, 200, 201, 203, 205, 208, 216, 218, 222, 232, 237, 241, 242, 244, 246, 247, 249, 255, 257, 262, 263, 265, 268, 269, 273, 288, 292, 305, 312, 313, 314, 316, 321, 322, 323, 359, 360, 361, 366, 367, 371, 373, 376, 383, 390, 397, 398, 399, 400, 404, 424, 455

Adaptation 74, 108, 109, 110, 287, 391, 399, 416, 449, 451, 453, 461, 462, 465

xiv, vi, 31, 37, 38, 44, 47, 49, 55, 70, 74, 94, 99, 102, 106, 108, 109, 110, 131, 132, 137, 138, 142, 153, 154, 167, 186, 189, 230, 238, 254, 257, 258, 277, 326, 349, 351, 391, 399, 416, 447, 448, 449, 450, 451, 452, 453, 454, 455, 456, 459, 461, 462, 463, 465

Adoration 79, 326, 376
20, 21, 80, 181, 189, 210, 326, 327, 361, 362, 363, 376, 424, 464

Advent 144, 157, 365, 375, 402, 408, 409, 427, 430, 432, 438
127, 144, 158, 374, 408, 409, 428, 429, 432, 434, 435, 438

Agnus Dei 123, 132, 184, 185, 255, 302, 303, 321, 322, 421
18, 185, 255, 321, 421

Alb 202, 233, 234, 289
33, 234, 280, 396, 397

All Saints 401
421

Alleluia 123, 130, 154, 155, 156, 241, 266, 290, 318
50, 124, 155, 156, 241, 242, 290, 318

Altar 130, 132, 138, 139, 164, 165, 166, 167, 168, 169, 193, 204, 209, 212, 218, 220, 289, 290, 292, 296, 302, 303, 304, 305, 306, 307, 316, 322, 323, 358, 359, 360, 361, 362, 363, 364, 365, 366, 367, 371, 376, 382, 398, 404, 450, 453
iv, viii, xv, 9, 18, 19, 21, 22, 24, 25, 36, 53, 55, 60, 63, 68, 107, 109, 124, 138, 139, 140, 165, 167, 168, 169, 193, 204, 205, 208, 209, 212, 213, 216, 218, 219, 226, 229, 230, 231, 235, 236, 237, 242, 244, 245, 246, 247, 248, 251, 254, 259, 260, 265, 266, 268, 269, 272, 274, 276, 280, 284, 290, 291, 292, 295, 302, 304, 305, 307, 311, 313, 316, 317, 318, 323, 325, 326, 327, 329, 331, 332, 333, 334, 345, 352, 355, 359, 360, 361, 362, 363, 364, 365, 366, 367, 368, 369, 370, 371, 373, 374, 376, 379, 383, 385, 389, 392, 398, 404, 427, 451, 453, 454

Altar Servers 398
212, 213, 216, 218, 219, 313, 398

Ambo 133, 150, 153, 161, 217, 231, 240, 241, 242, 243, 245, 266, 267, 276, 277, 318, 368, 369
124, 150, 153, 154, 165, 212, 214, 215, 216, 232, 237, 240, 242, 243, 244, 261, 266, 267, 317, 318, 359, 360, 367, 368, 369, 370, 371, 373, 383

Amen 131, 147, 170, 179, 191, 238, 239, 248, 249, 252, 254, 258, 261, 262, 266, 269, 307, 318, 348, 349
38, 56, 59, 103, 131, 145, 146, 162, 170, 179, 180, 192, 252, 253, 269, 318, 348, 350, 421

Amice 234, 397
234

Anamnesis 177
48, 58, 63, 65, 71, 175, 177

Annunciation of the Lord 137, 244
244

Apostles 78, 165, 176, 177, 204, 401, 412, 419
1, 2, 3, 49, 65, 159, 164, 177, 204, 412, 413, 431, 450

Art 107, 196, 223, 278, 354, 356, 392, 404, 461
x, xiii, xiv, 31, 99, 107, 109, 126, 229, 352, 354, 355, 356, 376, 377, 378, 391, 392, 400, 404, 451, 454

Ash Wednesday 409, 427, 430, 440
410, 428, 429

Assembly 102, 114, 118, 119, 123, 126, 149, 154, 159, 371, 358, 359
viii, 25, 33, 35, 39, 48, 49, 50, 51, 52, 53, 54, 55, 56, 57, 60, 68, 69, 70, 99, 100, 101, 102, 103, 104, 105, 106, 113, 114, 115, 118, 121, 122, 123, 124, 126, 127, 130, 133, 134, 136, 137, 138, 144, 145, 158, 159, 160, 161, 162, 168, 170, 172, 174, 190, 191, 192, 200, 201, 203, 204, 206, 207, 211, 214, 215, 216, 217, 219, 224, 226, 227, 228, 231, 235, 239, 240, 242, 243, 244, 245, 248, 254, 255, 261, 262, 270, 271, 272, 279, 281, 288, 289, 290, 291, 292, 293, 301, 302, 305, 306, 308, 311, 312, 313, 315, 316, 318, 319, 320, 324, 327, 329, 330, 343, 354, 355, 357, 359, 360, 361, 362, 363, 366, 368, 369, 371, 372, 373, 374, 405, 406, 407, 411, 412, 443, 449, 454

Baptism 102, 141, 168, 437
viii, 1, 2, 52, 68, 81, 82, 83, 90, 99, 101, 102, 142, 201, 206, 208, 230, 234, 385, 414, 427, 436, 437, 439, 449

Beauty 107, 129, 358, 378, 396, 400
99, 218, 289, 308, 309, 354, 365, 374, 378, 384, 397, 399, 400, 404

Bell 251
251

Benches 372
288, 373

Bible	149
	14, 239, 370, 385
Bishop	111, 112, 132, 137, 154, 157, 182, 189, 199, 201, 202, 218, 219, 222, 225, 229, 249, 250, 251, 254, 262, 267, 282, 284, 285, 287, 290, 325, 342, 356, 376, 399, 400, 428, 430, 449, 450, 451, 452, 453, 454, 456, 459, 460, 461, 463
	iii, vi, viii, x, xi, xiii, xvi, 2, 3, 4, 9, 11, 13, 17, 33, 34, 35, 37, 38, 50, 51, 54, 58, 60, 63, 70, 71, 81, 82, 99, 103, 104, 106, 107, 108, 109, 110, 111, 118, 121, 122, 123, 132, 133, 138, 139, 141, 142, 144, 157, 160, 165, 166, 168, 174, 176, 178, 180, 182, 183, 184, 186, 187, 188, 189, 200, 201, 202, 203, 204, 207, 208, 209, 212, 213, 219, 221, 224, 225, 226, 229, 230, 232, 237, 238, 250, 251, 260, 266, 275, 279, 280, 285, 286, 288, 290, 291, 312, 313, 314, 325, 326, 329, 330, 331, 334, 335, 336, 342, 344, 345, 346, 347, 349, 350, 352, 356, 357, 362, 376, 383, 384, 390, 392, 393, 394, 397, 398, 399, 400, 408, 413, 415, 427, 430, 431, 443, 447, 448, 450, 451, 452, 453, 454, 455, 456, 458, 459, 460, 461, 462
Blessing	112, 120, 141, 152, 192, 193, 202, 218, 247, 262, 263, 266, 267, 272, 282, 290, 296, 314, 329, 380, 381, 382, 395, 404
	xiii, 18, 21, 36, 54, 81, 142, 151, 163, 164, 176, 193, 213, 216, 217, 218, 219, 230, 236, 238, 245, 247, 261, 262, 266, 272, 283, 290, 291, 311, 315, 316, 336, 369, 371, 374, 375, 395, 397, 403, 424, 427, 443
Body and Blood	74, 76, 77, 79, 83, 101, 164, 165, 175, 176, 179, 180, 185, 186, 303, 306, 307, 349, 365
	19, 49, 56, 58, 59, 61, 63, 66, 67, 69, 71, 76, 80, 82, 177, 181, 185, 303, 305, 339
Book of the Gospels	133, 152, 229, 234, 235, 236, 242, 264, 265, 266, 267, 276, 325, 331, 366, 403, 453
	109, 124, 151, 230, 231, 232, 236, 237, 242, 264, 265, 266, 276, 325, 326, 328, 332, 366, 403, 453
Bow	132, 138, 193, 236, 241, 244, 247, 257, 263, 265, 266, 272, 276, 290, 296, 298, 299, 307, 316, 319, 323, 326, 327, 328, 329, 331
	viii, 139, 193, 236, 237, 242, 243, 244, 248, 258, 263, 265, 266, 272, 276, 290, 316, 317, 319, 323, 325, 326, 327, 328, 329, 330, 332, 348, 349

Bread 93, 163, 164, 165, 166, 168, 176, 181, 183, 184, 186, 203, 212, 231, 245, 246, 247, 256, 258, 268, 274, 296, 297, 298, 299, 330, 343, 385, 386, 388, 389, 390, 391, 393, 395

14, 43, 49, 57, 58, 64, 66, 69, 70, 71, 93, 116, 163, 164, 165, 166, 167, 168, 177, 181, 183, 184, 185, 186, 187, 188, 209, 213, 232, 233, 246, 252, 255, 258, 259, 260, 270, 302, 331, 336, 337, 338, 340, 343, 344, 345, 346, 347, 356, 383, 384, 385, 386, 387, 388, 389, 390, 392, 393, 395, 397

Calendar 136, 144, 153, 408, 409, 410, 411, 460, 466

xiv, 5, 17, 406, 408, 409, 410, 411, 429, 431, 432, 434, 460

Candles 212, 229, 234, 235, 242, 266, 273, 327, 361, 367

151, 213, 230, 235, 236, 237, 328, 361, 367, 404

Canon law **viii, 2, 29, 30, 34, 35, 36, 37, 38, 39, 40, 41, 44, 158, 187, 196, 280, 286, 313, 314, 315, 316, 336, 345, 346, 352, 439**

Canticle of praise 191, 261

191

Cantor 136, 142, 143, 153, 155, 159, 161, 185, 190, 216, 228, 244, 407

55, 127, 136, 143, 144, 159, 174, 185, 189, 211, 215, 216, 225, 228, 240, 245, 320, 369

Cathedra 381

360, 371

Celebrant 108, 119, 151, 157, 161, 219, 228, 246, 250, 259, 264, 289, 290, 291, 292, 293, 294, 295, 297, 298, 299, 300, 301, 302, 303, 304, 306, 307, 326, 358, 370, 371, 398, 432

viii, 5, 8, 21, 150, 192, 207, 220, 288, 289, 290, 291, 292, 293, 294, 295, 296, 297, 300, 301, 303, 305, 307, 315, 327, 334, 370, 390, 433, 447

Celebration 75, 78, 83, 87, 89, 91, 100, 101, 102, 103, 104, 105, 106, 107, 108, 109, 114, 115, 118, 121, 122, 125, 126, 129, 132, 133, 134, 136, 145, 150, 157, 161, 163, 170, 180, 199, 201, 204, 205, 206, 207, 210, 216, 217, 219, 220, 221, 226, 227, 228, 229, 245, 254, 263, 273, 275, 326, 327, 332, 347, 353, 357, 358, 361, 356, 366, 367, 371, 372, 376, 378, 385, 388, 389, 392, 396, 404, 406, 407, 414, 415, 416, 426, 427, 431, 432, 444, 449, 454, 457, 458, 460, 461, 462

vii, viii, ix, 1, 8, 18, 20, 21, 24, 25, 26, 27, 29, 31, 35, 38, 41, 45, 46, 47, 48, 49, 50, 51, 52, 53, 54, 55, 56, 60, 72, 75, 82, 88, 91, 92, 93, 99, 100, 101, 102, 103, 104, 106, 107, 108, 115, 118, 119, 121, 122, 125, 133, 134, 135, 136, 140, 145, 157, 159, 161, 162, 163, 171, 174, 199, 200, 202, 203, 204, 205, 208, 209, 212, 215, 216, 219, 220, 221, 222, 224, 225, 226, 227, 228, 230, 231, 232, 234, 236, 240, 244, 246, 254, 259, 263, 264, 266, 275, 280, 281, 283, 286, 288, 289, 291, 293, 296, 297, 302, 308, 309, 311, 315, 316, 320, 324, 328, 331, 333, 344, 351, 352, 353, 357, 361, 367, 374, 376, 378, 383, 384, 385, 386, 390, 396, 397, 405, 406, 407, 408, 409, 410, 423, 426, 427, 428, 429, 432, 435, 437, 438, 439, 440, 443, 449, 450, 451, 454, 455, 456, 460, 463

Chairs 139, 161, 231, 237, 243, 244, 260, 265, 268, 271, 274, 290, 316, 370, 372
288, 371, 373

Chalice 163, 165, 166, 184, 186, 187, 231, 245, 247, 251, 252, 255, 256, 260, 264, 268, 269, 271, 274, 288, 292, 296, 297, 298, 299, 303, 304, 305, 306, 307, 322, 323, 326, 330, 333, 343, 346, 347, 348, 349, 366, 391, 392, 404
xi, 9, 19, 21, 39, 58, 67, 69, 164, 165, 185, 186, 187, 205, 232, 233, 247, 248, 252, 255, 256, 269, 271, 304, 305, 306, 316, 321, 322, 323, 331, 333, 334, 335, 336, 337, 343, 344, 345, 346, 347, 348, 349, 350, 366, 386, 390, 392, 394, 395

Chalice veil 231
232, 233

Chant 127, 130, 135, 136, 137, 139, 142, 154, 155, 167, 188, 189, 236, 237, 241, 245, 247, 256, 266, 318
37, 109, 124, 126, 127, 128, 135, 136, 137, 139, 142, 143, 167, 168, 185, 188, 189, 190, 236, 239, 242, 245, 421

Chapel 376
317, 352, 376

Chasuble 233, 289, 397, 398
33, 234, 289, 396, 397, 398

Children 112, 420
43, 129, 146, 158, 159, 172, 211, 249, 300, 413, 418, 419, 436, 439, 451

Choir 136, 137, 142, 143, 144, 155, 159, 185, 190, 215, 216, 255, 293, 358, 371, 374, 375, 407

	106, 123, 127, 136, 138, 143, 144, 159, 185, 189, 190, 191, 215, 216, 225, 227, 359, 369, 374
Choir Dress	227, 371
	227
Chrism	81, 282, 285, 286
	4, 54, 81, 213, 282, 285, 286, 385
Christmas	286, 401, 408, 409, 432, 440
	63, 64, 244, 286, 408, 409, 420, 432, 434, 435
Church	75, 76, 77, 78, 83, 86, 88, 89, 94, 95, 96, 100, 101, 102, 103, 104, 106, 107, 111, 116, 121, 134, 140, 143, 145, 148, 158, 160, 162, 163, 166, 168, 174, 177, 178, 182, 199, 201, 203, 204, 217, 218, 221, 222, 225, 226, 245, 251, 277, 283, 285, 289, 294, 353, 354, 356, 357, 358, 359, 361, 362, 364, 368, 369, 372, 374, 375, 376, 377, 378, 382, 385, 386, 391, 396, 403, 404, 408, 409, 410, 412, 419, 425, 432, 434, 437, 446, 462, 465
	vii, viii, ix, x, xi, xiii, xv, 1, 2, 3, 4, 6, 9, 11, 12, 13, 14, 15, 16, 17, 18, 20, 25, 28, 29, 30, 31, 32, 33, 34, 35, 37, 38, 39, 40, 41, 42, 43, 44, 45, 46, 47, 48, 49, 50, 51, 52, 54, 55, 56, 57, 58, 59, 60, 61, 62, 63, 64, 65, 66, 68, 69, 70, 72, 73, 74, 75, 76, 77, 78, 79, 80, 81, 82, 83, 84, 86, 87, 88, 90, 94, 95, 99, 100, 101, 102, 103, 104, 105, 106, 107, 108, 114, 115, 116, 121, 122, 129, 131, 133, 134, 140, 141, 146, 150, 157, 158, 160, 162, 163, 166, 171, 174, 175, 176, 177, 178, 179, 181, 182, 187, 192, 199, 200, 202, 204, 207, 208, 209, 214, 215, 216, 218, 219, 225, 226, 229, 230, 231, 234, 239, 241, 244, 250, 251, 279, 280, 281, 282, 283, 284, 285, 286, 288, 289, 292, 297, 305, 311, 312, 335, 336, 338, 340, 351, 352, 353, 354, 355, 356, 357, 358, 359, 360, 361, 362, 363, 364, 366, 367, 369, 370, 371, 372, 373, 374, 375, 376, 377, 378, 379, 383, 384, 385, 386, 387, 391, 394, 398, 399, 400, 401, 403, 408, 409, 411, 413, 424, 425, 426, 428, 429, 432, 433, 436, 437, 438, 439, 440, 443, 444, 445, 448, 450, 455, 457, 458, 460, 463, 468
Ciborium	256, 260, 366, 393
	366
Cincture	234, 397
	234
Civil authorities	160
Clergy	371, 462
	viii, xiv, 12, 46, 50, 104, 107, 201, 211, 242, 255, 283, 330, 339, 351, 360, 369, 371, 390, 454, 462

Collect 118, 130, 134, 145, 146, 147, 239, 240, 318, 409, 417
145, 146, 239, 263, 318, 386, 409, 417, 418

Collection 137, 154, 189, 217, 417
5, 10, 14, 62, 137, 216, 245, 435, 464

Colors 231, 365, 400, 401, 402, 428, 453
230, 365, 400, 401, 429

Commentator 217, 407
216, 217, 369

Communication 371
106, 257, 371

Communion 83, 92, 93, 118, 121, 122, 123, 131, 133, 134, 135, 165, 175, 178, 180, 182, 183, 186, 187, 188, 189, 190, 191, 212, 231, 254, 255, 256, 257, 258, 259, 261, 264, 270, 271, 272, 274, 275, 277, 278, 301, 302, 304, 305, 306, 307, 321, 322, 323, 326, 333, 334, 337, 339, 341, 342, 343, 346, 347, 349, 372, 381, 382, 388, 390, 417, 422, 437, 442, 443, 450, 453
8, 15, 24, 26, 48, 49, 51, 53, 56, 57, 58, 60, 61, 65, 66, 67, 68, 69, 70, 71, 73, 82, 92, 93, 94, 109, 115, 118, 122, 133, 134, 136, 164, 165, 167, 175, 176, 179, 180, 181, 182, 183, 184, 186, 187, 188, 189, 190, 191, 192, 193, 203, 205, 209, 210, 212, 213, 215, 219, 233, 235, 247, 254, 255, 256, 257, 258, 259, 260, 264, 270, 271, 274, 275, 277, 279, 281, 301, 303, 304, 305, 306, 308, 321, 322, 323, 325, 327, 334, 335, 336, 337, 338, 339, 340, 341, 342, 343, 344, 345, 346, 347, 348, 349, 350, 359, 363, 377, 388, 395, 417, 418, 422, 434, 436, 437, 438, 442, 443, 444, 451, 452, 454, 463

Communion antiphon 190, 322
190, 322, 323

Communion-plate 231, 349
233, 258, 350

Communion under both kinds 93, 270, 306, 337, 341, 342, 346, 450
67, 73, 93, 94, 109, 187, 260, 271, 281, 322, 325, 334, 335, 336, 337, 339, 340, 341, 342, 349, 350, 451, 454

Community 95, 121, 122, 130, 140, 141, 161, 172, 181, 226, 227, 341, 342, 374, 378

2, 10, 31, 33, 38, 39, 41, 43, 45, 46, 48, 50, 53, 54, 58, 100, 101, 102, 103, 104, 105, 108, 118, 119, 126, 128, 130, 133, 139, 140, 141, 143, 145, 154, 157, 160, 163, 166, 168, 169, 172, 175, 178, 189, 192, 200, 202, 203, 204, 206, 207, 215, 216, 217, 221, 222, 224, 226, 227, 232, 240, 241, 242, 247, 254, 272, 280, 283, 285, 289, 310, 317, 336, 341, 353, 354, 355, 356, 357, 358, 363, 366, 371, 374, 378, 379, 384, 385, 394, 403, 407, 409, 430, 433, 439, 441, 445, 448, 459

Concelebration 282, 283, 284, 285, 287, 290, 450

xiv, 24, 26, 109, 122, 279, 280, 281, 282, 283, 284, 285, 286, 288, 289, 292, 295, 297, 300, 305, 307, 308, 309, 327, 366, 451

Conference of Bishops 109, 137, 154, 182, 189, 249, 254, 325, 399, 400, 449, 451, 452, 453, 454, 456, 459, 460, 461

70, 99, 138, 325, 345, 362, 392, 393, 394, 398, 399, 400, 413, 448, 451, 453, 454, 455, 456, 458

Confession 141

21, 141

Congregation 96, 111, 112, 144, 150, 153, 157, 160, 171, 172, 174, 185, 191, 194, 195, 196, 197, 221, 222, 223, 227, 255, 277, 278, 293, 309, 313, 320, 323, 350, 362, 367, 369, 375, 380, 381, 382, 388, 408, 410, 432, 466, 467

xiii, xiv, xv, xvi, 23, 24, 26, 27, 29, 32, 42, 50, 54, 58, 59, 65, 68, 71, 73, 105, 107, 109, 118, 119, 122, 136, 139, 144, 160, 171, 172, 174, 180, 185, 191, 226, 227, 238, 261, 275, 280, 281, 284, 293, 300, 310, 311, 313, 314, 315, 317, 320, 322, 324, 330, 335, 339, 344, 345, 346, 348, 377, 388, 408, 409, 419, 429, 433, 436, 439, 441, 442, 447, 448, 449, 453, 455, 458

Congregation for Divine Worship 112, 195, 197, 278, 436, 448, 466, 467

xiii, 27, 32, 42, 107, 109, 119, 238, 275, 284, 300, 335, 344, 345, 346, 377, 408, 453, 458

Consecration 79, 88, 132, 176, 249, 251, 252, 269, 329, 330, 390, 391, 395

8, 20, 21, 22, 23, 25, 58, 59, 79, 131, 173, 175, 176, 251, 252, 279, 280, 281, 293, 295, 297, 327, 336, 395, 450

Conversion **401**

Cope 202, 399
9, 36, 396, 399

Corporal 165, 231, 245, 246, 247, 252, 260, 271, 274, 306, 361, 366
9, 165, 232, 252, 361, 366

Creed 128, 158, 159, 244, 319, 329
55, 123, 158, 159, 244, 319, 329

Cross 76, 78, 114, 139, 140, 162, 168, 202, 212, 229, 234, 235, 236, 237, 238, 243, 248, 262, 265, 266, 268, 273, 274, 296, 317, 326, 327, 330, 331, 332, 360, 361, 367, 404
20, 25, 33, 56, 57, 62, 70, 76, 78, 139, 140, 151, 152, 162, 163, 169, 204, 213, 225, 230, 231, 236, 237, 248, 265, 273, 290, 316, 317, 327, 328, 329, 331, 332, 333, 361, 363, 367, 368, 379, 383, 392, 404, 413, 424, 431, 459, 464, 469

Cruets 231, 246
233, 246, 316

Culture 125, 126, 182, 325, 391, 406, 461, 462, 465
31, 70, 108, 110, 120, 125, 129, 133, 138, 183, 325, 326, 348, 354, 355, 357, 370, 374, 378, 379, 384, 400, 406, 447, 448, 445, 463

Dalmatic 233, 397, 398
396, 398, 399

Day 120, 140, 156, 157, 174, 178, 227, 229, 231, 238, 284, 286, 287, 296, 377, 402, 409, 410, 413, 417, 427, 428, 430, 438, 460
5, 6, 14, 17, 45, 64, 81, 100, 102, 117, 118, 137, 138, 139, 140, 141, 146, 152, 158, 178, 193, 216, 230, 233, 238, 279, 286, 312, 329, 336, 386, 402, 408, 413, 414, 417, 420, 421, 427, 429, 430, 434, 438, 440, 460

Deacon 124, 127, 129, 132, 133, 136, 138, 139, 140, 151, 157, 161, 166, 168, 183, 184, 193, 204, 209, 212, 218, 220, 228, 231, 233, 235, 263, 264, 265, 266, 267, 268, 269, 270, 271, 272, 274, 275, 277, 288, 290, 292, 301, 303, 304, 305, 306, 307, 314, 327, 329, 333, 341, 343, 358, 359, 371, 373, 395, 398, 399, 407
4, 9, 53, 123, 130, 139, 140, 150, 154, 157, 165, 167, 168, 169, 170, 183, 184, 193, 204, 205, 207, 211, 219, 224, 227, 228, 232, 234, 235, 236, 238, 242, 245, 246, 263, 264, 265, 266, 267, 268, 269, 270, 271, 272, 273, 274, 275, 276, 277, 288, 290, 291, 302, 303, 304, 305, 307, 308, 313, 314, 316, 320, 326, 327, 328, 334, 341, 343, 345, 350, 359, 371, 373, 395, 398, 399, 407

Dead	179, 296, 298, 402, 410, 420, 425, 437, 438, 439, 440, 443
	30, 33, 36, 59, 179, 298, 315, 401, 411, 421, 423, 435, 436, 437, 438, 439, 440, 441, 442, 443, 444, 445
Death	76, 297, 298, 439
	56, 57, 61, 65, 68, 69, 76, 77, 102, 177, 192, 230, 338, 368, 386, 435, 436, 437, 438, 440, 441, 443, 445
Dedication of a Church	382, 404
	355, 362, 363
Devotion	121, 354, 358, 378, 410, 431
	25, 54, 60, 63, 64, 65, 67, 68, 69, 104, 121, 310, 315, 359, 363, 368, 378, 411, 431, 435
Diaconate	204
	204, 314, 344, 397
Dialogue	121, 249
	xi, 8, 64, 122, 140, 149, 171, 172, 173, 178, 180, 250, 388, 430, 448, 458
Diocese	107, 218, 251, 284, 285, 342, 450, 460
	11, 17, 34, 38, 99, 107, 109, 111, 213, 250, 271, 285, 356, 357, 408, 430, 450, 451, 453, 460, 469
Dismissal	120, 193, 260, 263, 271, 323
	193, 261, 262, 272, 307, 323, 326, 443
Easter	141, 156, 157, 283, 286, 326, 369, 401, 408, 409, 410, 412, 427, 430, 432, 438
	xi, 9, 21, 22, 121, 142, 156, 220, 283, 327, 336, 368, 369, 408, 409, 410, 412, 427, 428, 429, 432, 434, 435, 459, 463, 464
Easter Triduum	438
	409
Easter Vigil	283, 286, 326
	9, 22, 220, 283, 327, 336, 427, 459, 464
Ecumenical	75, 96, 97, 111, 112, 193, 194, 195, 196, 197, 222, 223, 277, 309, 339, 380, 381, 382, 404, 422, 446, 449, 466, 467
	x, 4, 33, 64, 157, 178, 339, 340, 442, 468

Ember Days 460

Embolism 181, 182, 253, 320
8, 18, 123, 182, 253, 301

Entrance antiphon 316
168, 190, 317

Epiclesis 174, 269
48, 50, 58, 59, 64, 65, 66, 71, 131, 175, 176, 205, 251, 269, 295

Eucharist 75, 83, 85, 92, 96, 104, 105, 106, 107, 111, 115, 135, 159, 162, 164, 165, 178, 194, 196, 197, 201, 202, 203, 205, 209, 222, 225, 245, 246, 259, 260, 268, 274, 277, 283, 291, 309, 320, 350, 353, 359, 360, 361, 364, 375, 376, 377, 380, 381, 382, 385, 386, 389, 390, 396, 407, 425, 444, 449
vi, vii, viii, ix, xi, xiv, 1, 2, 5, 7, 8, 9, 14, 18, 20, 26, 38, 43, 46, 47, 48, 49, 50, 52, 53, 54, 55, 56, 57, 58, 59, 60, 61, 64, 65, 68, 69, 73, 74, 75, 76, 77, 78, 79, 80, 81, 82, 83, 85, 87, 88, 92, 93, 100, 101, 102, 103, 104, 105, 106, 107, 115, 116, 118, 120, 122, 123, 126, 128, 130, 131, 133, 134, 135, 137, 138, 139, 143, 144, 150, 156, 158, 159, 160, 162, 163, 164, 166, 171, 176, 179, 180, 181, 183, 184, 187, 188, 192, 199, 202, 209, 210, 213, 214, 219, 221, 222, 225, 226, 227, 228, 229, 230, 231, 232, 233, 234, 243, 244, 245, 255, 263, 264, 266, 268, 271, 273, 274, 280, 283, 284, 286, 289, 291, 312, 320, 324, 333, 335, 338, 339, 344, 351, 352, 353, 355, 359, 361, 364, 366, 368, 374, 375, 377, 383, 384, 385, 386, 387, 388, 389, 390, 396, 397, 399, 407, 423, 424, 426, 431, 435, 449, 450

Eucharistic Prayer 96, 117, 120, 131, 164, 169, 170, 172, 173, 174, 248, 249, 250, 251, 252, 269, 293, 294, 297, 298, 299, 300, 410, 418, 419, 420
2, 5, 7, 8, 18, 21, 31, 36, 38, 43, 48, 50, 51, 53, 57, 58, 59, 62, 63, 64, 66, 77, 106, 109, 117, 118, 120, 123, 124, 125, 130, 131, 132, 159, 168, 170, 171, 172, 173, 174, 175, 176, 177, 178, 179, 180, 207, 220, 247, 249, 250, 251, 253, 268, 269, 280, 292, 293, 294, 295, 296, 297, 298, 299, 301, 308, 313, 320, 330, 405, 406, 411, 417, 418, 419, 420, 421, 441

Experimentation 461
31

Explanations 91, 108, 119, 217, 264
46, 91, 119, 230, 447

Faith 75, 76, 78, 84, 86, 88, 96, 102, 104, 123, 130, 147, 148, 151, 155, 158, 159, 160, 193, 249, 252, 255, 302, 321, 339, 354, 378, 400, 444, 462

1, 15, 30, 32, 40, 44, 45, 46, 47, 48, 51, 55, 56, 69, 70, 71, 73, 76, 79, 86, 87, 88, 91, 103, 104, 105, 123, 134, 147, 151, 154, 157, 158, 159, 177, 209, 211, 214, 266, 319, 341, 353, 355, 363, 377, 378, 384, 392, 400, 402, 403, 424, 436, 437, 438, 463

Faithful 82, 88, 92, 93, 94, 96, 100, 101, 102, 103, 105, 107, 115, 120, 121, 122, 123, 125, 128, 130, 132, 133, 135, 137, 140, 142, 147, 148, 149, 152, 155, 160, 161, 165, 166, 172, 178, 180, 181, 182, 183, 186, 189, 190, 191, 196, 200, 203, 204, 205, 206, 207, 209, 210, 214, 215, 217, 218, 221, 223, 227, 231, 237, 238, 240, 244, 245, 246, 251, 254, 256, 257, 259, 264, 267, 268, 274, 277, 278, 282, 287, 288, 292, 300, 304, 314, 319, 333, 339, 340, 342, 343, 353, 357, 358, 362, 364, 367, 369, 372, 373, 374, 376, 378, 382, 388, 395, 406, 407, 410, 415, 416, 417, 425, 427, 430, 431, 442, 443, 449, 450, 453, 455, 457, 461, 462

vii, xi, 23, 25, 26, 28, 29, 32, 37, 38, 40, 41, 44, 45, 47, 48, 51, 52, 53, 54, 56, 57, 58, 59, 60, 61, 63, 64, 66, 67, 69, 70, 71, 73, 74, 77, 80, 81, 82, 85, 90, 92, 93, 95, 102, 103, 104, 105, 107, 109, 116, 118, 119, 120, 121, 122, 123, 124, 126, 128, 130, 131, 132, 134, 135, 136, 137, 138, 141, 142, 143, 146, 147, 149, 151, 152, 156, 158, 160, 161, 162, 164, 165, 166, 167, 169, 176, 178, 180, 182, 183, 184, 187, 188, 189, 191, 200, 201, 203, 204, 206, 207, 210, 211, 213, 214, 215, 216, 218, 219, 222, 224, 225, 226, 227, 228, 233, 235, 237, 238, 247, 249, 252, 253, 254, 255, 256, 257, 259, 262, 266, 267, 268, 277, 280, 283, 284, 289, 292, 294, 296, 300, 301, 302, 303, 305, 306, 308, 309, 311, 314, 315, 316, 319, 320, 324, 334, 336, 338, 339, 340, 343, 344, 345, 346, 347, 348, 349, 351, 359, 360, 367, 369, 372, 373, 374, 378, 379, 386, 387, 388, 390, 395, 403, 407, 415, 418, 424, 427, 429, 431, 433, 437, 438, 444, 449, 450, 451, 453, 454, 455, 456, 457, 462

Feasts 144, 365, 375, 401, 408, 412

21, 55, 144, 145, 212, 215, 244, 401, 402, 408, 413, 415, 426, 427, 432, 455, 464

Fixed altar 361, 362, 364

Food 180, 181, 388

2, 69, 180, 181, 346, 361, 388, 394

Formation 85

45, 91, 211, 214, 218, 222, 351, 357, 429

Funeral 161, 254, 402, 438, 441, 443, 444

135, 254, 263, 260, 436, 438, 439, 440, 441, 442, 443, 444, 445

Gathering 80, 114, 125, 140, 341, 364, 370

49, 52, 68, 81, 114, 115, 136, 140, 145, 179, 191, 225, 235, 255, 283, 289, 309, 341, 352, 354, 438

Genuflect 132, 244, 255, 302, 304, 306, 321, 326, 327

21, 139, 237, 244, 304, 321, 327, 328

Genuflection 326

19, 139, 305, 326, 327, 328, 330, 464

Gesture 81, 108, 129, 132, 133, 138, 140, 168, 169, 182, 183, 184, 186, 193, 203, 205, 206, 236, 237, 238, 239, 241, 242, 243, 244, 245, 246, 247, 248, 249, 250, 251, 252, 253, 254, 255, 257, 258, 261, 262, 263, 265, 266, 267, 268, 269, 270, 272, 276, 290, 293, 294, 296, 297, 298, 299, 300, 301, 302, 303, 307, 316, 317, 318, 319, 320, 321, 322, 323, 325, 327, 328, 329, 331, 332, 348, 349, 453

16, 129, 172, 207, 236, 246, 250, 253, 255, 257, 258, 270, 288, 295, 301, 308, 321, 330, 350, 424, 454

Gloria 123, 134, 143, 239, 243, 317

142, 143, 144, 174, 239, 317, 329, 421

God 77, 83, 86, 100, 106, 114, 115, 116, 117, 118, 119, 129, 134, 135, 143, 145, 146, 147, 148, 149, 150, 151, 152, 153, 158, 160, 164, 168, 172, 173, 178, 179, 191, 193, 200, 203, 204, 205, 206, 207, 225, 228, 230, 240, 241, 243, 247, 248, 250, 255, 262, 272, 282, 295, 296, 302, 303, 319, 321, 322, 329, 353, 358, 359, 360, 368, 377, 403, 406, 410, 412, 415

14, 26, 29, 30, 37, 44, 45, 46, 49, 50, 51, 52, 54, 55, 56, 57, 58, 59, 62, 63, 65, 66, 67, 68, 70, 77, 79, 80, 82, 86, 92, 100, 101, 102, 104, 105, 106, 108, 113, 115, 116, 117, 118, 120, 133, 134, 135, 141, 142, 143, 145, 147, 148, 149, 150, 153, 156, 158, 159, 160, 163, 164, 166, 169, 172, 173, 176, 178, 179, 188, 191, 192, 193, 199, 202, 205, 206, 207, 209, 211, 212, 214, 215, 216, 217, 218, 219, 221, 225, 228, 230, 235, 239, 240, 256, 257, 276, 283, 308, 309, 321, 329, 338, 348, 353, 359, 360, 361, 370, 377, 383, 384, 385, 391, 394, 403, 412, 424, 425, 434, 441, 442, 450, 455, 458

Good Friday 326, 401

161, 327, 368, 464

Gospel 116, 121, 123, 130, 131, 133, 151, 154, 155, 204, 210, 241, 242, 243, 264, 267, 276, 290, 319, 329, 330, 366, 412, 444, 461

21, 28, 39, 51, 55, 100, 103, 105, 117, 124, 132, 150, 151, 152, 154, 155, 156, 157, 158, 163, 165, 186, 211, 214, 215, 225, 231, 241, 242,

	243, 264, 266, 291, 318, 319, 324, 326, 394, 413, 414, 415, 416, 422, 441, 448
Gradual	137, 154, 155, 189
	12, 33, 50, 137, 138, 154, 168, 335
Greeting	120, 134, 138, 140, 192, 253, 263, 270, 317
	109, 124, 135, 138, 139, 140, 142, 193, 238, 242, 261, 266, 311, 317, 318, 326
Holiness	83, 358
	65, 66, 74, 82, 398
Holy days	89, 127, 157, 228, 438
	24, 39, 91, 127, 158, 187, 228, 336, 438, 451
Holy Spirit	100, 143, 145, 146, 149, 172, 174, 177, 203, 238, 244, 262, 299, 329
	28, 49, 50, 55, 56, 58, 59, 63, 64, 65, 66, 71, 72, 79, 86, 100, 131, 133, 146, 166, 172, 175, 176, 177, 178, 244, 384, 385, 424, 431, 455
Holy Thursday	79, 81, 283, 286, 438
	39, 54, 59, 61, 80, 81, 213, 280, 283, 336
Holy Week	409, 427, 430, 440
	26, 81, 410, 428, 429, 459
Homily	91, 117, 131, 134, 147, 149, 156, 157, 158, 159, 243, 264, 291, 369, 415, 441, 454
	24, 38, 39, 51, 53, 55, 91, 92, 102, 114, 116, 117, 119, 147, 148, 156, 157, 158, 159, 211, 212, 244, 266, 291, 324, 368, 369, 441, 442, 455
Host	184, 251, 252, 255, 257, 258, 269, 296, 297, 298, 299, 303, 306, 321, 322, 326, 330, 333, 334, 349
	15, 18, 20, 58, 233, 246, 252, 255, 256, 258, 302, 303, 304, 305, 321, 322, 333, 334, 335, 341, 346, 347, 348, 350, 387
Hymns	126, 154
	103, 153, 189, 190, 263, 455, 464
Incensation	248, 265, 268, 330, 331, 332
	139, 168, 169, 251, 269, 274

Inculturation 110, 125, 126, 182, 325, 391, 407, 461, 465, 466
ix, 30, 47, 49, 70, 71, 72, 102, 110, 127, 229, 241, 363, 407, 448, 457, 465, 468

Individualism 206
52, 206, 289

Institution narrative 176, 391
19, 20, 21, 58, 59, 131, 175, 176, 177, 186, 255, 330, 391, 420

Intinction 274, 303, 306, 307, 347, 349
275, 303, 306, 335, 336, 337, 347, 348, 349, 350

Introduction 75, 120, 134, 161, 195, 244, 252, 267, 277, 301, 461
ix, 3, 5, 6, 7, 10, 22, 31, 32, 34, 35, 36, 44, 46, 64, 73, 75, 90, 112, 113, 115, 118, 119, 120, 121, 123, 134, 138, 140, 141, 173, 187, 190, 205, 211, 238, 240, 244, 253, 281, 284, 312, 331, 336, 337, 399, 400, 406, 407, 416, 422, 424, 426, 438, 440, 447, 457

Jesus Christ 146, 172, 185, 243, 253, 255, 267, 302, 319, 320, 321
29, 31, 49, 72, 75, 92, 101, 106, 141, 143, 185, 209, 243, 253, 255, 367, 424

John Paul II 195, 196, 382, 467
xv, 42, 61, 99, 149, 156, 308, 338, 442, 448, 452, 458

Kiss 139, 237, 263, 265, 267, 272, 290, 307, 316, 319, 323, 325
139, 237, 265, 317, 319, 326, 330

Laity 95
xi, 12, 53, 59, 69, 104, 140, 150, 184, 200, 201, 206, 207, 208, 210, 215, 242, 249, 263, 271, 279, 335, 336, 339, 341, 342, 344, 346, 351, 360

Lamb of God 255, 303, 321, 322
58, 321

Lamp 376
376

Last Supper 76, 78, 162, 176, 183
48, 49, 56, 57, 76, 162, 163, 164, 177, 184

Latin 86, 90, 96, 111, 128, 193, 222, 277, 309, 350, 380, 386, 404, 422, 446, 452, 456, 466

x, 1, 2, 3, 4, 6, 9, 10, 11, 12, 14, 15, 16, 17, 18, 19, 20, 25, 27, 34, 42, 48, 49, 50, 59, 62, 74, 77, 81, 88, 90, 116, 121, 128, 129, 130, 140, 163, 184, 188, 203, 205, 207, 220, 221, 228, 239, 258, 280, 284, 294, 300, 302, 311, 313, 318, 319, 320, 321, 329, 335, 344, 350, 386, 387, 412, 425, 426, 437, 439, 440, 452, 456, 457, 458, 459

Law 196, 251, 284, 287, 377, 438, 451

viii, 2, 15, 16, 28, 29, 30, 31, 32, 33, 34, 35, 36, 37, 38, 39, 40, 41, 43, 44, 45, 46, 64, 65, 110, 154, 158, 187, 206, 219, 220, 280, 285, 286, 313, 314, 315, 316, 336, 345, 346, 352, 385, 394, 439, 451, 452, 458

Lay minister 132, 140, 151, 161, 190, 200, 207, 208, 209, 210, 212, 213, 214, 215, 216, 217, 218, 220, 221, 225, 228, 235, 242, 245, 246, 259, 274, 314, 343, 397, 398, 407

140, 228, 238, 241, 245

Lectern 318, 369

317, 318, 369, 370

Lectionary 152, 153, 154, 155, 195, 231, 235, 240, 403, 410, 413, 414, 416, 422

149, 153, 154, 156, 211, 232, 236, 239, 240, 246, 336, 368, 403, 406, 411, 412, 413, 414, 415, 417, 426, 435, 438, 455

Lector 124, 127, 137, 151, 161, 190, 209, 210, 213, 228, 235, 240, 241, 243, 244, 245, 267, 275, 276, 277

138, 150, 151, 208, 210, 211, 212, 213, 228, 236, 237, 238, 240, 241, 264, 267, 273, 275, 276, 277, 319, 320, 373

Lent 144, 155, 157, 356, 375, 402, 409, 427, 428, 430, 438

13, 24, 144, 154, 157, 158, 366, 368, 374, 408, 409, 426, 428, 429, 430, 435

Liturgical books 84, 85, 135, 216, 221, 395, 403, 463, 465

2, 5, 6, 7, 8, 10, 17, 18, 24, 30, 32, 34, 35, 37, 38, 42, 46, 50, 106, 109, 110, 221, 383, 403, 439, 447, 452, 465, 466

Liturgical reform 465

ix, 13, 16, 23, 28, 42, 48

Liturgical texts 85, 107, 108, 143, 146, 147, 149, 153, 163, 189, 190, 191, 288, 406, 407, 411, 412, 413, 414, 415, 416, 443, 452, 453, 454, 455, 456, 457

22, 34, 37, 106, 109, 119, 126, 454, 456, 457, 458

Liturgical Year 285, 400, 431, 458, 460, 466

xiv, 9, 10, 100, 101, 366, 374, 400, 401, 406, 408, 423, 429, 432, 459, 460, 463

Liturgy 79, 90, 91, 96, 97, 104, 108, 110, 111, 112, 115, 116, 120, 128, 130, 134, 147, 148, 149, 151, 152, 156, 162, 163, 165, 166, 193, 194, 195, 196, 197, 202, 222, 223, 240, 245, 265, 268, 274, 276, 277, 290, 291, 309, 318, 320, 356, 369, 373, 374, 375, 377, 380, 381, 382, 404, 422, 425, 434, 446, 449, 450, 458, 459, 461, 466, 467

vii, viii, ix, x, xiii, xiv, xvi, 1, 2, 3, 4, 5, 6, 7, 8, 9, 10, 11, 12, 13, 14, 15, 16, 17, 18, 19, 20, 23, 24, 25, 26, 27, 28, 29, 30, 31, 32, 33, 34, 35, 37, 38, 39, 41, 44, 45, 47, 49, 50, 51, 52, 53, 54, 55, 56, 60, 61, 62, 64, 65, 66, 69, 70, 71, 72, 73, 74, 75, 80, 83, 86, 89, 90, 91, 92, 95, 100, 101, 102, 103, 105, 107, 108, 109, 110, 111, 113, 114, 115, 116, 117, 118, 122, 123, 124, 125, 126, 127, 129, 130, 132, 133, 134, 135, 136, 137, 138, 139, 140, 144, 145, 146, 147, 149, 151, 152, 153, 155, 158, 159, 160, 161, 162, 163, 164, 166, 171, 180, 181, 184, 189, 191, 192, 199, 200, 201, 203, 204, 206, 207, 209, 210, 211, 212, 213, 214, 215, 216, 217, 219, 220, 221, 222, 224, 228, 230, 231, 232, 235, 239, 240, 241, 242, 244, 245, 249, 251, 257, 260, 261, 265, 268, 273, 275, 276, 280, 281, 284, 286, 290, 291, 307, 308, 310, 311, 312, 313, 315, 316, 317, 318, 320, 326, 327, 335, 337, 338, 342, 344, 345, 346, 349, 355, 356, 360, 364, 368, 370, 371, 372, 373, 374, 375, 376, 377, 379, 383, 384, 385, 386, 390, 397, 398, 399, 403, 404, 405, 406, 407, 408, 418, 423, 424, 434, 436, 438, 439, 442, 443, 444, 445, 447, 448, 449, 451, 455, 456, 457, 458, 459, 461, 463, 464, 465, 468, 469

Liturgy of the Word 115, 120, 134, 147, 148, 149, 151, 152, 202, 240, 265, 276, 290, 318, 369

47, 55, 56, 60, 115, 116, 124, 133, 134, 146, 147, 149, 151, 152, 153, 155, 208, 211, 214, 219, 231, 239, 240, 244, 265, 276, 290, 318, 386, 399, 418, 438, 444, 463

Lord's Prayer 123, 128, 181, 252, 253, 301, 320

8, 18, 180, 181, 253, 301, 320

Marriage 161

427, 429, 451, 463

Martyr	401
	106
Mary	112, 328, 378, 401, 410, 423, 431, 434
	xi, 73, 156, 310, 329, 325, 378, 384, 387, 411, 413, 430, 431, 432, 434, 345, 468, 469
Mass	75, 76, 77, 78, 79, 81, 83, 84, 87, 88, 89, 92, 96, 100, 101, 108, 109, 112, 114, 115, 116, 120, 121, 122, 126, 128, 130, 134, 135, 140, 147, 150, 153, 157, 169, 186, 191, 199, 201, 202, 204, 205, 216, 219, 221, 225, 226, 227, 228, 229, 235, 238, 240, 255, 260, 262, 263, 271, 272, 275, 282, 283, 285, 286, 287, 289, 303, 307, 312, 314, 316, 319, 320, 323, 325, 326, 327, 328, 330, 331, 333, 341, 358, 360, 362, 366, 374, 376, 381, 382, 385, 388, 392, 398, 402, 406, 407, 408, 409, 410, 411, 416, 417, 419, 420, 421, 422, 428, 430, 431, 432, 433, 438, 439, 441, 443, 449, 453, 454, 456, 457, 458
	vii, viii, xv, 5, 7, 9, 10, 11, 13, 17, 18, 19, 20, 21, 22, 24, 26, 32, 33, 39, 46, 47, 48, 50, 51, 52, 54, 55, 56, 57, 58, 59, 61, 63, 64, 65, 66, 67, 71, 73, 74, 76, 77, 78, 79, 81, 84, 85, 88, 89, 92, 100, 101, 104, 105, 108, 113, 114, 115, 116, 117, 118, 119, 120, 121, 122, 124, 127, 129, 131, 134, 136, 138, 140, 141, 142, 145, 146, 147, 149, 156, 159, 163, 173, 187, 192, 193, 199, 201, 211, 212, 213, 216, 221, 224, 225, 226, 227, 228, 229, 230, 232, 234, 235, 236, 237, 238, 239, 240, 242, 245, 246, 251, 256, 260, 263, 270, 271, 272, 275, 276, 279, 280, 281, 283, 284, 286, 288, 300, 302, 310, 311, 312, 313, 314, 315, 316, 317, 318, 320, 321, 322, 323, 324, 325, 326, 327, 328, 329, 330, 331, 333, 334, 335, 336, 337, 339, 341, 342, 344, 346, 347, 354, 362, 366, 368, 373, 376, 383, 384, 385, 389, 392, 397, 403, 405, 406, 407, 408, 409, 410, 411, 414, 415, 416, 417, 418, 419, 420, 421, 423, 424, 427, 428, 429, 430, 431, 432, 433, 435, 436, 437, 438, 439, 440, 441, 442, 443, 444, 445, 454, 455, 459
Mass for the Dead	439, 443
	437, 440
Masses with children	112
	43, 158, 159, 300, 413
Master of ceremonies	218
	10, 20, 217, 218
Meditation	148, 152, 153, 457
	53, 55, 113, 148, 149, 153, 214, 456

Memorial Acclamation 123
123

Memorials 408, 409, 410, 412, 417, 432, 440
408, 409, 410, 411, 413, 418, 431

Mercy 142, 255, 300, 302, 321, 420
44, 141, 143, 214, 429, 444

Minister(s) 101, 127, 129, 132, 136, 138, 140, 151, 168, 193, 200, 204, 209, 212, 218, 221, 228, 231, 233, 235, 236, 238, 242, 245, 246, 248, 252, 254, 257, 259, 260, 263, 264, 270, 273, 274, 275, 276, 278, 288, 312, 313, 314, 316, 317, 318, 319, 320, 321, 322, 323, 327, 343, 347, 348, 349, 358, 359, 369, 371, 395, 396, 397, 398, 409, 444
viii, 2, 5, 8, 15, 17, 21, 22, 24, 28, 30, 31, 32, 35, 39, 45, 50, 52, 53, 65, 79, 106, 108, 122, 125, 127, 129, 135, 136, 139, 140, 141, 167, 169, 193, 201, 203, 209, 210, 211, 213, 214, 215, 216, 217, 218, 219, 220, 221, 224, 225, 228, 229, 231, 233, 234, 235, 236, 237, 238, 240, 241, 242, 243, 245, 246, 248, 250, 252, 254, 256, 259, 260, 261, 263, 264, 267, 268, 269, 270, 271, 273, 274, 275, 225, 288, 293, 308, 310, 311, 312, 313, 314, 315, 316, 317, 318, 319, 320, 321, 322, 323, 324, 327, 328, 329, 330, 334, 335, 336, 343, 344, 345, 346, 348, 349, 350, 359, 362, 369, 370, 371, 372, 373, 374, 396, 397, 398, 407, 408, 409, 449, 450

Ministry 82, 96, 97, 111, 121, 168, 193, 194, 196, 197, 206, 209, 220, 222, 223, 227, 263, 274, 277, 278, 292, 380
xv, 15, 24, 27, 51, 54, 58, 82, 101, 157, 158, 162, 169, 183, 200, 202, 204, 207, 208, 209, 210, 211, 212, 213, 214, 215, 216, 217, 218, 220, 225, 226, 228, 244, 263, 264, 271, 272, 274, 275, 276, 288, 336, 345, 359, 363, 368, 369, 379, 397, 398, 450, 463, 468, 469

Missal 75, 78, 83, 84, 85, 86, 94, 95, 109, 119, 132, 137, 165, 189, 190, 195, 221, 231, 245, 249, 269, 274, 277, 292, 294, 316, 366, 402, 417, 418, 422, 425, 449, 452, 453, 454, 460, 465, 466
vii, viii, 10, 17, 18, 25, 26, 27, 36, 42, 46, 47, 48, 61, 64, 66, 70, 71, 73, 74, 75, 78, 83, 87, 94, 110, 119, 137, 138, 165, 172, 209, 231, 316, 342, 345, 352, 366, 406, 426, 428, 434, 436, 438, 448, 452, 457, 465, 466

Missale Romanum 94, 195, 418, 422, 452, 454, 466, 467
ix, xv, 1, 6, 10, 18, 22, 24, 25, 27, 63, 73, 74, 75, 106, 109, 112, 113, 114, 118, 121, 122, 221, 224, 238, 239, 281, 284, 311, 326, 327, 328, 385, 444, 447, 449, 458, 466

Movable altar 361, 362

361

Movement **24, 100, 102, 113, 129, 130, 145, 206, 222, 230, 242, 257, 280, 312, 332, 360, 373, 448**

Music 107, 128, 137, 142, 189, 194, 195, 221, 223, 277, 381

x, xv, 31, 71, 99, 107, 108, 118, 120, 124, 126, 127, 128, 129, 137, 138, 167, 168, 190, 191, 193, 211, 215, 216, 228, 245, 246, 247, 263, 356, 374, 407, 454, 468

Musical instruments 121, 374, 375

120, 374, 459

Musician **238**

Mysterium Fidei 96, 194, 252

26, 79, 310, 315

Mystery 75, 78, 83, 85, 89, 90, 91, 93, 107, 136, 140, 148, 157, 176, 191, 201, 247, 252, 268, 353, 415, 418, 425

vii, xi, 29, 32, 33, 41, 45, 47, 49, 53, 54, 55, 57, 58, 59, 60, 62, 64, 65, 70, 73, 79, 80, 82, 89, 90, 91, 93, 101, 103, 105, 106, 117, 136, 140, 156, 159, 163, 177, 192, 193, 230, 238, 268, 308, 367, 386, 413, 425, 431, 434, 436, 437, 441, 445, 463

New Testament 81, 414

28, 48, 82, 103, 163, 176, 181, 338, 414

Non-Catholics 444

Octave 409, 427, 430, 432, 440

428, 429, 432

Offering(s) 77, 78, 83, 96, 118, 130, 148, 164, 166, 168, 169, 172, 177, 179, 203, 206, 245, 246, 248, 291, 294, 295, 296, 297, 298, 299, 330, 331, 332, 417, 419, 424, 444, 445

viii, x, 9, 13, 18, 21, 49, 50, 52, 54, 57, 58, 59, 60, 61, 62, 63, 64, 65, 66, 67, 68, 69, 70, 71, 77, 78, 81, 82, 91, 101, 116, 118, 119, 124, 128, 161, 162, 166, 167, 168, 169, 170, 172, 175, 177, 178, 179, 183, 185, 205, 206, 207, 216, 234, 246, 248, 249, 270, 272, 279, 286, 310, 330, 332, 333, 335, 336, 341, 355, 363, 417, 418, 421

Opening Prayer **125, 145, 170, 192, 239, 318, 417, 418, 428**

Oration 118, 131, 417, 425, 433, 443, 454
162, 245, 433

Oratory 283, 355, 377
104

Order of Mass 83, 108, 419, 421, 449, 453, 457, 458
xv, 24, 46, 56, 65, 118, 149, 225, 232, 314, 315, 322, 324, 331, 407

Ordinary Time 402, 410, 417, 420, 431, 433, 440
22, 145, 409, 410, 413, 418, 421, 429, 431, 433, 434, 435

Ordination 204, 222, 249, 282, 285
2, 53, 157, 200, 202, 204, 207, 208, 212, 268, 279, 280, 281, 297, 310, 336, 341, 429, 451

Organ 121, 247, 374, 375, 381, 459
168, 374, 375, 459

Organist 215
215, 374

Pall and water 231, 245, 247, 274, 366
165, 232, 233, 245, 274, 366

Palm Sunday 401
263

Parish 226, 335
5, 6, 11, 38, 45, 108, 202, 217, 218, 221, 225, 226, 310, 342, 335, 377, 408, 435, 454

Participation 83, 92, 102, 103, 105, 122, 123, 128, 129, 157, 187, 199, 215, 227, 353, 364, 374, 409, 449, 461
viii, xi, 23, 31, 45, 48, 51, 52, 53, 54, 55, 60, 67, 69, 70, 73, 74, 81, 82, 83, 90, 91, 92, 93, 99, 101, 102, 103, 105, 107, 113, 119, 122, 123, 126, 129, 138, 141, 166, 172, 184, 188, 199, 200, 201, 206, 208, 213, 215, 216, 217, 225, 226, 228, 238, 249, 252, 280, 283, 289, 291, 294, 302, 308, 311, 312, 313, 322, 340, 353, 354, 359, 360, 367, 373, 374, 379, 403, 409, 437, 442, 449, 450, 458

Paschal candle 331

Paschal Mystery 425
29, 41, 49, 55, 58, 101, 106, 159, 230, 425, 436, 437, 441, 445

Passion 101, 177, 220, 367, 401
54, 60, 102, 142, 177, 230, 238, 263, 368, 398

Passover 74, 437
75, 164, 436, 437, 445

Pastor(s) 89, 218, 339
vii, x, 32, 105, 135, 207, 208, 216, 219, 221, 222, 226, 319, 335, 342, 450

Pastoral 87, 89, 93, 108, 111, 112, 152, 221, 227, 284, 285, 287, 341, 388, 406, 412, 415, 416, 419, 430, 432, 443, 454, 462
vii, viii, ix, x, 4, 10, 12, 14, 15, 18, 22, 26, 27, 28, 32, 33, 35, 38, 39, 41, 44, 46, 48, 51, 70, 72, 73, 74, 75, 87, 89, 93, 95, 102, 105, 108, 110, 115, 116, 121, 124, 125, 128, 135, 136, 150, 152, 154, 157, 158, 159, 161, 166, 171, 187, 189, 208, 212, 214, 217, 218, 222, 232, 236, 244, 252, 254, 258, 259, 261, 270, 280, 282, 284, 289, 294, 307, 308, 309, 314, 341, 352, 384, 387, 389, 405, 406, 407, 412, 413, 414, 415, 416, 417, 418, 420, 421, 429, 430, 433, 435, 436, 438, 440, 441, 443, 444, 445, 463, 465

Paten 186, 231, 246, 252, 255, 256, 260, 268, 269, 302, 303, 306, 321, 322, 333, 366, 393, 395, 404
186, 232, 233, 246, 252, 255, 306, 321, 333, 366, 392, 394, 395

Paul VI 96, 112, 193, 194, 222, 278, 446, 467
xv, 23, 24, 25, 26, 27, 50, 56, 75, 79, 90, 91, 117, 122, 124, 151, 156, 208, 209, 212, 310, 311, 315, 317, 337, 343, 345, 434, 466

Penance 95, 141, 428
60, 140, 141, 142, 429, 430, 463

People of God 83, 86, 100, 114, 129, 191, 205, 207, 225, 282
30, 44, 50, 51, 52, 54, 55, 68, 80, 82, 86, 102, 105, 108, 115, 118, 142, 191, 205, 206, 209, 215, 216, 221, 225, 228, 239, 283, 308

Polyphony 128

Pontifical 196, 222, 223, 362, 382, 404
12, 15, 208, 228, 281, 442, 468, 469

Poor 166, 245
95, 103, 165, 166, 167, 188, 328, 331, 384, 385, 394

Posture 129, 130, 131, 132, 138, 155, 162, 193, 203, 205, 206, 236, 240, 241, 242, 243, 244, 245, 247, 253, 255, 256, 257, 261, 263, 265, 266, 269, 270, 272, 276, 290, 292, 296, 298, 299, 304, 307, 316, 317, 319, 322, 323, 327, 328, 329, 331, 348, 362, 372, 453

viii, 19, 33, 93, 113, 128, 129, 130, 132, 172, 205, 207, 231, 241, 244, 245, 288, 308, 313, 330, 360, 453, 454

Praise 78, 134, 191, 243, 250, 261, 267, 319

49, 57, 62, 63, 64, 65, 66, 68, 69, 70, 71, 78, 101, 125, 141, 168, 173, 177, 178, 180, 181, 191, 218, 243, 383, 391, 424, 425, 441

Prayer 78, 86, 96, 117, 118, 120, 123, 125, 128, 130, 131, 145, 146, 147, 148, 149, 152, 160, 161, 162, 164, 168, 169, 170, 171, 172, 173, 174, 181, 182, 186, 191, 192, 203, 204, 210, 244, 245, 248, 249, 250, 251, 252, 253, 255, 261, 262, 264, 267, 268, 269, 270, 272, 274, 277, 291, 293, 294, 297, 298, 299, 300, 301, 302, 319, 320, 321, 323, 330, 369, 370, 375, 410, 417, 418, 419, 420, 428, 443, 462

viii, 2, 3, 5, 7, 8, 10, 17, 18, 19, 21, 31, 36, 38, 43, 45, 47, 48, 50, 51, 53, 57, 58, 59, 61, 62, 63, 64, 65, 66, 67, 68, 69, 71, 72, 76, 77, 78, 79, 85, 86, 87, 90, 94, 103, 106, 107, 108, 109, 114, 117, 118, 120, 121, 122, 123, 124, 125, 126, 130, 131, 132, 133, 134, 135, 145, 146, 147, 148, 149, 151, 159, 160, 161, 162, 166, 168, 169, 170, 171, 172, 173, 174, 175, 176, 177, 178, 179, 180, 181, 182, 186, 191, 192, 193, 204, 207, 209, 211, 214, 218, 220, 226, 239, 244, 245, 247, 249, 250, 251, 253, 255, 260, 261, 262, 266, 267, 268, 269, 272, 277, 280, 291, 292, 293, 294, 295, 296, 297, 298, 299, 300, 301, 308, 313, 318, 319, 320, 323, 324, 330, 369, 371, 375, 376, 385, 386, 405, 406, 411, 417, 418, 419, 420, 421, 424, 426, 428, 430, 431, 432, 436, 437, 441, 443, 444, 447, 455, 463, 464

Prayer of the Faithful 123, 130, 147, 148, 160, 204, 210, 244, 245, 264, 267, 268, 274, 277, 319, 369, 443

123, 147, 160, 161, 162, 204, 207, 211, 266, 267, 268, 277, 319, 320, 324, 369

Preface 81, 120, 173, 249, 250, 293, 420

vii, 5, 8, 16, 17, 22, 54, 63, 68, 81, 82, 118, 132, 168, 171, 173, 180, 250, 292, 377, 419, 421

Preparation of the Gifts 121, 131, 164, 165, 169, 291

9, 18, 21, 38, 66, 67, 109, 124, 131, 140, 165, 167, 168, 169, 170, 184, 189, 190, 231, 246, 247, 255, 274, 291, 320, 333

Presbyterate 106, 225

356

Presence 78, 84, 103, 140, 145, 203, 377

44, 48, 52, 53, 55, 61, 66, 73, 79, 80, 103, 104, 114, 115, 116, 124, 139, 140, 145, 147, 148, 150, 151, 154, 192, 203, 215, 218, 224, 225, 228, 230, 232, 240, 283, 288, 289, 291, 293, 309, 311, 316, 352, 363, 366, 368, 369, 372, 388, 390, 438

Presidential prayers 118, 456

5, 8, 117, 118, 120, 121, 145, 239

Priest 77, 80, 81, 92, 103, 104, 108, 114, 117, 118, 119, 121, 122, 124, 127, 129, 130, 132, 135, 136, 137, 138, 139, 140, 141, 143, 145, 151, 157, 159, 161, 162, 166, 168, 169, 171, 173, 174, 181, 183, 184, 186, 188, 190, 191, 192, 193, 203, 204, 205, 209, 212, 218, 219, 221, 228, 231, 233, 235, 236, 237, 238, 239, 240, 241, 242, 243, 244, 245, 246, 247, 248, 249, 250, 251, 252, 253, 254, 255, 256, 258, 259, 260, 261, 262, 263, 264, 265, 266, 267, 268, 269, 270, 271, 272, 273, 274, 275, 276, 277, 283, 286, 287, 290, 293, 312, 316, 317, 318, 319, 320, 321, 322, 323, 326, 327, 329, 330, 331, 332, 333, 342, 343, 349, 358, 359, 366, 370, 371, 373, 388, 390, 395, 398, 399, 406, 408, 409, 410, 414, 432, 450

viii, 5, 6, 7, 18, 33, 36, 50, 51, 52, 53, 57, 58, 59, 63, 64, 68, 69, 70, 71, 77, 81, 82, 92, 104, 107, 108, 114, 117, 118, 119, 120, 121, 125, 127, 130, 138, 139, 141, 142, 144, 145, 148, 150, 154, 157, 158, 159, 161, 162, 163, 167, 168, 169, 170, 172, 175, 179, 180, 181, 182, 184, 186, 187, 188, 189, 190, 192, 193, 202, 203, 204, 205, 207, 212, 219, 220, 221, 224, 226, 231, 232, 234, 236, 237, 238, 240, 241, 242, 243, 244, 245, 246, 247, 248, 249, 250, 252, 253, 254, 255, 256, 257, 259, 260, 261, 262, 263, 264, 265, 266, 268, 269, 270, 271, 272, 274, 276, 277, 280, 284, 286, 288, 291, 308, 310, 311, 312, 313, 314, 315, 316, 317, 318, 319, 320, 321, 322, 323, 324, 326, 327, 328, 330, 331, 332, 333, 334, 335, 336, 343, 345, 346, 347, 348, 350, 359, 366, 368, 370, 371, 373, 390, 398, 399, 406, 407, 408, 409, 411, 427, 429, 430, 433, 447, 451, 468, 469

Procession 136, 167, 188, 229, 231, 234, 235, 236, 256, 272, 273, 275, 289, 327, 330, 404

51, 124, 132, 135, 136, 142, 151, 154, 165, 166, 167, 188, 189, 190, 191, 230, 231, 232, 233, 234, 235, 236, 240, 242, 247, 256, 264, 273, 274, 276, 289, 328, 347, 368, 404

Profession of Faith 96, 123, 130, 147, 148, 158, 193
123, 134, 147, 154, 158, 266, 319

Psalms 126, 137, 153, 154, 189, 454
137, 138, 143, 153, 211, 370, 414, 455

Purification 169, 181, 306, 323, 333, 366, 396
169, 181, 182, 260, 323, 325, 333, 334, 345

Purificator 165, 231, 245, 260, 274, 307, 333, 348, 366
232, 260, 306, 334, 348, 366

Pyx 393
394, 403

Readings 108, 116, 120, 131, 147, 149, 150, 151, 156, 158, 210, 213, 214, 220, 229, 243, 267, 276, 318, 369, 406, 410, 412, 413, 414, 415, 422, 425, 426, 443, 453, 454
5, 17, 89, 102, 108, 109, 116, 117, 124, 147, 149, 150, 152, 156, 159, 211, 214, 216, 220, 230, 232, 239, 240, 243, 244, 267, 318, 319, 344, 405, 406, 411, 412, 413, 414, 415, 416, 417, 419, 422, 425, 426, 438, 447, 454, 455

Redemption 77, 100, 148, 179
53, 54, 57, 59, 61, 62, 65, 68, 100, 230, 413, 445

Reform 465
vii, ix, xiii, 1, 2, 11, 12, 13, 15, 16, 17, 22, 23, 24, 25, 28, 32, 34, 42, 48, 84, 135, 208, 217, 281, 311, 315, 317, 335, 337, 344, 357, 368, 431, 436

Relics 331, 363
332, 363, 364

Renewal 78, 449
ix, 22, 28, 32, 45, 47, 54, 57, 59, 64, 78, 149, 177, 217, 307, 384, 387, 427, 444, 449, 457

Reservation 260, 375, 377
260, 363, 364, 375, 376, 377

Response 90, 140, 149, 153, 196, 223, 240, 248, 254, 307

28, 30, 32, 56, 80, 90, 128, 140, 148, 149, 151, 152, 158, 159, 160, 161, 162, 170, 214, 215, 243, 248, 257, 284, 295, 320, 321, 403, 452

Rite(s) 75, 80, 84, 85, 86, 88, 90, 91, 96, 107, 108, 111, 115, 119, 123, 129, 134, 135, 141, 154, 166, 167, 169, 180, 182, 184, 185, 191, 192, 194, 195, 196, 197, 201, 221, 222, 223, 228, 235, 258, 259, 261, 263, 264, 270, 272, 273, 274, 275, 277, 282, 286, 289, 292, 301, 305, 306, 307, 309, 312, 316, 323, 339, 340, 342, 343, 350, 355, 362, 364, 369, 371, 375, 376, 380, 381, 382, 395, 397, 399, 407, 409, 416, 443, 458, 461, 462, 463, 465, 466

vii, viii, xiv, xv, xvi, 1, 2, 4, 5, 6, 7, 8, 9, 10, 12, 15, 20, 23, 24, 25, 26, 27, 29, 31, 32, 34, 35, 41, 45, 47, 48, 49, 51, 53, 57, 58, 61, 64, 66, 67, 71, 73, 74, 77, 81, 84, 85, 86, 90, 91, 100, 104, 106, 107, 109, 110, 113, 115, 119, 120, 121, 123, 124, 129, 132, 134, 135, 136, 137, 138, 139, 140, 141, 142, 143, 145, 157, 163, 164, 167, 169, 170, 172, 173, 175, 180, 181, 182, 183, 184, 185, 186, 190, 191, 192, 193, 200, 202, 209, 218, 222, 224, 226, 232, 233, 235, 237, 238, 239, 247, 255, 261, 263, 264, 265, 268, 270, 272, 273, 275, 276, 279, 280, 281, 282, 284, 289, 291, 292, 295, 296, 297, 300, 301, 302, 305, 307, 308, 310, 313, 315, 316, 317, 318, 322, 323, 324, 326, 327, 328, 329, 330, 333, 335, 337, 339, 340, 343, 345, 348, 350, 351, 352, 355, 356, 359, 362, 368, 384, 385, 389, 391, 395, 396, 419, 436, 438, 439, 440, 441, 442, 443, 444, 447, 448, 449, 454, 455, 459, 463, 464, 465, 466

Ritual 94, 112, 341, 371, 375, 376, 380, 381, 382, 402, 404, 414, 426, 427, 433, 446

vii, viii, 1, 3, 6, 8, 9, 10, 11, 12, 13, 16, 17, 18, 19, 20, 21, 22, 23, 25, 26, 27, 30, 47, 49, 58, 69, 70, 72, 94, 105, 106, 110, 119, 123, 124, 128, 129, 136, 137, 138, 139, 146, 151, 154, 156, 159, 160, 162, 166, 167, 169, 170, 171, 172, 175, 176, 179, 180, 182, 183, 184, 185, 186, 188, 190, 191, 192, 193, 199, 204, 209, 211, 217, 222, 239, 241, 242, 254, 255, 261, 262, 266, 270, 273, 280, 282, 288, 289, 293, 294, 295, 323, 341, 348, 355, 356, 360, 367, 368, 370, 378, 390, 402, 415, 416, 423, 426, 427, 428, 433, 435, 438, 454

Ritual Mass 94, 402, 414, 426, 427, 433

94, 402, 415, 426, 427, 433

Roman Ritual 75, 112, 129, 369, 371, 375, 376, 380, 381, 382, 397, 404, 446

Rubrics 119, 125, 154, 238, 248, 250, 262, 317, 319, 399

vii, viii, 8, 10, 18, 19, 21, 22, 27, 29, 35, 36, 43, 106, 141, 224, 225, 226, 227, 239, 251, 252, 300, 317, 322, 328, 333, 348, 429, 433

Sacrament 79, 141, 182, 188, 201, 256, 257, 258, 326, 327, 331, 339, 342, 349, 375, 425

21, 38, 54, 59, 60, 68, 69, 70, 76, 78, 79, 80, 100, 105, 139, 140, 141, 162, 184, 188, 209, 210, 234, 237, 258, 297, 327, 329, 332, 340, 364, 375, 376, 377, 414, 415, 451

Sacramental 78, 92, 93, 331, 332, 360, 374, 415, 425, 427, 462

2, 3, 26, 46, 48, 53, 57, 59, 60, 61, 63, 64, 66, 67, 68, 69, 70, 71, 73, 78, 92, 93, 105, 122, 129, 130, 160, 163, 177, 178, 188, 257, 280, 304, 336, 338, 346, 352, 354, 357, 363, 372, 377, 383, 390, 414, 427, 437, 442, 443, 450, 454, 463

Sacramentary 77, 85

3, 5, 6, 7, 8, 17, 18, 34, 39, 61, 67, 76, 77, 141, 238, 246, 262, 269, 314, 336, 384, 417, 418, 420, 434, 435

Sacristan 216

216, 390

Sacristy 134, 233, 275, 334, 396

234, 275, 355, 396

Saint 126, 194, 285, 328, 378, 410, 412, 414, 431

14, 20, 33, 36, 41, 60, 329, 363, 385, 413, 416, 420, 423, 426, 430, 431, 468, 469

Salvation 83, 103, 148, 150, 160, 164, 174, 175, 179, 183, 185, 203, 234, 339, 412, 418, 420

29, 41, 44, 46, 49, 54, 55, 56, 57, 58, 65, 68, 173, 174, 175, 179, 185, 310, 340, 412, 421, 424, 434

Seat 288, 290, 304, 307, 358, 371, 372

265

Sequence 156

6, 136, 156, 224, 226, 319, 338, 422

Service 108, 367

14, 32, 53, 54, 62, 63, 81, 105, 153, 199, 200, 207, 208, 209, 210, 213, 215, 216, 217, 218, 219, 274, 336, 345, 359, 370, 383, 403, 443

Sign of Peace 182, 184, 254, 270, 301, 320

133, 183, 254, 270, 320, 321, 324

Silence 131, 133, 134, 141, 145, 148, 149, 148, 162, 172, 240, 241, 243, 249, 260, 261, 323

viii, 50, 51, 55, 61, 113, 133, 141, 145, 147, 148, 158, 161, 162, 168, 172, 190, 191, 222, 232, 240, 241, 244, 247, 260, 261, 263, 290, 296, 318, 323

Sin 137, 181, 190

141, 181, 441

Singing 121, 125, 126, 127, 131, 136, 137, 148, 153, 167, 188, 190, 206, 214, 215, 216, 226, 227, 228, 241, 252, 266, 277, 375, 458

viii, 21, 50, 51, 52, 66, 103, 113, 118, 120, 125, 126, 127, 128, 136, 137, 138, 144, 147, 152, 154, 156, 167, 168, 170, 174, 182, 190, 193, 214, 215, 216, 232, 239, 241, 252, 261, 277, 294, 301, 308, 311, 318, 324, 369, 370, 374, 375, 454, 458

Species 78, 84, 93, 114, 176, 205, 206, 258, 259, 328, 339, 343, 371

19, 20, 22, 79, 80, 93, 177, 205, 252, 259, 279, 281, 335, 337, 339, 340, 343, 346, 348, 349, 350, 371, 372, 395, 454

Spiritual life 412

336, 413

Spoon 303

303, 306, 335, 337, 347, 350

Stational Mass 285

Stole 202, 233, 289, 397, 398, 399

33, 280, 396, 398, 399

Sunday 89, 91, 127, 141, 144, 156, 157, 159, 226, 228, 229, 234, 286, 365, 375, 401, 402, 408, 412, 416, 417, 419, 420, 427, 428, 430, 460

1, 21, 24, 26, 50, 106, 107, 126, 127, 144, 158, 159, 187, 216, 217, 221, 226, 230, 236, 239, 255, 263, 374, 389, 399, 408, 413, 415, 418, 420, 426, 429, 430, 438, 440, 460, 463

Symbol **33, 41, 139, 184, 202, 230, 235, 266, 305, 326, 338, 347, 349, 353, 372, 385**

Tabernacle 327, 371, 375, 376, 382

92, 139, 187, 236, 237, 327, 328, 329, 352, 371, 375, 376

Table 115, 149, 165, 166, 206, 231, 260, 267, 268, 271, 275, 288, 305, 307, 316, 323, 333, 360, 361, 362, 410
xi, 2, 52, 67, 71, 92, 101, 115, 116, 118, 134, 135, 140, 142, 163, 165, 167, 210, 231, 232, 237, 247, 256, 265, 268, 269, 288, 302, 309, 316, 318, 323, 333, 336, 345, 360, 361, 362, 363, 364, 366, 367, 368, 369, 386

Thanksgiving 78, 171, 173, 360, 418
49, 57, 58, 68, 69, 70, 71, 77, 78, 170, 171, 172, 173, 174, 176, 177, 178, 180, 191, 249, 360, 361, 362, 417, 424

Throne 371
65, 371

Thurible 212, 234, 235, 236, 241, 242, 243, 248, 265, 266, 269, 274, 290, 331, 332
235, 241, 265, 290, 331, 332, 333

Time 83, 84, 87, 94, 134, 136, 141, 185, 191, 204, 226, 239, 254, 261, 277, 283, 340, 396, 402, 410, 417, 420, 431, 433, 440, 449, 465
viii, x, 7, 8, 12, 13, 14, 15, 22, 25, 26, 30, 31, 32, 35, 36, 38, 39, 40, 46, 47, 48, 50, 56, 58, 61, 84, 85, 87, 89, 95, 105, 106, 110, 116, 118, 120, 126, 130, 133, 135, 136, 144, 145, 146, 147, 153, 166, 173, 176, 179, 189, 190, 193, 204, 218, 241, 243, 246, 247, 260, 261, 271, 272, 280, 281, 305, 327, 331, 333, 344, 345, 387, 391, 405, 409, 410, 411, 413, 418, 421, 424, 429, 430, 431, 432, 433, 434, 435, 436, 440, 441, 444, 448, 455, 464, 465

Tradition 75, 76, 83, 84, 87, 94, 95, 145, 150, 378, 386, 411, 412, 462, 465
vii, xiii, 2, 16, 29, 33, 37, 44, 46, 47, 48, 54, 56, 59, 60, 61, 64, 65, 69, 70, 71, 72, 73, 74, 75, 78, 83, 84, 87, 94, 95, 107, 110, 138, 139, 141, 146, 157, 174, 175, 176, 185, 208, 219, 224, 228, 229, 232, 237, 238, 239, 241, 279, 315, 329, 338, 354, 355, 379, 386, 434, 436, 445, 455, 460, 463, 464, 465

Transubstantiation 79
80

United States of America 74, 137, 189, 254, 342, 362, 365, 392, 393, 398, 402, 416, 428, 459
260, 271, 334, 342, 350, 394, 430

Unity 130, 136, 146, 150, 178, 182, 185, 188, 201, 206, 282, 285, 358, 389, 466

	31, 33, 34, 41, 52, 57, 58, 76, 86, 100, 105, 106, 110, 120, 122, 128, 129, 130, 136, 137, 138, 165, 166, 175, 178, 182, 185, 188, 190, 200, 202, 206, 230, 232, 235, 250, 279, 280, 281, 283, 284, 285, 286, 288, 291, 293, 294, 302, 307, 308, 351, 355, 359, 388, 389, 424, 428, 442, 448, 449, 465, 466
Vernacular	88, 89, 90, 91, 452
	23, 37, 44, 48, 73, 87, 88, 89, 90, 91, 109, 117, 137, 239, 251, 300, 436, 452, 455, 457, 465, 466
Vessels	209, 260, 264, 268, 271, 275, 316, 333, 343, 366, 392, 393, 394, 395, 396, 403, 453
	53, 109, 252, 255, 260, 264, 271, 275, 305, 314, 316, 325, 333, 334, 345, 347, 366, 383, 392, 393, 394, 395, 396, 397, 403, 404
Vestments	216, 277, 233, 235, 263, 289, 396, 399, 400, 401, 402, 403, 428, 453
	33, 203, 234, 264, 289, 308, 383, 385, 394, 396, 397, 399, 400, 401, 403, 430, 454
Voice	88, 121, 124, 125, 266, 293, 366
	127, 133, 136, 137, 170, 174, 189, 214, 232, 293, 295, 308
Votive Mass	94, 402, 410, 423, 426, 430, 431, 435
	410, 416, 423
Week	409, 413, 414, 428, 427, 430, 440
	26, 81, 101, 103, 389, 410, 429, 431, 459, 463
Weekdays	157, 408, 409, 410, 413, 417, 419, 431, 432, 433, 440
	21, 158, 342, 408, 409, 410, 413, 414, 418, 421, 431, 432, 433, 440
Wine	164, 166, 168, 176, 205, 212, 231, 245, 246, 247, 259, 268, 274, 333, 385, 389, 390, 391, 393
	18, 38, 43, 49, 64, 66, 69, 70, 71, 163, 164, 166, 167, 168, 177, 184, 185, 213, 233, 246, 247, 255, 258, 259, 268, 334, 335, 336, 337, 340, 343, 345, 346, 347, 356, 383, 385, 386, 389, 390, 391, 392, 393, 397
Word of God	116, 119, 149, 150, 151, 152, 153, 158, 160, 206, 359, 368, 403, 415
	29, 51, 52, 55, 56, 113, 116, 120, 133, 147, 148, 149, 150, 153, 158, 159, 160, 212, 214, 215, 216, 219, 276, 370, 403, 441

Work 77, 95, 164, 174, 185, 356, 412

x, xi, 3, 8, 10, 11, 13, 18, 22, 29, 34, 48, 49, 51, 56, 57, 58, 59, 61, 62, 72, 85, 86, 114, 118, 128, 166, 173, 174, 177, 185, 190, 192, 193, 199, 200, 209, 215, 216, 218, 262, 273, 312, 354, 355, 356, 378, 385, 386, 408, 412, 429, 444

World 77, 87, 95, 100, 148, 160, 183, 425, 428

31, 35, 36, 38, 40, 41, 42, 44, 57, 60, 65, 100, 102, 103, 109, 110, 160, 179, 192, 214, 230, 335, 338, 351, 384, 397, 430, 440

Worship 96, 100, 111, 112, 115, 194, 195, 196, 197, 277, 278, 309, 350, 353, 380, 381, 382, 466, 467

ix, x, xi, 1, 2, 3, 8, 12, 15, 17, 23, 27, 30, 32, 33, 34, 35, 38, 42, 45, 46, 47, 54, 57, 81, 89, 90, 96, 99, 100, 101, 102, 103, 105, 107, 108, 109, 111, 112, 114, 115, 118, 119, 120, 122, 124, 125, 126, 128, 131, 133, 135, 136, 138, 143, 166, 171, 191, 194, 196, 197, 199, 202, 203, 207, 215, 217, 218, 222, 229, 234, 238, 241, 242, 261, 275, 277, 279, 282, 284, 287, 290, 300, 305, 309, 328, 329, 335, 336, 339, 344, 345, 346, 350, 351, 352, 354, 355, 356, 357, 359, 360, 361, 362, 363, 364, 369, 371, 373, 376, 377, 378, 379, 380, 381, 382, 387, 391, 396, 397, 404, 408, 423, 425, 436, 439, 447, 448, 450, 451, 453, 455, 458, 460, 466, 467, 469